Sociology

Exploring the Architecture of Everyday Life

FOURTH EDITION

A companion anthology entitled

Sociology: Exploring the Architecture of Everyday Life
READINGS

accompanies this book and is available from
your instructor and college bookstore.

Sociology

Exploring the Architecture of Everyday Life

FOURTH EDITION

David M. Newman

Department of Sociology and Anthropology
DePauw University

Visual Essays edited by

Douglas Harper

Department of Sociology
Duquesne University

 PINE FORGE PRESS
An Imprint of Sage Publications, Inc.
Thousand Oaks, California • London • New Delhi

For information:

 Pine Forge Press
An imprint of Sage Publications, Inc.
2455 Teller Road
Thousand Oaks, California 91320
(805) 499-4224
E-mail: order@pfp.sagepub.com

Sage Publications Ltd.
6 Bonhill Street
London EC2A 4PU
United Kingdom

Sage Publications India Pvt. Ltd.
M-32 Market
Greater Kailash I
New Delhi 110 048 India

Printed in the United States of America

Library of Congress Cataloging-in-Publication Data
Newman, David M., 1958–.
    Sociology : exploring the architecture of everyday life / David M.
Newman. — 4th ed.
        p.   cm.
    Includes bibliographical references and index.
    ISBN 0-7619-8738-X (pbk.)
    1. Sociology.   I. Title.
    HM585 .N48 2002
    301—dc21

                                                    2001007231

This book is printed on acid-free paper.

02   03   04   05   06   10   9   8   7   6   5   4   3   2   1

Production Management: *Scratchgravel Publishing Services*
Copy Editor: *Linda Purrington*
Typesetter: *Scratchgravel Publishing Services*
Indexer: *James Minkin*
Cover Designers: *Ravi Balasuriya, Michelle Lee*

About the Author

David M. Newman (Ph.D., University of Washington) is an Associate Professor of Sociology at DePauw University. In addition to the introductory course, he teaches courses in research methods, family, social psychology, and deviance. He has won teaching awards at both the University of Washington and DePauw University.

About the Publisher

Pine Forge Press is an educational publisher, dedicated to publishing innovative books and software throughout the social sciences. On this and any other of our publications, we welcome your comments.

Please write to:

Pine Forge Press
An imprint of Sage Publications, Inc.
2455 Teller Road
Thousand Oaks, CA 91320-2218
(805) 499-0871
E-mail: info.pineforge@sagepub.com

Visit our World Wide Web site, your direct link to a multitude of online resources:

www.pineforge.com

For my Dad

Brief Contents

Detailed Contents

Preface

It was the first day of the fall semester in 1994. I had just finished making the final adjustments to the first edition of this book, which was due to be published the following January. I felt good, like I'd just accomplished something monumental. Even my two children were impressed with me (although not as impressed as the time we went to a professional hockey game and I leaped out of my seat to catch a speeding puck barehanded). I walked into the first meeting of my Contemporary Society class eager to start teaching wide-eyed, first-year students a thing or two about sociology.

In my introductory comments to the class that day I mentioned that I had just written this book. The panicked look in their eyes—a curious combination of awe and fear—calmed when I told them I wouldn't be using it that semester. I assured them that the process of writing an introductory text helped me immensely in preparing for the course and that I hoped to pass on to them the knowledge I had accumulated.

The next day after class one of the students—a bright, freshly scrubbed, 18-year-old—approached me. The ensuing conversation would leave a lasting, humbling impression:

Student: Hi. Umm. Professor Newman . . . I called my parents last night to, like, tell them how my first day in college went. I think they were, like, more nervous than I was. You know how parents can be.

Me: Yes, I sure do. I'm a parent myself, you know.

Student: Yeah, whatever. Anyway, I was telling them about my classes and my professors and stuff. I told them about this class and how I thought it would be pretty cool. I told them you were writing a book. I thought that would impress them, you know, make it seem like they were getting their money's worth and everything.

Me: Well, thanks.

Student: So, they go, "What's the book about?" [He laughed sheepishly.] I told them I didn't know, but I'd find out. So that's what I'm doing . . . finding out.

Me: Well, I'm glad you asked. You see, it's an introductory sociology textbook that uses everyday experiences and phenomena as a way of understanding important sociological theories and ideas. In it I've attempted to. . . .

Student: Wait, did you say it was a *textbook*?

Me: Why, yes. You see the purpose of the book is to provide the reader with a thorough and useful introduction to the sociological perspective. I want to convey. . . .

Student: [quite embarrassed now] Oh. Professor Newman, I'm really sorry. I misunderstood you. I thought you had written a *real* book.

Real book. *Real* book. *Real* book. Those words echoed in my head like some relentless church bell. At first I tried to dismiss the comment as the utterances of a naïve kid who didn't know any better. But the more I thought about it, the more I realized what his comment reflected. The perception that textbooks aren't *real* books is pervasive. I recently heard a radio ad for a local Red Cross book drive asking listeners to donate any unused or unwanted books *as long as they weren't textbooks.*

Sadly, these sorts of perceptions are not altogether unwarranted. Textbooks hover on the margins of the literary world, somewhere between respectful, intellectual, trailblazing research and Harlequin romance novels. Historically they've been less than titillating: thick, heavy, expensive, and easily discarded for a measly five bucks at the end-of-semester "book buy-back."

My goal from the start has been to write a textbook that reads like a *real* book. In the first three editions I wanted to capture simultaneously the essence of my discipline and the reader's interest. From what reviewers, instructors, and students who've read and used the book have said, I think I've been fairly successful. People seem to like the relaxed tone and appreciate the consistent theme that ties all the chapters together. Many instructors have commented on how the book enables students to truly understand the unique and useful features of a sociological perspective.

Features of the Fourth Edition

To my 12-year-old son, revising this book (now for the fourth time) is surely a sign of my incompetence. "Why do you keep writing the *same book* over and over? My math teacher makes me redo my homework when I get too many problems wrong. Is that what's going on here? Is your publisher making you write the book over because there's too much wrong stuff in it?" I told him "no" and that I'd make him read the book—cover to cover—if he continued criticizing it. He stopped.

Despite his concerns, sociology textbooks do need to be revised regularly. No book can be of lasting value if it remains static, locked into a particular style and content. I constantly keep my ears and eyes open, always looking for some new example or current issue to include in the book. My office overflows with boxes of newspaper articles, photocopied journal articles, and shreds of paper containing scribbled notes that I write to myself in the middle of the night when I have a flash of an idea.

When an author revises a book, it's easier to paste on new material than it is to cut out the old stuff. But simply adding on bits and pieces, here and there, tends to make books fat, messy, and unwieldy. So I've tried to streamline the book wherever possible. I've replaced outdated material with new information where appropriate, condensed or moved some sections, and combined Chapters 10 and 11 from the previous edition ("The Architecture of Stratification: Power, Class, and Privilege" and "The Architecture of Disadvantage: Poverty and Wealth") into one chapter.

Here are some of the specific changes I've made in this fourth edition to enhance the features that worked so well in previous editions.

Updated Examples and Statistical Information

As in the first three editions, each chapter is peppered with anecdotes, personal observations, and accounts of contemporary events. Many of the examples you will read are taken from today's news headlines; others are taken from incidents in my own life. All these examples are meant to show you the pervasiveness and applicability of sociology in our everyday experiences in a way that, I hope, rings familiar with you.

Throughout the book I've also tried to provide the most current statistical information possible. So I've updated all of the graphics and, in the process, changed many from statistical tables to more readable charts, making trends and relationships more obvious. Much of the new statistical data is drawn from the most recent 2000 Census.

New and Improved Visual Essays

This edition includes a larger, improved visual component. Many textbooks contain photographs, comic strips, and other types of pictures. But rarely does this material go beyond simply filling up space. I wanted the visual images in this book to paint detailed, informative sociological portraits. To that end, Douglas Harper, one of the foremost visual sociologists in the world today, produced several unique, vivid, and provocative visual essays for this edition. Doug is a master at using photographic images to tell powerful sociological stories. His essays—focusing on such diverse social phenomena as how we watch baseball games, the culture of tramps, transsexualism, family web sites on the Internet, images of social class, graffiti, global vegetable markets, the portrayal of women in Italian advertisements, immigrant funerals in Holland, and the depiction of the future in movies—provide a wonderful opportunity for you to "see" many of the concepts and ideas I've written about in the book. As you study the visual essays, you will become a much more visually astute observer of and participant in your own social world.

New Micro-Macro Connections and Research Features

In the first three editions I provided many in-depth features that focused either on a specific piece of sociological research or on some issue that illustrates the connection between the everyday lives of individuals and the structure of their society. These extended discussions link social institutions to personal experiences and, in the process, provide insight into the methods sociologists use to gather information and draw conclusions about how our world works.

Many instructors and students have found these features useful tools in generating classroom discussion. The features that I've updated from the previous edition include: trends in teen suicide, media censorship, the toy industry's role in gender socialization, the cultural impact of antidepressant drugs, the U.S. health care system, racism in professional sports, sexual harassment in the military, the shifting politics of immigration, and environmental justice. I've also added several new features that focus on such diverse topics as the sociological importance of chairs, ex-mental patients, virtual communities, social class differences in Internet access, the politics of multiracial identity, and racial profiling.

Increased Focus on Globalization and Technology

This edition also contains many more cross-cultural examples and discussions of globalization than did the previous editions, showing how our lives are linked to, and affected by, our increasingly global society. One of the most profound trends in the world today is the linking of heretofore disconnected societies and cultures. It is difficult, if not impossible, to provide a complete picture of sociology and social life without examining how our lives are intertwined with global events and processes.

I have also included more examples and analyses of new innovations in information and communication technology. In less than a decade, the Internet has dramatically changed the way we live our everyday lives. In the process, it has emerged as an important area of sociological study.

New Articles in the Companion Reader

Jodi O'Brien, a sociologist at Seattle University, and I have carefully edited a companion volume to this book consisting of short articles, chapters, and excerpts from other authors. These readings are provocative and eye-opening examples of the joys and insights of sociological thinking. Many of them vividly show how sociologists gather evidence through carefully designed research. Others are personal narratives that provide firsthand accounts of how social forces influence people's lives. The readings examine common, everyday experiences, important social issues, and distinct historical events that illustrate the relationship between the individual and society. We've taken great pains to include readings that show how race, social class, gender, and sexual orientation intersect to influence everyday experiences.

Of the 38 articles in the companion reader, 23 are new to this edition. The new selections touch on such important and relevant sociological issues as the ethical dilemmas posed by studying prostitutes, organized sports and the construction of male identities, women in the military, gay and lesbian parents, the public perception of poor women's and poor children's bodies, medicine as a means of social control, Americans' hectic work schedules, the social construction of whiteness, the millennial generation, Mexican immigration, and the lives of environmental activists.

Teaching Resources and Web Site to Accompany the Book and Companion Reader

David Yamane, sociologist at Notre Dame University, has edited a *Teaching Resources Guide,* available from Pine Forge Press in hard copy or on a disk. The manual provides comprehensive, thorough coverage of the material in both the text and the companion reader, including:

- *Chapter Summaries*
- *Class Exercises and Discussion Topics.* Suggestions for writing exercises, discussion topics, and student assignments to use both in and outside of class. This section also provides suggestions for how to utilize the text's Your Turn activities.
- *Literary and Visual Resources*
- *Selected Internet Resources*
- *Testing Materials.* Multiple-choice, short-answer, and essay questions. The test bank was developed to test students' understanding of the material, so instructors can encourage students to move beyond basic memorization of materials toward application and critique. The multiple-choice questions are organized as recall questions and

application questions. Recall questions are based more directly on the information presented in the textbook, and application questions assess students' comprehension of the material and their ability to apply concepts, theories, and research findings.

- *Summaries of Classic Sociological Studies*
- *Teaching Resource Materials: Annotated Bibliography.* An annotated bibliography of resources useful in preparing for and designing classes, suggestions for how to manage teaching interactions and elicit and evaluate student performance, and techniques for handling any challenges that arise in class.

David has also designed an Internet study site that can be accessed by students via the Pine Forge web site at www.pineforge.com. This site includes additional material not included in the book as well as test questions students can use to gauge their understanding of the information.

A Word About the "Architecture of Society"

I have chosen the image of architecture in the subtitle to convey one of the driving themes of this book: Society is a human construction. Society is not "out there" somewhere, waiting to be visited and examined. It exists in the minute details of our day-to-day lives. Whenever we follow its rules or break them, enter its roles or shed them, work to change things or keep them as they are, we are adding another nail, plank, or frame to the structure of our society. In short, society—like the buildings around us—couldn't exist were it not for the actions of people.

At the same time, however, this structure that we have created appears to exist independently of us. We don't usually spend much time thinking about the buildings we live, work, and play in as human constructions. We see them as finished products, not as the processes that created them. Only when something goes wrong—the pipes leak or the walls crack—do we realize that people made these structures and people are the ones who must fix them. When buildings outlive their usefulness or become dangerous to their inhabitants, people must renovate them or, if necessary, decide to tear them down.

Likewise, society is so massive and has been around for so long that it *appears* to stand on its own, at a level above and beyond the toiling hands of individual people. But here too when things begin to go wrong—widespread discrimination, massive poverty, lack of affordable health care, escalating crime rates—people must do something about it.

So the fascinating paradox of human life is that we build society, collectively "forget" that we've built it, and live under its massive and influential structure. But we are not "stuck" with society as it is. Human beings are the architects of their own social reality. Throughout this book I examine the active roles individuals play in planning, maintaining, or fixing society.

A Final Thought

One of the greatest challenges I face as a teacher of sociology is trying to get my students to see the personal relevance of the course material, to fully appreciate the connection between the individual and society. The true value of sociology lies in its unique ability to show the reciprocal connection between the most private elements of our lives—our characteristics, experiences, behaviors, and thoughts—and the cultures, groups, organizations, and social institutions to which we belong. The "everyday life" approach in this book uses real-world examples and personal observations as a vehicle for understanding the relationship between individuals and society.

My purpose is to make the familiar, unfamiliar—to make you critically examine the commonplace and the ordinary in your own life. Only when you step back and examine the taken-for-granted aspects of your personal experiences can you see that there is an inherent, sometimes unrecognized organization and predictability to them. At the same time you will see that the structure of society is greater than the sum of the experiences and psychologies of the individuals in it.

It is my conviction that this intellectual excursion should be a thought-provoking and enjoyable one. Reading a textbook doesn't have to be boring or, even worse, the academic equivalent of a trip to the dentist (although I personally have nothing against dentists). I believe that part of my task as an instructor is to provide my students with a challenging but comfortable classroom atmosphere in which to learn. I have tried to do the same in this book.

Your instructor has chosen this book, not because it makes his or her job teaching your course any easier, but because he or she wants you, the student, to see how sociology helps us to understand how the small private experiences of our everyday lives are connected to this thing we call society. I hope you learn to appreciate this important message, and I hope you enjoy reading this book as much as I enjoyed writing it.

Good luck,

David M. Newman
Department of Sociology and Anthropology
DePauw University
Greencastle, IN 46135
E-mail: DNEWMAN@DEPAUW.EDU

Acknowledgments

A book project such as this one takes an enormous amount of time to develop. I spent thousands of hours toiling away at the computer, holed up in my isolated third-floor office. Yet as solitary as this project was, it could not have been done alone. Many people provided invaluable assistance to make this book a reality. Without their generous help and support, it wouldn't have been written, and you'd be reading some other sociologist's list of people to thank. Because I have revised rather than rewritten this book, I remain indebted to those who have helped me at some point during the writing of all four editions.

First, I would like to thank the former publisher and president of Pine Forge Press, Steve Rutter. He pushed, prodded, and cajoled me into exceeding my expectations and overachieving. The numerous suggestions he has offered over the years made this book a better one. For that I am eternally grateful. I want to especially thank my long-time developmental editor Becky Smith for her years of patience and insightful guidance.

Likewise, the staff at Pine Forge—Sherith Pankratz, Paul O'Connell, Kirsten Stoller, and for past editions, Jean Skeels, Windy Just, and Rebecca Holland—must be thanked for helping me through the maze of details and difficulties that crop up in a project of this magnitude. My gratitude goes to Anne and Greg Draus at Scratchgravel Publishing Services for once again producing a quality book in record time. In addition, Linda Purrington provided firm but kind editorial hands in helping me polish the revised material. I would also like to express my thanks to David Yamane for creating an excellent instructor's manual and an impressive web site, Greg Draus for designing the graphic representations of statistical information, and to Veronica Oliva and Terri Wright for securing copyright permissions.

I appreciate the many helpful comments offered by the reviewers of the four editions of this book:

Sharon Abbott, Fairfield University
Deborah Abowitz, Bucknell University
Stephen Adair, Central Connecticut State
    University
Rebecca Adams, University of North
    Carolina, Greensboro
Ron Aminzade, University of Minnesota
Afroza Anwary, Carleton College
George Arquitt, Oklahoma State University
Carol Auster, Franklin and Marshall College
Ellen C. Baird, Arizona State University
David Bogen, Emerson College
Frances A. Boudreau, Connecticut College

Todd Campbell, Loyola University, Chicago
Wanda Clark, South Plains College
Thomas Conroy, St. Peter's College
Norman Conti, Cleveland State University
Doug Currivan, University of Massachusetts,
    Boston
Jeff Davidson, University of Delaware
Kimberly Davies, Augusta State University
Tricia Davis, North Carolina State University
James J. Dowd, University of Georgia
Charlotte Chorn Dunham, Texas Tech
    University
Donald Eckard, Temple University

Charles Edgley, Oklahoma State University

Rachel Einwohner, Purdue University

June Ellestad, Washington State University

Shalom Endleman, Quinnipiac College

Rebecca Erickson, University of Akron

Kimberly Faust, Fitchburg State University

Patrick Fontane, St. Louis College of Pharmacy

Michael J. Fraleigh, Bryant College

Barry Goetz, University of Dayton

Lorie Schabo Grabowski, University of Minnesota

Valerie Gunter, University of New Orleans

Roger Guy, Texas Lutheran University

Charles Harper, Creighton University

Doug Harper, Duquesne University

Peter Hennen, University of Minnesota

Max Herman, Oberlin College

Christine L. Himes, Syracuse University

Susan Hoerbelt, University of South Florida

Gary Hytreck, Georgia Southern University

Valerie Jenness, University of California, Irvine

Kathryn Johnson, Barat College

Richard Jones, Marquette University

Tom Kando, California State University, Sacramento

Steve Keto, Kent State University

Peter Kivisto, Augustana College

Marc LaFountain, State University of West Georgia

Melissa Latimer, West Virginia University

Joseph Lengermann, University of Maryland, College Park

Linda A. Litteral, Clark State Community College

Fred Maher

Kristen Marcussen, University of Iowa

Benjamin Mariante, Stonehill College

Joseph Marolla, Virginia Commonwealth University

Michallene McDaniel, University of Georgia

James R. McIntosh, Lehigh University

Jerome McKibben, Fitchburg State University

Ted P. McNeilsmith, Adams State College

Melinda Milligan, Tulane University

Susannne Monahan, Montana State University

Kelly Murphy, University of Pittsburgh

Elizabeth Ehrhardt Mustaine, University of Central Florida

Daniel Myers, University of Notre Dame

Anne Nurse, College of Wooster

Marjukka Ollilainen, Weber State University

Toska Olson, University of Washington

Larry Perkins

Bernice Pescosolido, Indiana University, Bloomington

Mike Plummer, Boston College

Edward Ponczek, William Rainey Harper College

Tanya Poteet, Capitol University

Sharon E. Preves, Grand Valley State University

Judith Richlin-Klonsky, University of California, Los Angeles

Robert Robinson, Indiana University, Bloomington

Mary Rogers, University of West Florida

Sally S. Rogers, Montgomery College

Wanda Rushing, University of Memphis

Michael Ryan, Upper Iowa University

Mark Shibley, Southern Oregon University

Thomas Shriver, Oklahoma State University

Katherine Slevin, College of William and Mary

Lisa White Smith, Christopher Newport University

Eldon Snyder, Bowling Green State University

Nicholas Sofios, Providence College

George Spilker, Clarkson College

Melanie Stander, University of Washington

Kandi Stinson, Xavier University

Richard Tardanico, Florida International University

Robert Tellander, Sonoma State University

Kathleen Tiemann, University of North Dakota

Steven Vallas, Georgia Institute of Technology

Tom Vander Ven, Hofstra University

John Walsh, University of Illinois, Chicago

Gregory Weiss, Roanoke College

Marty Wenglinsky, Quinnipiac College

Stephan Werba, Catonsville Community College

Cheryl E. Whitley, Marist College

Norma Williams, University of North Texas

Janelle Wilson, University of Minnesota, Duluth

Mark Winton, University of Central Florida

Cynthia A. Woolever, Lexington Theological Seminary

Ashraf Zahedi, Santa Clara University

Stephen Zehr, University of Southern Indiana

I also want to express my appreciation to the colleagues and friends who offered cherished assistance throughout the production of all four editions of this book and who put up with my incessant whining about how hard it all was. Some offered invaluable advice on specific topics; others provided general support and encouragement that helped me retain my sanity; and still others helped remind me that there's more to life than writing a book. In particular, I'd like to thank Nancy Davis, Rob Robinson, Andrew Williams, Nafhat Nasr, Tom Hall, James Mannon, Eric Silverman, Lakshmi Fjord, Rebecca Bordt, Carol Jones, Tom Chiarella, Lisa Chiarella, Bizz Steele, Jodi O'Brien, and Peter Kollock.

I would like to express special gratitude to my students who, throughout the years, have kept me curious and prevented me from taking myself too seriously.

Above all, I want to thank my wife Elizabeth and my sons Zachary and Seth for putting up with the frequent late nights, long faces, and lost confidences.

Sociology

Exploring the Architecture of Everyday Life

FOURTH EDITION

PART I

The Individual and Society

What is the relationship between your private life and the social world around you? Part I introduces you to the guiding theme of this book: Our personal, everyday experiences affect and are affected by the larger society in which we live. Chapters 1 and 2 discuss the sociological perspective on human life and the ways in which it differs from the more individualistic approaches of psychology and biology. You will read about what society consists of and get a glimpse into sociologists' attempts to understand the two-way relationship between the individual and society.

As you read on, keep in mind a metaphor that will be used throughout the book to help explain the nature of society: *architecture*. Like buildings, societies have a design discernable to the alert eye. Both are constructed by bringing together a wide variety of materials in a complex process. Both, through their structure, shape the activities within. At the same time, both change. Sometimes they change subtly and gradually as the inhabitants go about their lives; other times they are deliberately redecorated or remodeled. As you make your way through this book, see if you can discover more ways in which buildings and societies are alike.

Taking a New Look at a Familiar World

Sociology and the Individual

The Insights of Sociology

The Sociological Imagination

Andre was a model graduate student. His grades were excellent. He got along well with his professors and even collaborated on a published research paper with one of them. During his last two years of graduate school, he taught two introductory courses and proved to be a skilled and caring teacher. He completed his dissertation and was granted his PhD. Andre thought his future was clear: He would land a job at a top university, establish a national reputation as a top-notch researcher, and become a popular and beloved professor at a top university.

But when Andre entered the job market and began applying for faculty positions, he faced a surprising amount of difficulty. No one seemed willing to hire him for a full-time teaching position. The only way he was able to survive was by taking a temporary one-year replacement job. He became frustrated and began to question his own abilities: "Am I good enough to be a professor? Do I lack the sort of talent they're looking for? Maybe I'm not trying hard enough. What's wrong with me?" His friends and family tried to encourage him, but some of them secretly wondered if Andre wasn't as smart as they had thought he was.

Michael and Carole were both juniors at a large university. They had been dating each other exclusively for the past two years. Both on and off campus they were a loving couple, always reveling in each other's company. By all accounts, the relationship seemed to be going quite well. In fact, Michael was beginning to think Carole was "the one." He imagined them getting married, having children, and living happily ever after. Then one day out of the blue Carole dropped a bombshell. She told Michael she thought the relationship was going nowhere and perhaps they ought to start seeing other people.

Michael was stunned. "What did I do?" he asked her. "I thought things were going great. Is it something I said? Something I did?"

She said no, he hadn't done anything wrong, they had simply grown apart. She told him she just didn't feel as strongly about him as she once did.

After the breakup Michael was devastated. He turned to his friends for support. "She wasn't any good for you anyway," they said. "We always thought she was a little unstable. She probably couldn't get serious with anybody. It wasn't *your* fault, it was *hers*."

In both these stories the people involved, as well as outside observers, immediately try to explain the situation by focusing on individual characteristics and attributes. Andre blames himself for not being able to land a job; others question his intelligence. Michael wonders what he did wrong to sour his relationship with Carole; his friends question Carole's psychological stability. Such reactions are not uncommon. We have a marked tendency to attribute people's achievements and failures to their personal qualities (J. Miller, 1984).

Why can't Andre, our highly intelligent, well-trained, talented PhD, land a permanent job? It's possible that some inherent, personal flaw is preventing Andre from being employable: lack of drive, laziness, bad attitude, and so on. Or maybe he doesn't come across as friendly during job interviews.

But by focusing exclusively on such personal "deficiencies," we overlook the broader societal trends that can affect a person's job prospects. For instance, economic strains might limit the number of students in a society who can afford to go to college and thus the number of professors that universities need to hire. Faculty positions in higher education were abundant in the United States 25 years ago (National Center for Education Statistics, 1989). But in the 1990s, many university departments were forced to condense their faculty, thereby reducing the number of openings for new PhDs (see Exhibit 1.1). Today, the typical American with a PhD in history spends almost nine

Exhibit 1.1   **Declining Opportunities for University Professors**

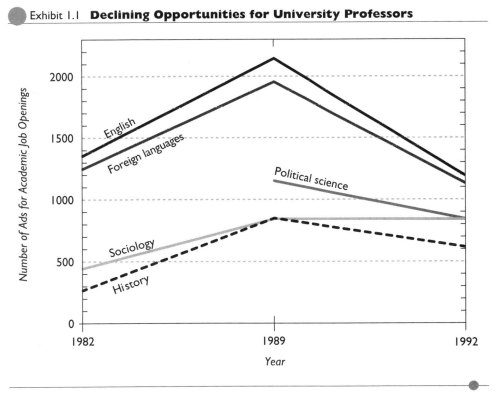

Source: B. Huber, 1994.

years in graduate school and faces a less than 50% chance of getting an academic job; nevertheless, the number of new PhDs increases by 10% each year (Menand, 1996). PhDs in mathematics have the highest unemployment rate ever, yet the number of new PhDs in the 1994–95 academic year was nearly 16% greater than the number the previous year (Worthington, 1996). As many as 38% of biology PhDs can't land anything but temporary jobs, even six years after receiving their degrees ("Too many biologists," 1998). So poorly perceived are faculty job opportunities that in a list of "Bottom 10" careers that once appeared in *USA Today*, college professor ranked eighth least desirable—ahead only of real estate agent and bartender.

So you see, Andre's employability is as much a result of the economic forces operating at the time as of any of his personal qualifications. Had he graduated 25 or even 5 years earlier, his prospects certainly would have been much brighter. For that matter, had he graduated 5 or 25 years later his prospects might also be better. Researchers predict that in the first decade of the 21st century, as the large number of professors hired in the United States in the 1960s reach retirement age and as the number of college-age Americans increases, there will be a shortage of university faculty and a subsequent abundance of openings once again. Indeed, after a decade of decline, there has already been a 20% increase in advertised teaching positions in sociology since the mid-1990s (American Sociological Association, 1999).

And what about our star-struck lovers, Michael and Carole? It seems perfectly reasonable to conclude that something about either of them or the combination of the two caused their breakup. We like to view dating relationships—not to mention marriages—as situations that succeed or fail solely because of the traits or behaviors of the two people involved: He does something that bothers her, she does something that annoys him, or they're simply incompatible.

But how would your assessment of the situation change if you found out that Donald—to whom Carole had always secretly been attracted—had just broken up with his longtime girlfriend and was now available? Relationships are not exclusively private entities; they're always being influenced by outside forces. They take place within a larger network of friends, acquaintances, ex-partners, co-workers, fellow students, and people as yet unknown who may make desirable or, at the very least, acceptable dating partners. When people believe they have no better alternative, they tend to stay with their present partners, even if they are not particularly satisfied. When people think that better relationships are available, they become less committed to staying in their present ones. As a character in the 2001 movie *The Wedding Planner* asks before leaving his fiancée for someone else, "What if a relationship you thought was great, really is great, but not as great as something that's even greater?" Indeed, according to research on the topic, people's perceptions of what characterizes a good relationship (such as fairness, compatibility, affection) are less likely to determine when and if it ends than the presence or absence of favorable alternatives (Felmlee, Sprecher, & Bassin, 1990). That is, couples may endure feelings of dissatisfaction until one partner sees a more attractive possibility elsewhere.

In addition, the sheer number of potentially available partners—a result of shifts in the birthrate 20 years earlier—could have indirectly affected Carole's decision. A surplus of men would increase the likelihood that she would eventually come across a suitable college-age alternative to Michael. A shortage of such men, in contrast, would make Michael look a lot better. Research shows that the risk of a relationship ending increases as the supply of potential alternative relationships increases (South & Lloyd, 1995). In sum, Michael's interpersonal value, and therefore the stability of his relationship with Carole, may have ended not because of anything he had done but because of forces over which he had little if any control.

Let's take this notion beyond their immediate dating network. Carole and Michael's relationship was certainly influenced by other social forces. For instance, the very characteristics and features that people consider attractive in the first place are determined by the values of the larger culture in which they live. Fashions and tastes are constantly changing, making particular characteristics (for example, hairstyles, body types, clothing), behaviors (smoking, drinking, exercising), or life choices (occupation, political affiliation) more or less desirable.

The moral of these two stories is simple: To understand phenomena in our personal lives, it is necessary to move past individual traits and examine broader societal characteristics and trends. External features beyond our immediate awareness and control often exert more influence on the circumstances of our day-to-day lives than our "internal" qualities. We can't begin to explain why relationships work or don't work without addressing the broader interpersonal network and culture in which they are embedded. We can't begin to explain an individual's employability without examining current and past economic trends and the resulting job structure. By the same token, we can't begin to explain the ordinary, everyday thoughts and actions of individuals without examining the social forces that influence them.

Sociology and the Individual

Herein lies the fundamental theme of sociology and the theme that will guide us throughout this book: Everyday social life—our thoughts, actions, feelings, decisions, interactions, and so on—is the product of a complex interplay between societal forces and personal characteristics. To explain why people are the way they are, we must understand the interpersonal, historical, cultural, organizational, and global environments they inhabit. To understand either individuals or society, we must understand both (C. W. Mills, 1959).

Of course, that's easier said than done. The United States is a society dominated by individualistic explanations of human behavior that seek to understand problems and processes by focusing exclusively on the personality, psychology, or even the anatomy of each individual. Consequently, most of us simply take for granted that what we choose to do, say, feel, and think are fiercely private phenomena. Everyday life seems to be a series of unabashedly free choices. After all, we choose what to major in. We choose what to wear. We choose what and when to eat. We choose our lifestyles, our mates, and so on.

But how free are these decisions? Think about all the times your actions have been impacted by social circumstances over which you had little control. Have you ever felt that because of your age or gender or race, certain opportunities were closed to you? Your ability to legally drive a car or drink alcohol is affected by your society's perception of age. When you are older you may be forced into retirement despite your ability and desire to continue working. Some occupations, such as bank executive and engineer, are still predominantly male, while others, such as nurse and administrative assistant, are almost exclusively female. In the United States, African Americans are conspicuously absent from the highest management positions in professional sports despite their overrepresentation as players.

Likewise, the doctrines of your religion may limit your behavioral choices. For a devout Catholic, premarital sex or even divorce is unlikely. A strict Muslim does not drink beverages containing alcohol. An Orthodox Jew would never drink milk and eat meat at the same meal.

Then there's the kind of hairstyle, clothing, or type of music you find appealing or unappealing. Large-scale marketing strategies can actually create a demand for particular products or images. Would the Backstreet Boys have become so popular without a tightly managed and slickly packaged publicity program designed to appeal to adolescent and preadolescent girls? Your tastes, and therefore your choices as a consumer, are often influenced by decisions made in corporate boardrooms. Furthermore, what you wear is dictated in part by the organizational setting in which you find yourself. For instance, appropriate attire for a stockbroker is very different from that for a college student.

Broad economic trends also influence your everyday life. You may lose your job or face a tightening job market as a result of economic fluctuations brought about by increased global competition or a recession. Or, because of the rapid development of certain types of technology, the college degree that may be your ticket to a rewarding career today may not qualify you even for a low-paying, entry-level position in 10 years. And if you don't get a good job after college, you may have to live at home for years after you graduate—not because you are emotionally incapable of separating from your parents but because you can't earn enough to support yourself. Indeed, according to the U.S. Bureau of the Census (1997b), the number of 25- to 34-year-olds who still live at home has increased steadily since the 1980s.

Certainly government and politics affect our personal lives too. A political decision made at the local, regional, national, or even international level might result in the closing of a government agency you depend on, make the goods and services to which you have grown accustomed either more expensive or unavailable, or change the amount of taxes you pay. Family leave policies established by the government may affect your decision whether and when to have a baby. If you are homosexual, the government can determine whether or not you have the right to legally marry your same-sex partner, whether or not you can be covered by your partner's insurance policy, or whether or not you can be fired from your job because of your sexual orientation. In the United States, decisions made by the Supreme Court can increase or limit your options for voluntarily ending a pregnancy, suing an employer for sexual harassment, or keeping the details of your life a private matter.

Our lives can be touched by events that occur in distant countries. In 1998 financial crises in Asia and Russia aroused fear that falling export prices would hurt U.S. companies. The result was a 10 to 15% fall in the U.S. stock market that directly affected many people's pocketbooks. At the same time, U.S. tobacco companies responded to the falling demand for cigarettes in this country by expanding their marketing in Eastern Europe and Asia, causing more respiratory ailments and straining the health care systems in those countries. Recently there has been a rash of protests in France and other countries against genetically modified crops (for example, corn and soybeans) imported from the United States. If these countries begin to ban such products, the economic consequences here may be measured in the billions of dollars. Of course, the attacks on the World Trade Center and the Pentagon on September 11, 2001, sent economic shock waves around the world that are still felt today.

The technologically interconnected nature of the world has made the effects of such international events almost instantaneous. In 2000 a virulent computer program dubbed the "I Love You" virus was created by a hacker in the Philippines. Within hours it had spread to Singapore, South Korea, Japan, Europe, and eventually across the Atlantic to the United States. The virus shut down computer systems in offices from Tokyo to Moscow to Rome to Atlanta. And it disabled e-mail networks in such powerful organizations as AT&T, the Pentagon, the U.S. State Department, and Britain's Parliament. Hundreds of thousands of home computers were also affected.

The Insights of Sociology

Sociologists do not deny that individuals make choices or that they must take personal responsibility for those choices. But they are quick to point out that we cannot fully understand things happening in our lives, private and personal though they may be, without examining the influence of the people, events, and societal features that surround us. The structure of our lives often is not immediately apparent. By showing how social processes can shape us, and how individual action can in turn affect those processes, sociology provides unique insight into the taken-for-granted personal events and the large-scale cultural and global processes that make up our everyday existence.

Other disciplines study human life, too. Biologists study how the body works. Neurologists examine what goes on inside the brain. Psychologists study what goes on inside the mind. These disciplines focus almost exclusively on structures and processes that reside *within* the individual. In contrast, sociologists study what goes on *among* people as individuals, groups, or societies. How do social forces affect the way people interact with one another? How do people make sense of their private lives and the social worlds they occupy? How does everyday social interaction create "society"?

Consider statistics from the National Basketball Association showing that overall shooting accuracy has decreased steadily over the past decade. As a result, teams don't score as many points as they used to. But has this happened because professional players aren't as talented as they once were? Hardly. Today's athletes are bigger, faster, and stronger than ever. Instead, broader social forces have changed the culture and economy of basketball. Exposed to the highly marketed images of superstars, younger players have devoted more time to developing flashy individual moves than to developing less glamorous but ultimately more valuable fundamental skills. The lure of multimillion-dollar contracts has created an enormous increase in players forgoing college—where traditionally they were able to improve their skills—to enter the pros. Today's young superstars are more likely to have an agent and an entourage than an influential coach-mentor.

Issues such as love, poverty, sex, age, and prejudice are also better understood within the appropriate societal context. For instance, we may feel that we marry purely for love, when in fact society pressures us to marry people from the same social class, religion, and race (P. L. Berger, 1963). Sociology, unlike other disciplines, forces us to look outside the tight confines of individual personalities to understand the phenomena that shape us. Consider, for example, the following situations:

- A young high school girl, fearing she is overweight, begins systematically starving herself in hopes of becoming more attractive.
- A 55-year-old college graduate, unable to find work for the past three years, sinks into a depression after losing his family and his home. He now lives on the streets.
- A 36-year-old professor kills herself after learning that her position at the university will be terminated the following year.
- The student body president and valedictorian of the local high school cannot begin or end her day without several shots of whiskey.

What do these people have in common? Your first response might be that they are all suffering or have suffered terrible personal problems—eating disorders, homelessness, suicidal depression, alcoholism. If you saw them only for what they'd become—an "anorexic," a "homeless person," a "suicide victim," or an "alcoholic"—you might think they have some kind of personality defect, genetic flaw, or mental problem that renders them incapable of coping with the demands of contemporary life. Maybe they simply lack the willpower to pick themselves up and move on. In short, your immediate tendency might be to focus on the unique, perhaps "abnormal," characteristics of these people to explain their problems.

But we cannot downplay the importance of their *social* worlds. The circumstances just described are all linked to larger phenomena. There is no denying that we live in a society that praises a lean body, encourages drinking to excess, and values individual achievement and economic success. Some people suffer under these conditions when they don't measure up. This is not to say, however, that all people exposed to the same social messages inevitably fall victim to the same problems. Some people overcome wretched childhoods; others withstand the tragedy of economic failure and begin anew; and some people are immune to narrowly defined cultural images of beauty. But to understand fully the nature of human life or of particular social problems, we must acknowledge the broader social context in which these things occur.

The Sociological Imagination

Unfortunately, we often don't see the connections between the personal events in our everyday lives and the larger society. People in a country such as the United States, which places such a high premium on individual achievement, have difficulty looking beyond their immediate situation. Someone who loses a job, gets divorced, or flunks out of school in such a society has trouble imagining that these experiences are somehow related to massive cultural or historical processes.

The ability to see the impact of these forces on our private lives is what the famous sociologist C. Wright Mills (1959) called the **sociological imagination**. The sociological imagination enables us to understand the larger historical picture and its meaning in our own lives. Mills argues that no matter how personal we think our experiences are, many of them can be seen as products of societywide forces. The task of sociology is to help us view our lives as the intersection between personal biography and societal history, to provide a means for us to interpret our lives and social circumstances.

Getting fired, for example, is a terrible, even traumatic private experience. Feelings of personal failure are inevitable when one loses a job. But if the unemployment rate in a community hovers at 25% or 30%—as it has in many places around the world and in many inner-city neighborhoods in the United States over the past several decades—then we must see unemployment as a social problem that has its roots in the economic and political structures of society. Being unemployed is not a character flaw or personal failure if a significant number of people in one's community are also unemployed. As long as the economy is arranged so that employees are easily replaced or slumps inevitably occur, the social problem of unemployment cannot be solved at the personal level (Lekachman, 1991; C. W. Mills, 1959).

The same can be said for divorce, which people usually experience as an intimate tragedy. But in the United States, close to one out of every two marriages will end in divorce, and divorce rates are increasing in many countries around the world. We must therefore view divorce in the context of broader historical changes occurring throughout society: the family, the law, religion, the economy, and the culture as a whole. It is impossible to explain significant changes in divorce rates over time by focusing exclusively on the personal characteristics and behaviors of divorcing individuals. Divorce rates don't rise simply because more individual spouses can't get along with one another, and they don't fall because more husbands and wives are suddenly being nicer to each other.

Mills did not mean to imply that the sociological imagination should debilitate us—that is, force us to fatalistically perceive our lives as wholly beyond our control. In fact, the opposite is true. An awareness of the impact of social forces or world history on our personal lives is a prerequisite to any efforts we make to change our social circumstances. Indeed, the sociological imagination allows us to recognize that the solutions to many of our most serious social problems lie not in changing the personal situations and characteristics of individual people but in changing the social institutions and roles available to them (C. W. Mills, 1959). Drug addiction, homelessness, sexual violence, hate crimes, eating disorders, suicide, and so on will not go away simply by treating or punishing a person who is suffering from or engaging in the behavior.

Émile Durkheim
A Sociological View of Suicide

Several years ago a tragic event occurred at the university where I teach. On a pleasant night a few weeks into the fall semester, a first-year student shot and killed himself in his dorm room. The incident sent shock waves through this small, close-knit campus. As you would expect in such a situation, the question on everyone's mind was, Why did he do it? Although no definitive answer was ever obtained, most people simply concluded that his was a "typical" suicide. He must have been despondent, hopeless, unhappy, and unable to cope with the demands of college and the pressures of contemporary social life. I heard students say that no one really knew much about him, that he was a bit of a loner. In other words, something was wrong with him.

As tragic as this incident was, it was not and is not unique. Since the 1950s the U.S. suicide rate (the percentage of people who die through suicide) has almost tripled for people between the ages of 15 and 24, becoming the third leading cause of death, behind accidents and homicides, among young Americans. The adolescent suicide rate is about 11.4 per 100,000 (Gaines, 1991; U.S. Bureau of the Census, 2000b). In one national survey, 15% of high school students admitted to at least one suicide attempt (cited in Mannon, 1997).

Focusing on individual characteristics such as depression and frustration doesn't tell us why so many people in this age group commit suicide, nor does it tell us why youth suicide has increased so dramatically over the past four or five decades. So, to understand "why he did it," we must look beyond the student's private mental state and examine the social and historical factors that might have affected him.

Clearly, life in contemporary developed societies is focused on individual achievement—being well-dressed, popular, and successful—more strongly than ever before. Young people are faced with almost constant pressure to "measure up" and define their identities, and therefore their self-worth, according to standards set by others (Mannon, 1997). Although most can adjust, a growing number cannot. In addition, as competition for scarce financial resources becomes more acute, young people are likely to experience unprecedented levels of stress and uncertainty about their own futures. As the quest to succeed begins earlier and earlier, the stakes increase.

Such changes may explain why suicide among African-American teenagers, once quite rare, has increased dramatically over the past two decades (see Exhibit 1.2). In some cities, such as Indianapolis, the suicide rate among young African Americans doubled in the second half of the 1990s (C. Williams, 2000). Some experts blame the increase on a growing sense of hopelessness and a long-standing cultural taboo against discussing mental health matters. Others, however, cite broader social factors brought about, ironically, by a growing economy. As more and more black families move into the middle class, there is increasing pressure to compete in traditionally white-dominated professions and social environments. Indeed, black teenagers who commit suicide are more likely to come from higher socioeconomic backgrounds than black teenagers in the general population (cited in Belluck, 1998a).

In other societies, different types of social changes may account for increases in suicide rates. In 1999, Japan saw its unemployment rate rise to record levels as companies grappled with a severe economic recession. The result was a 40% increase in one year in suicides among men in their 20s and a 53% increase in suicides among those aged 10 to 19 (Strom, 1999). In Ireland, which has the fastest-growing rate of suicide in the world, one in four suicides occur among those aged 15 to 24 (Clarity, 1999). Experts there attribute much of this increase to a weakening of religious proscriptions against suicide and an alteration of gender roles that has left many men unsure of their place in Irish society.

Sociology's interest in linking suicide to certain processes going on in society is not new. In fact, in one of the classic pieces of sociological research, the famous French

Exhibit 1.2 **Increasing Rates of Suicide Among Black Teens**

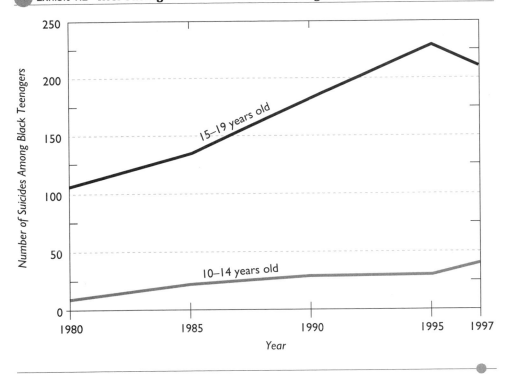

Source: U.S. Bureau of the Census, 2000b.

sociologist Émile Durkheim (1897/1951) argued that suicide is more likely to occur when the social ties that bind people to one another are either too weak or too strong. He was the first to see suicide as a manifestation of changes in society. In college a close friend of his, named Victor Hommay, committed suicide. Convinced that more was involved in Hommay's death than psychological shortcomings, Durkheim began to explore the sociological grounds for suicide.

How does one go about determining whether suicide—perhaps the most private act one can commit—is instigated by the structure of society? Durkheim decided to test his theory by comparing existing official statistics and historical records across groups, sometimes referred to as the **comparative method.** Many sociologists continue to follow this methodology, analyzing statistics compiled by governmental agencies such as the U.S. Bureau of the Census, the FBI, and the National Center for Health Statistics to draw comparisons among groups.

For about seven years Durkheim carefully examined the available data on rates of suicide among various social groups in Europe—populations of countries, members of religions or ethnic groups, and so on. Instead of simply describing the suicide rates of these different groups, Durkheim sought to discover and explain important social patterns. If suicide were purely act of individual desperation, he reasoned, one would not expect to find any noticeable changes in the rates from year to year or society to society. That is, the distribution of desperate, unstable, unhappy individuals should be roughly equal across time and culture. If, however, certain groups or societies had a significantly higher rate of suicide than others, something more than individual disposition would seem to be at work.

After compiling his figures, Durkheim discovered that, among other things, suicide rates in all the countries he looked at tended to be higher among widowed, single, and divorced people than among married people; higher among people without children than among parents; and higher among Protestants than among Catholics. Did this mean that unmarried people, childless people, and Protestants were more unhappy, depressed, or psychologically dysfunctional than other people? Durkheim didn't think so. Instead, he felt that something about the nature of social life among people in these groups increased the likelihood of suicide.

Durkheim argued that when group, family, or community ties are weak, people feel disconnected and alone. If a person lacks family ties and close friends or lives in a community that stresses individualism and de-emphasizes ties to a larger group, then that person is likely to lack a supportive network that could be a buffer against personal difficulties. Durkheim pointed out, for instance, that the Catholic Church emphasizes salvation through community and binds its members to the church through elaborate doctrine and ritual; Protestantism, in contrast, emphasizes individual salvation and responsibility. This individualism, he believed, explained the differences he noticed in suicide rates. Self-reliance and independence may glorify one in God's eyes, but they become liabilities if one is in the throes of personal tragedy.

Durkheim felt that life in modern society tends to be individualistic and dangerously alienating. Decades later, contemporary sociologists have found evidence supporting Durkheim's insight (for example, Bellah, Madsen, Sullivan, Swidler, & Tipton, 1985; Riesman, 1950). Many people in the United States today don't know and have no desire to know their neighbors. Strangers are treated with suspicion. In the pursuit of economic survival, we have become more willing to relocate, sometimes to areas completely isolated from previous family ties. As we spread out and become more insulated, we become more separated from those who could and would offer support in times of need. One recent study found that membership in voluntary organizations (PTA, Elks Club, Red Cross, League of Women Voters, and the like) has steadily declined in the United States over the past several decades. Over the same period the average number of hours a day that people watch television has increased (cited in S. Roberts, 1995).

The structure of our communities discourages the formation of bonds with others and not surprisingly, the likelihood of suicide increases at the same time. In the United States today the highest suicide rates are in the sparsely populated mountain states of Nevada, Utah, Idaho, Wyoming, and Montana. In these states divorce rates are also higher than those in other regions of the United States, and a larger proportion of new residents are not part of an established community (Doyle, 1994). The greater isolation of people in these regions makes them more individualistic, less likely to seek help or comfort from others in times of trouble, and therefore more susceptible to suicide.

Durkheim also felt, however, that suicide can become more likely when the ties to one's community are too strong. He suggested that in certain societies individuality is completely overshadowed by one's group membership; the individual literally lives for

Exhibit 1.3 **The Link between Suicide and Religious Ties**

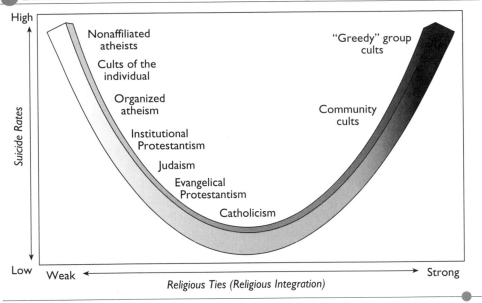

Source: Pescosolido & Georgianna, 1989.

the group, and personality is merely a reflection of the collective identity of the community. Religious cults, for example, require their members to reject their ties to outside people and groups and to live by the values and customs of their new community. When cult members feel they can no longer contribute to the group and sustain their value within it, they may take their own lives out of loyalty to group norms. Exhibit 1.3 maps the degree to which various religions encourage individuals to live for the group (religious integration) and shows the relationship to suicide. The lowest suicide rates occur with intermediate religious integration. The highest rates occur where there is very low integration (such as among nonaffiliated atheists) and very high integration (as found in "greedy" group cults that require a rejection of all outside network ties).

A terrible example of overly strong ties occurred in 1989 when four young Korean sisters, ranging in age from 6 to 13, attempted to kill themselves by ingesting rat poison. The three older sisters survived; the youngest died. The eldest provided startling sociological insight into this seemingly senseless act. Their family was poor—the father supported everyone on a salary of about $362 a month. The girl told the authorities that the sisters had made a suicide pact to ease their parents' financial burden and leave enough money for the education of their 3-year-old brother. Within the traditional Korean culture, female children are much less important to the family than male children. These sisters attempted to take their lives not because they were depressed or unable to cope but because they felt obligated to sacrifice their personal well-being to the success of their family's male heir ("Korean girls," 1989).

Just as the suicide pact of these young girls was tied to the social system of which they were a part, so, too, was the suicide of the young college student at my university. His choices and life circumstances were also a function of the values and conditions of his particular society. No doubt he had emotional problems, but these problems may have been part and parcel of his social circumstances. Had he lived in a society that didn't place as much pressure on young people or glorify individual achievement, he might not have chosen suicide. That's what the sociological imagination helps us understand.

CONCLUSION

In the 21st century, understanding our place within cultural, historical, and global contexts is more important than ever. The world is shrinking. Communication technology and the global economy bind us to people on the other side of the planet. Increasing ecological awareness opens our eyes to the far-reaching effects of environmental degradations. Upheavals in the former Soviet Union and Eastern Europe, the reunification of Germany, the reawakening of China, the collapse of Asian economies, and the overthrow of white rule in South Africa were perhaps the most significant political events at the end of the 20th century. The consequences of these colossal changes will continue to be felt around the world for many years to come.

When we look at how people's lives are changed by such events—as they sink into poverty or ascend to prosperity; stand in bread lines or work at a job previously unavailable; or find their sense of ethnic identity and sense of self-worth altered—we can begin to understand the everyday importance of large-scale changes.

However, we must remember that individuals are not just helpless pawns of societal forces. They simultaneously influence and are influenced by society. The next chapter provides a more detailed treatment of this theme. Then, in Part II, I examine how society and our social lives are constructed and ordered. I focus on the interplay between individuals and the people, groups, organizations, institutions, and culture that collectively make up our society. Part III focuses on the structure of society, with particular attention to the various forms of social inequality.

YOUR TURN

The sociological imagination serves as the driving theme throughout this book. It's not a particularly difficult concept to grasp in the abstract: Things that are largely outside our control affect our everyday lives in ways that are sometimes not immediately apparent; our personal biographies are a function of social history. Yet what does this actually mean? How can you see the impact of larger social and historical events on your own life?

One way is to find out what events were going on at the time of your birth. Go to the library and find a newspaper and a popular magazine that were published on the day you were born. It would be especially useful to try to find a newspaper from the town or city in which you were born. What major news events took place that day? What were the dominant social and political concerns at the time? What was the state of the economy? What was considered fashionable in clothing, music, movies, and so forth?

Ask your parents or other adults about their reactions to these events and conditions. How do you think those reactions affected the way you were raised and the values in your family? What have been the lasting effects, if any, of these historical circumstances on the person you are today?

In addition, you might want to check newspapers and magazines and the Internet to determine the political, economic, global, and cultural phenomena that were prominent when you entered high school. The emergence from adolescence into young adulthood is a significant developmental stage in the lives of most people. It often marks the first time that others—including parents and other adults—take us seriously. And it is arguably the most self-conscious time of our lives. Try to determine how these dominant social phenomena will continue to influence your life after college. Imagine how different your life might have been had these social conditions been different—for instance, a different political atmosphere, a stronger or weaker economy, a more progressive or repressive way of life, and so on.

CHAPTER HIGHLIGHTS

- The primary theme of sociology is that our everyday thoughts and actions are the product of a complex interplay between massive social forces and personal characteristics. We can't understand the relationship between individuals and societies without understanding both.

- The sociological imagination is the ability to see the impact of social forces on our private lives—an awareness that our lives lie at the intersection of personal biography and societal history.

- Rather than study what goes on *within* people, sociologists study what goes on *between* people, whether as individuals, groups, organizations, or entire societies. Sociology forces us to look outside the tight confines of our individual personalities to understand the phenomena that shape us.

KEY TERMS

comparative method Research technique that compares existing official statistics and historical records across groups to test a theory about some social phenomenon

sociological imagination Ability to see the impact of social forces on our private lives

2 Seeing and Thinking Sociologically

In 1994 ethnic violence erupted in the small African nation of Rwanda. The Hutu majority had begun a systematic program to exterminate the Tutsi minority. Soon gruesome pictures of the tortured and dismembered bodies of Tutsi men, women, and children began to appear on our television screens. When it was over, close to a million Tutsi had been slaughtered—half of whom died within a three-month period. Surely, we thought, such horror must have been perpetrated by bands of vicious, crazed thugs who derived some sort of twisted satisfaction from such unspeakable violence. Or maybe these were the extreme acts of angry soldiers, trained killers who were committed to destroying the enemy as completely as possible.

Actually, much of the responsibility lies elsewhere, in a most unlikely place: among the ordinary, previously law-abiding citizens of Rwanda. In 2001, two Benedictine nuns and a University of Rwanda physics professor stood trial for their role in the genocide. The nuns were accused of informing the military that Tutsi refugees had sought sanctuary in the church and standing by as the soldiers massacred them. One nun allegedly provided the death squads with cans of gasoline used to set fire to a building where 500 people were hiding. The professor was accused of drawing up a list of Tutsi employees and students at the university for the killers and killing at least seven Tutsis himself (Simons, 2001).

A report by the civil rights organization African Rights provides further evidence that members of the medical profession conceived, planned, and executed a great deal of the brutality ("Doctors implicated," 1996). The report details how doctors joined with militiamen to hunt down Tutsis, turning hospitals into slaughterhouses. Some helped soldiers drag sick and wounded refugees out of their beds to be killed. Others took advantage of their position of authority to organize road blocks, distribute ammunition, and compile lists of Tutsi colleagues, patients, and neighbors to be sought out and slaughtered. Many doctors who didn't participate in the actual killing refused to treat wounded Tutsis and withheld food and water from refugees who sought sanctuary in hospitals. In fact, the president of Rwanda and the Minister of Health were both physicians who were eventually tried as war criminals.

Ordinary, well-balanced people—teachers, nuns devoted to the ideals of charity and mercy, and members of a profession committed to healing and saving lives—had changed, almost overnight, into sadistic killers. How could this have happened? The answer to this question lies in the sociological claim that individual behavior is largely shaped by social forces and situational contingencies. The circumstances of large-scale ethnic hatred and war have the power to transform well-educated people with no previous history of violence into cruel butchers. Tragically, such forces were at work in many of the 20th century's most infamous examples of human brutality, such as the Nazi Holocaust during World War II and, more recently, ethnic massacres in Bosnia and Kosovo as well as Rwanda.

In this chapter, I examine the process by which individuals construct society and the way people's lives are linked to the social environment in which they live. The relationship between the individual and society is a powerful one—each affects the other.

How Individuals Structure Society

Up to this point I have used the word *society* rather loosely. Typically, sociologists define **society** as a population living in the same geographical area that shares a culture and a common identity and whose members are subject to the same political authority. Societies may consist of people from the same ethnic heritage or of hundreds of different groups who speak a multitude of languages. Some societies are highly industrialized and complex; others are primarily agrarian and relatively simple in structure. Some societies are highly religious; others are secular. Some societies are self-sufficient and produce most of the goods and services their people need; others rely mostly on trade with foreign countries for survival.

According to the 19th-century French philosopher Auguste Comte, all societies, whatever their form, contain both forces for stability, which he called "social statics," and forces for change, which he called "social dynamics." Sometimes, however, people use the term *society* only to mean a "static" entity—a natural, permanent, and historical structure. They frequently talk about society "planning" or "shaping" our lives and describe it as a relatively unchanging set of organizations, institutions, systems, and cultural patterns into which successive generations of people are born and socialized.

As a result, sociology students often start out believing not only that society is powerfully influential (which, of course, it is) but also that it is something that exists "out there," completely separate and distinct from us (which it isn't). It is tempting to view society simply as a "top down" initiator of human activity, a massive entity that methodically shapes the lives of all individuals within it, like some gigantic puppeteer manipulating marionettes. This characterization is not altogether inaccurate. Society does exert influence on its members through certain identifiable structural features and historical circumstances. The concept of the sociological imagination discussed in Chapter 1 implies that structural forces beyond our direct control do affect our personal lives.

But this view is only one side of the sociological coin. The sociological imagination also encourages us to see that each individual has a role in forming a society and influencing the course of its history. As we navigate our social environments, we respond in ways that may modify the effects and even the nature of that environment (House, 1981). As one sociologist has written,

> No [society], however massive it may appear in the present, existed in this massivity from the dawn of time. Somewhere along the line each one of its salient features was concocted by human beings. . . . Since all social systems were created by [people], it follows that [people] can also change them. (P. L. Berger, 1963, p. 128)

To fully understand society then, we must see it as a human construction made up of people interacting with one another. It consists of everyday *microsituations*—what we do, say, feel, and think when we're alone, in pairs, or in groups. When enough people alter their behavior, the nature of society changes (Collins, 1981).

Communication plays an important role in the construction of society. If we couldn't communicate with one another to reach an understanding about society's expectations, we couldn't live together. Through day-to-day communication, we construct, reaffirm, experience, and alter the reality of our society. By responding to other people's comments and gestures in the expected manner and by talking about social abstractions as real things, we help shape society (Shibutani, 1961).

Imagine two people sitting on a park bench who strike up a conversation. Their talk eventually turns to the "epidemic" of school shootings that has occurred all over this country over the past few years. One person is convinced that the causes of such tragedies are increased access to weapons and a youth culture that makes outsiders out of kids who are the least bit different; the other tags violent video games, lack of school discipline, and the breakdown of parental control as the culprits. The debate becomes heated: One thinks that the teen killers responsible for the shootings need help and guidance; the other feels that the killers (and maybe even their parents) should receive maximum criminal punishment. These two people obviously don't agree on the causes and solutions to the problem of "school violence." But merely by talking about it they are agreeing that the problem is real, that it indeed exists. In talking about such matters, people give shape and substance to society's ideals and values (Hewitt, 1988).

So you see, society is also a "bottom up" phenomenon. It might best be regarded as a work in progress, a becoming rather than a being. It is a succession of events, a flow of interchanges among people (Shibutani, 1961, p. 174). When we view society this way, we can begin to understand the role each of us has in altering it. Whenever we modify the expectations or behaviors associated with a social position we occupy, we are simultaneously modifying a part of our society. Individuals who occupy highly visible and influential positions are particularly effective. It is often argued, for instance, that Franklin D. Roosevelt's terms as U.S. president forever changed the nature of the presidency and the role of the federal government in people's lives (House, 1981).

It's not only powerful, influential people who can modify society, however. Sometimes the actions of ordinary individuals mobilize larger groups of people to collectively alter some aspect of social life. In 2000, for instance, Yugoslavian coal miners went on strike to protest what they considered voter fraud in the presidential election there. President Slobodan Milosevic had claimed victory, but the miners believed that his opponent, Vojislav Kostunica, had actually received more votes. When Milosevic sent police to quell the uprising, the miners used front-end loaders and other heavy mining machinery to ram through police blockades. This act of defiance ignited a nationwide revolt that eventually brought down the 13-year Milosevic regime.

In 1955, a black seamstress from Montgomery, Alabama, named Rosa Parks refused to give up her bus seat to a white man who had boarded the bus after her, although she was required to do so by law. The incident sparked a year-long citywide boycott of the public transit system and galvanized the entire civil rights movement of the 1950s and 1960s. Ms. Parks was an active member of the NAACP and had challenged the bus segregation laws many times before that day in December. And Montgomery's black community had been demanding changes in the transit system for some time (R. D. G. Kelley, 1996). Nevertheless, this single challenge to the broad societal expectations commonly associated with race at the time helped set in motion a massive restructuring of U.S. race relations. The repercussions continue to reverberate through our economic, educational, and political systems today.

Even something so apparently unchangeable as our collective past can be shaped and modified by individuals. We usually think of history as a fixed, unalterable collection of social events that occurred long ago; only in science fiction can one "go back" and change history. No one would question that King John of England signed the Magna Carta in 1215 or that the Declaration of Independence was signed in 1776 or that the Civil War ended in 1865 or that John F. Kennedy was assassinated on November 22, 1963.

Although historical events themselves don't change, their meaning and relevance can. Consider the celebration in 1992 of the 500th anniversary of Columbus's voyage to the Americas. Schoolchildren once were taught that Columbus's 1492 voyage represented a triumphant step forward for Western civilization. However, increasing sensitivity to the social value of all racial and ethnic groups and the acknowledgment of their past persecution forced many people to reconsider the historical meaning of Columbus's journey. In fact, some historians now consider it one of history's most dismal examples of wanton and deadly prejudice.

In sum, we live in a world in which our behaviors are largely a product of societal and historical processes. Society is an objective fact that coerces, even creates, us (Berger, 1963). At the same time, we are constantly creating, maintaining, reaffirming, and transforming society. Hence society is part and parcel of human interaction (Collins, 1981). But although we create society, we then collectively "forget" we've done so, believe it is independent of us, and live our lives under its influence.

Social Influence: The Impact of Other People in Our Everyday Lives

We live in a world with other people. I know that's not the most profound statement you've ever heard, but it is key to understanding the sociology of human behavior. Our everyday lives are a collection of brief encounters, extended conversations, intimate interactions, chance collisions, and superficial contacts with other people. In our early years we may have our parents, siblings, uncles, aunts, and grandparents to contend with. Soon we begin to form friendships with others outside our families. Our lives also become filled with connections to other people—classmates, teachers, co-workers, bosses, spiritual leaders, therapists—who are neither family nor friends but who have an enormous impact on us. And, of course, we have daily encounters with total strangers: the clerk at the supermarket, the server at the restaurant, the cashier at the video rental store, the people who sit next to us on airplanes. If you think about it, even being alone requires that we know what it's like to be with other people. As I discuss in Chapters 5 and 6, much of our private identity—what we think of ourselves, the type of people we become, and the images of ourselves we project in public—is derived from our contact with others.

Sociologists tell us that these encounters have a great deal of *social influence* over our lives. Whether we're aware of their doing so or not, other people affect our thoughts, perceptions, and behaviors. We take into account their feelings and concerns before acting. Perhaps you've decided to date someone only to be stopped dead in your tracks by the question, What would my mother think of this person? The others who influence us may be in our immediate presence or hover in our memories. They may be real or imagined, loved or despised. And their effects on us may be deliberate or accidental. Our lives are spent forming or dissolving attachments to other people; we may seek them out one moment, avoid them the next.

Imagine for a moment what your life would be like if you had never had contact with other people (assuming you could have survived this long!). You'd lack the key experiences that make you a functioning human being. You wouldn't know what love is, or hate or jealousy or compassion or appreciation, for that matter. You wouldn't know if you were wealthy or poor, bright or dumb, witty or boring. You'd also lack some important and basic information. You wouldn't know what day it is, how much a pound weighs, where Belgium is, or which plants and animals are edible. Furthermore, you'd have no language, and because we use language to think, imagine, predict, plan, wonder, and reminisce, you'd lack these abilities as well.

Contact with people is essential to a person's social development. But there is more to social life than the mere fact that it involves other people. We act and react to things and people in our environment as a result of the meaning we attach to them. A squirrel instinctively runs away at the sight of a dog barreling toward it. A human, however, does not have such an automatic reaction. We don't have very many instincts. We've learned from past experiences that some animals are approachable and others aren't. So we can think, "Is this dog friendly or mean? Does it want to lick my face or tear me limb from limb?" and respond accordingly. Similarly, when someone gently touches our shoulder during a conversation, we must define this gesture before we respond: Is this person being friendly or flirtatious? In short, we usually interpret events in our environment before we act.

The presence of other people may motivate you to improve your performance—for example, when the quality of your opponent makes you play the best tennis match of your life. But their presence may at other times inhibit you—as when you forget your lines in the school play because your entire family is staring at you from the audience.

Other people also have a direct and personal effect on our behavior. I'm sure you've been in situations in which other people have tried to persuade you to do things against your will or better judgment. Perhaps a friend convinced you to buy a

Kia instead of a Honda. Or perhaps someone persuaded you to steal a candy bar, cheat on your taxes, or disregard the speed limit. On occasion, such social influence can be deadly.

Stanley Milgram
Ordinary People and Cruel Acts

If a being from another planet were to read the history of human civilization, it would probably conclude that we are tremendously cruel, vicious, and evil creatures. From countless wars and crusades to ethnic genocides and terrorist attacks, from backwater lynchings and violent crimes to schoolyard bullying and extreme wrestling, humans have always shown a powerful tendency to ferociously turn on their fellow humans.

The curious thing is that people involved in such acts often show a profound capacity to deny responsibility for their actions by pointing to the influence of others: "My friend made me do it" or "I was only following orders" or "That's what the audience wants to see." Can an ordinary, decent person be pressured by another to commit an act of extreme cruelty? Or do cruel actions require inherently cruel people?

In one of the classic pieces of social research, social psychologist Stanley Milgram (1974) set out to answer this question. He wanted to know how far people would go in obeying the commands of an authority. He set up an experimental situation in which a subject, on orders from an authoritative figure, flips a switch, apparently sending a 450-volt shock to an innocent victim.

Subjects were told they would be participating in a study of the effects of punishment on learning. On a specified day each subject arrived at the laboratory with another person who, unknown to the subject, was actually an accomplice of the experimenter. Each subject was informed that he or she would play the role of "teacher," and the other person would be the "learner." The teacher was taken to a separate room that held an ominous-looking machine called a shock generator. The learner was seated in another room out of the sight of the teacher and was supposedly strapped to an electrode from the shock generator.

The teacher read a series of word pairs (for example, *blue–sky, nice–day, wild–duck*) to the learner. After reading the entire list, the teacher then read the first word of a pair (for example, *blue*) and four alternatives for the second word (for example, *sky, ink, box, lamp*). The learner had to select the correct alternative. Following directions from the experimenter, who was present in the room, the teacher flipped a switch and shocked the learner whenever he or she gave an incorrect answer. The shocks began at the lowest level, 15 volts, and increased with each subsequent incorrect answer all the way up to the 450-volt maximum.

As instructed, all the subjects shocked the learner for each incorrect response. (Remember the learner was an accomplice of the experimenter and was not actually being shocked.) As the experiment proceeded and the shocks became stronger, the teacher could hear cries from the learner. Most of the teachers, believing they were inflicting serious injury, became visibly upset and wanted to stop. The experimenter, however, ordered them to continue—and many did. Despite the tortured reactions of the victim,

65% of the subjects complied with the experimenter's demands and proceeded to the maximum, 450 volts.

Milgram repeated the study with a variety of subjects and even conducted it in different countries, including Germany and Australia. In each case about two-thirds of the subjects were willing, under orders from the experimenter, to shock to the limit. Milgram showed that out of deference to authority ordinarily nice people would do terrible things that they wouldn't do under other circumstances.

Milgram's research raises questions not only about why people would obey an unreasonable authority but also about what the rest of us think of those who do. A contemporary study of destructive obedience in the workplace—investigating such actions as dumping toxic waste in a river or manufacturing a defective automobile—found that the public perceives people as less responsible for such acts when the transgressors are believed to be conforming to company policy or obeying the orders of a supervisor than when they are thought to be acting on their own (Hamilton & Sanders, 1995).

Milgram's study has generated a tremendous amount of controversy. For three decades, this pivotal piece of research has been replicated, discussed, and debated by other social scientists (Miller, Collins, & Brief, 1995). Since the original study, other researchers have found that in small groups people sometimes collectively rebel against what they perceive as unjust authority (Gamson, Fireman, & Rytina, 1982). Nevertheless, Milgram's findings are discomforting. It would be much easier to conclude that the acts of inhumanity we read about in our daily newspapers are the products of defective or inherently evil individuals. All society would have to do then is identify, capture, and separate them from the rest of us. But if Milgram is right, if most of us could become evil given the "right" circumstances or influences, then the only thing that separates us from evildoers is our good fortune and our social environment.

Societal Influence: The Effect of Social Structure on Our Everyday Lives

Social life is more than just individual people affecting one another's lives. Society is not just a sum of its human parts; it's also the way those parts are put together, related to each other, and organized (Coulson & Riddell, 1980). Statuses, roles, groups, organizations, and institutions are the building blocks of society. Culture is the mortar that holds these blocks together. Although society is dynamic and constantly evolving, it has an underlying *macro-level* structure that persists.

Statuses and Roles

One key element of any society is its collection of **statuses**—the positions that individuals within the society occupy. When most of us hear the word *status,* we tend to associate it with prestige. You might hear someone say that an army general has more status than a corporal. But here we're talking about a status as any socially defined position that a person can occupy: cook, daughter, professor, husband, student, alcoholic, computer nerd, electrician, shoplifter, and so on. Some statuses may, in fact, be quite prestigious, such as president. But others carry very little prestige, such as gas station attendant. Some statuses require a tremendous amount of training to enter, such as physician; others, such as movie lover, require little effort at all.

We all occupy many statuses at the same time. I am a professor, but I am also a department chair, husband, son, nephew, uncle, father, brother, friend, consumer, second baseman, homeowner, neighbor, author, and runner. My behavior, of course, is dictated to a large degree by the status that is most salient at a particular point in time. When I am running, my status as husband or professor is not particularly relevant. On the other hand, if I want to run in a 10K race on my wedding anniversary, I may be in trouble!

Sociologists often distinguish between ascribed and achieved statuses. An **ascribed status** is a social position that we acquire at birth or enter involuntarily later in life. Our race, sex, ethnicity, and status as someone's child or grandchild are all ascribed statuses. As we get older, we become teenagers and, eventually, old people. These aren't positions we choose to occupy. An **achieved status**, in contrast, is a social position we take on voluntarily or acquire through our own efforts or accomplishments, such as being a student or a spouse or an engineer.

Of course, the distinction between ascribed and achieved status is not always so clear. Some people become college students not because of their own efforts but because of their parents' influence. Chances are that the religion with which you identify is the one your parents belong to. However, many people decide to change their religious membership later in life. Moreover, as we'll see later in this book, certain ascribed statuses (sex, race, ethnicity, and age) influence our access to desirable achieved statuses.

Statuses are important sociologically because they all come with a set of rights, obligations, behaviors, and duties that people occupying a certain position are expected or encouraged to perform. These expectations are referred to as **roles**. For instance, a "professor" is expected to teach students, answer their questions, be impartial, and dress appropriately. Any out-of-role behavior may be met with shock or suspicion. If a professor consistently showed up for class in a bathing suit, that would certainly violate his or her "scholarly" image and call into question his or her ability to teach.

Each person, as a result of her or his own skills, interests, and interactional experiences, defines roles differently. Students enter a class with the general expectation that their professor is going to teach them something. Each professor, however, may have a different method. Some professors are very animated, others remain stationary behind a podium. Some will not allow questions until after the lecture, others demand constant discussion and probing questions from students. Some are meticulous and organized, others scattered and absent-minded.

People engage in typical patterns of interaction based on the relationship between their roles and the roles of others. Employers are expected to interact with employees in a certain way, as are dentists with patients and salespeople with customers. In each case actions are constrained by the responsibilities and obligations associated with those particular statuses. We know, for instance, that lovers and spouses are supposed to interact with each other differently from the way acquaintances or friends are supposed to interact. In a parent–child relationship, both members are linked by certain rights, privileges, and obligations. Parents are responsible for providing their children with the basic necessities of life—food, clothing, shelter, and so forth. These expectations are so powerful that not meeting them may constitute the crime of negligence or abuse. Children, in turn, are expected to abide by their parents' wishes. Thus interactions within a relationship are functions not only of the individual personalities of the people involved but also of the role requirements associated with the statuses they occupy.

We feel the power of role expectations most clearly when we occupy two conflicting statuses simultaneously. Sociologists use the term **role conflict** to describe situations in which people encounter tension in trying to cope with the demands of incompatible roles. People may feel frustrated in their efforts to do what they feel they're supposed to do when the expectations of one role clash with the expectations of another. Someone may have an important out-of-town conference to attend (status of sociologist) on the same day her 10-year-old son is appearing as a talking pig in the school play (status of parent). Or a teenager who works hard at his job at the local ice cream shop (status of employee) is frustrated when his buddies come and expect him to give them free ice cream (status of friend).

In 1998, Barry Elton Black, the leader of a branch of the Ku Klux Klan in Pennsylvania, was arrested for burning a cross at a Klan rally. Although the owner of the property had given the Klan permission to hold the rally on his land, the burning cross was about 30 feet tall and clearly visible from a nearby state highway. Local police testified that the sight of the burning cross caused a car with black passengers to flee the area and some white residents to seek protection from sheriff's deputies (Holmes, 1998). Believing that cross burning was a form of free speech protected by the U.S. Constitution, Mr. Black contacted the American Civil Liberties Union to defend him. The attorney who agreed to represent Mr. Black was David Baugh, a black man. In doing so, Mr. Baugh had to choose between the beliefs associated with his racial status (that cross burning is an act designed to terrorize and intimidate and that one should not assist an organization committed to your destruction) and those of his occupational status (that everyone, no matter how distasteful their actions are, has a constitutionally guaranteed right to free expression). Black was originally found guilty and sentenced to five years in prison. But in 2001 the Virginia Supreme Court overturned the conviction, ruling that such acts of bigotry are a protected form of free speech. The important point for us here is the controversy raised by Mr. Baugh's decision to represent a Klan member, which illustrates the powerful effects of role conflict.

Groups

Societies are not simply composed of people occupying statuses and living in accordance with roles. Sometimes individuals form well-defined units called groups. A **group** is a set of people who interact more or less regularly with one another and who are conscious of their identity as a group. Your family, the people you regularly work with, any clubs or sports teams to which you belong are all social groups.

Groups are not just collections of people who randomly come together for some purpose. They have a structure that defines the relationships among members. Often each individual within a group occupies some named position or status—father, president, treasurer, supervisor, linebacker, and so forth. Group membership can also be a powerful force behind one's future actions and thoughts. For instance, a girl who is not a member of the popular clique at school but wants to be is likely to structure much of her daily activities around gaining entry into that group.

A **primary group** consists of a small number of members who have direct contact over a relatively long period of time. Emotional attachment is high in such groups, and members have intimate knowledge of each other's lives. Families and close friends would be considered primary groups. A **secondary group**, in contrast, is much more formal and impersonal. The group is established for a specific task, such as the production or sale of consumer goods, and members are less emotionally committed to one another. Their roles tend to be highly structured. Primary groups may form within secondary groups, as when close friendships form among co-workers, but in general secondary groups require less emotional investment than primary groups.

Like societies, groups have a reality that is more than just the sum of their members; a change in a group's membership doesn't necessarily alter its basic structure. Change in primary groups, though, perhaps through divorce or death, produces some dramatic effects on the nature and identity of the group although the group still exists.

Secondary groups, however, can endure changing membership relatively easily despite the fact that some, or even all, individuals leave and new ones enter—for example, when the senior class in a high school graduates and is replaced in the school the following year by another group of students.

Statuses related to race, gender, ethnicity, and religion can serve as important sources of a person's group identity. Although these attributes are not social groups in the strictest sense of the term, they function like groups in that members share certain characteristics and interests. For instance, members of a particular racial or ethnic group may organize into a well-defined unit to fight for a political cause. The feelings of "we-ness" or "they-ness" that are generated by such group membership can be constructive or dangerous, encouraging pride and unity in some cases, and anger, bitterness, and hatred in others.

Like statuses and roles, groups come with a set of general expectations. Actions within a group are judged according to a conventional set of ideas about how things ought to be. For example, a co-worker who always arrives late for meetings or never takes his or her turn working an undesirable shift is violating the group's expectations.

Organizations

At an even higher level of complexity exist **organizations**, networks of statuses and groups created for a specific purpose. Doctors Without Borders, Honda Motors, the International Brotherhood of Teamsters, Oxford University, Microsoft, the National Organization for Women, and the Catholic church are all examples of organizations. Organizations contain groups as well as individuals occupying clearly defined statuses.

Some of the groups within organizations are transitory, some are more permanent. For instance, a university is composed of individual classes that disband at the end of the semester as well as of more permanent groups such as the faculty, administration, secretarial staff, maintenance staff, and alumni.

Large, formal organizations are often characterized by a *hierarchical division of labor*. Each person in an organization occupies a position that has a specific set of duties and responsibilities, and those positions can be "ranked" according to power and importance. At General Motors, for instance, assembly line workers typically don't make decisions about personnel or budgetary policies, and the vice president in charge of marketing doesn't spray-paint the underbodies of newly assembled Buicks. In general, people occupy certain positions in an organization because they have the skills to do the job that is required of them. When a person can no longer meet the requirements of the job, he or she will be replaced without seriously affecting the functioning of the organization.

Organizations are a profoundly common and visible feature of everyday social life, as you'll see later in Chapter 9. Most of us cannot acquire food, get an education, pray, undergo life-saving surgery, or earn a salary without coming into contact with or becoming a member of some organization. To be a full-fledged member of modern society is to be deeply involved in some form of organizational life.

Social Institutions

When stable sets of statuses, roles, groups, and organizations form, they provide the foundation for addressing fundamental societal needs. These enduring patterns of social life are called **social institutions**. Sociologists usually think of institutions as the building blocks that organize society. They are the patterned ways of solving the problems and meeting the requirements of a particular society. Although there may be conflict over what society "needs" and how best to fulfill those needs, all societies must have some systematic way of organizing the various aspects of everyday life. Key social institutions in modern society include the family, education, politics, the economy, and religion. Some sociologists would add health care and the military to the list.

Family: All societies must have a way of replacing their members, and reproduction is essential to the survival of human society as a whole. Within the institution of family, sexual relations among adults are regulated, people are cared for, children are born and socialized, and newcomers are provided an identity—a "lineage"—that gives them a sense of belonging. Just how these activities are carried out varies from society to society, but family, whatever its form, remains the hub of social life in virtually all societies (J. H. Turner, 1972).

Education: New members of a society need to be taught what it means to be a member of that society and how to survive in it. In small, simple societies the family is the primary institution responsible for socializing new members into the culture. However, as societies become more complex, it becomes exceedingly difficult for a family to teach its members all they need to know to function within that society. Hence, most modern, complex societies have an elaborate system of schools—primary, secondary, college, professional—that not only create and disseminate knowledge and information but also train individuals for future careers and teach them their "place" in society.

Politics and law: All societies face the problem of how to preserve order, avoid chaos, and make important social decisions. The legal system provides explicit laws or rules of conduct and mechanisms for enforcing those laws, settling disputes, and changing outdated laws or creating new ones (J. H. Turner, 1972). These activities take place within a larger system of governance that allocates and acknowledges power, authority, and leadership. In a democracy the governance process includes the citizens, who have a say in who leads them; in a monarchy kings or queens can claim that their birthright entitles them to positions of leadership. In some societies the transfer of power is efficient and mannerly; in others it is violent.

Economy: From the beginning of human societies, the problems of securing enough food and protecting people from the environment have existed (J. H. Turner, 1972). Today, modern societies have systematic ways of gathering resources, converting them into goods and commodities, and distributing them to members. In addition, societies provide ways of coordinating and facilitating the operation of this massive process. For instance, banks, accounting firms, insurance firms, stock brokerages, and computer networks don't produce goods themselves but provide services that make the gathering, producing, and distributing of goods possible. To facilitate the distribution of both goods and services, economic institutions adopt a system of common currency and an identifiable mode of exchange.

Religion: All societies also face the problem of providing their members with a sense of purpose and meaning in their lives. Religion gives individuals a belief system for understanding their existence as well as a network of personal support in times of need. Although many members of a given society—and, in fact, some entire societies—may actively reject religion, it remains one of the most enduring and powerful institutions in human societies. In some societies it provides enormous comfort to people; in others, it has created irreparable divisions.

Health care: One of the profoundly universal facts of human life is that people get sick. Most modern societies have established a complex system of health care to disseminate medical treatments. Doctors, nurses, hospitals, pharmacies, drug and medical equipment manufacturers, patients, and others all play an active role in the health care institution.

Military: To deal with the possibility of attack from outside, many societies maintain an active military defense. However, militaries are used not only to defend societies but also, at times, to attack other countries in order to acquire land, resources, or power.

The social institutions within a society are highly interrelated. Debates over the state of the U.S. health care system make people aware of its links to the economy and politics. People's family experiences are intimately bound to economic, political, educational, and religious spheres. Although much dissemination of information occurs in schools, religion and politics can play a major role in what gets taught there. For instance, in 1999 the Kansas Board of Education, in response to pressure from religious organizations, voted to delete virtually any mention of evolution from the state's science curriculum (the decision was reversed two years later).

To individual members of society, social institutions appear natural and inevitable. Most of us couldn't imagine life without a family. Nor could most of us fathom what society would be like without a stable system of government, a common currency, or schools to educate our children. It is very easy, then, to think that institutions exist independently of people.

We each have a role to play, however, in maintaining or changing social institutions. For instance, in 1999 people in 11 European nations voted to adopt a common form of currency, the euro. As a result, travel and trade between these countries, as well as the options available to their individual workers and consumers, will surely take on a different look in the future. Although the effects of these changes will be felt at the organizational and institutional level, they are ultimately initiated, implemented, and, most importantly, experienced by individual people.

Culture

The most ubiquitous and pervasive element of society is **culture**, which consists of the language, values, beliefs, rules, behaviors, and physical artifacts of a society. Think of it as a society's "personality." Culture gives us codes of conduct—the proper, acceptable ways of doing things. We usually don't think twice about it, yet it colors everything we experience.

Culture is particularly apparent when someone questions or violates it. Those who do not believe what the majority believes, value what the majority values, or obey the same rules the majority obeys are likely to experience punishment, psychiatric attention, or social ostracism. I discuss the power of culture in more detail in Chapter 4, but here we should look at two key aspects of culture that are thoroughly implicated in the workings of social structure and social influence: values and norms.

Values. Perhaps no word in the English language carries more baggage than *values.* Terms such as *moral values, traditional values,* and *homespun American values* are bandied about unthinkingly. Sociologically speaking, a **value** is a standard of judgment by which people decide on desirable goals and outcomes (Hewitt & Hewitt, 1986). Values represent general criteria on which our lives and the lives of others can be judged. They justify the social rules that determine how we ought to behave. For instance, laws against murder clearly reflect the value we place on human life.

Different societies emphasize different values. Success, independence, and individual achievement are seen as important values in U.S. society. In other societies, such as Japan, people are more likely to value group obligation and loyalty to family.

Values within a society sometimes come into conflict. The value of privacy ("stay out of other people's business") and the value of generosity ("help others in need") may clash when we are trying to decide whether to help someone who appears to need assistance. Similarly, although the value of cooperation is held in high esteem in contemporary U.S. society, when someone is taking a final exam in a sociology class cooperation is likely to be defined as cheating. When the key values that characterize a particular social institution come into conflict, the result may be widespread legal and moral uncertainty among individuals.

Micro-Macro Connection
Parental Rights versus Children's Welfare

One such conflict involves the value of family privacy. Contemporary U.S. life is built on the assumption that what a family does in the privacy of its home is or at least should be its own business. Family life, many people believe, is best left to family members, not the neighbors, the government, the courts, or other public agencies. Consequently, American families are endowed with significant autonomy—the right to make decisions about their future or about treatment of their members (see Chapter 8).

The value of privacy has not always characterized American families. Before the 19th century people didn't feel at all uncomfortable about entering others' homes and telling them what to wear or how to treat their children. The development of the ideal of family privacy and autonomy emerged with the separation of home and work and the growth of cities during the late 19th century (Parsons, 1971). Innovations in the amenities available within the home—indoor plumbing, refrigerators, telephones, radios, televisions, central heating and air conditioning, backyard swimming pools, video players, and computers—have all increased the privacy and isolation of American households. Our need to leave home for entertainment, goods, or services has been considerably reduced. Air conditioners, for instance, allow us to spend hot, stuffy summer evenings inside our own homes instead of on the front porch or the local ice cream parlor. Today, with the Internet and home shopping networks, a family can purchase all it needs without ever leaving home. The institution of family has become increasingly self-contained and private.

But the value of family privacy has always varied along social class lines. In poor households, dwellings are smaller and more crowded than more affluent homes, making privacy more difficult to obtain. Thin walls separating cramped apartments hide few secrets. Mandatory inspections by welfare caseworkers and housing authorities further diminish privacy. And poor families must often use public facilities (health clinics, laundromats, public transportation, and so on) to carry out the day-to-day tasks that wealthier families can carry out privately.

The large-scale commitment to the value of family privacy has not been without its problems. For instance, the value we place on the welfare of children has come into direct conflict with the value of family privacy. At what point should a state agency intervene and violate the privacy of the family to protect the welfare of a child? Does it better serve society's interests to protect family privacy or to protect children?

Parents never have had complete freedom to do as they wish with their children. We're horrified at the thought of a parent beating his or her child to the point of injury or death. But we're equally horrified, it seems, at the thought of the state intruding on parents' right to treat their children as they see fit. The infliction of severe physical punishment on children by their parents has become as much an issue of parents' rights, as it is an issue of child welfare. In the United States, parents have the legal right to direct the upbringing of their children, to determine the care they receive, and to use physical means to control their children's behavior. From a sociological perspective, injuring children is simply the extreme outcome of the widely practiced and accepted belief that parents have the right to punish their children.

The Parental Rights and Responsibilities Bill, introduced in Congress in 1996, would have, if enacted, forbidden state and local governments from "interfering with or usurping the right of a parent" to direct the upbringing of a child. The bill would have allowed parents to sue teachers, librarians, school counselors, police officers, and social workers for interfering with parents' ability to control the education, health, discipline, and religious teaching of their children. The bill never came to the floor of Congress. Nevertheless, it and similar bills introduced in several states signal a growing concern among some parents that their autonomous ability to raise their children is being eroded.

Indeed, the state has on many occasions violated the privacy of a family when that family's religious or cultural beliefs conflicted with the values of the larger society. For instance, in 1995 an Anderson, Indiana, couple who postponed medical treatment for their 6-year-old son because of their religious beliefs were charged with homicide and neglect of a dependent when he died of streptococcus pneumonia meningitis (Labalme, 1995). In 1996, the U.S. Supreme Court let stand a ruling by the Minnesota Court of Appeals that awarded $1.5 million to the father of an 11-year-old boy who died after his mother, stepfather, and two Christian Science practitioners tried to use prayer to heal his diabetes. In its ruling, the Court stated, "Although one is free to believe what one will, religious freedom ends when one's conduct offends the law by, for example, endangering a child's life" (Greenhouse, 1996, p. A12).

Ironically, concern over increases in juvenile violence has led some cities and states to enact laws that make parents more responsible for disciplining their children (Applebome, 1996b). In West Virginia, for example, parents of a child caught defacing a public building can be liable for up to $5,000 in fines. If their child associates with a convicted felon, drug dealer, or members of a street gang, Louisiana parents can be found guilty of "improper supervision of a minor" and fined up to $1,000 and imprisoned for up to 6 months.

Sometimes state intervention into the private affairs of families is influenced by broader political concerns. Consider, for example, the highly-publicized case of the 6-year-old Cuban boy Elián Gonzalez. In 1999, Elián and his mother were attempting to flee Cuba for the United States when the boat they were on capsized, drowning the mother. Elián was taken in by relatives living in Florida. Although his father in Cuba wanted him returned, Elián's U.S. relatives felt he would be better off living in the democratic United States than in communist Cuba and kept him here despite court orders to relinquish him. To these relatives, the desire to prevent Elián from being raised under communism outweighed the parental rights of his father. Five months later, U.S. officials finally removed Elián at gunpoint from his uncle's home in Miami and returned him to his father. Although the images of armed officials pointing weapons at a frightened boy were upsetting, most U.S. citizens thought the state did the right thing by stepping in to reunite the boy with his father.

All the cases described here illustrate the profound effects of cultural and political values on the everyday lives of individuals. Situations such as these pit the privacy and autonomy of families against society's institutional responsibility to protect children and create new citizens.

Norms. **Norms** are culturally defined rules of conduct. They specify what people should do and how they should pursue values. They tell us what is proper or necessary behavior within particular roles, groups, organizations, and institutions. Thousands of norms guide the minute and the grand details of our lives, from the classroom to the dining room to the bedroom, from how we should act in elevators to how we should address our boss.

Norms make our interactions with others reasonably predictable. Americans expect that when they extend a hand to another person, that person will grasp it and a handshake will follow. They would be shocked if they held out their hand and the other person grabbed it and wouldn't let go, or spit on it. In contrast, people in some societies commonly embrace or kiss each other's cheek as a form of greeting, even when involved in a formal business relationship. A hearty handshake in those societies might be interpreted as an insult. In Thailand, people greet each other by placing the palms of their hands together in front of their bodies and slightly bowing their heads. This greeting is governed by strict norms. Slight differences in the placement of one's hands reflects the social position of the other person—the higher the hands, the higher the position of the person being greeted. You can see, then, that norms serve as the fundamental building blocks of social order. Without them, "living with others" in a relatively harmonious way would be utterly impossible (see Chapter 4).

Social Structure in Global Context

A discussion of social structure would not be complete without acknowledging the fact that statuses, roles, groups, organizations, social institutions, and culture are sometimes influenced by broad societal and historical forces in today's world. One broad societal force with deep implications for contemporary society is **globalization**, the process through which people's lives all around the world become increasingly interconnected—economically, politically, environmentally, and culturally (see Chapter 9 for more detail).

For instance, international financial institutions and foreign governments often provide money to support the building of hydroelectric dams in poor countries. According to the World Commission on Dams, 1,600 such dams are currently under construction in 40 countries (Bald, 2000). These projects are meant to provide additional energy sources in areas where energy is dangerously deficient. However, they frequently transform individual lives, social institutions, and indigenous cultures in the process. A dam along the Moon River in Thailand destroyed forests that for centuries were villagers' free source of food, firewood, and herbal remedies. With the dam flooding, local farmers not only lost their farmland but also lost the value of their knowledge of farming methods that had developed over centuries to adapt to the ebb and flow of the river. A massive system of 22 dams along the Euphrates River in southern Turkey will displace 100,000 people with similar expertise and living patterns and submerge countless cultural treasures in an area known worldwide as "the cradle of civilization." Neither of these dams would have been built without the funding and political clout of global organizations and foreign corporations.

Cultures have rarely been completely isolated from outside influence, because throughout human history people have been moving, spreading goods and ideas. What is different today, though, is the speed and scope of these changes. Overnight mail service and direct long-distance telephone dialing have increased the velocity of cross-national interaction. Advances in transportation technology have made international trade more cost effective and international travel more accessible to ordinary citizens. And the Internet has given people around the world instantaneous access to the cultural artifacts and ideals of other societies. "It took television 13 years to acquire 50 million users; the Internet took only five" (Zwingle, 1999, p. 12).

To some sociologists, the outcome of today's globalization will be nothing short of a single "global culture," where traditional geographic, political, economic, and cultural boundaries eventually become obsolete (Featherstone, 1990).

> Once I started looking for them, these moments were everywhere: That I should be sitting in a coffee shop in London drinking Italian espresso served by an Algerian waiter to the strains of the Beach Boys singing "I wish they all could be California girls. . . ." Today we are in the throes of a worldwide reformation of cultures, a tectonic shift of habits and dreams called . . . "globalization." (Zwingle, 1999, p. 12)

Clearly, societies are more interdependent than ever, and that interdependence matters for individual lives. Sometimes these effects are positive. Pharmaceutical breakthroughs in the United States, for instance, can save lives around the world. Other times global influence can have disastrous consequences. The establishment of a toy factory in Southeast Asia or a clothing factory in Mexico may mean the loss of hundreds of manufacturing jobs in Kentucky or California.

In short, it is becoming increasingly difficult, if not impossible, to consider ourselves members of a single society. We are all citizens of a world community. Many of today's most pressing societal problems—widespread environmental devastation, large- and small-scale wars, economic crises, and so on—are a function of globalization. But so are expanding opportunities to learn about other societies and to learn from them.

Three Perspectives on Social Order

A society is a complex system, much like a living organism. Just as the heart, lungs, and liver work together to keep an animal alive, so, too, do all the elements of a society's structure work together to keep society alive. All societies require certain things to survive. They must ensure that the goods and services people need are produced and distributed; they must provide ways of dealing with conflicts between individuals; they must provide ways to ensure that individuals are made a part of the existing culture. The question of what holds all these elements of society together and how they combine to create social order has concerned sociologists for many years. Sociologists use three major theoretical orientations to address this question: the structural-functionalist perspective, the conflict perspective, and symbolic interactionism.

The Structural-Functionalist Perspective

According to sociologists Talcott Parsons and Neil Smelser (1956), two theorists typically associated with the structural-functionalist perspective, social institutions play a key role in keeping a society alive and stable. Institutions allow societies to attain their goals, adapt to a changing environment, reduce tension, and recruit individuals into social roles. Economic institutions, for instance, allow adaptation to dwindling supplies of natural resources or to competition from other societies. The family controls and regulates reproduction. Likewise, educational institutions train people for the future statuses they will have to fill to keep society going. Religions help maintain the existence of society by reaffirming people's values and maintaining social ties among people (Durkheim, 1915/1954).

Sociologist Robert Merton (1957) distinguishes between manifest and latent societal functions. **Manifest functions** are the intended, obvious consequences of activities designed to help some part of the social system. For instance, the manifest function of going to college is to get an education and acquire the credentials necessary to establish a career. **Latent functions** are the *unintended*, sometimes unrecognized, consequences of actions that coincidentally help the system. The latent function of going to college is to meet people and establish close, enduring friendships. In addition, college teaches students how to live on their own, away from their parents. It also provides important lessons in negotiating the intricacies of large bureaucracies—registering for classes, filling out forms, learning important school policies—so that students figure out how to "get things done" in an organization. These latent lessons will certainly help students who enter the equally large and bureaucratic world of work after they graduate (Galles, 1989).

From the structural-functionalist perspective, if an aspect of social life does not contribute to society's survival—that is, if it is *dys*functional—it will eventually disappear. Things that persist, even if they seem to be disruptive, must persist because they contribute somehow to the survival of society. Take prostitution, for example. A practice so widely condemned and punished would appear to be dysfunctional for society. But prostitution has existed since human civilization began. Structural-functionalists suggest that prostitution satisfies sexual needs that may not be met through more socially acceptable means, such as marriage. Customers can have their physical desires satisfied without having to establish the sort of emotional attachment to another person that would destroy a preexisting marriage, harm the institution of the family, and ultimately threaten the entire society (K. Davis, 1937).

The Conflict Perspective

Structural-functionalism was the dominant theoretical tradition in sociology for most of the 20th century, and it still shapes sociological thinking to a certain degree. But it has been criticized for accepting existing social arrangements without examining how they might exploit or otherwise disadvantage certain groups or individuals within the society. The conflict perspective addresses this deficiency by viewing the structure of society as a source of inequality, which always benefits some groups at the expense of other groups.

Hence conflict sociologists are likely to see society not in terms of stability and acceptance but in terms of conflict and struggle. They focus not on how all the elements of society contribute to its smooth operation and continued existence but on how these elements promote divisions and inequalities. Social order arises not from the societal pursuit of harmony but from dominance and coercion. The family, government, religion, and other institutions foster and legitimate the power and privilege of some individuals or groups at the expense of others.

Karl Marx, perhaps the most famous conflict theorist, focused exclusively on economic arrangements. He argued that all human societies are structured around the ways they produce the goods that people need to live. The individuals or groups who control the means of production—land in an agricultural society, factories in an industrial society, computer networks and information in a postindustrial society—have the power to create and maintain social institutions that serve their interests. Hence, economic, political, and educational systems in a modern society support the interests of those who control the wealth (see Chapter 10).

Marx believed that conflict between the "haves" and the "have-nots" is inevitable and creates a situation in which those in power must enforce social order. He said this conflict is not caused by greedy, exploitative individuals; rather, it is a by-product of a system in which those who benefit from inequality are thus motivated to act in ways that maintain it.

Contemporary conflict sociologists are interested in various sources of conflict and inequality. For instance, feminist theorists focus on gender as the most important source of conflict and inequality in social life. Compared with men, women in nearly every contemporary society have less power, influence, and opportunity. In families, women have traditionally been encouraged to perform unpaid household labor and child care duties whereas men have been free to devote their energy and attention to earning money and power in the economic marketplace. Women's lower wages when they do work outside the home are often justified by the assumption that their paid labor is secondary to that of their husbands. But as women in many societies seek equality in education, politics, career, marriage, and other areas of social life, their activities inevitably affect social institutions (see Chapter 12 for more details). Feminist theory helps us understand the difficulties men and women face in their everyday lives as they experience the changes taking place in society.

Because this perspective focuses so much on conflict, it tends to downplay or overlook the elements of society that different groups and individuals share. In addition, its emphasis on inequality has led some critics to argue that it is a perspective motivated by a particular political agenda and not the objective pursuit of knowledge.

Symbolic Interactionism

The structural-functionalist and the conflict perspectives differ in their assumptions about the nature of society, yet both analyze society mostly at the *macro-*, or structural, level, focusing on societal patterns and the consequences they produce. In contrast, symbolic interactionism attempts to understand society and social structure through an examination of the *micro*-level, personal, day-to-day interactions of people as individuals, pairs, or groups.

These forms of interaction take place within a world of symbolic communication. The symbols we use—language, gestures, posture, and so on—are influenced by the larger context of a group or society (see Chapter 5). A society would be utterly unmanageable if the people in it didn't share a language or agree on what certain gestures meant. But the agreement is never complete. When we interact with others, we constantly attempt to interpret what they mean and what they're up to. Most human behavior, then, is determined not by the objective facts of a given situation but by the subjective meanings people attach to the facts (Weber, 1947). A gentle pat on the cheek means one thing if it comes from someone with whom you are romantically involved but something quite different if it comes from your mother or your boss.

Society, therefore, is not a structure that exists independent of human action. It emerges from the countless symbolic interactions that occur each day between individuals. Each time I refer to "U.S. society" or "the global economy" or "the Newman family" in my casual conversations with others, I am doing my part to reinforce the notion that these are real things. By examining how and why we interact with others, symbolic interactionism reveals how the everyday experiences of people help to construct and maintain social institutions and, ultimately, society itself.

This perspective helps us remember that for all its structural elements, society is, in the end, people interacting with one another. But by highlighting micro-level experiences, symbolic interactionism runs the risk of ignoring large social patterns and structures.

You can see that each of these perspectives has its advantages and shortcomings. Each is helpful in answering particular types of questions. For instance, symbolic interactionism is helpful in explaining how individuals construct meaning to make sense out of their social surroundings. Structural-functionalism is useful in showing us how and why large, macro-level structures, such as organizations and institutions, develop. And the conflict perspective sheds light on the various sources of social inequality that exist in this and other societies. At times the perspectives complement one another; at other times they contradict one another. In subsequent chapters, I use all three to examine the relationship between the individual and society.

CONCLUSION

Living with others, within a social structure, influences many aspects of our everyday lives. But we must be cautious not to overstate the case. Although the fundamental elements of society are not merely the direct expressions of the personalities of individuals, we must also remember that people are more than "robots programmed by social structure" (Swanson, 1992).

The lesson I want you to take from this chapter—and, in fact, from this book—is that the relationship between the individual and society is a reciprocal one. One cannot be understood without accounting for the other. Yes, "society" touches our lives in intimate, important, and sometimes not altogether obvious ways. And yes, this influence is often beyond our immediate control. But society is not simply a "forbidding prison" that mechanically determines who we are and what we do (P. L. Berger, 1963). We as individuals can affect the very social structure that affects us. We can modify role expectations, change norms, create or destroy organizations, revolutionize institutions, and even alter the path of world history.

YOUR TURN

Alcohol occupies an important but problematic place in many societies. We decry its evils, yet we are encouraged to turn to it in times of celebration, despair, disappointment, anger, and worry.

Behavior "under the influence" is a biological consequence of the presence of alcohol in the body. Among the physical effects are vomiting, hangovers, and liver damage. When a person's blood alcohol level reaches a certain point, that person will have trouble walking and talking; at a higher level he or she will pass out.

But is the social behavior we see in drunken people reducible to a chemical reaction in the body? The traditional explanation for drunken behavior is that the chemical properties of alcohol do something to the brain that reduces inhibitions. If this were true, though, drunken behavior would look the same everywhere. The fact is, social behavior under the influence of alcohol can vary from culture to culture. The way people handle themselves when drunk "is determined not by alcohol's toxic assault on the seat of moral judgment, conscience, or the like, but by what their society makes of and imparts to them concerning the state of drunkenness" (MacAndrew & Edgerton, 1969, p. 165).

Ask people who grew up in a culture different from yours (for example, students who grew up in a different country or in a different socioeconomic class or geographic region) how people behaved when drunk. Do these behaviors differ from those you've observed? Have them describe their first drunken experience. Are there similarities or differences in how people are introduced to alcohol?

Also ask people from different sexes, races, ethnic groups, and ages the same questions. Are there variations in the "drunken experience" within a society? What do these differences illustrate about the norms and values of these different groups? You might also ask some young children to describe how drunk people act. Are there any similarities in the images they have of drunkenness? Do you consider their ideas about drunkenness accurate? Where do you think their ideas about alcohol come from?

Use the results of these interviews to explain the role of social and societal influence on people's personal lives. Do you think your conclusions can be expanded to other private phenomena, such as sexual activity or religious experiences? Why or why not?

CHAPTER HIGHLIGHTS

- Although society exists as an objective fact, it is also created, reaffirmed, and altered through the day-to-day interactions of the very people it influences and controls.

- Humans are social beings. We look to others to help define and interpret particular situations. Other people can influence what we see, feel, think, and do.

- Society consists of socially recognizable combinations of individuals—relationships, groups, and organizations—as well as the products of human action—statuses, roles, culture, institutions, and broad societal forces such as globalization.

- There are three major sociological perspectives. The structural-functionalist perspective focuses on the way various parts of society are structured and interrelated to maintain stability and order. The conflict perspective emphasizes how the various elements of society promote inequality and conflict among groups of people. Symbolic interactionism attempts to understand society and social structure through the interactions of people and the ways in which they subjectively define their worlds.

KEY TERMS

achieved status Social position acquired through our own efforts or accomplishments or taken on voluntarily

ascribed status Social position acquired at birth or taken on involuntarily later in life

culture Language, values, beliefs, rules, behaviors, and artifacts that characterize a society

globalization The process through which people's lives all around the world are economically, politically, environmentally, and culturally interconnected

group Set of people who interact more or less regularly and who are conscious of their identity as a unit

latent function Unintended, unrecognized consequences of activities that help some part of the social system

manifest function Intended, obvious consequences of activities designed to help some part of the social system

norm Culturally defined standard or rule of conduct

organization Large, complex network of positions, created for a specific purpose and characterized by a hierarchical division of labor

primary group Collection of individuals who are together over a relatively long period, whose members have direct contact with and feel emotional attachment to one another

role Set of expectations—rights, obligations, behaviors, duties—associated with a particular status

role conflict Frustration people feel when the demands of one role they are expected to fulfill clash with the demands of another role

secondary group Relatively impersonal collection of individuals that is established to perform a specific task

social institution Stable set of roles, statuses, groups, and organizations—such as the institution of education, family, politics, religion, health care, or the economy—that provides a foundation for behavior in some major area of social life

society Population of people living in the same geographic area who share a culture and a common identity and whose members fall under the same political authority

status Named social position that people can occupy

value Standard of judgment by which people decide on desirable goals and outcomes

The Old Ball Game

Douglas Harper

To watch a professional baseball game is to experience the world both as an individual and as a member of a larger social structure. A baseball game offers a good example of how individuals participate in creating social life and, conversely, how social structure shapes our everyday experience.

Consider two forms of the baseball audience experience: attending a game in a stadium and viewing the game on television. If we attend a game in person, we become actively involved in constructing the "audience experience." We watch carefully to keep track of the players and the progress of the game; perhaps we keep inning-by-inning records, using the arcane symbols of scoring. The actions of all the players, all the other members of the crowd, and all the stadium personnel (hot dog vendors,

● In what sociologists might call a macro-level, structural view of baseball, we can see the entire game and see the players in relationship to one another. We can observe the setting of the game (a park) and many of the elements (such as fans and advertisements) that give the game meaning in a larger context. But this photograph does not provide a complete view of the structural characteristics of the game of baseball, of course. It would be impossible to show in a single photograph how baseball's media and financial concerns extend into the entire society and even cross national borders.

security guards, announcers, and so on) become part of our experience of the game. We also take part in repeated events—called *rituals*—that define the audience experience in the park. Some rituals are specific to an individual setting; for example, at Yankee Stadium the grounds-keepers groom the infield while marching in unison to the song "YMCA." Other rituals are universal: Halfway through the seventh inning, at all professional baseball games in the United States, the crowd stands and sings "Take Me Out to the Ball Game." Like all rituals, the song connects the individual with the history of baseball and with all fans who have attended ball games before. These rituals help define what it means to be an audience and contribute to the overall experience of the game.

If we watch the game on television, however, TV personalities take over much of the task of constructing the social reality of the game. We are directed to notice one set of events rather than another; we are told "how to be an audi-ence." The photographic style used to broadcast the game (especially the close-up) emphasizes the individual players and their accomplish-ments. Thus in watching baseball on TV, we do not get as broad a view of the game experience or even see the way that several players partici-pate on a given play. Because the televised event emphasizes the individual player-as-hero, we often overlook the social context—namely, the team—that gives his heroic actions meaning. The home run glorifies the batter and is exciting to witness, but the sacrifice fly may allow a run to score that is just as meaningful to the team.

For this essay, I photographed baseball games in several parks. I tried to see through the camera lens as a sociologist rather than a typical spectator. I studied how the symbols found in baseball parks suggest mythical histories of larger-than-life heroes and looked at aspects of the fan experience that would not normally be photographed by a sports photographer.

● This photograph was taken from roughly the same vantage point as the previous photo but with a different camera lens (and in a different ballpark). The perspectives created by these lenses (and the one in the next photo as well) may be viewed as metaphors for different sociological perspectives. If the previous photo suggested a structural, macro level of analysis, this one suggests a middle range. Middle-range theory seeks explanation of social phenomena at a higher order than person-to-person interaction but lower than the whole system. Typical units of analysis are statuses, roles, and norms.

Here we can see the coordination of several social statuses, including first baseman, baserunner from the opposing team, first base coach who will guide that runner's actions, and two umpires. The roles that these people play in the game are aligned with the roles of people occupying the statuses of pitcher, batter, and catcher. The positions of the players are determined by norms, or rules of behavior.

● At what sociologists call a micro level of analysis, we can focus on the creation and coordination of social interaction. In this photo several individuals carefully coordinate their actions, hoping to achieve different ends. The umpire, symbol of social control, defines actions as good or bad, successful or unsuccessful. The batter wants to drive the approaching ball into the outfield; the catcher wants the ball in his mitt after it crosses the strike zone. Their interactions with each other (and with the pitcher, who is not in the picture) involve actions, gestures, and words.

The game of baseball, seen from this perspective, consists of individuals acting on their interpretations of the actions of others. These interpretations require that people agree on the meaning of certain symbols, including words, gestures, and material objects such as uniforms. Even an argument between the umpire and a player is socially choreographed: Only certain words, gestures, and forms of touch are allowed.

Symbols of Heroism

To be a baseball fan is to internalize messages about the history of the game. Symbols communicate some of this history.

● In Baltimore the areas just outside the ballpark are a fan's delight, featuring pedestrian-friendly zones, ready food and drink, and symbols of Oriole lore. The oversized number sculptures you see here refer to team players so great that their numbers were "retired." No players may use them again. Obviously having your number retired is a great honor, because all teams have only the numbers 00 to 99 to assign to players.

● For Pittsburgh Pirates fans, few if any heroes can compare to Roberto Clemente, who is poised, larger than life, outside the Pirates' stadium. Outside the Metrodome, home of the Minnesota Twins, the sculptures are silhouetted abstractions. Perhaps the Twins' heroes, such as Kirby Puckett, are not long enough departed from the game to justify a full-blown, realistic monument. (Note also the young fan wearing a jersey representing Paul Molitor, a brief hero for the Twins.) Inside New York's Yankee Stadium, one of the great old stadiums, the greatest player of all time, Babe Ruth, needs only a photograph and a neon sign to evoke a heroic tradition.

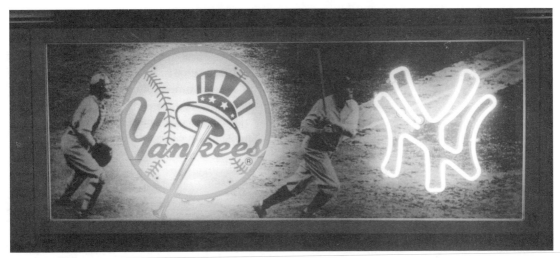

● Fans also claim symbols as part of their own identity. Wearing a copy of the uniform of a hero is certainly a common form of fan behavior. But here we see an unusual degree of fan dedication: a tattoo indicating loyalty to the game of baseball itself.

The Fan Experience

Macro-level, structural aspects of professional baseball have a significant effect on the fan experience. Just consider its history: Baseball was originally played in a narrow band of cities, such as New York, Pittsburgh, Chicago, and St. Louis. But it soon expanded to both the north and the south, to such cities as Minneapolis, Montreal, and Tampa, and the season lengthened to accommodate a three-step playoff and World Series schedule. Because of more extreme weather conditions, it became difficult to play the game outdoors all season long in some areas. The solution was to build many stadiums with permanent or retracting roofs and to replace the grass field with plastic carpet. The new parks, built from the mid-1960s through the 1980s, also accommodated football. However, these dual-purpose parks have been a failure. Most of these stadiums have been torn down and replaced or are in the process of being replaced.

What is the sociological significance of this failed experiment? First, sociologists have noted that leisure activities and sports emerge natu-rally from material environments and culture. Baseball first developed where the seasons invited outside activities from April to October. And because baseball is leisurely, it is a perfect summer event. Where it first emerged, baseball took on the rhythm of a daily activity between the beginning of spring and the end of fall. The baseball season announced summer and its promise and ended as the fall reached its peak. When baseball was removed from these meteo-rological and calendrical dimensions, it lost its natural pace and meaning. It is certainly less enjoyable to sit outside and watch a game in a steam bath summer of the southern United States or the deep freeze of a northern fall day.

The extension of baseball into regions where it cannot easily be played, and the creation of stadiums to fit both baseball and football, can also be seen as an example of something that the 19th-century sociologist Max Weber warned us about: focusing so much on rationality and efficiency that we lose sight of our real goals. It may seem quite practical to build a facility for both baseball and football and

● The walkway toward the Hubert H. Humphrey Metrodome in Minneapolis, home of the Minnesota Twins, is perhaps the most failed park currently operating in baseball. On beautiful fall afternoons in the 2000 season, some games had fewer than 1,000 fans in attendance.

to cover a facility to keep out the weather. But the main point of baseball—a pleasurable fan experience—is diminished by these decisions. Similarly, plastic carpet may be more economically rational than grass, but it is ugly and changes the way the game is played.

Finally, the extension of major league baseball to regions with extreme climates is a clear attempt to transform a leisure activity into an economic enterprise. Major league baseball

(and other national-level sports) are huge financial concerns. They will likely continue to expand to new regions as long as they can be financially viable, whether this expansion makes sense for the game or for fans.

So much for some macro-level observations about professional baseball. Other details of the game point up more individual, micro-level aspects of the fan experience.

● Most teams draw fans to the "sports experience" by staging events such as live music before the games. Here a fan dances with an even younger fan, on whom the typical barrage of beer advertising is wasted.

● For an hour before the game, fans are allowed to enter the seating area closest to the field of play, to temporarily sit where the wealthy patrons sit. (These most desirable seats are increasingly owned by corporations and given as favors to business partners.) Fans who can talk their way past the ushers who guard the passageway to the hitting area call greetings and good wishes to their heroes. The players seldom look up as they trot back and forth to the dugout, but sometimes a player will toss a ball to a fan or meander to a designated area where the fan and player can intersect—the end of the dugout—to sign autographs.

Being part of the crowd is exhilarating as well as nerve racking. In sociological terms, it is an example of mass behavior, which offers fascinating insights into the power of group expectations and norms. As I mentioned earlier, ritual is also an important element of the fan experience. Among the formal rituals of all games are the singing of the National Anthem at the beginning of the game and the "seventh-inning stretch," where all fans stand and rock back and forth while singing "Take Me Out to the Ball Game." Like all rituals, these must be performed correctly. All men are instructed to remove their hats before singing the National Anthem, and everyone must stand. But there is some flexibility in the ritual as well: At Camden Yards, for example, home of the Baltimore Orioles, the crowd yells out a resounding "O" at the beginning of the phrase: "Oh say, does that star-spangled banner yet wave . . ." It was startling to a visiting fan until I realized that the faithful were calling out for their home team, the Orioles.

● The last game at Three Rivers Stadium, Pittsburgh, October 2000, drew a sold-out crowd of 54,000. Fans gathered to say good-bye to a stadium that was still functional but about to be torn down to be replaced with, ironically, a park resembling the park that Three Rivers replaced in 1970. This photograph shows how thousands upon thousands of people can crowd together to partake of an experience where order is maintained through well-understood expectations and norms.

● In the 1970s fans began a strange ritual called "the wave." To start such a wave, a group of fans stand simultaneously and throw their hands into the air. If they are successful, the wave moves around the stadium as adjoining sections take their turn. One watches the wave move around the stadium and then engulf one's own section. Here young girls are trying unsuccessfully to initiate a wave. A more compelling ritual is the singing of "Take Me Out to the Ball Game" during the seventh-inning stretch. Projecting the words of the song onto a screen, as at Camden Yards, home of the Baltimore Orioles, gives the ritual an "official" imprint that encourages participation.

PART II
The Construction of Self and Society

Part II examines the architecture of individual identities and of society: how reality and truth are constructed; how social order is created and maintained; how culture and history influence our personal experiences; how societal values, ideals, and norms are instilled; and how we acquire our sense of self. The tactical and strategic ways in which we present images of ourselves to others are also addressed. You will see how we define "acceptable" behavior and how we respond to those who "break the rules." The section closes with a look into how we form relationships and interact within small, intimate groups.

3 Building Reality: The Social Construction of Knowledge

The year was 1897. Eight-year-old Virginia O'Hanlon became upset when her friends told her that there was no Santa Claus. Her father encouraged her to write a letter to the *New York Sun* to find out the truth. The editor's reply—which included the now famous phrase "Yes, Virginia, there is a Santa Claus!"—has become a classic piece of American folklore. "Nobody sees Santa Claus," the editor wrote, "but that is no sign that there is no Santa Claus. The most real things in the world are those that neither children nor men [sic] can see" ("Is There a Santa Claus?" 1897).

In his book *Encounters with the Archdruid*, John McPhee (1971) examines the life and ideas of David Brower, one of the most successful and energetic environmentalists in the United States. McPhee recalls a lecture in which Brower claimed that the United States has 6% of the world's population and uses 60% of the world's resources and that only 1% of Americans use 60% of those resources. Afterward McPhee asked Brower where he got these interesting statistics:

> Brower said the figures had been worked out in the head of a friend of his from data assembled "to the best of his recollection." . . . [He] assured me that figures in themselves are merely indices. *What matters is that they feel right* [emphasis added]. Brower feels things. (p. 86)

What do these two very different examples have in common? Both reflect the fickle nature of "truth" and "reality." Young Virginia was encouraged to believe in the reality of something she could and would never perceive with her senses. She certainly learned a different sort of truth about Santa Claus when she got older, but the editor urged the young Virginia to take on faith that Santa Claus, or at least the idea of Santa Claus, exists despite the lack of objective proof. That sort of advice persists. A survey of 200 child psychologists around the United States found that 91% of them advised parents not to tell their young children the truth when asked about the existence of Santa Claus (cited in Stryker, 1997).

Likewise, David Brower is urging people to believe in something that doesn't need to be seen. What's important is that the information "feels right," that it helps one's cause even if it is not based on hard evidence.

Such precarious uses of truth might appear foolish or deceitful. Yet much of our everyday knowledge is based on accepting as real the existence of things that can't be seen, touched, or proved— "the world taken-for-granted" (P. L. Berger, 1963, p. 147). Like Virginia, we learn to accept the existence of things such as electrons, the ozone layer, black holes, love, and God, even though we cannot see them. And like David Brower, we learn to believe and use facts and figures provided by "experts" as long as they sound right or support our interests. I would guess that you are more likely to trust the predictions of a meteorologist about tomorrow's weather than predictions made by a fortune teller.

How do we come to know what we know? How do we learn what is real and what isn't? In this chapter I examine how sociologists discover truths about human life. But to provide the appropriate context, I must first present a sociological perspective on the nature of reality. How do individuals construct their realities? How do societal forces influence the process?

Understanding the Social Construction of Reality

In the previous chapter you learned that the elements of society are human creations that provide structure to our everyday lives. They also give us a distinctive lens through which we perceive the world. For example, because of their respective occupational training and the different social spheres they occupy, an architect, a real estate agent, a police officer, and a firefighter can each look at the same building and see different things: "a beautiful example of Victorian architecture," "a moderately priced fixer-upper," "a target of opportunity for a thief," or "a fire hazard."

What we know to be true or real is always a product of the culture and historical period in which we exist. In some cultures the existence of spirits, witches, and demons is a taken-for-granted part of everyday reality that others might easily dismiss as "unrealistic." It takes an exercise of the sociological imagination, however, to see that what we ourselves "know" to be true today—the laws of nature, the causes and treatments of certain diseases, and so forth—may not be true for everyone everywhere or may be replaced by different truths tomorrow (Babbie, 1986). To some cultures, our faith in the curative powers of little pills—without the intervention of spiritual forces—might seem naïve. Or consider how ideas about reality change over time. In 1900 a doctor might have told a patient with asthma to go to the local tobacconist for a cigarette. An alcoholic might have been prescribed opium. People with colds may have been told to inhale formaldehyde. Tuberculosis was treated with strychnine; diabetics received a dose of arsenic (Zuger, 1999). Quite possibly people 100 years from now will look back at the beginning of the 21st century and regard some of our taken-for-granted truths as mistaken, misguided, or downright laughable.

The process through which facts, knowledge, truth, and so on are discovered, made known, reaffirmed, and altered by the members of a society is called the **social**

construction of reality (P. L. Berger & Luckmann, 1966). This construction starts with the simple foundation of knowledge as a human creation. However, most of us live our lives from a different assumption—that of an objective reality, independent of us, that is accessible through our senses. We assume that this reality is shared by others and can be taken for granted as reality (Lindesmith, Strauss, & Denzin, 1991). We are quite sure that trees and tables and trucks don't exist simply in our imagination.

Yet at times what we define as real seems to have nothing to do with what our senses tell us is real. Picture a 5-year-old child who wakes up in the middle of the night screaming that monsters are under her bed. Her parents comfort her by saying, "There aren't any monsters. You had a nightmare. It's just your imagination." The next day the child comes down with the flu and wants to know why she is sick. The parents respond by saying, "You've caught a virus, a bug."

"A bug? You mean like an ant or a beetle?"

"No. It's the sort of bug you can't see—but it's there."

Granted, viruses can be seen and verified with the proper equipment, but without access to such equipment the child has to take the parents' word for it. In fact, most of us accept the reality of viruses without ever having seen them for ourselves. The child learns to accept the authoritative claims of her parents that something that was "seen" (the nightmare monster) is not real, although something that was not seen (the virus) is real.

Hence, reality may be more a matter of agreement than something inherent in the natural world. Sociologists, particularly those working from the perspective of symbolic interactionism and conflict theory, strive to explain the social construction of reality in terms of both its causes and its consequences. Their insights help explain many of the phenomena that influence our daily lives.

Laying the Foundation: The Bases of Reality

Think of society as a building constructed by the people who live and work in it. The building's foundation, its underlying reality, determines its basic shape and dimensions. And the foundation is what makes that building solid and helps it stand up through time and weather. For students of architecture as well as sociology, the first thing to understand is the way the foundation is prepared.

Symbolic interactionism encourages us to see that people's actions toward one another and interpretations of situations are based on their definitions of reality, which are in turn learned from interactions with those around them. What we know to be real we share with other members of our culture. Imagine how difficult it would be to believe in something that no one else believed in. Psychiatrists use such terms as *hallucination* and *delusion* to describe things experienced by people who see, hear, or believe things that others don't.

The social construction of reality is a process by which human-created ideas become so firmly accepted that to deny them is to deny common sense. Of course, some features of reality are grounded in physical evidence—fire is hot, sharp things hurt. But other features of reality are often based not on hard evidence but on such forces as culture and language, self-fulfilling prophecies, and faith.

Culture and Language

We live in a symbolic world and interact through symbolic communication—that is, through language. Language makes people, events, and ideas meaningful. In fact, language reflects and often determines our reality (Sapir, 1949; Whorf, 1956). Thus language is a key tool in the construction of society.

Within a culture, words evolve to reflect the phenomena that have practical significance. The Solomon Islanders have nine distinct words for "coconut," each specifying an important stage of growth, but they have only one word for all the meals of the day (M. M. Lewis, 1948). The Aleuts of northern Canada have 33 words for "snow" that allow them to distinguish differences in texture, temperature, weight, load-carrying capacity, and the speed at which a sled can run on its surface (E. T. Hiller, 1933). The Hanunóo people of the Philippines have different names for 92 varieties of rice, allowing them to make distinctions all but invisible to English-speakers, who lump all such grains under a single word: *rice* (Thomson, 2000). Yet a traditional Hanunóo coming to this country would be incapable of seeing the distinctions between a *Ford* and a *Toyota* or between a *hatchback* and a *station wagon*.

Language is such a powerful filter that it can even influence sensory perception. All human beings with normal eyesight see the same spectrum of colors because all colors exist in the physical world. Color consists of visible wavelengths that blend imperceptibly into one another (Farb, 1983). There are no sharp breaks in the color spectrum that distinguish, say, red from orange. But when Americans look at a rainbow they see six different colors: red, orange, yellow, green, blue, and purple. Not everyone in the world sees those same colors, though. Some people who speak non-European languages have different ways of partitioning the color spectrum. As Exhibit 3.1 shows, the Shona of Zimbabwe divide the spectrum into three colors and the Bassa of Liberia have only two color categories (Gleason, 1961). These basic categories provide convenient labels from which people of these cultures can describe variants of color that matter in their lives. When a Shona says *citema*, others know immediately that she is referring to a color we would consider either green or blue. For the Bassa, purple, blue, and green are different shades of *ziza*, just as pink is a shade of red in English.

In addition to affecting perceptions of reality, language influences our attitudes toward specific problems and processes (Sapir, 1929). The use of words reinforces

Exhibit 3.1 **Cross-Cultural Differences in Color Terms**

English	red	orange	yellow	green	blue	purple
Shona	cipsuka		cicena		citema	cipsuka
Bassa	hui			ziza		

Source: Farb, 1983

prevailing ideas and suppresses conflicting ideas about the world. In a highly specialized market economy such as the United States, for example, the ability to distinguish
linguistically between "real" work and "volunteer" work allows us to telegraph our attitudes about a person's worth to society. In small, agricultural societies, where all
people typically work to provide the basic necessities and to ensure the survival of
their tight-knit community, labor is not characterized according to its worth in the
marketplace. In such societies, work is work whether you're paid to do it or not.

Within a culture, certain professions or interest groups develop a distinctive language, known as *jargon*, that allows members of the group to communicate with one
another clearly and quickly. Surfers and snowboarders have a specialized vocabulary
(not understandable to most nonsurfers or nonsnowboarders) through which they can
efficiently convey information about ocean or snow conditions to others. At the same
time, jargon can sometimes create boundaries and therefore mystify and conceal
meaning from outsiders (Farb, 1983). For instance, by using esoteric medical terminology when discussing a case in front of a patient, physicians define who is and who isn't
a member of their group and reinforce their image as highly trained experts.

The fact that the meanings of words can be so slippery often makes interaction
difficult and sometimes leads to catastrophe. Imagine that a night watchman enters the
storage room of a chemical plant and notices some gasoline drums in the corner under
a sign that says "Empty Barrels." The watchman lights a cigarette and throws the match
into one of the empty barrels, resulting in a terrible explosion. The immediate cause of
the explosion, of course, was the gasoline fumes that remained in the drum. But, as
one anthropologist points out,

> It could be argued that a second cause of the explosion was the English language. The
> barrels were empty of their original contents and so belonged under the empty sign.
> Yet they were not empty of everything—the fumes were still present. English has no
> word—no single term—that can convey such a situation. Containers in English are ei-
> ther empty or they are not. . . . There is no term in the language for . . . "empty of the
> original contents but with something left over." There being no word for such an in-
> between state, it did not occur to the watchman to think of the explosive fumes.
> (Thomson, 2000, p. 80)

Language is sometimes used to purposely deceive as well. A *euphemism* is an inof-
fensive expression substituted for one that might be offensive. On the surface such
terms are used in the interests of politeness and good taste, such as saying "perspira-
tion" instead of "sweat." However, euphemisms also shape perceptions. Political regimes routinely use them to cover up, distort, or frame their actions in a more positive
light. Here are a few examples of euphemisms, followed by their real meanings:

- *Reconditioned*—used
- *Sanitation engineer*—garbage collector
- *Collateral damage*—civilian deaths during military combat
- *Ethnic cleansing*—deportation and massacre of the people of one culture by those of
  another culture
- *Tactical redeployment*—retreat during battle

- *Economically nonaffluent*—poor
- *Revenue enhancement*—tax increase
- *Achieve a deficiency*—flunk a test
- *Urban camper*—homeless person
- *Negative patient outcome*—death
- *Postconsumer waste material*—garbage
- *Meal replacement*—junk food
- *Deselected, involuntarily separated, downsized, nonretained, vocationally relocated*, or *dehired*—fired

In sum, language helps frame or structure social reality and gives it meaning. Language also provides people with a cultural and group identity. If you've ever spent a significant amount of time in a foreign country or even moved to a new school, you know that you cannot be a fully participating member of a group or a culture until you share its language.

Self-Fulfilling Prophecies

As you will recall from Chapter 2, we do not respond directly and automatically to objects and situations; instead, as the symbolic interactionist perspective points out, we use language to define and interpret them and then act on the basis of those interpretations. By acting on the basis of our definitions of reality, we often create the very conditions that we believe exist. A **self-fulfilling prophecy** is an assumption or prediction that, purely as a result of having been made, causes the expected event to occur and thus confirms its own "accuracy" (Merton, 1948; Watzlawick, 1984).

Every holiday season we witness the stunning effects of self-fulfilling prophecies on a national scale. It goes something like this: In September or so, the toy industry releases the results of an annual survey of retailers indicating what are predicted to be the top-selling toys at Christmas. Usually one toy in particular is hailed as the most popular, can't-do-without, hard-to-get gift of the year. In the 1980s it was Cabbage Patch Dolls; in the early 1990s Mighty Morphin Power Rangers and Ninja Turtles claimed the title; more recently, Beanie Babies, Furbies, Pokemon or Harry Potter paraphernalia, and Razor scooters filled the bill. In November or so we begin to hear the hype about unprecedented demand for the toy and the likelihood of a shortage. Powerful retail store chains—like Toys 'R' Us or WalMart—may announce the possibility that if things get out of hand they may have to start rationing: one toy per family. Fueled by the fear of seeing a disappointed child's face at Christmas, thousands of panicked parents rush the stores to make sure they're not left without. Some hoard extras for other parents they know. As a result, the supply of the toy—which wasn't perilously low in the first place—is severely depleted, thereby bringing about the predicted shortage. The mere belief in some version of reality creates expectations that can actually bring about a reality that never existed.

Self-fulfilling prophecies are particularly powerful when they become an element of social institutions. In schools, teachers can subtly and unconsciously encourage the performance they expect to see in their students. For instance, if they believe their students to be especially intelligent they may spend more time with them or uninten-tionally show more enthusiasm when working with them. As a result, these students may come to feel more capable and intelligent and actually perform accordingly (Rosenthal & Jacobson, 1968).

Self-fulfilling prophecies can often affect people physically. For years doctors have recognized the power of the "placebo" effect—the tendency for patients to improve be-cause they have been led to believe that they are receiving some sort of treatment (which they are not). For instance, in one study, 42% of balding men taking a placebo drug either maintained or increased the amount of hair on their heads. Doctors in Texas studying knee surgery found similar levels of pain relief in patients whether the surgery was real or faked (cited in Blakeslee, 1998). It's estimated that between 35% and 75% of patients benefit from taking dummy pills in studies of new drugs (Talbot, 2000b). In 1999, a major pharmaceutical company halted development of a new anti-depressant drug it had been promoting, because studies showed that placebo pills were just as effective in treating depression (Talbot, 2000b).

The inverse of the placebo effect is the creation of expectations that make people worse. Anthropologists have documented numerous mysterious and scientifically difficult-to-explain deaths that follow the pronouncement of curses or evil spells (Watzlawick, 1984). Recently, medical researchers have begun to examine this phe-nomenon, sometimes referred to as the "nocebo" effect. For instance, in Japan, re-searchers carried out an experiment on 13 people who were extremely allergic to poi-son ivy. The experimenters rubbed one of their arms with a harmless leaf and told them it was poison ivy; the experimenters rubbed the other arm with poison ivy and told the subjects it was a harmless leaf. All 13 broke out in a rash where the harmless leaf had touched their skin; only 2 reacted to the real poison ivy leaves (cited in Blakeslee, 1998). Another study found that patients with heart disease who expected their condition to worsen had on average 1.6 times as many episodes of the disease and were 1.5 times as likely to die from it as patients who had a more positive outlook (cited in Hilts, 1995). In other words, in many cases when people expected to get worse, they did. Once again, we see how reality is shaped by human beings, as much as reality shapes them.

Faith and Incorrigible Propositions

Suppose you leave your house one morning with 75 cents in your pocket. When you arrive at your destination, you have only 50 cents. Objectively, 25 cents has disap-peared, but you "know better." Even though your eyes tell you that the money isn't there, you have learned that it couldn't possibly have vanished. Rather than abandon this lesson, you come up with a series of "reasonable" explanations: "I must have mis-counted." "A quarter must have fallen out of my pocket somehow." "Someone picked my pocket." To acknowledge the possibility that the money literally disappeared would be to challenge the reality on which your everyday life is based. It is an article of faith that an object cannot disappear into thin air.

Such an unquestionable assumption, called an **incorrigible proposition,** is a belief that cannot be proved wrong and has become so much a part of common sense that one continues to believe it even in the face of contradictory evidence. By explaining away contradictions with "reasonable" explanations, we strengthen the correctness of the initial premise (Watzlawick, 1976). In the process, we participate in constructing a particular version of reality.

Even belief systems that most of us might consider unconventional can be quite resilient and invulnerable to contradiction (Snow & Machalek, 1982). For instance, practitioners of Scientology strive to attain a perfect level of mental functioning called "clear." Yet there is no evidence that any Scientologists have ever achieved such a state. Does this historical failure contradict the group's claims? No. Instead, individual members focus on their individual deficiencies: They have not yet attained the "appropriate mental level" necessary to reach clear. Note how such an explanation allows practitioners to maintain the belief that such a mental state really exists while at the same time reinforcing the hope that someday they may be able to achieve it.

Sociologists Hugh Mehan and Houston Wood (1975) furthered our understanding of incorrigible propositions by examining the research of the anthropologist E. E. Evans-Pritchard (1937). Evans-Pritchard described an elaborate ritual practiced by the Azande, a small African society located in southwestern Sudan. When faced with important decisions—where to build a house, whom to marry, and so on—the Azande consulted an oracle or a powerful spirit. They prepared for the consultation by following a strictly prescribed ceremony. A substance was extracted from the bark of a certain type of tree and prepared in a special way during a seancelike ritual. The Azande believed that a powerful spirit would enter the potion during this ceremony. They then posed a question to the spirit in such a way that it could be answered either yes or no and fed the substance to a chicken. If the chicken lived, they would interpret the answer from the spirit as yes; if the chicken died, the answer was no.

Our Western belief system tells us that the tree bark obviously contains some poisonous chemical. Certain chickens are physically able to survive it, others aren't. But the Azande had no knowledge of the bark's poisonous qualities or of chicken physiology. In fact, they didn't believe the tree or the chicken played a part in the ceremony at all. The ritual of gathering bark and feeding it to a chicken transformed the tree into the spirit power. The chicken lived or died not because of a physical reaction to a chemical but because the oracle "hears like a person and settles cases like a king" (Evans-Pritchard, 1937, p. 321).

But what if the oracle was wrong? What if an Azande was told by the oracle to build a house by the river and the river overflowed its banks, washing away the house? Evans-Pritchard observed several cases of Azande making bad decisions based on incorrect "advice" from the oracle. How could they reconcile these sorts of inconsistencies with a belief in the reality of the oracle?

To us the answer is obvious: There was no spirit, no magic, just the strength of the poison and the health of the chickens. We see these bad decisions as contradictions, because we view them from the reality of Western science. We observe this ritual to determine if in fact there is an oracle, and of course we're predisposed to believe there isn't. We are looking for proof of the existence of something of which we are highly skeptical.

For the Azande, though, the contradictions were not contradictions at all. They *knew* the oracle existed. This was their fundamental premise, their incorrigible proposition, just like our fundamental premise that things don't disappear into thin air. It was an article of faith that could not be questioned. All that followed for the Azande was experienced from this initial assumption. The Azande had ways of explaining contradictions to their truths, just as we do. When the oracle failed to provide them with proper advice, they would say, "A taboo must have been breached" or "Sorcerers must have intervened" or "The ceremony wasn't carried out correctly."

Protecting incorrigible propositions is essential for the maintenance of reality systems. By explaining away contradictions we are able to support our basic assumptions and live in a coherent and orderly world.

Building the Walls: Conflict, Power, and Social Institutions

We, as individuals, play an important role in coordinating, reproducing, and giving meaning to society in our daily interactions. But our ability to define social reality is limited. We are certainly not completely free to create whatever version of social reality we want to create. We are, after all, born into a preexisting society with its norms, values, roles, relationships, groups, organizations, institutions, and so forth. Just as the walls of a building constrain the ability of the inhabitants to move about, directing them through certain predetermined doorways and corridors, these features of society influence our thoughts and deeds and consequently constrain our ability to freely construct our social world (Giddens, 1984). As Karl Marx wrote, "[People] make their own history, but they do not make it just as they please; they do not make it under circumstances chosen by themselves, but under circumstances directly encountered, given and transmitted from the past" (Marx, 1869/1963, p. 15).

Like contemporary conflict theorists, Marx was particularly interested in how inequality of economic conditions shape people's ability to act. Certain people or groups of people are more influential in defining reality than others. Think of all the times you have done something just because someone with more influence, authority, or expertise—a parent, an instructor, a boss, a scientist, or a politician—has decided you should.

As the conflict perspective points out, in any modern society—where classes, ethnic and religious groups, age groups, and political interests struggle for control over resources—there is also a struggle for the power to determine or influence that society's conception of reality (Gans, 1971). Those who emerge successful gain control over information, define values, create myths, manipulate events, and influence what the rest of us take for granted. Conflict theorists therefore argue that reality doesn't simply emerge out of social interaction but is based on the interests and visions of powerful people, groups, organizations, and institutions. People with more power, prestige, status, wealth, and access to high-level policy makers can make their perceptions of the world the entire culture's perception. In other words, "He who has the bigger stick has the better chance of imposing his definitions of reality" (P. L. Berger & Luckmann, 1966, p. 109). That "bigger stick" can be wielded in several ways. Various social institutions and the people who control them play a significant role in shaping and sustaining perceptions of reality. If you wish to develop the sociological imagination, you need to understand the role of not only individuals but also these larger forces in shaping private lives.

Moral Entrepreneurs

Certain groups have moral concerns they passionately want translated into law. These **moral entrepreneurs** (H. Becker, 1963) need not be wealthy or influential individuals. Instead, by virtue of their initiative, access to decision makers, skillful use of publicity, and success in neutralizing any opposing viewpoints, they are able to turn their interests into public policy (Hills, 1980). Just as a financial entrepreneur is in the business of selling a product to the public, a moral entrepreneur is in the business of selling a particular version of reality to the public. Groups that seek to outlaw pornography, sexually explicit lyrics in rock music, abortion, gambling, and homosexuality, as well as groups that promote gun control, literacy, awareness of domestic violence, and support for AIDS research, are crusading for the creation of a new public conception of morality. For the moral entrepreneur the existing "reality" is not satisfactory: "He [*sic*] feels that nothing can be right in the world until rules are made to correct it. . . . Any means is justified to do away with it. The crusader is fervent and righteous, often self-righteous" (H. Becker, 1963, pp. 147–148).

Clearly, moral entrepreneurship is closely linked to certain social institutions. Religion, for example, provides many people with values that dictate what is right and wrong, proper and improper, good and bad (J. H. Turner, 1972). These values are sometimes formally written into a religious code (for example, the Ten Commandments or the Koran) that provides direct guidance for day-to-day life and the rationale that drives attempts to change the beliefs and behaviors of others.

If they have the political savvy to insinuate their belief systems into the legislative process, moral entrepreneurs can often exert significant influence over a society's definition of reality. In the early 20th century, for instance, the actions of a small group of women, the Women's Christian Temperance Union, led to the passage of the Eighteenth Amendment to the U.S. Constitution, which prohibited the use, possession, and sale of alcoholic beverages (Gusfield, 1963). These women used strong, religiously inspired arguments against the "evils" of alcohol to convince legislators it ought to be outlawed.

However, although religious codes of conduct provided the supportive ideology for the temperance movement in the United States, it was—on closer inspection—a political struggle among various interest groups. The struggle symbolized the conflict between the values of rural, middle-class Protestants and the values of immigrant, urban, lower-class Catholics (Gusfield, 1963). Alcohol consumption was part of the everyday lives of these immigrants, and the temperance movement became a symbolic crusade for rural Protestants trying to maintain their position in a rapidly changing society. This interpretation is supported by the fact that temperance advocates were less concerned with the enforcement of Prohibition laws than with their passage, which is why the Eighteenth Amendment was eventually repealed. Through such issues of reform, a group of moral entrepreneurs can defend its perception of reality within the total society (Gusfield, 1963).

The Economics of Reality

Definitions of reality often reflect underlying economic concerns and interests. Ideas that become socially "popular" often reinforce the interests of wealthy individuals and organizations, allowing them to control the activities of others. The key concerns from the perspective of conflict theory are who benefits economically and who loses from dominant versions of reality.

Take mental illness, for example. The number of problems officially defined by the American Psychiatric Association (APA) as mental diseases and defects increases each year (Caplan, 1995; S. A. Kirk & Kutchins, 1992; Szasz, 1990). In defining what is and is not mental illness, the APA unwittingly reflects the economic organization of U.S. society. In the United States individuals rarely pay the total costs of medical services out of their own pockets. Most of the money for health care services comes from the federal and state governments or from private insurance companies. Only if disorders such as alcoholism, gambling, depression, anorexia, and cocaine addiction are formally defined as illnesses is their treatment eligible for medical insurance coverage.

Economic interests are frequently served by the manner in which language is used to define reality. For example, the 1992 Children's Television Act requires local broadcasters to demonstrate their commitment to the educational needs of children in order to have their licenses renewed (Andrews, 1992). The intent of the law was to improve the quality of children's programming. But instead of adding more educational programs, which are traditionally less lucrative than commercial programs, many stations kept the programs that were already in place and simply redefined "educational" and "informational." One television station, for example, considered the cartoon *Super Mario Brothers* educational because it taught children self-confidence. Another said that *Yogi Bear* teaches moral and ethical values by showing children the consequences of doing "stupid things" or "taking what doesn't belong to you" (Kunkel, 1998). Other stations scheduled their educational programs at unpopular hours, such as 5:30 or 6:00 A.M. Because of such lax compliance, a Federal Communications Commission ruling in 1996 tightened the definition of educational and required television stations to air three hours of educational programming a week, between 7 A.M. and 10 P.M. Broadcasters complain that it's difficult to make educational programs (as they are now defined) that children want to watch. With billions of dollars at stake, broadcasters prefer to redefine what an educational program is in order to protect their financial interests.

The Politics of Reality

The institution of politics is also linked to societal definitions of reality. To a great extent, politics is concerned with controlling public perceptions of reality so that people will do things or think about issues in ways that political leaders want them to. During important political campaigns we can see such attempts to influence public perception. Mudslinging, euphemistically called "negative campaigning," has become as common an element of the U.S. electoral process as speeches, debates, baby kissing, and patriotic songs. Most politicians know that if you say something untrue or unproven about an opponent often enough, people will believe it. Ironically, constant public denials by the victim of the charges often reinforce the reality of the charges and keep them in the news. The actual validity of the claims becomes irrelevant as the accusations are transformed into "fact" and become solidified in the minds of the voting public.

However, the relationship between politics and reality goes beyond the dirty campaigns of individual candidates. The social construction of reality itself is a massive political process. Governments, both national and local, live or die by their ability to manipulate public opinion so they can reinforce their claims to legitimacy. Information is selectively released, altered, or withheld in an attempt to gain public approval and support. Such shaping of reality is accomplished most notably through the media.

The Medium Is the Message

The mass media—television, radio, books, newspapers, magazines, the Internet—are the primary means by which we are entertained and informed about the world around us. But the messages we receive from the media also reflect dominant cultural values (Gitlin, 1979). In television shows and other works of fiction, the way characters are portrayed, the topics dealt with, and the solutions imposed on problems all link entertainment to the prevailing societal tastes in consumption and the economic system.

The media also play a key role in any political system. They are our primary source of information about local, national, and international events and people. News broadcasts and newspapers tell us about things we cannot experience directly, making the most remote events meaningful (Molotch & Lester, 1974). The way we look at the world and define our lives within it is therefore shaped and influenced by what we see on the news, hear on the radio, and read in our daily papers.

Because the news is the means by which political realities are disseminated to the public, it is an essential tool in maintaining social order (Hallin, 1986; Parenti, 1986). In many societies, most news sources don't even try to hide the fact that they are mouthpieces of one faction or another. In repressive societies, the only news sources allowed to operate are those that represent the government. In China, for instance, the flow of news information is clearly controlled by the government. People who live in societies with a cultural tradition of press independence, in contrast, assume that news stories are purely factual—an accurate, objective reflection of the "world out there" (Molotch & Lester, 1975). Like everything else, however, news is a constructed reality (Molotch & Lester, 1974).

Hundreds, perhaps thousands of potentially newsworthy events occur every day. Yet we'll see maybe 10 of them on our favorite evening broadcast. These events exist as news not because of their inherent importance but because of the practical, political, or economic purposes they serve. The old newsroom adage, "If it bleeds, it leads," attests to the fact that events with shocking details—which appeal to the public's fondness for the sensational—are the ones most likely to be chosen. At its most independent, the news is still the product of decisions made by reporters, editors, network executives, and corporation owners, all of whom have their own interests, biases, and values (Molotch & Lester, 1974).

Often complex issues are presented in simplified and sometimes clichéd ways to serve broader political interests. In 1996, a 6-year-old boy in Lexington, North Carolina, was charged by school administrators with sexual harassment for kissing a classmate. News stories focused on the absurdity of such a charge, and the story was used by some social critics to support their contention that "political correctness" had gone too far and that sexual harassment wasn't a serious social problem. What wasn't presented was the information that the boy had been bothering several classmates for a long time, that he had resisted less extreme efforts to discipline him, that the school had been sued previously for not taking action against an older boy who had engaged in similar behavior, and that the boy's parents refused to cooperate in disciplining him (Schwalbe, 1998). Had this information accompanied the story, many people might have drawn very different conclusions about the case.

Although "freedom of the press" is a core American value, official censorship has been not only tolerated but encouraged in some situations. Take the media coverage of the Persian Gulf War in 1991. This was the first war to be covered in a live, around-the-clock format. More than 100 countries around the world received reports from CNN, making the war a truly global media event (Barker, 1997). But the most striking feature of the coverage of this war was the reliance on studio-based coverage and stage-managed events. Most of what the viewing public saw consisted of journalist recaps, analyses by consultants and experts, military press conferences, and tapes provided by the military. Journalists were permitted to cover the war only if they were in organized "pools" escorted by military personnel (Pratkanis & Aronson, 1991). Reporters were never allowed unsupervised access to the battle lines or to the soldiers. Military escorts had the authority to stop any interview or photograph if they felt it endangered the operation. Any journalist who attempted to operate independently was subject to arrest. Military officials decided which army units could be visited by reporters, which reporters could make the visits, which soldiers they could talk to, what the television cameras could show, and what could be written (Cummings, 1992). Reporters were completely dependent on official statements and government-issued videotapes. The public was told that such tight restrictions were necessary to ensure the physical safety of the war correspondents, protect the well-being of our soldiers, and promote the war effort.

Not surprisingly, media reports during the war were congratulatory and optimistic: the low number of Allied casualties, the spectacular success of the air campaign and ground attacks, the effectiveness of U.S. high-tech weaponry, the carefully calibrated pressure that kept the Iraqis from unleashing chemical weapons, and so on. Only 1% of the visual images on television were of death and injury (Barker, 1997). Press briefings gave the impression that the Allied forces were trying hard to maintain a high moral ground in the war (Lopez, 1991). Indeed, one of the most enduring images of the war was that of technologically "smart" weapons that were able to hit targets with pinpoint accuracy, thereby minimizing unnecessary destruction and casualties to civilians.

Such tightly controlled reporting served the interests of the TV networks as well as the military. The Persian Gulf War blurred the boundary between military action and media event, creating what one commentator called "twenty-four-hours-a-day, eye-burning, blood-pumping, high-tech, all-channel" entertainment (Engelhardt, 1992, p. 147). It provided the kind of programming that television networks crave.

Only after the war ended did we hear another side to the story:

- More bombs were dropped on Iraq than were dropped during all of World War II, and only 7% of the bombs were "smart bombs."
- More than 150,000 civilians were killed, and Iraqi casualties approached a quarter of a million.

- The Iraqi army, often represented as the highly trained "Elite Republican Guard," was largely made up of unwilling conscripts forced to serve in the war.
- Electric, water, and sewage facilities in northern Iraq were destroyed, returning the country to a preindustrial level of development.
- Western armies slaughtered the retreating Iraqi army in what some observers called a "turkey shoot."
- Many of the American soldiers who were killed died not at the hands of the enemy but as an accidental consequence of "friendly fire" (Lopez, 1991; Mowlana, Gerbner, & Schiller, 1992).
- The official control of information allowed the war to be defined in terms that were favorable to the military and to the government.

For everyday news stories, such official censorship is usually unnecessary, even in societies that restrict the press. Because of the economic pressures to attract audiences and keep their attention, TV networks and newspapers usually censor themselves (Bagdikian, 1991). Reporters pursue particular stories, particular governmental activities, and particular foreign scenes. Less exciting, more complicated stories end up in the wastebasket or on the cutting-room floor.

Micro-Macro Connection
Missing from the News

The problem with the daily distillation of information is not so much what is false but what is missing (Bagdikian, 1991). We usually have no way of knowing what events have not been selected for inclusion in the day's news or what plausible alternatives are kept out of the public eye. Each year Project Censored, a media watchdog group, publishes its list of the top news stories that never made the news in the United States and hence never came to the public's attention (Jensen & Project Censored, 1995; Phillips & Project Censored, 1997, 2000). Here are some stories the mainstream media never covered:

- The U.S. government currently sells over half of all the weapons sold in the global arms market—compared to 16% in 1988. In fact, the George H. W. Bush and Bill Clinton administrations gave away about $7 billion worth of excess weapons between 1990 and 1995. In the 1990s, Turkey used U.S. weapons to destroy 3,000 Kurdish villages.
- The Food and Drug Administration has refused to take steps to protect consumers from known carcinogens found in some toothpaste, shampoo, sunscreen, makeup, and other personal care products.
- Studies carried out in the 1980s by the National Institute for Occupational Safety and Health found that 240,450 American workers were exposed to hazardous materials in the workplace. Of those, about 170,000 were never told about serious health risks from on-the-job exposure.
- The world's fishing fleets waste about 60 billion pounds of fish and seafood every year—enough for 120 billion meals.

- Tuberculosis has reemerged as a deadly communicable disease, threatening more people worldwide than AIDS, cholera, dengue fever, and other infectious diseases combined—even though it is largely curable.
- The U.S. Justice Department rejected a study, which it had originally commissioned, that found that the most popular school-based drug prevention program in the country—Drug Abuse Resistance Education (DARE)—was an extremely expensive failure.

The economic and political motivation for such selectivity becomes apparent when we consider who owns the media. In 1983, 50 companies controlled over half of all U.S. media outlets; in 1999, six companies—General Electric, Viacom, Disney, Time Warner, Bertelsmann, and Rupert Murdoch's News Corporation—controlled over half of all media outlets (Bagdikian, 2000).

> ABC is a subsidiary of Disney, which also owns theme parks, an oil and gas company, cable channels, magazines, newspapers, record companies, an insurance company, and even a hockey team. Time Warner owns Turner Broadcasting, parent company of CNN, [TNT, and TBS], as well as sports teams, cable companies, film studios, retail stores, utility companies, and much more. NBC is now owned by General Electric, while CBS [Showtime and MTV] belong to [Viacom]. Fox Television is part of Rupert Murdoch's media empire, which also includes HarperCollins publishing, newspapers, magazines, and television stations. (Iggers, 1997, p. 46)

Many observers fear that corporation-owned media will twist the news to promote the parent company's narrow economic interests (M. C. Miller, 1996). For instance, how likely is it that ABC would run a news story critical of hiring practices at Disney theme parks? What are the chances that NBC would air a series of stories critical of nuclear weapons, given that its parent company, General Electric, is a huge defense contractor involved in nuclear production?

In addition, most journalists are white and come from upper-middle-class families. Almost all have college degrees, and a majority have attended graduate school (Parenti, 1986). Because common social class interests make for common political perspectives, a remarkable degree of ideological uniformity exists among those responsible for assembling and presenting the news. This is not to say that all the news we receive is knowingly misrepresented. On the contrary, reporters, editors, and producers most likely present the news "as they see it." The problem is that "as they see it" is to some extent determined by their class background and political perspective.

As the viewing public, our recourse is difficult. To criticize faulty government policies and consider solutions to difficult social problems, we need solid information, which is frequently unavailable. The challenge we face is to recognize the processes at work in the social construction of reality and to take them into account as we "consume" the news. A critical dimension of the sociological imagination is the ability to "read silences" —to be attentive to what the mass media don't say. Fortunately, one of the purposes of sociology is to scientifically amass a body of knowledge that we can use to assess how our society really works.

Appreciating the Art of Social Research

Up to this point, I've been describing how individuals, groups, and various social institutions go about constructing reality. We've seen that these realities sometimes shift with time, place, and individual perception. Faced with this type of fluctuation, sociologists, as well as scholars in other disciplines, attempt to identify a more "real" reality through systematic, controlled research. The rules sociologists abide by when conducting research give them confidence that they are identifying more than just a personal version of reality. Instead, they hope to determine a reality as it exists for some group of people at a particular point in time.

Moving beyond the level of individual conclusions about the nature of social reality is crucial if we are to escape the distortions of personal interests and biases. A danger of relying on individual perceptions is that we are likely to conclude that our experiences are what everyone experiences. For example, the famous psychiatrist Sigmund Freud used his own childhood as the ultimate "proof" of the controversial concept, the Oedipus conflict (the belief that male children are secretly in love with their mothers and jealous of their fathers). He wrote to a friend in 1897, "I have found, in my own case too, being in love with the mother and jealous of the father, and I now consider it a universal event of early childhood" (quoted in Astbury, 1996, p. 73).

To avoid the risk of such distortions, sociologists focus on what most people believe or how most people behave. But in doing so, sociologists run the risk of simply restating what people already know. Indeed, a common criticism of sociology you hear sometimes is that it is just a fancy version of common sense. A lot of the things that we think are obvious based on our personal observations, however, turn out not to be so straightforward under the closer scrutiny of social research. Consider the following "commonsense facts":

- Rape, assault, and murder occur most often between total strangers.
- School violence is the most dangerous threat to children's well-being in the United States today.
- Because of the high divorce rate in the United States, people are reluctant to get married.
- American children today are more likely to live in a single-parent household than they were 100 years ago.

Most of us probably believe these statements are true. Given what you've read or seen on television, they probably make a lot of sense. But how accurate are they?

According to the Federal Bureau of Investigation (1991), approximately half of all murder victims each year are related to or know their murderers. And the Justice Department reports that more than half of the 1.4 million victims of violence treated in hospital emergency rooms were hurt by someone they knew: a spouse, a boy- or girlfriend, a parent, a friend, or an acquaintance ("Many victims of violence," 1997). Although people close to us provide a great deal of pleasure in our lives, they are also the ones who can frustrate and hurt us the most. Few people can make us as angry as a loved one.

Although the rash of deadly school massacres—most notably the one in Littleton, Colorado, in 1999—has touched off a torrent of fear and anxiety about school safety, these incidents are the statistical equivalent of a needle in a haystack. According to the Centers for Disease Control and Prevention, homicide is the second leading cause of death among youngsters today. However, fewer than 1% of these killings occur in or around schools (cited in Stolberg, 1999). In fact, children are much more likely to die violently in their own homes than in their schools.

Close to 90% of Americans marry at least once by the time they're 40. In fact, about two-thirds of divorced women and three-fourths of divorced men eventually re-marry (Cherlin, 1992). Although we have become increasingly willing to end a bad marriage, we still tend to place a high value on the institution of marriage itself.

The percentage of children who live with one parent is roughly the same as it was a century ago. At that time life expectancy was much lower than it is today, so it was highly likely that a child would lose one parent to death before he or she reached adult-hood (Kain, 1990).

As you can see, sometimes commonsense "facts" don't hold up under the weight of evidence provided by social research.

The Nature of Social Research

Research is all around us. Throughout our lives we are flooded with statistics that are supposedly the result of scientific research—which detergents make clothes brighter, which soft drinks are preferred by most people, which chewing gum is recommended by four out of five dentists. Many of the important decisions we make, from purchas-ing a car to voting for a presidential candidate, are supported by some sort of research.

In addition, a significant proportion of our own lives is spent doing casual re-search. Every time we seek out the opinions of others, gauge the attitude of a group, or draw conclusions about an event, we engage in a form of research. Say, for example, that you thought your exam scores would improve if you studied with others. You then formed a study group. After the exam you compared your grade with the grade you re-ceived on the previous exam to see if there was any significant improvement. If there was, you would likely attribute your better performance to the study group. This is the essence of research: You had an idea about some social process, and you went out and tested it to see if you were correct.

Although useful and common, personal research like this is fraught with prob-lems. We may make inaccurate or selective observations, overgeneralize on the basis of a limited number of observations, or draw conclusions that protect our own interests (Babbie, 1992). Maybe your exam score would have improved even without the study group because you had a better understanding of the material this time and had a bet-ter sense of what the instructor expected.

The Empirical and Probabilistic Aspects of Research

In contrast to the casual way we carry out our personal research, sociologists attempt to define reality through a careful process of collecting information and answering questions. Sociological researchers methodically record observations across a variety of situations; they design and choose questions in advance and ask them in a consistent way of a large number of people; they use sophisticated techniques to ensure that the characteristics of the people in a study are similar to those of the population at large; and they use computers to generate statistics from which confident conclusions can be drawn.

Furthermore, sociological research is subjected to the scrutiny of peers who will point out any mistakes and shortcomings. Researchers are obligated to report not only their results but also the methods they used to collect data and the conditions surrounding the study. Such detailed explanation allows other researchers to replicate a study—that is, to perform it themselves to see if the same results are obtained. The more a particular research result is replicated, the greater its acceptance as fact in the sociological community.

Sociological research, then, is a more sophisticated and structured form of the sort of individual inquiry we use every day. First and foremost, it is an empirical endeavor. **Empirical research** operates on the assumption that answers to questions about human behavior can be ascertained only through controlled, systematic observations in the real world. Great scholars can spend years thinking about human life and developing logical explanations about particular social phenomena. But for most sociologists, the strength of an explanation depends on how much empirical support it has.

Another important characteristic of social research is that it is **probabilistic**. Instead of making absolute predictions, claiming that *X* always causes *Y*, most sociologists prefer to state that under certain conditions *X* will probably cause *Y* in most people—in other words, that human behavior operates within the laws of probability. Whenever sociologists set out to find the reasons, for example, why people hold prejudiced beliefs, why some religious groups are more opposed to abortion than others, or why some countries have a higher birthrate than others, they are searching for the factors that would explain these phenomena most but not all of the time.

Theories, Variables, and Hypotheses

In addition to being empirical and probabilistic, social research is purposeful. Unlike personal research, which may be motivated by a hunch, whim, or immediate need, most social research is guided by a particular theory. A **theory** is a set of statements or propositions that seeks to explain or predict a particular aspect of social life (Chafetz, 1978). Theory is not, as is popularly thought, conjecture or speculation. Ideally, theories deal with the way things are, not the way they ought to be.

Research and theory closely depend on each other. Research without any underlying theoretical reasoning is simply a string of meaningless bits of information (C. W. Mills, 1959); theory without research is abstract and speculative.

Some theories—such as structural functionalism, conflict theory, or symbolic interactionism—are quite broad, attempting to explain why social order exists or how societies work overall. Other theories are more modest, attempting to explain more narrowly certain behaviors among specific groups of people. For example, Travis Hirschi (1969) developed a theory of juvenile delinquency called "social control theory," in which he argued that delinquent acts occur when an individual's bond to society is weak or broken. These bonds are derived from a person's attachments to others who obey the law, the rewards one gains by acting nondelinquently (commitments), the amount of time a person engages in nondelinquent activity (involvements), and the degree to which a person is tied to society's conventional belief system.

To test theories, sociologists must translate abstract theoretical propositions into testable hypotheses. A **hypothesis** is a researchable prediction that specifies the relationship between two or more variables. A **variable** is any characteristic, attitude, behavior, or event that can take on two or more values or attributes. For example, the variable "marital status" has several categories: never married, cohabiting, married, separated, divorced, widowed. The variable "attitudes toward capital punishment" has categories ranging from very favorable to very unfavorable. Hirschi was interested in why juveniles engage in delinquent behavior. Such a question is far too general to study, so he developed a clear, specific, empirically testable prediction or hypothesis, specifying a relationship between two variables: Strong *social bonds* will be associated with low levels of *delinquency*.

In developing their theoretical explanations, sociologists distinguish between independent and dependent variables. An **independent variable** is the factor that is presumed to influence or create changes in another variable. The **dependent variable** is the one assumed to depend on, be influenced by, or change as a result of the independent variable. If we believe that gender affects people's attitudes toward abortion (that is, women will hold more favorable attitudes than men), then "gender" would be the independent variable and "attitudes toward abortion," the dependent variable. For Hirschi's theory of juvenile delinquency, the strength of the social bond was the independent variable and level of delinquency was the dependent variable.

The problem for social researchers, like Hirschi, is that the concepts that form the basis of theories are often abstract and not amenable to empirical observation. We can't directly observe concepts such as "social bonds." So these variables must be translated into something that can be observed or measured: **indicators**.

In his survey of 1,200 boys in grades 6 through 12, Hirschi derived a set of indicators for his independent variable, the strength of the social bond. To determine the degree to which young people are attached to law-abiding others, Hirschi measured their attraction to parents, peers, and school officials. To determine the degree to which they derived rewards from acting nondelinquently, he asked them to assess the importance of such things as getting good grades. To determine the proportion of their lives spent in conventional activities, he asked them how much time they spent in school-oriented activities. Finally, to determine their ties to a conventional belief system, he asked them questions about their respect for the law and the police.

Hirschi measured the dependent variable, delinquent activity, by asking the boys if they'd ever stolen things, taken cars for rides without the owners' permission, banged up something on purpose that belonged to somebody else, or beaten up or hurt someone on purpose. In addition, he used school records and police records to measure acts that had come to the attention of authorities.

The data he collected supported his hypothesis and therefore strengthened the power of his original theory.

Modes of Research

Although the answers to important sociological questions are not always simple or clear, the techniques sociologists use to collect and examine data allow them to draw informed and reliable conclusions about human behavior and social life. The most common techniques are experiments, field research, surveys, and unobtrusive research.

Experiments. An **experiment** is typically a research situation designed to elicit some sort of behavior under closely controlled laboratory circumstances. In its ideal form, the experimenter will randomly place subjects into two groups, then deliberately manipulate or introduce changes into the environment of one group of subjects (called the "experimental group") and not the other (called the "control group"). Care is taken to ensure that the groups are relatively alike except for the variable that the experimenter manipulates. Any observed or measured differences between the groups can then be attributed to the effects of the experimental manipulation (Singleton, Straits, & Straits, 1993).

Experiments have a significant advantage over other types of research because the researcher can directly control all the relevant variables. Thus conclusions about the independent variable causing changes in the dependent variable can be made more convincingly. The artificial nature of laboratory experiments, however, may make subjects behave differently than they would in their natural settings, leading some people to argue that experimentation in sociology is practically impossible (Silverman, 1982).

To overcome this difficulty, some sociologists have created experimental situations outside the laboratory. In 1979 Arthur Beaman and his colleagues (Beaman, Klentz, Diener, & Svanum, 1979) conducted an experiment to see whether self-awareness decreases the likelihood of engaging in socially undesirable behavior—in this case, stealing. The researchers set up situations in which children arriving at several homes on Halloween night were sent into the living room alone to take candy from a bowl. The children were first asked their names and ages and then told, "You may take one of the candies." For the experimental group, a large mirror was placed right next to the candy bowl so that the children couldn't help but see themselves. For the control group, there was no mirror. In the control group, 37% of the children took more than one candy, but only 4% of the children in the experimental group took more than one candy. The researchers concluded from this experiment that self-awareness can have a significant effect on honesty.

Field Research. In **field research**, sociologists observe events as they actually occur, without selecting experimental and control groups or purposely introducing any changes into the subjects' environment. Field research can take several forms. In **nonparticipant observation**, the researcher observes people without directly interacting with them and without their knowledge that they are being observed. Sociologist Lyn Lofland (1973), for example, studied how strangers relate to one another in public places by going to bus depots, airports, stores, restaurants, and parks and secretly recording everything she saw.

Participant observation requires that the researcher interact with subjects. In some cases the researcher openly identifies him- or herself. For instance, to gain insight into how people balance work and family, sociologist Arlie Russell Hochschild (1997) observed and interviewed 130 or so employees at a large public relations company she called "Amerco" over a period of three years. She was particularly interested in why employees tend not to take advantage of available family leave policies. At Amerco, only 53 of 21,000 employees—all of them women—chose to switch to part-time work in response to the arrival of a new baby. Less than 1% of the employees shared a job or worked at home, even though the company permits it. Most of the workers worked a lot of overtime, coming in early and staying late.

So why were these workers so unwilling to change their work lives to spend more time with their families even when the company would have supported them in doing so? Through her long-term observations of Amerco, Hochschild came to believe that the explanation could be found in the meanings people attach to their jobs and their families. She felt that for many people, work has become a form of "home" and home has become "work." Home has traditionally been defined as a soothing place where people should feel secure, relaxed, and comforted. Work, on the other hand, has traditionally been defined as a harried and insecure place where people often feel dehumanized ("just a cog in a machine") and where their worth is judged not by who they are but by how much they produce. But for many people at Amerco, home had become a place of frenzied activity and busy schedules whereas work had become a sort of nurturing refuge where they could relax and share stories with friends. So they prefer spending more time at work.

This type of field research is quite time-consuming. Researchers can conduct only a limited number of interviews and can observe only a limited number of people. Hochschild collected rich information about people's work/family tradeoffs, but she studied only one corporation. It's risky to generalize from the experiences of a small group of workers in one company in one society to all workers in all sorts of work environments.

In more delicate situations the researcher must conceal his or her identity. The researcher attempts to become a member of the group being observed and behaves as naturally as possible. In the mid-1950s a social psychologist named Leon Festinger set out to examine how groups protect their beliefs in the face of undeniable contradictory evidence (Festinger, Riecken, & Schacter, 1956). He chose to study a "doomsday" cult that had organized around the belief that a substantial chunk of the Western Hemisphere would be destroyed by a cataclysmic flood on December 21, 1955. He knew that studying such a group would be quite difficult. Highly sensitive to the public's skepticism, members would probably be unwilling to answer an interviewer's questions about their activities and beliefs. So Festinger and his assistants decided to pose as individuals interested in joining the group. Eventually they became full-fledged members, participating in all the group's activities.

When the great flood didn't occur on December 21, the group had to find some way to reconcile their beliefs with the failed prophecy. As the fateful day was ending, their leader began to make importance out of seemingly irrelevant recent news events. For instance, the Associated Press had reported that over the prior few days earthquakes had occurred in Nevada, California, and Italy. The damage brought about by these disasters became "proof" to the group members that cataclysms were actually happening. Members claimed that because of the group's efforts, their area had been spared from these upheavals.

Surveys, When it is impossible or impractical to carry out field observations or to set up a controlled experimental situation, social researchers use the survey. **Surveys** require that the researcher pose a series of questions either orally or on paper. The questions should be understood by the respondent the way the researcher wants them to be understood and measure what the researcher wants them to measure. In addition, the respondent is expected to answer the questions honestly and thoughtfully.

All of us have experienced surveys of one form or another. Every 10 years people who live in the United States are required to fill out questionnaires for the U.S. Census Bureau. At the end of some college courses you've probably filled out a course evaluation. Or perhaps you've been interviewed in a shopping mall or answered questions during a telephone survey.

Surveys typically use standardized formats. All subjects are asked the same questions in roughly the same way, and large samples of people are used as subjects. When sociologists Philip Blumstein and Pepper Schwartz (1983) undertook a massive study of intimate couples in the United States, they sent questionnaires to people from every income level, age group, religion, political ideology, and educational background. Some of their respondents were cohabiting, others were married. Some had children, others were childless. Some were heterosexual, others homosexual. All couples filled out a 38-page questionnaire that asked questions about their leisure activities, emotional support, housework, finances, sexual relations, satisfaction, relations with children, and so forth. More than 6,000 couples participated. From these surveys Blumstein and Schwartz were able to draw conclusions about the importance of money, work, sexuality, power, and gender in couple's lives.

Unobtrusive Research. All the methods I've discussed so far require the researcher to have some contact with the people being studied: giving them tasks to do in an experiment, or watching them (with or without their knowing that they are participating in social research), or asking them questions. The problem with these techniques is that the very act of intruding into people's lives may influence the phenomena being studied. Asking people questions about their voting intentions prior to an election, for instance, may affect their eventual voting behavior. Simply observing people can dramatically alter their behavior. In the late 1930s two sociologists (Roethlisberger & Dickson, 1939) were hired to study working conditions and worker productivity at an electric company in Hawthorne, Illinois. They were interested in finding out whether changing certain physical conditions in the plant could improve workers' productivity and satisfaction. They quickly discovered that when they brightened the lighting in the workroom, workers produced more. Increasing the brightness of the lights some more increased productivity more. To bolster their conclusion, they decided to dim the lights to see if productivity dropped. Much to their dismay, productivity *increased again* when they darkened the room. They soon realized that the workers were responding more to the attention they were receiving from the researchers, than to changes in their working conditions. This phenomenon has come to be known as the "Hawthorne effect."

To avoid such influence, sociologists sometimes use another research technique, unobtrusive research, which requires no contact with people at all. **Unobtrusive research** is an examination of the evidence of social behavior that people create or leave behind. Suppose you wanted to know what exhibits are most popular at a museum (Webb, Campbell, Schwartz, Sechrest, & Grove, 1981). You could poll people, but they might tell you things that make them appear more intellectual and sophisticated than they really are. You could stand there and watch people, but they might become self-conscious. Perhaps a better way would be to wait until the museum is empty and check the wear and tear on the floor in front of the exhibits. Those exhibits where the carpeting is worn down are probably the most popular. This would be an example of unobtrusive research.

There are several types of unobtrusive research. One type is the analysis of statistics gathered by someone else for some other purpose. Émile Durkheim used this technique when he examined different suicide rates for different groups to gain insight into the underlying causes of suicide (see Chapter 1). This sort of analysis is still used extensively by sociologists today. One of the most popular and convenient sources of data is the U.S. Census. Studies that examine broad, nationwide trends (for instance, marriage, divorce, or premarital childbearing rates) typically use existing census data.

Another form of unobtrusive research, called **content analysis,** is the study of recorded communications—books, speeches, poems, songs, television commercials, Web sites, and so forth. For example, sociologists Bernice Pescosolido, Elizabeth Grauerholz, and Melissa Milkie (1997) analyzed close to 2,000 children's picture books published from 1937 to 1993 to see if there were any changes in the way African Americans were portrayed. They believed that these depictions could tell a lot about the shifting nature of race relations in the larger society. The researchers looked not only for the number of black characters in these books but also at whether they were being portrayed positively or negatively. They found, among other things, that in times of high uncertainty in race relations and substantial protest and conflict over existing societal norms, blacks virtually disappeared from picture books. Furthermore, depictions of intimate, equal interracial interactions and portrayals of blacks as primary characters remain rare.

A third type of unobtrusive research is **historical analysis,** which relies on existing historical documents as a source of research information. Sociologist Kai Erikson (1966) was interested in how communities construct definitions of acceptable and unacceptable behavior. For his book *Wayward Puritans,* he studied several "crime waves" among the Puritans of the Massachusetts Bay Colony in the late 17th century. Erikson examined diaries, court records, birth and death records, letters, and other written documents of the period. Because a key piece of data was the number of criminal convictions, court records were an important source of information.

Piecing together fragments of information 300 years old was not easy. One problem Erikson faced was the fact that the Puritans didn't observe any consistent rules of spelling. The name of one man was spelled 14 different ways. In some instances it wasn't clear whether two people with similar names were actually the same person. Erikson solved the problem by inspecting birth and death certificates and other records to distinguish one life span from another.

Erikson was able to draw some conclusions about the nature of human life and shifting cultural definitions of reality. He found that each time the colony was threatened in some way—by opposing religious groups, a crisis of faith in the authority of the community leaders, or the king of England's revocation of its charter—the numbers of convicted criminals and the severity of punishments significantly increased. Erikson believed that these fluctuations occurred because the community needed to restate its moral boundaries and reaffirm its authority.

Another form of unobtrusive research that is becoming increasingly popular is **visual sociology**, a method of studying society through photographs, video, and film. Some visual sociologists use these media to gather sociological data—much as documentary photographers and filmmakers do. The visual images they create are meant to tell a sociological story. Other visual sociologists analyze the meaning and purpose of existing visual texts, such as sports photographs, film advertisements, and the photographic archives of corporations (Harper, 1996). The visual essays that appear throughout this book use this methodology to examine important issues of sociological interest.

The Trustworthiness of Social Research

Most sociologists see research as not only personally valuable but central to human knowledge and understanding. However, as informed consumers we must ask, How accurate is this information? We tend to believe what we read in print or see reported on television or on the Internet. Unfortunately, much of what we see is either inaccurate or misleading. To evaluate the results of social research, we must examine the researcher's samples, indicators, values, and interests.

Samples. Frequently, researchers are interested in the attitudes, behaviors, or characteristics of large groups—college students, women, sports enthusiasts, Brazilians, and so on. It would be impossible to interview, survey, or observe all these people directly. Hence, researchers must select from the larger population a smaller **sample** of respondents for study. The characteristics of this subgroup are supposed to approximate the characteristics of the entire population of interest. A sample is said to be **representative** if the small group being studied is in fact typical of the population as a whole. For instance, a sample of 100 students from your university should include roughly the same proportion of first-year students, sophomores, juniors, and seniors that characterizes the entire school population. Sampling techniques have become highly sophisticated, as illustrated by the relative accuracy of polls conducted to predict election results.

In the physical sciences sampling is not an issue. Certain physical or chemical elements are assumed to be identical. One need only study a small number of test tubes of nitrogen because one test tube of nitrogen should be the same as any other. Human beings, however, vary widely on every imaginable characteristic. One could not make a general statement about all Americans on the basis of an interview with one person. For that matter, one could not draw conclusions about all people from observing a sample consisting only of Americans, men, or teenagers. Samples that are not representative can lead to inaccurate and misleading conclusions.

Note the sampling problems revealed in the following letter to the editor of a small-town newspaper in the rural Midwest:

> I went to a restaurant yesterday for lunch. I began to feel guilty, when I reached into my pocket for a cigarette. . . . I was thinking of the government figures which estimated cigarette smokers at 26% of the population of the United States. But everywhere I looked inside that room, people were smoking. I decided to count them. There were 22 people in the room. . . . I was surprised to discover that the government's figures were an outright fabrication. . . . Seventeen people out of the 22 were cigarette smokers . . . that accounts for over 77% of the people in that restaurant. . . . The government's figures are understated by 51% and just plain wrong! (*Greencastle Banner Graphic*, 1992)

This letter writer assumes that the 22 people who frequented a small restaurant in a small, relatively poor rural town on a single day were an adequate representation of the entire U.S. population. Such a conclusion overlooks some important factors. Government studies show that the lower a person's income, the greater the likelihood that person will be a smoker. Furthermore, people in blue-collar or service jobs are more likely to smoke than people in white-collar jobs. Finally, the prevalence of smoking is higher in the Midwest than in other parts of the country (U.S. Department of Health and Human Services, 1988).

Indicators. As you recall, one problem sociologists face when doing research is that the variables they are interested in studying are usually difficult to see. What does powerlessness look like? How can you "see" marital instability? How would you recognize alienation or social class? Sociologists thus resign themselves to measuring indicators of things that cannot be measured directly. Researchers measure events and behaviors commonly thought to accompany a particular variable, hoping that what they are measuring is a valid indicator of the concept they are interested in.

Suppose you believe that people's attitudes toward abortion are influenced by the strength of their religious beliefs, or "religiosity." You might hypothesize that the more religious someone is, the less accepting she or he will be of abortion rights. To test this hypothesis you must first figure out what you mean by "religious." What might be an indicator of the strength of someone's religious beliefs? You could determine if the subjects of your study identify themselves as members of some organized religion. But would this indicator tell how religious your subjects are? Probably not, because many people identify themselves as, say, Catholic or Jewish but are not religious at all. Likewise, some people who consider themselves quite religious don't identify with any organized religion. So this measure would focus on group differences but would fail to capture the intensity of a person's beliefs or the degree of religious interest.

Perhaps a better indicator would be some quantifiable behavior, such as the frequency of attendance at formal religious services. Arguably, the more someone attends church or synagogue, the more religious that person is. But here, too, we run into problems. Church attendance, for instance, may reflect family pressure, habit, or the desire to visit with others rather than religious commitment. Furthermore, many very religious people are unable to attend services because they are sick or disabled.

Frequency of prayer might be a better indicator. Obviously people who pray a lot are more religious than people who don't pray at all. But some nonreligious people pray for things all the time. As you can see, indicators seldom perfectly reflect the concepts they are intended to measure.

Surveys are particularly susceptible to inaccurate indicators. A loaded phrase or an unfamiliar word in a survey question can dramatically affect people's responses in ways unintended by the researcher. The National Opinion Research Center asked in an annual survey of public attitudes if the United States was spending too much, too little, or about the right amount of money on "assistance to the poor." Two-thirds of the respondents said the country was spending too little. But in a different study the word *welfare* was substituted for "assistance to the poor" in the question. This time nearly half of the respondents said the country was spending too much money (Kagay & Elder, 1992).

Values and Interests. In addition to samples and indicators, the researcher's own values and interests can influence social research. Ideally, research is objective and nonbiased and measures what is and not what should be. However, the questions researchers ask and the way they interpret observations always take place in a particular cultural, political, and ideological context (Ballard, 1987; Denzin, 1989). If prevailing social values identify an intact nuclear family as the best environment for children, then most researchers will be prone to notice the disadvantages and perhaps ignore the advantages of other family arrangements. Furthermore, research is sometimes carried out to support a narrowly defined political or economic interest, as when tobacco companies fund studies that show no relationship between smoking and cancer.

We must remember that sociologists are people too, with their own biases, preconceptions, and expectations. Sociologists' values determine the kinds of information they gather about a particular social phenomenon. If you were conducting research on whether the criminal justice system is fair, would you study criminals, politicians, law enforcement personnel, judges, or victims? Each group would likely provide a different perception of the system. The most accurate picture of reality is likely to be based on the views of all subgroups involved.

In fact, values can influence the questions that researchers find important enough to address in the first place (Reinharz, 1992). For instance, research on families has historically reflected the interests of men by viewing the female-headed household as dysfunctional or deficient (Thorne & Yalom, 1982). Similarly, the male bias affects the questions that are researched in the study of women's work (Acker, 1978). The term *labor force* has traditionally referred to those working for pay and has excluded those doing unpaid work such as housework and volunteer jobs—areas that are predominantly female. Thus, findings on labor force participation are more likely to reflect the significant elements of men's lives than of women's lives. You can see that a lack of data does not necessarily indicate that a phenomenon or a problem doesn't exist. Perhaps all it indicates is that no researcher has yet undertaken a systematic study of it.

Ethics in Research

Research, as I mentioned earlier, often represents an intrusion into people's lives—it may disrupt their ordinary activities and it often requires them to reveal personal information about themselves. Ethical researchers agree, therefore, that they should protect the rights of subjects and minimize the amount of harm or disruption subjects might experience as a result of being part of a study. Ethical researchers agree that no one should be forced to participate in research, that those who do participate ought to be fully informed of the possible risks involved, and that every precaution ought to be taken to protect the confidentiality and anonymity of subjects. Sociologists almost always conduct their research under the scrutiny of university review committees for the protection of human subjects.

At the same time, however, researchers must attempt to secure the most accurate information possible. Sometimes this requirement conflicts with ethical considerations. Recall from Chapter 2 that when social psychologist Stanley Milgram studied obedience to authority he deceived his subjects into thinking they were actually administering painful shocks to others. His results would have been severely flawed—and crucial information about the power of authority would have been lost—had he informed his subjects that the fellow "subject" wasn't really being shocked, that it was all a fabrication. The question then, as always, was at what point does our need to acquire important sociological knowledge override the obligation to protect subjects?

Laud Humphreys
The Tearoom Trade

Most sociologists agree that the psychological anguish Milgram's subjects experienced was worth the information that was obtained. There is less agreement and more controversy, however, over situations in which researchers misrepresent their identities in order to gather information. Consider Laud Humphreys's 1970 study called *The Tearoom Trade,* a study many sociologists found ethically indefensible. Humphreys was interested in studying anonymous and casual homosexual encounters among strangers. He decided to focus on interactions in "tearooms," which are places, such as public restrooms, where male homosexuals go for anonymous sex. (This study was done well before the AIDS epidemic significantly curtailed such activity.)

Because of the secretive and potentially stigmatizing nature of the phenomenon he was interested in, Humphreys couldn't just come right out and ask people about their actions. So he decided to engage in a secretive form of participant observation. He posed as a lookout, called a "watchqueen," whose job was to warn participants of intruders as they engaged in sexual acts with one another in public restrooms. In this way he was able to conduct very detailed observations of these encounters.

Humphreys also wanted to know about the regular lives of these men. Whenever possible he wrote down the license numbers of the participants' cars and tracked down their names and addresses with the help of a friend in the local police department. About a year later he arranged for these individuals to be part of a simple medical survey being conducted by some of his colleagues. He then disguised himself and visited their homes, supposedly to conduct interviews for the medical survey. He found that most of the men were heterosexual, had families, and were rather respected members of their communities. In short, they led altogether conventional lives.

Although this information shed a great deal of light on the nature of anonymous homosexual acts, some critics argued that Humphreys had violated the ethics of research by deceiving his unsuspecting subjects and violating their privacy rights. Some critics also noted that Humphreys might have been sued for invasion of privacy if he had not been studying a group of people rendered powerless by their potential embarrassment. Others, however, supported Humphreys, arguing that he could have studied this topic in no other way. In fact, his book won a prestigious award. But 30 years later, the ethical controversy surrounding this study remains.

CONCLUSION

In this chapter I have described some of the processes by which reality is constructed, communicated, manipulated, and accepted. Reality, whether in the form of everyday observations or formal research, is ultimately a human creation. Different people can create different conceptions of reality.

This issue can be raised from a personal level to a global one. Every culture believes that its reality is the paramount one. Who is right? Can we truly believe that a reality in direct conflict with ours is equally valid? If we profess that everyone should have the right to believe what she or he wants, are we acknowledging the socially constructed nature of reality or merely being tolerant of those who are not "smart enough" to think as we do? Do we have the right to tell other people or other cultures that what they do or believe is wrong only because it conflicts with our definition of reality? Exasperating and complex, these questions lie at the core of everyday life, international relations, and global commerce.

YOUR TURN

The reality we take for granted is a social construction. This is particularly apparent when we look at the information presented to us as fact through published academic research, word of mouth, or the media. Reality is influenced by the individuals and organizations who are responsible for creating, assembling, and disseminating this information.

Choose an event that is currently making national headlines. It could be a story about the president or Congress, a major national tragedy or disaster, or a highly publicized criminal trial. Over the course of a week analyze how this story is being covered by the following:

- Your local newspaper
- The major national newspapers (*USA Today*, the *New York Times*, the *Washington Post*)

- Mainstream news magazines (*Time, Newsweek, U.S. News & World Report*)
- Alternative magazines (*Utne Reader, Mother Jones, In These Times*, and so on)
- A local TV station
- The major networks (NBC, CBS, ABC, Fox, CNN)
- The Internet (chat rooms, Web sites, discussion lists, and so on)

Pay particular attention to the following:

- The amount of time or space devoted to the story
- The "tone" of the coverage (Supportive or critical? Purely factual or reflective of certain political opinions? Specific, objective language or biased, inflammatory language?)

Summarize your findings. What were the differences in how the story was covered (for example, local versus national media, print versus electronic media, one TV network versus another, mainstream versus alternative press)? What were the similarities?

Interpret your findings. What do these differences and similarities suggest about the people who run these organizations? Whose political or economic interests are being served or undermined by the manner in which the story is being presented to the public? Which medium do you think is providing the most accurate, objective coverage? Why?

CHAPTER HIGHLIGHTS

- The social construction of reality (truth, knowledge, and so on) is the process by which reality is discovered, made known, reinforced, and changed by members of society.

- Language is the medium through which reality construction takes place. It enables us to think, interpret, and define. Linguistic categories reflect aspects of a culture that are relevant and meaningful to people's lives.

- Not all of us possess the same ability to define reality. Individuals and groups in positions of power have the ability to control information, define values, create myths, manipulate events, and ultimately influence what others take for granted.

- The purpose of a discipline such as sociology is to amass a body of knowledge that provides the public with useful information about how society works. This is done through systematic social research—experiments, field research, surveys, and unobtrusive research.

KEY TERMS

content analysis   Form of unobtrusive research that studies the content of recorded messages, such as books, speeches, poems, songs, television shows, Web sites, and advertisements

dependent variable   Experimental variable that is assumed to be caused by, or to change as a result of, the independent variable

empirical research   Research that operates from the ideological position that questions about human behavior can be answered only through controlled, systematic observations in the real world

experiment   Research method designed to elicit some sort of behavior, typically conducted under closely controlled laboratory circumstances

field research Type of social research in which the researcher observes events as they actually occur

historical analysis Form of social research that relies on existing historical documents as a source of data

hypothesis Researchable prediction that specifies the relationship between two or more variables

incorrigible proposition Unquestioned cultural belief that cannot be proved wrong no matter what happens to dispute it

independent variable Experimental variable presumed to cause or influence the dependent variable

indicator Measurable event, characteristic, or behavior commonly thought to reflect a particular concept

moral entrepreneur Group that works to have its moral concerns translated into law

nonparticipant observation Form of field research in which the researcher observes people without directly interacting with them and without letting them know that they are being observed

participant observation Form of field research in which the researcher interacts with subjects, sometimes hiding his or her identity

probabilistic Capable of identifying only those forces that have a high likelihood, but not a certainty, of influencing human action

representative Typical of the whole population being studied

sample Subgroup chosen for a study because its characteristics approximate those of the entire population

self-fulfilling prophecy Assumption or prediction that in itself causes the expected event to occur, thus seeming to confirm the prophecy's accuracy

social construction of reality Process through which the members of a society discover, make known, reaffirm, and alter a collective version of facts, knowledge, and "truth"

survey Form of social research in which the researcher asks subjects a series of questions, either verbally or on paper

theory Set of statements or propositions that seeks to explain or predict a particular aspect of social life

unobtrusive research Research technique in which the researcher, without direct contact with the subjects, examines the evidence of social behavior that people create or leave behind

variable Any characteristic, attitude, behavior, or event that can take on two or more values or attributes

visual sociology Method of studying society that uses photographs, video, and film either as means of gathering data or as sources of data about social life

4 Building Order: Culture and History

In Madagascar, the harvest months of August and September mark the *famadi-hana*—the "turning of the bones." Families receive messages from their dead loved ones, who may say that they are uncomfortable or need new clothes. In an elaborate ceremony that includes feasting and singing, the family digs up the graves of the deceased. The bodies are wrapped in shrouds and seated at the dinner table. Family news is whispered to them, and toasts are drunk. Widows and widowers can often be seen dancing with the bones of their dead spouses. The exhumed bones are then oiled and perfumed and laid back onto their "beds" inside the family tomb (Perlez, 1991).

In the late 19th and early 20th centuries, dating and courtship in North America were based on a ritualized system known as "calling." Although the process varied by region and social class, the following general guidelines were involved:

> When a girl reached the proper age or had her first "season" (depending on her family's social level), she became eligible to receive male callers. At first her mother or guardian invited young men to call; in subsequent seasons the young lady . . . could bestow an invitation to call upon any unmarried man to whom she had been properly introduced at a private dance, dinner, or other "entertainment." . . . Other young men . . . could be brought to call by friends or relatives of the girl's family, subject to her prior permission. . . . The call itself was a complicated event. A myriad of rules governed everything: the proper amount of time between invitation and visit (two weeks or less); whether or not refreshments should be served . . . ; chaperonage (the first call must be made on mother and daughter . . .); appropriate topics of conversation (the man's interests, but never too personal); how leave should be taken (on no account should the woman accompany [her caller] to the door nor stand talking while he struggles with his coat). (B. L. Bailey, 1988, pp. 15–16)

How could anybody dig up the body of a dead relative? Why would young men and young women follow such elaborate rules just so they could go on a date? Such practices seem peculiar, silly, or backward to most of us, but to the people involved, they are or were simply the taken-for-granted, "right" ways of doing things.

Some of the things you do may seem equally incomprehensible to an outside observer. For instance, you may not think twice about eating a juicy steak, but someone from a culture that views cows as sacred may be horrified at the thought. You may routinely shave your face, legs, or armpits, but imagine what these practices would look like in a culture where such acts are blasphemous. You may think a Spaniard's fondness for bullfighting is "absurd," yet millions of people in the United States shell out a lot of money each year to watch large men in brightly colored helmets and uniforms knock each other down while they chase, throw, carry, and kick an object made out of the hide of a dead pig. You may pity the turn-of-the-century woman who squeezed her body into ultra-tight corsets in order to achieve the figure men admired (Ehrenreich & English, 1979). Yet many women today (as well as some men) routinely coat their skin with flesh-colored makeup, use harsh chemicals to color their hair, pay to have someone cut into their faces to decrease the size of their noses or tighten the skin around their chins, and even starve themselves in the interests of becoming slender.

The legitimacy of certain practices and ideas can be understood only within the unique context of the group or society in which they occur. What is considered abnormal in one case might be perfectly normal, even necessary, in another. It takes sociological imagination to see that time and place have a great influence on what people consider normal.

Ancestor worship in Madagascar is a custom that has been around for centuries, impervious to the arrival of Christian churches and Western ideals. To the people who practice it, the ritual of burial and disinterment is more important than marriage. Life is seen as a mere transition. They believe that through one's ancestors an individual can communicate with God. The Malagasy people believe that spirits stay with the bones and have needs for earthly goods like food and clothing. It's up to the living to provide these things. In exchange, the dead take care of the living by determining health, wealth, and fertility. In short, the custom is quite rational and beneficial: Their own earthly well-being and spiritual salvation depend on it.

Likewise, the practice of calling played an integral part in turn-of-the-century U.S. culture. It maintained the social class structure by serving as a test of suitability, breeding, and background (B. L. Bailey, 1988). Calling enabled the middle and upper classes to protect themselves from what many at the time considered the "intrusions" of urban life and to screen out the effects of social and geographical mobility that reached unprecedented levels at the turn of the century. It also allowed parents to control the relationships of their children, thereby increasing the likelihood that their pedigree would remain intact.

These phenomena illustrate the important role played by culture and history in creating social order. Whether we're talking about our own ordinary rituals or those practiced by some distant society, the normative patterns that mark the millions of seemingly trivial actions and social encounters of our everyday lives are what make society possible. They tell us what to expect from others and what others should expect from us. In this chapter I examine how order is created and maintained in society by looking at the various taken-for-granted aspects of culture that lend structure to our daily lives. In the process I compare specific aspects of our culture to others, past and present.

Dimensions of Culture

In everyday conversation, the term *culture* is often used only when discussing something "foreign." We rarely feel the need to question why we do certain things in the course of our everyday lives—we just do them. It's other people in other lands whose rituals and beliefs need explaining. What we fail to realize is that culture is "doing its job" most effectively when it is unnoticed. It's what we take for granted that we're least likely to speak about; and it's those cultural silences that are most familiar to members and most important for social order to endure (Perin, 1988). Only in times of dramatic social change and moral uncertainty, or when circumstances force us to compare our society to another (for example, when traveling abroad) do we become aware that we, too, are influenced by a distinct set of cultural rules and values.

We can know a lot about someone just by knowing something about his or her culture:

> Even those of us who pride ourselves on our individualism follow most of the time a pattern not of our own making. We brush our teeth on arising. We put on pants—not a loincloth or a grass skirt. . . . We sleep in a bed—not a hammock or on a sheep pelt. I do not have to know the individual and his [or her] life history to be able to predict these and countless other regularities. (Kluckholm, 2000, p. 83)

To a large degree, we are products of the culture and historical epoch in which we reside. From a very young age we learn, with a startling amount of accuracy, that certain types of shelter, food, tools, clothing, music, sports, and art characterize our culture and make it different from others. Without much conscious effort, we also learn what to believe, what to value, and which actions are proper or improper in both public and private.

Material and Nonmaterial Culture

Culture consists of all the products of a society that are created over time and shared. These products may be tangible or intangible. The term **nonmaterial culture** refers to all the nonphysical products of society that are created over time and shared: knowledge, beliefs, customs, values, morals, symbols, and so on. Nonmaterial culture also includes common patterns of behavior and the forms of interaction appropriate in a particular society. It is a "design for living" that distinguishes one society from another. Like an owner's manual for social life, nonmaterial culture tells us how our society works, what we are to believe is possible, how we are to conduct our everyday lives, and what to do if something breaks down. Without an understanding of a society's nonmaterial culture, people's behaviors—not to mention the symbolic significance of their material world—would be thoroughly incomprehensible.

Material culture includes the physical artifacts that shape the lives of members of a particular society: distinctive clothing, buildings, inventions, food, artwork, literature, music, and so on. Some of the most important elements of material culture are technological achievements, which are the ways members of a society apply knowledge to adapt to changing social, economic, or environmental conditions. For instance, plastic products have provided people with cheaper and more convenient packaging of needed goods—and in the process altered shopping and consumption patterns.

Similarly, the advent of the automobile gives people greater mobility to take advantage of economic opportunities elsewhere and thereby dramatically changes some of their values and the way they live. In advanced industrialized countries such as the United States and Canada, the automobile has been widely available since the early 20th century, so we have become accustomed to the social changes associated with it, such as suburban living and unchaperoned teen dating. But the changes are more noticeable today in places such as Nepal and rural China, where the automobile is just beginning to impact people's lives.

Changes in material culture often change the physical environment. The enormous amount of nonbiodegradable plastic piling up in overflowing landfills has spawned a vast array of advances in recycling technology. Likewise, heavy reliance on the automobile has created several serious problems in urban areas throughout the world: air pollution, depletion of fossil fuel reserves, traffic, and suburban sprawl. These problems, in turn, have created the need for further material developments, such as mechanical devices to reduce pollution, alternative fuel sources, and more efficient highway systems.

Micro-Macro Connection
The Chair

Even the simplest and most taken-for-granted material objects carry enormous cultural weight. Take, for example, the common chair. We spend a huge chunk of our lives sitting in chairs—in dining rooms, kitchens, living rooms, classrooms, libraries, offices, patios, cars, buses, movie theaters, restaurants, and so on. You're probably sitting in one at this very moment.

Chairs supposedly make our lives comfortable. To be able to relax, kick off your shoes, and plop down on the old La-Z-Boy after a hard day's work is one of life's great pleasures. But such comfort has a steep cost. Ironically, lower back pain, often caused by bad sitting posture or poorly designed chairs, is second only to the common cold as the leading cause of absenteeism from work (Cranz, 1998). And our sedentary lifestyle has created a nation of people who are woefully out of shape.

Like all pieces of material culture, chairs are human creations. But once they're built, they start to shape us. The type of chair you use in your sociology class immediately places you in the role of student. And whether these chairs are arranged in rows or in a circle determines the degree of interaction expected of you in class. Children's first institutional lessons in controlling their bodies typically involve the chairs they are told to "sit still" in. Sitting quietly in rows of hard straight chairs is not a natural state of being for young children. But it certainly helps teachers maintain authority and keep disruptive behaviors safely contained.

Chairs often take on important cultural significance beyond their functionality. For instance, the chair a person sits in may define that person's social status. In antiquity, only the most powerful and prestigious members of a society had access to chairs;

the throne is one of the most enduring symbols of royalty worldwide. When the Pope issues an authoritative decree to Catholics around the world, he is said to be speaking *ex cathedra*, which literally means "from the chair." In some families children learn very quickly the consequences of sitting in or otherwise sullying "Dad's chair." The "chair" of an academic department can wield a great deal of power. On the other end of the spectrum, the "electric chair" is reserved for the lowest and most despicable of citizens, whose heinous crimes have led society to pronounce them unfit to live.

The right-angled posture required to sit in a chair, which we assume to be the universally proper way to sit, is used by only a third to half of the people worldwide (Cranz, 1998). In many parts of the world people sit on floors, mats, carpets, or platforms. A Chinese man will likely squat when waiting for a bus; a Japanese woman kneels when eating; an Arab might sit cross-legged on the floor when reading.

Regardless of whether we use a chair or what sort of chair we use, one thing is clear: this habit was created, modified, nurtured, and reformed in response to cultural—and not anatomical—forces. Our subjective experiences of comfort are socially constructed and our bodies respond accordingly. For the American it *really is* more comfortable to sit in a chair; for the Arab it *really is* more comfortable to sit on the floor. The fact that these choices are experienced subjectively as personally pleasant doesn't mean that culture isn't at work here.

Global Culture

Although culture gives a society its distinctive character, cultural "purity" is all but obsolete (Griswold, 1994). Transnational media, global communication and transportation systems, and massive immigration have contributed to the worldwide homogenization of some cultural elements. For instance, American pizza, which originated in Naples, Italy, has migrated to every corner of the globe. Domino's Pizza now has over 2,000 stores in 61 countries; Pizza Hut has close to 4,000 stores in over 90 countries (Crossette, 2000a). What were once unique features of U.S. material culture—such as action films, blue jeans, and designer coffee houses—can now be found on nearly every continent. It wouldn't be particularly surprising to find people wearing Levi's in a remote village in the Andes Mountains of Peru or watching MTV in Bangkok. In 2000, Starbucks opened a coffee shop in Beijing's Forbidden City, across from the former Imperial Palace.

In some societies, imported elements of culture are seen as dangerous encroachments on long-held traditions and national unity. Approximately two-thirds of French respondents to a recent survey felt that the United States exerted too much cultural influence on Europe (Daley, 2000). A French sheep farmer named José Bové has become something of a national hero for vandalizing McDonald's restaurants, a symbol of what many French consider to be the unwanted intrusion of U.S. food culture. In 1998, culture ministers from 20 different countries on four continents met to discuss how best to maintain their own cultures in a global environment dominated by U.S. media (Croteau & Hoynes, 2000).

Emotions can run especially high when the integrity of a culture's language is at stake. About 60% of all existing languages have fewer than 10,000 speakers. These languages are highly vulnerable to disappearance in a global culture. Indeed, each year about 30 languages around the world become extinct. Australia once had 250 different languages; today there are about 20 (J. Raymond, 1998). One linguist recently predicted that at least half of the world's roughly 6,500 languages will die during the next century. Taking their place will be a handful of dominant languages that, in a technologically connected world, are seen as "linguistic passports" to education and a successful economic future (P. H. Lewis, 1998b).

Foremost among these major languages is English, which today shapes communication all over the world. The word for home run in Spanish is *jonrón*. The French word for weekend is *le week-end*. People are recognizing that in a world of collapsing borders a common language is useful. And because of pervasive U.S. cultural influences and technologies, English is an understandable choice. For instance, English remains the default language of the Internet, even though almost half of the 280 million people worldwide who use the Internet speak languages other than English (Kushner, 2000).

The growth of English—and especially American English—as a sort of "world" language has had a profound effect on the way people in other countries go about their business. For example, the Swiss government recently decreed that all Swiss children above the age of 6 must learn English. But not everyone is happy about such developments. In 1994 the French culture minister proposed a law that would have required that 3,000 English words widely used in France be replaced by their French equivalents. The government now requires civil servants to use French terms instead of English slang while on the job. Similarly, in an effort to limit the influence of American popular music, the Israeli Parliament approved a bill requiring that half of the songs on national radio stations must be in Hebrew. According to the sponsor of the bill, "We are putting up a protective wall against the flood of foreign culture" (quoted in Greenberg, 1998, p. 10).

Subcultures

Sociologists and anthropologists usually speak of culture as a characteristic of an entire society. But culture can also exist in smaller, more narrowly defined units. A **subculture** consists of the values, behaviors, and physical artifacts of a group that distinguishes itself from the larger culture. Think of it as a culture within a culture. Racial and ethnic groups, religions, age groups, even geographic areas often develop their own distinct subcultures.

Consider life at your university. You are probably well aware of the material and nonmaterial culture that is unique to your campus. Perhaps some landmark—a bell tower or an ornate archway—is the defining symbol of the university, or maybe some area or piece of art occupies a hallowed place in campus life. I'm sure you know what your school mascot is and what the school colors are. In addition, when you arrived on campus, you probably had to learn a tremendous amount of new information about the nonmaterial culture just to survive—how to register for courses; how to address a professor; where to eat and study; what administrators, faculty, and fellow students expect of you. You may have even been required to learn an entirely new vocabulary of terms that only students at your university understand. On my campus, the student newspaper publishes a glossary of terms at the beginning of each academic year to aid first-year students in their adjustment to life here. Just as you had to learn how to be a member of your society, you had to learn how to be a member of your university subculture.

But placing a label on a subculture sometimes forces people to ignore its complexity and diversity. For instance, you often hear people talk about the U.S. "teen subculture" as if it were a single, self-contained entity that is the same everywhere. But such a characterization overlooks the multitude of subgroups within that subculture:

> On any sustained wander through the world of American youth, one meets . . . an endless array of ardent skaters, skins, rockers, ravers, rebels, heshers, punks, Goths, jocks, Rude Boys, hippies, preps, rappers, neo-Nazis, cheerleaders, Satanists, and straightedged anarchists. This is just an arbitrary, incomplete catalogue of a few high-profile formations—the kind that tend to have their own magazines, Web sites, fashion lines, and music playlists, not to mention "beliefs." There are thousands of smaller sects and splinters and tendencies, gangs and subgangs and cliques, rising and falling all the time, each with a party line on a range of cultural issues, large and small. (Finnegan, 1998, p. 349)

Although certain subcultures may appear to dramatically conflict with the beliefs and values of the dominant culture, they never exist completely independent of that culture. For instance, alienated youth may adorn themselves in the angry and rebellious fashion trappings of gangsta rappers or antiglobal anarchists, but they still must conform to many of the dictates of the larger culture by exchanging money for necessary goods and services, going to school, and eventually getting a job so they can support themselves.

History: The "Archives" for Everyday Living

Like culture, history is simultaneously ubiquitous and invisible. We rarely see the connection between our personal lives and the larger historical context in which we live. Just as culture tends to be equated with the foreign, history tends to be equated with the past.

It is all too easy to use contemporary criteria to try to understand the thoughts and actions of people who lived long ago. For example, in 1997 the New Orleans School Board voted unanimously to change the name of George Washington Elementary School. The board as a matter of policy opposes naming schools for former slave owners, no matter what their other accomplishments, or for persons who didn't believe in equal rights for all. When Washington died in 1799, he owned 316 slaves (Sack, 1997). Abraham Lincoln, one of history's most influential proponents of liberty and equality, once said, "There is a physical difference between the white and black races which I believe will forever forbid the two races living together on terms of social and political equality" (quoted in Gould, 1981, p. 35). Similar views of racial separation were voiced by such important historical figures as Benjamin Franklin, Thomas

Jefferson, and Charles Darwin. Such comments today would be taken as indications of a deeply held prejudice.

However, we must understand such beliefs and behaviors not merely as signs of personal bigotry but as reflections of the dominant belief system of the times. In other words, they are social constructions. As repugnant as we might find these attitudes, they were taken as undeniable truths by the scientific communities of their era. Innate "racial inferiority" was as much an established "scientific fact" then as the expansion of the universe is today. (See Chapter 11 for more detail on the belief in innate racial inferiority.)

The norms and values that govern everyday life in a given society are also likely to change over time. Some cultural practices that were wholly unacceptable in the past have now become commonplace. Premarital sex and househusbands do not incite the sort of moral outrage or suspicion they once did. However, many actions have become less acceptable over time, at least among certain subcultures. I read a while ago that showering after gym class—a mandatory, military-like ritual two decades ago—has become virtually obsolete among U.S. high school students today (D. Johnson, 1996a). Some cite insecurities about body image, heightened sexual awareness, and lack of time in a busy schedule as possible reasons for a phenomenon that would have been unheard of and even punishable a generation ago.

Other acts have not just become less acceptable, they've become criminal. In the United States, there was a time when people could smoke cigarettes anywhere and anytime they pleased—in hospitals, supermarkets, restaurants, movie theaters. Now, with the increase in health awareness, smoking in public has been severely restricted and even outlawed in some locales. In New York, talking on a cell phone while driving is now a crime.

Historical shifts in the cultural acceptance of certain behaviors involve more than just a societal realization of the danger of such behaviors. Actually, as conflict theory would point out, such designations are greatly influenced by social and economic concerns. Take, for instance, the criminalization of opium—the substance from which heroin is derived. During the 19th century, the use of opium was permitted in many parts of the world without legal sanction; it was commonly used for therapeutic purposes as a pain reliever, a cold medicine, and a cough suppressant (Inciardi, 1992). The typical "heroin addict" at the time in the United States was a white middle-class housewife.

By the early 20th century, however, things had changed considerably. In the United States, there was a growing fear, particularly on the West Coast, of economic competition from Chinese laborers who had been "imported" to work on the railroads. Workers began to see Chinese immigrants as a direct threat to their material interests. At the same time, these immigrants became equated with opium use (Hagan, 1985). What followed must have made perfectly logical sense at the time: If a despised group characteristically engages in a particular behavior, there must be something wrong with that behavior. A moral consensus soon emerged that focused on the presumed link between the Chinese and narcotics (Bonnie & Whitebread, 1974). It wasn't long before opium use became the dreaded "Oriental dope problem." By 1914 tight legislative controls restricted the U.S. distribution of opium to authorized medical prescriptions only. By 1925 it was completely outlawed (Becker, 1963).

Cultural Expectations and Social Order

Despite periodic shifts in the acceptability of specific acts, culture and history provide people with a common bond, a sense of shared personal experiences. That we can live together at all depends on the fact that we share a tremendous amount of cultural knowledge. This knowledge allows us to predict, with a fair amount of certainty, what most people will do in a given situation. I can assume that when I say, "Hi, how are you?" you will say, "Fine." You probably would not go into some long-winded explanation of your mental, physical, and emotional condition at that precise moment because doing so would violate the cultural rules governing casual greetings.

The actions of individuals are not simply functions of personality types or psychological predispositions; rather, they are also a reflection of shared cultural expectations. Culture provides us with information about which of these actions are preferred, accepted, disapproved, or unthinkable at a given time (McCall & Simmons, 1978). Recall from Chapter 2 that norms are the rules that govern the routine social encounters in which we all participate. Although everyday norms are sometimes difficult to identify and describe, they reflect commonly held assumptions about conventional behavior—what is considered good and bad, moral and immoral, appropriate and inappropriate. Without norms, individual behaviors in any given situation would vary widely, and a lot more of our time would be spent trying to figure out other people's behavior so we could frame our responses accordingly.

Consider the unspoken norms in a situation we've all experienced, shopping at a supermarket:

> There is a customer role to be played in grocery stores. There generally is a standard of orderliness. Shoppers are not seen pushing each other out of the way, picking things out of each other's shopping carts, or sitting on the floor eating from a recently opened can. How does one "know" how the role of customer is to be played? Aside from the "No Shirt. No Bare Feet" sign on the door . . . there is no clear listing of shopping rules.
>
> Evidence of the implied existence of such rules can be found in the way people react to a fellow shopper dressed in a gorilla suit or to someone who violates the norms for waiting in line at the checkout counter. One may feel that rules are being broken when one finds oneself standing in line with melting ice cream behind a grandmother who takes out her grandchildren's photographs to show the clerk. Such behavior violates the norms of universalism (all customers are to be treated equally) and efficiency; the grocery store is not a context in which one shares one's private self with others, particularly anonymous others. (Kearl & Gordon, 1992, p. 274)

Norms can be generalized in similar situations within a culture. That is, we can be reasonably certain that grocery store behavior that is appropriate in Baltimore will be appropriate in Houston as well. The grocery store experience itself would be chaotic if there weren't a certain degree of agreement over how we should act. Without such unspoken rules, every situation would have to be interpreted, analyzed, and responded to as if it were an entirely new occasion. Social life (not to mention preparing meals) would be utterly unmanageable.

Micro-Macro Connection
The "Right" Emotions

To illustrate the enormous power of cultural norms, I turn to a common element of social life—emotions. We all experience emotions as physical, sometimes instantaneous responses to life events. Thus we're inclined to see emotions as natural and universal. Yet emotional display comes under the strict control of cultural norms. When people "instinctively" hide or alter their emotions to fit the situation, they are playing a significant role in maintaining social order.

Take televised beauty pageants, for example. As the field of contestants is reduced to the final two, the camera zooms in on both of them. Usually they're standing on stage hugging each other in shaky anticipation of the final verdict. When the winner is announced, the runner-up is the picture of grace and charm, all smiles and congratulations. But we all know better. She has just lost the contest of her life on national television and has got to be sad, angry, or at the very least disappointed. Why does the runner-up suppress the urge to show her true emotions? Part of the reason is that she feels compelled to obey the cultural norms regarding the expression of emotions in that context. There's more at stake than her feelings. Imagine what would happen to the multimillion-dollar beauty contest industry if the losers suddenly began to display their bitterness and discontent on stage—arguing with judges, showing disdain for winners, and so forth.

Ironically, the powerful norms that govern the expression of emotions in most situations do not exist in any explicit form. We have many unwritten rules about which emotions are appropriate to feel, which are appropriate to display, and how intense the emotional display should be under specific circumstances. For instance, we're supposed to be sad at funerals, happy at weddings, and angry when we are insulted. We're supposed to feel joy when we receive good news but not show too much of it if our good fortune is at someone else's expense. We're supposed to be mildly upset if we get a B– instead of a B+ in a course but not sink into severe depression. In extreme cases the violation of such norms can lead to grave sanctions, such as being diagnosed as mentally ill (Pugliesi, 1987; Thoits, 1985).

Cultural norms about expressing emotions are often linked to organizational concerns and needs. In her book *The Managed Heart*, Arlie Russell Hochschild (1983) describes the feeling rules required by occupations in which employees have a great deal of contact with the public. To satisfy these rules, workers must either express or suppress their private feelings on demand. Flight attendants, for example, must constantly be good-natured and calm under dangerous conditions. They must make their work appear effortless and handle other people's feelings as deftly as their own. This ability is not just a matter of living up to social expectations—it is part of their job description. A "smile" becomes an economic asset and a public relations tool.

Likewise, doctors and nurses are trained to show kind concern for their patients, not disgust or alarm. Furthermore, they cannot become too emotionally involved with patients, because they see pain, suffering, and death every day. It is difficult not to become attached to patients but such emotional outlay would inevitably lead to burnout, making effective job performance impossible. Doctors and nurses are more successful in their jobs when they can keep their emotions under control.

Some companies now include explicit instructions on emotional control and display as part of their training programs for new employees. This is especially true in service sector jobs where contact with customers occurs over the phone:

> Remember, smiling can be heard as well as seen. . . . Have a smile in your voice and avoid sounding abrupt. . . . Try to make the caller feel you are there for them . . . [avoid] a disinterested, monotonous tone to voice. . . . Use language which conveys understanding of and empathy for the caller's individual situation, e.g., "are you OK?" "was anyone hurt?" "that must have been very distressing for you." (Telephone performance guidelines, insurance company) (Cameron, 1999)

> You must never sound bored on a call. Your telephone manner should convey the impression that you have been waiting for that individual call all day. . . . Our commitment is to give the caller an impression of excitement, friendliness, helpfulness, and courtesy. (Manual for directory assistance operators) (Cameron, 1999)

> If a customer comes across as cold and diffident, convince yourself that beneath the surface is a warm, caring, loving human being. Try to reach that suppressed warmth by injecting emotional warmth into your own words. (Freemantle, 1998)

The ability to enact convincing performances has become even more important given the rise of management techniques that use customer or client input as a means of assessing employees. Many service sector companies now survey customers and use undercover "secret shoppers" or other forms of surveillance to gather information on workers, making appropriate emotional display even more important. Hochschild warns that this kind of "emotional labor" eventually takes a heavy psychological toll on the workers, who are required to adopt a display of emotions that reflects corporate needs and not their own. These people become increasingly estranged from their true feelings (Hochschild, 1983).

Although it is not surprising that organizations would have an interest in emotional displays by members, it is perhaps less obvious that particular emotions are linked to larger societal concerns such as politics and economics, often as a method of social control (Kearl & Gordon, 1992). For instance, conflict theory points out that some political and religious regimes may use fear to quell dissent and enforce obedience. Earlier in this century, in response to the increasing political and economic strength of African Americans, many white southerners used fear to control blacks, through the threat of lynching and other forms of violence. Similarly, religious leaders often use the fear of eternal damnation to make sure their followers cooperate.

The effectiveness of invoking emotions such as guilt, anxiety, and shame waxes and wanes as social climates change. In the past, when communities were smaller and more interdependent, social behavior could be easily regulated by the threat of shame. If people broke a law or violated some norm of morality, they would bring humiliation on themselves, their families, and the community at large. But as societies became more complex, such close ties began to disappear. Today, the political control of behavior through emotion is more likely to be directed inward, in the form of guilt and anxiety. For instance, if working mothers are implicated by politicians as contributing to the "breakdown" of the traditional family, more and more mothers will experience guilt when they seek employment outside the home (Berg, 1992). Likewise, more stringent restrictions on abortion would increase the anxiety experienced by women who are considering it.

Norms such as those governing the expression of emotions give us a way to communicate and maintain social order. They keep us in line by creating powerful cultural expectations that are difficult to violate.

Social Institutions and Cultural Norms

Large social institutions are closely related to culture. For one thing, some institutions reflect deeply held cultural values. A free-market economy, for instance, reflects the values of achievement, competition, material acquisition, and so on. A democratic government reflects the values of freedom and citizen participation. Other institutions—such as education, religion, and family—provide the mechanisms through which culture is transmitted across generations.

Institutions are also strongly supported by cultural norms. When a particular pattern of behavior becomes widely accepted and taken for granted in society, sociologists say that it has become an **institutionalized norm** (DiMaggio & Powell, 1991). For instance, the institutionalized (that is, culturally acceptable) way of becoming financially successful in many societies is to get a college degree (and perhaps an advanced degree after that), start out in an entry-level position somewhere, and eventually work your way to the top. Even things that most of us would condemn have, at times, been institutionalized and encouraged by society. Slavery, for example, was for several hundred years a culturally, politically, and economically acceptable practice in the United States. The buying and selling of slaves were strongly approved by the nation's most powerful forces as well as by many ordinary people (Birenbaum & Sagarin, 1976).

Institutionalized norms constrain people's behavior by making some lines of action unthinkable. But they don't just limit options, they also establish the setting in which people discover their preferences and begin to see the world in a particular way (DiMaggio & Powell, 1991). The orientation and training sessions people are expected to participate in when they start a job, for example, clearly indicate the organization's expectations and each person's new responsibilities. The fact that other employees accept these expectations as legitimate reinforces the idea that organizational norms shouldn't be questioned. Similarly, the military ritualizes the process of becoming a full-fledged member through training, oaths of allegiance, and recognition of the passage from one rank to another. In doing so it ensures conformity to military norms. Religious congregations reinforce "appropriate" lifestyles and downplay inappropriate ones through collective worship services.

When institutions change so, too, do institutionalized norms. Changes in the institution of the U.S. family, for instance, have created some new expectations: Children are now expected to be more independent; fathers are expected to be more involved in the nurturing of children. In the political realm, shifting public opinion as well as political necessity eventually led to the abolition of slavery.

Shifts in one institution are often linked to shifts in another. In Russia, for example, the collapse of communism has strengthened the role of religious organizations in providing people with normative guidelines. In the United States, the fact that mothers are no longer expected to be the sole caretaker of children has meant an increase in the number of mothers who enter the paid labor force, which in turn has created higher demand for organized day care. The abolition of slavery meant that the entire economic system of the U.S. South had to be restructured, from a plantation economy to one characterized by smaller landholdings and more industry.

Norms and Sanctions

Most norms provide only a general framework of expectations; rarely do they tell us exactly how to act, and rarely are they obeyed by all people at all times. Furthermore, norms may be ambiguous or contradictory. It is no surprise, then, that behavior sometimes departs markedly from normative expectations. When it does, negative **sanctions** may be applied. A sanction is a direct social response to some behavior; a negative sanction is one that punishes or otherwise discourages violations of social norms and symbolically reinforces the culture's values and morals.

Different norms evoke different sanctions when violated. **Mores** (MORE-ayz) are norms, sometimes codified into laws, that are taken very seriously by society. Violation of some mores can elicit severe, state-sponsored punishment, such as serving time in prison for armed robbery. Other mores may be equally serious but are much less formally stated. Sanctions for violating these norms may be in the form of public ostracism or exclusion from the group, as when one is excommunicated for going against the moral doctrine of one's church.

The vast majority of everyday norms are relatively minor, however; violation of these norms, called **folkways**, carries much less serious punishment. For instance, if I chew with my mouth open and food dribbles down my chin, others may show outward signs of disapproval and consider me a "disgusting pig." I may receive fewer dinner invitations, but I won't be arrested or banished from the community.

According to the structural-functionalist perspective, each time a community moves to sanction an act, it strengthens the boundaries between normative and nonnormative behavior (Erikson, 1966). In the process the rest of us are warned of what is in store if we, too, violate the norms. In the 17th century, for example, criminals and religious heretics were executed at high noon in the public square for all to see. The spectacle was meant to be a vivid and symbolic reaffirmation of the community's norms. Today, of course, such harsh sanctions are likely to be hidden from the public eye. However, the publicity surrounding executions, as well as the visibility of less severe sanctions of norm violations, serves the same purpose—to declare to the community where the line between acceptable and unacceptable behavior lies. By sanctioning the person who violates a norm, society informs its members what type of person cannot live "normally" within its boundaries (Pfohl, 1994).

In-Groups and Ethnocentrism

As children, most of us were taught, explicitly or implicitly, that we live in the greatest place on Earth. We may also have been taught to have pride in our religious, racial, or ethnic group. But the belief that our group is the "best" means that other groups are "not the best." Distinguishing between our in-group and out-groups is not unusual; people tend to evaluate other cultures in comparison to their own. This tendency is called **ethnocentrism.**

Ethnocentrism is a consequence of the nature of human interaction itself. Much of our everyday lives is spent in groups and organizations. By their very character these collectivities are composed of individuals with some, though not necessarily all, shared interests. The same is true for larger cultures. To the extent that a majority of our time is spent with others "like us," our interactions with others "not like us" will be limited, and they will remain "foreign" or "mysterious" to us. Similarity breeds comfort; difference breeds discomfort. For example, despite laws against the practice, many Japanese stores continue to have policies of refusing to serve foreigners (French, 1999a). In fact, when Japanese citizens who have lived abroad return to Japan, they find that they are no longer regarded as fully Japanese and are treated with the sort of cold disdain that foreigners there often experience (French, 2000a).

Another reason for the existence of ethnocentrism is the loyalty we develop to our particular culture (Charon, 1992). Different values, beliefs, and actions come to be seen not merely as different ways of thinking and doing but as threats to what we hold dear. For example, in 1996, the national convention of Southern Baptists—the largest Protestant denomination in the United States—adopted a resolution calling for a major campaign to convert Jews to Christianity. To some Baptists, Christianity is the natural, necessary culmination of Jewish history, making Judaism unnecessary. The persistence of Jews who choose to remain Jews poses a challenge to this idea of inevitability, creating the need for intensive conversion (Garment, 1996). More recently some Southern Baptist congregations have targeted Hindus, Moslems, Mormons, and Jehovah's Witnesses for conversion ("Baptists Seek to Convert," 2000).

Cultural loyalty is encouraged by institutional ritual. Saying the Pledge of Allegiance at the beginning of the school day, playing the "Star-Spangled Banner" at sports events, and observing holidays such as Memorial Day and the Fourth of July all reinforce loyalty to U.S. culture. These are the "sacred objects" of U.S. society (Durkheim, 1915/1954). Religious artifacts and symbols, uniforms and team colors, and distinctive ethnic clothing all foster a sense of pride and identity and hold a community of similar people together, often to the exclusion of others. Sometimes these symbols evoke extreme emotions, as we've witnessed over the past few years when blacks and whites angrily clashed over the flying of the Confederate battle flag atop the State Capitol in South Carolina.

Cultural Variation and Everyday Experience

As populations grow more ethnically and racially diverse and as the people of the world become linked more closely by commerce, transportation, and communication, the likelihood of individuals from different cultures and subcultures living together increases. An awareness of cultural differences helps ease everyday interactions in a multicultural society and can be crucial in international relations. Consider, for example, the way people look at each other. Some meanings of certain gazes appear universal. For instance, in most societies people convey positive attitudes and emotions with longer gazes and convey negative attitudes and emotions with shorter ones. In all cultures, people notice when someone is gazing inappropriately. But just what is considered "inappropriate" varies from culture to culture. For instance, Japanese speakers tend to focus on the listener's neck, rather than the eyes, during conversations. Swedes, when conversing, are likely to gaze at one another for long periods of time. But in most of Latin America it is considered rude and disrespectful to gaze too long at one's superior. When a Latino child in an American school is admonished by a teacher, the child will lower his or her eyes as a sign of respect. But what do American teachers demand of the child they are scolding? "Look at me! Pay attention!" (Argyle, 2000).

Many of the clashes we hear about can be traced to a lack of awareness of differences in cultural expectations. For example, in 1997 a Danish woman visiting New York City was arrested and charged with child neglect for leaving her infant child alone on the sidewalk outside a restaurant while she ate lunch inside. In Denmark such a practice is common and considered appropriate. In 1999, an Afghan refugee was charged with child abuse when he was seen kissing his son's penis, a traditional expression of love in Afghanistan. He lost custody of the boy.

Other cultural conflicts have potentially more serious repercussions. Several years ago, a Chinese immigrant living in New York City bludgeoned his wife to death with a hammer after she confessed she was having an affair. The facts of the case were clear. The man freely admitted that he had killed his wife. Instead of being convicted of murder, however, the man was convicted of the lesser charge of second-degree manslaughter. He received a sentence of five years' probation. The defense attorney argued that the man's overwhelming sense of shame brought on by his wife's adultery put him in a frame of mind in which he could no longer control his actions. According to one anthropologist who testified in the case, adultery in China is an "enormous stain" that reflects not only on the aggrieved husband but also on his ancestors and all future generations of his family. The judge ruled that the man's actions, though tragic and unfortunate, were nonetheless understandable from the point of view of the man's cultural training (Bohlen, 1989).

Cultural variation reflects more than simply differences in people's habits and customs. It indicates that even the most taken-for-granted truths in our lives, the things that we assume to be universal and unambiguous, are subject to different interpretations and definitions worldwide. Two important examples of such variation are beliefs about health and illness and definitions of sex.

Health and Illness

Medical beliefs and practices always reflect the cultural values of a society (Coe, 1978). We can't claim to have a disease that doesn't exist in our culture. In Malaysia a man may be diagnosed with *koro*, a sudden intense anxiety that his sexual organs will recede into his body, causing death. In some Latin American countries a person can suffer from *susto*, an illness tied to a frightening event that makes the soul leave the body, causing unhappiness and sickness (Goleman, 1995). Neither of these conditions exists as a medical diagnosis in other parts of the world. But they are not simply anthropological curiosities. They show that notions of health and illness are shaped by culture.

What are even more compelling, though, are the dramatic cultural differences in medical treatment among societies that share many values, beliefs, norms, and structural elements. In the United States medical treatment tends to derive from an aggressive, "can do" spirit. Doctors in the United States are much more likely than European doctors to prescribe drugs and resort to surgery (Payer, 1988). U.S. women are more likely than their European counterparts to undergo radical mastectomies, deliver their babies by cesarean section, and undergo routine hysterectomies while still in their 40s. People in the United States see their bodies as machines that require annual checkups for routine maintenance. Diseases are enemies that need to be conquered (for example, people here try to "beat" cancer).

In contrast, British medicine is much more subdued. British physicians don't recommend routine examinations, seldom prescribe drugs, and order about half as many X rays as U.S. doctors do. British patients are also much less likely to have surgery. These attitudes also influence the perceptions of patients. People who are quiet and withdrawn—which U.S. doctors might consider symptoms of clinical depression—tend to be seen by British psychiatrists as perfectly normal.

The French are keenly sensitive to bodily appearance, which is why French physicians are more likely to treat breast and other types of cancer with radiation rather than surgery. The French believe that a patient's "constitution," or physical makeup, is as important in the onset of disease as germs and bacteria. They are more likely to prescribe vitamins to bolster the body than antibiotics to fight germs.

In addition to determining the nature of illness, cultural attitudes also determine what it means to be sick. Each society has a **sick role**, a widely understood set of rules about how people are supposed to behave when sick (Parsons, 1951). When someone is sick, the illness is considered to be beyond the person's control, and she or he is excused from normal social role responsibilities.

The sick role entails certain obligations, too. For instance, a sick person is duty-bound to want to get better as quickly as possible, to seek competent help, and to cooperate in the process of recovery. In the United States the obligation to seek competent help usually means following a doctor's instructions: undergoing the recommended technical procedures, taking the prescribed medication, resting, exercising, drinking fluids, and so on. Most people in the United States do not go to witch doctors or exorcists for cures. And many are reluctant to use holistic healers, chiropractors, homeopaths, osteopaths, or any other alternative approach outside mainstream medicine.

Failure on the part of sick people either to exercise their rights or to fulfill the obligations of the sick role may elicit sanctions from the group (Coe, 1978). For instance, those who do not appear to want to recover or who seem to enjoy being sick quickly lose certain privileges, such as sympathy. A person may also give up legal rights by not seeking or following expert advice. Parents have been arrested for not acquiring traditional medical assistance for their sick children. If you are hospitalized and your attending physician doesn't think you ought to be discharged, but you leave anyway, your records will indicate that you have left "A.M.A."—against medical advice. This designation protects the doctor and the hospital from any liability should your condition worsen.

The dimensions of the sick role are, of course, relative to the nature and severity of the illness (Segall, 1987). Compare the "rights" of a person with cancer to those of a person with strep throat. For certain illnesses we are entitled to stay in bed, free from all our usual obligations. For other illnesses we are expected to carry on with our usual activities. But of course, those expectations are culturally influenced. Anthropologists describe a practice found in parts of Japan, China, India, Estonia, and Spain called the *couvade,* from a French term meaning "cowardly inactivity." During childbirth, the father may lie down beside the mother and scream with pain. Following the birth of the child, the mother is expected to return to her normal duties right away, whereas the father goes to bed, sometimes for up to 40 days! It is the father, not the mother, who is relieved of ordinary social responsibilities and who is eligible for sympathy from the village.

Sex

The culture we grow up in shapes our most fundamental beliefs, even about what most people would consider to be the basic universal facts of life. For instance, we take for granted that humans can be divided into two clearly identifiable sexes—males and females—that are determined at the time of conception. If you asked someone how to distinguish between males and females, the response would probably focus on observable physical characteristics—body shape, hair, voice, facial features, and so on. When biologists distinguish between the sexes, they, too, refer to physical traits—chromosomes (XX for female, XY for male), sex glands (ovaries or testes), hormones (estrogen or testosterone), internal sex organs (uterus or prostate gland), external genitalia (vagina or penis), reproductive capacities (pregnancy or impregnation), germ cells produced (ova or sperm), and secondary sex characteristics (hips and breasts or facial hair and deep voice).

These characteristics, and hence the two biological sex categories, male and female, are usually assumed to be universal (found in all cultures throughout all of human history), exhaustive (that is, there's no third sex), and mutually exclusive (that is, a person cannot be both or be neither). There may be differences across time and cultures as to how we *expect* the two sexes to act and look (what sociologists call gender, as you will see in Chapter 5), but every society has some way of determining who is male and who is female.

Yet the truth about sex is much more complex. Hermaphrodites (or intersexuals), for instance, are individuals in whom sexual differentiation is either incomplete or ambiguous. They may have the chromosomal pattern of a female but the external genitalia of a male, or they may have both ovaries and testicles. Experts estimate that 1 baby in 2,000 is born with sex organs that don't fit either of the standard sex categories (Cowley, 1997).

According to one prominent biologist, instead of two sexual categories there are actually many gradations of sex running from female to male, and along that spectrum lie at least *five* sexes (Fausto-Sterling, 1993). In addition to males and females, there are "true hermaphrodites," people who possess one testis and one ovary; "male pseudo-hermaphrodites," people who have testes and some aspects of female genitalia but no ovaries; and "female pseudohermaphrodites," people who have ovaries and some aspects of male genitalia but no testes.

It is interesting to note that the medical response to intersexuals supports the cultural reality that there are two and only two sexes. Hermaphroditism is usually defined by biologists as a combination of the two existing categories and not as a third, fourth, or fifth category unto itself. Furthermore, on the diagnosis of hermaphroditism, a decision is always made to define the individual as either male or female. In societies with advanced medical technology, surgical and chemical means may be used to establish consistency between anatomy and the social label. Every month dozens of sexually ambiguous newborns are "assigned" a sex and undergo surgery to confirm the designation (Cowley, 1997). About 90% are designated as female, because creating a vagina is considered surgically easier than creating a penis (Angier, 1997b).

An increasingly vocal group of intersexuals protest that many of the surgical techniques used to "correct" the problem of anomalous genitalia are mutilating and potentially harmful. They cite cases of people with ambiguous genitals being robbed of any sexual sensation in the attempt to surgically "normalize" them—that is, give them the physical appearance of either a male or a female. The founder of the Intersex Society of North America eloquently summed up her organization's frustration: "They can't conceive of leaving someone alone" (quoted in Angier, 1997a, p. A10).

The medical profession can't leave these individuals alone because to do so would undermine our *cultural understanding* of sex. The drastic surgical intervention that ensues is undertaken not because the infant's life is threatened but because our entire social structure is organized around having two and only two sexes (Lorber, 1989). The male–female dichotomy in our culture is so essential to our way of life that those who challenge it are considered either crazy people or cultural heretics who are being disloyal to the most fundamental of biological "facts." To suggest that the labels "male" and "female" are not sufficient to categorize everyone is to threaten a basic organizing principle of social life.

But the cross-cultural evidence indicates that not every society has two and only two categories:

- In traditional Navajo culture, one could be male, female, or *nadle*—a third sex assigned to those whose sex-typed anatomical characteristics were ambiguous at birth (M. K. Martin & Voorhies, 1975). Physically normal individuals also had the opportunity to choose to become nadle if they so desired. Nadle were allowed to perform the tasks of both men and women.
- The Mohave have four categories. A boy who shows preferences for female clothing and activities undergoes an initiation at puberty and becomes an *alyha*. He would then adopt a female name, paint his face as a woman, and marry a man. When married, he cuts his upper thigh every month to signify a menstrual period. Girls who prefer male activities can become a *hwame* at puberty. Afterward, such a girl is allowed to hunt, farm, and assume paternal responsibilities for children (Kimmel, 2000).

- Among the Hua of Papua New Guinea, sex is thought to change throughout a person's life (Gailey, 1987). The Hua believe that women lose some of their femininity each time they have a child. After three births a woman has lost enough femininity to be allowed to participate in the discussions and rituals of men and to share their higher status and authority. Men gradually lose their masculinity by giving it to young boys during developmental rituals. Consequently, older men come to acquire the same social status as young women.
- The *hijras* of India are neither men nor women (Nanda, 1990). They are born as men but by choice they have their genitals surgically removed. This transforms them not into women but into hijras, who live as women—dressing, standing, walking, and sitting as women. There are many figures in Hindu mythology who are neither male nor female. Hence Indian culture not only accommodates the hijras but views them as meaningful, even powerful beings.

These cross-cultural examples illustrate that our taken-for-granted beliefs about sex are not held worldwide. In other cultures sex is not dichotomous, exhaustive, or permanent.

CONCLUSION

Over the span of a year or two, most cultures seem to have a stable set of norms about the acceptability of certain behaviors. This stability is illusory, however. From the perspective of a generation or even a decade, that sense of order would be replaced by a sense of change (McCall & Simmons, 1978). Behaviors, values, beliefs, and morals fluctuate with startling frequency. Thus, comparisons across eras, in addition to comparisons across cultures, can provide rich insight into shifting definitions of acceptability, the nature of everyday life, and ultimately large-scale social change and stability.

The cultural and historical underpinnings of our private lives help us see the relationship between the individual, society, and social order. Cultural practices add continuity and order to social life.

To an individual, culture appears massive and unrelenting, but at the same time it cannot exist without people. Norms govern our lives, whether we live by them or rebel against them. But to fully understand the relationship between the individual and society we must look beyond the fact that culture and history shape our lives; we must see them as human constructions as well.

YOUR TURN

Although everyday norms underlie all we do, they remain largely unnoticed and unquestioned. The best proof of the existence of these norms lies in our reactions when they are violated. The following suggestions for proving the existence of norms are based on an exercise used by Jodi O'Brien at Seattle University. If you like, choose a different unspoken norm that lends order and predictability to daily social interactions, and try breaking it.

- Make a purchase in a department store and offer to pay more than the listed price. Try to convince the clerk that you think the merchandise is worth the price you are offering.
- Send a close family member a birthday card months away from his or her actual birthday.
- Talk to yourself in a public place.
- Stand or sit close to a stranger or stand far away from a good friend or lover during the course of an ordinary conversation.
- Select an occasion—going to class, going on a date, going to the library—and dress differently from the expected "uniform." Treat your attire as absolutely appropriate to the circumstances.
- Whenever someone says to you "See you later," ask him or her probing questions: "When?" "Do you have some plans to get together later?" "What do you mean by 'see'?" and so on. Or when someone says, "How's it going?" ask, "What do you mean by 'it'?" "What do you mean by 'going'?"
- In a restaurant offer to pay for your meal before you order it, or order dessert first, then the main course, then appetizers, then drinks.

It is particularly important that this behavior be neither flagrantly bizarre—such as going to class dressed as a chicken—nor a violation of the law. Such acts do not address the power of the subtle, unspoken norms that, symbolic interactionism argues, make social life orderly. Also, do not do anything that might seriously inconvenience or humiliate someone else or put you in danger. Finally, make sure the norm has something to do with keeping order in face-to-face interactions. For instance, coming to class 10 minutes late violates a social norm, but it doesn't disrupt interactional order. Above all, remember to treat your violation as perfectly normal. You must give the impression that what you are doing is perfectly acceptable and ordinary.

As you conduct your experiment, record your own feelings and reactions as well as those of the subjects. What were people's initial reactions? What did they do to try to "normalize" your behavior? How did you feel breaching this norm? Was it uncomfortable? If so, why? If possible, try to debrief your subjects afterward: Tell them what you were really doing, and then interview them regarding their interpretations of the experience. This will provide you with information on how people attempt to "explain away" unusual and strange circumstances and how they attempt to restore order to the situation. What are the implications of these sorts of "experiments" for understanding human behavior and the nature of social order in this society?

CHAPTER HIGHLIGHTS

- Culture provides members of a society with a common bond, a sense that we see certain facets of society in similar ways. That we can live together at all depends on the fact that members of a society share a certain amount of cultural knowledge.

- Norms—the rules and standards that govern all social encounters—provide order in our lives. They reflect commonly held assumptions about conventional behavior. Norm violations mark the boundaries of acceptable behavior and symbolically reaffirm what society defines as right and wrong.

- The more ethnically and culturally diverse a society is, the greater the likelihood of normative clashes between groups.

- Over the span of a few years, most cultures present an image of stability and agreement regarding normative boundaries. This agreement is illusory, however. Over a generation or even a decade, that sense of order is replaced by a sense of change.

KEY TERMS

ethnocentrism Tendency to judge other cultures using one's own as a standard

folkway Informal norm that is mildly punished when violated

institutionalized norm Pattern of behavior within existing social institutions that is widely accepted in a society

material culture Artifacts of a society, which represent adaptations to the social and physical environment

more Highly codified, formal, systematized norm that brings severe punishment when violated

nonmaterial culture Knowledge, beliefs, customs, values, morals, and symbols that are shared by members of a society and that distinguish the society from others

sanction Social response that punishes or otherwise discourages violations of a social norm

sick role Set of norms governing how one is supposed to behave and what one is entitled to when sick

subculture Values, behaviors, and artifacts of a group that distinguish its members from the larger culture

A Culture of Tramps

Douglas Harper

People typically see their own culture as normal and may be startled to learn that other people around them have a different culture. That may especially be the case for subcultures that are defined by mainstream society as "deviant," such as the "tramp" culture pictured here.

Like any other culture, however, even the tramp culture has a clear set of norms. For example, after a tramp has worked for weeks or months, within the tramp culture it is appropriate to drink up one's wages in a drunken binge that may last for days or even weeks. Excessive drinking causes problems for tramps, but they define it as a normal part of their culture, like a football player who regards his injuries as inevitable.

● I met this tramp, Carl, in Minneapolis. Suffering through a hangover after a three-week drunk, he was heading 2,000 miles to the apple harvest in Washington State. He accepted my company because I had a sack of food. We "buddied up," which is a tramp expression noting a relationship of limited but specific commitment.

● Carl's gear for a 2,000-mile migration to the apple harvest included a razor and a mirror. He was finished with his drunk, and he knew he needed to shave and clean up to get a job. After he shaved, he handed me the razor and told me that either I shaved or I'd be heading the rest of the way by myself. The tramp understood that his life consisted of several identities and that the shift from a skid row drunk to a worker required specific attention to his appearance.

Freight trains are a particularly important and challenging part of tramp culture. They are complicated and dangerous. Tramps watch others ride trains and are quick to point out amateurs who don't know the cultural ropes or failures in the culture who may be smart but remain incompetent in the ways of tramps.

● Tramps know where and how to ride freights. Here we rode on an exposed auto carrier, which is one of the least desirable places on a freight train. Riders are exposed to the elements, but worse than that, they are visible to yard police. Tramps prefer to ride inside empty boxcars or under the truck trailers bolted onto flatcars, called "piggybacks." There are at least 20 different places a tramp may ride a freight, and tramps spend a great deal of time arguing the comparative advantages of such locations.

● There were eventually 38 men in this boxcar, as it approached the towns where the apple orchards were situated. During the hot afternoon a tramp entered the car with a bottle of wine, but most tramps shied away. It is a strong tramp norm not to get drunk on a freight train, because to do so places the rider in great danger. Most tramps remembered the norms and passed on a tempting cold drink.

The culture of tramps is connected to what has been called the "macro" or structural aspect of society. We look at homeless people and see only a social problem or evidence of individual failure. But the tramps I met on trains and during apple harvests are homeless only some of the year, and then they ride a freight perhaps thousands of miles to become workers somewhere else. In the Pacific Northwest tramps pick fruit. They usually leave their wages in the harvest towns, where they either spend it getting drunk or have it stolen by "jack-rollers" or the police. Tramps define this way of spending money as normal, and their behavior services an agricultural economy that needs intensive but intermittent labor. We take for granted that our fruits and vegetables await us in clean and orderly stores, but these products have come to us because a culture of probably homeless workers have labored for paltry wages in circumstances where they have little if any social power. In the case of tramps, their own cultural definition of their lives and fate justifies what is, in fact, an exploitative labor situation.

● While waiting to be hired for the apple harvest, tramps assembled at one of many "jungles" in the area. In the jungles tramps lived by norms: food was shared, the camp was kept clean, and firewood was replaced. But when we were hired to work in an orchard, we were given a one-room cabin in which to live. Suddenly we had transformed from tramps to workers. We got an advance on our wages, bought cans of beans and Spaghetti-O's, and began living under a roof. The change in Carl was remarkable. Suddenly he was master of a different world.

Note that I refer to these men as "tramps" because that is how they define themselves. The existence of a distinctive culture is often signaled by words that have meaning only within the framework of that culture. When tramps see another man in a freight car, they see a *bindle-stiff*, an *Airedale*, a *mission-stiff*, a *rubber tramp*, a *jack-roller*, or one of many other categories of tramps. Each of these labels defines a certain set of actions, possessions, behaviors, and beliefs. In other words, they are not casual definitions but definitions that indicate an individual's identity. They are no less important or socially powerful than our own cultural definitions.

● Tramps define themselves by how they travel and what they do. This man is a "bindle-stiff" because he carries his gear in an old-fashioned manner, tied into what are called *bindles*. A bindle-stiff usually spends his time in the less-threatening environments of smaller cities or freight yards in the American West. His identity is made complete by his dog on a hand-made leash. Here he enters the relatively hostile environment of Seattle, where many will prey on an elderly tramp. He may be visiting family, because many tramps keep family connections. Or he may be on his way to the freight yard to catch a train to an orchard or another city.

● When a tramp can no longer take care of himself on the open road, he retires to a mission. He then becomes a "mission stiff," like the tramp in this photograph. Because tramps value independence, the admission that one must leave the road to retire to a mission is a radical redefinition of oneself. Tramps talk of retiring to a small cabin in the woods but seldom accumulate enough money to do it. Rather, they end their days in a home-made shack by a freight yard or in a mission when the weather turns too cold to live outside. It is at the ends of their lives that the inconsistencies in their self-definitions and their actual situations become most apparent.

● The tramps pictured here live in Boston. On the surface they appear to be the same as the tramps pictured earlier. Yet their culture is profoundly different. In the East single homeless men are not an agricultural labor force, and it is more difficult for them to ride freights. Without work and mobility, the tramp becomes a stationary homeless man, reduced to begging and scavenging. Still, the homeless man lives in a culture. These two men are in a "bottle gang," furtively sharing a pint of cheap wine they have purchased from a day's work panhandling and scavenging for spare change.

To study culture one must participate as well as observe. To study tramps I rode freight trains, lived in hobo jungles and skid row missions, and picked apples in orchards where all the workers were tramps. I became something of an expert in tramp culture, which eventually made these arcane cultural situations part of my own understanding of the world.

Source: Excerpted from Douglas A. Harper, *Good Company* (Chicago: University of Chicago Press, 1982).

5 Building Identity: Socialization

My family once lived in a suburb just outside New York City. One day, when I was 9 years old, my parents sat me down and told me that we were going to be moving. They had narrowed down our ultimate destination to two possibilities: Laredo, Texas, or Burbank, California. After some rather intense debate, they chose Burbank. And so we headed "out West," where from age 9 to age 18 I lived in the shadow of the entertainment industry and all its glamour, glitz, and movie stars. It wasn't long before I became a typical sun-worshiping, Frisbee-throwing, southern California kid.

I often wonder how differently I would have turned out if my parents had chosen Laredo and I had spent my formative years in the heart of Texas instead of in the middle of Tinsel Town. Would I have a fondness for 10-gallon hats and snakeskin boots instead of tennis shoes and shorts? Would I have grown up with country music instead of the Beach Boys? Would my goals be different? In short, would I be a different person?

Try to imagine what your life would be like if you had grown up under different circumstances. What if your father had been a harpsichord enthusiast instead of a Cubs fan? What if your family had been Jewish instead of Episcopalian? What if you had had an older brother instead of a younger sister? What if you had lived on a farm instead of in a big city? What if you had been born in the 1940s instead of the 1980s? Your tastes, preferences, and hobbies, as well as your morals, values, ambitions, and aspirations, would no doubt be different. But more profoundly, your self-concept, self-esteem, personality—the essence of who you are—would be altered.

Consider the broader social and historical circumstances of your life. What kind of impact might they have had on the type of person you are? Talk to people who grew up in the 1930s and they will speak of the permanent impact that the Great Depression had on them (Elder & Liker, 1982). Imagine spending your childhood as a Jew in Nazi Germany. That couldn't help but shape your outlook on life. The same can be said for growing up black in South Central Los Angeles in the 1990s or white in Beverly Hills during the Bush presidency.

Becoming the person you are cannot be separated from the people, historical events, and social circumstances that surround you. In this chapter I examine the process of socialization—how we learn what's expected of us in our families, our communities, and our culture and how we learn to behave according to those expectations. The primary focus will be on the development of identity. **Identity** is our most essential and personal characteristic. It consists of our membership in social groups (race, ethnicity, religion, gender, and so on), the traits we show, and the traits others ascribe to us. Our identity locates us in the social world, thoroughly affecting everything we do, feel, say, and think in our lives. Most people tend to believe that our self-concept, our sense of "maleness" or "femaleness," or our racial and ethnic identities are biologically or psychologically determined and therefore permanent and unchangeable. But as you will discover, these characteristics are social constructions: as much a product of our social surroundings and the significant people in our lives as a product of our physical traits and innate predispositions.

Social Structure and the Construction of Human Beings

The question of how we become who we are has for centuries occupied the attention of biologists, psychologists, anthropologists, sociologists, philosophers, and novelists. The issue is commonly framed as an ongoing debate between *nature* (we are who we are because we were born that way) and *nurture* (we are who we are because we grew up that way). Are we simply a product of our genes and biochemistry, or are we "created" from scratch by the people and the social institutions that surround us?

The answer to this question swings back and forth depending on the dominant cultural values. In the late 19th and early 20th centuries genetics became a popular explanation for human behavior, including a variety of social problems such as crime, poverty, and mental deficiency. Scientists, borrowing from the selective breeding practices used with racehorses and livestock, advocated programs of *eugenics,* or controlled mating to ensure that the "defective" genes of troublesome individuals would not be passed on to future generations. Theories of genetic inferiority became the cornerstone of Hitler's horrors in Nazi Germany during World War II. After the war, most people wanted to get as far away from such "nature" arguments as possible. So in the 1950s and 1960s people heavily emphasized environmental influences on behavior, especially the role of early family experiences in shaping children's futures (Gould, 1997).

Today, because of the growing cultural emphasis on scientific technology, genetic explanations have again become fashionable. In recent years researchers have claimed that such diverse social phenomena as shyness, impulsiveness, intelligence, aggression, obesity, risk taking, alcoholism, and addiction to gambling are at least partly due to heredity. The success of the Human Genome Project—meant to identify all the 100,000 genes in human DNA—will no doubt add fuel to "nature" arguments in the years to come.

Recently, a psychologist named Judith Harris (1998) achieved significant notoriety for her rather stunning suggestion that the home environment has virtually no effect on children. She claims that the only thing that parents contribute to their child's development is their genetic material; that nothing parents do or say makes much of a difference at all as to what sort of adult the child will eventually become. But even Harris acknowledges that nature alone isn't sufficient to predict a child's development. She points out that later on in life peer groups play a powerful role in shaping a child's personality. Although Harris's book has been roundly criticized, it does ultimately support the view that, when all is said and done, both nature and nurture are responsible for who we become. Both inheritance and environment matter.

Most sociologists would argue that human beings are more than just a collection of physical and psychological characteristics. But that's not to say that inborn traits are of absolutely no importance. Certainly our physical attractiveness and strength, genetic predisposition to sickness, and so on have some effect on our personal development. Furthermore, our every thought and action is the product of a complex series of neurological and electrochemical events in our brains and bodies. Males and females obviously differ anatomically and hormonally and may even see the world differently as a result. When we eat we are reacting to a physiological sensation—stomach contractions—brought about by a lowering of blood sugar. Satisfying hunger is clearly a biological process.

But the issue is not so much whether these innate differences or physiological events exist; rather, it is how they are shaped by culture and whether people define them as significant. The way we react to the sensation of hunger cannot be predicted by physiology alone. What, when, how, and how often we eat are all matters of cultural forces that we learn over time. Likewise, society can magnify physiological differences or cover them up. We've collectively decided that some differences are socially irrelevant (for example, eye color) and that some are important enough to be embedded in our social institutions (for example, gender and race), giving rise to different rights, duties, expectations, and access to institutional opportunities.

Who we become is influenced by the behaviors and attitudes of significant people in our lives as well as by cultural and institutional forces. As these things change, so do we. This proposition is not altogether comforting. It implies that who we are may in some ways be "accidental," the shaky result of a series of social coincidences, chance encounters, decisions made by others, and of political, economic, and historical events that are in large measure beyond our control, such as living in California rather than Texas.

Socialization: Becoming Who We Are

The fundamental task of any society is to reproduce itself—to create members whose behaviors, desires, and goals correspond to those that are deemed appropriate and desirable by that particular society. Through the powerful and ubiquitous process of **socialization** the needs of society become the needs of the individual.

Socialization is a process of learning. To socialize someone is to train that person to behave appropriately. It is the means by which people acquire important social skills, such as driving a car, converting fractions into percentages, speaking the language correctly, or using the little fork instead of the big fork at the right times. But socialization is also the way we learn how to perceive our world; how to interact with others; what it means to be male or female; how, when, why, and with whom to be sexual; what we should and should not do under certain circumstances; what our society defines as moral and immoral; and so on. In short, it is the process by which we internalize all that cultural information discussed in the previous chapter.

Although socialization occurs throughout our lives, the basic, formative instruction of life occurs early on. Young children must be taught the fundamental values, knowledge, and beliefs of their culture. Some of the socialization that occurs during childhood—often referred to as **anticipatory socialization**—is the primary means by which young individuals acquire the values and orientations found in the statuses they will likely enter in the future (Merton, 1957). Household chores, a childhood job, sports, dance lessons, dating, and many other types of experiences give youngsters an opportunity to rehearse for the kinds of roles that await them in adulthood.

The Acquisition of Self

The most important outcome of the socialization process is the development of a sense of self. The term **self** refers to the unique set of traits, behaviors, and attitudes that distinguishes one person from the next.

The self is both the active source of behavior and its passive object (G. H. Mead, 1934). As an active source, the self can initiate action, which is frequently directed toward others. Imagine, for example, that Curt and Mary are having dinner in a restaurant. Mary has a self that can perceive Curt, talk to him, evaluate him, perhaps even try to manipulate or persuade him to act in a way that is consistent with her interests. Mary also has a self that is a potential object of others' behavior: She can be perceived, talked to, evaluated, manipulated, or persuaded by Curt.

Mary can also direct these activities toward herself. She can perceive, evaluate, motivate, and even talk to herself. This is called **reflexive behavior**. To have a self is to have the ability to plan, observe, guide, and respond to one's own behavior (G. H. Mead, 1934). Think of all the times you have tried to motivate yourself to act by saying something such as "All right, if I read 20 more pages of this boring textbook, I'll give myself a hot fudge sundae." To do this you must simultaneously be the motivator and the one being motivated—the seer and the seen.

At this very moment you are initiating an action: reading this book. But you also have the ability (now that I've mentioned it!) to be aware of your reading behavior, to observe yourself reading and even evaluate how well you are doing. This sounds like some sort of out-of-body experience, but it isn't. Nothing is more fundamental to human thought and action than this capacity for self-awareness. It allows us to control our own behavior and interact smoothly with other self-aware individuals.

Human babies possess no sense of self at birth. This is not to say that infants don't act on their own. Anyone who has been around babies knows that they have a tremendous ability to initiate action, ranging all the way from Kodak-moment cute to downright disgusting. They cry, eat, sleep, play with squeaky rubber toys, and eliminate waste, all with exquisite panache and regularity. They respond to the sounds, sights, smells, and touches of others from the very first days of life.

But this behavior is not characterized by the sort of self-consciousness that characterizes later behavior. Babies cannot say to themselves, "I can't believe how loud I can cry" or "I wonder if Mom will feed me if I scream." As children grow older, though, they begin to exert greater control over their conduct. Part of this transformation is biological. As they mature they become more adept at muscle control. But physical development is only part of the picture. Humans must acquire certain cognitive capacities through interactions with others, including the abilities to differentiate between self and others, to understand and use symbolic language, and to take the roles of others.

The Differentiation of Self. To distinguish between oneself and others, one must be able to recognize oneself as a distinct entity (Michener, DeLamater, & Schwartz, 1986). The first step in the acquisition of self, then, is learning to distinguish our own faces and bodies from the rest of the physical environment. Surprisingly, we are not born with this ability. Not only are newborns incapable of recognizing themselves, they also cannot even discriminate the boundaries between their bodies and the bodies of others. Infants will pull their own hair to the point of excruciating pain but will not realize that the hair they're pulling and the hair that they feel being pulled is the same hair.

With cognitive growth and social experience, infants gradually recognize themselves as unique physical objects. Most studies in this area indicate that children usually develop this ability at about 18 months (Bertenthal & Fischer, 1978). If you make a large mark on a child's forehead with a washable marker, hold the youngster up to a mirror, and observe whether the child reaches up to wipe away the smudge, you can tell if the youngster knows that the image in the mirror is his or her own.

Language Acquisition and the Looking-Glass Self. The next important step in the acquisition of self is the development of speech (Hewitt, 1988). Symbolic interactionism points out that mastery of language is critical in children's efforts to differentiate themselves as distinct social as well as physical objects (Denzin, 1977). Certainly language acquisition relies on neurological development. But the ability to grasp the nuances of one's own language requires input from others. Most parents talk to their children from the start. Gradually, children learn to make sounds, imitate sounds, and use sounds as symbols for particular physical sensations or objects. Children learn that the sounds "Mama" and "Dada" are the sounds associated with two important objects in their life. Soon children learn that other objects—toys, animals, foods, Aunt Donna—have unique sounds associated with them as well.

This learning process provides the child access into the preexisting linguistic world in which his or her parents and others live (Hewitt, 1988). The objects named are not only those recognized within the larger culture but also those recognized within the family's particular social group (defined by race and ethnicity, class, or religion). The child learns the names of concrete objects (balls, buildings, furniture) as well as abstract ideas that cannot be directly perceived (for example, God, happiness, and idea).

By learning that people and other objects have names, the child also begins to learn that these objects can be related to one another in many named ways. Depending on who is talking to whom, the same person can be called several different names. The object "Daddy" is called, by various other people, "David," "Dave," "Dr. Newman," "Professor Newman," "Honey," and "Dummy." Furthermore, the child learns that different people can be referred to by the same name. All those other kids at the park have someone they also call "Mama."

Amid these monumental discoveries young children learn that they too are objects that have names. A child who learns that others are referring to her when they use the word "Nancy," and that she too can use "Nancy" to refer to herself, has taken a significant leap forward in the acquisition of self. The child is now able to visualize herself as a part of the named world and the named relationships to which she belongs.

The self that initially emerges from this process is a rather simple one. "Nancy" is just a name associated with a body, which explains why very young children just learning to form sentences may refer to themselves by their name instead of the first-person pronoun (for example, "Nancy is hungry" instead of "I am hungry"). A more sophisticated sense of self is derived from the child's ability to learn the meaning of this named object.

Children learn the meaning of named objects in their environment by observing the way other people act toward those objects. They learn what "chair" means by observing people sitting on one. Parental warnings allow them to learn that a "hot stove" is something to be avoided. Similarly, they learn the meaning of themselves by observing how people act toward them. People treat children in a variety of ways: care for them, punish them, love them, teach them. If parents, relatives, and other significant people perceive a child as smart, they act toward him or her that way. Thus the child eventually comes to believe he or she is a smart person. Sociologist Charles Horton Cooley (1902) referred to this process as acquisition of the **looking-glass self**. We use the actions of others toward us as mirrors in which we see ourselves and determine our self-worth.

How the child-as-named-object is defined by others is linked to larger societal considerations as well. Every culture has its own way of defining individuals at various stages of the life cycle. Children are not always defined, and have not always been defined, as a special subpopulation that requires nurturing and protection (Ariès, 1962). In some societies they are expected to behave like adults and are held accountable for their actions just as adults would be. Under such cultural circumstances, a 5-year-old's self-concept might be derived from how well she or he contributes economically to the family, not from how cute or playful she or he is. Moreover, every society has its own standards of beauty and success. If thinness is a culturally desirable characteristic, a thin child is more likely to garner positive responses and develop a positive self-image than a child who violates this norm (that is, an obese child).

The Development of Role Taking. This process would be pretty simple if everyone in our lives saw us in exactly the same way. But different people expect or desire different things from us. Children eventually pick this up and learn to modify their behavior to suit different people. Four-year-old Rafael learns, for instance, that his 3-year-old sister loves it when he sticks green beans up his nose, but he also knows that his father doesn't find this behavior at all amusing. So Rafael will avoid such conduct when his father is around but will proceed to amuse his sister with this trick when Papa is gone. The ability to use other people's perspectives and expectations in formulating one's own behavior is called **role taking** (G. H. Mead, 1934).

Role-taking ability develops gradually, paralleling the increasing maturation of linguistic abilities. George Herbert Mead (1934) identified two major stages in the development of role-taking ability and, ultimately, in the socialization of the self: the play stage and the game stage. The **play stage** occurs when children are just beginning to acquire language. Role taking at the play stage is quite simple in form, limited to taking the perspective of one other person at a time. Very young children cannot see themselves from different perspectives simultaneously. They have no idea that certain behaviors may be unacceptable to a variety of people across a range of situations. They know only that this particular person who is in their immediate presence will approve or not approve of this conduct. Children cannot see that their mother's disapproval of public nose picking reflects the attitudes of a larger group and is generally unacceptable. This more sophisticated form of self-control develops at the next stage of the socialization process: the game stage.

The **game stage** occurs about the time that children first begin to participate in organized activities such as school events and team sports. The difference between role taking at the play and game stages parallels the difference between childhood play behavior and game behavior. Play is not guided by a specific set of rules. Play has no ultimate object, no clearly organized competition, no winners and losers. Children playing baseball at the play stage have no sense of strategy and may not even be aware of the rules and object of the game. They may be able to hit, catch, and throw the ball but have no idea how their behavior is linked to that of their teammates. If a little girl is playing third base and the ball is hit to her, she may turn around and throw the ball to the left fielder, not because it will help her team win the game but because that's where her best friend happens to be.

At the game stage children do have a sense of the object of the game. They realize that each player on the team is part of an organized network of roles determined by the rules of the game. Children know they must continually adapt their behavior to the team's needs in order to achieve a goal. To do so, they must predict how both their teammates and the opponents will act under certain circumstances.

The ability to imagine the group's perspective characterizes the game stage of self-development. With regard to social behavior, not only does the child learn to respond to the demands of many people, but he or she can also respond to the demands of the community or even society as a whole. The perspective of society and its constituent values and attitudes is known as the **generalized other.**

To take the role of the generalized other is to perceive one's behavior from the point of view of the group, not just one particular person. "Mama doesn't like it when I pick my nose in restaurants" (play stage) becomes "It's never acceptable to pick one's nose in public" (game stage). This ability is crucial because it enables the person to resist the influence of specific people who happen to be in his or her immediate presence. The boy who defies his peers by not joining them in an act of petty shoplifting is showing the power of the generalized other. During the game stage, the attitudes and expectations of the generalized other are incorporated into one's self-concept.

Real life is not that simple, though. The generalized other becomes larger as a child matures, growing to include family, peer group, school, and finally the larger social community. People from markedly different backgrounds are likely to internalize different sets of group attitudes and values. A Catholic contemplating divorce, for instance, is taking the role of a different generalized other than an atheist contemplating divorce. Likewise, the social worlds and social standards of men and women are different, as are those of children and adults, parents and nonparents, middle-class and working-class people, and people who grew up in different societies.

As we move from one institutional context to another, we adopt the perspective of the appropriate group and can become, for all intents and purposes, a different person. At work we behave one way, at church another, at a family gathering still another. We are as many different people as there are groups and organizations of which we are members.

Common sense suggests that people who have greater knowledge and experience should be better role takers. For example, parents should be more sensitive to their children's views than vice versa, because the parents were children once themselves. However, given the conditions of power and dependence, this is often not the case. People in superior positions are not required to conform their behavior to—nor even to be aware of—the wishes and desires of underlings. First-year college students are typically more aware of the actions and interests of upper-class students than vice versa. Low-level employees must be sensitive to the behaviors and preferences of those above them if they want to achieve occupational success and mobility. It could even be argued that less powerful nations must have heightened sensitivity to the activities of their more powerful neighbors. I have heard some Canadians complain that they are "required" to know virtually everything about the United States—its culture as well as its economic and political systems—whereas most people in the United States tend to be rather oblivious to even the most accessible elements of Canadian society and culture.

In sum, the ability to imagine another person's attitudes and intentions and thereby to anticipate that person's behavior is essential for everyday social interaction. Through role taking we are able to envision how others perceive us and what their response may be to some action we're contemplating. Hence, we can select behaviors that are likely to meet with the approval of the person or persons with whom we are interacting and can avoid behaviors that might meet with their disapproval. Role taking is thus a crucial component of self-control and social order. It is fundamental in the development of a social being who is capable of normative behavior. It is the means by which culture is incorporated into the self.

Resocialization

Socialization does not end in childhood; it continues throughout our lives. Adults must be **resocialized** into a new set of norms, values, and expectations each time they leave behind old social contexts or roles and enter new ones (Ebaugh, 1988; Pescosolido, 1986; I. H. Simpson, 1979). For instance, we have to learn how to think and act like a spouse when we marry (Berger & Kellner, 1964), a parent when we have kids (A. Rossi, 1968), and a divorced person when a marriage ends (Vaughan, 1986). Every new group or organization we enter, every new friendship we form, every new life-changing experience we have, requires the formation of new identities and socialization into new sets of norms and beliefs.

Sometimes resocialization is forceful and comprehensive. In prisons, mental hospitals, monasteries, military training camps, and other **total institutions** (Goffman, 1961), groups of individuals are cut off from the broader society and forced to lead an enclosed, formally administered life. Previous socialization experiences are systematically destroyed and new ones developed to serve the interests of the group. In an army boot camp, for instance, the individual must shed his or her identity as a civilian and adopt the new identity of soldier. He or she must learn to look, act, and think like a soldier and learn to see the world from the soldier's perspective. To aid in this transformation, recruits are stripped of old identity markers (clothes, personal possessions, hairstyle) and forced to take on new ones designed to nullify individuality (uniforms, identification numbers, similar haircuts).

Soon the individual learns to identify with the ideology of the total institution. In the boot camp, the uniformity of values and appearance is intended to create a sense of solidarity among the soldiers and thereby make the military more effective in carrying out its tasks. Part of the reason for all the controversy over diversity in the military—first with the inclusion of African Americans, then with women, and now with homosexuals—is that it introduces a variety of beliefs, values, appearances, and lifestyles into a context where, from an institutional perspective, similarity is essential.

The mechanisms of resocialization have been tragically exploited from time to time. Four noteworthy examples are the 1978 mass suicide of 911 members of Jim Jones's People's Temple in Jonestown, Guyana; the 1993 armed standoff and subsequent destruction of David Koresh's Branch Davidian compound in Waco, Texas; the 1995 sarin gas attack on the Tokyo subway system by members of the Japanese religious group Aum Shinrikyo; and the mass suicide of 39 followers of Marshall Herff Applewhite and the Heaven's Gate religious sect in 1997. Koresh, Jones, Asahara Shoko (Aum's leader), and Applewhite told their followers that in order to achieve better and more meaningful lives, they would have to isolate themselves, severing all ties to their previous lives—all previous values, relationships, emotional bonds, and so on. The members abandoned their past "disreputable" selves so totally and were resocialized and indoctrinated by their leaders so completely that their ability to make decisions on their own behalf was impaired (Coser & Coser, 1993). When people are physically and emotionally cut off from their friends and family, they lose their personalities and can be influenced, cajoled, or threatened into doing virtually anything, even injuring others or giving up their own lives.

Less drastically, but no less deliberately, certain occupations resocialize new entrants. Often the purpose is simply to make sure people who work in the occupation share the same professional values, methods, and vocabulary. Many large companies, for example, have orientation programs for new employees to teach them what will be expected of them as they begin their new jobs. Sometimes the purpose is to make new entrants abandon their original expectations and adopt a more realistic view of the occupation. Police recruits who believe their job is to protect people must learn that deadly force is appropriate and sometimes necessary in the line of duty (J. Hunt, 1985). Many medical students' ideals become more realistic as they learn about the exhausting demands of their profession (H. S. Becker & Geer, 1958; Hafferty, 1991). Such resocialization is especially important in occupations that deal with highly emotional matters, such as the funeral industry.

Spencer Cahill
The Professional Socialization of Funeral Directors

Funeral directors must routinely deal with death and corpses. They are exposed to sights, smells, and sounds that most people would find repulsive. And they must discuss cold, practical matters, such as prices and methods of payment, with grief-stricken clients, without appearing callous. Thus the occupational socialization of funeral directors is as important as that in any other profession that deals with human tragedy (clergy, doctors, nurses, police detectives, and so on). But unlike these other professionals, for whom death is merely one aspect of the job, funeral directors exist solely for the purpose of dealing with death.

To study the process of becoming a funeral director, sociologist Spencer Cahill (1999) spent five months as a participant observer in a mortuary science program at a community college. In most states, funeral directors must complete an accredited program in mortuary science before getting their license to practice. Cahill regularly attended classes on such topics as health and sanitation science, psychology of grief, and embalming. He also talked informally with the other students and interviewed eight of them formally. What was especially unique about his research approach was that instead of taking the stance of the detached, objective researcher, Cahill incorporated his own feelings and emotional reactions into his analysis.

He found that the entire mortuary science education program serves to *normalize* the work, so that students become comfortable with death. Reminders of death are a constant presence. Nothing is hidden. For instance, all the classrooms contain some artifacts of death, such as refrigerated compartments that hold corpses, stainless steel embalming tables, and caskets. All the instructors Cahill observed spread their lecture notes on a body gurney, forgoing the traditional lectern and table. It was also common practice for instructors to leave the door open between the classroom and the embalming laboratory, allowing the lingering smell of decomposing bodies to drift into the classroom.

Because they tend to be shunned by other students, the mortuary science students tend to stick together, providing an almost constant network of support. From these casual interactions (as well as their conversations with instructors) these students learn an occupational language that communicates professional authority and calm composure toward things most of the public would find upsetting. For example, the students learn to see the corpse not as an individual person with a history and a family, but as a series of technical puzzles and problems posed by the cause of death (for example, ingested substances, chemical changes, injuries sustained before death).

However, Cahill points out that professional socialization is not enough to create funeral directors. He notes that students for whom death has always been a mystery or students who are predisposed to becoming queasy don't last very long in the program.

In contrast, those who are familiar with death or who have somehow worked with the dead previously (such as the sons or daughters of funeral directors) were the ones most likely to succeed.

Eventually the mortuary students who complete the program adopt the identity of funeral director. They learn to normalize death and acquire the perceptions, judgments, and emotional management skills required of this occupation. As one well-socialized student put it, "What we do is far less depressing than what nurses and doctors do. We only get the body after the death and do not have to watch all the suffering" (quoted in Cahill, 1999, p. 109).

The Self in Cultural Context

When we imagine how others will respond to our actions, we choose from a limited set of alternative lines of conduct that are aspects of the wider culture. In the United States, the self is likely to incorporate key virtues such as self-reliance and individualism. Hence personal goals often take priority over allegiance to groups (Bellah et al., 1985). In the United States, people readily change their group membership as it suits them—switching churches or even religions, leaving one employer for another, moving from neighborhood to neighborhood, and so on (Goleman, 1990).

In most non-Western countries, however, the self is more likely to be *collectivist*; that is, personal identity is completely subsumed under group identity (K. J. Gergen, 1991). In India, for instance, feelings of self-esteem and prestige derive more from strong identification with the reputation and honor of one's family than from individual achievements (Roland, 1988). In such a setting, a high value is placed on preserving one's public image so as not to bring shame on one's family, tribe, or community (Triandis, McCusker, & Hui, 1990). Overcoming personal interests and temptations to show loyalty to one's group and other authorities is celebrated. During the 1998 Winter Olympics observers noted that most players on the Japanese hockey team didn't want to score too many goals, for fear of singling themselves out from the team.

In *individualist* cultures such as the United States, personal accomplishments are a key ingredient of one's self-concept. The amount of respect we deserve is determined in large part by our level of expertise. For example, before a public speech a guest lecturer will likely be introduced to her audience as "a distinguished scholar, a leader in her field" along with a list of her scholarly achievements. In Asia, however, people would consider such pronouncements self-centered and egotistical. Asian lecturers usually begin their talks by telling the audience how *little* they know about the topic at hand (Goleman, 1990). Not only does this example show some interesting cultural differences in "appropriate" public behavior, but it also indicates vast differences in how people see themselves and the worlds they inhabit.

When we acquire a self, we are simultaneously acquiring a repertoire of behaviors that are culturally defined. Our cultural belief systems determine whether we see ourselves as a bundle of individual traits and accomplishments or as an extension of a dense network of social relations and group affiliations. But even in an individualist society such as the United States, our personal identities are inseparable from the various groups and organizations to which we belong. Consider the network revealed in Exhibit 5.1, which shows the contents of a person's wallet.

To fully understand how we become who we are, we must know the norms and values of our society, family, peers, co-workers, and so forth. Beyond that, though, we must also understand our position in the social structure. We must know to what extent our race and ethnicity, social class, and religion set limits on the kinds of social relationships we can and will form. And we must know how institutions affect the way we're socialized. All affect our identity, as well as our ability to take the roles of people who are different from us.

Socialization and Stratification: Growing Up with Inequality

Socialization does not take place in a social vacuum. Your social class, your race and ethnicity, and your gender all become significant features of your social identity. Were you born into a poor or a well-to-do family? Are you a member of a racial minority or a member of the dominant group? Are you male or female? These elements of identity shape your experiences with other people and the larger society and will direct you along a certain life path. In most societies, social class, race and ethnicity, and gender are the key determinants of the opportunities people have access to throughout their lives.

Social Class

Social classes consist of people who occupy similar positions of power, privilege, and prestige. People's positions in the class system affect virtually every aspect of their lives, including political preferences, sexual behavior, religious affiliation, diet, and life expectancy (M. L. Kohn, 1979). Conflict theory points out that even in a relatively open society such as the United States, parents' social class consigns children to certain educational, occupational, and residential opportunities. In addition, the values and orientations children learn are influenced by their parents' class standing.

In Chapter 10 you will learn more about how social class affects attitudes and opportunities. The important point here is that social class and socialization are linked. Sociologist Melvin L. Kohn (1979) interviewed 200 American working-class and 200 middle-class couples who had at least one child of fifth-grade age. He found that the middle-class parents were more likely to promote such values as self-direction, independence, and curiosity than were the working-class parents. Other researchers have found this tendency especially strong among middle-class mothers (Xiao, 2000). Conversely, working-class parents were more likely to emphasize conformity to external authority, a common characteristic of the blue-collar jobs they're likely to have. They want their children to be neat and clean and to follow the rules. Of course, not all middle-class parents, or working-class parents, raise their children the same way and many factors other than social class influence parental values (Wright & Wright, 1976). Nevertheless, Kohn found that these general tendencies were consistent regardless of the sex of the child or the size and composition of the family. Moreover, others have found that despite cultural differences, this relationship between social class standing and socialization exists in non-Western (Japan) and formerly noncapitalist (Poland) societies (Schooler, 1996).

Exhibit 5.1 **A Sociological Portrait of Identity**

What can you tell about the owner of the wallet whose contents are shown here? More important, what can you tell from the wallet's contents about the importance of groups, organizations, and institutions in our lives? To lose a wallet is to lose tangible evidence of personal identity and our connections to the social structure.

Depending on whom you talk to, money ❶ is either "the root of all evil" or "what makes the world go 'round." There's no denying that money is vitally important in the lives of most people. The entire structure of Western societies is built around it. But the money in our wallets has no intrinsic value. It is merely paper. It is valuable only because we, as a collective, agree to give it symbolic value. In fact, the dollar bill is one of the most internationally recognized symbols, readily accepted throughout the world.

We need identification cards to use the services of many of the organizations and groups to which we belong. Forget your membership card, and you can't work out in your local gym; forget your meal card, and you can't eat in your campus dining hall; forget your video store card, and you can't rent that movie you were dying to see. Some office buildings, in the interest of security, have issued identification cards that employees must use just to get into the building.

Most of us carry a variety of credit cards for department stores or other retail outlets ❷. But credit cards do more than simply enable us to make purchases without having to pay cash right away. They represent power, status, and prestige. Credit card companies have created a whole system of hierarchy and privilege. If you have a regu-

lar credit card, you're just a regular citizen; own a gold card and you have access to more money and more privileges; a platinum or titanium card puts you at the top of the heap, giving you even more opportunities. Other organizations have tried to use this status system. The Preferred Reader card ❸ you see here is an example.

Your driver's license ❹ is the most frequently asked-for identification card. What does this say about the cultural importance of automobiles in our lives? What are some of the reasons people ask to see our driver's licenses? The necessity of having this identification card has caused many people who don't need or want to drive to take a driving test.

The library card ❺, like many identification and credit cards, encodes information about you into its bar code. Magnetic strips and bar codes connect you to huge data banks that keep track of your creditworthiness and your record of payments (not to mention whether you have any overdue books). Some of these data banks also sell your name to marketing organizations that provide information about your patterns of consumption—maybe not always accurately—for future marketing campaigns. The catalogs that multiply in your mailbox can probably be traced back to an identification strip on one of your cards.

The contents of a wallet reflect important sociological ideas. As you make your way through this book, notice how concepts such as social identity, deviance, socialization, power, organizations, institutions, race, gender, class, and family can be "seen" by taking a peek inside your wallet.

Class differences in socialization are also directly related to future goals. Working-class parents tend to believe that eventual occupational success and survival depend on their children's ability to conform to and obey authority (Kohn, 1979). Middle-class parents believe their children's future success will result from assertiveness and initiative. Hence, middle-class children's feelings of control over their own destiny are likely to be much stronger. In a study of African-American women, those from middle-class backgrounds reported that their parents had higher expectations for them and were more involved in their educations than women from working-class backgrounds reported (Hill, 1997).

Race and Ethnicity

In 1999, shortly after an unarmed West African immigrant was shot and killed by four white police officers in Bronx, New York, some of my students became embroiled in a heated discussion of the incident. One student, who was white, expressed concern that because of the terrible actions of these individual officers, young children of all races would now grow up mistrusting or even hating the police. As a child she had been taught that the role of the police is to help people and that if she were ever in trouble or lost she could approach an officer for assistance. She never questioned whether or not the police could be trusted.

Some of the African-American students in class quickly pointed out that their socialization experiences had been quite different. Parents and others in their neighborhoods had taught them never to trust the police because officers were just as likely to exploit and harass them as to help them. They were taught to seek out neighbors, not the police, if they ever needed help. To them the police were not knights in shining armor but bullies with badges. Indeed, two years after racially motivated riots occurred in South Central Los Angeles, a survey of 227 black residents there found that over half of the respondents felt that unnecessary force by the Los Angeles Police Department was increasing; many respondents felt that it could have easily been them being beaten instead of Rodney King, the black man whose beating touched off the riots (Murty, Roebuck, & Armstrong, 1994).

In the wake of several other incidents around the country where police killed people of color, some parents and civic leaders now teach black and Latino children how to respond safely when approached by the police. The NAACP, the Allstate Insurance Company, and the National Organization of Black Law Enforcement Executives have published brochures and held community forums on "guidelines for interacting with law enforcement officials." Among other things, children are being taught to speak when asked to speak, to stop when ordered to stop, to never make any sudden movements, and to always display their open hands to show they aren't armed (Barry, 2000; Herbert, 1999).

Although the two perspectives of my students are not representative of every white or every black person in the United States, the interchange illustrates the stark impact race and ethnicity can have on socialization. For white children, the values they are taught when growing up are likely to be the mainstream view. Chances are that schools and religious organizations will reinforce the socialization messages expressed to them in their families—for example, that "hard work will pay off in the long run."

For racial and ethnic minorities, however, socialization occurs within a more complex social environment (R. J. Taylor, Chatters, Tucker, & Lewis, 1990). Minority children live simultaneously in two different worlds: their ethnic community, which values them, and "mainstream" society, which may not. Hence, children must become knowledgeable of the dominant culture as well as their own.

In ethnic groups that have been able to overcome discrimination and achieve at high levels—such as some Asian-American groups—ethnic socialization typically focuses on the values of their culture of origin. But among other groups, such as African Americans, parents' discussion of race is more likely to focus on preparing their children for prejudice (McLoyd, Cauce, Takeuchi, & Wilson, 2000). Parents often feel obligated to teach their children how to deal with the realities of racism or ethnic hatred in a society set up to ignore or actively exclude them (Staples, 1992). These children are likely to be taught that "hard work" alone might not be enough to get ahead in this society. Even African-American children from affluent homes in integrated neighborhoods need reassurances about the racial issues they will encounter (Comer & Poussaint, 1992). You will learn more about the effects of race and ethnicity on social life in Chapter 11.

Gender

As you will recall from Chapter 4, the belief that there are two and only two sexes—male and female—does not exist worldwide. Cultures are even more likely to differ in what is expected of people based on their sex and in how male and female children are to be socialized. Before discussing this aspect of socialization, it's necessary to distinguish between two concepts: sex and gender. **Sex** is typically used to refer to a person's biological maleness or femaleness. **Gender** designates masculinity and femininity, the psychological, social, and cultural aspects of maleness and femaleness (Kessler & McKenna, 1978). This distinction is important because it reminds us that male–female differences in behaviors or experiences do not spring naturally from biological differences between the sexes (Lips, 1993).

The gender socialization process begins the moment a child is born. A physician, nurse, or midwife immediately starts that infant on a career as a male or female by authoritatively declaring whether it is a boy or girl. In most U.S. hospitals the infant boy is wrapped in a blue blanket, the infant girl in a pink one. From that point on, the developmental paths of males and females diverge. The subsequent messages that individuals receive from families, books, television, and schools not only teach and reinforce gender-typed expectations but also influence the formation of their self-concepts. Parents are their children's first source of information about gender. However, if you were to ask parents whether they treated sons any differently from daughters, most would probably say no. Yet there is considerable evidence that what parents do and what they say they do are two different things (Lips, 1993; Lytton & Romney, 1991; Renzetti & Curran, 1989). In fact, gender-typed expectations are so ingrained that parents are often unaware that they are behaving in accordance with them (S. Goldberg & Lewis, 1969; Will, Self, & Datan, 1976).

In one study, 30 first-time parents were asked to describe their recently born infants (less than 24 hours old). They frequently resorted to common gender stereotypes.

Those with daughters described them as "tiny," "soft," "fine-featured," and "delicate." Sons were seen as "strong," "alert," "hardy," and "coordinated" (J. Z. Rubin, Provenzano, & Luria, 1974). A replication of this study two decades later found that U.S. parents continue to perceive their infants in gender-stereotyped ways, although to a lesser degree than in the 1970s (Karraker, Vogel, & Lake, 1995). Parents also tend to engage in rougher physical play with infant sons than with infant daughters and use subtle differences in tone of voice and different pet names, such as "Sweetie" versus "Tiger" (MacDonald & Parke, 1986; Tauber, 1979).

New parents, understandably proud of their new status, can be very sensitive about the correct identification of their child's sex. Even parents who claim to consider sex and gender irrelevant may nevertheless spend a great deal of time ensuring that their child has the culturally appropriate physical appearance of a boy or girl. This is not surprising in cultures where sex and gender are centrally important and sexual ambiguity is distasteful. Others' misidentification of the sex of their baby can be an embarrassing, even painful experience for some parents, which may explain why parents of a girl baby who has yet to grow hair (a visible sign of gender in many cultures) will often tape pink ribbons to the bald baby's head. In many Latin American countries, families will have baby girls' ears pierced and earrings placed in them to provide an unmistakable indicator of the child's sex.

Beyond its importance to parents, proper gender identification of babies has a lot to do with maintaining social order. When my elder son was an infant, I dressed him on several occasions in a pink, frilly snowsuit in order to observe the reactions of others. (Having a sociologist for a father can be rather difficult from time to time!) Invariably someone would approach us and start playing with the baby. Some variation of the following interchange inevitably ensued:

"Oh, she's so cute! What's your little girl's name?"
"Zachary."
"Isn't Zachary a boy's name?"
"He's a boy."

At this point the responses would range from stunned confusion and awkward laughter to dirty looks and outright anger. Clearly people felt that I had emotionally abused my son somehow. I had purposely breached a fundamental gender norm and thereby created, in their minds, unnecessary trauma (for him) and interactional turmoil (for them).

Both boys and girls learn at a very young age to adopt gender as an organizing principle for themselves and the social world in which they live (Howard & Hollander, 1997). They begin to distinguish the female role from the male role, learn to see a broad range of activities as "appropriate" for only one gender or the other, and come to identify themselves accordingly. According to most developmental psychologists, by the age of 3 or so most children can accurately answer the question "Are you a boy or a girl?" (see, for example, Kohlberg, 1966). But to a young child, being a boy or a girl means no more than being named Juan instead of Juanita. It is simply another characteristic, like having brown hair or 10 fingers. The child at this age has no conception that gender is a category into which every human can be placed (Kessler & McKenna, 1978).

At around age 5 the child begins to see gender as an invariant characteristic of the social world—something that is fixed and permanent. Likewise, these young children exhibit a high degree of gender typing in their preferences for particular activities (Kohlberg, 1966). Children at this age express statements such as "Doctors are men" and "Nurses are women" as inflexible, objective "truths." Only later will the child be able to realize that gender roles are not as inflexible as once believed.

These early lessons of gender are provided by parents, siblings, and other significant people in the child's immediate environment. Often these individuals serve as observational models whom the child can identify with and ultimately imitate. Other times the lessons are more purposive and direct, as when parents provide their children with explicit instructions on proper gender behavior, such as "Big boys don't cry" or "Act like a young lady."

Evidence suggests that the instructions are particularly rigid and restrictive for U.S. boys (Franklin, 1988). Indeed, the social costs for "gender-inappropriate" behavior are disproportionately severe for boys. The "sissy" in U.S. society has much more difficulty during childhood than the "tomboy." This discrepancy, which is clearly linked to the different social values ascribed to men and women, is discussed in more detail in Chapter 12.

As children grow older, parents tend to encourage more gender-typed activities. One study found that household tasks differ along gender lines. American boys are more likely to mow the lawn, shovel snow, take out the garbage, and do the yard work, whereas girls tend to clean the house, wash dishes, cook, and babysit the younger children (White & Brinkerhoff, 1981).

Parents maintain their children's gender identity through the things they routinely provide for them: clothes, adornments, books, videos, and so forth. Clothes, for example, not only inform others about the sex of an individual, they also send messages about how that person ought to be treated and direct behavior along traditional gender lines (Shakin, Shakin, & Sternglanz, 1985). Frilly dresses do not lend themselves easily to rough and dirty play. Likewise, it is difficult to walk quickly or assertively in high heels and tight miniskirts. Clothes for boys and men rarely restrict physical movement in this way. Toys and games are an especially influential source of gender information parents provide their children.

Micro-Macro Connection
Girls' Toys and Boys' Toys

Like most people over the age of 40, I can remember a time when toys played a very different role in American children's lives from the role they play today. When I was a child, my friends and I didn't have many toys. When we did receive a new one it was usually a special occasion, such as a birthday, a holiday, or a cavity-free dental checkup. Every once in a while we'd save up enough money, walk down to the local toy shop, and buy some toy for ourselves that we'd been coveting for months. The toys were simple and straightforward—wagons, fire engines, dolls, balls, trains, board games, and so on—and we'd use them and use them until they broke or wore out. When our parents detected a significant spurt in our maturity, they might get us a toy that required special caution: a chemistry set, an Easy Bake oven, an electric racing car set.

Today toys have changed. Toy making is now a multibillion-dollar business, part of a giant transnational, interconnected industry. It's virtually impossible to buy a toy these days that's not linked to some new film, television show, fast food restaurant, or other high-powered marketing campaign. Toy companies now commonly produce TV cartoons based on their own toy lines. By 1985, the top 10 best-selling toys all had their own cartoons. Parents find it difficult to resist their children's wishes, which are likely to be formed by television advertisements. Try taking a child to McDonald's without having to purchase a toy there. The quaint toy shop of the past has been replaced by the massive toy mega-warehouse filled with endless aisles stocked floor to ceiling with boxes sporting eye-popping colors and screaming images. Toys, it seems, have lost their innocence.

But the current state of the toy industry is not simply a result of profit-hungry corporations trying to find new ways to exploit the child market (Cross, 1997). Toys have always played a significant role in teaching children about prevailing cultural conceptions of gender. In the 1950s—a time in U.S. history when most adults had endless faith in the goodness of technological progress—Erector sets were supposed to encourage boys to be engineers and scientists. Dollhouses and baby dolls taught girls to be modern homemakers and mothers during a time when girls were expected to occupy those roles in adulthood.

You may be surprised to learn that today, in an era of greater gender equality, dolls, makeup kits, and toy kitchens continue to be the most profitable items for girls. The vocabulary of girls' toys consists of such terms as *nurturing, love,* and *magic* (Lawson, 1993). The highly stereotypical "Barbie" doll has been the best-selling girls' toy for decades. In 1993 Barbie topped $1 billion in sales. Ninety-five percent of girls aged 3 to 11 own at least one Barbie, the average number being eight (Cross, 1997).

Toy manufacturers also continue to make fortunes promoting action and violence to young boys. War toys, competitive games of strategy, and sports paraphernalia are long-standing staples of the toy industry's boy market. The words *hero, warrior, battle,* and *speed* characterize boys' toys. In 1983 the popular action figure GI Joe got his own TV show; by 1988, two-thirds of American boys between the ages of 5 and 11 owned Joes (Cross, 1997). Today, the boys' toy market is saturated with plastic descendants of Joe: high-tech soldiers, muscle-bound action figures, and intergalactic warriors.

Gender-specific toys foster different traits and skills in children and thereby serve to further segregate boys and girls into different patterns of social development. "Boys' toys" encourage invention, exploration, competition, and aggression. "Girls' toys" encourage creativity, nurturing, and physical attractiveness (C. L. Miller, 1987).

In some cases manufacturers have attempted—usually only half-heartedly—to blur the lines between boys' and girls' toys. A few years ago, the Hasbro toy company tried to interest boys in troll dolls, which are traditionally popular among girls. What they came up with were old-fashioned action figures in the shape of a troll having such names as "Troll Warrior" and "Battle Troll" (Lawson, 1993). Other companies have tried to sell girls action figures and dinosaurs, which are typically the province of boys, but have drifted into traditional gender stereotypes. Meritus Industries' "Darlin'

Dinos," for example, are pink and have full heads of hair that can be combed. Mattel's "Wonder Woman" action figure fights not with swords or machine guns but with a wand that sprays bubbles.

Moreover, toy manufacturers are still quick to exploit the gender-distinct roles children are encouraged to pursue when they become adults. "My Bundle Baby," manufactured by Mattel, is a 10-inch infant doll in a padded pouch that can be worn around a child's abdomen. By pressing a button hidden inside the pouch, the child can feel the baby inside "kick" and can hear its heartbeat (Lawson, 1992). The "Judy" doll, manufactured by the Judith Corporation, looks like any other 11-inch doll except that she is pregnant. She comes with a distended tummy that, when removed, reveals the presence of a cute baby nestled comfortably inside the doll's plastic uterus. The baby can be bloodlessly removed and a flat, nonpregnant tummy inserted in its place. The advertisement reads, "Judy is more than a toy, she's a natural way for your child to learn while playing." In other words, the Judy doll teaches young girls the cultural value of motherhood.

The gender stereotypes associated with toys persist in the computer age. In 2000, Mattel released the Barbie PC, a pink, Barbie-themed computer for girls. At the same time, the company also released a companion computer for boys, the Hot Wheels PC. The Barbie PC comes loaded with only about half of the educational software found in the Hot Wheels PC, leading critics to argue that Mattel was perpetuating harmful stereotypes by assuming that girls are only interested in fashion and boys are more interested in intellectual pursuits (Headlam, 2000a). A company spokesperson denied that the distribution of software was unfair to girls. She said that Mattel wanted the two computers to have roughly the same amount of software, but the larger number of popular Barbie programs, such as *Barbie Fashion Design* and *Detective Barbie,* left less room for educational titles on the girls' computer.

Institutions and Socialization

It should be clear by now that becoming who we are is a complex process embedded in the larger social structure. We are much more than the sum of our anatomical and neurological parts. Not only can cultural attitudes toward race, class, and gender dramatically affect our personal identities, but various social institutions—in particular, the educational system, religious organizations, and the mass media—exert considerable influence on our self-concept, our values, and our perspectives as well.

Education

In contemporary industrial societies the most powerful institutional agent of socialization, after the family, is education. In fact, according to the structural-functionalist perspective, the primary reason that schools exist is to socialize young people. Children formally enter the school system around age 5 when they begin kindergarten, although many enter earlier in preschool or nursery school. At this point, the "personalized" instruction of the family is replaced by the "impersonalized" instruction of the school, where the children in most developed countries will remain for the next 13 years or longer. No other institution has such extended and consistent access to a person's social growth.

Although schools are officially charged with equipping students with the skills they need to fulfill various roles in society (for example, reading, writing, mathematics), they also teach students important social, political, and economic values. When students set up simulated grocery stores or banks, they are learning about the importance of free enterprise and finance in a capitalist society; when they hold mock elections, they are being introduced to a democratic political system; when they spend time tending a school garden, they are learning to nurture the earth.

More subtly, schools teach students what they can expect for themselves in the world. Ironically, although individual accomplishment is stressed in U.S. schools, through grades and the like, students learn that their future success in society may be determined as much by who they are as by what they achieve. Ample evidence shows that teachers react to students on the basis of race, religion, social class, and gender (L. C. Wilkinson & Marrett, 1985). It is in school that many children are first exposed to the fact that people and groups are ranked in society, and soon they get a sense of their own relative standing in the social hierarchy.

Some sociologists argue that schooling in most cultures is designed not so much to provide children with factual information and encourage creativity but to produce passive, nonproblematic conformists who will fit into the existing social order (Gracey, 1991). This training in conformity involves several different dimensions (Brint, 1998). First, there is *behavioral* conformity. Teachers in the early grades typically keep children in line by controlling their bodily movements, such as making them sit still or forcing them to raise their hands before speaking. Second, schools teach *moral* conformity. Teachers often instruct children about the importance of such moral virtues as honesty, courage, kindness, fairness, and respect. Finally, schools teach children to conform to *culturally* approved styles and outlooks. In some societies, teachers reward their students for showing a quick wit; in other societies children are rewarded for demonstrating thoughtfulness and asking deep, probing questions. Such training socializes students to adopt traits that are considered culturally desirable within that society.

Sometimes these different dimensions overlap. Rules against arguing with the teacher, for instance, teach children the moral "goodness" of respecting authority. But they can also foster passivity and give students their first taste of control by authoritative adults other than their parents. Such classroom regulations, then, help impose discipline while at the same time they prepare children for what they will face in the larger culture. Obeying the kindergarten teacher today prepares the individual for obeying the high school teacher, college professor, and boss tomorrow.

Many of these lessons vary by gender. Schools subtly create children's conceptions of gender by teaching them that teachers expect different things from boys and girls. In an observational study of five preschool classrooms in the United States, sociologist Karin Martin (1998) found, among other things, that teachers tend to discourage girls from speaking loudly and place tighter restrictions on their movement than they do on boys. In addition, preschool teachers are more likely to physically restrain boys—for example, by holding them to stop them from running—than girls. Such actions go a long way in telling boys and girls, even at this early age, that they are being perceived differently. And because such instructions are so common, they make any differences between boys' and girls' physical activity look and feel natural.

Teachers are also likely to treat their older male and female students differently. It is not uncommon for teachers to ask boys to run the film projector or rearrange desks and ask girls to water the plants or dust the tables (Thorne & Luria, 1986). A nation-wide survey of 3,000 boys and girls between the ages of 9 and 15 found that boys received far more attention from teachers than girls. Teachers were also more likely to encourage assertive behavior in boys (American Association of University Women, 1991). This differential treatment is often reinforced in high school by textbooks and other curricular materials that frequently consign women to stereotypical roles in U.S. society (for example, nurse or spouse) or to ignore their contributions to the shaping of history.

College professors, like their elementary and high school counterparts, may treat men and women differently in the classroom as well. Disparaging comments about women, the use of gender-stereotyped examples, and the use of the generic "he" are some examples of behavior that sends young women the message that they are over-reaching societal expectations (R. M. Hall & Sandler, 1985).

It may seem that the educational system is overwhelmingly dedicated to fitting every student into preordained roles. However, some teachers and alternative schools instill values that are at odds with existing social arrangements. The point is that because of the primacy of formal education in the everyday lives of most children, the institutional agenda of a particular school system can have important consequences for the types of people they will eventually become.

Religion

As the structural-functionalist perspective tells us, religion is the social institution that tends to the spiritual needs of individuals and serves as a major source of cultural knowledge. It plays a key role in the development of people's ideas about right and wrong. It also helps in the formation of people's identities by providing coherence and continuity to the episodes that make up each individual's life (Kearl, 1980). Religious rites of passage, such as baptisms, bar and bat mitzvahs, confirmations, and weddings, reaffirm an individual's religious identity while impressing on her or him the rights and obligations attached to a new status (Turner, 1972).

Religion occupies a complex and curious place in U.S. life. Structural changes in society have made religious affiliation somewhat unstable in recent years. For instance, economic circumstances have forced large numbers of families to relocate, loosening connections to extended family and friendship networks. As the United States becomes a society of people moving from city to city or state to state, many of the ties that bind people to the same religion are broken. Only about 43% of adults attend religious services regularly (U.S. Bureau of the Census, 2000b). Many of our most powerful religious groups (Lutherans, Methodists, Episcopalians, Presbyterians, Roman Catholics, Jews, and so on) have seen their memberships decline steadily over the past several decades (Jacquet & Jones, 1991; Shorto, 1997).

But the membership decline in mainline religions does not necessarily mean that religion is losing its influence as a major socializing force in U.S. society. Indeed, at the same time that membership in mainline religions has declined, that of "evangelical" churches (Mormons, Jehovah's Witnesses, Seventh Day Adventists, Assemblies of God, Church of God in Christ) has increased (Finke & Stark, 1992; Jacquet & Jones, 1991; Shorto, 1997). And new religions are constantly emerging. Of the 1,600 religions and denominations in the United States today, 800 were founded after 1965. Furthermore, immigration has helped fuel an increase in non-Christian religions. The number of Hindus in the United States has grown from 70,000 in 1977 to 800,000 today. There are now as many Muslims in the United States as there are Presbyterians. Religion may not look the same as it did 50 years ago, but it still remains a fundamental socializer in most people's lives.

Compared to most other Western democracies, such as Germany and Great Britain, people in the United States stand out for the depth of their religious beliefs (Kelley & DeGraaf, 1997). Consider these facts (respectively from Greeley & Hout, 1999; Niebuhr, 1996; Shorto, 1997; U.S. Bureau of the Census, 2000b):

- Seventy percent of U.S. residents belong to a church or synagogue.
- Sixty-two percent of U.S. residents have no doubts that God exists; only 2% express outright disbelief.
- Nine out of every 10 homes contain at least one Bible. About one-third of U.S. residents believe the Bible is the actual word of God, and more than 80% believe it was divinely inspired.
- Among U.S. adults, 90% believe in heaven, 65% believe in the devil, and 75% believe that angels exist and affect human lives. A greater percentage of U.S. adults, no matter what their religious affiliation, believe in life after death today than in the 1970s.

In short, religion remains a significant part of U.S. life. After all, we still consider ourselves to be "one nation under God" and our money still proclaims our trust in God. Religion can be found in every corner of social life. It's virtually impossible to watch a sporting event these days without seeing a baseball player cross himself before batting, a football player point skyward after scoring a touchdown, or a basketball player thank God for a victory in a postgame interview. Sales of Christian books, computer games, and videos, and toys are going up each year. The contemporary Christian music genre, alone, is a $1-billion-a-year business. Enrollment in evangelical colleges grew 24% between 1990 and 1996, and the number of families choosing to homeschool their children for religious reasons has increased at an annual rate of 15 to 20% since 1985 (Talbot, 2000a).

Mass Media

Another powerful institutional socializer is the media. It's estimated that by the time the average U.S. student graduates from high school, she or he will have spent more time watching television than in the classroom (Croteau & Hoynes, 2000). Newspapers, magazines, radio, and film, as well as television, transmit persuasive messages on the nature of reality. They also tell us the type of person we "should" be, from how we should perform our jobs to how different social classes live to what our intimate relationships and families are supposed to look like. The media teach us about prevailing values, beliefs, myths, stereotypes, and trends (Gitlin, 1979) and provide an avenue through which we learn new attitudes and behavior (Bandura & Walters, 1963). Sociologists, psychologists, and, of course, politicians continue to debate the degree to which sex and violence in film, television, and video games influence behavior, particularly among young people.

These lessons begin early. Children's books, for instance, teach youngsters what other little boys or girls in their culture do and what is expected of them. In the early 1970s Lenore Weitzman and her colleagues studied the portrayal of gender in popular U.S. preschool books (Weitzman, Eifler, Hodada, & Ross, 1972). They found that boys played a more significant role in the stories than girls by a ratio of 11 to 1. Boys were more likely to be portrayed in adventurous pursuits or activities that required independence and strength; girls were likely to be confined to indoor activities and portrayed as passive and dependent. The prevalence of gender stereotypes in children's books has decreased only slightly over the past several decades (S. B. Peterson & Lach, 1990). Males still tend to be portrayed as adventurous, competent, and clever; females are depicted as fearful, incompetent, and dependent (A. J. Davis, 1984). In addition, recent attempts to neutralize the stereotypical portrayal of gender through nonsexist children's books have had little impact on the overall market.

These images of males and females have a strong influence on children's perceptions and behaviors. One study found that children's own writing reflects the same sort of gender stereotypes found in the books they read. In stories written by 180 boys and girls in the first through sixth grades, male characters predominated. Furthermore, the male characters were depicted in stereotypically male occupations: doctor, astronaut, dentist, professor, police officer. Female characters were shown largely in traditional female occupational roles: cook, teacher, babysitter, nurse (Trepanier & Romatowski, 1985).

The effects of televised images on children's notions of gender are especially powerful. Children who watch a lot of television are more likely to hold stereotypical attitudes toward gender, exhibit gender-related characteristics, and engage in gender-related activities than children who watch little television (M. Morgan, 1987; Signorielli, 1990). In one study, girls who did not have stereotypical conceptions of gender to begin with showed a significant increase in such attitudes after two years of heavy television watching (M. Morgan, 1982). In another study, 4- to 6-year-old children refused to play with a particular toy after watching two Muppets on TV who said the toy was OK only for the other sex (Cobb, Stevens-Long, & Goldstein, 1982).

These effects are not surprising given the programming that children encounter. Despite some notable exceptions (for example, *Sesame Street*), most children's television shows continue to portray males and females in stereotypical gender roles (Signorielli, 1990). A study of 41 Saturday morning cartoons found that though things have improved since 1980, both male and female cartoon characters are still portrayed stereotypically. Male characters are more likely than female characters to occupy leadership roles, act aggressively, give guidance to or come to the rescue of others, express opinions, ask questions, and achieve their goals. In addition, males are more likely to be portrayed in some kind of recognizable occupation, whereas females are more likely to be cast in the role of caregiver (Thompson & Zerbinos, 1995).

Television commercials also perpetuate stereotypes. In an analysis of over 500 U.S. and Australian commercials targeting children, boys were more likely to be depicted in dominant and active roles than were girls. Girls tended to be portrayed as shyer, giggly, and passive. The differences were less pronounced in Australia where there's been a more active movement to counter gender stereotypes in the media. Such images are not trivial, given that U.S. children watch over 20,000 TV commercials a year (Browne, 1998).

But the socializing influence of the media can be much more subtle. Consider the role that televised sports play in teaching people in the United States certain cultural values (Gitlin, 1979). Television has reduced the sports experience to a sequence of individual achievements. For instance, coverage of the Olympic Games every four years focuses almost exclusively on the efforts, obstacles, successes, and failures of individual athletes (Hilliard, 1994). Likewise, media coverage of professional sports concentrates on the achievements of individuals rather than teams. The 1998 Major League baseball season was dominated by the individual quests of Mark McGwire and Sammy Sosa to break the single-season home run record. Their teammates were reduced to supporting-cast members. Few fans seemed to care how the respective teams were doing. And many observers credited this duel for individual glory for resurrecting sagging public interest in baseball.

We have grown used to hearing such descriptions as "best," "superstar," and "greatest of all time." Praise is heaped not only on individuals and the occasional "dynasty" team, but also on more specific actions: "best jump shot," "best backhand," "best at hitting with two outs and runners in scoring position," "best open field tackler," "best chip out of a sand trap." Such characterizations not only perpetuate the importance of individual achievement—a cultural value on which the entire U.S. social structure is based—but also give the impression that it is always possible to find something, however narrowly defined, at which one can be "best" (Gitlin, 1979).

CONCLUSION

Becoming the people we are is a complex social process. Those intimate characteristics we hold so dear—our self-concept, our gender, and our racial and ethnic identity—are reflections of larger cultural attitudes, values, and expectations. Yet we are not perfect reflections of society's values. With all the powerful socializing institutions that pull our developmental strings, we continue to be and will always be individuals.

Sometimes we ignore our generalized others and strike out on our own with complete disregard for community standards and attitudes. Sometimes we form self-concepts that contradict the information we receive from others about ourselves. Sometimes we willingly violate the expectations associated with our gender or our race. Societal influence can go only so far in explaining how we become who we are. The rest—that which makes us truly unique—remains a fascinating mystery.

YOUR TURN

Being a child or an adolescent is not simply a biological stage of development. It is a *social* identity. People's experiences with this identity emerge from a particular cultural and historical context as well as the process of socialization that takes place within their families. But many other social institutions assist in the process of raising children, often in ways that aren't immediately apparent.

To see firsthand how such socialization works, visit a large shopping mall. Most malls today have children's clothing stores (for example, *Baby Gap*). If yours doesn't, go to one of the large department stores and find the children's clothing section. Start with the infants' clothes. Is there a difference between "girls' clothes" and "boys' clothes"? Note the differences in the style, color, and texture of boys' versus girls' clothes. Collect the same information for clothes designed for toddlers, preschoolers, and elementary school age children.

Now find a store that specializes in clothes for preteens and teenagers. How do clothing styles differ along gender lines at this age level?

After collecting your data, try to interpret the differences you noticed. Why do they exist? What do these differences say about the kinds of social activities in which boys and girls are expected or encouraged to engage? For instance, which clothes are "rugged" and which are "dainty"? How do such differences reinforce our cultural conceptions of masculinity and femininity? Turning your attention to teenagers, how do popular clothing styles encourage sexuality?

The next stop on your sociological shopping trip is a toy store. Can you detect a boys' section and a girls' section? How do you know? How do the toys differ? What sorts of interactions with other children do the toys encourage? Competition? Cooperation? Which toys are designed for active play? Which seem to encourage passive play? For what sorts of adult roles do the toys prepare children? Provide specific examples.

Finally, find a bookstore that has a children's book section. Which books are more likely to interest boys? Which will interest girls? Are there different sections for "boy" and "girl" books? What are the differences in the sorts of characters and plots that are portrayed? Does the bookstore have a section that contains books designed to help adolescents through puberty? If so, do these books offer different advice to adolescent boys and girls?

Use your findings in all these areas—clothing, toys, and books—to analyze the role that consumer products play in socializing children into "appropriate" gender roles. Is there more or less gender segregation as children get older? Do you think manufacturers, publishers, retail outlets, and so on are simply responding to market demands (that is, do they make gender-specific products because that's what people want), or do they play a role in creating those demands?

CHAPTER HIGHLIGHTS

● Socialization is the process by which individuals learn their culture and learn to live according to the norms of a particular society. It is how we learn to perceive our world, gain a sense of our own identity, and interact appropriately with others. It also tells us what we should and should not do across a range of situations.

- One of the most important outcomes of socialization for an individual is the development of a sense of self. To acquire a self, children must learn to recognize themselves as unique physical objects, master language, learn to take the roles of others, and, in effect, see themselves from another's perspective.

- Socialization is not just a process that occurs during childhood. Adults must be resocialized

into a new galaxy of norms, values, and expectations each time they leave or abandon old roles and enter new ones.

- We learn the social expectations that go with our social class, racial or ethnic group, and gender through socialization.

- Socialization occurs within the context of several social institutions—family first, and then schools, religious institutions, and the mass media.

KEY TERMS

anticipatory socialization Process through which people acquire the values and orientations found in statuses they will likely enter in the future

game stage Stage in the development of self during which a child acquires the ability to take the role of a group or community (the generalized other) and to conform his or her behavior to broad, societal expectations

gender Psychological, social, and cultural aspects of maleness and femaleness

generalized other Perspective of the larger society and its constituent values and attitudes

identity Essential aspect of who we are, consisting of our sense of self, gender, race, ethnicity, and religion

looking-glass self Sense of who we are that is defined by incorporating the reflected appraisals of others

play stage Stage in the development of self during which a child develops the ability to take a role, but only from the perspective of one person at a time

reflexive behavior Behavior in which the person initiating an action is the same as the person toward whom the action is directed

resocialization Process of learning new values, norms, and expectations when an adult leaves an old role and enters a new one

role taking Ability to see oneself from the perspective of others and to use that perspective in formulating one's own behavior

self Unique set of traits, behaviors, and attitudes that distinguishes one person from the next; the active source and passive object of behavior

sex Biological maleness or femaleness

socialization Process through which one learns how to act according to the rules and expectations of a particular culture

total institution Place where individuals are cut off from the wider society for an appreciable period and where together they lead an enclosed, formally administered life

A Matter of Sexual Identity

Douglas Harper

In our society the delineation of people of different sexes (physical characteristics) and genders (psychological, social, and cultural aspects of maleness and femaleness) is strongly enforced. We discourage ambiguous sexual or gender definitions. Thus people who want to redefine their sexual or gender identity are often viewed as deviants who are going against nature. Most societies, but U.S. society in particular, deal rigidly with people who violate gender norms. These people pay a heavy price: social isolation, ostracism, and other problems that accompany social rejection.

It is possible to redefine one's sexual identity through surgery and hormone treatment, but the shift in self-concept is usually hidden from public view.

There is a quiet revolution, however, in the universe of what is now called transgendering. People are publicly claiming a gender different from the one they were born with or, even more radically, shifting from one sex identity to another as the situation warrants. A number of prominent figures have publicly switched sexes or genders or defied the rigid two-gender model.

UPI/BETTMANN

DAVID HURN/MAGNUM

● A courageous early pioneer in the transgendering revolution was James/Jan Morris. As a well-respected travel writer, Morris lived into his adulthood as Jim. He then became Jan through a process that was both surgical and social. Jan's professional life continued the career begun by Jim; the transformation was public and unabashed.

● The Italian film actress Eva Robbins is a hermaphrodite, meaning that she has both male and female reproductive organs—a genetic variation that occurs naturally in a small percentage of people (see Chapter 4). She has starred as a gorgeous woman in more than 10 Italian movies. In *Belle of the Bar,* Eva plays Giulia, a seductive hermaphroditic prostitute who captures the eye of Leo, a conservative heterosexual male. The Italian advertisement for the film reads, "But when she—quite graphically—turns out to be Leo's male cousin, Eva is simply sublime." What is striking about this film is not that a transgendered individual is portrayed; the film *The Crying Game* popularized the idea of falling in love by mistake with a person of the "wrong" sex. What is remarkable in Eva Robbins's case is that by playing her own sexual biography she has sensitized Italian viewers to the realities of natural sexual variation.

● The 2000 Democratic convention included Minnesota delegate Jane Fee, a 73-year-old World War II–era veteran who was a long-standing military officer, a member of the National Rifle Association, and father of four children. For 62 years she had been James Fee, who had had a successful career and a secret life as a transgendered person. For the last decade, Jane Fee has been a vocal defender of the rights of transgendered people and an advocate for public acceptance. Like Eva Robbins, her goal has been to normalize the transgender experience.

6 Building Image: The Presentation of Self

Forming Impressions of Others

Managing Impressions

Mismanaging Impressions: Spoiled Identities

On Christmas Day 1981 I met my soon-to-be wife's family for the first time. For this group of important strangers, I knew I had to be on my best behavior and say and do all the right things. I wanted to make sure the impression they formed of me was that of a likable fellow whom they'd be proud to call a member of the family.

As people busily opened their presents, I noticed the wide and gleeful eyes of my wife's 14-year-old sister as she unwrapped what was to her a special gift—her very own basketball. Being the youngest in a family of eight kids, she didn't have much she could call her own, so this was a significant moment for her. She had finally broken away from a life filled with hand-me-downs and communal equipment. She hugged that ball as if it were a puppy.

I saw my chance to make the perfect first impression. "I'm not a bad basketball player," I thought to myself. "I'll take her outside to the basketball hoop in the driveway, impress her with my shooting skills, become her idol, and win family approval."

"Hey, Mary," I said, "let's go out and shoot some hoops." After we stepped outside I grabbed the new ball from her. "Look at this," I said as I flung it toward the basket from about 40 feet away. We both watched as the ball arced gracefully toward its destination, and for a brief moment I actually thought it was going to go in. But that was not to be.

As if guided by the taunting hand of fate, the ball struck an exposed bolt that protruded from the base of the supporting pole of the hoop. There was a sickeningly loud pop, followed by a hissing sound as the ball fluttered to the ground like a deflated balloon. It sat there lifeless, never having experienced the joy of "swishing" through a net. For that matter, it had never even been bounced on the ground in its short-lived inflated state.

For a few seconds we both stood numb and motionless. Then I turned to apologize to the 14-year-old girl whose once cheerful eyes now harbored the kind of hate and resentment usually reserved for ax murderers and IRS auditors. In a flash she burst into tears and ran into the house, shrieking, "THAT GUY popped my ball!" It was hardly the heroic identity I was striving for. As the angry mob poured into the backyard to stare at the villainous and still somewhat unknown perpetrator, I became painfully aware of the fragile nature of the self-images we try to project to others.

We all have been in situations—a first date, a job interview, a first meeting with a girlfriend or boyfriend's family—in which we feel compelled to "make a good impression." We try to present a favorable image of ourselves so that others will make positive judgments of us. This phenomenon is not only an important and universal aspect of our personal lives but a key element of social structure as well.

In this chapter I examine the social creation of images. How do we form impressions of others? What do we do to control the impressions others form of us? I also discuss broader sociological applications of these actions. What are the institutional motivations behind individuals' attempts to control others' impressions of them? How do groups and organizations present and manage collective impressions? Finally, what happens when these attempts fail and images are spoiled, as mine was in the story I just told?

Forming Impressions of Others

When we first meet someone we form an immediate impression based on observable cues, such as age, ascribed status characteristics like race and sex, individual attributes, and verbal and nonverbal expressions. All these cues help us form an initial assessment of the other person's identity.

Keep in mind that the importance of this information—the value attached to a certain age, race, or sex; the particular physical or personality traits that are defined as desirable; the meaning of certain words and gestures—varies across time and place. Hence the impressions that people form of others—good, bad, or indifferent—must always be understood within the appropriate cultural and historical context. For instance, an expressive person in the United States may give the impression of being energetic and outgoing; in Thailand or Japan that person may be considered dangerous or crazy; and in Great Britain such a person may seem boorish and rude.

Social Group Membership

Age, sex, race, and to a certain degree ethnicity can often be determined merely by looking at a person; social class is less obvious but sometimes becomes known early in an encounter with another person, through the person's language, mannerisms, or dress. As you saw in the previous chapter, our socialization experiences provide us with a sense of the cultural significance of belonging to certain social groups: male or female, black or white, upper class or working class, and so on. We learn to expect certain things from certain types of people. For instance, if all you know about a person is that she's female, you may assume she's compassionate, emotional, and nurturing. Likewise, if all you know about a person is that she is 85 years old, you might predict that she has low energy, poor memory, and conservative political attitudes. Think about your expectations when you learn that a classmate is from a different country—or, for that matter, from a different region of your own country. Of course, such expectations are rarely completely accurate. Nevertheless, we begin social interactions with these culturally defined conceptions of how people from certain social groups are likely to act, what their tastes and preferences might be, and what values and attitudes they are likely to hold.

This information provides the initial backdrop to all social encounters between people who have little if any prior knowledge of one another. It is so pervasive and so quickly processed that we usually notice it only when it isn't there. If you spend much time in Internet chat rooms, you may have noticed how difficult it can be to form a friendship or carry on a discussion when you don't know whether you are interacting with someone of the same sex or with someone of a different sex.

When the only thing we know about an individual, is his or her social group characteristics, we structure our impressions of the person around those few facts. We have a tendency to ignore other details. A few years ago, then–U.S. Secretary of State Madeleine Albright made headlines after discovering that, despite being raised all her life as a Roman Catholic, her parents had been Jewish at one time. Her Czechoslovakian parents had secretly decided to convert to Christianity in the 1930s to avoid Nazi persecution. Immediately, newspapers here and abroad began speculating on whether or not this new piece of information about her family's religious identity would affect her ability to deal fairly in foreign affairs, particularly in the Middle East. That is, some wondered whether her approach to matters concerning Israel and its surrounding Arab neighbors might be compromised by this new light on her personal history. She had not changed. But her social group membership had enlarged, and people now saw her differently and therefore judged her differently.

Physical Appearance

We confirm or modify early impressions based on social group membership by assessing other characteristics that are easily perceivable, such as a person's physical appearance (Berndt & Heller, 1986). The way people dress and decorate their bodies communicate their feelings, beliefs, and group identity to others. People's clothes, jewelry, hairstyles, and so on can also indicate their ethnicity, social class, age, cultural tastes, morality, and political attitudes.

But again, these impressions can be influenced by our cultural background. Physical appearance is enormously important in U.S. culture. Everywhere we turn, it seems, we are encouraged to believe that if our skin isn't free of blemishes, if we are too short or too tall, if we are over- or underweight, if our hair isn't stylish, if our clothes don't reflect the latest fashion trend, we have fallen short. Although we readily acknowledge that using a person's physical attractiveness to form an impression is shallow and unfair, we usually do it anyway.

Research confirms that physical appearance affects our perceptions and judgments of others. For instance, the impressions that adults form of young children are heavily influenced by the child's physical attractiveness (Clifford & Walster, 1973; Dion, 1972). Attractive men are perceived as more masculine and attractive women more feminine than their less attractive counterparts (Gillen, 1981). We assume that physically attractive people possess other desirable traits, such as sensitivity, kindness, strength, and sexual responsiveness (Dion, Berscheid, & Walster, 1972). Research on jury deliberations in legal trials suggests that attractive defendants are treated better (for example, receive shorter jail sentences) than less attractive defendants (Stewart, 1980).

Physical attractiveness is still a more salient issue for women than it is for men. The cultural norms used to evaluate overall female beauty in the United States continue to be so narrow and unrealistic that many women have a sense of perpetual deficiency as a result (Schur, 1984). Women have more money, political clout, and legal recognition today than ever, but they are still judged primarily in terms of their physical appearance. For instance, without having won a major tournament Anna Kournikova has become the highest-earning player in women's tennis today. According to a *Sports Illustrated* story on her, "a hot body can count as much as a good backhand" (quoted in Dowd, 2000, p. 19).

Even women in positions of power and influence are likely to be evaluated by their looks. As one author puts it, "The more legal and material hindrances women have broken through, the more strictly and heavily and cruelly images of female beauty have come to weigh upon us" (Wolf, 1991, p. 10).

In the 2000 presidential election, Katherine Harris, the Florida secretary of state, became perhaps *the* most controversial figure in one of the most important political events in U.S. history. She made headlines when she refused to acknowledge disputed hand-recounted ballots in some counties and certified George W. Bush as the winner in Florida, paving the way for his election. Although some people criticized her for her partisan politics and her narrow interpretation of Florida election laws, many others focused on her use of heavy makeup and taste for austere business suits. She was called "Cruella de Vil" and "Vampira on a bad night." It's hard to imagine any male figures in this controversy described the way a reporter for the *Washington Post* described Ms. Harris:

> Her lips were overdrawn with berry-red lipstick—the creamy sort that smears all over a coffee cup and leaves smudges on shirt collars. Her skin had been plastered and powdered to the texture of pre-war walls in need of a skim coat. And her eyes, rimmed in liner and frosted with blue shadow, bore the telltale homogenous spikes of false eyelashes. (quoted in Scott, 2000, p. 3)

At the individual level such an emphasis on physical appearance devalues a person's other attributes and accomplishments; at the institutional level it plays an important role in the nation's economy by sustaining several multibillion-dollar industries, including advertising, fashion, and cosmetics (Schur, 1984).

Micro-Macro Connection
Obesity

In U.S. society, and in most industrialized societies, the negative effects of being considered unattractive are perhaps felt most strongly by those whose body size does not meet cultural standards (Allon, 1982; English, 1991). People are likely to judge an overweight person as lacking in willpower and as being self-indulgent, personally offensive, and even morally and socially unfit (Millman, 1980). Obesity can affect economic opportunities as well. Research has found significant discrimination against obese people at every stage of the employment cycle, including hiring, placement, compensation, promotion, discipline, and discharge (Roehling, 1999). One study of young women in Britain found that the heaviest 10% of their age group earned 7.4% less than their nonobese peers and that the heaviest 1% earned 11.4% less (cited in "Physical traits," 1994).

In high-visibility occupations such as public relations and sales, overweight people are often regarded as unemployable because they might project a negative image of the company they are working for. Ironically, however, in a society that celebrates thinness, approximately one-fifth of all Americans (and one-fourth of those under age 19) are overweight (Critser, 2000).

In some societies being overweight does not devalue a person in the eyes of others. In Mexico, for example, people are significantly less concerned about their own weight and are more accepting of overweight people than individuals in the United States (Crandall & Martinez, 1996). In Niger, being overweight is considered an essential part of female beauty, so women sometimes take steroids to gain bulk or even ingest feed and vitamins that are meant to be consumed by animals (Onishi, 2001). In earlier eras in U.S. society as well, being robust was considered attractive.

Although the distaste for obesity usually applies to both sexes, it is felt particularly strongly by women. Since the 1920s cultural standards have idealized increasingly thinner female bodies (Freedman, 1986). In one study 70% of U.S. college women felt they were overweight, although fewer than 40% actually were (T. M. Miller, Coffman, & Linke, 1980). Furthermore, U.S. women are becoming weight conscious at increasingly younger ages. A survey of 500 elementary school children found that more than half the girls thought they were too fat, even though only 15% were actually heavier than the norm (Goleman, 1991b). At any one time, half of U.S. women are on a diet; and half of all 9-year-old girls have been on a diet at least once in their lives ("The facts," 1996).

Weight concerns are not shared equally by all U.S. women, however. In one study, 90% of white junior high and high school girls voiced dissatisfaction with their bodies, whereas 70% of black teens were satisfied with their bodies (Parker, Nichter, Nichter, Vuckovic, Sims, & Ritenbaugh, 1995). Young white women are likely to want to achieve an appearance featured in the media, even when they regard such images as unrealistic and largely artificial (Milkie, 1999). In contrast, research has consistently shown that despite powerful media images, African-American women worry less than women of other races about weight, dieting, or being thin (Molloy & Herzberger, 1998).

In one study, 64% of African-American women stated that they'd rather be "a little overweight" than "a little underweight." Indeed, black adolescents tend to perceive themselves as thinner than they actually are, whereas white adolescents tend to perceive themselves as heavier than they actually are. When black women do diet, their efforts to lose weight are more realistic and less extreme than white women's attempts (Parker et al., 1995). These attitudes and behaviors are especially true among poor and working-class African-American women. More affluent black women are more likely to be exposed to dominant white preferences, attitudes, and ideals about beauty and weight. But in general, black women are less dissatisfied with their body weight than white women and therefore have higher self-esteem, have a more positive body image, and suffer from fewer eating disorders.

Female weight concern has large-scale implications because of the role it plays in the growth and success of the multibillion-dollar diet "industry": low-calorie foods, diet books, weight-loss organizations, and so forth. Today, the number of readers of *Weight Watchers Magazine* is the same as that of the *New York Times* ("Harper's Index," 1996).

With the growth in global communication technology, images of thin U.S. women have infiltrated the global community (Croteau & Hoynes, 2000). For instance, a few years after the introduction of U.S. television shows like *Melrose Place* and *Beverly Hills, 90210,* eating disorders among teenage girls in Fiji rose dramatically. Before 1995, few girls on Fiji dieted. In fact, the concept of "calories" was foreign to them. By 1998, however, 69% of girls said they had been on a diet at some point in their lives and 15% had induced vomiting to control their weight. Fijian girls who said they watched television three or more hours a night were 50% more likely to describe themselves as "too big or fat" than girls who didn't watch much television (cited in Goode, 1999b).

Unnecessary concern over weight shows how powerful cultural beliefs are in the formation of self-concepts. At best, the failure to meet broad cultural standards of thinness can generate antagonism toward one's own body and lowered self-esteem. At worst, it can lead to life-threatening eating disorders (Chernin, 1981). Such drastic responses indicate the importance of body size—and physical appearance, in general—in creating impressions in social interaction.

Verbal and Nonverbal Expression

Another important piece of information we use in forming impressions of others is what people express to us verbally or nonverbally. Through speech, movement, posture, and gestures, people provide cues about their values, attitudes, sentiments, personality, and history (G. P. Stone, 1981). Sometimes these forms of communication are used purposely to convey meaning. However, some physical expressions, such as a shaky voice, a flushed face, and trembling hands, are difficult to control. They convey an impression whether we want to or not.

Most of us are quite proficient at "reading" even the subtlest nonverbal messages. We learn early that a raised eyebrow, a nod of the head, or a slight hand gesture can mean something important in a social encounter. So crucial is this ability in maintaining orderly interactions that some psychologists consider a deficiency in it to be a learning disability akin to severe reading problems (Goleman, 1989).

Managing Impressions

People form impressions of others and create impressions of themselves at the same time. This ability to create impressions is the defining feature of human interaction. Naturally, we try to create impressions of ourselves that give us advantages—by making us seem attractive or powerful or otherwise worthy of people's attention and esteem. That's what I was trying to do when I attempted the ill-fated jump shot with my future sister-in-law's new basketball.

The process by which people attempt to present a favorable public image of themselves is called **impression management.** Erving Goffman (1959), the sociologist most responsible for the scholarly examination of impression management, portrays everyday life as a series of social interactions in which a person is motivated to "sell" a particular image to others. The primary goal of impression management is to project a particular identity that will increase the likelihood of obtaining favorable outcomes from others in particular social situations (E. E. Jones & Pittman, 1982; Stryker, 1980). To do so, we can strategically furnish or conceal information. We may need to advertise, exaggerate, or fabricate our positive qualities and hide behaviors or attributes that we believe others will find unappealing.

A person can occupy various identities: student, sibling, child, employee, wealthy person, trusted friend, future lawyer, cyclist. As a general rule, the more important an identity is to an individual's overall self-concept, the more time she or he will spend on activities expressing that identity (McCall & Simmons, 1978). For instance, if you aspire to be a marriage counselor, you may spend a great deal of time listening to people's problems or commenting on people's relationships.

Often people try to present a favorable image by altering their physical appearance. Clothing and body adornment can be used to manipulate and manage the impressions others form of us. People can dress to convey the impression that they are worthy of respect or, at the very least, attention (Lauer & Handel, 1977). Businesspeople are acutely aware of and usually conform to a corporate dress code; even if the code is "business casual," those who dress too casually are not taken seriously. Children often signal their entry into the world of adolescence by wearing the clothing of their peers and refusing to wear the clothing chosen by their parents (G. P. Stone, 1981). The purveyors of rap, hip-hop, industrial, ska, and goth music use clothing and hairstyle as an expression of subcultural identity and social rebellion. And as you are well aware, fashion is a significant element of the student culture on most college campuses (Moffatt, 1989). In short, by what they wear people tell one another who they are, where they come from, and what they stand for.

The desire to manage impressions by controlling physical appearance motivates people to do far more than buy a new outfit or two. People in the United States are willing to spend huge amounts of money to improve their looks. In 1999 alone they spent $6 billion on fragrance, $6 billion on makeup products, and $8 billion on hair and skin care products (cited in C. Newman, 2000). Some people take even more extreme measures. According to the American Society of Plastic and Reconstructive Surgeons, an estimated 2.1 million Americans underwent plastic surgery in 1998, up 50% from 1992; and people are having these surgeries performed at younger and younger ages (cited in K. Hamilton & Weingarden, 1998). Procedures such as breast augmentations, collagen injections, eyelid surgeries, liposuction, tummy tucks, and nose jobs are becoming increasingly common, even among adolescents (J. Gross, 1998). Although most cosmetic surgery is performed on women, more and more men are opting for it; between 1992 and 1997, the number of men who had face-lifts more than doubled (Fraser, 1999). Exhibit 6.1 shows how broadly popular cosmetic surgery has become.

The growing popularity of these procedures reflects pervasive discontent among people in the United States over the way they look. According to one study, 85% of American women and 72% of American men are dissatisfied with at least one aspect of their looks (cited in Goleman, 1991a). Such dissatisfaction can have long-lasting effects. People who don't like the way they look report higher levels of overall unhappiness than people who are satisfied with their appearance (Berscheid & Walster, 1974). Psychiatrists estimate that between 2% and 10% of the U.S. population suffer from a

Exhibit 6.1 **The Popularity of Cosmetic Surgery in the United States**

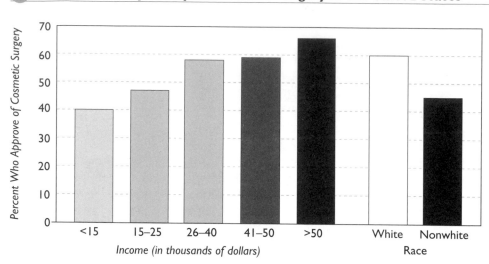

Source: American Society for Aesthetic Plastic Surgery, 1999.

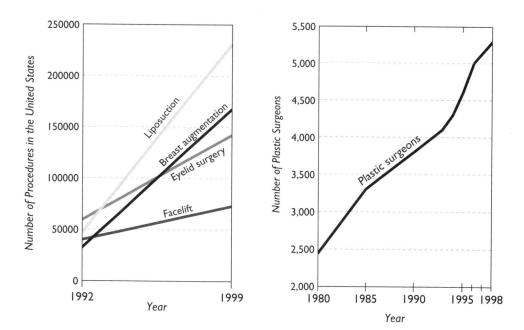

Source: American Society of Plastic and
Reconstructive Surgeons, 2001.

Source: U.S. Bureau of the Census, 2000b.

"disorder," called *body dysmorphic disorder,* which has become more common over the last decade or so (Goleman, 1991b). These individuals are so self-conscious about their looks that their lives are constricted in some significant way, from feeling inhibited during lovemaking to becoming homebound or suicidal. Perhaps not surprisingly, 15% of women and 11% of men in a recent survey said they'd sacrifice more than five years of their life to be at their ideal weight (cited in C. Newman, 2000).

When the stakes are high, impression management is especially important. If you have ever seen a U.S. political party's national convention, you have witnessed the careful and strategic staging of an event designed to help the party's presidential candidate manage an image that will be attractive to voters. Music, balloons, lighting, colors, even individual delegates are all transformed into stage props that are manipulated to project images of patriotism, unity, organization, and effectiveness.

The candidate must also personally present an image that will appeal to the public:

> In 1976, Gerald Ford's aides insisted on a neutral background for debates to camouflage the President's thinning gray hair. . . . During the 1988 Presidential primary campaign . . . Representative Richard Gephardt took a pencil to his ghostly eyebrows to give them more definition. During the same campaign, an adviser to Bruce Babbitt recommended he do "eyebrow pushups" to gain control of his sometimes ungainly facial expressions. [President George H. W.] Bush reportedly tried to exchange his karate-like hand gestures for a more Presidential-looking set. (Kolbert, 1996, p. E5)

George W. Bush grew up in a wealthy family. He was educated at an elite, East Coast prep school and a prestigious Ivy League university. His father was a lifelong politician and president himself. Yet during the presidential campaign of 2000, Bush, with the help of his advisers and handlers, decided that the best strategy for winning the election was to present himself as an anti-intellectual, down-to-earth, "likable guy" who was more interested in slapping backs and telling jokes than with discussing the nuances of foreign and domestic policy. This strategy was specifically designed to highlight the contrasts between Bush and his opponent, Al Gore, a candidate whose preference for formal policy speeches made him appear stiff, serious, and aloof.

Political impression management continues past election day. The president, with the help or hindrance of the media, must play simultaneously to an external and internal audience (P. Hall, 1990). The external audience is composed of foreign allies and adversaries, who must be convinced of his authority and his ability to fulfill commitments. The internal audience is the voting public, whom he must impress through the portrayal of "presidential character": good health, decisiveness, a stable home and family life, and so forth. Like all politicians, a president must be prepared to use impression management to get a favorable result in an opinion poll or a desired vote in Congress.

Goffman argues that impression management is not used just to present false or inflated images of ourselves. Many real attributes we possess are not immediately apparent to others, or our actions may be misinterpreted. Imagine yourself taking the final exam in your sociology course. You look up from your paper and make brief eye contact with the instructor. You are not cheating, but you think the instructor may interpret your wandering eyes as an indication of cheating. Chances are you will consciously overemphasize your noncheating behavior by acting as though you're in deep thought or by glancing at the clock to highlight your "law-abiding" image.

Obtaining favorable outcomes through impression management is usually associated with social approval—that is, with being respected and liked by others. However, different circumstances may require projecting different identities (E. E. Jones & Pittman, 1982). Perhaps you've been in situations where you tried to appear helpless in order to get someone else to do a task you really didn't want to do, or maybe you tried to be as powerful and fearsome as you could to intimidate someone into doing something for you. Perhaps you "played dumb" to avoid challenging a superior (Gove, Hughes, & Geerkin, 1980). As social beings we have the ability to tailor our images to fit the requirements of a particular situation.

Micro-Macro Connection
Managing Impressions in Cyberspace

The Internet has transformed social institutions as profoundly as the telephone, radio, and television did in previous eras (Chapman, 1996). What is particularly interesting is its effect on the way people perceive and interact with others. In the disembodied world of e-mail, newsgroups, discussion lists, chat rooms, and bulletin boards, identity claims are difficult to prove (Donath, 1997). Without being able to check the other person's physical features, facial expressions, tone of voice, body language, clothing, biographical information, or any other interactional cues that aid in forming impressions, Internet participants must rely on written words alone for information about the trustworthiness of someone they know only through electronic communication (Rheingold, 1994; Sproull & Kiesler, 1991).

In some ways these limitations make electronic interactions more honest and straightforward. People often end up revealing far more about themselves than they would be inclined to do face to face. For instance, some observers have noted that people participating in bulletin boards and chat rooms are increasingly likely to express their true, sometimes virulent, feelings about such things as race relations and affirmative action, issues they would otherwise be reluctant to discuss in the presence of someone who might be offended (Marriot, 1998). In a university study, 3% of students who filled out a paper-and-pencil version of a survey admitted using illegal drugs at least once a week for recreational purposes. Of those who received the same survey via electronic mail, 14% made the same admission (Sproull & Kiesler, 1991). Internet discussion groups are particularly popular among gay men and lesbians, who feel that in such venues they can openly discuss issues of importance to the gay community or even "come out of the closet" without being condemned or harassed by neighbors and coworkers ("Gay men and lesbians," 1996).

Moreover, people with physical characteristics that might impede face-to-face interactions or negate their authority can communicate effectively over the Internet without immediately being judged by others. As one participant in a computer conference system bluntly put it,

All messages have an equal chance because they all look alike. The only thing that sets them apart is their content. If you are a hunchback, a paraplegic, a woman, a black, fat, old, have two hundred warts on your face, or never take a bath, you still have the same chance. (quoted in Zuboff, 1988, p. 371)

Thus, computer interaction has the capacity to eliminate or at least reduce the types of social inequalities that are often based on physical appearance.

Ironically, computer interaction also allows people to lie about who they are. The identities people can claim on the Internet appear unlimited: one person can create multiple identities, a man can claim to be a woman, a high school dropout can claim to be a senior citizen surviving on Social Security; "the plain can experience the self-presentation of great beauty; the nerdy can be elegant; the obese can be slender" (Turkle, 1994, p. 162).

There has been a great deal of speculation in recent years on the extent and implications of gender switching, the online practice of pretending to be someone of the opposite sex. One study surveyed 400 participants in online communities called MOOs (multiuser, object-oriented systems), which are populated by cartoon characters, called avatars, chosen by each participant to represent him or her. The study found that 40% of MOO participants had engaged in some form of gender switching, but about half of them soon gave it up (cited in Headlam, 2000b). Most engaged in the practice out of curiosity or for fun and gave it up when it stopped being interesting.

Such deception is not as easy as it may sound, however. Gender affects language patterns, perspective, and interpretations of experiences. A man may write, "I am a female," but using a "female voice" and providing convincing responses to others' questions might be quite difficult for a man to do over time (Donath, 1997).

Furthermore, the medium itself limits identity deception. For instance, all posted messages on electronic bulletin boards contain a header that includes an account or user name and a domain name or address. Although all identifying information can be stripped from a message so it can be sent anonymously or with a pseudonym, many user groups frown on or prohibit anonymous postings. The domain name, which indicates the organization that provides the account from which the person is writing, functions very much like a company letterhead. It tells whether a person is writing from a university, a research lab, a private corporation, a government agency, or a commercial Internet service provider. Hence, this name may offer contextual information about the writer, such as his or her educational status or occupation. In addition, the idiosyncratic language style people use online—jargon, phrases, and abbreviations common to particular groups or communities—may either reinforce or negate a claimed identity.

The Internet is a world of complex interactions, unmatched in its ability to bring together people from different real-world cultures (see Chapter 8 for more on virtual communities). Despite the potential problems arising from attempts to manipulate identity on the Internet, it offers the possibility of reducing differences between social groups by de-emphasizing information about race, ethnicity, occupation, gender, disability, and other ascribed social statuses. We can only imagine what the social implications will be as large numbers of people around the world escape the physical, geographical, political, racial, and ethnic constraints that have always governed human interaction.

Dramaturgy: Actors on a Social Stage

"All the world's a stage, and all the men and women merely players. They have their exits and their entrances, and one man in his time plays many parts," wrote William Shakespeare in *As You Like It*. The study of social interaction as theater is called **dramaturgy**. Goffman (1959) argues that people in everyday life are like actors on a stage. The "audience" consists of people who observe the behavior of others, the "roles" are the images people are trying to project, and the "script" consists of their communication with others. The goal is to enact a performance that is believable to a particular audience and that allows us to achieve the goals we desire. Every aspect of social life can be examined dramaturgically, from the ritualized greetings of strangers to the everyday dynamics of our family, school, and work lives.

Front Stage and Back Stage. A key structural element of dramaturgy is the distinction between front stage and back stage. In the theater, front stage is where the performance takes place. In contrast, back stage is where makeup is removed, lines are rehearsed, performances are rehashed, and people can fall "out of character."

In social interaction, **front stage** is where people maintain the appropriate appearance as they interact with others. For workers in a restaurant, front stage is the dining room where the customers (the audience) are present. Here the servers (the actors) are expected to present themselves as upbeat, happy, competent, and courteous. **Back stage**, however, is the region where people can knowingly violate their impression management performances. In the restaurant, back stage is the kitchen area where the once courteous servers now shout, shove dishes, and even complain about or make fun of the customers.

The barrier between front and back stage is crucial to successful impression management because it blocks the audience from seeing behavior that would ruin the performance. During a therapy session (front stage), psychiatrists usually appear extremely interested in everything their patients say and show considerable sympathy for their problems. At a dinner party with colleagues or at home with family (back stage), however, they may express total boredom and disdain for the patients' disclosures. If patients were to see such back stage behavior, not only would the performance be disrupted, but the psychiatrist's professional credibility and reputation would suffer as well. One study found that beneath their mask of neutrality, many psychiatrists harbor strong and professionally inappropriate feelings—including hatred, fear, anger, and sexual arousal—toward their patients (cited in Goleman, 1993).

Peter Ubel
Elevator Talk among Doctors and Nurses

We all take for granted, when visiting a doctor's office or a hospital, that the doctors and nurses will protect the confidentiality of their patients. Yet the temptation to talk about patients behind their backs ("back stage") is often hard to resist. Dr. Peter Ubel and his colleagues (Ubel, Zell, Miller, Fischer, Peters-Stefani, & Arnold, 1995) sent observers to five Pennsylvania hospitals to determine the frequency and nature of inappropriate talk about patients among hospital personnel. The researchers were particularly interested in conversations that could easily be overheard by people who shouldn't be privy to such information. They decided to focus on elevator talk.

Of the 259 elevator rides they observed during which passengers had a chance to converse, inappropriate comments were made 14% of the time. The observers found that the remarks fell into four distinct categories:

- *Comments violating patient confidentiality:* The majority of back stage comments inappropriately disclosed factual information about a patient's condition. These remarks were usually simple declarations, such as "Mr. X was readmitted last night for more chemo." In other situations the comments exposed professional disagreement over a particular course of action. For instance, in one case two physicians had a heated debate over the merits of removing parts of either one or two lungs from a patient.
- *Unprofessional remarks and motivation:* Another category of comments consisted of remarks that raised questions about medical personnel's ability or desire to provide quality care. For instance, doctors or nurses sometimes complained that they were too tired or too sick to do their jobs well. On some occasions, physicians were heard talking about how they were just biding their time in the hospital until they could go elsewhere and make large amounts of money. Such comments clearly call into question their primary motivation.
- *Comments raising questions about quality of patient care:* Some conversations consisted of personnel complaining about hospital resources and facilities, thereby raising doubts about whether or not the institution offered good patient care. Other times, nurses or doctors would question the qualifications of a colleague. Although the motivation behind such remarks is not always clear, people coming to visit their loved ones in a hospital who overhear these casual conversations are not always capable of weighing unsubstantiated information.
- *Derogatory comments about patients or their families:* The last category of inappropriate back stage comments were direct insults about patients, focusing on such traits as weight or body odor. Such comments reflect poorly on the compassion of health care workers. In addition, visitors' anxiety about the quality of care may increase if visitors are led to believe that the staff doesn't like them or their loved ones.

This research points to the institutional importance of maintaining boundaries between front and back stage. Health care workers will always talk about patients behind their backs. But in a field such as medicine, which deals with extremely delicate personal information and life and death decisions, the credibility of the profession depends on workers' ability to correctly determine when a location is, in fact, private back stage. Public awareness of these sorts of remarks can have serious economic, political, and perhaps even legal consequences. The problem has become so bad that elevators in some California hospitals now carry posted warnings reminding medical personnel to refrain from talking about patients.

Props. Successful impression management also depends on the control of objects, called *props*, that convey identity. In the theater props must be handled deftly for an effective performance. A gun that doesn't go off when it's supposed to or a chair that unexpectedly collapses can destroy an entire play. The same is true in social interaction. For instance, college students might make sure their school books are in clear view and beer bottles disposed of as they prepare for an upcoming visit from their parents. Similarly, someone might spend a great deal of time setting a romantic mood for a dinner date at home—the right music, the right lighting, pictures of former lovers hidden from view, and so on.

Recently researchers in England, observing patrons in an upscale pub, discovered that men were much more likely than women to use their cellular phones as props designed to advertise their social worth. Whereas women with cell phones tended to keep them in their purses, only bringing them out when needed, men tended to set theirs on the bar counter or table, where they drew attention to the phones by constantly picking them up and moving them around. According to the researchers, what's being advertised is not wealth, per se, but social importance—the fact that one is important enough to be reachable at all times (cited in Angier, 2000).

Sometimes people use props to create an environment that reinforces some individuals' authority over others. Note the way props were used to intimidate this professor as he testified before Congress about children and violence:

> And then I was called to the witness stand. Now, the chair is something nobody talks about. It is low and extremely puffy. When you sit in it your butt just keeps sinking, and suddenly the tabletop is up to your chest. The senators peer down at you from above, and the power dynamic is terrifying. (Jenkins, 1999, p. 21)

Viewing impression management from a dramaturgical perspective reminds us that our everyday actions rarely occur in a social vacuum. Indeed, our behaviors are often structured with an eye toward how they might be perceived by particular "audiences."

Social Influences on Impression Management

Up to this point I've described dramaturgy and impression management from the point of view of individual people driven by a personal desire to present themselves in the most favorable light possible. But social group membership may also influence the sorts of images a person tries to present in social interaction. The elements of a person's identity—age, gender, race and ethnicity, religion, social class, occupational status—influences others' immediate expectations, which can be self-fulfilling. In other words, members of certain social groups may manage impressions somewhat differently from nonmembers because of society's preconceived notions about them. Race or ethnicity and social status are among the most notable influences on impression management.

Race and Ethnicity. People of racial or ethnic minorities are often forced to present self-images that are consistent with the expectations or stereotypes of others. In a society in which race is a primary source of inequality, living up (or down) to such expectations may be one of the few means by which people can participate actively in public life while retaining their own cultural identity. Individuals from oppressed groups may appear to fit common racial or ethnic stereotypes in public (front stage), but an analysis of private (back stage) behavior often indicates that they are keenly aware of the roles they have been forced to play. Impression management is obviously an important survival tactic.

Elijah Anderson
Streetwise

Throughout the 1980s sociologist Elijah Anderson carried out observational research in a racially, ethnically, and economically diverse area of Philadelphia he called Village-Northton. The area was home to two communities: one black and very poor, the other middle- to upper-income and predominantly white. Anderson was particularly interested in how young black men—the overwhelming majority of whom were civil and law-abiding—managed public impressions to deal with the assumption of Village residents that young black men are dangerous.

Anderson discovered that a central theme for most area residents was maintaining safety on the streets and avoiding violent and drug-related crime. Incapable of making distinctions between law-abiding black males and others, people relied for protection on broad stereotypes: Whites are law-abiding and trustworthy; young black men are crime-prone and dangerous.

Residents of the area, including black men themselves, were likely to defer to unknown black males on the street. Women—particularly white women—clutched their purses and edged up closer to their companions as they walked down the street. Many pedestrians crossed the street or averted their eyes from young black men who were seen as unpredictable and menacing.

Some of these men in the Village developed certain interactional strategies to overcome the immediate assumption that they were dangerous. For instance, they often used friendly greetings as a kind of preemptive peace offering, designed to advise others of their civil intentions. Or they went to great lengths to behave in ways contrary to the presumed expectations of whites:

> I find myself being extra nice to whites. A lot of times I be walking down the streets . . . and I see somebody white. . . . I know they are afraid of me. They don't know me, but they intimidated. . . . So I might smile, just to reassure them. . . . At other times I find myself opening doors, you know. Holding the elevator. Putting myself in a certain light, you know, to change whatever doubts they may have. (E. Anderson, 1990, pp. 185–186)

Such impression management requires an enormous amount of effort and places responsibility for ensuring social order on this man. He feels compelled to put strangers at ease so he can go about his own business. He understands that his mere presence makes others nervous and uncomfortable. He recognizes that trustworthiness—an ascribed characteristic of whites—is something blacks must work hard to achieve.

Other young black men, less willing to bear the burden of social order, capitalized on the fear they knew they could evoke. Some purposely "put on a swagger" or adopted a menacing stance to intimidate other pedestrians. Some purposely created discomfort in those they considered "ignorant" enough to be unnecessarily afraid of them.

According to Anderson, law-abiding youths have an interest in giving the impression that they are dangerous: It is a way to keep others at bay. The right looks and moves ensure safe passage on the street. Notice how this young man used such a strategy as a protective device:

> When I walk the streets, I put this expression on my face that tells the next person I'm not to be messed with. That "You messing with the wrong fellow. You just try it. Try it." . . . I'll put my hand in my pocket, even if I ain't got no gun. Nobody wants to get shot. . . . Some guys go to singing. They try to let people know they crazy. 'Cause if you crazy [capable of anything], they'll leave you alone. And I have looked right in they face [muggers] and said, "Yo, I'm not the one." Give 'em that crazy look, then walk away. . . . They catch your drift quick. (E. Anderson, 1990, p. 177)

The irony of such survival tactics is that they make it even more difficult for others to distinguish between those who are law-abiding and those who are crime prone. By exhibiting an air of danger and toughness, the young black man may avoid being ridiculed or even victimized by his own peers, but he risks further alienating law-abiding whites and blacks. Members of racial or ethnic minorities face many such special dilemmas in impression management, whether they attempt to contradict stereotypes or embrace them.

Social Status. A person's relative position in society can also influence impression management. Like the young black men in Anderson's study, some working-class youths, frustrated by their lack of access to the middle-class world and their inability to meet the requirements of "respectability" as defined by the dominant culture, may present themselves as malicious or dangerous. A tough image helps them gain attention or achieve status and respect within their group (Campbell, 1987; A. K. Cohen, 1955).

Conversely, those who occupy the dominant classes of society can get the attention and respect we all want with very little effort (Derber, 1979). They get special consideration in restaurants, shops, and other public settings. They monopolize the starring roles in politics and the public arena and also claim more than their share of attention in ordinary interactions. By displaying the symbolic props of material success—large homes, tasteful furnishings, luxury cars, expensive clothes—social strivers know that they can impress others and thereby reinforce their own sense of worth and status.

Similar dynamics permeate the world of work. Those at the very top of an organization need not advertise their high status because it is already known to people with whom they interact regularly. Their occupational status is a permanently recognized "badge of ability" (Derber, 1979, p. 83). Other people, however, must consciously solicit the attention to which they feel they are entitled. For example, physicians may wear stethoscopes and hospital garb to communicate their high-status identity to others outside the hospital; female doctors often wear white coats to ensure that they will not be mistaken for nurses. In societies that place a high value on work, those who have no way of exhibiting an occupational badge or whose occupation is seen as inferior find their social worth constantly in question, particularly in interactions with high-status others. They must resort to alternative strategies, such as subtly or blatantly disclosing their status, talking constantly or shifting the conversation to a topic about which they have some expertise (Trudgill, 1972).

Impression management plays a prominent role in the socialization process within many professions (A. Hochschild, 1983). Managers and CEOs in large companies, for instance, are acutely aware of the corporate image they must exude through their dress and demeanor. If you've ever worked as a salesperson, you know the economic importance of presenting yourself as knowledgeable, trustworthy, and above all honest. Medical school students must learn how to manage their emotions in front of patients and to present the image of "competent physicians." New teachers must learn what images are most effective in getting students to comply. One teacher described the importance of impression management this way:

> You can't ever let them get the upper hand on you or you're through. So I start out tough. The first day I get a new class in, I let them know who's boss. . . . You've got to start off tough, then you can ease up as you go along. If you start out easygoing, when you try to be tough, they'll just look at you and laugh. (Goffman, 1959, p. 12)

Subtle details of ordinary social encounters also reveal a great deal about a person's ability to successfully manage an impression. In any given situation, one person is likely to have more power, a greater ability to intentionally influence others to act in a way consistent with the person's wishes (Wrong, 1988). When we first hear the word *power,* we think of it in terms of orders, threats, and coercion. But noncoercive forms of power—the signs and symbols of dominance, the subtle messages of threat, the gestures of submission—are much more common (Henley, 1977). The humiliation of being powerless is felt by people who are ignored or interrupted, are intimidated by another's presence, are afraid to approach or touch a superior, or have their privacy freely invaded by another.

The norms that govern the way people address each other reflect underlying power differences. For instance, the conversations that take place between friends or siblings are commonly marked by the mutual use of such informal terms as first names or nicknames. When status is unequal, though, the lower-status person is often required to use terms of respect such as *Sir* or *Ma'am* or *Doctor*. In the South in years past, every white person had the privilege of addressing any black person by first name and receiving the respectful form of address in return. President Bush's fondness for making up funny nicknames for people on his staff or members of Congress may appear amiable and friendly, but it also reinforces power differences. These people are still required to refer to him as "Mr. President."

Another example of the symbolic power of forms of address is the way that child actors often change their names when they reach adulthood—for instance, from Ricky to Rick—to convey a desired sense of maturity. Similarly, an uncle's habit of calling me "Davey" is irritating not because I don't like the name but because it doesn't fit with my professional self-concept.

Status differences are even more clearly institutionalized in some languages. In Spanish, *tu* is the familiar word for "you," which is used when one is talking to a subordinate or to a person of equal status. *Usted* also means "you," but it is the formal version, used when one is addressing a person of superior status. The terms we use to address others may on the surface appear simply to be forms of etiquette. However, forms of address convey a great deal of information about who we think we are in relation to the others we encounter.

Collective Impression Management

We often find ourselves in situations that require a "couple" image, a "group" image, or an "organizational" image of some sort. These impressions are more complex than individual ones, and their management often requires the help and cooperation of others. For example, business partners often present a united front and a joint image of trustworthiness to their clients. Goffman (1959) uses the term **performance team** to describe those individuals who intimately cooperate in staging a performance that leads an audience to form an impression of one or all of the team members.

Team members are highly dependent on one another and must show a fair amount of trust and loyalty, because each member has the power to disrupt or "give away" the performance at any moment. Individuals who cannot be trusted—such as political advisers who have worked for another party or people who are emotionally unstable and unpredictable—thus make poor teammates.

One of the most obvious teams is the married couple. Couples are socially obligated to present a believable and cooperative image, particularly if the audience does not know them very well. Nothing is more uncomfortable than being present when a couple is fighting, bickering, or putting each other down. We, as the audience, feel as if we are watching something not meant for our eyes. The cultural value of marriage—and, by extension, the institution of family—is publicly reinforced by the ability of couples to collectively project contented images of their relationship.

Like individual impression management, successful teamwork depends on maintaining the boundary between front and back stage. If a couple's teamwork is cohesive and the performance believable, the partners can give the impression that they are happy and content even if they have had a bitter fight moments before going out in public. But the boundary between front and back stage is fragile, and third parties may undermine the best efforts at impression management. Imagine a dinner guest being informed by a precocious 4-year-old that "Mommy and Daddy stopped yelling and screaming at each other when you came over." Young children who can speak but are not yet schooled in the social conventions of everyday interaction are not, from the dramaturgical perspective, trustworthy performance teammates. They are often too honest to maintain a front. They are naturally inclined to let audiences back stage, thereby disrupting both the order of the situation and the identities the actors have attempted to claim.

The ability to go back stage periodically is critical to the maintenance of a sound team relationship. Not only does it give the team a place to rehearse public performances, but it also provides a refuge from outside scrutiny. For married couples, tensions can rise if they must constantly be "on" for an audience. This is precisely why out-of-town guests become a burden after a long visit or why living with one or the other partner's parents becomes so difficult. The couple has no back stage, no chance for privacy, no place to go to escape the demands of audience expectations.

Organizations must carefully manage their impressions, too. Some professional situations—gynecological examinations, for instance—require individual and team impressions to be managed with finesse so that clients do not become embarrassed, humiliated, or threatened and take their business elsewhere (Henslin & Biggs, 1978). Organizations that depend on public approval for their survival have also developed team performances to manage public perceptions (S. J. Taylor & Bogdan, 1980). Take, for instance, the way U.S. law enforcement organizations present high-profile crime suspects to the public. The suspect being transported from one place to another is usually in shackles with armed officers on either side. Occasionally the officers try to hide the alleged perpetrator's face with a coat or a hat, even though we are likely to know who he or she is. The "perp walk," as it is known, is a decades-long tradition designed not only to satisfy the press but to give police an opportunity to gloat over their latest capture and, in the process, humiliate the suspect (Labaton, 1996). Moreover, if staged well, the perp walk makes the suspect look dangerous, the kind of person who would mail letter bombs, blow up federal office buildings, or commit serial murder. If prisoners are left unshaven, unkempt, and presented in orange prison jumpsuits, the public gets the impression that they've already been convicted.

Individual impression management and organizational impression management are governed by the same principles (A. Hochschild, 1983). Take, for instance, the management of props and physical space. The walls of a hospital are usually lined with soothing paintings designed to calm, not agitate; children's wards are often filled with colorful images of familiar cartoon characters. Airplanes are meticulously designed to manage a collective impression that distracts passengers from the potential danger:

> The Muzak tunes, the TV and movie screens, and the smiling flight attendants serving drinks are all calculated to "make you feel at home." Even fellow passengers are considered part of the stage. At Delta Airlines, for example, flight attendants in training are advised that they can prevent the boarding of certain types of passengers—a passenger with "severe facial scars," for example. The instructor elaborated: "You know, the other passengers might be reminded of an airplane crash they had read about." The bearer of a "severe facial scar," then, is not deemed a good prop. His or her effect on the emotions of other money-paying passengers might be all wrong. (A. Hochschild, 1983, pp. 51–52)

In any society, people often find themselves in situations where they must depend on others for the successful performance of the roles they play as individuals. Without teamwork, many performances would fail, interactions would fall apart, and ultimately social order would be threatened (Henslin, 1991).

Mismanaging Impressions: Spoiled Identities

We sometimes fail miserably in our attempts to project favorable images of ourselves to others. We may mishandle props, blow our lines, mistakenly allow the audience back stage, or otherwise destroy the credibility of our performances. Some of us manage to recover from ineffective impression management quite quickly; others suffer an extended devaluation of their identities. What happens when impression management is unsuccessful? What do we do to regain identities and restore social order?

Embarrassment

A common emotional reaction to impression mismanagement is **embarrassment**, the spontaneous feeling we experience when the identity we are presenting is suddenly and unexpectedly discredited in front of others (Gross & Stone, 1964). An adolescent boy trying to look "cool" in front of his friends may have his tough image shattered by the unexpected arrival of his mother in the family station wagon. We can see his embarrassment in the fixed smile, the nervous hollow laugh, the busy hands, and the downward glance that conceals his eyes from the gaze of others (Goffman, 1967). Embarrassment can come from a multitude of sources: lack of poise (for example, stumbling, spilling a drink, inappropriate bodily exposure), intrusion into the private settings of others (a man walking into a women's restroom), improper dress for a particular social occasion, and so on.

Embarrassment is sociologically important because it has the potential to destroy the orderliness of a social situation. Imagine being at your graduation ceremony. As the class valedictorian is giving the commencement address, a gust of wind blows her note cards off the podium. As she reaches down to collect them, she knocks over the microphone and tears her gown. In front of hundreds of people she stands there, flustered, not knowing what to say or do. The situation would be uncomfortable and embarrassing not only for her but for you and the rest of the audience as well.

Because embarrassment is disruptive for all concerned, it is in everyone's best interest to cooperate in eliminating it. To call attention to such an act may be as embarrassing as the original episode itself, so we may pretend not to notice the faux pas (Lindesmith, Strauss, & Denzin, 1991). By suppressing signs of recognition, we make it easier for the person to regain composure (Goffman, 1967). A mutual commitment to supporting others' social identities, even when those identities are in danger, is a fundamental rule of social interaction.

At times, however, embarrassment is used strategically to disrupt another person's impression management. Practical jokes, for instance, are intentional attempts to cause someone else to lose identity. More seriously, groups and organizations may use embarrassment or the threat of embarrassment (for example, hazing) to encourage a preferred activity or discourage behavior that may be damaging to the group. Such embarrassment reasserts the power structure of the group, because only certain people can legitimately embarrass others. A low-status employee has much less freedom to embarrass a superior than vice versa.

Groups and organizations, as entities, may also be embarrassed. A few years ago, the entire New Zealand health care industry suffered an embarrassing blow to its image when it was discovered that a con artist professing to be a psychiatrist and Harvard graduate had been practicing medicine there for more than a year.

Most government agencies and large corporations now have public relations departments that carefully manage the corporate image by controlling negative publicity (E. Gross, 1984). In 1999 the International Olympic Committee hired a public relations firm to repair an image tarnished by reports that members of the organizing committee for the 2002 Winter Olympics in Salt Lake City had bribed international officials. There is even an insurance company that, as part of its corporate liability policy, pays policyholders up to $50,000 for the emergency hiring of an image consultant to help manage embarrassing public relations disasters (Landler, 1996).

Sometimes a single rumor causes massive corporate embarrassment. In 1993, for example, a rash of reports surfaced around the United States from people who claimed to have found hypodermic needles and syringes in cans of Diet Pepsi. Investigators eventually found the claims to be unsubstantiated. Nevertheless, stores in many parts of the country began to pull the product off their shelves or offer refunds to worried customers. The Food and Drug Administration advised consumers to buy Pepsi in glass or plastic bottles. The phenomenon was a public relations nightmare for Pepsi. Facing severe financial losses, the company mounted a massive and expensive media campaign—which included TV commercials, talk show appearances, full-page newspaper ads, and a toll-free consumer hotline—to counteract the embarrassment and costly fallout of a spoiled public image.

Remedies for Spoiled Identities

Organizations and governments can enlist the aid of experts to overcome the debilitating effects of negative images, but individuals are left to their own devices. Fixing a spoiled identity is not easy. The mere knowledge that we are being evaluated negatively can impede our thought, speech, and action. Nevertheless, the major responsibility for restoring order lies with the person or group whose actions disrupted things in the first place.

To restore social order and overcome a spoiled identity, the transgressor will use an **aligning action** (Stokes & Hewitt, 1976). Sometimes aligning can be done easily and quickly. If you step on a person's foot while standing in line at a cafeteria, a simple apology may be all that's needed to bring order back. By apologizing you acknowledge that such an act is wrong and send the message that you are not ordinarily a breaker of such social norms. Other situations, however, call for more detailed repairs:

- An **account** is a verbal statement designed to explain unanticipated, embarrassing, or unacceptable behavior (C. W. Mills, 1940; M. Scott & Lyman, 1968). For example, an individual may cite events beyond her or his control ("I was late for the wedding because there was a lot of traffic on the highway") or blame others ("I spilled my milk because so-and-so pushed me"). An alternative is to define the offending behavior as appropriate under the circumstances, perhaps by denying that anyone was hurt by the act ("Yeah, I stole the car, but no one got hurt"), claiming that the victim deserved to be victimized ("I beat him up, but he had it coming"), or claiming higher, unselfish motives ("I stole food, but I did it to feed my family").
- A **disclaimer** is a verbal assertion given before the fact to forestall any complaints or negative implications (Hewitt & Stokes, 1975). If we think something we are about to do or say will threaten our identity or be used by others to judge us negatively, we may use a disclaimer. Phrases such as "This may sound crazy to you, but . . ." or "I probably don't know what I'm talking about, but . . ." or "This may sound racist, but . . ." introduce acts or expressions that ordinarily might be considered undesirable. As long as a disclaimer is provided, a person claiming to be nonracist feels he

or she can go ahead and make a racist statement, and a self-proclaimed nonexpert can pretend to be an expert.

Accounts and disclaimers are important links between the individual and society. We use them to explicitly define the relationship between our questionable conduct and prevailing cultural norms. That is, by using them we publicly reaffirm our commitment to the social order that our conduct has violated and thereby defend the sanctity of our social identities and the "goodness" of society.

In some cases, the provision of accounts has become a lucrative business. In Britain, a company called the Alibi Agency offers detailed accounts for people who want to keep their extramarital relationships secret. For a fee, they will create an elaborate and credible alibi for the customer:

> If someone tries to contact you, our receptionist will take the call as a hotel receptionist, for example, or a golf-club secretary. We will let the caller hear us try to page you, then offer to take a message when you can't be found. If we know where you are, we can even ring you while the caller is on hold, then patch the call through as if it were to your "room." We also take care of payments for hotels, meals, or gifts, then bill your credit card for car repairs or software purchases. (The Alibi Agency, 2001)

Other people may also try to deal with a transgressor's spoiled identity through a process called **cooling out** (Goffman, 1952), gently persuading someone who has lost face to accept a less desirable but still reasonable alternative identity. People engaged in cooling out seek to persuade rather than force offenders to change. It's an attempt to minimize distress. The challenge is to keep the offender from realizing that he or she is being persuaded.

Cooling out is a common element of social life; it is the major function of consumer complaint personnel, coaches, doctors, and priests. Cooling out also plays a major part in informal relationships. A partner who terminates a dating or courting relationship might persuade the other person to remain a "good friend," thereby gently pushing the person into a lesser role without completely destroying his or her self-worth.

Cooling out is often motivated by institutional pressures. Consider the environment of higher education. The aspirations of many people in U.S. society are encouraged by open-door admissions policies in some universities and most community colleges (Karabel, 1972). There is a widely held cultural belief that higher education is linked to better employment opportunities and that anyone can go to college. Discrepancies, however, inevitably arise between people's aspirations and their ability to succeed. If educational institutions simply kicked unqualified students out of school, the result would likely be widespread public pressure and anxiety over the system itself. Hence, most community colleges opt for a "soft response" of cooling out the unqualified student (B. Clark, 1960). A counselor may direct a poor student toward an alternative major that would be easier but still "not that different" from the student's original goal—for example, nurse's aide instead of registered nurse. Or the counselor might encourage the student to seek employment after graduation from a two-year program rather than transfer to a four-year university. That is, the student is gently persuaded to redefine him- or herself.

Institutional cooling-out processes such as these are inherent in an educational system that doesn't have clear selection criteria. In the United States, acceptance into college is based on a combination of achievement (tests, grades), aptitude (standardized test scores), and personality traits (interviews, letters of recommendation). In contrast, educational selection in Japan is based on a single criterion: achievement as measured by exams and grades. Selections are made on admission to senior high school. National universities do not allow any exceptions. Because career paths are clearly and quickly defined, Japanese higher education has no need for an institutionalized cooling-out process (Kariya & Rosenbaum, 1987).

Stigma

The permanent spoiling of someone's identity is called **stigma**. A stigma is a deeply discrediting characteristic, widely viewed as an insurmountable obstacle preventing competent or morally trustworthy behavior (Goffman, 1963). Stigmas spoil the identities of individuals regardless of other attributes those individuals might have. According to Goffman, the three types of stigma are defects of the body (for example, scars, blindness, paralyzed or missing limbs); defects of character (for example, dishonesty, weak will, unorthodox beliefs inferred from a known record of mental illness, imprisonment, or substance abuse); and membership in particular social groups, such as races, religions, or ethnicities that are devalued in society. The impression management task when faced with stigma is not so much to recapture a tarnished identity as to minimize the social damage.

Some stigmas are worse than others. For instance, the use of eyeglasses to compensate for a sensory deficiency (poor vision) is usually considered far less stigmatizing than the use of hearing aids to compensate for a different sensory deficiency (poor hearing). Stigma varies across time and culture as well. Being a Christian in the 21st century is very different from being one in A.D. 100, and being a Christian in the United States is different from being one in the Middle East (Ainlay, Becker, & Coleman, 1986). As we saw earlier in this chapter, obesity is stigmatized in contemporary Western societies but was seen as desirable, attractive, and symbolic of status and wealth in the past (Clinard & Meier, 1979).

Interactions between the stigmatized and the nonstigmatized—called "mixed contacts"—are often uneasy. We have all felt uncomfortable with people who are "different" in appearance or behavior. Stigma initiates a judgment process that colors impressions and sets up barriers to interaction (E. E. Jones et al., 1984).

Whether intentionally or not, nonstigmatized individuals often pressure stigmatized people to conform to inferior identities. A person in a wheelchair who is discouraged from undertaking certain activities or a blind person who is dissuaded from venturing out of the house alone is not given the chance to develop important skills and is subsequently kept dependent.

The anticipation of discomfort can lead people to arrange their lives to avoid mixed contacts (Goffman, 1963). Research shows that people terminate interactions sooner, are more inhibited, and are more rigid when interacting with a physically disabled person than with a physically normal person (Kleck, 1968; Kleck, Ono, &

Hastorf, 1966). Such discomfort probably stems from uncertainty as to what behavior is appropriate. On the one hand, the nonstigmatized may fear that if they show direct sympathy or interest in someone's condition they will be regarded as rude or intrusive. On the other hand, ignoring it may make the interaction artificial and awkward or create impossible demands (Michener, DeLamater, & Schwartz, 1986).

As for people with stigmatizing conditions, Goffman argues that they usually have some sense that others are evaluating them negatively. Consider the case of Mark Breimhorst, a Stanford University graduate. Mr. Breimhorst has no hands. When he was applying to business schools in 1998, he received permission to take the Graduate Management Admissions Test on a computer and was given 25% more time to accommodate his disability. His results were mailed out to prospective graduate schools with the notation "*Scores obtained under special circumstances.*" Mr. Breimhorst was not admitted to any of business schools to which he applied. He filed a federal lawsuit against the testing service, challenging the way they flag scores of students who need accommodations. Such notations, he argued, are stigmatizing because they create suspicion that the scores are less valid than others (Lewin, 2000a). In 2001, the testing service announced it would no longer flag the results of students who receive special accommodations.

Faced with such discrimination, people with stigmatizing conditions often use drastic coping strategies to establish the most favorable identity possible. One strategy is to try to hide the stigmatizing condition. People who are hard of hearing, for instance, may learn to read lips or otherwise interact with people as if they could hear perfectly; those with bodily stigmas may opt for surgical remedies.

Michael Petrunik and Clifford Shearing (1983) studied the coping strategies used by people who stutter. They observed and took part in weekly therapy groups over a period of 13 years. In addition they conducted in-depth interviews with stutterers, their families and friends, speech therapists, and other medical practitioners. Common public reactions to stutterers include pity, condescension, ridicule, and impatience. Some stutterers hide their stigma by avoiding speaking situations or by not using particularly troublesome words. Others structure situations so that someone else does the talking. For example, in a restaurant stutterers may encourage others to order first. As soon as an acceptable item is mentioned, they simply duplicate the order by saying, "Me, too" or "Same here."

Some stigmatized individuals, particularly those whose conditions are not immediately observable, use a policy of selective disclosure and concealment. Sociologist Charlene E. Miall (1989) interviewed and surveyed 70 infertile women to see if they felt stigmatized. Nearly all the respondents categorized infertility as something negative, an indication of failure, or an inability to function "normally." Furthermore, most of the women were concerned that an awareness of their infertility would cause others to view them in a new and damaging light. Consequently, most of these women engaged in some form of information control. Many simply concealed the information from everyone except medical personnel and infertility counselors. Others used medical accounts, saying, "It's beyond my control." Some disclosed the information only to people they felt would not think ill of them. Some even used the disclosure of their infertility to gain control of a situation by deliberately shocking their "normal" audience (Miall, 1989).

Of course, not all stigmas can be hidden. Some individuals can only minimize the degree to which their stigmas intrude on and disrupt the interaction. One tactic is to use self-deprecating humor to relieve the tension felt by the nonstigmatized. Others may try to focus attention on attributes that are unrelated to the stigma. For instance, a person in a wheelchair may carry around esoteric books in a conspicuous manner to show others that she or he can perform well in intellectual matters.

But some people with stigmas boldly call attention to their condition by mastering areas thought to be closed to them (such as mountain climbing for an amputee) or by organizing a movement to counter social oppression. For instance, the National Association to Advance Fat Acceptance helps fat people ("fat" is the preferred adjective, by the way) cope with a society that hates their size and lobbies state legislatures to combat "size discrimination." In 1999, they staged a "million pound march" in Santa Monica, California, to support an antidiscrimination law there. Similarly, a disabled singing group routinely performs a song titled "Let the Children Stare," to convey the message that no good comes from ignoring disabilities (D. Martin, 1997). Hardly self-pitying, such individuals embrace their disabilities as a vital and important part of their identity. Many say they would reject being cured, even if it were possible. Rather, they want the world to adapt to their needs. As one disabled person put it, "We will not change to fit the mold. Instead, we will destroy the mold and change the world to make sure there is room for everyone" (quoted in D. Martin, 1997, p. E1).

But overcoming the problems created by stigma cannot be accomplished solely through individual impression management or collective demonstrations. Long-lasting improvements can be accomplished only at the societal level through the alteration of cultural beliefs about the nature of stigma (Link, Mirotznik, & Cullen, 1991). As long as we hold stigmatized individuals solely responsible for overcoming their condition, social problems will continue to be perceived only in individual terms.

CONCLUSION

After reading this chapter, you may have an image of human beings as cunning, manipulative, and cynical play actors whose lives are merely a string of phony performances carefully designed to fit the selfish needs of the moment. The impression manager comes across as someone who consciously and fraudulently presents an inaccurate image in order to take advantage of a particular situation. Even the person who seems not to care about his or her appearance may be consciously cultivating the image of "not caring."

There's no denying that people consciously manufacture images of themselves that allow them to achieve some desired goal. Most of us go through life trying to create the impression that we're attractive, honest, competent, and sincere. To that end we carefully manage our appearance, present qualities we think others will admire, and hide qualities we think they won't. When caught in an act that may threaten the impression we're trying to foster, we strategically use statements that disclaim, excuse, or justify it.

So who is the real you? If people freely change their images to suit the expectations of a given audience, is there something more stable that characterizes them across all situations?

If you are aware that the impression you are managing is not the real you, then you must have some knowledge of what *is* the real you. And what you are may, in fact, transcend the demands of particular situations. Some basic, pervasive part of your being may allow you to choose from a repertoire of identities the one that best suits the immediate needs of the situation. As you ponder this possibility, realize that your feelings about impression management reflect your beliefs about the nature of individuals and the role society and others play in our everyday lives.

YOUR TURN

Impression management is a tool most of us use to present ourselves as likable people. Occasionally, however, our attempts fail. Survey several friends or classmates and have them describe their most embarrassing moment. What were the circumstances surrounding the incident? What identities were they trying to present? How did the attempt to claim these identities fail? How did these people immediately react, physically and behaviorally, to the embarrassment? How did they try to overcome the embarrassment and return order? Did they offer some sort of account? Were the consequences of the failed impression management temporary or permanent? What did the witnesses to the embarrassing incident do? Did their reactions alleviate or intensify the embarrassment?

Once you've gathered a substantial number of stories (about 12 or 15), see if you can find some common themes. What are the most frequent types of embarrassing situations? What are the most frequent reactions? If your class is large, your instructor can have you report your results to a small group of fellow students or to the entire class. What kinds of patterns can you identify in the embarrassing stories people tell? Are there gender, ethnic, or age differences in what people find embarrassing?

Sociologists Edward Gross and Gregory Stone have written, "In the wreckage left by embarrassment lie the broken foundations of social transactions" (1964, p. 2). What do you suppose they mean by that? Discuss the sociological importance of embarrassment (and, more important, the reactions to embarrassment) in terms of the maintenance of interactional and social order.

CHAPTER HIGHLIGHTS

- A significant portion of social life is influenced by the images we form of others and the images others form of us.

- Impression formation is based initially on our assessment of ascribed social group membership (race, age, gender, and so on), individual physical appearance, and verbal and nonverbal messages.

- While we are gathering information about others to form impressions of them, we are fully aware that they are doing the same thing. Impression management is the process by which we attempt to control and manipulate information about ourselves to influence the impressions others form of us. Impression management can be both individual and collective.

- Impression mismanagement can lead to the creation of damaged identities that must be repaired in order to sustain social interaction.

KEY TERMS

account Statement designed to explain unanticipated, embarrassing, or unacceptable behavior after the behavior has occurred

aligning action Action taken to restore an identity that has been damaged

back stage Area of social interaction away from the view of an audience, where people can rehearse and rehash their behavior

cooling out Gently persuading someone who has lost face to accept a less desirable but still reasonable alternative identity

disclaimer Assertion designed to forestall any complaints or negative reactions to a behavior or statement that is about to occur

dramaturgy Study of social interaction as theater, in which people ("actors") project images ("play roles") in front of others ("audience")

embarrassment Spontaneous feeling experienced when the identity someone is presenting is suddenly and unexpectedly discredited in front of others

front stage Area of social interaction where people perform and work to maintain appropriate impressions

impression management Act of presenting a favorable public image of oneself so that others will form positive judgments

performance team Set of individuals who cooperate in staging a performance that leads an audience to form an impression of one or all team members

stigma Deeply discrediting characteristic that is viewed as an obstacle to competent or morally trustworthy behavior

7 Constructing Difference: Social Deviance

In 1984, 22-year-old Kelly Michaels moved to New York to pursue her dream of becoming an actress. She was a mild-mannered, devout Catholic who loved children. To support herself she began working at the Wee Care Preschool in a New Jersey suburb, and by all accounts the kids there loved her (Hass, 1995).

Two weeks after Michaels left Wee Care for a better-paying job at another nursery school, a 4-year-old boy who was enrolled at Wee Care was taken to a doctor. A nurse rubbed his back and explained that she was going to take his temperature rectally. He said something like "That's what teacher [Michaels] does to me at nap time."

"What does your teacher do?" the nurse asked.

"She takes my temperature," he replied. Although it was unclear exactly what he meant by this—Michaels sometimes rubbed children's backs to get them to sleep and did take their temperature with a plastic forehead strip—the boy's alarmed mother, who happened to be the daughter of a local judge, called the school and the police (Michaels, 1993). The police questioned the child as well as other children at Wee Care, searching for evidence that Michaels had sexually abused them. As word spread of the investigation, worried parents phoned other parents to share stories about the latest allegations. The police encouraged parents to seek state-funded psychological help for themselves as well as their children. In turn, the therapists encouraged the parents to cooperate with authorities in prosecuting Michaels.

That casual comment made by a little boy in a doctor's office touched off a 16-month investigation by the Division of Youth and Family Services that eventually ended in a 235-count indictment against Michaels. During the investigation, scores of parents became convinced that Michaels had raped their children with silverware, wooden spoons, LEGOs, and light bulbs; that she had played "Jingle Bells" on the piano while naked; that she had licked peanut butter off children's genitals, made them drink her urine, and forced them to eat excrement off the floor (Hass, 1995).

The 10-month trial was filled with a host of inconsistencies and questionable legal tactics. Prosecutors never provided any substantiated evidence of abuse, yet they portrayed Michaels as "actressy" and "deviously charming." None of the other teachers at the day care center had heard or seen anything, even though most of the alleged abuse took place during children's nap time in a room set off only by a plastic curtain. The judge in the trial allowed the children to testify on closed-circuit TV while sitting on his lap and denied the defense experts the opportunity to cross-examine the children. One of the prosecution's witnesses—a child therapist—testified that the children who denied being molested by Ms. Michaels suffered from something called "child sexual abuse accommodation syndrome," which made them deny the abuse. In fact, the more the children denied it, the more certain the child therapist was that the abuse had actually happened.

Michaels was found guilty of 115 counts of assault, sexual abuse, and terrorist threats and sentenced to 47 years in prison. In 1993, after she had spent five years in prison—including an 18-month stint in solitary confinement—a state appellate court overturned the conviction. Later, the New Jersey State Supreme Court upheld the appellate court's decision, decrying the original conviction with outrage. The court wrote that all 20 children who testified against Michaels had been led, bribed, or threatened (Hass, 1995). Michaels filed a $10 million lawsuit against the county, the state, and virtually every person involved in her prosecution, stating that they had maliciously made up crimes that had never occurred. She said, "I'm out to destroy the mythical monster of their creation, a drooling, dark beast that never was" (quoted in Hass, 1995, p. 38). Her lawsuit was eventually thrown out.

You might think that a formal declaration of innocence from such a powerful body as a state supreme court would change people's feelings about Kelly Michaels. Yet she remains a target of hate. Eight civil suits are pending against Michaels by parents who still believe their children—aged 3 to 5 at the time—were sexually abused. As one parent put it, "I know in my heart that Kelly Michaels sexually molested my child, and I will believe that until the day I go to my grave" (quoted in Hass, 1995, pp. 40–41). Another mother said she might try to kill Michaels with her bare hands if she had the chance.

Why was it so hard for people to admit that Michaels was innocent? For one thing, this case, dealing with such a frightening crime as child molestation, symbolized the disorder that many people felt was plaguing society. The terrifying message was that our children could be hurt not only by creepy, middle-aged men but also by seemingly safe, 22-year-old college women. At a time when child abuse was becoming a national obsession, the case reflected our darkest collective fears. In the frenzy over children's safety, no one seemed willing to defend the principle of reasonable doubt.

Even more striking about this case is what it says about the way individuals think. Once people in the community had concluded that Kelly Michaels committed these horrible acts, no amount of conflicting evidence was going to sway them to believe otherwise. As you know, our responses to other people are often based on our expectations of them. Well before her legal conviction, Michaels had been pronounced a deviant; even the New Jersey State Supreme Court could not convince people otherwise. Such labels and what they imply in people's minds can overshadow everything else about a person. When Michaels was formally tagged a criminal at the conclusion of her trial, the public degradation acquired its legal legitimacy. From that point on, she would never again be able to reclaim a normal life and in many people's minds would forever be a "child molester." Indeed, a recent Associated Press news release about Michaels's attempted lawsuit was titled "Sex offender's case denied in court" (2001).

Wrongly spending five years in prison as a convicted child molester is not the sort of thing most of us have experienced. Keep in mind, though, that the process of affixing deviant labels and judging people on the basis of them can be found not only in such systems as criminal courts but in everyday social interchanges as well. Perhaps there have been times in your life when you acquired some sort of reputation that you could not shed.

In this chapter I focus on several questions that have been addressed by many sociologists but still arouse widespread disagreement: What is deviance? How do people become deviant? Who gets to define what is and is not deviant? What are the consequences of being identified as deviant by others?

Defining Deviance

For the most part, the term *deviance* refers to socially disapproved behavior—the violation of some agreed-on norm that prevails in a community or in society at large. Staring at a stranger in an elevator, driving over the speed limit, talking to oneself in public, wearing outlandish clothes, robbing a bank, or sending deadly anthrax spores through the mail can all be considered deviant acts. Some deviant acts are assaults on taboos, the most serious of a society's norms. But most deviance is rather trivial—even "normal." Most of us, at some point in our lives, occupy statuses or engage in behaviors that could be regarded by others as deviant.

The determination of which behaviors or characteristics are deviant and which are normal is complex. We usually assume that people agree about what and who is deviant. For instance, no one would challenge the notion that child abuse is bad and that child abusers ought to be punished. But the level of agreement within a given society over what is deviant—what specific acts constitute child abuse—is subject to much disagreement and even overt conflict. What is a perfectly acceptable method of discipline to one parent may be a cruel form of abuse to another.

To make the issue more complicated, some sociologists identified with structural-functionalism (for example, Durkheim, 1958; Erikson, 1966) argue that deviance is not always bad for society and may actually serve a useful purpose. As you may recall from Chapter 4, norm violations help define the cultural and moral boundaries that distinguish right from wrong, increase feelings of in-group togetherness for those who unite in opposition to normative threats, and encourage society to revise itself and respond to new concerns. At the surface level, acts of deviance are disruptive and generate varying degrees of social disapproval, but at a deeper level they can contribute to the maintenance and continuity of every society.

Before examining the theoretical explanations and the social implications of deviance, let's look at two different approaches to defining deviance: absolutism and relativism. I use these terms here to describe the strategies that people employ when analyzing deviants and deviance, not to describe philosophical positions on morality. In other words, sociologists aren't judging whether a given behavior should or shouldn't be considered deviant; instead, they are examining whether people respond to deviance from the perspective that all human behavior can be classified as good or bad (absolutists) or from the perspective that definitions of deviance are socially created (relativists).

Absolutist Definitions of Deviance

According to **absolutism**, there are two fundamental types of human behavior: that which is inherently proper and good and that which is obviously improper, immoral, evil, and bad. The distinction is clear and identifiable. The quality of deviance can be found in the very nature of the act. Right and wrong exist prior to socially created rules, norms, and customs and independent of people's subjective judgments (E. Goode, 1994).

Absolutist definitions of deviance are often accompanied by strong emotional reactions. The absolutist view holds that no normal, decent person would willingly violate norms and participate in a deviant lifestyle, be it violent crime, drug use, or nontraditional sexuality. For instance, when asked whether homosexuality is a sin, a prominent U.S. senator answered, "Yes, it is. In America right now there's an element that wants to make that alternative lifestyle acceptable. . . . Others have a sex addiction or are kleptomaniacs. There are all kinds of problems and addictions and difficulties and experiences of this kind that are wrong" (quoted in Berke, 1998, p. A19). A nationwide study found that although people in the United States seem to be showing increasing tolerance for and acceptance of people of different religions and different racial and ethnic groups, they still remain decidedly intolerant of homosexuality, commonly describing it as "sick," "immoral," "sinful," "perverted," and "abnormal" (A. Wolfe, 1998).

Such attitudes are sometimes reflected in people's actions toward those considered deviant. Hours after Matthew Shepard, a gay college student at the University of Wyoming, died from injuries sustained in a savage beating, two gay rights organizations received telephone messages applauding the killing and closing with the words, "I hope it happens more often." Protesters arrived at his funeral carrying signs saying, "God Hates Fags!" Indeed, surveys of gay college students show that between 16% and 26% have been threatened with violence and as many as three-quarters have been verbally harassed (cited in Brooke, 1998, p. A17).

An absolutist definition of deviance implies something about society's relationship with the person committing the deviant act. Many people within society consider deviant people to be morally, psychologically, and perhaps even anatomically different from ordinary, conforming people. The attribute or behavior that serves as the basic reason for defining a person as deviant in the first place is considered pervasive and essential to his or her entire character (Hills, 1980). Respectable, conventional qualities become insignificant. It doesn't matter, for instance, that the "sexual deviant" has an otherwise ordinary life, that the "schizophrenic" has recovered, or that the violent act of the "murderer" was completely atypical of the rest of his or her life. In short, the deviant act or trait becomes a sort of moral identity, signifying a judgment about the overall worth of the individual (Katz, 1975). Being defined as deviant means being identified as someone who cannot and should not be treated as an ordinary human being.

Here the absolutist approach runs into some problems. People often make judgments of deviance and deviants on the basis of stereotypes. If you ask someone to imagine what a typical drug addict looks like, chances are the response will describe a dirty, poor, strung-out young man living on the streets and resorting to theft to support his habit. The image probably wouldn't be one of a middle-class alcoholic housewife or a clean-shaven, hardworking physician hooked on prescription drugs, even though these groups constitute a higher percentage of drug addicts than any other in U.S. society (Pfohl, 1994). The other side of the coin is that people who commit deviant acts may not be sanctioned harshly if they are otherwise perceived as "respectable." When sociologists William Chambliss and Richard H. Nagasawa (1969) compared the arrest rates of white, African-American, and Japanese-American youths in Seattle, they found that ethnic stereotypes led police to overestimate the involvement of African Americans in criminal activities and to underestimate the involvement of Japanese Americans.

As this study indicates, in U.S. society the consequences of stereotypes regarding deviance fall heavily on members of racial and ethnic minorities. The Sentencing Project, a nonprofit research and advocacy organization, found that one in three black men in their 20s and one in eight Latino men are under the supervision of the criminal justice system—prison, probation, or parole—on any given day. Although some might see such a figure as clear evidence of higher rates of minority involvement in crime, other statistics seem to suggest something different. For instance, African Americans make up 12% of the nation's population and constitute roughly the same percentage (13%) of all illegal drug users; yet they represent more than 40% of arrests for drug possession, 56% of all convictions for drug possession, and 74% of all prison sentences for drug possession (Butterfield, 1995; U.S. Bureau of Justice Statistics, 1993). In 75% of cases in which a federal prosecutor sought the death penalty between 1995 and 2000 the defendant was a member of a minority group; and in half the cases, the defendant was black (cited in Bonner & Lacey, 2000). Exhibit 7.1 shows the black–white disparity in arrests, convictions, and length of sentence for different types of crime. Such biases can distort the official records regarding who makes up the population of deviants in this country and can reinforce public perceptions of what typical deviants look like (Archer, 1985; Pfohl, 1994; Reiman, 1998).

Oversimplified images of deviants always fall short of accounting for every individual. The vast majority of African Americans do not commit crimes, just as the vast majority of gay men are not sexual predators, the vast majority of Italians are not involved in the Mafia, and the vast majority of Muslims are not terrorists. Nevertheless, the degree to which such images are thought to characterize an entire group is important because it determines individual and societal responses. If affluent housewives or businesspeople who abuse drugs are not considered typical drug addicts, they will never be the focus of law enforcement attention, collective moral outrage, political rhetoric, or public policy.

Relativist Definitions of Deviance

An absolutist perspective on deviance can lead to narrow and often inaccurate perceptions of many important social problems. This shortcoming can be avoided by employing a second approach to analyzing deviance, **relativism**, which draws from symbolic interactionism. This perspective states that deviance is not a property inherent in any particular act, belief, or condition; instead, it is socially constructed, a creation of collective human judgments and ideas. Like beauty, deviance is in the eye of the beholder. The relativist approach is useful when the focus of study is the process by which some group of people or some type of behavior is defined as deviant.

Exhibit 7.1 **Racial Differences in Arrests, Convictions, and Sentencing**

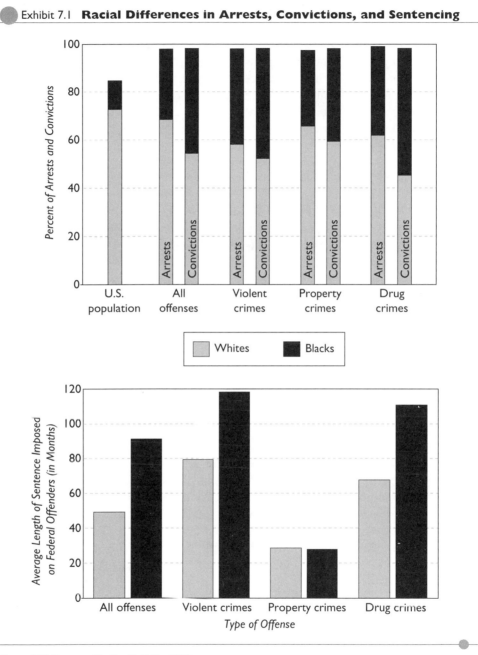

Source: U.S. Bureau of Justice Statistics, 1999.

For the relativist, complex societies consist of different groups with different values and interests. Sometimes these groups agree and cooperate to achieve a common goal, as when all segments of society join together to fight a foreign enemy. But more often than not there is conflict and struggle among groups to realize their own interests and goals.

Different people can thus have dramatically different interpretations of the same event. In 1995, a 35-year-old white man named William Masters was taking his usual armed, late-night walk through a barren neighborhood in Los Angeles. He came upon two young Latino men spray-painting graffiti beneath a freeway overpass. Masters wrote down the license number of their car on a small piece of paper. When the men saw him and demanded the paper, Masters pulled out his 9-millimeter pistol and shot them—wounding one and killing the other. He told police that the men threatened him with a screwdriver and that he acted in self-defense, even though both were shot in the back. He was not charged with murder. Eventually he was found guilty of one count of carrying a concealed gun in public and one count of carrying a loaded gun in public—charges that carried a maximum of 18 months in jail and a $2,000 fine.

Shortly after his arrest, Masters claimed that his actions shouldn't be defined as deviant. In fact, his statements indicated that he felt the killing should be seen as appropriate, even desirable. He told one interviewer he was sure people were glad that as an intended victim he had gotten away, and that no jury would ever convict him (Mydans, 1995).

Many people agreed. Callers to talk radio shows and letters to newspapers described him as a hero and a saint. Some applauded him for his vigilant anti-graffiti efforts and for his foresight in carrying a weapon for self-protection. A few suggested that society would be better off with more people like William around (Mydans, 1995).

But others defined the event and Masters quite differently, expressing dismay at the verdict and arguing that he was simply a racist out looking for trouble. They felt he was not a considerate fellow who was doing his part to clean up the streets but a deviant who literally got away with murder.

All those who expressed opinions on this case would likely agree on one thing: Murder is a deviant act at the far end of spectrum of social acceptability. They would probably all want to punish a murderer severely. However, their perceptions of whether William Masters was a murderer were quite different. Was he a "hero" or a "killer"? An "avenging angel" or a "dangerous deviant"? The answers to these questions lie not in moral judgments of the objective act of taking another's life but in the way it was defined and responded to by others.

To fully understand the societal and personal implications of deviance designations, we must look at how these definitions are created and perpetuated. One of the key factors is who is doing the defining. If an act is deviant only because someone sees it that way, then the definition of deviance becomes rather arbitrary. One person's crime is another person's act of moral conscience; one group's evil is another group's virtue; one culture's freedom fighter is another culture's terrorist. When we try to see certain acts from another group's perspective, even our most solidly held ideas about deviance become perplexing.

Definitions of deviance are always relative to particular cultural standards. In Singapore a young vandal is a serious deviant (punishable by caning), as is a person who leaves chewed gum where it can be stepped on. And the fine for simply bringing one stick of gum into Singapore is $10,000. A blasphemer in a fundamentalist Islamic society may be put to death for questioning the existence of God, an "offense" most Westerners would probably consider trivial. Making a large profit on a business transaction is highly acceptable in the United States but until recently was considered "profiteering" in China—a crime punishable by death (G. Stephens, 1994).

Even within the same country, one community's standards can differ from another's, creating conflict. For example, the sacramental use of peyote—a cactus that contains the hallucinogenic substance mescaline—has been a part of the religious rituals of certain Native American groups for centuries. In 1990 the Oregon State Supreme Court ruled that the First Amendment's protection of free exercise of religion allowed the use of peyote for religious purposes. But the U.S. Supreme Court later overturned this ruling, stating that government policies and laws must be upheld even to the disadvantage of some religious groups (Greenhouse, 1990). Even though people in the United States who use peyote for religious purposes don't consider themselves deviant, they were defined and treated that way by the dominant culture.

The absolutist approach assumes that certain individual characteristics are typical of all deviants, but the relativist approach acknowledges that there is no typical deviant. In fact, the same act committed by two different people may be defined very differently. For example, the police regularly harass, arrest, and jail street prostitutes. In the 1980s, however, Sydney Biddle Barrows, a wealthy descendant of an original Plymouth colonist, established a high-class brothel as a business enterprise and became known as the "Mayflower Madam." Instead of spending time in prison for breaking the law, she made the talk show circuit and wrote a best-selling book. Clearly, her socioeconomic status and pedigree influenced public definitions regarding the deviant nature of her activities. When *she* did it, somehow it wasn't so bad.

Immediate situational circumstances can also influence definitions of deviance. Drinking liquor in a bar is more acceptable than drinking in a college classroom; drinking on the weekend is more acceptable than drinking during the week; drinking in the evening is more acceptable than drinking in the morning, and so on.

Even acts of extreme violence may be defined as acceptable under certain circumstances. Killings committed in self-defense, as some defined William Masters's actions, and killings committed under the auspices of the government—shooting looters during a riot, killing enemy soldiers during wartime, or executing convicted murderers—fall outside the category of behaviors deemed deviant and problematic in society. Under certain circumstances, then, the act of purposely taking a human life may be seen by some as justified (E. Goode, 1994).

It's important to keep in mind that a relativist approach to defining deviance doesn't mean that every act under any circumstance should be celebrated:

> Relativity does not require moral indifference, and it does not mean that one can never be upset or horrified by what one experiences in another group or culture. . . . [It] just reminds us that our personal beliefs or our cultural understandings are not necessarily found everywhere. (Curra, 2000, p. 13)

In sum, then, to a relativist, the main concerns in analyzing deviance are who commits the act, who labels it, and where and when it occurs, as much as what act is committed. Some people have the wherewithal to avoid having their acts defined as deviant. Definitions of deviant behavior change over time, and certain acts are acceptable to some groups and not others. But relativists, like absolutists, acknowledge that every society identifies certain individuals and certain behaviors as bothersome and disruptive and therefore as justifiable targets of social control, whether through treatment, punishment, spiritual healing, or correction.

The Elements of Deviance

The two perspectives on deviance raise some complex and controversial issues. Nevertheless, the general definition of deviance we're left with goes something like this: **Deviance** is an individual's or group's behavior (how people act), ideas (how people think), or attributes (how people appear) that some people in society find offensive, wrong, immoral, sinful, evil, strange, or disgusting.

This definition consists of three elements (Aday, 1990):

- *Expectation:* Some sort of behavioral expectation must exist, a norm that defines appropriate, acceptable behavior, ideas, or characteristics. The expectations may be implicit or explicit, formal or informal, and more or less widely shared.
- *Violation:* Deviance implies some violation of normative expectations. The violation may be real or alleged; that is, an accusation of wrongdoing may be enough to give someone the reputation of deviance.
- *Reaction:* An individual, group, or society must react to the deviance. The reaction is likely to lead to some sort of response: avoidance, criticism, warnings, punishment, or treatment. The reaction may accurately reflect the facts, or it may bear little resemblance to what really happened, as when people are punished or ostracized for acts they did not commit.

Deviance, then, cannot exist if people don't have some idea of what's appropriate, if someone hasn't been perceived as violating some social norm, and if others haven't reacted.

Explaining Why People Become Deviant

This question of how certain acts and certain people come to be defined as deviant is different from the question of why people do or don't commit acts that are considered deviant. Most sociological theories addressing the question of why people become deviant focus on their personal characteristics, the environmental forces on them, and the effectiveness of various methods of social control.

The structural-functionalist perspective, for instance, tells us that it is in society's interest to socialize everyone to strive for success so that the most able and talented people will come to occupy the most important positions. Sociologist Robert Merton (1957) argues that the probability of committing deviant acts increases when people experience a contradiction between these culturally defined goals and access to the legitimate means by which they can achieve those goals. Those who believe that being wealthy and achieving the "American Dream" are important goals but who have no money, no employment opportunities, and no access to higher education, Merton argues, are more inclined than others to try to achieve the goal of success through illegitimate means. In this sense, people who sell, say, stolen TVs to get rich are motivated by the same desires as people who sell real estate to get rich. People who lack access to legitimate means may also reject the culturally defined goal of success and retreat from society altogether. According to Merton, such deviants as vagrants, chronic drunks, drug addicts, and the mentally ill fall into this category.

Another sociologist, Edwin Sutherland (Sutherland & Cressey, 1955), bases his theory of deviance on the symbolic-interactionist principle that we all interpret life through the symbols and meanings we learn through our interactions with others. Sutherland argues that individuals learn deviant patterns of behavior from the people with whom they associate on a regular basis: friends, family members, peers. Through our associations with these influential individuals we learn not only the techniques for committing deviant acts (for example, how to pick a lock or how to snort cocaine) but also a set of beliefs and attitudes that justify or rationalize the behavior (Sykes & Matza, 1957). To commit deviant acts, we must learn how to perceive those acts as normal.

Deterring Deviance

Some sociologists have turned away from the issue of why some people violate norms to the issue of why more people don't (see, for example, Hirschi, 1969). Their concern is with the mechanisms society has in place to control or constrain people's behavior. **Deterrence theory** assumes that people are rational decision makers who calculate the costs and benefits of behavior before they act. If the benefits of a deviant act (for instance, monetary wealth or psychological satisfaction) outweigh the costs (for instance, the severity of punishment or the likelihood of getting caught), we will do it. Conversely, if the costs exceed the potential benefits, the theory predicts that we'll decide it's not worth the risk (van den Haag, 1975). Some research shows that states with a high certainty of punishment (estimated by the percentage of convicted offenders sentenced to state prisons) tend to have lower crime rates. However, with the exception of homicide, increasing severity of potential punishment (measured by the average prison sentence for a given offense) tends not to be related to decreases in crime rates (Tittle, 1969).

The current controversy surrounding capital punishment is, essentially, a debate over its true capacity to deter potentially violent criminals. According to deterrence theory, a punishment, in order to be effective, must be swift as well as certain and severe. However, capital punishment is anything but swift. Currently, more than 3,500 inmates are on death row in the United States, but fewer than 500 prisoners have been executed since 1976, when the death penalty was reinstated. The average length of time spent by a convict on death row is 8.8 years (Butterfield, 1998).

In addition, opponents of the death penalty argue that violent offenders are often under the influence of drugs or alcohol or are consumed by passion when they commit an act of violence. Hence, they may not be thinking rationally (that is, weighing the potential benefits of the act against the costs of punishment) at the time of the crime. The threat of being condemned to death may not deter such people at the time they are committing the act. Researchers have, indeed, found little empirical support for the argument that the publicized threat of capital punishment reduces murders (W. C. Bailey, 1990). Nor have they found that well-publicized executions deter homicides (R. D.

Peterson & Bailey, 1991). In fact, recent figures show that over the last two decades, the homicide rate in the 38 states with the death penalty has been 48 to 100% *higher* than that in the 12 states without the death penalty (Bonner & Fessenden, 2000).

Most societies around the world have abandoned the use of capital punishment for both moral and practical reasons: It isn't humane, and it doesn't deter crime. For instance, in 1998, the European Union adopted policy guidelines stating that the "abolition of the death penalty contributes to the enhancement of human dignity and the progressive development of human rights" (Amnesty International, 1998, p. 4). Nevertheless, the majority of U.S. citizens continue to favor the death penalty and believe it is a useful tool in fighting crime. Recent legislative efforts to increase the number of offenses punishable by the death penalty and reduce the number of "death row" appeals an offender can file reflect this popular attitude.

Labeling Deviants

These theories help us explain why some people engage in deviant acts whereas others don't, but they bypass the question of why certain acts committed by certain people are considered deviant in the first place. **Labeling theory** attempts to answer this question by characterizing deviance as the consequence of the application of rules and sanctions to an offender (see, for example, Becker, 1963; Lemert, 1972). A deviant person is not someone who is fundamentally different from a nondeviant but rather someone—such as preschool teacher Kelly Michaels—to whom the label "deviant" has been successfully applied (Becker, 1963).

According to this theory, the process of being singled out, defined, and reacted to as deviant changes a person in the eyes of others and has important life consequences for the individual. A deviant label suggests that the person holding it is someone who is habitually given to the types of undesirable motives and behavior thought to be typical of others who possess the label. The "ex-convict" is seen as a cold-blooded and ruthless character without hope of reform, the "mental patient" as dangerous and unpredictable, the "alcoholic" as weak-willed, the "prostitute" as dirty and immoral. The problem, of course, is that such labels can be misleading. For instance, a study by two marketing professors found that convicted felons showed just as much integrity as students in a program leading to the degree of master of business administration on a test of ethics related to difficult business situations. In fact, the convicts were *less* likely to indicate that they'd steal employees from competitors or scrimp on customer service ("MBA vs. prison," 1999). Nevertheless, a deviant label influences others' feelings and reactions toward the person—commonly rejection, suspicion, withdrawal, fear, mistrust, and hatred (A. K. Cohen, 1966).

The effects of deviant labels are so powerful that many judges around the country are now realizing that the public humiliation associated with these labels can be used as an alternative to incarceration. For example, an Illinois man convicted of assault was required to place a large sign at the end of his driveway that reads, "Warning: A Violent Felon Lives Here. Travel at Your Own Risk." In some states, convicted drunk drivers have to put special license plates on their cars; convicted shoplifters must take out ads in local newspapers, use their photograph, and announce their crimes. In Minneapolis, people arrested for soliciting prostitution are forced to stand, handcuffed, in front of community members, who verbally shame them. In Kansas City, a municipal cable TV channel broadcasts the names, mug shots, birth dates and home towns of men arrested for trying to buy sex (Belluck, 1998b). Such penalties are designed to shame the labeled individuals into behaving properly. They also satisfy the public's need for dramatic moral condemnation of deviants (Hoffman, 1997).

Deviant labels can impair an individual's eligibility to enter a broad range of socially acceptable roles. Consider the impact on convicted sex offenders of the 1994 Federal Crime Bill. This law requires states to register and track convicted sex offenders for 10 years after their release from prison and to privately notify police departments when the sex offenders move into a new community. Two years later the U.S. Senate approved a measure requiring all states to make public the whereabouts of paroled sex offenders. In Louisiana, homeowners can sign up for a service that notifies subscribers by e-mail when registered sex offenders move to within a mile of their homes; the service provides maps showing where the sex offenders live ("Site warns of new neighbors," 2001). In California a CD-ROM, available for public viewing in sheriffs' offices and police departments statewide, contains the names, physical descriptions, criminal histories, residential zip codes, and in some cases photographs of nearly 64,000 sex offenders convicted in the state; almost all these people must register every year for the rest of their lives (Purdum, 1997). Sixteen states have "sexually violent predator" statutes that give officials the power to commit violent sex offenders to mental hospitals involuntarily or retain them in prison indefinitely *after* their prison terms are up (Goldberg, 2001). These are men who have "paid their debt" to society by serving their mandated prison sentences. However, under these laws, convicted sex offenders can never fully shed their deviant identity and be above suspicion. Finding a decent place to live or a decent job may be a problem for the rest of their lives.

All ex-convicts experience the "stickiness" of labels to some degree. Potential employers, for instance, often refuse to hire ex-convicts, even when the crime had nothing to do with the job requirements. Like the public at large, many employers believe that prisons do not rehabilitate but actually make convicts more deviant by teaching them better ways to commit crime and by providing social networks to criminal activity on the outside (R. Johnson, 1987). In addition, being labeled as deviant may actually increase the probability that the behavior itself will stay the same or become worse (Archer, 1985). Thus a great many ex-convicts in the United States do return to prison. Roughly two-thirds of all ex-convicts will be rearrested within three years, and 40% will end up behind bars again ("Coming to a neighborhood," 2001).

A mere charge of criminal activity can conjure up suspicions of tainted character. The labeling process is powerful enough, even in the absence of wrongdoing, to produce a durable loss of status for the individual (R. D. Schwartz & J. H. Skolnick, 1962). You may recall the case of Richard Jewell, the security guard originally suspected of setting off the bomb that killed two people and injured more than a hundred during the 1996 Summer Olympics in Atlanta. Newspapers and television news shows "convicted" him even though no criminal charges were ever filed. Operating on unsubstantiated tips and hearsay, the FBI launched a full investigation of Jewell's life and character. Three months later the Justice Department sent him a letter stating that he was no longer a suspect. Jewell sued a newspaper, a radio station, and a television network for the stigmatizing effect their stories had on his life. He eventually settled out of court and built a satisfactory life for himself. But it took years.

Nancy Herman
Becoming an Ex-Crazy

Sociologist Nancy Herman (1993) was interested in how labeling can weaken a person's self-image, create "deviant" patterns of behavior, and lead to social rejection. She was especially concerned with how former mental patients are reintegrated into society after their release from a psychiatric hospital.

Herman's own personal history influenced her decision to study this topic. Her father was an occupational therapist at a large psychiatric institute in Ontario, Canada. She spent most of her childhood and adolescence roaming the halls talking to patients. From time to time patients would spend Thanksgiving and Christmas with her family.

For this study, she conducted in-depth interviews with 146 nonchronic (hospitalized in short intervals for less than two years) and 139 chronic former mental patients (hospitalized continuously for two or more years). She interviewed them in a variety of settings, such as coffee shops, malls, and their own homes. Many subjects invited her to their self-help group meetings, therapy sessions, even protest marches.

Herman found that these ex-patients, on release, noticed right away that friends, neighbors, co-workers, and family members were responding to them on the basis of their "mental illness" label and not on the basis of their identity prior to hospitalization. Despite the fact that their treatment was complete (that is, they were "cured" of their "illness"), others still saw them as defective. They were often made to feel like failures for not measuring up to the rest of "normal" society. As one woman put it,

> When I was released, I presumed that I could resume with the "good times" once again. I was treated—I paid my dues. But I was wrong. From the first moment I set foot back onto the streets of "Wilsonville" and I tried to return to my kids, . . . I learned the hard way that my kids didn't want nothing to do with me. They were scared to let me near the grandkids—that I might do something to them. They told me this right to my face. . . . Having mental illness is like having any other illness like heart troubles, but people sure do treat you different. If you have heart troubles, you get treated, and then you come out good as new and your family still loves you. But that's not so with mental illness . . . you come out and people treat you worse than a dog! (quoted in Herman, 1993, p. 303)

On release, some of the former patients Herman interviewed were quite open about their illness and attempted to present themselves in as "normal" a way as they could. Others became political activists who used their "ex-mental patient" label to try to dispel common myths about mental illness or to advocate for patients' rights.

But most of the former patients spent a great deal of time selectively concealing and disclosing information regarding their past history of hospitalization. Most of them wanted to protect themselves from the negative consequences they felt would surely result from revealing information about their illness and treatment. Strategies of concealment included such techniques as avoiding certain individuals, redirecting conversations so that the topic was less likely to come up, lying about their absence, and withdrawing from social interaction. Constant concern with people "finding out" created a great deal of anxiety, fear, and frustration, as described by this 56-year old woman:

> It's a very difficult thing. It's not easy to distinguish the good ones from the bad ones. . . . You've gotta figure out who you can tell about your illness and who you better not tell. It is a tremendous stress and strain that you have to live with 24 hours a day! (quoted in Herman, 1993, p. 306)

The stickiness of the "crazy" label is difficult for former mental patients. However, Herman's research shows that ex-patients are not powerless victims of negative societal reactions, passively accepting the deviant identity others attribute to them. Rather, they are strategists and information managers who play active roles in transforming themselves from "abnormal" to "normal."

Linking Power and the Social Construction of Deviance

Because deviance is socially defined, the behaviors and conditions that come to be called "deviant" can at times appear somewhat arbitrary. However, according to the conflict perspective the definition of deviance is often a form of social control exerted by more powerful people and groups over less powerful people and groups. In U.S. society, the predominant means of controlling deviants—those whose behavior does not conform to the norms established by the powerful—are criminalization and medicalization. Labeling people as either criminals or as sick people gives the socially powerful a way to marginalize and discount certain people who challenge the status quo. Criminalization and medicalization also have economic and other benefits for certain powerful groups.

The Criminalization of Deviance

One of the most important constructed realities is what we regard as legal or illegal behavior. Certain acts are defined as crimes because they offend the majority of people in a given society. Many of us trust our legal institutions—legislators, courts, and police—to regulate social behavior in the interest of the common good.

According to conflict theory, most societies ensure that those offenders who are processed through the criminal justice system are members of the lowest socioeconomic class (Reiman, 1998). Poor people are more likely to get arrested, be formally charged with a crime, have their cases go to trial, get convicted, and receive harsher sentences than more affluent citizens (Parenti, 1995; Reiman, 1998). In 2000, the governor of Illinois called for a moratorium on executions in his state after 13 men on death row—all of whom were poor and were represented in their trials by public defenders—were proven innocent. Another 33 who were sentenced to die had lawyers who were later disbarred or suspended for incompetence. In Alabama, the public defender representing a man facing the death penalty had never tried a capital case and had no money to hire an investigator. The man was sentenced to death. Cases like these have intensified the national debate over the quality of legal representation provided to poor people accused of capital crimes.

Such imbalances in the justice system go beyond the way poor people are treated by police, judges, attorneys and juries. If that were the case, the situation would be relatively easy to deal with. Instead, they occur because the actions of poor individuals are more likely to be **criminalized**—that is, officially defined as crimes in the first place. Poor people sometimes commit acts—car theft, burglary, assault, illegal drug use, and so on—that fit commonly held definitions of what a crime is. As a result, they become "typical criminals" in the public eye.

The Social Reality of Crime. Conflict theory points out that powerful groups often try to foster a belief that society's rules are under attack by deviants and that official action against them is needed. The strategy has worked well. In polls taken in the United States in the 1980s and early 1990s, an average of 83% of respondents felt that the justice system was not harsh enough in dealing with criminals (Gaubatz, 1995). Governments at the state and federal level have responded to the popular sentiment by "getting tough on crime"—cracking down on drug users and dealers, reviving the death penalty, scaling back parole eligibility, lengthening prison sentences, and building more prisons. By 1999, 15 states had abolished parole boards and early release programs, resulting in more prisoners serving their full sentences (Butterfield, 1999). Not surprisingly, the inmate population has swelled. According to the Justice Department, the number of inmates in U.S. prisons has grown exponentially over the past several decades. In 1970 there were less than 200,000 people in state and federal prisons; by 1999 that figure had swelled to almost 1.3 million, not including over 600,000 more held in local jails (cited in Haberman, 2000). Nearly 1 of every 150 people in this country is in prison or jail, a figure no other industrialized country comes close to (Egan, 1999). There's some evidence that these "get tough" actions may be working. The FBI reports that rates of violent crime and property crime have been dropping steadily for seven consecutive years (U.S. Bureau of the Census, 2000b). Exhibit 7.2 shows the statistical relationship between incarceration rates and crime rates.

But because many states have sharply curtailed education, job training, and other rehabilitation programs inside prison, newly released inmates—who are likely to be poor—are significantly less likely than their counterparts of two decades ago to find jobs and stay out of the kind of trouble that leads to further imprisonment (Butterfield, 2000b). In addition, parole officers are quicker to rescind a newly released inmate's parole for relatively minor infractions, like failing a drug test. In California, for instance, four out of five former inmates returned to prison *not* for committing new crimes, but for violating the conditions of their parole.

According to conflict theory, the law is not a mechanism that merely protects good people from bad people; it is a political instrument used by specific groups to further their own interests, often at the expense of others. The law, they argue, is created by economic elites who control the production and distribution of major resources in society (Chambliss, 1964; Quinney, 1970). Law is, of course, determined by legislative action.

Exhibit 7.2 **Rising Incarceration Rates, Decreasing Crime Rates**

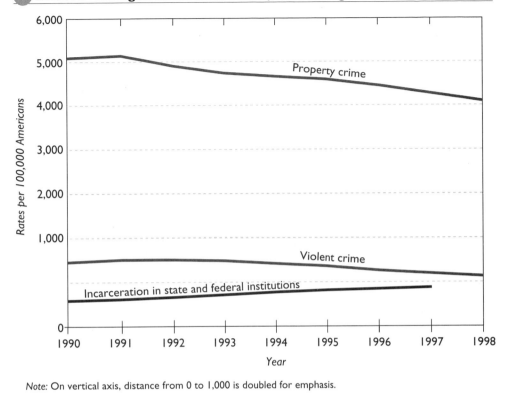

Note: On vertical axis, distance from 0 to 1,000 is doubled for emphasis.

Source: U.S. Bureau of the Census, 2000.

But legislatures are greatly influenced by these powerful segments of society via lobbying groups, political action committees, individual campaign contributions, and so on. The acts that conflict with the economic or political interests of the groups that have the power to influence public policy are more likely to be criminalized; for example,

> Two wealthy contractors, who pocketed $1.2 million in government contracts for work they never did, were ordered to pay $5,000 in fines and do 200 hours of community service. But a Norfolk, Virginia, man got ten years for stealing 87 cents; a youth in Louisiana received fifty years for selling a few ounces of marijuana; a Houston youth was sentenced to fifty years for robbing two people of $1 as they left a restaurant; a five-time petty offender in Dallas was sentenced to *one thousand* years in prison for stealing $73. A man caught trying to break into a house in Florida, thus violating his probation for shoplifting a pair of shoes, was sentenced to life in prison. (Parenti, 1995, p. 127)

Through the mass media, dominant groups influence the public to look at crime in ways that are favorable to them. The selective portrayal of crime plays an important role in shaping public perceptions of the "crime problem" and therefore its "official" definition. When politicians talk about fighting the U.S. crime problem, or when news shows report fluctuations in crime rates, they are almost always referring to street crimes (illegal drug use, robbery, burglary, murder, assault, and so on) rather than corporate crimes, governmental crimes, or crimes more likely to be committed by people in influential positions:

> Press coverage focuses public attention on crime in the streets with scarcely a mention of "crime in the suites," downplaying such . . . crimes as briberies, embezzlements, kickbacks, monopolistic restraints of trade, illegal uses of public funds by private interests, occupational safety violations, unsafe consumer goods, and environmental poisonings. (Parenti, 1986, p. 12)

Furthermore, how crime is defined and reported is largely determined by the race and social class of the victim and victimizer. Affluent victims receive more press coverage than poor victims, leaving the public with the incorrect impression that most crime victims are from middle- and upper-class backgrounds. Conversely, racial minority and low-income lawbreakers are more likely to be publicized as criminals than are wealthy corporate leaders, whose law-breaking activity may actually be more harmful to the common good (Parenti, 1986).

Such exposure creates a way of perceiving crime that becomes social reality. We accept the "fact" that certain people or actions are a threat to the well-being of the entire society and therefore a threat to our own personal interests. Consequently, many of us are willing to tolerate the violation of others' civil rights in the interests of controlling crime. For instance, over the past several years, New York City has seen a 44% decrease in murder, rape, and robbery cases. During the same time, however, there has been a 43% increase in the number of allegations of excessive force made against the city's police ("Harper's Index," 1998a). In the months following the attacks of September 11, 2001, the federal government eased restrictions on the surveillance, apprehension, interrogation, and detention of suspected terrorists. To many people, this is the price we must pay in order to control "the crime problem" or to ensure public safety.

Others, however, worry that such abuses are disproportionately directed toward people of color or people at the lower end of the socioeconomic spectrum. For instance, lower-class convicts in state prisons are often subjected to treatment that wouldn't be tolerated if it were directed toward more affluent convicts in medium-security prisons. For four years, some inmates in the Alabama prison system—who are predominantly poor and black—were chained to metal "hitching posts" for as long as 7 hours at a time no matter what the weather. They were denied food and water and bathroom privileges and were sometimes subjected to verbal and physical abuse by prison guards (Nossiter, 1997). In 1997 a judge ruled that the hitching post could no longer be used. He stated, "With deliberate indifference for the health, safety, and indeed the lives of inmates, prison officials have knowingly subjected them to all hazards of the hitching posts, then observed as they suffered pain, humiliation, and injuries as a result" (quoted in Nossiter, 1997, p. A10). It's hard to imagine such a tactic being used on middle-class convicts.

Corporate Crime. People in the United States take for granted that street crime is the worst social problem and that corporate crime is not as dangerous or as costly

(Reiman, 1998). U.S. citizens shake their heads over the exploitive practices of corporations or wealthy despots in such places as the rain forests of Brazil and Indonesia and the sweatshops of Southeast Asia. However, unsafe work conditions; dangerous chemicals in the air, water, and food; faulty products; unnecessary surgery; and shoddy emergency medical services actually put people who live in the United States into more constant and imminent physical danger than do ordinary street crimes. Approximately 19,000 people are murdered every year in the United States. At the same time, 56,000 Americans die each year on the job or from occupational diseases such as black lung and asbestos. Tens of thousands more die from pollution, contaminated foods, hazardous consumer products, and hospital malpractice (Mokhiber, 1999). Corporate crime also poses greater economic threats to Americans. The FBI estimates that burglary and robbery cost the United States $3.8 billion a year. In contrast, auto repair fraud alone costs an estimated $40 billion and health care fraud an additional $100 to $400 billion a year (Mokhiber, 1999).

The general public actually views certain types of corporate crime (such as knowingly manufacturing defective products) as more serious than street crimes (Mokhiber, 2000). Yet the individuals and corporations responsible for these dangers rarely receive heavy criminal punishment (Reiman, 1998). Their offenses tend not to be treated as "real" crimes:

- In 1994 six U.S. airlines—American, Delta, Northwest, TWA, Alaska, and Continental—settled federal antitrust charges that they had collaborated illegally to raise airline ticket fares between 1988 and 1992. The price-fixing arrangement cost consumers some $4 billion in excess fares. No criminal charges were filed, however, and the airlines received no formal punishment. Under the settlement, they simply agreed not to use a computerized fare system to negotiate ticket-price changes anymore.
- In 1997 justice officials in Florida concluded that the Prudential Insurance Company of America, the nation's largest insurer, engaged in a deliberate scheme to cheat its customers for more than a decade. Instead of criminal prosecution, the company settled with the state for a fine of $15 million—a fraction of the $2 billion earned by defrauding customers for so long (Treaster & Petersen, 1997).
- In the 1980s and 1990s thousands of car owners complained to Ford Motor Company that their cars unexpectedly stalled, sometimes on highways and while making left turns across oncoming traffic. During this period there were numerous reports of serious, sometimes fatal accidents. Top Ford executives assured regulators that they didn't know what was causing the problem and that there was no reason compelling enough to warrant a costly recall of some 22 million cars manufactured between 1983 and 1995. However, internal documents discovered in 2000 showed that the company was well aware at the time that a faulty computerized ignition system would shut down the engine if it got too hot. A judge ordered a recall, but Ford continues to appeal that decision. Almost 15 million of these vehicles remain on the road today (Labaton & Bergman, 2000).

If you were an individual who had stolen millions of dollars from a bank, a shop owner who had defrauded your customers of billions of dollars, or a small businessperson who had knowingly manufactured a potentially lethal product, it's highly unlikely that you would be allowed to carry on with life as usual. Yet large corporations engage in such activities every day without much public outcry, moral panic, or legislative action. Most of them aren't even prosecuted under criminal statutes. Instead, we direct massive law enforcement efforts at "typical" street criminals such as beggars, thieves, prostitutes, and drug dealers.

The War on Drugs. Different cultures show varying levels of tolerance when it comes to drug use. For instance, throughout the South Pacific people commonly chew betel nuts for their stimulant effects; in the Bolivian and Peruvian Andes people chew coca leaves during their ordinary workday. The Huichol of central Mexico ingest peyote—a small cactus that produces hallucinations—as part of their religious rituals. And in the United States we wink at the use of substances that alter people's states of mind, such as coffee, chocolate, and alcohol.

But when it comes to illegal drugs, American attitudes change dramatically. The United States has been in an ill-defined, undeclared, but highly publicized "war" against illegal drugs for many years. There is a widespread belief on the part of the American public that drug users and drug dealers are enemies who are destroying the country and need to be stopped (E. Goode, 1989). Indeed, the term *drugs* itself has become an easy and safe scapegoat on which to focus collective hatred. More people are behind bars in the United States for drug offenses than are in prison for all crimes in England, France, Germany, and Japan combined (Egan, 1999b).

What prompts us to devote so much effort and so many resources to the war on drugs? For one thing, the United States has been described as a *temperance culture* (H. G. Levine, 1992)—one in which self-control and industriousness are perceived as desirable characteristics of productive citizens. In such an environment, drug-induced states of altered consciousness are likely to be perceived as a loss of control and thus feared as a dangerous threat to the economic and physical well-being of the population.

Many sociologists also argue that antidrug campaigns and legislative activities are driven chiefly by political and economic interests (see, for example, E. Goode, 1989). The war on drugs in the United States has permitted greater social control over groups perceived to be threatening, such as young minority men, and has mobilized voter support for candidates who profess to be "tough" on drugs. Capitalizing on the "drug menace" as a personal and societal threat is a common and effective political tactic (Ben-Yehuda, 1990).

Take, for instance, the highly publicized U.S. "crack epidemic." Crack, a smokeable form of cocaine, more potent and less expensive than the powdered form, appeared in late 1984 and early 1985 primarily in impoverished African-American and Latino inner-city neighborhoods. By 1986, terms such as the "crack epidemic" and the "crack plague" had seeped into the vocabulary of U.S. politicians and the news media. *Newsweek* called crack "the most addictive drug known to man." *U.S. News and World Report* proclaimed that it was "the No. 1 problem we face" (Reinarman & Levine, 1997). Television shows depicted the uncontrollable violence of "crackheads" and the tragedy of "crack babies." Congress toughened drug laws in response to crack.

In truth, however, most of the people who have tried crack have not become addicted to it. Crack has always been used heavily by the same population that has always used heroin heavily: the urban poor. Daily crack smoking occurs mostly among a small minority of the poorest segment of the population. Even at the height of the crack "epidemic," only a small percentage of people used it. Crack never became a wildly popular drug in the United States—or anywhere else, for that matter (Reinarman & Levine, 1997).

Furthermore, crack cannot be blamed for all the violence in U.S. society. In 1997, 3% of all violent crimes were committed by people under the influence of crack or cocaine; 21% were committed by people under the influence of alcohol ("Harper's Index," 1998b).

So a decade after crack became identified as the single most dangerous drug in U.S. society, it has all but disappeared from our cultural radar. Nevertheless, the social construction of the crack epidemic left its mark. It prompted the United States to make its drug laws more severe, lock up record numbers of people, and shift federal money from schools to prisons. Between 1986 and 1996, the number of people imprisoned for drug offenses grew by more than 400%, twice the rate of growth for violent offenders (Egan, 1999b).

The drug war is also big business. Budgets for drug law enforcement at home and abroad increased from about $1 billion in 1981 to more than $10 billion in 1996 (Bertram & Sharpe, 1998). In 1999, the Clinton administration proposed that federal antidrug budget be increased to close to $18 billion. This huge budget increase benefits not only the employees of drug enforcement agencies but also the employees and stockholders of companies that supply police and military equipment, build and run prisons, and produce antidrug advertising.

The very definition of which substances are "drugs" is influenced by powerful interests. Behind the phrase "the war on drugs" is the assumption that illegal drugs (marijuana, crack, cocaine, heroin, and so forth) are the most dangerous substances and the ones that must be eradicated. However, the difference between legal and illegal drugs is not necessarily a function of their relative danger. The National Commission on Marijuana and Drug Abuse defines a drug as any chemical that affects the structure and function of a living organism (cited in Fine, 1990). Such a definition includes alcohol, nicotine, caffeine, all types of prescription and over-the-counter medication, herbal remedies, and perhaps even salt and sugar. These substances, even though they can be harmful and addictive, are either completely legal or legal under certain restrictions.

Tobacco, for example, is a clearer health risk than either alcohol or marijuana but has only recently been discussed in terms of drug abuse. Not counting the death and sickness caused by inhaling secondhand smoke and by chewing it, tobacco is estimated to kill approximately 400,000 U.S. residents annually—the equivalent of three fully loaded jumbo jets crashing each day for an entire year (Paulos, 1995). For every U.S. resident who dies from illegal drug use, 21 die from smoking-related illnesses ("Harper's Index," 1996). However, knowing the hazards of cigarette smoking has not prompted our society to outlaw it entirely, as we have outlawed marijuana smoking and cocaine use. Criminalizing tobacco would have a disastrous impact on several large corporations and on several states whose economies depend on this crop.

The treatment of drug users also shows how conceptions of deviance are socially constructed. Society does not stigmatize and scorn "respectable" people addicted to legal substances. Police don't harass abusers of prescription drugs, ransack their homes, or develop creative ways of apprehending and arresting them. Yet such tactics—not to mention illegal searches and seizures, wiretapping, surveillance of the U.S. mail, and other invasions of privacy (Wisotsky, 1998)—may be used against "typical" addicts or suspected drug sellers, even if such measures cross the line of ethics and individual, constitutional rights. In 1991, for example, a Los Angeles woman and her three children were awakened in the middle of the night by a hand grenade exploding outside the front door of their apartment. As the windows shattered, several men in black hoods charged into the apartment with guns drawn. They were looking for the woman's cousin, a suspected drug dealer. The U.S. Supreme Court has upheld the constitutionality of such actions as long as the officers act in "good faith" (Duke, 1994).

The "drug courier profile" is another reflection of how the war on drugs has affected social relations. The profile is a set of characteristics used to identify drug smugglers in public facilities such as airports, train stations, bus depots, and interstate highways. Officers look for people who are obviously in a hurry, have bought a one-way ticket or paid for the ticket with cash, have changed travel plans at the last minute, are the first to get off the plane, or fly to or from Miami or Detroit or any other city with heavy drug traffic. The U.S. Supreme Court ruled in 1989 that such factors, as well as a person's physical appearance, can amount to a "reasonable suspicion." Hundreds of people are stopped and interrogated each week in the United States as they are boarding, arriving, or simply passing through an airport (Belkin, 1990). In addition, law enforcement agencies commonly recruit hotel managers and employees to act as confidential informers about people who fit the profile. Front desk clerks, bellhops, and porters are trained to be suspicious of people who ask for corner rooms, who haul trailers behind their cars, or who frequently move from room to room (Kocieniewski, 1999). Hotel managers routinely allow state troopers, without warrants, to look at the credit card receipts and registration information of all the guests. In return, the managers are assured that any searches or arrests will occur off hotel premises.

For all the reliance on the profiles, they have proved relatively ineffective. Statistics on airport searches in Denver, Pittsburgh, and Buffalo show that only about 3% of these searches result in an arrest (cited in Duke, 1994). Critics also argue that damaging stereotypes, particularly racial ones, are a key element of the drug courier profile. For instance, hotel informants are trained to pay particular attention to guests who speak Spanish. In 1991 the *Pittsburgh Press* examined 121 cases in which travelers were searched and no drugs were found. Of these people, 77% were black, Latino, or Asian. In Memphis about 75% of the air travelers stopped by Drug Enforcement agents were black, yet only 4% of the flying public is black. A Rutgers University statistician found that on a stretch of the New Jersey Turnpike, only 4.7% of all traffic consisted of late-model cars with out-of-state license plates driven by African-American men. However, more than 80% of the cars that were stopped and drivers who were interrogated on the highway fit that description (cited in Duke, 1994).

Meanwhile, little has been accomplished in the way of stopping the illegal activities of the rich and powerful interests that participate in the drug industry. Established financial institutions often launder drug money, despite laws against it (Parenti, 1995). Massive international crime organizations that ensure the flow of illicit drugs into the country have grown bigger and richer, despite a decades-long attempt to stop them

(Bullington, 1993). Unlike low-status users and small-time dealers of illegal drugs, these organizations wield tremendous economic power and political influence (Godson & Olson, 1995).

The Medicalization of Deviance

Given the fact that deviance designations are related to the economic and political power arrangements in society, how does a particular way of thinking about deviance become dominant? In Chapter 3 I described the actions of moral entrepreneurs—people or groups of people who crusade to have their versions of reality accepted by society at large. Moral entrepreneurs are usually interested in a single issue, be it abortion, drunk driving, child abuse, or offensive art. Occasionally, however, certain institutions become particularly influential in constructing an entire belief system that proposes causes of and solutions to a wide range of social problems. Instead of fighting for one particular issue, some institutions create an entire worldview.

Perhaps the most obvious and powerful force in defining deviance in the United States today is the medical establishment. The field of medicine has been extremely successful in presenting a conception of deviance that equates it with illness. Each time we automatically refer to bizarre or troublesome behavior as "sick," we help to perpetuate the perception that deviance is diseaselike. **Medicalization** is the definition of behavior as a medical problem or illness and the mandating or licensing of the medical profession to provide some type of treatment for it (Conrad, 1975). Many physicians, psychologists, psychiatrists, therapists, insurance agents, and the entire pharmaceutical industry in the United States benefit from a medicalized view of deviant behavior.

Conduct that was once categorized simply as misbehavior is now redefined as a psychiatric disease, disorder, or syndrome. Between 1952 and 1994 the number of mental disorders officially recognized by the American Psychiatric Association increased from 110 to 374 (Caplan, 1995). To accommodate the growing number of "illnesses," the number of psychiatric professionals and the number of people seeking psychiatric help have almost tripled over the last two decades. The U.S. government has estimated that the economic cost of mental health care is close to $55 billion a year (S. A. Kirk & Kutchins, 1992). The Surgeon General of the United States estimates that one in five U.S. residents can be diagnosed as having some sort of mental disorder in a given year and that half of all U.S. residents have such disorders at some time in their lives (cited in Pear, 1999a). Along with alcoholism, drug addiction, and mental illness, these disorders now include overeating, undereating, learning disabilities, shyness, violence, child abuse, addiction to using the Internet, and excessive gambling, shopping, and sex.

Why has the medical view of deviance become so dominant? One reason is that medical explanations of troublesome social problems and deviant behaviors are appealing to a society that wants simple explanations for complex social problems. If violent behavior is the result of a dysfunction in a person's brain, it then becomes a problem of defective, violent individuals, not of the larger societal context within which violent acts take place. Likewise, when our doctor or therapist tells us our anxiety, depression, crabbiness, and insecurity will vanish if we simply take an antidepressant drug, we are spared the difficult task of looking at the social complexities of our lives or the structure of our society.

The medicalization of deviance also appeals to humanitarian values. The designation of a problem as an illness removes legal and moral scrutiny or punishment in favor of therapeutic treatment (Zola, 1986). The alcoholic is no longer a sinner or a criminal but a victim, someone whose behavior is an "illness," beyond his or her control. Children who have trouble learning in school aren't disobedient and disruptive, they are "sick." If people are violating norms because of a disease that has invaded their bodies, they should not be held morally responsible. Medicalization creates less social stigma and condemnation of people labeled deviant.

But despite its enormous appeal, the tendency to medicalize deviance has serious social consequences (Conrad, 1975). These include the individualization of complex social issues and the depoliticization of deviance.

Individualizing Complex Social Issues. U.S. society often emphasizes the individual over the social structure. Instead of seeing certain deviant behaviors as symptomatic of a faulty social system—blocked economic opportunities, neighborhood decay, repressive social institutions, or unattainable cultural standards—people in the United States tend to see such behaviors as expressions of individual traits or shortcomings. Depression, alcoholism, eating disorders, and so on are "diseases" that lie within the person and hence can be remedied only through actions aimed at the individual (Kovel, 1980).

Individualistic medical explanations of deviance are not necessarily wrong. Many violent people do have brain diseases, and some schizophrenics do have chemical imbalances. But when we focus exclusively on these explanations, the solutions we seek focus on the perpetrator alone, to the exclusion of everything else.

Consider the problem of a disorder now commonly diagnosed in U.S. children—attention deficit hyperactivity disorder (ADHD). A child with ADHD is difficult to deal with at home and in the classroom. He or she fidgets and squirms, has difficulty remaining seated, can't sustain attention in tasks or play activities, can't follow rules, talks excessively, and is easily distracted (American Psychiatric Association, 1994).

Forty years ago these children were considered bad or troublesome and would have been subjected to punishment or expulsion from school. Today, however, most hyperactive behavior is diagnosed as a symptom of a mental disorder, and drugs are prescribed to treat it. It is estimated that 3 to 4 million children in the United States are taking drugs to curb their overactivity or inattentiveness (cited in Alessio & Condor, 1999). In one school district in the southeastern United States, 18–20% of fifth-grade boys were taking such drugs (cited in Koch, 1999). Production of Ritalin, the most popular of these drugs, has increased by nearly 500% since 1990 (Kolata, 1996; McGinnis, 1997).

Despite occasional adverse side effects, the drugs are generally successful in quieting unruly and annoying behavior (Whalen & Henker, 1977). In this sense the medicalization of hyperactivity is useful. As Peter Conrad (1975) writes, everyone involved benefits from the medical diagnosis and treatment of the problem:

Both the school and the parents are concerned with the child's behavior; the child is very difficult at home and disruptive in school. No punishments or rewards seem consistently to work in modifying the behavior; and both parents and school are at their wits' end. A medical evaluation is suggested. The diagnosis of hyperkinetic behavior leads to prescribing . . . medications. The child's behavior seems to become more socially acceptable, reducing problems in school and at home. (p. 19)

But are we ignoring the possibility that these actions may be a child's adaptation to his or her social environment? Hyperactive behavior may be a response to an educational system that is set up to discourage individual expression (Conrad, 1975). Narrowly defined norms of acceptable behavior make it difficult if not impossible for children to pursue their own desires and needs. Some pediatricians argue that the symptoms of ADHD may just be children's natural reaction to living in a fast-paced, stressful world (Diller, 1998). Critics of the use of drugs also worry about the mixed messages children receive when they are handed a daily pill to medicate away their troublesome behavior, while at the same time they're being told to say "no" to drugs (Koch, 1999).

I'm not suggesting that all children who are diagnosed with ADHD are disruptive because they are bored in school or because their individual creativity and vitality have been discouraged. The point is that from an institutional perspective, the labeling of disruptiveness as an individual disorder serves the interests of the school system by protecting its legitimacy and authority. The institution could not function if disruptiveness were tolerated (Tobin, Wu, & Davidson, 1989). But if the educational system promoted and encouraged free individual expression instead of obedience and discipline, overactivity wouldn't be considered disruptive and wouldn't be a problem in need of a solution.

When inconvenient behavior is translated into an individual sickness, medical remedies (that is, drugs) become a convenient tool for enforcing conformity and upholding the values of society. Indeed, we have come to rely on drugs not just to cure infections or fight pain but to help us through many of our common problems in living, such as anxiety, sleep problems, overeating, sadness, fears and so on. The drug Prozac, in particular, has become so popular that it has become a prominent feature of the culture.

● **Micro-Macro Connection**
Prozac and the Pharmaceutical Personality

Since its introduction in 1987, close to 35 million people worldwide have taken the antidepressant drug Prozac. Almost as soon as it hit the market, it was being hailed as a miracle drug. Not only was it effective in treating depression and easy to prescribe, it was relatively free of side effects such as the weight gain, low blood pressure, irregular heart rhythms, and so on common with other drug treatments. By 1990 Prozac had become the top-selling antidepressant in the world, a position it continues to hold. Although sales have stabilized in the past few years as similar antidepressants entered the market, Prozac still brings in close to $3 billion in annual revenues (Zuckoff, 2000).

Prozac has grown to be more than just a treatment for depression, however. It is now regularly prescribed for people with eating disorders, obsessive-compulsive disorders, anxiety disorders, social phobias, obesity, gambling addiction, premenstrual syndrome, and family problems. Some people use it to enhance job performance, improve their alertness and concentration, overcome boredom, think more clearly, become more assertive, or get along better with their mates. Perhaps the fastest-growing market for Prozac is among children. In the United States, prescriptions for Prozac and Prozac-type drugs for people under 18 rose from 410,000 in 1994 to 735,000 in 1996, an increase of 80% (Crowley, 1997). In 1999, physicians wrote 3,000 prescriptions for Prozac for infants under a year old ("Top 10 drugs," 1999). It's even used to treat the behavior problems of dogs and cats.

Clearly, Prozac's initial realm of clinical depression has expanded to include more of what were once thought of as ordinary life stresses. In his book *Listening to Prozac* (1997), psychiatrist Peter Kramer—an avid proponent and energetic prescriber of the drug—argues that Prozac can (and perhaps should) also be used to remove aspects of our personality we find objectionable. He likens the use of Prozac in overcoming undesirable psychological traits to the use of cosmetic surgery in overcoming undesirable physical ones.

Most people who have benefited from Prozac describe it in adoring, almost worshipful terms. They weren't healed, they were transformed. Shy introverts report turning into social butterflies, mediocre workers turn into on-the-job dynamos, the bored become interested and alert, even the unattractive begin to feel more beautiful. One woman, referring to this apparent change in physical appeal, reported that "people on the sidewalk [now] ask me for directions!" (Kramer, 1997, p. 8). Some people see Prozac as nothing short of a divine creation:

> As my husband and I watched the results of Prozac, we knew that the medication was God's gift to us. Breakthroughs . . . like Prozac are evidence of His grace. I now *feel* God's love for me as I never have before. . . . I believe that it is helping me be more true to the person God created me to be [emphasis in original]. (quoted in "Christian faith," 1995, p. 17)

According to Kramer, his patients feel "better than well" shortly after they begin taking the drug. They report noticeable improvement in their popularity, business sense, self-image, energy, and sexual appeal (Kramer, 1997). One patient was having trouble at work and had recently broken up with her boyfriend. Kramer prescribed Prozac. Within weeks she was dating several men and handling her job demands smoothly. She even received a substantial pay raise. So enthusiastic was her loyalty to the drug that she happily referred to herself as "Ms. Prozac."

Prozac is appealing for economic reasons as well. Because traditional psychotherapy (patients talking to therapists about their problems) is time consuming and expensive, efforts to cut health care costs work against its use. A psychiatrist may charge over $150 for an hour-long session. Prozac, which is one of the most expensive antidepressants, still costs only about $15 a week. Many prepaid health care plans have begun to limit or exclude extensive talk therapy in their coverage, thereby indirectly encouraging greater use of such drugs as Prozac (Cooper, 1994).

In light of these benefits, we should perhaps not be surprised that Prozac has become a cultural icon. I recently saw a bumper sticker that said, "Mean people need Prozac." The drug pops up in magazine cartoons and David Letterman jokes. In 1993 a picture of the pill made the cover of *Newsweek*. A popular cocktail drink, "Cranzac," combines Prozac and cranberry juice for those unable to tolerate full doses of the drug. Even the word *Prozac* has become a metaphor for a quick-relief cure-all. Commenting on the effectiveness of job training programs in helping the unemployed and underemployed, the editor of the *Washington Post* once said, "Employment training programs are no Prozac for an anxious age" (quoted in Sorohan, 1995, p. 11). One writer noted that "Prozac has attained the familiarity of Kleenex and the social status of spring water" (Crowley, 1994, p. 41).

Prozac certainly has helped millions of people in serious need. However, its popularity raises fundamental sociological questions about the role drugs ought to play in everyday life. Critics fear that Prozac—as well as other drugs that can modify character—is aimed not so much at "sick patients" as at people who already function at a high level and want enriched memory, enhanced intelligence, heightened concentration, and a transformation of bad moods into good ones (Begley, 1994).

If Prozac does make people "better than well," how might its growing popularity affect social life? In a fast-paced, achievement-oriented society such as the United States, the motivations for gaining a competitive edge—whether in school, on the job, or in interpersonal relations—are obvious. Those who earn higher grades, sell more cars, or come across as more charming and attractive can reap enormous financial and social benefits.

But once people begin to use a drug to chemically enhance performance, those who do not use the drug—whether for reasons of principle or because they can't afford it—risk losing out and becoming the less rewarded and less valuable members of the community (D. J. Rothman, 1994). Would we, as a society, have to resort to legal regulation—much like the ban on athletic performance enhancers such as anabolic steroids—to prevent a desperate race to keep up?

On a more profound level, if we can use existing pharmaceutical technology to chemically eradicate sadness and despair—to create a world in which pain can be "erased as easily and fully as dirty words on a school blackboard" (Mauro, 1994, p. 46)—why would anyone ever put up with emotional discomfort? In the past, people simply assumed that despair was part of the human condition. Suffering made us stronger. Just as physical pain prevents us from burning ourselves if we get too close to a fire, perhaps mental pain, too, serves a purpose, such as motivating us to change life situations that are getting us into trouble. But people today are more inclined to believe they have a right not to be unhappy. Sadness is inconvenient and prevents us from reaching our potential. Yet do we want a society free of undesirable emotions, where people are "shiny and happy" all the time?

Such questions, of course, are hypothetical. Prozac hasn't yet completely redefined society. Surely depression, unlike polio or smallpox, will never be totally eradicated. But the technological possibilities raise important issues about the role of medicine in defining deviance, controlling behavior, constructing personality, and ultimately determining social life and the culture that guides it.

Depoliticizing Deviant Behavior. The process of individualizing and medicalizing social problems robs deviant behavior of its power to send a message about malfunctioning elements of society. The legitimacy of disruptive behaviors or statements is automatically destroyed when they are seen as symptoms of individual defects or illnesses. We need not pay attention to the critical remarks of an opponent if that opponent is labeled as mentally ill. Political dissidents in totalitarian countries are often declared insane and confined to hospitals in an attempt to quiet dangerous political criticism. The Chinese government, for instance, has forcibly hospitalized and medicated hundreds of followers of the outlawed spiritual movement, Falun Gong, which it has condemned as a dangerous cult (Eckholm, 2001).

Such practices are not found only in foreign countries. In 1945 the famous U.S. poet Ezra Pound, who was living in Italy, was brought back to the United States to stand trial for treason. He was accused of making anti–United States radio broadcasts from Rome during World War II. But the court, prosecution, and defense, together with several psychiatrists, agreed that he was mentally unfit to stand trial. He was committed to St. Elizabeth's Mental Hospital in Washington, DC, where he remained for the next 13 years. Although some have argued that confining Pound in a mental hospital helped him avoid an almost certain prison sentence, others suggest that declaring him "mentally ill" not only punished him for subversive conduct but also allowed the government to discount statements he had made that attempted to undermine the U.S. war effort.

Nor is the political use of medicalization restricted to the distant past. A *Dallas Morning News* investigation discovered that high-ranking U.S. military commanders have tried to discredit and intimidate subordinates who report security and safety violations or military overpricing by ordering them to undergo psychiatric evaluations or by sending them to a mental ward (Timms & McGonigle, 1992). One West Point cadet spent a month in a psychiatric ward for reporting widespread illegal drug use at the academy. He met officer patients in the ward who had objected to army policy and who were involuntarily receiving electric shock treatments. And a chief petty officer in the air force contends that his forced hospitalization was part of a retaliation for reporting payroll abuses at Dallas Naval Air Station. He insightfully describes the power of medical labels to discredit his political criticism: "What happened was nobody would speak to me. Let's face it. After someone has gone to a mental ward, you kind of question what's going on. It was a nice ploy, and it worked. What they did was totally neutralize me" (quoted in Timms & McGonigle, 1992).

Portraying deviants as sick people who must be dealt with through medical therapies is a powerful way for dominant groups in society to maintain conformity and protect themselves from those whom they fear or who challenge the way "normal" social life is organized (Pfohl, 1994). The seemingly merciful medical labels not only reduce individual responsibility but also reduce the likelihood that such potentially contagious political behavior will be taken seriously (Hills, 1980).

CONCLUSION

When we talk about deviance, we usually speak of extreme forms: crime, mental illness, substance abuse, and so on. These activities are indeed troublesome, but for most people they remain comfortably distant phenomena. I think most of us would like to cling to the belief that deviants are "them" and normal people are "us."

The lesson I want you to take away from this chapter, however, is that the issue of deviance is, essentially, an issue of social definition. As a group, community, or society, we decide which differences are benign and which are devalued. Standards and expectations change. Norms come and go. The consequence is that each of us could be considered deviant to some degree by some audience. We have all broken unspoken interactional norms; many of us have even broken the law. To a lesser degree, we are all potentially like Kelly Michaels, subject to being erroneously labeled deviant and unfairly treated as a result. Given the right—or wrong—circumstances, all of us run the risk of being negatively labeled or acquiring a bad reputation.

This chapter has examined deviance as both a micro- and a macro-level sociological phenomenon, as something that plays a profound role in both individual lives and in society as a whole. Although sociologists are interested in the broad social and political processes that create cultural definitions of deviance, they are also interested in the ways these definitions are applied in everyday life. Societal definitions have their most potent effect when expressed face to face. We can talk about such powerful institutions as medicine creating definitions of deviance that are consistent with broader political or economic interests, but if these definitions aren't accepted as appropriate to some degree by a majority, they will be ineffectual. Again, we see the value of developing the sociological imagination, which helps us understand the complex interplay between individuals and the culture and community within which they live.

YOUR TURN

People's perceptions of deviant acts and individuals are a crucial element of our understanding of deviance. From a conflict perspective, these perceptions are usually consistent with the goals and interests of those in power. But what exactly are people's perceptions of deviance?

Make copies of the following list, and find 20 to 30 people who would be willing to read it and answer a few questions. Try to get an equal proportion of males and females and younger and older people. Have each person rank the following "deviant" acts in order from 1 to 15, with 15 being the most serious and 1 the least serious. Do not define for them what is meant by "serious."

- Catching your spouse with a lover and killing them both
- Embezzling your employer's funds
- Robbing a supermarket with a gun
- Forcibly raping a stranger in a park
- Selling liquor to minors
- Killing a suspected burglar in your home
- Practicing medicine without a license

- Soliciting for prostitution
- Hitting your child
- Selling cocaine
- Manufacturing and selling cars known to have dangerous defects
- Forcibly raping a former spouse
- Being drunk in public
- Killing a person for a fee
- Conspiring to fix the prices of machines sold to businesses

After the volunteers are finished, ask them how they decided on their rankings. What criteria did they use for judging the seriousness of each act? Where did their perceptions come from? Why do they think the "less serious" acts on the list are against the law?

After collecting all your data, compute the average ranking for each of the 15 items. (For each item, add all the ranking scores and divide by the number of responses.) The larger the average score, the more the perceived seriousness of that act. Which acts were considered the most serious and which the least serious? Was there a fair amount of agreement among the people in your sample? Were there any differences between the ratings of men and women? Between older and younger people? Between people of different racial or ethnic groups? Use the conflict perspective to discuss the role these perceptions play in the nature and control of deviance.

Source: The 15 items in this exercise are adapted from Rossi, Waite, Bose, and Berk, 1974.

CHAPTER HIGHLIGHTS

- According to an absolutist definition of deviance, there are two fundamental types of behavior: that which is inherently acceptable and that which is inherently unacceptable. In contrast, a relativist definition of deviance suggests that it is not a property inherent in any particular act, belief, or condition. Instead, deviance is a definition of behavior that is socially created by collective human judgments. Hence, like beauty, deviance is in the eye of the beholder.

- According to conflict theory, the definition of deviance is a form of social control exerted by more powerful people and groups over less powerful ones.

- The labeling theory of deviance argues that deviance is a consequence of the application of rules and sanctions to an offender. Deviant labels can impede everyday social life by forming expectations in the minds of others.

- The criminal justice system and the medical profession have had a great deal of influence in defining, explaining, and controlling deviant behavior. Criminalization is the process by which certain behaviors come to be defined as crimes. Medicalization is the depiction of deviance as a medical problem or illness.

KEY TERMS

absolutism Approach to analyzing deviance that rests on the assumption that all human behavior can be considered either inherently good or inherently bad

criminalization Official definition of an act of deviance as a crime

deterrence theory Theory of deviance positing that people will be prevented from engaging in deviant acts if they judge the costs of such an act to outweigh its benefits

deviance Behavior, ideas, or attributes of an individual or group that some people in society find offensive

labeling theory Theory stating that deviance is the consequence of the application of rules and sanctions to an offender; a deviant is an individual to whom the identity "deviant" has been successfully applied

medicalization Definition of behavior as a medical problem and mandating the medical profession to provide some kind of treatment for it

relativism Approach to analyzing deviance that rests on the assumption that deviance is socially created by collective human judgments and ideas

Graffiti and the Eye of the Beholder

James Prigoff

Most people would consider graffiti an ugly form of deviant expression that defaces property. Yet the deviant nature of graffiti is a matter of judgment and evaluation. The identity of the individual or group responsible for creating graffiti may be more relevant to its being called "deviant" than are the painted drawings or words themselves.

● These murals are by "Twist" (Barry McGee), a graffiti artist in San Francisco. Twist's work has also been displayed at the San Jose Art Museum (1994).

The world of the graffiti artist is a diverse subculture with its own well-defined language, roles, and standards of excellence:

> Kids call it tagging. To most adults, it is nothing but ugly, hostile graffiti, as unavoidable as a scream . . . insistent and rude as rap from a boom box. . . . Whatever else it is, this is lettering on public display, far different from the dismal scrawling on a public toilet. This is script as stylized as the uniform of teen urban life—the bandanna, the baseball cap worn backwards, the Raiders football jacket. (Richard Rodriguez)

New York–style graffiti—and its artistic outgrowth, spraycan art, which originated in the train yards of New York City in the 1960s—has come to communicate everything from simple group identity and political ideology to messages about anger, rebellion, and power. Recognition motivates many. Says Alex Alvarez, a graffiti painter,

> I write my name up there and then maybe paint a little extra picture around it and— KA POW!—I'm famous. It's a real rush.

● Mural in San Francisco by Omega, Hex, Raevyn, Crayone, Picasso, Toons, Benz, and Ink.

● Lask with his mural "Wine" in Staten Island, New York.

● Painted by Apolonari in Oakland, California.

Is graffiti always deviant? Is it art or vandalism? At contemporary art shows, large pieces of graffiti art can sell for as much as $100,000. Well-known artists like Keith Haring and Jean-Michel Basquiat spray-painted graffiti on doors before they became famous. What is the difference between graffiti sprayed on a garbage truck, a commissioned mural carrying the name of a political candidate during a campaign, and a soft drink advertisement painted on the side of a city bus? Who gets to write and draw on public property?

● Without permission youths practiced their calligraphy and design skills on this sanitation truck.

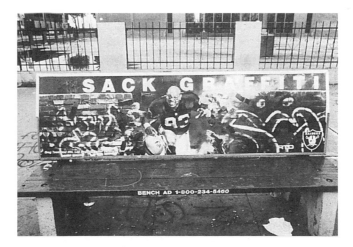

● Cities and private groups still fight graffiti, but mainstream culture sends conflicting messages.

● Jerry Brown commissioned Frame, a spray can artist, to paint a mural on a bus to advertise Brown's presidential candidacy.

● Corporate "graffiti": A Pepsi ad completely covers this San Francisco bus.

● Chrysler created its own "graffiti": altered ads for its Plymouth Neon. The ads started out with a plain white background, an image of the car, and the simple message "Hi." In subsequent weeks, the advertisers added letters, graffiti-style, to spell out "Hip" and "Chill." The outcry from antigraffiti organizations prompted the public relations manager for the Chrysler Corporation to issue a formal statement: "We don't promote or condone graffiti or the destruction of property. The campaign [has been] successful. It's given the car a personality."

8

Building Social Relationships: Intimacy and Families

Life in Groups

Family Life

Family and Social Structure

Family Dilemmas

The end of the 20th century was a strange and highly public time for the type of social relationships that are normally considered private:

- Celebrities such as Jack Nicholson, Eddie Murphy, Anthony Quinn, Madonna, Jodie Foster, Michelle Pfeiffer, Rosie O'Donnell, and Warren Beatty became unwed parents at a time when over 30% of all births are to unmarried mothers.
- A Virginia woman made national headlines for months after she sliced off her husband's penis after he had allegedly repeatedly raped her. That same year, 3 to 4 million women were battered by their husbands.
- The top-rated prime-time television show for the week of April 3, 2000, was *Who Wants to Marry a Millionaire?*—a show in which 50 women competed to marry a wealthy man they had never seen.
- On a Web site established in 1999, the eggs of fashion models were put up for auction to those who want to create beautiful babies from a stranger's genetic material.
- A member of the 1996 gold medal U.S. Olympic gymnastics team sued for independence from her parents, alleging that they had squandered her fortune and oppressed her for years.
- While legislators in Vermont and Hawaii engaged in heated debate over granting gay couples the legal right to marry, a Canadian court overturned the definition of "spouse" as heterosexual.

Some people might see these events as proof of the demise of the "traditional" family and the breakdown of society; others see them as a neutral sign of changing societal circumstances.

Like every other aspect of our individual lives, close relationships must be understood within the broader contours of our society. We often fail to realize that laws, customs, and social institutions regulate what we can and can't do with our intimate partners, relatives, friends, and associates (Cherlin, 1978). This chapter takes a sociological peek into the private and public aspects of social relationships. Specifically, it explores the role that social relationships, especially family bonds, play in our daily lives and some of the social processes that take place within small, close-knit groups. How are these relationships established? Why are they so important to us? How do societal factors such as social institutions, gender, race, and social class affect our perceptions of intimacy and belonging? And why are the desirable aspects of these relationships so often outweighed by the negative, such as family violence?

Life in Groups

The quality and quantity of our social relationships—whether they link associates, friends, or family members—are the standard against which many of us judge the quality and happiness of our lives (Campbell, Converse, & Rodgers, 1976). We spend a tremendous amount of time worrying about present relationships, contemplating new ones, obsessing over past ones, or fretting over the fact that we are currently not part of one. Three of the most popular films of 2000—*What Women Want, Family Man,* and *Cast Away*—all focused on characters whose career choices had left them psychologically isolated from their loved ones. Indeed, the search for a sense of belonging and closeness has become one of the prime obsessions of the 21st century. Popular magazines, self-help books, advice columns, supermarket tabloids, Web sites, chat rooms, and television talk shows overflow with advice, warnings, and pseudoscientific analyses of every conceivable aspect of a relationship.

Not surprisingly, at a time when we hunger for intimacy and sometimes pay tidy sums of money attempting to get it, our social relationships are fraught with difficulty. People who live in complex, urban, industrial or postindustrial societies have gradually become less integrated and connected to others. We're more mobile in our careers, more willing to relocate, and thus more likely to break ties with friends and fellow members of religious, sports, and social groups than people were, say, a century ago. In the United States, the proportion of people who socialize with neighbors more than once a year has steadily declined over the last two decades. Membership in church-related groups, civic organizations (such as the Red Cross, Boy Scouts, and PTA), and fraternal organizations (such as the Lions, Elks, and Shriners) has likewise decreased. Between 1980 and 1993 the total number of bowlers in the United States increased by 10%, but team bowling in organized leagues decreased by 40% (Putnam, 1995). During the same period, the number of U.S. adults living alone almost doubled; single people who have never married now make up about one-fourth of the adult population in this country (U.S. Bureau of the Census, 2000b).

Some sociologists attribute these trends to U.S. culture's emphasis on individualism. It takes away a sense of community, diminishing the ability to establish ties with others and making it easier for people to walk away from groups that they see as unfulfilling (Bellah et al., 1985; Sidel, 1986). In a national poll, 25% of Americans said that for $10 million they'd abandon their entire family (J. Peterson & Kim, 1991). The high value that contemporary society places on individual achievement and success sometimes makes social relationships, even family relationships, seem expendable.

By contrast, in collectivist societies such as India and Japan, group ties play a more substantial role in people's everyday lives. Duty, sacrifice, and compromise are considered more desirable traits than personal success and individual achievement.

Group connections are assumed to be the best guarantee for an individual's well-being. Hence, feelings of group loyalty and responsibility for other members tend to be strong.

Even in most individualistic cultures, however, social relationships play an important societal role: They help to control the actions of individuals by socializing group members to a particular set of norms and values. Perhaps you've expressed an opinion or engaged in some behavior that met with disapproval from your friends or class-mates. Or maybe you expressed an unpopular political sentiment at the family dinner table or dated someone your parents despised. If so, you certainly know the discomfort of standing out and violating a group's standards. Whenever a member says or does something that is out of line with group norms, other members may increase their communication with that person in an effort to change her or his mind (Rodin, 1985). Or they may simply reject him or her, either blatantly or subtly (Schacter, 1951). Rejecting the "deviant" is a means of reestablishing equilibrium within the group and ensuring that its values and perceptions remain dominant.

Despite the inevitable conflicts in close groups and the difficulties of maintaining ties in an individualistic, mobile, high-tech society, people place a high value on belonging and intimacy. We are spending more time than ever at work, sometimes to the detriment of our relationships with families, neighbors, and the community. But we are also seeking closer ties with the people in our workplace (Wuthnow, 1994). In small groups of colleagues and like-minded co-workers, people may find the sense of belonging that is harder to come by these days from more traditional sources.

Micro-Macro Connection
Virtual Communities in the Global Village

Ironically, we are learning to use the very technology that has physically separated us—cars, planes, phones, e-mail—to establish and maintain relationships over long distances (Wellman & Gulia, 1999). For instance, **virtual communities** are groups of people who communicate with one another electronically, not face-to-face. Usually virtual communities are populated by people who share a common interest, even though they've never met in person and may reside in different countries. They can take the form of a mailing list on a particular topic, or they can be Web sites with chat rooms for real-time discussions. Such communities can overcome the time and place constraints that limit the establishment of more traditional face-to-face groups. So, for instance, if you are unable to sleep at 3 o'clock in the morning, you can go on-line, where you're bound to find someone to talk to or exchange ideas.

These connections usually don't require huge investments of time, money, or energy. You can participate for any length of time at your own convenience. And they are long term in that they aren't disrupted, as real-world communities tend to be, when people relocate.

In contrast with in-person situations—where people are typically reluctant to speak, let alone share deep secrets, with a stranger—in virtual communities people often find quick social support and a sense of camaraderie. For instance, whereas most elderly users of "SeniorNet" joined to gain access to information, most stay because of the companionship. The most popular activity among participants at this site is "chatting with others" (Wellman & Gulia, 1999).

But to what extent do virtual communities approximate real ones? Can relationships formed on-line ever completely substitute for those established in the physical world? Can a cyberhug be as gratifying as a face-to-face hug? According to one sociologist, virtual communities can reach the highest levels of intimacy if the number of participants is kept relatively small, admission to the group is controlled to foster friendliness and trust, and people present themselves honestly (Etzioni, 2000). Indeed, people in virtual communities can do many of the things they'd do together in a face-to-face relationship—fight, flirt, console, criticize, nurture, share, grieve, and so forth. Much of the research on this question shows that strong ties established on-line have many characteristics similar to strong "real world" ties, such as encouraging frequent contact and being mutually supportive (Wellman & Gulia, 1999). Some people report that their closest friends are members of their electronic group. And I'm sure you've heard stories about people marrying someone they first met on the Internet.

However, virtual communities do have some disadvantages. For one thing, the interaction between individuals occurs exclusively in the domain of written words. As you saw in Chapter 6, in everyday life a great deal of information is provided through nonverbal communication, something absent from computer-based conversation. In addition, lacking the sense of commitment that traditionally binds groups together, a member of a virtual community can simply leave an interaction whenever she or he wants simply by "exiting" the session.

Furthermore, virtual communities cannot provide the sort of subtle biographical knowledge that is often established in traditional communities. Here's how one author contrasts the real-world community of her father, who had recently died in a plane crash, with virtual communities:

> [His neighbors] knew his comings and goings, his eccentricities. They had been to his house for dinner and heard his stories, his endless repertory of jokes, his theories. They had known when he had visitors and when he was out of town. They knew that he had been growing tomatoes and that he had worried that the tomatoes wouldn't ripen before the first frost. They argued with him at town meetings and read the letters he sent to the local paper. . . . Even if they hadn't known him well, they had seen him in his everyday life. (Hafner, 1999, p. D10)

For this person, virtual communities could not provide the same relationships that real-world communities provide. But for others, the ties that people develop in cyberspace can sometimes be just as fulfilling and just as supportive. Indeed, on-line relationships established with people worldwide may be more stimulating than relationships established in a local neighborhood, because they encourage the crossing of ethnic, racial, class, and cultural barriers. The irony, of course, is that in the process of establishing such global connections, community interaction has moved out of public spaces, making people's lives more physically isolated than ever before.

Family Life

Groups are obviously important to social functioning. But of all the groups we belong to, the most important is the family. Family provides the relationships that give us a sense of identity and personal history. Perhaps no facet of human existence is more familiar to us or occupies more time, effort, and emotion. Most of us spend our childhood and adolescence in some kind of family, go through the sometimes painful rituals of dating, fall in love, and become spouses, parents, and grandparents. Many of us have seen the dark side of these relationships, too: divorce, abuse, and violence.

Historical Trends in Family Life

Many functionalist sociologists have voiced concern over the current state of the family as an important social institution. Over time, they argue, the family has been losing many, if not all, of its traditional purposes (Lasch, 1977). Historically, the family was the center of many important activities. It was where children received most of their education and religious training. It was where both children and adults could expect to receive emotional nurturing and support. It was the institution that regulated sexual activity and reproduction. And it was also the economic center of society, where family members worked together to earn a living and support one another financially.

But as an economy shifts from a system based on small, privately owned agricultural enterprises to one based on massive industrial manufacturing, the role of the family changes. Economic production moves from the home to the factory, and families become more dependent on the money that members earn outside the home. The teaching of skills and values that were once a part of everyday home life begin to take place almost exclusively in the schools. Even the family's role as a source of emotional security and nurturing disappears as it becomes less able to shield its members from the harsh realities of modern life (Lasch, 1977).

For all these reasons many people, from research scholars to politicians to everyday people on the street, are concerned about the survival of the contemporary family. Anxiety over the future of families has generated some strident calls, in societies throughout the world, for a return to the "good ol' days" of family life. The belief in a lost "golden age" of family has led some to depict the present as a period of rapid decline and inevitable family breakdown (Coontz, 1992; Hareven, 1992; Skolnick, 1991). However, although concern over the state of the family is particularly acute today, it is important to realize that each succeeding generation has been concerned about a "crisis of the family" (Hareven, 1992; Skolnick, 1991). Families have always been diverse in structure and have always faced difficulties protecting members from economic hardship, internal violence, political upheaval, and social change.

According to sociologist William J. Goode (1971), the traditional family of the past that people in the United States speak so fondly of and want to re-create never existed. He calls the idealized image of the past "the classical family of Western nostalgia":

> It is a pretty picture of life down on grandma's farm. There are lots of happy children, and many kinfolk live together in a large rambling house. Everyone works hard. Most of the food to be eaten during the winter is grown, preserved, and stored on the

farm. . . . Father is stern and reserved and has the final decision in all important matters. . . . All boys and girls marry, and marry young. . . . After marriage, the couple lives harmoniously, either near the boy's parents or with them. . . . No one divorces. (p. 624)

Like most stereotypes, this one is not altogether accurate. Because 19th-century American adults had a shorter life expectancy than adults today, children were actually *more* likely to live in a single-parent home at that time, because of the death of a parent (Kain, 1990). Even children fortunate enough to come from intact families usually left home to work as servants or apprentices in other people's homes. Furthermore, though close to 20% of U.S. children live in poverty today, about the same proportion lived in orphanages at the turn of the century—and not just because their parents had died. Many were there because their parents simply couldn't afford to raise them. Rates of alcohol and drug abuse, school dropouts, and domestic violence were all higher a century ago than they are today (Coontz, 1992).

Perhaps the most pervasive myth is that of the primacy of the **extended family**—several generations living under the same roof. Today's more isolated **nuclear family**, consisting only of mother, father, and children, is often compared unfavorably to the image of the huge, happy family of the past with its massive and perpetually available support network. Research shows, however, that U.S. families have always been fairly small and primarily nuclear (Blumstein & Schwartz, 1983; W. J. Goode, 1971; Hareven, 1992). This country has no strong tradition of large extended families. In fact, the highest proportion of extended family households ever recorded was only around 20%, between 1850 and 1885 (Hareven, 1978). Because people didn't live as long as they do today, most died before ever seeing their grandchildren. Even in the 1700s the typical family consisted of a husband, a wife, and approximately three children.

When households of the past were large, it was probably due to the presence of nonfamily members: servants, apprentices, boarders, and visitors. The reduction in average household size we've seen over the last several centuries was not caused by a decline in the number of extended relatives but by a decrease in nonfamily members living in a household, a reduction in the number of children in a family, and an increase in young adults living alone (Kobrin, 1976).

As people immigrated to the United States from countries that did have a tradition of extended families, such as China or Italy, often their first order of business was to surrender their extended families so they could create their own households. Reducing the size of their families was seen as a clear sign that they had become Americans. Large, multigenerational families simply didn't make economic sense anymore. Being able to move to a different state to pursue a job would be next to impossible with a bunch of grandparents, aunts, uncles, and cousins in tow.

In addition, it's not at all clear that families today are as isolated as some people make them out to be. More U.S. residents than ever have grandparents alive, and the ties between grandparents and grandchildren may be stronger than ever. Today, most adults see or talk to a parent on the phone at least once a week (Coontz, 1992). Extended family members may not live under the same roof, but they do stay in contact and provide advice, emotional support, and financial help when needed (Cicirelli, 1983).

Another oft-cited indicator of the demise of the U.S. family that is based on faulty conceptions of the past is the current high divorce rate. Most of us assume that the divorce rate in this country was always very low until it accelerated with unprecedented speed during the 1960s and 1970s. Many observers fear that the intact middle-class lifestyle depicted in 1950s television shows such as *Ozzie and Harriet, Father Knows Best*, and *Leave It to Beaver* has crumbled away forever. The rise in the divorce rate has been attributed to the free-love movement of "swinging singles, open marriages, alternative lifestyles, and women's liberation" (Skolnick, 1991). True, the 1960s and 1970s were a revolutionary period in U.S. history. Norms governing all aspects of social life were certainly changing.

What these conclusions overlook, however, is the longer historical trend in divorce. People were comparing divorce rates in the 1960s and 1970s to the abnormally low rate of the 1950s. From this narrow perspective the divorce rate did, indeed, appear to shoot up. But divorce in this country had been increasing steadily since 1900 (see Exhibit 8.1). It rose sharply right after World War II, most likely because of short courtships before the young men shipped out and the subsequent stress of separation. In the 1950s the rate dropped just as sharply. The high divorce rates of the 1960s and 1970s, then, represented somewhat of a return to a national trend that had been developing since the turn of the century. Indeed, in the 1990s, the rate actually decreased.

Furthermore, the rate of "hidden" marital separation a hundred years ago was probably not that much less than the rate of "visible" separation today (Sennett, 1984).

Exhibit 8.1 **Historical Trends in American Divorce**

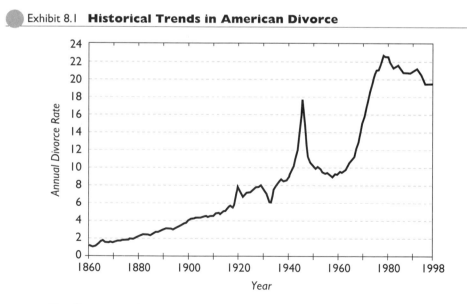

Note: Divorce rate for 1860–1920 is number of divorces per 1,000 existing marriages; for 1920–1996, divorces per 1,000 married women ages 15 and older.

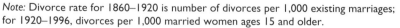

Sources: Cherlin, 1992; U.S. Bureau of the Census, 1998c, 2000b.

For financial or religious reasons, divorce was not an option for many people in the past. For instance, divorce rates actually fell during the Great Depression of the 1930s. Did this mean that economic hardships were bringing more couples closer together so that spouses could provide one another with love and support that would get them through tough times? Hardly. With jobs and housing scarce, many couples simply couldn't afford to divorce. Rates of marital unhappiness and domestic violence actually increased. A significant number of people turned to the functional equivalents of divorce—desertion and abandonment—which have been around for centuries. So you can see that the divorce rate may have been lower in the past, but families found other ways to break up.

In sum, the image of a warm, secure, stable family life in past times is at odds with the actual history of U.S. families (Skolnick, 1991). Calls for a return to the "good ol' days" are, in the end, calls for a return to something that has never truly existed. By glorifying a mythical and idealized past, we artificially limit ourselves to an inaccurate image of what we think a "normal" family ought to look like.

The Culture of Intimacy and Family

Families can be found in every human society, and from a functionalist perspective, they all address similar societal needs: regulating sexual behavior, creating new members of society to replace those who die, and protecting and socializing the young. However, the way families go about meeting these needs—their structure, customs, patterns of authority, and so on—differ widely across cultures. Thus ideas about what a family is and how people should behave within it are culturally determined.

Cultural Variation in Family Practices. Most of us take for granted that **monogamy**, the marriage of one man and one woman, is the fundamental building block of the family. Some families do exist without a married couple, and some people may have several spouses over their lifetimes. But monogamous marriage is undeniably an integral part of our image of the family.

In the United States, monogamous marriage continues to be the only adult intimate relationship that is endorsed by the Internal Revenue Service, legally recognized, and culturally approved. It is still the one relationship in which sexual activity is not only acceptable but expected. Monogamous marriage, like the family in general, is an institution, a patterned way of life that includes a set of commonly known roles, statuses, and expectations:

> People know about it; they can describe it; and they have spent a lifetime learning how to react to it. The *idea* of marriage is larger than any individual marriage. The *role* of husband or wife is greater than any individual who takes on that role. (Blumstein & Schwartz, 1983, p. 318)

No other relationship has achieved such status. Despite its alleged state of disrepair and public concern with its disintegration, monogamous marriage remains the pinnacle of committed intimacy in the United States. It is the cultural standard against which all other types of intimate relationships are judged. For instance, the campaign to legally recognize permanent homosexual relationships is, in essence, a campaign to elevate those unions to the status of marriage.

It's hard to imagine a society that is not structured around the practice of monogamy, but many cultures allow an individual to have several husbands or wives at the same time. This type of marriage is called **polygamy**. Some anthropologists estimate that about 75% of the world's societies prefer some type of polygamy, although few members within those societies actually have the resources to afford more than one spouse (Murdock, 1957; Nanda, 1994). Even in the United States, certain groups practice polygamy. Between 20,000 and 60,000 members of a dissident Mormon sect in Utah live in households that contain one husband and two or more wives (McCarthy, 2001). Although these marriages are technically illegal—as a condition of statehood Utah outlawed polygamy in 1896—few polygamists are ever prosecuted. In fact, 2001 marked the first time in 50 years that a person was convicted on polygamy charges. However, this case shouldn't be taken as an indicator that Utah is cracking down on polygamy. It involved a man—with five wives and twenty-five children—who decided to discuss his polygamous marriage openly on national talk shows, violating an unwritten rule that such arrangements would be quietly tolerated if the participants didn't speak publicly about them.

Cultures differ in other taken-for-granted facets of family life. Take living arrangements, for example. In U.S. society, families tend to follow rules of **neolocal residence**—that is, young married couples are expected to establish their own households, separate from their respective families, when financially possible. Cross-culturally, however, this arrangement is somewhat uncommon. Only about 5% of the world's societies are neolocal (Murdock, 1957; Nanda, 1994). In most societies married couples live with or near either the husband's relatives (called "patrilocal" residence) or the wife's relatives (called "matrilocal" residence).

The belief that members of a nuclear family ought to live together is not found everywhere either. Among the Kipsigis of Kenya, for instance, the mother and children live in one house and the father lives in another. The Kipsigis are polygamous, so a man might have several homes for his several wives at one time (W. N. Stephens, 1963). Among the Thonga of southern Africa, children live with their grandmothers once they stop breastfeeding. They remain there for several years and are then returned to their parents. On the traditional Israeli kibbutz, or commune, children are raised not by their parents but in an "infants' house," where they are cared for by a trained nurse (Nanda, 1994).

Child-rearing philosophies vary cross-culturally as well. Most people in the United States believe that young children are inherently helpless and dependent. They feel that if parents attend to the child's drives and desires with consistency and affection, that child will learn to trust the parents, adopt their values, develop a sturdy self-concept, and turn out to be a well-rounded, normal individual. In contrast, the traditional Japanese parent views the young infant not as dependent and helpless but as a willful creature whose natural instincts need to be tamed (Kagan, 1976). Any excitement on the part of the child must be suppressed. In the highlands of Guatemala, parents believe that their child's personality is determined by the date of birth. The parents are almost entirely uninvolved in the child's life, standing aside so he or she can grow as nature intended. In many societies—Nigeria, Russia, Haiti, the Dominican Republic, and Mexico, to name a few—parents think that the best way to teach children to be respectful and studious is to beat them. In contrast, most American child development experts believe that physical punishment can deaden the child's spirit and lead to violence later in life (Dugger, 1996). Despite these dramatic differences, most children in all these cultures grow up equally well adapted to their societies.

The U.S. Definition of Family. The official definition of family used by the U.S. Bureau of the Census is "two or more persons, including the householder, who are related by birth, marriage, or adoption, and who live together as one household." If we accept this narrow definition, then other arrangements—homosexual relationships, nonmarital cohabitation, and various forms of group living—cannot be considered families in the strict sense of the word. They become deviant lifestyles that require condemnation, alternative arrangements that require tolerance, or sociological curiosities that require explanation. Nevertheless, the structure of U.S. households is quite diverse, as shown in Exhibit 8.2.

Having living arrangements legally recognized as a family has many practical implications. Benefits such as inheritance rights, insurance coverage, eligibility to live in certain apartment complexes, savings from joint tax returns, and visitation rights in prisons and hospital intensive care units are determined by marital or family status. Members of other kinds of relationships are not eligible. In 1999 Samer Yahya, an Italian man attending college in Hartford, Connecticut, was attempting to return from a month-long visit with relatives in Rome. He never made it on the flight. Immigration

Exhibit 8.2 **The Diversity of American Households**

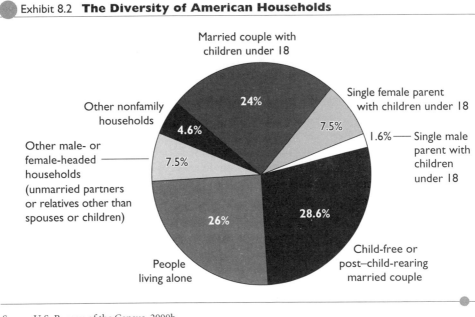

Source: U.S. Bureau of the Census, 2000b.

agents in Rome determined that he had a flawed visa. He was strip-searched and shackled to a bench overnight in the airport. The American embassy in Rome denied him a new visa, saying that although he was a legitimate student, it was likely that after graduation he would stay in the United States illegally because of his long-term relationship with an American man. This relationship was not a legal marriage, and so it gave Yahya no protection against deportation. Had they been a heterosexual married couple, Yahya would have automatically gained residency rights as the spouse of an American citizen. U.S. immigration law considers foreign nationals whose work or student visas have expired to be "illegal immigrants," even though they and their American partners may share mortgages, businesses, homes, and even children. Immigration lawyers estimate that tens of thousands of relationships have been broken apart by this law (Jacobs, 1999).

Although acceptance of gays and lesbians, in general, seems greater than ever, most people still perceive homosexual unions as a threat to the "family." According to one poll, nearly 70% of U.S. residents oppose homosexual marriages (cited in "Marriage and divorce," 1996).

Currently, no state grants homosexuals the right to legally marry. In 1993, the Hawaii State Supreme Court ruled that the state's failure to recognize gay marriage amounted to gender discrimination. But this ruling was rendered moot in 1998 when voters overwhelmingly approved an amendment to the state constitution limiting marriage to opposite-sex couples. Utah, Delaware, South Carolina, Alaska, New Hampshire, and California have also passed laws banning same-sex marriage. In 1996 President Clinton signed into law the Defense of Marriage Act, which formally reaffirms the definition of marriage as the union of one man and one woman; authorizes all states to refuse to accept same-sex marriages from other states if they ever become legal; and denies federal pension, health, and other benefits to same-sex couples.

Nevertheless, some noteworthy attempts have been made to give some legal recognition to homosexual unions. In 2000, Vermont became the first state to approve "civil unions," legally recognized relationships that give gay couples all the benefits of marriage. But it stopped short of calling same-sex unions *marriage*. Similar laws have been on the books for years in such cities as San Francisco and West Hollywood, California; Ithaca, New York; and Madison, Wisconsin. The city of Seattle, Washington, extends full medical, dental, and life insurance benefits to the "domestic partners" of city workers. In addition, thousands of employers—including over 100 Fortune 500 companies—now grant the partners of homosexual employees some of the same benefits traditionally granted to spouses, an increase of 25% from the previous year ("Employers offer gays more benefits," 2000).

Heterosexual cohabitors have also faced difficulty achieving cultural recognition. Between 1990 and 2000 the number of cohabiting couples nearly doubled, from 3.2 million to 5.5 million (U.S. Bureau of the Census, 2001b). They now comprise over 7% of all U.S. households (Caplow, Hicks, & Wattenberg, 2001). But although public attitudes have grown more tolerant of unmarried adults living together, the law sometimes has been slower to adjust. In New Mexico "unlawful cohabitation" is a crime, the punishment for which is six months in jail. In 2000, efforts in Arizona to repeal that state's 80-year-old anticohabitation law failed. Massachusetts did repeal a 1784 law banning "lewdly and lasciviously associating and cohabitating without the benefit of marriage"—but not until 1987 (Yardley, 2000b).

Obviously, whatever a culture decides to define as the legitimate characteristics of a family has important consequences for people's lives.

Family and Social Structure

All of us have experience with families, so it's very tempting to look at this topic in individualistic, personal terms. However, the sociological imagination encourages us to think about how social forces affect this aspect of our private lives. As you will see, a focus on the influence of social structure—social institutions and sources of social inequality, such as gender, race, and class—can help us understand some of the dilemmas facing contemporary families.

Institutions Influencing Family

As a social institution, family is connected to other institutions in important ways. The legal, political, economic, and religious forces that shape society are perhaps the institutions that most influence the actions of individuals within family relationships. Keep in mind that individuals within families can act to influence society as well.

Law and Politics. The relationship between the family and the law is obvious. Marriage, for instance, is a legal contract. In the United States, each state determines the legal age at which two people can marry, the health requirements, the length of the waiting period required before marriage, rules determining inheritance, and the division of property in case of divorce (Baca-Zinn & Eitzen, 1996). In the case of homosexual unions, the law's power to either forbid or grant family rights and privileges is especially obvious.

Politics and family are interconnected in other ways too. Many of today's most pressing political issues—affordable child care, parental leave, teen pregnancy, the aging population, abortion, homelessness, poverty—are fundamentally family problems. For example, abortion didn't become a significant political issue until the late 1960s, when it became part of the larger movement for women's rights and reproductive freedom. Later the right-to-life movement framed the abortion debate not only as a moral and political issue but also as a symbolic crusade to define (or redefine) the role of motherhood and family within the larger society (Luker, 1984).

Family has taken on enormous symbolic importance in American social life and has become a highly emotional political buzzword. Over the past two decades many politicians have defined as one of their primary goals the restoration of "traditional family values." Unfortunately, what exactly "traditional" or "family" means in the context of political debates is never made clear.

Strictly speaking, *traditional family* refers to people living together who are related by blood, marriage, or adoption. Politically, however, the term usually has more to do with family authority, the moral obligations of parenting and marital commitment, and sexual expression (Hunter, 1991). Conservative critics deplore not only the greater visibility of cohabiting and homosexual couples but also the increasing numbers of single and working mothers and the rising rates of divorce. Despite all the political rhetoric, however, some women will continue to raise children alone, wives and mothers will continue to work outside the home, sex will never be confined to marriage, and gays will not all return to the closet.

Religion. Religion can play a role in virtually every stage of family life: dating, marriage, sexuality, childbearing decisions, parenthood, child discipline, responses to illness and death, household division of labor, and so on. One of the key aspects of religion is to constrain human behavior or at the very least to encourage members to act in certain ways. This normative aspect of religion has important consequences for people's family experiences. For instance, all the major religions in the United States are strong supporters of marriage. In recent years, more churches have begun requiring couples to participate in premarital counseling and education programs before the wedding. In addition, religions almost universally prohibit sexual relations outside marriage. Some religions prohibit divorce or don't permit remarriage after divorce. Some oppose the use of contraceptives and encourage large families. In highly religious families, a sacred text such as the Bible, the Koran, or the Talmud may serve not only as a source of faith but as a literal guidebook for every aspect of family life.

Religion's influence on family life needn't be so direct, however. For example, among Muslims and certain Christian denominations families are expected to tithe, or donate, a certain amount of their income (10%, in most cases) to support their religious establishment. Although it is a charitable thing to do, tithing can create problems for families that are already financially strapped.

Most evidence suggests that religious involvement has a positive effect on family life, including higher levels of marital commitment (Larson & Goltz, 1989), more positive parent–child relationships (Pearce & Axinn, 1998), less permissive sexual attitudes (Thornton & Camburn, 1989), lower rates of cohabitation (Thornton, Axinn, & Hill, 1992), and lower rates of voluntary childlessness (Heaton, Jacobson, & Fu, 1992). "Spiritual wellness" is often cited as one of the most important qualities of family well-being (Stinnett & DeFrain, 1985).

However, in some situations the link between religious beliefs and actual family behavior may not be as strong as we might think. Even in highly religious families, the practical demands of modern life make it difficult to always subscribe to religious teachings. For instance, although fundamentalist Christians believe wives should stay at home and submit to the authority of their husbands, many fundamentalist women do work outside the home and exert powerful influence over family decisions (Ammerman, 1987). Moreover, although many religions stress the value of keeping families intact, increased religious involvement does not do much to strengthen troubled marriages (Booth, Johnson, Branaman, & Sica, 1995). Increased religious involvement does seem to slightly decrease thoughts about divorce, but it doesn't enhance marital happiness or stop spouses from fighting.

Economics. The world of economics affects virtually every aspect of family life, from the amount of money coming into the household to the day-to-day management of finances and major purchasing decisions. Money matters are closely related to feelings of satisfaction within family relationships. When couples are disappointed with how much money they have or how it is spent, they find all aspects of their relationships less satisfying (Blumstein & Schwartz, 1983).

Such financial problems are not just private troubles. Rather, they are directly linked to larger economic patterns. Major alterations in an economy almost always have a profound impact on the family. Between 1989 and 1995, for example, per capita income in the United States was stagnant. Incomes have improved a bit in recent years, but many adults in the United States still have difficulty supporting a family. It now costs two-parent, middle-class families over $165,000 to raise a child to the age of 17, up from $25,230 in 1970 (U.S. Department of Agriculture, 2001).

At the global level, the competitive pressures of the international marketplace have forced many businesses and industries to make greater use of so-called disposable workers—those who work part-time or on temporary contract. These jobs offer no benefits and no security and therefore make family life less stable (Kilborn, 1993; Uchitelle, 1993). Other companies have reduced their costs by cutting salaries, laying off workers, or encouraging early retirement. Some businesses are relocating either to other countries or to other parts of the United States where they can pay lower wages (see Chapter 10 for a more detailed discussion). Some 4,000 U.S.–owned manufacturing plants are now located in northern Mexico, employing nearly a million Mexican workers and contributing about $7 billion to the local economy ("Good fences," 1998). The companies obviously benefit, the Mexican workers may benefit, but displaced U.S. workers and their families do not.

Financial uncertainty makes a stable family life very difficult. Sustaining a supportive, nurturing family environment is nearly impossible without adequate income or health care. When economic foundations are weak, the emotional bonds that tie a family together can be stretched to the breaking point (Newman, 1988).

Micro-Macro Connection
Dual-Earner Parents

One of the most significant economic facts to emerge in the early 21st century is that in most married-couple families, both partners work. In 1999, 57% of U.S. families with at least one child under the age of 6 had two working parents. That figure was up from 32% in 1976. Of those families with children between the ages of 6 and 17, 70% consisted of an employed mother and father (U.S. Bureau of the Census, 2000b). The dual-earner family is now the most common type of U.S. family. By 1990, the percentage of households that consisted of a married couple dependent on a sole male breadwinner had dropped to less than 14%, from a high of almost 60% in 1950 (Gerson, 1993).

The financial strains of modern living have made it difficult for young couples to survive on only one income. The image of the "traditional" family—where Dad goes off to work and Mom stays home to raise the kids—does not reflect reality for most people today. Nevertheless, for the most part social institutions are still built around the outdated belief that only one partner (typically the father) in a couple should be working. Such beliefs have created serious burdens for working parents.

Exhibit 8.3 **Compromises to Balance Work and Family**

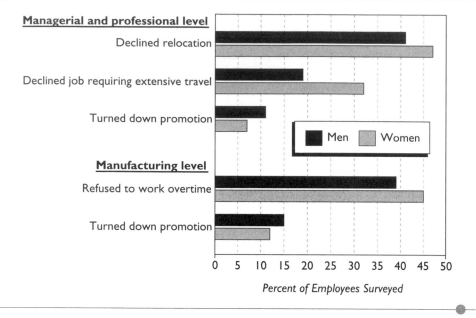

Source: Lewin, 1995b.

Many couples find they must make career tradeoffs to try to balance their work and family lives. Exhibit 8.3 shows the results of a survey of more than 6,000 employees of a major chemical company on the compromises they had made in order to maintain a home life. Women and men alike, at the managerial/professional level and on the shop floor, refused various career- or income-enhancing opportunities that would have meant less time for family.

Some experts feel that the single most important step society could take to help dual-earner families would be to help them deal with child care demands. The Family and Medical Leave Act, signed into law by President Clinton in 1993, is a step in that direction: It guarantees some workers up to 12 weeks of unpaid sick leave per year for the birth or adoption of a child or to care for a sick child, parent, or spouse. However, it has some important qualifications that seriously limit its usefulness to the working population:

- The law covers only workers who have been employed continuously for at least one year and who work at least 25 hours a week. As a result, temporary or part-time workers are not eligible.
- The law is of no value to parents who can't afford to take unpaid leave.
- The law exempts companies with fewer than 50 workers; hence only about 40% of the full-time workforce is covered.
- The law allows an employer to deny leave to any employee who is in the highest paid 10% of its workforce, if allowing that person to take the leave would create "substantial and grievous injury" to the business's operations.

Between 1994 and 1995, less than 4% of employees in companies covered by this law actually took leave from their jobs ("Impact of the Family and Medical Leave Law," 1997). Employees themselves are partly responsible for this low level of participation, but evidence has also surfaced that employers are not always in complete compliance with the law. In 1998, the U.S. Department of Labor required employers to pay over $4.5 million to some 2,400 workers who had filed complaints about being denied family leave ("Employers hit with $4.5 million," 1999). For instance, a Maryland state trooper was awarded $375,000 in 1999 because he was refused extended leave to care for his newborn daughter (Lewin, 1999).

Although this law represents an improvement over past conditions, the United States still lags behind other countries. According to a United Nations survey of 152 countries, the United States is one of only six—along with Australia, New Zealand, Lesotho, Swaziland, and Papua New Guinea—that does not have a national policy requiring paid maternity leave (cited in Olson, 1998). Consider the policies of a few other industrialized nations (Bell-Rowbotham and Lero, 2001):

- In France, mothers are provided 16 weeks off work at 84% pay for the first and second children, and 24 weeks for the third and subsequent children. They also receive up to 3 years of unpaid leave with job protection.
- In Norway, parents can take 42 weeks leave at 100% pay or 52 weeks at 80%. Fathers are entitled to 4 weeks of this leave. Parents can also combine part-time work and partial parental benefits. For example, one parent could take full leave at 100% pay for 42 weeks and the other could combine 80% work and 20% leave for nearly 2 years.
- In the United Kingdom, parents receive 18 weeks of maternity leave at 90% of their salary and 12 weeks at a flat rate. They can also take up to 40 weeks of unpaid family leave.

If we are truly concerned about preserving families, we too need to find a better way to reconcile work life and family life.

Gender

We cannot talk about structural influences on the family without discussing the role of gender. Gender roles in the family are certainly changing. But men and women are still likely to enter relationships with vastly different expectations, desires, and goals. Gender explains a variety of phenomena in intimate relationships, such as the way people talk to one another, how they express themselves sexually, how they deal with conflict, and what they feel their responsibilities are. As a result, gender influences how men and women go about creating, maintaining, and thinking about family relationships.

Traditional gender role socialization encourages women to be sensitive, express affection, and reveal weakness, whereas men are taught to be competitive, strong, and emotionally inexpressive. These stereotypes have some basis in fact. Research has consistently shown that women have more close friends than men and are more romantic in their intimate relationships (Perlman & Fehr, 1987). Furthermore, women have been shown to be more concerned about, attentive to, and aware of the dynamics of their relationships than men are (see, for example, Fincham & Bradbury, 1987; Rusbult, Zembrodt, & Iwaniszek, 1986). Women even think more and talk more about their relationships than men do (Acitelli, 1988; Holtzworth-Munroe & Jacobson, 1985).

Ironically, such attentiveness and concern do not necessarily mean that women get more out of family relationships than men do. In fact, the opposite may be true. According to one sociologist, every marriage actually contains two marriages: "his" and "hers"—and "his" seems to be the better deal (Bernard, 1972). Married men derive more satisfaction from marriage than married women do (Skolnick, 1981). Marriage even seems to benefit men's health and well-being. Married men get sick less, live longer, and have fewer emotional problems than single men (Gove, Style, & Hughes, 1990; Ross, Mirowsky, & Goldstein, 1990). Women's family experiences can be quite different. Three times as many married women as single women show signs of anxiety, depression, and emotional distress (Carr, 1988).

Because of the continued pressures of gender-typed family responsibilities, women are more likely than men to experience the stresses associated with parenthood and running the household. Men have historically been able to feel they are fulfilling their family obligations by simply being financial providers. Most people still interpret a man's long hours on the job as an understandable sacrifice for his family's sake. Fathers rarely spend as much time worrying about the effect their work will have on their children as mothers do. In contrast, even in the relatively "liberated" United States, women's employment outside the home is usually perceived as optional or, more seriously, as potentially damaging to the family. Some people think that women with children simply shouldn't work, even at part-time jobs, if they can afford to stay at home. In 1998 Deborah Eappen, the doctor whose baby son died while under the care of a British nanny, was severely criticized in the newspapers and on radio talk shows because she worked three days a week. Stories such as these force many working women to agonize over whether their financial well-being and personal independence are being purchased at the cost of their families.

Social Diversity and Family Life

Most people in the United States assume that love is all they need to establish a fulfilling, long-lasting relationship. But their intimate choices are far from free and private. The choices they make regarding whom to date, live with, or marry are governed by two important social rules that limit the field of eligible partners: exogamy and endogamy.

Exogamy rules specify that an individual must marry outside certain groups. In almost all societies, exogamy rules prohibit people from marrying members of their own nuclear family—siblings, parents, and children. Rules of exogamy extend to certain people outside the nuclear family to include cousins, grandparents, and, in some societies, stepsiblings. Opposition to granting cultural and legal "legitimacy" to homosexual marriages springs, in part, from some people's belief that a person should only be allowed to marry someone outside his or her sex.

Less obvious are the rules of **endogamy**, which is marriage within one's social group. In some countries, such as India and Pakistan, the rules of endogamy are rigidly enforced. Most marriages are arranged by families to preserve group identities, with little thought for the compatibility or shared affection of the partners. In contrast, the choice of marital partners in the United States and most other Western countries is supposedly more open, a matter of personal preference. But the vast majority of intimate relationships in the United States—and, indeed, throughout the world—occur between people from the same religion, racial or ethnic group, and social class. To be sure, similar backgrounds—and thus similar beliefs, values, and experiences—increase the likelihood that two individuals will be attracted to each other. However, the rules of endogamy reflect a cultural distaste for relationships that cross group boundaries.

Differences in family structure, sexual division of labor, child rearing, and so on that are based on social differences have been well documented (see, for example, L. Rubin, 1976; Shon & Ja, 1992; Staples & Mirande, 1980). The more interesting question for sociologists today is whether the increasing diversity of the population is likely to alter conceptions of the "typical" family in years to come. Whether families become more similar or more diverse in the future depends on whether the formation of families across racial, religious, or social class lines becomes more common than it is today.

Religious Background. Marrying outside one's religion is more common than it once was in industrialized countries, where greater mobility and freer communication bring people from diverse religious backgrounds into contact. In the United States, over one-quarter of all marriages occur between people of different religions (Glenn, 1982).

Although the traditional norms that once obligated people to marry within their faith have diminished, most religions still actively discourage interfaith marriages. Their concern is that such marriages may further weaken people's religious beliefs and values, lead to the raising of children in a different faith, or take religion out of the family entirely. Religious leaders often worry about the bigger problem of maintaining their ethnic identity within a diverse and complex society (M. M. Gordon, 1964).

American Jews provide a good example of the consequences of interfaith marriage. The percentage of Jews in the U.S. population has declined from 4% to 2.3% in the past 50 years (Safire, 1995). Although only 1 Jew in 10 married a non-Jew in 1945, 1 in 2 does so today. A lower birthrate among Jews compared to other groups, coupled with the propensity to not raise children as Jews in interfaith families, explains, in part, why the Jewish population is dropping so precipitously.

A statement issued in 1973 by Reform Judaism's Central Conference of American Rabbis (the most liberal, and therefore the most tolerant, branch of U.S. Judaism) defined interfaith marriages as "contrary to Jewish tradition" and discouraged rabbis from officiating at them (Niebuhr, 1996). Indeed, most rabbis today refuse to perform interfaith weddings, even though there is some evidence that interfaith couples who have been married by rabbis are likely to raise their children as Jews.

Many Jewish leaders fear that the outcome of this growing trend will be not only the shrinking of the Jewish population but also the erosion and perhaps extinction of an entire way of life. They believe that the survival of U.S. Jewry itself depends on maintaining the integrity of traditional Jewish values and institutions. Young people who decide to marry outside the faith "are threatening to transform Judaism into a religion of half-remembered rituals, forgotten ancestors and buried beliefs" (Rosen, 1997, p. 7).

Race and Ethnicity. Marriages that cross racial lines have become more common in U.S. society, increasing from 310,000 in 1970 to 1.3 million in 1999 (U.S. Bureau of the Census, 2000b). Still, this figure constitutes only 2.3% of all U.S. marriages. Of all interracial marriages, 23% are black–white unions, accounting for just 0.5% of all marriages (U.S. Bureau of the Census, 2000b). Racial and ethnic endogamy is a global phenomenon, forming the basis of social structure in most societies worldwide (Murdock, 1949).

The issue of racial and ethnic endogamy is an especially emotional one in U.S. society. Fear and condemnation of interracial relationships have been a part of culture, politics, and law since the first settlers arrived close to 400 years ago. The first law against interracial marriage was enacted in Maryland in 1661, prohibiting whites from marrying Native Americans or African Americans. Over the next 300 years or so, 38 more states put such laws on the books, expanding their coverage to include Chinese, Japanese, and Filipino Americans. These laws were supported by biological and evolution-based theories of race, which spelled out essential differences (and therefore implied superiority or inferiority) between the races. Laws were enacted to prevent a mixing of the races (referred to as "mongrelization") that would destroy the racial purity (and superiority) of whites. The irony, of course, is that racial mixing had been taking place since the very beginning, much of it through coercive sexual activity between white slave owners and black slaves.

Legal sanctions against interracial marriage persisted well into the 20th century. In 1958, for example, when white Richard Loving and his new wife, black Mildred Jeter Loving, moved to their new home in Virginia, a sheriff arrived to arrest them for violating a state law that prohibited interracial marriages. The Lovings were sentenced to 1 year in jail but then learned that the judge would suspend the sentence if they left the state and promised not to return for 25 years. They agreed but, after leaving town, filed suit. In 1967 the U.S. Supreme Court ruled in their favor, concluding that using racial classifications to restrict freedom to marry was unconstitutional.

More than 40 years later, people are no longer banished for marrying people of a different race. Nevertheless, even though attitudes are becoming more tolerant, discomfort with interracial relationships still lingers. Two states—South Carolina and Alabama—had laws against interracial marriage on the books until the mid-1990s. Even today, rural judges can sometimes make it difficult for interracial couples to marry (Staples, 1999).

People involved in interracial relationships state that the most difficult problem they face, both before and after marriage, is racism (Rosenblatt, Karis, & Powell, 1995). Some interracial couples describe how they must be on "constant alert" in public places for disapproving stares, subtly insulting comments, and blatant indignities, such as being spat on or refused services (Pierre-Pierre, 1998; Wilkerson, 1991a). Others, fearful of family ostracism, never tell their own parents that they are married to someone of a different race or that they have children. In one survey 66% of whites said they'd oppose a close relative's marriage to a black person; only 4% said they'd favor it (Wilkerson, 1991b). So pervasive are these feelings that many people involved in interracial homosexual relationships report finding it more difficult being an interracial couple in U.S. society than being a gay couple (Gillings, 1996).

Social Class. If we were to base our ideas about the formation of romantic relationships on what we see in movies, we might be tempted to conclude that divisions based on social class don't matter in U.S. society or perhaps don't exist at all. Films such as *Titanic, Good Will Hunting, Fools Rush In,* and *Inventing the Abbotts,* as well as such older ones as *Pretty Woman, White Palace, Pretty in Pink,* and *Love Story,* send the message that when it comes to love we're all really alike. In these stories the power of love is strong enough to blow away differences in education, pedigree, resources, and tastes. When it comes to love, Hollywood's United States is a classless society.

In reality, however, social class is a powerful factor in whom we choose to marry. Around the world, people face strong pressures to choose marital partners from the same social class (Carter & Glick, 1976; Kalmijn, 1994). Even if two individuals from different races or religions marry, chances are they will have similar socioeconomic backgrounds. Certainly some people do marry a person from a different social class, but the class tends to be an adjacent one—for instance, an upper-class woman who marries a middle-class man. Marriages between people of vastly different class rankings are quite rare. The reason is that individuals from similar social classes are more likely to come into contact and to share values, tastes, goals, expectations, and educational background.

The U.S. education system plays a particularly important role in bringing people from similar class backgrounds together. Neighborhoods—and thus neighborhood schools—tend to be homogeneous in social class. College continues class segregation. People from upper-class backgrounds are considerably more likely to attend costly private schools, whereas those from the middle class are most likely to enroll in state universities and those from the working class are most likely to enroll in community colleges. These structural conditions increase the odds that the people whom college students meet and form intimate relationships with will come from a similar class background.

Social class doesn't only influence people's marital choices, it affects the ways families function as well. In many ways all families must face the same issues: work, leisure, child rearing, and interpersonal relations (L. Rubin, 1994). But beneath the similarities we see dramatic differences in how these issues are handled. Because of heightened concern over class boundaries, ancestry, and maintenance of prestige, upper-class parents exert much more control over the dating behaviors of their children than lower-class parents do (Domhoff, 1983; M. K. Whyte, 1990). Upper-class families are also better able to use their wealth and resources in coping with some of the demands of family life. Finding adequate child care arrangements will probably not pose much of a dilemma to parents who can afford a full-time, live-in nanny. The picture for working-class families, though, is quite different.

Lillian Rubin
Working-Class Families

For more than two decades, sociologist Lillian Rubin (1976, 1994) studied social class differences in U.S. family life. In 1976 she conducted in-depth interviews with 50 working-class families. For purposes of comparison she also interviewed 25 professional, middle-class families. The differences she found give a personal face to the effects of social class on family life in U.S. society. Among the differences she discovered were that working-class people are more likely than middle-class people to marry early, have large families, have premarital pregnancies, and experience marital unhappiness and divorce.

Working-class youth, living in the confined space of their parents' homes, must often forgo college and make significant economic contributions to the family. For them, marriage often represents an attractive escape from the hardships and restrictions of their lives with their parents. But the women Rubin interviewed were almost unanimous in their belief that many of their marital troubles came from marrying too early. Many expressed hope that their daughters would not make the same mistake they had made.

Another noticeable characteristic of working-class marriages is a severe split between masculine and feminine cultures. Working-class couples tend to be more traditional in their perceptions of gender roles. Working-class wives seem to be more willing than middle-class wives to grant legitimacy to their husbands' authority. Furthermore, Rubin found little communication between working-class husbands and wives, especially regarding personal or emotional matters:

> They talk *at* each other, *past* each other, or *through* each other—rarely *with* or *to* each other. He blames her: "She's too emotional." She blames him: "He's always so rational." . . . The problem lies in the fact that they do not have a language with which to communicate, with which to understand each other. (p. 116)

In perhaps the most telling illustration, Rubin asked the wives what they valued most in their husbands. The professional, middle-class subjects tended to focus on such issues as intimacy, sharing, communication, and the comforts and prestige that their husbands' occupations provided them. Working-class wives were more dismal in their assessments, focusing on the absence of such problems as unemployment, alcoholism, and violence. As one 33-year-old housewife put it,

> I guess I can't complain. He's a steady worker; he doesn't drink; he doesn't hit me. That's a lot more than my mother had, and she didn't sit around complaining and feeling sorry for herself, so I sure haven't got the right. (L. Rubin, 1976, p. 93)

This is not to say that working-class women are not concerned with the emotional side of their marriages. But when the material aspects of life are problematic, they become dominant, all-consuming issues that require immediate solutions.

Yet however dismal their lives were, Rubin noticed that the families she talked to still clung to the belief that the future promised progress and that the solutions to their problems were within their grasp. The sacrifices they were making would somehow pay off in the future.

In 1994, she visited the homes of 162 working-class families in a variety of cities across the country to see how the economic downturn of the 1980s and early 1990s had affected them. Many of these families were ones she had interviewed for the first study. The title of this follow-up study, *Families on the Fault Line,* suggests a precarious life on the edge of disaster. These families aren't considered officially "poor." Nevertheless, the hope that had sustained them through bad times two decades earlier—the belief that if they just worked hard enough and played by the rules they'd eventually grab a piece of the American Dream—no longer existed. It wasn't so much the possibility of becoming destitute that worried them. It was the fear that they might never be able to move up.

Rubin also found that these working-class families seem significantly more concerned with race than they were 20 years earlier. Racial hostility was a recurrent theme in people's discussions, often arising spontaneously as they complained about the current state of their lives. Among these families, economic anxieties had combined with the changing face of the United States to create profound uneasiness about people from different racial or ethnic groups as well as recent immigrants:

> If we keep letting all them foreigners in, pretty soon there'll be more of them than us and then what will this country be like? I mean, this is *our* country, but the way things are going, white people will be the minority in our own country. Now does that make any sense? (p. 173)
>
> If our people were as hard working and disciplined as the Asians, we'd be a lot better off. I'm not a racist, but sometimes they give me the creeps. You've got to watch out for them because they'll do anything for a buck, anything. I guess what bothers me the most is you can't get away from them. . . . You go to the bank, they're working there. You go to a store, they're behind the counter. It's like they're gobbling up all the jobs in town. (pp. 188–189)

From these sentiments we can see that the more economically precarious people's lives are, the more likely they are to focus on differences between themselves and others.

Family Dilemmas

Throughout this chapter you've seen the vital role that family plays in our everyday lives. But given all the pressures on families from the society around them, it should be no surprise that some families experience serious problems. Those problems include divorce and its aftereffects, and family violence.

Divorce

Although it is more common and more acceptable in some places than in others, virtually all societies have provisions—legal, communal, or religious—for dissolving

Exhibit 8.4 **Divorce Rates in Selected Developed Countries**

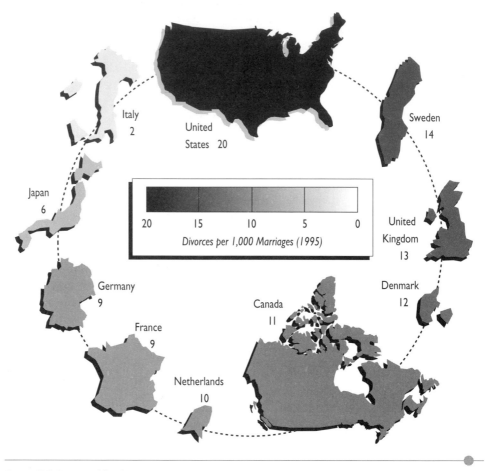

Italy 2

United States 20

Sweden 14

Japan 6

United Kingdom 13

Germany 9

Denmark 12

Canada 11

France 9

Netherlands 10

20   15   10   5   0

Divorces per 1,000 Marriages (1995)

Source: U.S. Bureau of the Census, 1998c.

marriages (McKenry & Price, 1995). Worldwide, divorce rates tend to be associated with socioeconomic development. The developing countries of Latin America (for example, Ecuador, Nicaragua, and Peru) and Asia (for example, Thailand, Malaysia, Sri Lanka) have substantially lower divorce rates than the developed countries of Western Europe and North America (Trent & South, 1989). Furthermore, practically every industrialized country in the world experienced an increase in divorces between 1950 and 1990 (W. J. Goode, 1993), although their divorce rates vary quite a bit, as Exhibit 8.4 shows.

Even in societies that we would consider modern and developed, powerful religious forces can suppress divorce rates. For instance, in 1995, the Irish government began a campaign against the Catholic Church over the country's constitutional ban on divorce. The government estimated that at least 80,000 people were locked in broken marriages and that they deserved the right to remarry. But the Catholic bishops launched a massive advertising counterattack, arguing that even unhappily married people have an obligation to keep their marriages intact to provide a good example for society. The referendum was passed by a minuscule margin, and in 1997, for the first time, people in Ireland had the right to legally divorce.

Despite the fact that the dissolution of marriage is virtually universal, no society places a positive value on divorce. In fact, in most societies people who divorce are somehow penalized, either through formal controls such as fines, prohibitions against remarriage, excommunication, and forced alimony and child support or through informal means such as censure, gossip, and stigmatization.

The Normalization of Divorce. Most people in the United States have seen the end of a marriage, either their own or that of someone close to them. In an average year there are over 1.1 million divorces in the United States, a rate of almost 20 divorces per 1,000 existing marriages (U.S. Bureau of the Census, 2000b). This rate has more or less stabilized over the past few years, but it is still quite high, considering that the rate was about 14 per 1,000 marriages in 1970 and 4 per 1,000 in 1900 (refer back to Exhibit 8.1). Experts project that close to one out of every two marriages that begins in a given year will eventually end in divorce (T. C. Martin & Bumpass, 1989). Such figures terrify people who are about to enter a "lifetime" relationship and distress those already married who want some sense of permanence for their children (Blumstein & Schwartz, 1983).

The causes of the high divorce rate in Western societies include such things as the weakening of the family's traditional economic bonds, a reduction in the influence of religion, and the stress of shifting gender roles (Popenoe, 1993). One particularly influential factor has been a cultural shift in the perception of marriage. Marriage has become a voluntary contract system that can be ended at the discretion of either spouse. In the past, when economic needs—not to mention such constraints as parental expectations or religious norms—held couples together, people "made do" with loveless, unsatisfying marriages because they had to. But when these constraints do not exist, people are less willing to make do (Skolnick, 1996). Increasing earning power and decreasing economic dependence on men have made it easier for women to end a marriage that is unsatisfying.

In addition, people's overall attitudes toward divorce have become more accepting over the past several decades (Thornton, 1989). In the 1960s, a divorced politician didn't stand a chance of being elected in the United States. Today many of our most influential lawmakers are divorced. In the 1980s Ronald Reagan's divorce and remarriage didn't prevent him from being elected—twice. In the 2000 election, people barely mentioned vice presidential candidate Joseph Lieberman's divorce and remarriage. Most people now recognize that a divorce may be preferable to an unhappy marriage. In short, divorce is as much a part of U.S. family life as, well, marriage.

Changing perceptions of marriage and changing cultural attitudes toward divorce are typically accompanied by other structural changes. In the United States, modifications of existing divorce laws in the past two decades have made it easier for people in an unsatisfying marriage to end it. In the past, evidence of wrongdoing—adultery, desertion, abuse, and so forth—was required for courts to grant a divorce. But in the past

25 years every state has adopted a form of no-fault divorce. No-fault laws have eliminated the requirement that one partner be found guilty of some transgression. Instead, marriages are simply declared unworkable and are terminated.

Many critics argue that these laws have made divorce too easy and too quick, although whether or not they actually have is a matter of some debate. Nevertheless, as a result there seems to have been a shift back to less tolerant public attitudes toward divorce. One survey found that 55% of U.S. citizens favor making it harder to leave a marriage when one partner wants to maintain it (cited in Leland, 1996). In some states—Iowa, Idaho, Georgia, Michigan, and Pennsylvania, to name a few—legal measures have been debated that would impose mandatory waiting periods for couples contemplating divorce or restore the old requirement of proving fault in cases where only one spouse is seeking divorce (D. Johnson, 1996b). Other states are toying with the idea of providing financial incentives—in the form of discounted marriage licenses—for couples who participate in premarital counseling. In 1997, the Louisiana State Legislature passed a measure forcing engaged couples to choose between a standard marriage contract, which permits no-fault divorce, and a "covenant marriage," which could be dissolved only by a mutually agreed-on two-year separation or proof of fault, chiefly adultery, abandonment, or abuse (Loe, 1997). Critics of such measures note that instead of having a positive impact on family life, the result might be an increase in contentious, expensive, potentially child-harming divorces and in unhappy, perhaps even dangerous marriages.

Children, Divorce, and Single Parenting. Over a million U.S. children each year see their parents divorce (U.S. Bureau of the Census, 2000b). In 1960, 9% of children under 18 lived with a single parent; by 1998, the figure had increased to 32% (U.S. Bureau of the Census, 2000b). If the divorce rate remains high and out-of-wedlock birth continues its upward trend—nearly one-third of all births in the United States are to unmarried women (U.S. Bureau of the Census, 2000b)—perhaps as many as 60% of U.S. children born in the early 2000s will live in a single-parent family before the age of 16 (Furstenberg & Cherlin, 1991). Moreover, the odds of growing up in a single-parent family are higher for some racial groups than others (see Exhibit 8.5).

Although divorce can be traumatic for adults, most recover after a period of years. Children, however, have a more difficult time adjusting. For them, divorce sets a series of changes in motion, each with the potential to disrupt their lives. They may have to move to a new home in a new neighborhood, make new friends, and go to a new school. Because the overwhelming majority of children of divorce live with their mothers, they may also experience a decline in their standard of living. The earning capacity of women is lower than that of men to begin with. Furthermore, noncustodial fathers do not always pay child support. In almost two-thirds of divorces, fathers are required to pay child support. Of these, 40% pay the full amount, 30% pay a partial amount, and 30% pay nothing (U.S. Bureau of the Census, 2000b). About a half of divorced mothers with custody of children therefore don't receive any financial assistance at all. Award rates are especially low for African-American and Latina women, who suffer from higher rates of poverty to begin with (Klawitter, 1994).

The relationship that children have with their noncustodial parent also tends to diminish over time. One national study found that half of U.S. children whose parents

● Exhibit 8.5   **Family Composition and Race**

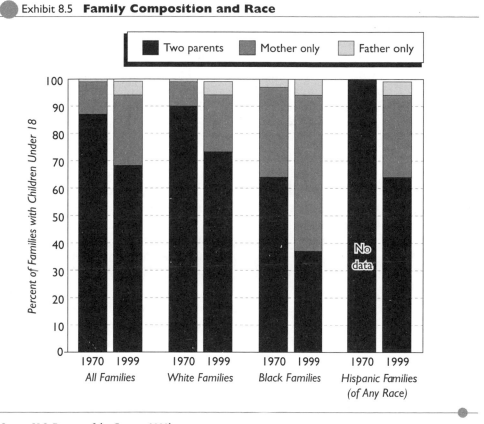

Source: U.S. Bureau of the Census, 2000b.

were divorced and who were living with their mothers hadn't seen their fathers in the last year, and only one out of six had regular, weekly contact with their noncustodial father. Children were most likely to see their fathers immediately after the separation. But after several years, contact dropped off sharply (Furstenberg & Nord, 1985). Another study found that 75% of noncustodial fathers never attend their child's school events, 85% never help them with their homework, and 65% never take their children on vacations (Teachman, 1991). Fewer than one in five noncustodial fathers have significant influence over their children's health care, education, religion, and so forth (Arendell, 1995).

What are the long-term effects of divorce on children? A substantial body of research shows that regardless of race or education of parents, children raised in single-parent homes fare worse at every stage of life than children from two-parent families. An extensive review of studies published during the 1990s found that children from divorced families fare worse in terms of academic success, psychological adjustment, self-concept, social competence and long-term health than children from intact, two-parent families (Amato, 2000). In adulthood, they are at greater risk of low socioeconomic attainment, increased marital difficulties and divorce (Diekmann & Engelhardt, 1999).

These differences are typically attributed to factors such as the absence of a father, increased strain on the custodial parent to keep the household running, and emotional stress and anger associated with the separation. However, the causes of these problems are more likely to be factors that can also be found in two-parent families: low income, poor living conditions, and lack of parental supervision (Cherlin, 1992).

Some critics argue that the standard research design in studies on the impact of divorce on children—comparing children whose parents have divorced to children in happy, intact families—is flawed. Indeed, if we compare kids from divorced families to kids from intact families whose parents are unhappily married or whose families experience a great deal of conflict, we find that the frequency of such problems is similar for both sets of children (Cherlin et al., 1991). In fact, children who grow up in intact families marked by frequent conflict may actually have more problems. This research suggests that these behavioral problems are caused not by the divorce itself but by exposure to conflict between the parents both before and after the divorce (Stewart, Copeland, Chester, Malley, & Barenbaum, 1997). In short, the simple fact of growing up in a single-parent family may not be as important in the development of a child as the way parents relate to each other and to the child.

Remarriage and the Reconstituted Family. Close to half of all marriages in the United States today involve at least one partner who was previously married (U.S. Bureau of the Census, 2000b). This statistic suggests that although people are quite willing to escape a bad marriage, they have not necessarily given up on the concept of marriage entirely.

Although they are fairly common, remarriages are not without their problems. The divorce rate for remarriages is actually higher than the rate for first marriages. In the United States, 39% of remarriages end within the first 10 years, compared to 33% of first marriages (Bramlett & Mosher, 2001).

Some sociologists describe remarriage as an "incomplete institution," meaning that it lacks the guiding norms, values, and role expectations that first marriages typically have (Cherlin, 1978). Remarriage disrupts the conventional family structure so that the traditional roles, relationships, and norms no longer apply. We have no set of institutional expectations for relationships between former and current spouses, between stepparents and stepchildren, between step- and half-siblings, and with extended kin (Ahrons & Rodgers, 1987). Laws and customs have been slow to catch up. For instance, do stepchildren have legal claims to their stepparents' property? Do incest rules apply to stepsiblings? An increasing number of people face such issues, finding themselves in a marital structure quite different from the kind with which they are familiar (Goetting, 1982).

Remarriage is particularly difficult when children are involved. Although most stepparents are able to build strong, durable, loving relationships with their partner's children, others face difficulties. Guidelines for stepparents are much less clear than they are for parents. When a new stepparent enters the former single-parent family, the entire system may be thrown out of balance. He or she may be seen as an outsider, or worse, an intruder. Stepsiblings may be asked to share bedrooms or other possessions. They may see their connection to their biological parent as giving them greater claim on that parent's affection and resources. Rules and habits change and, for a time, confusion, resentment, and hostility may be the norm. Conflict is common in all types of families, but such issues as favoritism, divided loyalties, the right to discipline, and financial responsibility are particularly likely to occur in reconstituted families.

The high divorce rate of remarriages and the high levels of conflict within some reconstituted families are not simply an outgrowth of people's psychological inability to sustain intimate relationships, as some analysts have claimed. The fact that remarriages are not fully institutionalized is what makes them susceptible to failure. The lack of clear role definitions, the absence of established societal norms, and the increased complexity of the family structure itself increase the likelihood of tension and turmoil. Perhaps in the future, as we develop standard ways of defining and coping with reconstituted families, remarriage may become more institutionalized and less problematic. Until then remarriage will continue to create a great deal of tension and confusion.

Family Violence

Every day in this country, four women are killed by their spouses or lovers; and in any given year more women are abused by their husbands than get married in the same period. In the United States the likelihood that a man will be assaulted by someone in his own family is 20 times higher than the odds that he will be assaulted by a stranger; women are 200 times more likely to be assaulted by a family member than by an outsider (Straus, 1991). One in seven U.S. adults claim to have been sexually abused as a child, and one in six claim to have been physically abused (cited in Coontz, 1992). The irony is that, outside of wars and riots, the home—that loving place that nourishes us when the outside world has sucked away our life energy—can also be one of the most violent places in a society.

Some sociologists claim that U.S. women are just as likely to hit their husbands as men are to hit their wives (Straus, 1993). However the surveys on which such conclusions are based tend not to ask what acts were done in self-defense, who initiated the act, or who was injured. So mild acts of violence are sometimes lumped together with life-threatening forms of violence. When such information is available, we see that violence directed toward women tends to be far more severe and more difficult to escape than domestic violence directed toward men (Kurz, 1998). The U.S. Bureau of Justice Statistics estimates that close to 900,000 women were attacked by their intimate partners in 1998, down from 1.1 million in 1993 (Rennison & Welchans, 2000). These figures are based on a national survey of crime victims and not on cases reported to the police, which are significantly lower. Indeed, the Bureau of Justice Statistics reports that only a little over half of incidents of violence between intimates are ever reported to the police. Even so, because of the private nature of these acts, a more accurate number of women who are beaten by their intimate partners each year may be over 2 million (Blackman, 1994; A. R. Roberts, 1996).

Children are even more likely to be victims of domestic violence and neglect. In some poverty-stricken countries, children may be consigned to unpleasant and dangerous labor, sold to buy food for the rest of the family, or even murdered in infancy. In the United States, close to 2 million cases of child abuse are reported annually, though some surveys place the figure closer to 7 million. In a given year 1,300 children will die of abuse or neglect (Gelles & Cornell, 1990; U.S. Bureau of the Census, 2000b). If we include slapping and spanking a child in our definition of child abuse, then approximately 9 out of every 10 children under the age of 3 in the United States has been the object of some sort of physical violence on the part of their parents (Straus & Gelles, 1990). Because of the private nature of this violence and the desire of family members to keep it hidden, all these figures are almost certainly underestimates.

Although it would be comforting to believe that domestic violence is rare and occurs only in families that harbor a "sick" parent or spouse, actually it happens with alarming frequency and is likely to be committed by people we would otherwise consider normal. Spouse abuse and child abuse—not to mention elder abuse and violence between siblings—are found in every culture, class, race, and religion. Domestic violence is not an aberration; it is a fundamental characteristic of the way we relate to one another in family settings.

Public Tolerance of Domestic Violence. To understand why domestic violence is so common in this country, we must look at public perceptions and attitudes toward it. In one national survey, one in four wives and one in three husbands said that hitting a partner was "necessary, normal, or good." When the same sample was asked about "slapping or spanking" a 12-year-old child, the figure rose to about 75% (Straus, Gelles, & Steinmetz, 1980).

Being violent with a stranger in public has clear, definite, and punishable consequences. But being violent with a family member in the privacy of one's own home has few. Traditionally we have perceived domestic violence, particularly wife abuse, as somehow less bothersome and more tolerable than other types of violence.

To investigate public tolerance of family violence, psychologists Lance Shotland and Margaret Straw (1976) performed an experiment that involved staging what appeared to be heated altercations between a man and woman as they emerged from an elevator. The researchers set up two scenarios that were identical except for one important detail. In the first, the woman, who is the object of the man's verbal and physical threats, shouts, "Get away from me! I don't even know you!" In the second (with identical actors and identical behaviors), she says, "Get away from me! I don't know why I ever married you!" In the first situation, bystanders intervened 65% of the time (that is, they attempted to stop the apparent fight). In the second, bystanders intervened only 19% of the time. Clearly, the second case was being defined by observers as a domestic dispute between spouses, conjuring up a different set of norms that stopped them from "getting involved" in the private affairs of a couple. The perception of an intimate relationship prevented most people from seeing the incident as a potentially violent and dangerous situation.

Similar perceptions exist at the organizational level. Police departments are often reluctant to get too involved in domestic disputes. Some have arrest policies called "stitch rules," which specify how serious an injury a victim must sustain, measured by how many stitches are required, to justify the arrest of the assailant (Gillespie, 1989). One study found that the majority of domestic disputes and family violence incidents reported to the police resulted in no arrest; either the police did nothing or the offender was referred to other agencies (D. J. Bell & S. L. Bell, 1991). Given this sort of response, it is not surprising that only about 15% of battered women ever contact the police (Straus & Gelles, 1986).

But things are changing. More and more police departments in the United States are revising their unspoken "hands off" policies toward domestic violence cases. In Indianapolis, for example, where the number of domestic violence cases doubled between 1990 and 1991, officers are now required to make an arrest even if they don't directly witness the assault. In addition, officers must have 30 hours of in-service domestic violence training each year. In other cities, domestic violence victims are prohibited from dropping assault charges once they are filed.

Family Violence in Cultural Context. Individual-level factors such as frustration over money, stress, and alcohol and drug use are frequently implicated as major causes of domestic violence. To some analysts, batterers are either psychopaths or people who are just plain prone to violence. But to fully understand domestic violence, we must take a look at some important characteristics of a society.

The United States, one of the most violent industrialized countries on earth, is fundamentally committed to the use of violence to achieve desirable ends (Straus, 1977). It is in our streets, our schools, our movies, our television shows, our toy stores, our spectator sports, and our government. It's even in our everyday language: We *assault* problems, *conquer* fears, *beat* others to the punch, *pound* home ideas, and *shoot down* opinions (Ewing, 1992). For many people in the United States, violence is the appropriate means by which to resolve certain problems. Not surprisingly, then, such cultural patterns of violence spill into the family.

In addition, most societies in the world are dominated by and built around the interests of men. Men occupy the high-status positions, exercise decision-making and political power, tend to dominate interpersonal relationships, and occupy the roles society defines as most valuable (Frieze, Parsons, Johnson, Ruble, & Zellman, 1978). Domestic violence not only is a consequence of male domination but also reinforces it:

> The act of violence is many things at once. At the same instant it is the individual man acting out relations of sexual power; it is the violence of a society—a hierarchical, authoritarian, sexist, class-divided . . . crazy society—being focused through an individual man onto an individual woman. . . . These acts of violence are like a ritualized acting out of our social relations of power: the dominant and the weaker, the powerful and the powerless . . . the masculine and the feminine. (Kaufman, 1987, p. 1)

Male dominance has a long and infamous history (Gelles & Cornell, 1990). Roman law, for instance, justified a husband's killing his wife for reasons such as adultery, wine drinking, and other so-called inappropriate behaviors (Steinmetz, Clavan, & Stein, 1990). The "rule of thumb" in English common law recognized a husband's right to beat his wife with a stick that was no bigger than the circumference of his thumb.

The laws relating to rape in most countries around the world—and in some states in the United States—include what is commonly known as the marital rape exemption. These laws typically define rape as "the forcible penetration of the body of a woman, *not the wife of the perpetrator*," making rape in marriage a legal impossibility (Russell,

1998, p. 71). In eight states, husbands cannot be prosecuted for raping their wives unless they are living apart or legally separated. In 26 other states, they can be prosecuted under certain circumstances but are totally exempt in others (Russell, 1998).

Male dominance has sometimes led to a double standard of acceptable violence. In 1994 a Maryland man who killed his wife with a hunting rifle four hours after finding her in bed with another man pleaded guilty to voluntary manslaughter and was sentenced to 18 months in prison. The sentence was half as long as the prosecution recommended. The judge in the case said afterward that he wished he didn't have to send the man to prison at all. A day after this case, another judge handed down a three-year sentence to a woman who pleaded guilty to voluntary manslaughter for killing her husband after 11 years of abuse. Her sentence was three times longer than what the prosecutors in that case had sought (Lewin, 1994).

Men who beat their partners are not necessarily psychotic, deranged, "sick" individuals. Rather, they are often men who believe that male dominance is their birthright. Such men are actually living up to cultural prescriptions that are cherished in many societies—aggressiveness, male dominance, and female subordination (Dobash & Dobash, 1979). We have a deeply entrenched tendency to perceive domestic violence as "normal" violence, as something that, though not necessarily desirable, is not surprising or unexpected either. Consequently, much of the research in this area has focused on the victims rather than on the perpetrators.

Personal and Institutional Responses to Abuse. One question that has captured the attention of many marriage and family researchers is, Why do women stay in abusive relationships in societies that have made divorce relatively simple? During the 1960s the *masochism thesis*—that is, that women like being humiliated and hurt—was the predominant reason offered by psychiatrists (see, for example, Saul, 1972). Even today many psychiatrists believe masochism—or "self-defeating personality disorder," as it is now called—should be a "legitimate" medical explanation for women who stay in abusive relationships. Other contemporary explanations focus on the woman's character flaws, such as a weak will or pathological emotional attachment.

All these explanations wrongly focus on the victim while paying little attention to her social situation. From a conflict perspective we can see that in a society reluctant to punish abusers, many women may perceive that they have no alternatives and feel physically, economically, and emotionally trapped in their relationships. Indeed, the broader economic structure conspires to keep women in abusive relationships. Women who are unemployed and cannot support themselves financially are significantly less likely to leave an abusive marriage than women who are employed and who therefore have their own source of income (Strube & Barbour, 1983).

The perception that battered women simply sit back and take the abuse, thinking they somehow deserve it, is inaccurate. One study of 1,000 battered and formerly battered women nationwide found that they tried a number of active strategies to end the violence directed against them (Bowker, 1993). They tried to talk men out of beating them, extracted promises that the men wouldn't batter them anymore, avoided their abuser physically or avoided certain volatile topics, hid or ran away, and even fought back physically. Many of these individual strategies had limited effectiveness, however, and so most of these battered women eventually turned to people outside the relationship for informal support, advice, and sheltering. From these informal sources, the women generally progressed to organizations in the community, such as police, social service and counseling agencies, women's groups, and battered women's shelters. Some of these women were able, eventually, to end the violence; others weren't. The study points out that most women actively try to end their victimization.

In some cases, the social organizations and institutions that are designed to help battered women are ineffective. As recently as 10 years ago, for instance, emergency room workers routinely interviewed battered women about their injuries with their husbands present. The courts, too, have historically treated spousal violence less seriously than other crimes, making it even more difficult for women to seek help. In 1978, for instance, an Indiana prosecutor refused to prosecute for murder a man who beat and kicked his ex-wife to death in the presence of a witness and raped her as she lay dying. Filing a manslaughter charge instead, the prosecutor said, "He didn't mean to kill her. He just meant to give her a good thumping" (quoted in Jones, 1980, p. 308).

Sometimes the resources in place to assist battered women are simply inadequate. In rural areas with no public transportation, shelters exist but may be inaccessible to women who live miles away and don't own a car. In small towns, confidentiality is virtually impossible. The fact that people tend to know one another can dissuade a woman from calling a local sheriff's office for help, because the person answering might be a friend or relative of her abusive partner.

The problem of inadequate resources is not limited to scarcely populated rural areas, however. In New York City, for instance, the mayor recently launched a massive campaign against domestic violence. Most buses and subways now display posters encouraging battered women to come forward and seek help from city-supported shelters and other services. Every day about 65 battered women who feel they're in danger call the Victim Services hotline requesting shelter. But every day about 60 of them are told no spaces are available (Sontag, 1997). Some of these women are so desperate that they agree to be bused hundreds of miles away to a place where shelter is available. This remedy may get them out of harm's way, but it may also wreck their work lives, endanger welfare checks, and disrupt their children's schooling.

In sum, the decision to stay in an abusive relationship is the result not of irrationality or mental dysfunction but of rational choices women make in response to an array of conditions, including fear of and harassment by the abuser, the everyday realities of dependence, and the lack of institutional support (Baker, 1997). In that respect, battered women are no different from any other individuals seeking to negotiate the complexities of social life.

CONCLUSION

Social relationships form the center of our personal universes. Life in groups provides us with the sense of belonging that most of us need. However, though these relationships are the principal source of identity, community, happiness, and satisfaction for many, they can be the source of tremendous anguish and suffering for others.

Perhaps the most important group to which we belong is family, a public as well as a private institution. True, most intimate and family behavior occurs away from the watchful eyes of others; we alone have access to our thoughts, desires, and feelings regarding those with whom we are intimately involved. But other people do care about what goes on in our relationships. People around us, the government, even society as a whole, have a vested interest in what happens in our intimate lives.

The social institutions and culture that make up our society also shape the very nature and definition of "family." Today the boundaries of that definition are being pushed by rapidly increasing numbers of "nontraditional" families—dual-earner couples, single-parent households, cohabitors, the voluntarily single, same-sex couples, and so on.

Every family relationship, whether it violates or conforms to current social norms, reflects the dominant ideals and beliefs about what a marriage or a family ought to look like. Although each relationship is unique, this uniqueness will always be bounded by the broader constraints of our cultural, group, and institutional values.

YOUR TURN

There is no universal definition of "family." Our ideas about what a family is depend on the culture we grew up in. Within a particular culture, people may also debate what a family is and which groups get to be defined as a family.

With so much disagreement, it would be interesting to find out how people actually define a family. Go to a spot on campus with a lot of foot traffic and ask passersby for their definition of the word *family*. See if you can find any patterns in people's responses. Do you see a tendency to focus on blood relations, or is the emotional component of family more important? Is the presence of children necessary to definitions of family?

To delve deeper into the diversity of family definitions and experiences, pose the following questions to several friends or classmates. Try to acquire as diverse a sample of respondents as possible by talking to people from different cultural, racial, ethnic, religious, gender, and age groups:

- How many brothers and sisters do you have?
- If they are younger, did your parents expect you to help take care of them?
- Did you share a room with any of them while you were growing up?
- How many different houses and/or apartments did you live in while growing up?
- How often do you see your grandparents?
- Did you ever have grandparents or other relatives live in your house?
- Do you address your relatives by family terms ("Uncle Bob," "Aunt Beth," "Grandpa," "Grandma") or by first name?
- Do you expect to help support your parents when you are older?

Did you notice any interesting trends in people's responses? What do their answers say about the structure of their families? Did you find any consistent differences across cultural, gender, class, race, or age lines? For instance, does the likelihood of sharing a room with a sibling differ for people of different age groups? Do members of different ethnic groups maintain different degrees of contact with grandparents or other relatives? Do they have different expectations about supporting their parents in the future? What do these different responses tell us about the broader structural context within which we live our family lives?

A variation on this exercise would be to examine the content of the personal home pages that more and more families are now posting on the Internet. (If you are using a search engine such as Yahoo, narrow your search by going to the following subcategories: society and culture → people → personal home pages → families.) When I last checked, there were close to 3,000 such sites listed alphabetically. Randomly select 50 or so (or more if you have time or are able to work in groups), and try to document the different categories of information families include about themselves—factual information (for example, size and location of family), likes and dislikes, opinions on political or social issues, links to other Web sites, and so on. Do these pages tend to focus on nuclear families, or do they include information about extended family members? Are certain racial, ethnic, or religious groups over- or underrepresented? Did you notice any differences in the home pages of U.S. families versus families from other societies? What do the content and design of these home pages tell us about the nature and importance of family in people's lives? How can you explain the willingness of these families to expose such private aspects of their lives to the vast, public domain of cyberspace?

CHAPTER HIGHLIGHTS

- In this culture, close relationships are the standard against which we judge the quality and happiness of our everyday lives. Yet in complex, individualistic societies they are becoming more difficult to establish and sustain.

- Many people in the United States long for a return to the "golden age" of the family. But the image of the U.S. family of the past is largely a myth.

- Although monogamous marriage is the only sexual relationship that has achieved widespread cultural legitimacy in the United States, other forms of intimacy (for example, extra- and premarital sex, polygamy) are considered legitimate in other societies.

- Although we like to think that the things we do in our family relationships are completely private experiences, they are continually influenced by large-scale political interests and economic pressures. Furthermore, our choices of romantic partners are governed to some degree by cultural rules that encourage us to form relationships within certain social groups and outside others.

- Divorce is not a solely private experience. It occurs within a cultural, historical, and community context. The high rate of remarriage after divorce indicates that people still view the institution of marriage as desirable.

- Instead of viewing domestic violence (spouse abuse and child abuse) as a product of "sick" individuals, sociologists are likely to view it as the product of a culture that tolerates violence in a variety of situations, traditionally grants men authority over women in family roles, and values family privacy and autonomy over the well-being of individual members.

KEY TERMS

endogamy Marriage within one's social group

exogamy Marriage outside one's social group

extended family Family unit consisting of the parent–child nuclear family and other relatives, such as grandparents, aunts, uncles, and cousins

monogamy Marriage of one man and one woman

neolocal residence Living arrangement in which a married couple sets up residence separate from either spouse's family

nuclear family Family unit consisting of at least one parent and one child

polygamy Marriage of one person to more than one spouse at the same time

virtual community Group of people who use computers to regularly communicate with one another in lieu of face-to-face interaction

Families on the Web

Luc Pauwels

You might feel that there's nothing more boring than looking at someone else's family photo album, Christmas slide show, or vacation video. But for sociologists, family photographs are very important. They represent a valuable source of information about family structure and dynamics. The family photo album allows us to present to the world, and to posterity, an idealized, culturally approved image of our family.

Although family members may value their photographs as a perfect representation of their family and family life, we must understand that in truth these pictures are always a *preferred* image of family life. Nearly every family has a collection of similar shots from the same sorts of events, the happy moments that we consider "normal" landmarks of human success. Birthday parties, weddings, and holiday trips are typical times when we keep the camera at hand.

Meanwhile, we tend not to bring cameras to the sadder or less valued moments of family life (separations, divorces, deaths, and so on). We see family members when they are healthy more often than when they are sick. We favor photographs of people when they are young over those of very old family members. We tend not to take pictures when someone is emotionally upset or angry, when children are fighting with one another, when family members are using the bathroom, or during other moments culturally defined as "unphotogenic." In reality, these moments are much more common and would provide a much more accurate picture of family life than the "happy" moments that grace the pages of family photo albums.

In short, family photographs are thus like all other representations: They never include everything; they are biased and highly selective.

Na

Voor

● "Disagreement in the family?" a Belgian camera retailer's catalog asks in bold lettering. "By just pushing a few buttons, Auntie is removed from the picture in no time." Until now, unhappy moments simply went unrecorded. But today opportunities exist to rewrite memories of happy moments. Unwanted elements—such as an ex-lover in a memorable group picture—can be digitally removed without sacrificing the whole or degrading the original.

The desire to construct and present ideal images of the family has survived a number of innovations in photographic technology. All sorts of manipulations and alterations were already common practice in the 19th century— both at the prephotographic level (for example, staging events and selecting moment and subject) and at the postphotographic level (for example, framing, cropping, soft focusing, retouching, creating photo montage). When portrait studios mushroomed in the 1840s, photographers customized the setting and the costume of their clients to match the status,

profession, or aspirations they wished to emphasize, thus imitating the portrait painters before them. Many photographic studios offered a broad range of painted backgrounds, furniture, and clothing from which a client could choose.

The many new features of digital technology facilitate and even seem to stimulate the creative treatment of reality. Family photographers can digitally adjust their "visual diaries" to reflect certain desires, ideals, or feelings. A new reality can easily be produced through insertions, omissions, recolorings, morphing, and other digital manipulations.

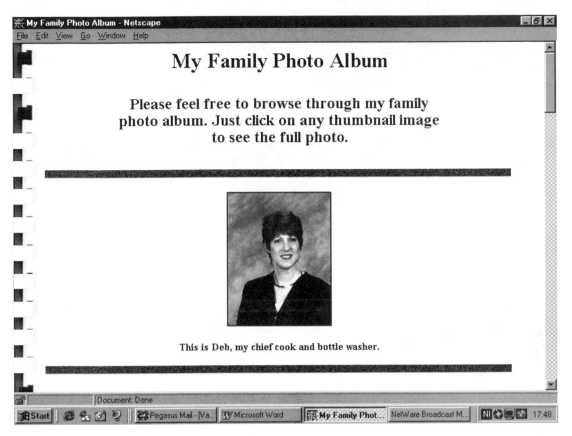

My Family Photo Album

Please feel free to browse through my family photo album. Just click on any thumbnail image to see the full photo.

This is Deb, my chief cook and bottle washer.

● The "electronic" photo album is the latest manifestation of a long-standing social practice, revitalized and upgraded for a digital age.

The World Wide Web is also a new technology being discovered as a vehicle for displaying and disseminating what were once private family stories. A growing number of families have created Web sites dedicated to advertising their successes and sharing their domestic highlights. The traditional family photo album's emphasis was on internal "public relations," directed toward friends, family members, and potential family members. Now, however, a favorable self-image may potentially be displayed to a limitless number of external and anonymous visitors.

Not all family Web sites consciously embrace the opportunity to present themselves to the world at large. Some use the Web primarily as a cheap, slick, and easy-to-update way to maintain contact with distant friends and relatives. They tend to take the public implications and the potential for a wider audience as an unavoidable consequence of posting family information on the Web rather than as an intended forum for communicating their family values. Some of them are well aware of the boring effect their Web site might have on strangers. One disclaimer I found read: "This is a very personal Web page I made for our family so please don't put it on any 'worst of the Web' sites!"

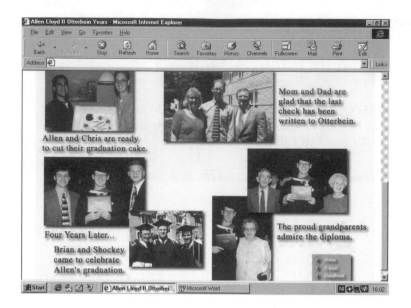

Mom and Dad are glad that the last check has been written to Otterbein.

Allen and Chris are ready to cut their graduation cake.

Four Years Later...
Brian and Shockey came to celebrate Allen's graduation.

The proud grandparents admire the diploma.

The fact that a growing number of families choose to disclose their own private lives to the greedy gaze of anonymous Web surfers is somewhat puzzling. However, whether they are or are not digitally manipulated, family photos remain very vivid expressions of family values (such as happiness, domesticity, loyalty, solidarity) and norms. Most of the time they try to foster a favorable image of the family.

Private Web sites often provide a lot of information about prevailing values in a particular culture. Pictures and stories about love and caring (for grandparents, parents, children, pets), material possessions (cars, houses), achievements in education and sports, and the military "tour of duty" are typical on family Web sites. Inasmuch as family Web site creators are aware of the extended audience, the issues they choose to cover seem to expand far beyond domestic activities and values. Some private Web sites also contain—explicitly or more implicitly—verbal and visual statements about gender relations and roles, politics, religion, sexual orientation, and leisure and sports.

Allen and Brenda's

Welcome To The Upper Ohio Valley

Cat's Meow	Circus	Genealogy	Sherlock Holmes	Guestbook
Flowers	Travel	Boy Mechanic	Pipes	Allen II
Needlework	Ohio Valley	Golf Courses	Cigars	Abigail
Yearbooks	US Navy	WEB Notes	Railroading	Chips
WEB Rings	Trivia Games	E-Mail Us	Links	Searches

How will your site be found in the crowd?

Fahey Family Guestbook

Guestbook by TheGuestBook.com

Sign my GuestBook

Shows: 602. Inputs: 35. Last show: Thu May 25 10:08:33 2000 . Last input: Sat May 20 22:14:07 2000 .

Name: gordon fahey (Homepage)
Country: USA   **Date:** Mon Feb 28 14:17:57 2000
Comment: I like your site very much, especially the web cams....pretty neat.

Gordo

Name: Brian Fahey (Homepage)
Country: england   **Date:** Sat Jan 29 18:53:57 2000
Comment: nice site have you done much geneology contact me if you want any info on my family

Name: Pattie Fahey Castro (Homepage)
Country: U.S.A.   **Date:** Fri Jan 21 09:50:35 2000

● Although the producers and consumers of electronic "family albums" are physically apart, the technology allows them to interact. Often feedback is prompted by asking visitors to sign the "guest book" and to add some phrases of appreciation, suggestions, and other comments. Many family Web sites offer the opportunity to exchange e-mail. Some Web site owners also go to great lengths trying to entertain the visitor with all sorts of games and topics of general interest. These devices are additional attempts to raise interest with the extended audience and to forge a relationship.

Family Web sites also create opportunities to forge links among people all over the world who might have something in common. As one family Web site creator explained:

Although I do not like to use too much personal information or information that would indicate our location or daily routine, I guess I feel that people can find out just about anything that they want in one way or another if they wish to. We have communicated with many interesting people because of the site.... We are looking for people who share our interests or who need information about things

which we know about. It is also a way to share with family and old friends.

The multimedia context of the Web is providing private image makers with an increasingly flexible medium for constructing and disseminating fact and fiction about their lives. The many visual and verbal communication features help channel visitors' possible interpretations in a direction preferred by the Web site creator. Thus families that want to visually reorganize and reinterpret their private experiences and share them with an international audience now have the means.

PART III

Social Structure, Institutions, and Everyday Life

Up to this point you have learned how our everyday lives are constructed and ordered. But this is only part of the picture. What does social life look like from the top down? Once the architecture is constructed and in place, what influence does it exert on our everyday lives? To answer these questions the remaining chapters investigate the organizational and institutional pressures on everyday life and the various sources of structural inequality in society: social class and wealth, race and ethnicity, and gender. Population trends are another structural influence on everyday life. These facets of society may seem ominous and impenetrable. However, you will see that our lives don't completely fall under the control of the social structure. As the concept of the sociological imagination suggests, the collective actions of individuals often bring about fundamental changes in society.

The Structure of Society: Organizations and Social Institutions

The 2000 presidential election will no doubt go down in U.S. history as one of the closest and most bizarre political events of all time. We all witnessed the chaos of election night. Early on Al Gore, the Democratic candidate, was projected as the winner of Florida's 25 electoral votes, giving him the inside track to the presidency; a few hours later that projection was rescinded and Florida was labeled "too close to call." In the early morning hours of the following day, George W. Bush, the Republican candidate, was projected as the winner of Florida, and therefore the election, only to have that projection withdrawn when Florida, again, was declared "too close to call." The ensuing month or so brought a daily dose of street protests; charges of voter fraud; machine and manual recounts; debates over absentee votes, dimpled chads, and butterfly ballots; lawsuits and countersuits; controversial political decisions and legal rulings. On December 13, the U.S. Supreme Court made its final ruling, essentially declaring George W. Bush the next president, even though he received several hundred thousand fewer votes nationwide than his challenger.

To listen to the newspapers and television news programs tell it, here and abroad, the most powerful country in the world was in a state of utter political confusion. The situation was being described in either derisive or apocalyptic terms. U.S. citizens were losing their moral authority to lecture other countries about the virtues of democracy. We were about to face a "constitutional crisis." We were going to be a country without a leader. We were on the brink of anarchy.

Of course, none of that happened. As one journalist put it, "[T]he apparatus of government is still in place, skilled politicians and career civil servants still keep things running, and ultimately nothing apocalyptic is likely to happen. . . . The system will work and life will go on" (Belluck, 2001, p. A9). Indeed, to the average U.S. citizen, nothing was really all that different during the electoral struggle in Florida. Buses and trains and planes still ran on time. Food was still being delivered to grocery shelves. People were still doing their holiday shopping. The stock market remained solid. Government services were still being provided. We all simply went about our business, pausing now and then to witness the political spectacle or to debate with friends and family at the dinner table or with co-workers at the water cooler.

Why didn't the country collapse during this 36-day electoral soap opera? Why didn't violence erupt in the streets and some well-armed faction attempt to forcefully resolve the impasse? To answer that question we must turn to one of the key concepts of this book: social structure. Despite the strong emotions, dire predictions, and sometimes confrontational behavior of the more partisan individuals, the system remained intact. Whether we agreed with the ultimate outcome or not, the legal and political institutions functioned as they were designed to. From local precincts and campaign organizations to state legislatures to the highest court in the land, the system hummed along. To be sure, the motives of some of the individual players were questionable. But the structure itself rose above the actions of these individuals and prevented the sort of large-scale catastrophe that media personalities and pundits predicted.

It remains to be seen what lingering effects this election will have on U.S. society. Things will no doubt change. But for now our everyday lives remain largely unaffected by an event that had the potential for disaster. Indeed, had this election not been as close as it was, most of us would have gone on unaware of the intricacies of the massive political and legal structure that picks our leaders.

One of the great sociological paradoxes of human existence is that we are capable of producing a social structure that can so quietly influence our daily lives but then experience this structure as something other than a human product. It is ironic that we spend most of our lives either within or responding to the influence of larger structural entities—particularly in a society such as the United States that so fiercely extols the virtues of rugged individualism and personal accomplishment.

This chapter focuses on our relationship with the social structure we construct and maintain. This focus requires us to examine the structure not only from the individual's perspective but also from the macro-sociological perspective of the organizations and institutions themselves. Many important social issues look quite different depending on the perspective we use to understand them.

Social Structure and Everyday Life

As you may recall from Chapter 2, social structure is the framework of society that exists above the level of individuals and provides the social setting in which individuals interact with one another to form relationships. The concept of structure is important because it implies a patterned regularity to the way we live our individual lives and in the way societies work.

All scientific disciplines have some notion of structure: Chemists assume the existence of atomic structure; microbiologists rely on molecular structure; physicians couldn't practice medicine if they didn't have a sense of anatomical structure; even astronomers take for granted the structure of the universe (Smelser, 1988). There may be uncertainty about its nature, but members of all these disciplines rely on the concept of structure.

Likewise, structure occupies an important place in sociology. Although sociologists may disagree about its origin, constituent elements, or power over everyday life, few would argue that **social structure**—the social institutions, organizations, groups, statuses and roles, values, and norms that add order and predictability to our private lives—doesn't exist at all. We could not draw any meaningful conclusions about human behavior if we started with the notion that society is haphazard and that things happen by chance alone.

If you know what to look for, you will see that social structure is ubiquitous. Consider, for instance, the components of social structure that affect the experience of going to school. Within the broad U.S. educational institution, there are examples of every component of social structure:

- *Organizations:* National Education Association, National Teachers' Association, state teachers' associations, local school boards, local administrative boards, and so on
- *Groups:* faculty, student body, classes, cafeteria staff, and so on
- *Statuses:* teacher, student, principal, custodian, coach, librarian, and so on
- *Roles:* teaching, learning, disciplining, making and taking tests, coaching, and so on
- *Cultural beliefs:* for example, the belief that education is the principal means of achieving financial success, that it makes possible a complex division of labor, and that it makes a technologically advanced society possible
- *Institutionalized norms:* the expectation that everyone attend school until the age of 16, school rules that determine acceptable behavior (such as not running in the halls, not screaming in class, staying on the school grounds until classes are over), and so on (Saunders, 1991).

The massive structure of the educational system is a reality that determines life chances and choices. You may choose which science class to take in high school, whether to go on to college, and what to major in once you get there, but the availability of jobs to people without a college education and the admissions policies of potential colleges are factors beyond your control. You're reading this book right now not because of your fondness for fine literature but because of the structural requirements of being a college student. You know you must graduate in order to get a good job. To graduate you must get good grades in your classes. To get good grades in your classes, you must keep up with the material so you are prepared for exams. You might rather be doing a number of other things right now—reading a better book, swimming, making love, watching TV, doing nothing, sleeping—but these personal preferences must take a back seat to the more immediate structural demands of college life.

Often the needs of individuals and the needs of the institution are incompatible. Suppose your instructor told you that she or he was going to give everyone in the class an *A* as long as they showed up every day. Your immediate reaction might be joy, because such a grade would no doubt improve your personal grade point average. And, after all, that's something every student wants, right? But what if all instructors in all courses at your school decided to do the same thing? Everybody who simply showed up for class would graduate with a perfect GPA. How would you feel then? Certainly your joy might be tempered by the knowledge that such a campus-wide grading policy would destroy the reputation of your school. As long as the institution of education is structured on the assumption that only the smartest or hardest-working students earn the top grades, such changes—personally beneficial though they may be—will be perceived by others as a sign that your school is academically inferior. Hence your long-term interests may actually be best served by a highly competitive system that ensures that some students will fail.

Although social structure is an essential element in the organization of everyday life, it can at times create problems. Mistakes are often the end result of a chain of events set in motion by a social structure that either induces errors or makes them difficult to detect. What appear to be obvious errors in human judgment are often, on closer inspection, linked to broader system failures. For instance, a study by the Institute of Medicine (1999b) found that serious errors by health professionals are one of the leading causes of death in the United States. In hospitals alone, mistakes—drug mix-ups, surgical errors, misdiagnoses, and so forth—kill as many as 98,000 people a year. More people die from these errors than from traffic accidents, breast cancer, or AIDS. The tendency to sue individual doctors for malpractice in such cases demonstrates an overwhelming cultural perception that these errors are caused by individual incompetence.

But a closer look reveals structural, not just individual, problems. An analysis of 334 drug errors in hospitals found that system failure was responsible for most of them—for example, poor dissemination of drug knowledge to doctors, inadequate availability of patient information, faulty systems for checking correct dosage, inefficient hospital procedure (Leape & Bates, 1995). The Institute of Medicine report recognizes that the problem lies at a level above individual health care workers. It recommends that the health care system build safety concerns into its operations at all levels. It suggests creating a national center for patient safety, establishing a mandatory nationwide reporting system, placing greater emphasis on safety and training in licensing and accreditation evaluations, and developing a "culture of safety" that would help make the reduction of medical errors a top professional priority. Safety procedures in other industries—the commercial airline industry, for example, where co-pilots are required to make sure pilots are performing at a top level—have already proved that structural solutions can reduce problems for individuals.

Social Dilemmas: Individual Interests and Structural Needs

Although social structure can clearly affect the lives of individuals, individual actions can also have an enormous effect on the structure and stability of an entire group or community. We often take for granted that groups of individuals with common interests will attempt to further those interests. Let's say residents want to make sure that their neighborhood is free of crime. It follows logically that each individual would, as a rational person, act to achieve that objective. For instance, everyone would volunteer at some point to "patrol" his or her street at night, or neighbors might all chip in money to improve street lighting.

In actuality, though, the opposite appears to be true (Cross & Guyer, 1980; Messick & Brewer, 1983; Olsen, 1965). People often do not voluntarily act to achieve a common objective unless some sort of device coerces their behavior. Instead, they usually act to ensure their own personal interests. For example, some may not donate money for a new streetlight because they believe others will do so. Such a phenomenon is known as a **social dilemma** (Messick & Brewer, 1983). If each person in a group pursues his or her self-interests, the result may be ruin for everyone. If every person individually decides not to donate money, the new streetlight will never be purchased, and everyone will suffer.

The phenomenon of social dilemmas illustrates how unfettered individualism can have disastrous consequences for the larger society. Major social problems such as environmental pollution can be understood as stemming, at least in part, from the decisions made by people acting in their own interest as opposed to the collective interest. My flinging one bag of trash onto the highway may not seem so significant or destructive. But large numbers of people doing the same thing would be very destructive. If we think of nations as individual actors and the planet as the community to which they belong, many problems that have global significance—including inadequate recycling, failure to conserve energy, and species extinction—can also be understood from this perspective. Two important types of social dilemmas are the tragedy of the commons and the free-rider problem.

The Tragedy of the Commons

The term *commons* was originally used to describe the pasture ground, often located in the center of colonial towns, where all the local herders brought their animals to graze. The land was a public good available to anyone. When everyone used the commons in moderation, the grass was allowed to regenerate, resulting in a perpetual supply of food for the herds (Hardin & Baden, 1977).

However, each herder could increase his or her profits by increasing the size of the herd and letting the animals eat as much as they wanted. Each animal represented a profit for the individual herder whereas the cost of grazing was shared by all the herders. Thus, each herder might rationally decide to increase the size of his or her herd. But when many of the herders allowed their growing herds to eat as much of the grass as they wanted for as long as they wanted, the grass in the commons could not regenerate fast enough to feed them all. The tragic result was that the commons collapsed and the herds that grazed on it died or were sold. Tragedy ensued because the short-term needs of the individual overshadowed the long-term collective needs of the group.

In this illustration, the common resource was grass, and the group was relatively small. However, the "tragedy of the commons" model can be applied to any situation in which common resources can be used by a number of people and are available to all. For example, people have traditionally considered oceanic fish stocks as part of a global commons belonging to no person or nation. They are a seemingly inexhaustible resource available for the taking. Individual nations do have total control over any resources found within their territorial waters (which, for the United States, stretch 200 miles from either coast). But beyond territorial waters everyone has an unrestricted right to fish (Nickler, 1999). Fishers in an open-access system often attempt to catch as many fish as possible, using ever-more-efficient tracking devices and ever-bigger nets.

But the overfishing of these areas eventually results in a decreased population of fish, which can cause the commercial extinction of particular species.

Situations become particularly troublesome when individuals begin to panic. In the flood-prone summer of 1993 a river overflowed its banks in Des Moines, Iowa, wiping out a filtration system and making the municipal water supply unsafe. To restore full water service, the system had to be refilled with clean water. The situation was urgent. Without full water pressure in the city's water pipes, not only were residents without regular water service, but fire engines weren't able to use hydrants. Local officials asked everyone to voluntarily refrain from using tap water in their homes and businesses for a few days. If all the city's residents had limited their water use as asked, everyone in the community would have had water within a couple of days. For some individuals, however, the temptation to use water secretly in the privacy of their own homes was too hard to resist. So many residents violated the city's request that the resumption of full water service was delayed for many more days (Bradsher, 1993). As a result of individuals seeking their own'»ort-term benefits, the entire community suffered.

Why do such dilemmas occur? Part of the problem is a lack of communication and a lack of trust among individual members of a community. I may want to conserve water by using it sparingly but if I think my neighbors are hoarding, I too will hoard to make sure I don't go without. Hence I may follow a line of action that results in a positive outcome for me but that may eventually have a negative outcome for the community. A "sensible" strategy for the common good—that is, one of moderation and conservation—is quite easy to abandon at the first sign of someone else satisfying his or her short-term gains.

The problem is made worse when individuals think that meeting their individual needs w l not affect the community. "Is my using an extra gallon of water *really* going to harm the community?" The dilemma arises when everyone, or at least a substantial number of people, concludes that it will not. As we collectively ignore or downplay the consequences of our actions, we collectively overuse the resource and pave the way for disasters that none of us has caused individually (Edney, 1979).

The Free-Rider Problem

Social dilemmas can also occur when people refrain from contributing something to a common resource because the resource is available regardless of their contribution. Why pay for something that's available for free? For example, it is irrational, from an individual's point of view, to donate money to public television. I can enjoy *Sesame Street, Nova,* and *Masterpiece Theater* without paying a penny. My small personal donation wouldn't be more than a tiny drop in public television's budgetary bucket and would have no noticeable impact on the entire amount needed to run a network anyway. From my point of view, I have no incentive to incur any costs when I don't have to. If everyone acted this way, however, we would all eventually lose the resource. If public television depended solely on voluntary donations—corporate grants and sponsorships actually keep it going—it would have disappeared a long time ago.

Sociologists sometimes refer to this situation as the **free-rider problem** (Olsen, 1965). As the term implies, a free rider is an individual who acquires a good or service without risking any personal costs or contributing anything in return. Free-rider behavior can be seen in a variety of everyday activities, from reading a magazine at a newsstand, without buying, to photocopying a chapter from a book one has not bought. We all enjoy the benefits our tax dollars provide—police, firefighters, smooth roads, and other municipal services. But if taxes were voluntary, would anyone willingly pay for these services?

We can see evidence of the free-rider problem at the institutional level. People often talk about children as a vital resource on whom the future of the country and the planet depend. The care and education of these children can be seen as a public resource. All society benefits when children are in good physical, social, and psychological health. Yet taxpayers often don't see that increasing taxes to improve schools, raise teachers' salaries, or hire more youth social workers will benefit them in the long run.

Solutions to Social Dilemmas

The tragedy of the commons and the free-rider problem can be solved or at least decreased in several ways (Messick & Brewer, 1983). Establishing communication among individuals helps because it allows people to know what others are up to. When individual actions are identifiable, feelings of personal responsibility are likely to increase (Edney & Harper, 1978). However, this solution is not very practical when the group or community is quite large, such as an entire country, for instance.

Another solution is to use coercion through restrictive rules or laws to prevent people from seeking their self-interested goals. Requiring people to pay taxes is one example. Another example is setting up union "closed shops," meaning that to work at a company an employee must join the union and pay union dues. Without this requirement, individual employees would be able to enjoy the benefits provided by the union—higher wages, better working conditions—without having to pay anything for them.

These types of solutions have worked. Many nations with commercial fishing industries have agreed to reduce the harvest of certain species so that stocks could be replenished. And the city of Des Moines set up an emergency hot line that people could call and anonymously turn in violators of the water rules. A work crew would go to a reported home or business and check for unauthorized water use. If the crew found the water meter running, the valve at the curb would be turned off for a week. No appeals were allowed, and water users were never told who turned them in. In addition, the offenders' names and addresses were immediately made known to reporters under Iowa's open records rules and spread across the state by newspapers, radio, and television (Bradsher, 1993). It was a drastic step, but the long-term welfare of the entire community was at stake.

The Structure of Organizations

Social life is far more complex than simply trying to balance individual and collective interests. Those of us who live in a complex society are all, to varying degrees, organizational creatures. We're born in organizations, educated in them, spend most of our adult lives working for them, and will most likely die in them (E. Gross & Etzioni, 1985). Organizations help to meet our most basic needs.

Think about the food that graces your table. The farm where the food is produced is probably a huge organization, as are the unions that protect the workers who produce the food and the transportation companies that bring it to your local stores. And all this is controlled by a vast network of financial organizations that sets prices and by governmental agencies that ensure the food's safety.

To prepare the food that is produced, delivered, and sold, you have to use products made by other organizations—a sink, a refrigerator, a microwave, a stove. To use those appliances you have to make arrangements with other organizations, such as the water and power departments, the gas company, and the electric company. And to pay these bills, you must use still other organizations—the postal service, your bank, and credit companies.

Where does the money to pay the bills come from? Most likely your job. If you are employed, you probably work for yet another organization. And when you receive a paycheck, the government steps in to take its share.

What about the car you use to get to that job? No doubt a huge multinational corporation manufactured it. Huge multinational corporations produced the fuel on which the car runs. The roads you travel on to your destinations are built and maintained by massive organizations within the state and federal governments. You aren't even allowed to drive unless you are covered by insurance, which is available only through an authorized organization.

What if things aren't going well? Say you become sick, or you have an accident, or you have a dispute with someone. Here, too, organizations come into play. You have to use hospitals, insurance companies, police departments, and courts.

You get the picture? Life in a complex society is a life touched by public and private organizations at every turn. In such a society things must be done in a formal, planned, and unified way. For instance, the people responsible for producing our food can't informally and spontaneously make decisions about what to grow and when to grow it. The people responsible for selling it to us can't make its availability random and unpredictable. Imagine what a mess your life would be if you didn't know when your local supermarket would be open or what sorts of food would be available for purchase. What if one day it sold nothing but whole wheat flour, the next day only plums, and the day after that just packaged lunch meats?

In a small-scale community where people grow their own food and the local mom-and-pop store provides everything else, the lack of structure might not be a problem. But this type of informal arrangement can't work in a massive society. There must be a relatively efficient and predictable system of providing goods and services to large numbers of people. The tasks that need to be done just to keep that system going are too complex for a single person—accounting, sales, marketing, research and development, public relations, insurance, maintenance, shipping and receiving, and so on. This complexity makes bureaucracy necessary.

Bureaucracies: Playing by the Rules

The famous 19th-century sociologist Max Weber (VAY-ber) was vitally interested in understanding the complexities of modern society. He noted that human beings could not accomplish such feats as building cities, running huge enterprises, and governing large and diverse populations without bureaucracies. Bureaucracies were certainly an efficient and rational means of managing large groups of people, although Weber acknowledged that these qualities could easily dehumanize those who work in and are served by these organizations.

Today we tend to see bureaucracies primarily as impersonal, rigid machines that trespass into our personal lives. Bureaucracies conjure up images of rows of desks occupied by faceless workers, endless lines and forms to fill out, and frustration over "red tape." Indeed, the word *bureaucrat* has taken on such a negative connotation that to be called one is an insult. Keep in mind, however, that in a sociological sense **bureaucracy** is simply a large hierarchical organization that is governed by formal rules and regulations and that has a clear specification of work tasks.

This specific type of organization has three important characteristics:

- *Division of labor:* The bureaucracy has a clear-cut **division of labor**, which is carefully specified by written job descriptions for each position. The bureaucracy theoretically becomes more efficient because it employs only specialized experts, with every one of them responsible only for the effective performance of her or his narrowly defined duties (Blau & Meyer, 1987). The division of labor enables large organizations to accomplish larger goals than would be possible if everyone acted independently. Tasks become highly specific, sometimes to the point that it is illegal to perform someone else's task. In hospitals, for instance, orderlies don't prescribe drugs, nurses don't perform surgery, and doctors don't help patients with their insurance forms.

- *Hierarchy of authority:* Not only are tasks divided in a bureaucracy, but they are also ranked in a **hierarchy of authority** (Weber, 1946). Most U.S. bureaucracies are organized in a pyramid shape with a few people at the top who have a lot of power and many at the bottom who have virtually none. People at one level are responsible to those above them and can exert authority over those below. Authority tends to be attached to the position and not to the person occupying the position, so that the bureaucracy will not stop functioning in the event of a retirement or a death. When President Bill Clinton took office in 1993, he automatically became the commander-in-chief of the military. But because of his lack of military service, some high-ranking military officials privately expressed their mistrust of him. And yet those officers never questioned their obligation to follow his directives. For example, in 1998 no one disobeyed his command to bomb suspected terrorist outposts in Afghanistan and the Sudan. The hierarchy of authority in bureaucracies not only allows some people to control others, it also justifies paying some people higher salaries than others.

- *Impersonality:* Bureaucracies are governed by an elaborate system of rules and regulations that ensure a particular task will be done the same way by each person occupying a position. With a system of rules, people don't have to "reinvent the wheel" each time a problem arises. Furthermore, rules help ensure that bureaucrats perform their tasks impartially and impersonally. Ironically, the very factors that make the typical bureaucrat unpopular with the public—an aloof attitude, lack of genuine concern—actually allow the organization to run more efficiently. We may want the person administering our driver's license examination to acknowledge us and care about us, but doing so would seriously impede the smooth functioning of the entire system. Think of how you'd feel if the road-test examiner had decided to stop for a cup of coffee with the person who was taking the driver's test before you.

Your university is a clear example of a bureaucracy. It has a definite division of labor that involves janitors, secretaries, librarians, coaches, professors, administrators, and students. The tasks people are responsible for are highly specialized. Professors in the Spanish department don't teach courses in biology. In large universities the specialization of tasks is even more narrowly defined. Sociology professors who teach social deviance probably don't teach demography.

Although the power afforded different positions varies from school to school, all universities have some sort of hierarchy of authority. Usually this hierarchy consists of janitors, groundskeepers, and food service workers at the bottom, followed by students, staff employees, teaching assistants, part-time instructors, professors, and department chairs. At the administrative level are associate deans, deans, vice presidents, and ultimately the president of the university and the board of trustees.

In addition, universities are governed by strict and sometimes exasperating sets of rules. There are rules regarding when and how students can register for classes, rules about when grades must be turned in by professors, graduation requirements, and behavioral policies. Strict adherence by university employees to these rules and policies—sometimes to the chagrin of the frustrated student who can't register for the one political science class he or she needs to graduate—is likely to give universities their final bureaucratic characteristic: impersonality.

As people are fit into roles within bureaucracies that completely determine their duties, responsibilities, and rights, they often become rigid and inflexible and are less concerned with the quality of their work than with whether they and others are playing by the rules. In the 1999 film *Fight Club* the main character, Jack, is driven to destructive rebellion by the mind-numbing nature of his job, illustrated in interchanges like the following:

Boss: I'm going to need you out-of-town a little more this week. We've got some "red-flags" to cover.

Jack's voiceover: It must've been Tuesday. He was wearing his "cornflower-blue" tie.

Jack: [in listless "management speak"] You want me to de-prioritize my current reports until you advise of a status upgrade?

Boss: You need to make these your primary "action items." Here are your flight coupons. Call me from the road if there are any snags. Your itinerary . . .

[Jack hides a yawn and pretends to listen]

Such mechanistic jargon and excessive concern over product movement are the hallmarks of the dehumanizing bureaucracy. They are the source of frustrating procedures and practices that often seem designed to *prevent* things from happening (G. Morgan, 1986). It's not surprising that in such environments people become oriented more toward conformity and getting through the day than toward problem solving and critical thinking.

Although he stressed the functional necessity of bureaucracies in complex Western societies, Weber warned that they could take on a life of their own, becoming impersonal "iron cages" for those within them. He feared that bureaucracies might one day dominate every part of society, locking people in a system that allows movement only from one dehumanizing bureaucracy to another. Weber's fears have been largely realized. The bureaucratic model pervades every corner of modern society. The most successful bureaucracies not only dominate the business landscape, but they have also come to influence our entire way of life.

George Ritzer
The McDonaldization of Society

Sociologist George Ritzer (2000) uses the McDonald's restaurant chain as a metaphor for some of the harmful effects of bureaucratization on society. Each day about 45 million people eat at a McDonald's restaurant. In 2000 alone, McDonald's cash registers rang up more than $40 billion in sales (McDonald's Corporation, 2001). The 28,000 McDonald's restaurants in the United States and in 119 other countries can be found in every corner of life—in airports, shopping malls, movie theaters, and college campuses—in nearly every significant town or city across the United States to the main thoroughfares in major foreign cities such as London, Paris, Bangkok, and Moscow. Dining cars on the Swiss Federal Railroads serve McDonald's meals. China has 63 McDonald's restaurants, even though only 10% of the population can afford a Big Mac. Because of its international appeal, McDonald's fed all the 1996 Olympic athletes in Atlanta (Drucker, 1996).

McDonald's phenomenal success has spawned countless other fast-food chains that emulate its model: Kentucky Fried Chicken, Taco Bell, Domino's Pizza, Long John Silver's, and so on. Its formula has also influenced other types of businesses, among them Toys "R" Us, Starbucks, Econo-Lodge motels, Pearle Vision Centers, Jiffy Lube, Barnes & Noble bookstores, and Blockbuster Video. These organizations have adopted McDonald's system of streamlining processes, offering uniform goods or services, speeding up transactions with customers, and keeping tight control of costs and thus profit margins.

But the success of McDonald's is more than just a story about hamburgers, profits, and business savvy. McDonald's has become a sacred institution, occupying a central place in popular culture. The "golden arches" of McDonald's are among the most identifiable symbols in society today. They're everywhere. When we're not driving past them, we see them on television.

McDonald's appeals to us in a variety of ways:

> The restaurants themselves are depicted as spick-and-span, the food is said to be fresh and nutritious, the employees are shown to be young and eager, the managers appear gentle and caring, and the dining experience itself seems to be fun-filled. We are even led to believe that we contribute, at least indirectly, to charities by supporting the company that supports Ronald McDonald Houses for sick children. (Ritzer, 2000, pp. 7–8)

According to Ritzer, McDonald's has been so successful primarily because it fits Weber's model of the classic bureaucracy. It has a clear division of labor and a uniform system of rules that make it highly efficient and predictable. No matter where you are, you know what to expect when you go into a McDonald's. You know that the ketchup will always be in the same place on the sandwich. French fries cook in precisely 3 minutes and 10 seconds; hamburger patties in 108 seconds. As one observer put it, McDonald's customers "are not in search of 'the best burger I've ever had' but rather 'the same burger I've always had' " (Drucker, 1996, p. 47).

In addition, if you've ever watched the workers behind the counter, you know that each has specialized tasks that are narrowly defined:

> By combining twentieth-century computer technology with nineteenth-century time-and-motion studies, the McDonald's corporation has broken the jobs of griddleman, waitress, cashier and even manager down into small, simple steps. . . . The corporation has systematically extracted the decision-making elements from filling french fry boxes or scheduling staff. . . . They relentlessly weed out all variables that might make it necessary to make a decision at the store level, whether on pickles or on cleaning procedures. (Garson, 1988, p. 37)

McDonaldization is likely to continue, and even spread, for several reasons:

- *It is impelled by economic interests:* Profit-making enterprises will go on emulating the McDonald's bureaucratic model because it leads to higher profits. When McDonald's reaps greater efficiency and therefore higher profits through the increased use of nonhuman technology or the uniformity of its product, others quickly follow suit.
- *It has become a culturally desirable process:* We live in a culture that treasures efficiency, speed, predictability, and control. Our desire for these values often blinds us to the fact that fast foods (as well as their household equivalent, microwaved foods) actually cost us more financially and nutritionally than meals we prepare ourselves. Moreover, for many people the commitment to McDonald's is more emotional than economic. We all have memories of McDonald's: It's where we went after Little League games, it's where we hung out as teenagers, it's where we stopped on the way to the hospital for the birth of a first child, and so on. Because of the hallowed place it occupies in our society, people are willing to overlook its disadvantages.
- *It parallels other changes occurring in society:* With the increasing number of dual-earner couples, families are less likely to have someone with the time or the desire to buy the ingredients, prepare the meal, bring everyone together to eat it, and clean up afterward. Furthermore, a society that emphasizes mobility is one in which the fast-food mentality will thrive.

But McDonaldization does have a downside. Although the efficiency, speed, and predictability of this model may be appealing and comforting to some, the system as a whole has made social life more homogeneous, more rigid, and less personal. The smile on the face of the employee taking your order is a requirement of the position, not a sign of sincere delight in serving you. The fast-food model has robbed us of our spontaneity. Our creativity and desire for uniqueness have been reduced, trapping us in Weber's "iron cage"—a bureaucratic culture that requires little thought about anything and leaves virtually nothing to chance.

The Hierarchical Makeup of Organizations

Given the previous descriptions, you might think that everyone within a bureaucracy feels alienated, depersonalized, or perhaps even exploited. But a person's experience in a large bureaucracy depends in part on where she or he fits in the overall hierarchy of the organization. As the conflict perspective points out, although some people are dehumanized by their place in the hierarchy, others may actually benefit from theirs.

The Upper Echelons. People at the top of large organizations have come the furthest within the bureaucracy, are the fewest in number, and get the most out of their position.

One interesting and disturbing characteristic of bureaucracies is that the executives tend to be extremely homogeneous; that is, they are similar to one another in terms of relevant social characteristics (DiMaggio & Powell, 1983; Kanter, 1977; W. H. Whyte, 1956). Despite the recent influx of women and minorities into executive positions around the world, executives still tend to be predominantly male, members of the dominant ethnic group, and middle or upper class (Zweigenhaft, 1987). Within Fortune 500 companies in the United States, for example, women and minorities hold fewer than 10% of top management positions (cited in Oldham, 2000). In addition, executives' educational, social, and familial experiences are remarkably similar (Kanter, 1977; C. W. Mills, 1956). This homogeneity is caused by not only historical prejudices in hiring and promotion practices but also by the nature of top-level jobs.

The higher one's place is in the bureaucracy, the more ambiguous one's job description becomes. Upper-level executives don't have clearly bounded jobs with neatly defined responsibilities. The executive must be prepared to use his or her discretion and be flexible enough to deal with a variety of different problems at all times. However, although discretion is the defining feature of an executive's position, the bulk of his or her time is not spent in making major decisions, creating, and planning but in attending meetings, writing memos, responding to phone messages and faxes, and participating in company-related social gatherings.

Because the role of the executive is, by nature, vague, no clear-cut criteria exist by which to evaluate whether a person is performing the job effectively. Such things as sales and production records or profit margins can provide only indirect indicators of an executive's competence. Asked what makes an executive effective, top-level employees indicated such vague factors as the ability to communicate and to win acceptance as the most important criteria (Kanter, 1977).

In such an environment, rapid communication, common language, and common understanding are important. From the perspective of the organization, the best way to ensure efficiency, then, is to limit top-level jobs to people who are similar to one another, who have had similar experiences, and who come from similar backgrounds. The result is a closed circle of executives who resemble one another but who are insulated from the rest of the organization. Because of the structure of their occupational roles, white male executives are sometimes uncomfortable with people seen as different, such as racial and ethnic minorities and women.

A self-fulfilling prophecy is embedded in this structure as well. The more closed and exclusive the network of executives, the more difficult it is for "outsiders" to break in. Their very difficulty gaining access to the top level of the organization is then perceived as a sign of their incompetence and an indicator to the insiders that they were right to close their ranks in the first place.

The Middle Ground. The view from the middle is quite different. The middle is in some ways the most depressing part of a bureaucracy (Kanter & Stein, 1979). Those at the top set the organizational agenda and dictate policy, and those at the bottom solely follow orders and directives from above. The people in the middle are caught between those below, whose cooperation they need, and those above, who selectively grant them the authority to implement organizational policy. Hence, middle-level employees are sometimes trapped in a world of conflicting role expectations.

Often the morale of people in the middle is sustained by the belief that they have a shot at the top. If I believe I have a chance to be promoted at some point in the future, my boring and unfulfilling job as a middle-level manager will hold different meaning for me than it would if I expect to remain in the same position forever (McHugh, 1968). It becomes a step on the ladder of success, a necessary but temporary stage in my upward mobility. Unpleasant tasks may be minor inconveniences, but they are the price I have to pay. This hope of future promotion may drive people in the middle to concentrate on accumulating bits of status and privilege so they can make enough of an impact to gain recognition from those above.

For most middle-level employees, however, the hope of upward mobility is just that—hope. Because of the pyramid structure of most bureaucracies, the vast majority of middle-level employees will not move up. Many simply fail in the increasingly competitive push for advancement into the upper echelons of the organization. Others are stuck in jobs that provide little or no opportunity for advancement. Some people are able to develop a comfortable niche in the middle (Kanter & Stein, 1979), but others are likely to harbor a bitterness that creates feelings of alienation and anger and may manifest itself in attempts to retaliate and punish the company.

The structure of most large organizations often forces middle-level managers to become cautious in their approach to their jobs. Unwilling to jeopardize the limited privileges they have attained, middle-level managers may become controlling, coercive, and demanding in their relationships with the people they supervise, ruling their narrow domain with an iron hand, "like a school teacher more concerned about the neatness of the paper than its ideas" (Kanter & Stein, 1979, p. 95).

For some people in the middle, membership in the organization becomes their life, often to the detriment of other roles and relationships. Almost 50 years ago sociologist William H. Whyte (1956) described how the personal lives of rising young executives were often overshadowed by their desire to succeed in the corporate world. Large organizations instilled in their employees a corporate social ethic, a belief that "belongingness" to the group was the ultimate need of the individual. Such beliefs encouraged total commitment to the organization, making a person's private life irrelevant for smooth organizational functioning.

Whyte's depiction of the private costs of organizational life ring true today. Organizations still value team players, middle-level employees who place organizational interests above their own (Jackall, 1988). To be a good team player one must avoid expressing strong political or moral opinions, sacrifice one's home life by putting in long hours, and be forever obedient to one's superiors. Being seen as a loyal and effective group member and sticking to one's assigned position are also important. Distinctive characteristics, such as being abrasive or pushy or not knowing when to back off, are dangerous in the bureaucratic world. According to one study, one of the most damaging things that can be said about a middle-level manager is that she or he is brilliant. This judgment usually signals that the individual has publicly asserted her or his intelligence and is perceived as a threat to others (Jackall, 1988).

Interestingly, although organizations still value the ideal of team play, individuals today seem to be less willing to sacrifice their personal lives and beliefs for the organization. Two sociologists, Paul Leinberger and Bruce Tucker (1991), interviewed the sons and daughters of the original "organizational men" whom Whyte had interviewed back in the 1950s. Leinberger and Tucker found that these individuals were very different from their parents in values and attitudes. They tended to be individualists, more inclined to pursue self-fulfillment than a feeling of belongingness to the organization. Given recent social trends, this finding is not surprising. In an era when corporate mergers, relocations, and downsizing are commonplace, organizational loyalty makes less sense for the individual.

Although few desire to go back to a past when middle-level employees sacrificed everything for their career aspirations, Leinberger and Tucker (1991) point out that today's cultural emphasis on individualism has also created other problems, such as feelings of isolation, the inability to commit to others, and the absence of a sense of community.

The Lower Echelons. A discussion of the everyday experience of bureaucracy would be incomplete without discussing what it looks like from the bottom. Those who stand lowest in the organization's hierarchy are paid the least, valued the least, and considered the most expendable (Kanter & Stein, 1979). The real sign that one is at the bottom is the degree to which he or she is controlled by others. People at the bottom don't have the right to define their occupational tasks themselves. They have little discretion, little autonomy, little freedom, and little influence. In the university bureaucracy, for example, students usually don't have much say over the content of their courses, the curriculum of their major, or the requirements necessary for graduation.

Most corporations are still organized in terms of ideas developed in the early 1900s. The fundamental principle is that a highly specific division of labor increases productivity and lowers costs. Hence, the low-level work tasks in a bureaucratic organization are usually subdivided into small parts that can be performed repetitively by unskilled workers. This structure provides management with the maximum control over workers' jobs, and the workers themselves become "an indistinguishable swarm" (Kanter & Stein, 1979, p. 178).

Technological advancements often coincide with the subdivision of low-level jobs and a decline in the level of skills required to do them (Hartmann, Kraut, & Tilly, 1989). For example, in the insurance industry, the skilled work of assigning risks and assessing people's claims has been increasingly incorporated into computer software programs. What once required a great deal of human judgment and discretion is now almost completely routinized. Less-skilled, less-experienced, lower-paid clerks can now perform the work once performed by skilled workers and professionals (Hartmann, Kraut, & Tilly, 1989).

This process, called **de-skilling**, creates jobs that require obedience and passivity rather than talent and experience. De-skilling provides the organization with clear financial benefits but creates low levels of job satisfaction among the employees. Dull and repetitive tasks that offer little challenge, such as assembly line work, account for a substantial amount of the discontent experienced by workers at the bottom of large bureaucracies (U.S. Department of Health, Education, and Welfare, 1973). In one study, assembly line workers in textile and automobile plants were compared to skilled technicians in the chemical industry. Because the skilled workers had jobs that involved the exercise of judgment and initiative, they were much less alienated and found their jobs much more rewarding than did the assembly line workers (Blauner, 1964).

Attempts at enriching the otherwise dull work lives of people at the bottom have been somewhat successful. Workers at the Motorola Company had to assemble a portable telephone beeper that consisted of 80 small parts. In the traditional way, each worker made a small change and passed the unit to the next worker. In the revised procedure, each worker assembled an entire unit, and the worker's name appeared on the completed beeper. Although the assembly costs were higher, the company claimed that the quality of the product was also higher and absenteeism and turnover rates were lower (E. Gross & Etzioni, 1985).

Without such workplace innovations, the task facing many workers at the bottom is to make their occupational lives tolerable by exerting some kind of control over the work they do. You might think that the top-down flow of authority in bureaucratic organizations would make such a task relatively impossible. In reality, though, lower-level employees are rarely completely powerless and can be somewhat autonomous, even creative, in their positions.

For one thing, the sheer size of large corporations makes it next to impossible for middle- and upper-level managers to supervise directly and therefore exert continuous authority over lower-level workers. Substantial opportunities exist, even in the most highly structured and repetitive jobs, for workers either to redefine the immediate nature of their tasks or to willingly and secretly violate the expectations and orders of superiors. For instance, one study found that clerical, service, and manual workers often figure out ways to do required chores in less than the time allotted by management. They can then spend the rest of their time doing what they want (Hodson, 1991).

In sum, lower-level workers are not necessarily powerless automatons whose lives are totally structured from above. In fact, the authority of middle-level managers thoroughly depends on their subordinates' willingness to cooperate and abide by management's directives. People who don't care about the organization because they feel it doesn't care about them can allow mistakes to go through, put in the minimum amount of time possible, or engage in deliberate sabotage. Such worker resistance can be disastrous for the manager and for the organization as a whole (Armstrong, Goodman, & Hyman, 1981). When they are organized, lower-level workers can even exert tremendous influence over the policies of a company, through strikes, slowdowns, and collective bargaining arrangements.

The Creation of Organizational Reality

Organizations are more than just structure, rules, policies, goals, job descriptions, and standard operating procedures. According to the symbolic interactionist perspective, their formal, structural characteristics are created, maintained, and changed through the everyday actions of their members (G. Morgan, 1986).

The language of an organization is one of the ways it creates its own reality. At one level, new members must learn the jargon of the organization to survive within it. To function within the military system, for example, a recruit must learn the meaning of a dizzying array of words, phrases, acronyms, abbreviations, slang, sounds, and symbols that are unintelligible to outsiders (Evered, 1983). More important, language helps generate and maintain the organization by marking boundaries between insiders and outsiders.

The organizations that work well are those in which everyone internalizes the same rules, values, and beliefs. The best-selling managerial book *In Search of Excellence* states that building a strong corporate culture requires "shaping norms," "instilling beliefs," "inculcating values," and "generating emotions" (Peters & Waterman, 1982). Corporate slogans such as "Quality is Job 1" (Ford), "Progress is our most important product" (General Electric), "Just do it" (Nike), and "Think different" (Apple) communicate the values around which organizations build and symbolize important aspects of the corporate philosophy (G. Morgan, 1986). In some organizations new members are told stories about the founding of the organization, its charismatic leaders, or some other significant event that becomes a metaphor for the culture of that organization.

Whatever the official rules, beliefs, and values of the organization, people have their own ideas and may develop their own informal structure within the larger formal structure of the organization (Meyer & Rowan, 1977). For example, restricting output is one norm that frequently emerges in factory settings (P. Thompson, 1989). Employees collectively decide, implicitly or explicitly, not to produce as much as they are physically capable of producing. This informal system of productivity norms develops partly out of a mistrust of management and the belief that increased productivity would result in higher expectations, not higher rewards (Roethlisberger & Dickson, 1939). Those who produce too much or who work too quickly are considered "rate busters," deviants within the factory subculture. Indeed, rate busters are likely to be employees whose skill and seniority place them in relatively strong positions. Only a worker with such status can escape the sanctions of fellow workers (Burawoy, 1979).

Restricted output can also be seen in the college classroom. Most instructors tell their students that classroom discussion is important and that they may even use it as a criterion for assigning a final grade. Yet rarely does every student in a class, or even a majority of students, participate. Most college students know that a small group of people—perhaps 3 or 4 in a class of 40—can be counted on to respond to questions asked by the professor or to comment on any issue raised in class. These students relieve the remainder of the class from the burden of having to talk at all (Karp & Yoels, 1976). But although these talkative students are carrying the discussion for the entire class, they tend to be disliked by others. A strong norm among many students says that people shouldn't talk too much in class (Karp & Yoels, 1976). Such linguistic "rate busting" upsets the normative arrangement of the classroom and, in the students' eyes, may increase the instructor's expectations, thereby hurting everyone in the long run. Other students indicate their annoyance by audibly sighing, rolling their eyes, rattling their notebooks, or openly snickering when a classmate talks too much.

One of the fascinating ironies of large organizations is that if everyone followed every rule exactly and literally, the organization would eventually self-destruct. For example, the goal of the highly bureaucratized criminal court system is to ensure justice by punishing those who have violated society's laws. Each person accused of committing a serious crime is constitutionally guaranteed a trial by a jury of peers. The jury trial is considered the epitome of justice and has been played out in movies and television so often that we all know what it looks like even if we haven't directly experienced it ourselves. However, the day-to-day operations of the criminal court system bear little resemblance to this common media image. Public defenders, district attorneys, private attorneys, and judges actually work closely together to move offenders through the system in an orderly fashion (Sudnow, 1965). Only a tiny percentage of criminal cases—between 10% and 20%—ever go to trial (D. C. Gibbons, 1992). The rest are either dismissed or, more commonly, settled through plea bargaining, an arrangement whereby, in exchange for a less severe punishment, the accused pleads guilty to a less serious crime than the original charge. Over 93% of criminal convictions in federal cases result from guilty pleas rather than trials (U.S. Sentencing Commission, 1998).

If judges and attorneys followed the procedural rules to the letter and provided all their clients with the jury trial that is their constitutional right, the system would break down. The courts, already overtaxed, would be incapable of handling the volume of cases. Thus the informal system of plea bargaining has taken root, allowing the courts to continue functioning. Those individuals who play exclusively by the rules, such as a young, idealistic public defender who wants to take all her or his cases to trial, are subject to informal sanctions by judges and superiors, such as inconvenient trial dates or heavier caseloads.

In sum, organizational life is a combination of formal structural rules and informal patterns of behavior. Codified rules are sometimes violated and new, unspoken ones created instead. Stated organizational goals often conflict with the real ones. Despite what may appear to be a clear chain of command, the informal structure—friendships, coalitions, and so on—often has more of an impact on how things are done.

Organizations and Institutions

Understanding the influence of organizations on our everyday lives tells only part of the story. Organizations themselves exist within a larger structural context, acting as a sort of liaison between people and major social institutions such as the economic system, government, religion, health care, and education. As we saw in Chapter 2, institutions are stable sets of statuses, roles, groups, and organizations that provide the foundation for behavior in certain major areas of social life. They are patterned ways of solving the problems and meeting the needs of a particular society.

Organizational Networks within Institutions

Like individual people, organizations are born, grow, become overweight, slim down, migrate, form relationships with others, and die. They interact with one another, too, cooperating on some occasions and competing on others, depending on the prevailing economic and political winds. Just as we can talk about a hierarchy of people or groups within an organization, we can also talk about a hierarchy of organizations within an institution. As with people, some organizations are more powerful than others and can dictate the manner in which others live their lives. When giant corporations such as General Electric, Microsoft, Coca-Cola, and IBM change their operations or come up with an innovative new product, they immediately influence the practices of other organizations throughout their respective industries. If one of these titans decides to downsize or expand its operations, the effects are felt throughout the entire financial community.

But even powerful organizations like these cannot stand alone. Massive networks of organizations are linked by common goals and needs. The networks are often so complex that organizations from very different fields find themselves dependent on one another for survival.

Micro-Macro Connection
The U.S. Health Care System

Consider the U.S. health care system, a major social institution. Think about the vast network of organizations that are necessary for a single hospital to operate. First of all, the hospital is tightly linked to all the other hospitals in the area. A change in one, such as a reduction in the number of patients treated in the emergency room or the opening of a new state-of-the-art trauma center, would quickly have consequences for all the others. The linkage among hospitals enables the transfer of equipment, staff, and patients from one hospital to another when necessary.

The hospital must also link to formal training organizations such as medical schools, nursing schools, and teaching hospitals. These organizations usually affiliate with larger universities, thus expanding the links in the network. And, of course, the American Medical Association and various licensing agencies oversee the establishment of training policies and credentials.

To survive financially, the hospital must also make connections to funding organizations. Hospitals have traditionally been owned and operated by a variety of governmental, religious, nonprofit, and for-profit organizations. They must operate under a set of strict regulations, which means they must also link to the city, state, and federal governmental agencies responsible for certification, such as the Joint Commission on Accreditation of Hospitals (Perrow, 1986). Add to these the links to the medical equipment industry, the drug industry, insurance companies, the legal profession, charities, political action committees working on health care reform, and patients' rights groups, and the system becomes even more complex.

The fact that each of these parts of the health care system is a part of its own complex bureaucratic network is mind-boggling. Yet despite this institution's size and importance, when patients go to a hospital they don't see it as a node in the vast health care network. They see it in terms of the individuals they encounter. Patients are obviously much less interested in the hospital's organizational links than they are in whether their nurse treats them compassionately or not.

Thus the need for good person-to-person links guides the policies of the whole institution. For example, the costs of medical miscommunication can be severe—patients sometimes don't follow treatment regimens they don't understand, pass on infectious diseases because they don't know how often to take their medication, or miss appointments for follow-up care. Doctors miss diagnoses or get people to agree to procedures they don't fully understand.

In an increasingly diverse society, where people speak a variety of languages, governments and hospitals are scrambling for ways to deal with the problem of poor communication. Some states require hospitals to provide interpreters for patients with little or no English skills or risk losing Medicaid and Medicare reimbursements, but the rules are vague and enforcement difficult. Hiring full-time interpreters can be costly, especially in large cities such as New York, where hundreds of languages are spoken. So some hospitals compile comprehensive lists of existing staff members who speak other languages. But for most hospitals the ability to treat non-English-speaking patients relies on the hit-and-miss use of volunteers, patients' relatives, even bystanders to act as interpreters (Fein, 1997). They go to such lengths because they realize that the well-being of the entire institutional network can sink or swim on the actions of individual people.

Institutional Pressures toward Similarity

If you think about how many varieties of organizations exist in the world, you may be tempted to focus on their obvious differences. Some are large, others small. Some are formal and complex, others informal and simple. Some have a pyramid-shaped chain of command, others are more egalitarian (E. Gross & Etzioni, 1985). Sociologists have long been interested in the unique ways different organizations adapt to changing political, economic, cultural, or environmental circumstances. However, organizations seem to be more similar than different and even tend to imitate one another's actions as they become established in a particular institution (DiMaggio & Powell, 1983).

Organizational similarity is not really that surprising. Because of the nature of the problems that organizations in the same industry have to address, they come to adopt similar methods of dealing with them. For instance, the major U.S. commercial television networks—NBC, ABC, CBS, and Fox—see the success that one has with a particular type of program and try to attract viewers in much the same way. As you well know, the perceived popularity of a certain type of television show—such as the greedy game show where people can win millions of dollars; the sitcom revolving around the lives of good-looking, single, urban, young adults; or the "reality-based" show where ordinary people are filmed 24 hours a day—creates an avalanche of similar shows on other networks. In short, instead of adjusting directly to changes in the social environment—such as the shifting tastes of the television viewing public—organizations end up adjusting to what other organizations are doing (DiMaggio & Powell, 1983).

The surprising fact is that the imitated practices are not necessarily more effective. After once-novel strategies have spread throughout an industry, they no longer improve the organization's performance. Viewers eventually get sick of funny home video shows, hospital dramas, or shows where ordinary people are plopped down in some exotic locale and are filmed getting on each other's nerves and betraying one another for a lot of money. The net effect of the imitations is to reduce innovation within the industry.

The tendency for organizations to emulate one another is heightened in times of institutional uncertainty (DiMaggio & Powell, 1983). When new technologies are poorly understood, when the physical environment is undergoing dramatic changes, or when local, state, and federal governments are creating new regulations or setting new agendas, organizations are likely to be somewhat confused about how things ought to be done. Just as individuals look to one another to help define ambiguous situations and determine an appropriate course of action, so do organizations.

Take changes in the field of higher education, for instance. Many colleges and universities across the country are being forced to address the problem of how to attract more students. Such was the case several years ago at the university where I teach. An outside consultant was called in to design a new marketing strategy for the school. He had some clear strategies for "packaging" the school's image to make it more attractive to prospective students: redesigned brochures, a new recruitment video, a flashy Web site, state-of-the-art bulk mailing techniques, and so on. But he was doing the same thing for several other schools competing for the same shrinking pool of students. He admitted that many of the "novel" strategies he advised us to use were things other universities were already using. We were addressing a new and uncertain dilemma by replicating the practices of other organizations in the network.

Organizations also resemble one another because those who run them, particularly professionals, tend to come from similar training backgrounds. In many institutions the professional career track is so closely guarded that the individuals who make it to the top are virtually indistinguishable from one another (DiMaggio & Powell, 1983). Medical schools are important centers for the development of organizational norms among doctors. Furthermore, the fact that most doctors belong to the American Medical Association creates a pool of individuals with similar attitudes and approaches across a range of organizations. When these doctors become administrators, they will likely bring this common approach to running a hospital.

In sum, certain organizational forms dominate not necessarily because they are the most effective means of achieving goals but because social forces such as institutional uncertainty and the power of professions to provide individuals with a single normative standard create pressures toward similarity. Such similarity makes it easier for organizations to interact with one another and to be acknowledged as legitimate and reputable within the field (DiMaggio & Powell, 1983). But this homogeneity is not without its costs. When organizations replicate one another, institutional change becomes difficult, and the iron cage of bureaucracy becomes harder to escape.

Globalization and Social Institutions

You've seen throughout this book so far the enormous effect that globalization is having on everyday life. Many of our important social institutions have become international in scope—notably communications, economics, education, and religion. How do such global institutions meet the needs of human beings around the world?

Communication Media

Electronics and telecommunications give people worldwide, immediate access to other cultures, making it practically impossible for societies to exist in complete isolation. Certainly the Internet has done more to bring people from disparate cultures together than any other communications device. But the computer isn't the only electronic globalizing force. Consider the impact that television has had on the world.

No other medium can match television for the size of its audiences and its access to people's homes. Between 1980 and 1995 the number of households with television sets worldwide increased by 100 million, with the most dramatic growth occurring in Africa, Asia, and Latin America (see Exhibit 9.1). Television is now watched by close to 3 billion people a day (Barker, 1997). Two billion people watched France defeat Brazil in soccer's 1998 World Cup (Croteau & Hoynes, 2000).

But the global impact of television is not just a matter of numbers. For instance, in the late 1980s Soviet and East European governments were unable to prevent the reception of Western television broadcasts. Street protests taking place in one country were watched by millions of people in others, many of whom took to the streets themselves. The 1989 revolutions that marked the fall of the Soviet Union and other regimes in the Soviet bloc have been called the first "television revolutions" (Giddens, 2000).

Television's global growth has also occurred along commercial lines. That is, television doesn't simply provide people around the world with useful, practical information. It provides a commercial outlet for an ever-expanding international market. You can find U.S.–made sitcoms, dramas, music videos—and, above all, commercials—in virtually every corner of the world today. U.S. media corporations control 60% of the film distribution networks in Europe, and over half the movies shown on European television are made in the United States. MTV reaches over 200 million households in 71 countries; CNN broadcasts to over 800 million people in 210 nations and territories around the world (Croteau & Hoynes, 2000).

That's not to say that people elsewhere watch only U.S. television shows. The top-rated shows in almost any country are, by and large, local products. But even locally produced television shows may be influenced by U.S. television. In China, for example, Shanghai TV airs a Chinese version of *Sesame Street,* backed by General Electric ("World view," 1998). *America's Funniest Home Videos* is copied as *Smile, Please* in Germany and *Beadle's About* in England (Croteau & Hoynes, 2000). In Mexico, a New York–based advocacy group joined with sociologists and television producers to create a U.S.–style soap opera called *Acompáñame* (*Come Along with Me*). However, instead of the standard soap opera fare, where characters lead lives of corruption and intrigue, this show depicts a lower-class family that practices family planning. In one episode,

Exhibit 9.1 **Global Growth in Television Ownership**

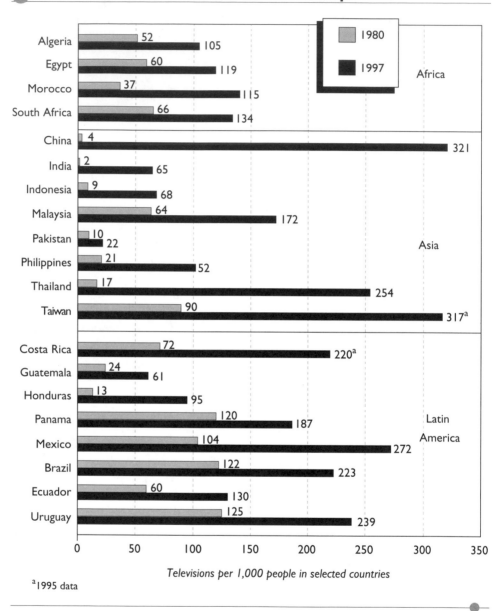

Televisions per 1,000 people in selected countries

[a] 1995 data

Source: U.S. Bureau of the Census, 2000b.

the husband accompanies his wife to a birth control clinic. In the six months following this episode, registration at Mexico's family planning clinics jumped by 33% (cited in Steiner, 1998a).

Economics

Looking around my office, I notice that my telephone, radio, and computer were made in Japan; my desk and chair in the United States; my watch in the Philippines; my stapler in Great Britain; my calculator in Taiwan; my shoes in Korea; my pants in Hong Kong; my bottled water in France; the frame holding a picture of my kids in Thailand; and my briefcase, paper clips, and tea kettle in China. Because of the rapid increase in recent years in the economic links among producing nations, your life is probably similarly filled with products made in other countries. Global trade grew from $380 billion in 1950 to $5.86 trillion in 1997, a 1500% increase (L. R. Brown & C. Flavin, 1999).

Economic globalization is more than just a matter of more goods being shipped from one place to another, however. Businesses that once operated exclusively in their home country now are **multinational corporations,** extending their markets and production facilities globally. For instance, the Sony Corporation—for years a symbol of the successful Japanese corporate model—has relocated so many of its factories to countries outside of Japan that 60% of its workforce is now non-Japanese (Greider, 1997). The biggest Japanese auto makers, including Toyota, Honda, Mazda, Nissan, and Subaru, now manufacture many of their cars in the United States. As a result, many aspects of the "Japanese model of production"—which places heavy emphasis on teamwork and cooperation—have become an integral part of the U.S. economy (L. Graham, 1995).

If a product wasn't manufactured in another country, chances are that some of its component parts were (such as Japanese computer chips in U.S.–made cars). Almost 40% of all the parts used in U.S. manufacturing, for example, are imported from other countries (Cetron, Rocha, & Luckins, 1991). In 1997 the U.S. Federal Trade Commission established a policy whereby a product can bear the label "Made in the U.S.A." if "substantially all" of it was made in the United States. The Boeing 777 wide-body airplane is a shining example of U.S. dominance in advanced aeronautical technologies, but sections of the aircraft are actually manufactured in 12 different countries (Greider, 1997).

The social, political, and economic processes involved in globalization have made national boundaries all but irrelevant. Multinational corporations don't owe their allegiance to any one country's political authority or culture. At the same time, national governments and international financial organizations such as the World Bank, the World Trade Organization, and the International Monetary Fund loan money to countries all over the world to finance development and reconstruction projects. (For more on the global economic impact of international financial organizations and multinational corporations, see Chapter 10.)

In many ways, the world is becoming a single economic unit. For instance, in 1999 eleven Western European countries agreed to adopt a common currency, the euro. Furthermore, with the costs of communication and computing falling rapidly, barriers of time and space that traditionally separated national markets have also been falling. Cultural differences aside, most countries today share a similar language, the language of money (Bradshaw & Wallace, 1996). Even the most remote rural villagers are linked to the world economy as they carry out transactions over the Internet and send and receive goods around the world. The very idea of a "national border," in all but the most obvious geographic sense, is becoming less relevant as labor and commerce flow from one country to another (Aronowitz & DiFazio, 1995).

A global economy has its everyday advantages. Goods and services manufactured in a country where wages are lower are less expensive for consumers in other countries. Universally accepted credit cards such as Visa and MasterCard make international travel more convenient. Snack bars in Toyko's Narita Airport accept American money. Global economic influence has enabled a significant portion of the world's population to be healthier, eat better, and live longer than the royalty of past civilizations (Kurtz, 1995).

But global trade has also created some interesting everyday dilemmas. For instance, financial institutions must keep close track of holidays around the world to avoid trying to do business on nonbusiness days. In some countries, holidays are determined by the lunar calendar, which not only varies from year to year but may vary from area to area within a country based on local customs. In other countries, such as France, the dates of some bank holidays are a matter of negotiations between the banks and the unions that represent their employees. Even weekends are defined differently in different countries. In Taiwan, the weekend consists of every Sunday and the second and fourth Saturday of each month. In Malaysia, it is every Sunday and only the first Saturday of every month. And in Lithuania, one-day weekends are occasionally followed by four-day weekends (Henriques, 1999).

Globalization has fostered some more serious social problems as well, including higher levels of unemployment in countries with labor and environmental protections and the exploitation of workers in poor, developing countries. The result is a world-wide system of inequality whose problems are often invisible to consumers. For instance, most of the lace that goes into making the shawls, curtains, doilies, and under-garments sold in many Western societies is imported through a vast network of traders and exporters. Yet the fabric itself is produced by a small group of poor "housewives" in a few secluded villages in India, who work more than 8 hours a day making the lace in addition to the 8 hours they spend each day doing housework (Mies, 1982). As you'll see in more detail in the next chapter, not everyone is an equal player in the global economy. But because the origin of products is seldom clear-cut, it is difficult to boycott manufacturers that profit from exploiting poor laborers or countries with inadequate policies protecting workers and the environment.

Critics also argue that pressure to compete in the global marketplace will erode the ability of governments to set their own economic policies and protect national interests. One hundred and fifty years after Karl Marx and Friedrich Engels wrote their famous *Communist Manifesto,* their predictions about the divisive and painful consequences of globalization sound like a description of the contemporary global economy:

> All old-established national industries have been destroyed or are daily being destroyed. They are dislodged by new industries whose introduction becomes a life or death question for all civilized nations . . . industries whose products are consumed not only at home but in every quarter of the globe. . . . The intellectual creations of individual nations become common property. (Marx & Engels, 1848/1982, pp. 12–13)

Marx and Engels could easily have been talking about the dominance of the 21st-century consumer culture, where Nike, Coca-Cola, McDonald's, Starbucks, and other corporate icons have truly become universal symbols. To many, economic globalization is homogenizing cultures and values around the world:

> A few decades ago, it was still possible to leave home and go somewhere else: the architecture was different, the . . . language, lifestyles, dress, and values were different. That was a time when we could speak of cultural diversity. But with economic globalization, diversity is fast disappearing. . . . When global hotel chains advertise to tourists that all their rooms in every city of the world are identical, they don't mention that the cities are becoming identical too: cars, noise, smog, corporate highrises, violence, fast food . . . Nikes, Levi's, Barbie Dolls, American TV. . . . What's the point of leaving home? (Turning Point Project, 1999, p. A7)

Finally, the pressures of global economic competition can have serious ramifications for private lives everywhere. For example, the *Calophyllum lanigerum* tree, which grows in the rain forests of Malaysia, produces a substance that may destroy the HIV virus. Thus the Malaysian rain forests may contain the cure for AIDS. But multinational logging companies are fighting with multinational pharmaceutical companies, international medical researchers, and the Malaysian government to continue highly profitable heavy cutting in these rich forests (Bradshaw & Wallace, 1996). A medical treatment that could possibly benefit millions of people worldwide is being destroyed as people and companies in another country try to carve out their piece of the economic pie.

Education

The prospect of international economic competition can also foster change in a country's educational system. For instance, students in other countries consistently outperform U.S. students in such fields as math and science, causing alarm among many educational experts and political leaders. One cross-national study found that the United States ranks below the international average on math scores of eighth-graders (National Center for Education Statistics, 1999). U.S. 13-year-olds spend an average of 178 days a year in school, compared to 198 in Russia, 220 in Japan, 222 in Korea, and 222 in Taiwan (National Center for Education Statistics, 2000).

Japanese schools, in particular, are famous for producing high achievers. Even 3-year-olds may spend hours a day memorizing stories, learning vocabulary, making calendars, and taking achievement tests (WuDunn, 1996). But their achievement may come at a steep price. Some Japanese sociologists blame the intense competitive pressures children face for the dramatic rise in youth crime over the past few years. As they get older, many Japanese children attend classes all day, then go to one of the many private "cram" schools where they study for entrance exams until 10 or 11 P.M. Historically, passing these grueling exams and getting into the top high schools and elite colleges was a virtual guarantee of a prestigious job. But Japan's recent economic stagnation and record unemployment have begun to shatter the implicit social contract that, in the past, justified all the hard work and sacrifice. Many Japanese youth rebel and turn to crime when they discover that not only do they not have much of a social life, they have no job opportunities either (French, 1999b).

Few people in the United States would argue that we should emulate the pressurized Japanese educational model. In fact, some critics feel we already place far too much emphasis on performance and achievement in this society (Mannon, 1997). Nevertheless, concern over our ability to compete in the global marketplace has led to nationwide calls for such educational reforms as heavier emphasis on math and science, more time spent on foundational skills such as reading and writing, increased computer literacy, and training in political geography and international relations. Many school districts around the country have adopted longer school days and a year-round schedule to improve student performance. In one Houston school district, for instance, students attend classes everyday from 7:25 A.M. to 5 P.M., two or three Saturdays a month, and several weeks during the summer (Wilgoren, 2001). In 1998 the Atlanta public school system eliminated recess in its elementary schools, calling it a waste of time that would be better spent on academics.

Religion

Another institution influenced by globalization is religion. Despite the enormous variety of cultures and ethnicities that exist today, nearly two-thirds of the world's population belongs to just three major religions—Christianity, Hinduism, and Islam—which have successfully crossed national boundaries for centuries. Exhibit 9.2 shows how dominant these world religions are.

Today, some denominations are globalizing to deal with shrinking domestic memberships:

- In 1980, three-quarters of Mormons were U.S. residents; by 1997, less than half lived in the United States.
- Ten times as many members of the Assemblies of God, a Pentecostal denomination, live overseas as live in the United States, its birthplace.
- The Methodist church lost 1 million U.S. members between 1980 and 1995 but gained about 500,000 elsewhere, mostly in Africa (Niebuhr, 1998b).
- The Anglican church is growing faster in Africa than in its traditional bases, Britain and North America (Niebuhr, 1998a).

Technological advances are making many of the world's religions even more international: "Jews from around the world can now fax their prayers to the Wailing Wall in Jerusalem. Fortune-tellers in China provide computer-generated astrological charts. . . . American television offers its viewers Christian preachers and Buddhist teachers" (Kurtz, 1995, p. 1).

This globalization of religion is ironically creating crises for religious communities. Exposure to competing worldviews challenges traditional beliefs. In some cases, religions have reacted with a forceful revitalization of ancient, fundamentalist traditions (Kurtz, 1995). Witness the growing trend toward governments defining themselves in narrowly religious terms. The ascension of fundamentalist Islamic govern-

Exhibit 9.2 **Dominance of World Religions**

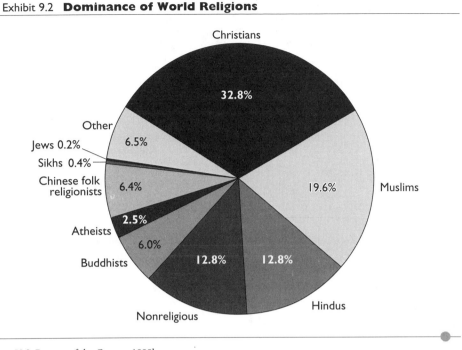

Source: U.S. Bureau of the Census, 1999b.

ments in Iran and Afghanistan, the growing influence of Orthodox Jews in Israeli politics, and the continuing conflict between Christians and Muslims in Bosnia and Kosovo attest to the fact that many people today believe religion cannot be separated from a nation's social and political destiny.

The rise of religious nationalism around the world has created a threat to global security. The values and institutions of Western countries are frequently blamed for a society's moral decline. The possibility of violence by supporters of religious nationalist movements has brought down political regimes, changed the outcomes of elections, strained international relations, and made some parts of the world a dangerous place for Western travelers (Juergensmeyer, 1996).

But religion has also played a positive role in world affairs and created dramatic social changes. According to Max Weber, the spread of Protestant beliefs throughout Europe made the growth of modern capitalism possible. Protestantism maintained that worldly achievements, such as the accumulation of wealth through hard work, are a sign of God's favor. But early Protestants also believed that God frowns on vulgar displays of wealth, such as big houses, fancy clothes, and so forth. So people were motivated to save and reinvest their wealth rather than spend it frivolously. You can see how such beliefs made large-scale and long-term economic growth possible (Weber, 1904/1977).

The influence of religious movements on social life continues. In the 1960s television pictures of Buddhist monks setting themselves on fire in Vietnam to protest the war fed the growing antiwar movement in the United States. In the 1970s and 1980s images of Catholic priests and nuns challenging government policies in Central and South America provoked a heightened awareness worldwide of the plight of indigenous people there. Today, followers of the Dalai Lama are raising global awareness of the plight of Tibetans who seek independence from China. Their actions have led to the establishment of organizations such as the International Campaign for Tibet, which has growing support worldwide.

CONCLUSION

More than three centuries ago, John Donne wrote, "No man is an island, entire of itself; every man is a piece of the continent, a part of the main." The same can be said of contemporary social life. We are not isolated individuals whose lives are simply functions of personal characteristics and predispositions. We are social beings. We are part of aggregations of other social beings. We have a powerful need to belong to something larger than ourselves. As a result, we constantly affect and are affected by our associations with others, whether face to face or in well-structured groups, massive bureaucratic organizations, or all-encompassing social institutions.

Throughout Part II of this book, I discussed how society and culture affect everyday experiences and how those experiences help to construct and maintain social order. The development of self and self-controlled behavior, the influence of cultural norms, responses to deviance, and so on are all topics that provide insight into how we are able to live together in a relatively orderly and predictable way. In this chapter, however, you can see that the social structure, though created and maintained by the actions of individuals, is more than just the sum of those actions. Organizations interact at a level well above the individual; institutions are organized in a massive, global system.

Social structure is bigger than any of us, exerts enormous control over our lives, and is an objectified reality that appears to exist independently of us. But it cannot exist without us. I'm reminded of a skit from the old British comedy show *Monty Python's Flying Circus,* in which a high-rise apartment building stood erect only because its inhabitants believed in it. When they doubted its existence, it began to crumble. Like that building, social structure requires constant human support. Once we as a society are no longer able to sustain our organizations or believe in our institutions, they fall apart.

YOUR TURN

One of the major criticisms of complex contemporary society is its sometimes dehumanizing way of life. To see this consequence of routinization firsthand, visit several fast-food restaurants close to your home (McDonald's, Taco Bell, Kentucky Fried Chicken, Long John Silver's, and the like). Observe the overall structure of the establishment. How is the work area situated in regard to the customer area? Are the cooking facilities hidden from public view? Note the number of employees and the gender and age configuration of the staff. Observe the way the customers are processed. Can you detect a "script" that the employees follow? How do they address customers? How are orders filled? Is there any room for "ad-libbing"? Does each worker seem responsible for a single task (grilling burgers, bagging fries, operating the cash register, cleaning tables)? Do male employees seem to work in different areas from female employees? Is there an apparent hierarchy among the workers? What is the manager's role? Were you able to detect the ways in which ordinary workers "resist" on a daily basis (rate-busting norms, sabotage, labor–management conflicts)?

Compare your findings across the different restaurants you observed. How much similarity in routine is there? Is some common procedure characteristic of all fast-food restaurants, or does each restaurant have a unique way of running? How do such things as diversity and creativity fit into the procedure?

Drawing from this chapter's discussion of the features of bureaucracies and the notion of McDonaldization, discuss how the systems employed in these restaurants maximize efficiency at the cost of dehumanizing the people involved, both workers and customers.

CHAPTER HIGHLIGHTS

- Social structure is both a source of predictability and a source of problems in everyday life. Sometimes individual interests coincide with structural needs; other times they conflict.

- By virtue of living in society, we are all organizational creatures. We are born in organizations, educated in them, spend most of our adult lives working in them, and will probably die in them.

- A common form of organization in a complex society is the bureaucracy. A bureaucracy is a large hierarchical organization that is governed by a system of rules and regulations, has a clear specification of work tasks, and has a well-defined division of labor.

- The everyday experience of bureaucratic organizations is determined by where one fits into the hierarchical structure. Bureaucracies look very different depending on whether one is situated at the top, middle, or bottom.

- Organizations are more than structures, rules, policies, goals, job descriptions, and standard operating procedures. Each organization, and each division within an organization, develops its own norms, values, and language.

- Organizations exist within highly interconnected networks. In times of institutional or environmental uncertainty, organizations tend to imitate one another, adopting similar activities, policies, and goals.

- As national borders become increasingly permeable, cultures and social institutions become more global in nature.

KEY TERMS

bureaucracy Large hierarchical organization governed by formal rules and regulations and having clearly specified work tasks

de-skilling Subdivision of low-level jobs into small, highly specific tasks requiring less-skilled employees

division of labor Specialization of different people or groups in different tasks, characteristic of most bureaucracies

free-rider problem Tendency for people to refrain from contributing to the common good when a resource is available without requiring any personal cost or contribution

hierarchy of authority Ranking of people or tasks in a bureaucracy from those at the top, where there is a great deal of power and authority, to those at the bottom, where there is very little power and authority

multinational corporation Company that has manufacturing, production, and marketing divisions in multiple countries

social dilemma Potential for a society's long-term ruin because of individuals' tendency to pursue their own short-term interests

social structure Social institutions, organizations, groups, statuses and roles, values, and norms that add order and predictability to our private lives

The Trail of the Tomato

Deborah Barndt

The life cycle of a tomato reveals how globalization touches us daily. In a collaborative cross-border research project, we followed the trail of a tomato from a Mexican field to a Canadian fast-food restaurant. The key characteristic of this process is the many steps between production and consumption. Most of us are unaware of who has planted, picked, sorted, packed, processed, transported, prepared, and sold the food we eat. The trail of the tomato also reflects power relationships between the north and the south (in this case, between Mexico in the south and the United States and Canada in the north), as well as inequalities based on gender, race, and class.

As a northern "gringa" researcher documenting Mexican women, I too reflected and reinforced power differences. When I photographed women picking and packing tomatoes, my camera was a symbol of my privilege.

Although it was an awkward reminder of the differences in our social power, some women workers befriended me and invited me to visit them later in their rural community.

Returning to Mexico four months later (the picking season abruptly ended by a premature freeze), I found these women in their homes, no longer salaried workers in a multinational operation. With camera and tape recorder, I followed Teresa through her day as she prepared food for her family. Teresa is a salaried worker for an agro-export company based on monocultural (one-crop) production, which has an impact on the health of both the land and the people who work it. Her story reflects the shifting role of women in the new global economy. It also illustrates how subsistence and market economies coexist and how family economies remain the economic and social base for Mexican peasants.

● When I first met Teresa in December, she was picking tomatoes and supervising workers in an agribusiness tomato plantation outside of Sayula, in the state of Jalisco, Mexico.

With 40 pails to fill for the 28-peso ($5–6) daily wage, she couldn't talk much then, so she invited me to visit her sometime in her village, half an hour away.

When I returned to Mexico four months later, the tomato harvest had prematurely ended due to a freeze. I found Teresa, her family, and many co-workers at home in Gomez Farias.

● *Teresa:* I was born in 1930 in a family of five kids. My papa died when I was 2, so my mama had to raise us on her own. I never went to school. They brought books into the rancho, and my brothers taught themselves to read. But not me, I didn't learn; I'm like a *burrito* (little donkey).

● *Teresa:* We got married when I was 17, and I kept doing the same work. Now I'm 67, and Pedro's 72, five years older than me.

We had 16 children—imagine! The oldest is 47 and the youngest is 21. Nine of them are still alive; seven died of illness, of bronchitis (from the cold).

Our two oldest daughters are married and live in Tlapapa; three married sons and two daughters live here. They visit often and help; we share what we have. While we are alive, as long as God offers us the gift of life, we help each other.

We get eggs from our chickens. From time to time, we eat beef, chicken, squash, carrots, lettuce.

When the day dawns, with God's blessing, we find things to eat, even if it's just beans.

270

● *Teresa:* Our grandchildren are studying, but when they're not in school, they come to work in the fields on the weekends and during vacations; they get the same pay as others.

● *Teresa:* Everyone has their job. My husband and I are the *cabos* (foremen) for our *tabla* (field). Some are *piscadores* (pickers), others are *vaciadoras* (who empty the pails), others are *aquadores* (they bring us water) and *apuntadoras* (who record the number of pails).

● *Pedro:* Before, we worked harder, we worked with animals. We cultivated three crops to-gether—corn, squash, and beans—in the same field. We rotated from one lot to another.

Before, the tomatoes and corn grew well without chemicals. We used the waste of animals as fertilizer; we put it on the plants; it was very good and would last for two to three years.

The fertilizer we use now only lasts for one season. It's expensive and very strong. It kills the squash, and the *milpa* (field) becomes very sad. The corn grows well, it grows tall, but the fertilizer damages the squash and the beans.

● *Teresa:* The chemicals bother us, if they get into our lungs. Those who don't cover themselves suffer more. We put one handkerchief in the back, one in the front, just leaving a slot open for the eyes. This protects us from the pesticides, the insects, the sun.

● *Teresa:* We all feel the economic crisis. The work in Sayula stopped in February because of the freeze. There is no *chamba* (work) now. We can't keep working, so we don't earn any money. It's very depressing; we're sad when we're not working.

When we find work, we're happy.

In a broader sense, this visual essay exposes only one piece of a globalized food system: Teresa doesn't know where the tomatoes she picks end up, and she can contribute only a small part of the story about where they come from. This has been one of the most powerful and recurring themes in our efforts to trace the trail of the tomato: No one has the whole picture, and most actors in the system understand only their small piece of the long and complex process. Nonetheless, Teresa's story begins to fill a void in our distanced, northern understanding of where our food comes from and what impact its production has on other people and lands.

● *Teresa:* I've seen big trailer trucks on the highway; I've wondered where they're going. They come from far away and they go far away; we don't know where.

The tomatoes don't stay here.

● When I showed these photos to Teresa, she wasn't aware of the work of 500 women in the packing plant just five minutes from where she picks tomatoes.

At the other end of the food chain, Teresa's photo story became a catalyst for conversations with Susan, one of hundreds of supermarket cashiers in Canada who eventually sell these tomatoes to consumers. Susan's responses reflect her curiosity about and empathy with the women working at the other end of the food chain:

> We live in different cultures, with different climates and different life experiences, and yet we're going through the same things. [For example,] Teresa used to make her own tortillas but now she has to go and work. And she's feeling that pull just like the North American women are: Should I stay at home with the kids? Should I go to work? She's feeling the economic thing, obviously because everybody has to survive, everybody has to eat. She's taking care of the family, that's a priority in her life; I'd like to think that in my life that's a priority.

Teresa had mentioned the freeze that cut short their harvest season and left them unemployed; Susan remembers the impact the freeze in the south had on prices in her store. Signs were posted in the produce department explaining why the vegetables were suddenly so expensive.

The Mexican pickers, when hearing about the Canadians who receive and sell the fruits of their labor, raised this question: "I often wonder what happens to our tomatoes. I wonder if they realize the work we have done so they can eat tomatoes." This, at least, is a connection between women workers nurtured by a red fruit that makes a long journey, passing from one hand to another. As a photographer of both ends of the process, I became a conduit between them, and the photographs became a medium for connecting them.

10

The Architecture of Stratification: Social Class and Inequality

---

Stratification Systems

Sociological Perspectives on Stratification

Inequality in the United States

Global Development and Inequality

The *Titanic* was the most magnificent vessel of its time. If you've seen the recent Hollywood film, you know that the ship had every amenity and comfort: Turkish baths, the finest orchestras, intricately tiled walls, the best cuisine. What it didn't have were enough lifeboats. There was room for only 1,178 of the 2,207 passengers and crew members on board. Over the span of two hours on that cold April night in 1912, as the "unsinkable" ocean liner was engulfed by the frigid waters of the North Atlantic, more than 1,500 people lost their lives.

This part of the story is well known. What is less well known is that some of the passengers actually had much better survival chances than others. More than 60% of the people from the wealthy first-class deck were saved; 36% of the people from the second-class deck were saved; and 24% of the people from the lowest, or "steerage," class were saved. The figures were even more striking for women and children, who, by virtue of chivalrous tradition, were entitled to be spared first. In first class, 97% of the women and children survived; in second class, 89% survived. However, only 42% of the women and children in steerage were saved (W. Hall, 1986).

One of the reasons so many of the wealthier passengers survived was that access to the lifeboats was from the higher first- and second-class decks. The locked doors and other barriers that kept the third-class passengers from venturing up to the upper decks during the cruise were not removed when disaster struck. In addition, little effort was made to save the people in steerage. Some were forcibly kept down by sailors standing guard.

For the passengers on the *Titanic*, social inequality meant more than just differences in the comfort of their accommodations or the quality of the food they ate. It literally meant life or death. This situation is a metaphor for what many people face in today's society. Those at the top have easy access to various "lifeboats" in times of social or economic disaster; others face locked gates, segregated decks, and policies that make mere survival exceedingly difficult (Sidel, 1986).

Let's turn the clock ahead to 1995, when a record-setting summer heat wave took the lives of more than 700 people in Chicago. Most of the victims were poor and elderly

277

people who had suffocated in their closed, stifling apartments. Most couldn't afford air conditioners or fans. Some died behind boarded windows, afraid of being invaded by predators and thieves in their high-crime neighborhoods if they left their windows open (Terry, 1995). Furthermore, the city's heat emergency plan was inadequate to deal with the reality of poor communities, where large numbers of people have no way of escaping the heat. Again we see how the lack of economic resources can have direct, physical consequences for people's lives.

In this chapter I look at the basic issues of inequality and stratification. Why do some people have more of a society's resources and opportunities than other people do? How is inequality felt at the individual and institutional levels? Finally, what does inequality look like at the global level? In subsequent chapters I explore two other facets of inequality: race and gender. Although sociologists disagree on many other points, they concur on this one: Various forms of social inequality do in fact exist in all contemporary societies, including the United States.

Keep in mind as you read the next three chapters that individuals create these social structures in addition to living under their influence. Inequality is often felt most forcefully and reinforced most effectively in the everyday interactions that make up our ordinary private experiences. People bring with them into all social encounters different levels of conversational, emotional, physical, institutional, and cultural resources that create and reinforce the status differences between them. Although social inequalities may be built into the structure of society, they are not fixed and unyielding. They ultimately emerge from the actions of real people.

Stratification Systems

Inequality is woven into the fabric of all societies through a structured system of **stratification**, the ranking of entire groups of people that perpetuates unequal rewards and life chances in a society. Just as geologists talk about strata of rock that are layered one on top of another, the "social strata" of people are arranged from low to high. All societies, past and present, have had some form of stratification, although societies may vary in the degree of inequality between strata. The four main forms of stratification that sociologists have identified—all of which continue to exist in contemporary societies—are slavery, caste systems, estate systems, and social class systems.

Slavery

One of the most persistent forms of stratification in the world is slavery. **Slavery** is an economic form of inequality in which some people are the property of others. They are owned, controlled, coerced, and restricted. One can become a slave in a variety of ways: through birth, military defeat, debt, or, as in the United States up until the mid-19th century, capture and commercial trade (Kerbo, 1991). Because slaves are considered possessions, they are denied the rights and life chances other people take for granted.

Slavery has occurred in some form or another almost everywhere in the world at some time:

It was common in ancient Babylon, Persia, Egypt and the Roman Empire. It was found in Asia and Africa. It did not disappear in Western Europe until late in the Middle Ages, and was still present in the Western Hemisphere when the early Spanish explorers arrived. Press-gangs rowing ancient Mediterranean war boats, captive victims in pre-Columbian sacrificial rites, Africans brought to the Americas in chains—all are recognizable, indisputable examples of enslavement. (Crossette, 1997b, p. D4)

But slavery is not just a horrible vestige of a distant past. Today, children in Togo and Benin (in West Africa) are sometimes seized from their villages and sold into servitude in Nigeria, Gabon, and elsewhere. Debt bondage is still practiced in certain parts of South Asia. In India, children are sometimes mutilated, enslaved, and transported to Saudi Arabia to plead for money outside mosques (Crossette, 1997b).

A form of slavery exists in the United States as well. The CIA estimates that as many as 50,000 women and children from Asia, Eastern Europe, and Latin America are brought to the United States each year, held in bondage, and forced to work as prostitutes, laborers, or servants (Brinkley, 2000). In 1997 federal agents in North Carolina and New York found more than 70 illegal Mexican immigrants—most of whom were deaf—who were being held in bondage and forced to peddle trinkets at local shopping centers and in subway stations. They were crowded into apartments, monitored while working, forced to turn over all their earnings, and prevented from leaving. In 1998 federal prosecutors charged 16 people with running a prostitution ring that enslaved dozens of Mexican women in agricultural migrant camps in Florida and South Carolina. The women who tried to escape were tracked down, beaten, and raped.

Caste Systems

Some societies today, such as India and Pakistan, retain a second form of stratification: a **caste system.** Traditionally, one's caste, which determines one's lifestyle, prestige, and occupational choices, was fixed at birth and couldn't be changed. Ancient Hindu scriptures, for instance, identified the strict hierarchy of elite, warrior, merchant, servant, and untouchable castes. And even today, cultural rules specify that people should take the occupation of their parents and marry within their caste (Weber, 1970). The rights and duties associated with membership in each caste were clear. In India, "untouchables"—members of the lowest caste—were once required by law to hide from, or, if that wasn't possible, to bow in the presence of anyone from a higher caste. They were routinely denied the right to enter Hindu temples or to draw water from wells reserved for members of the higher castes, who feared they would suffer ritual pollution if they touched or otherwise came in contact with an untouchable.

Things are beginning to change in India. The poorest Indians are now voting and joining political parties in record numbers. In fact, more "untouchables" vote than members of the upper caste (Dugger, 1999a). But the caste system still serves as a powerful source of stratification and oppression. In 1999, 22 "untouchables" were massacred by wealthy landowners in retaliation for their participation in political protests (Dugger, 1999c).

Estate Systems

A third form of stratification is the **estate system**, or **feudal system**, which develops when high-status groups own land and have power based on their noble birth (Kerbo, 1991). Estate systems were most commonly found in preindustrial societies. In medieval Europe, the highest "estate" in society was occupied by the aristocracy, who derived their wealth and power from large-scale land holdings. The clergy formed the next estate. Although they had lower status than the aristocracy, they still claimed considerable status because the Church itself owned a great deal of land and exerted influence over people's lives. The last, or "third," estate was reserved for commoners: serfs, peasants, artisans, and merchants. Movement between estates was possible though infrequent. Occasionally a commoner might be knighted or a wealthy merchant might become an aristocrat.

Some vestiges of the estate system can still be seen today. In Great Britain, for instance, Parliament's House of Lords is still occupied primarily by people of "noble birth" and a small group of aristocratic families still sits at the top of the social ladder, where they enjoy tremendous inherited wealth and exercise significant political power.

Social Class Systems

Although all three of the other systems still exist, stratification systems in contemporary industrialized societies are most likely to be based on social class. A **social class** is a group of people who share a similar economic position in society based on their wealth and income. It is essentially, therefore, an economic stratification system. Throughout this book so far I have mentioned the effects of social class on a variety of experiences—child rearing, deviance, family relations, and so forth. But social class is more than a characteristic that distinguishes one group's pattern of behavior from another's. It is a means of ranking people or groups that determines access to important resources and life chances.

Closely related to the concept of class is socioeconomic status. In Chapter 2, I defined *status* simply as a social position. But with regard to stratification, **socioeconomic status** refers to the prestige, honor, respect, and power associated with different class positions in society (Weber, 1970). Socioeconomic status is obviously influenced by wealth and income, but it can also be derived from *achieved characteristics,* such as educational attainment and occupational prestige, and from *ascribed characteristics,* such as race, ethnicity, gender, and family pedigree. Hence, wealth and income do not alone determine a person's socioeconomic status. For instance, the occupational prestige of high school teachers is far higher than that of carpenters, plumbers, and mechanics (J. A. Davis & Smith, 1986), yet teachers often earn substantially less. Organized criminals may have a lot of money and live in large houses, but they obviously lack prestige and honor.

Class systems differ from other systems of stratification in that they raise no legal barriers to **social mobility**, the movement of people or groups from one level to another. Theoretically, in a class system anybody, no matter how destitute they are, can rise to the top. In practice, however, mobility between classes may be quite difficult.

Much as we'd like to believe otherwise, the opportunities to move from one class level to another are not equally available to everyone. Often the families we're born into exert as much influence on our class standing as our personal achievements—or more. Likewise, race and gender have historically determined a person's access to educational, social, and employment opportunities.

To determine a person's class standing, contemporary sociologists usually compile information on measurable factors such as annual income, wealth, occupation, and educational attainment. But the boundaries between classes tend to be rather fuzzy. Some have argued that there aren't any discrete classes with clearly defined boundaries but rather a socioeconomic continuum on which to rank individuals (P. M. Blau & Duncan, 1967).

Nevertheless, discrete class designations remain a part of everyday thinking, political initiatives, and social research. The **upper class** is usually thought to include owners of vast amounts of property and other forms of wealth, owners of large corporations, top financiers, rich celebrities and politicians, and members of prestigious families. The **middle class** is likely to include managers, supervisors, executives, small business owners, and professionals (for example, lawyers, doctors, teachers, and engineers). The **working class** typically includes industrial and factory workers, office workers, clerks, and farm and manual laborers. Finally, the "poor" consist of people who work for minimum wages or are chronically unemployed. They are sometimes referred to as the **lower class** or **underclass**. These are the people who do society's dirty work, often for very low wages (Walton, 1990; E. O. Wright, Costello, Hachen, & Sprague, 1982).

Class standing can determine a whole host of life chances, including access to education, high-paying jobs, even levels of physical comfort. For instance, several airlines have removed rows of coach seats to make room for more affluent passengers in the first-class section. In fact, first-class and business-class seats now account for more than 22% of airlines' passenger revenue, up from 9% in 1987 (Reich, 1998). This change is not just a matter of bigger seats. First-class sections contain more flight attendants per person than coach sections, and the first-class attendants respond more quickly to call buttons. Such exclusive personal attention reinforces feelings of power and privilege and can make coach passengers feel like second-class citizens.

Conversely, as you may recall from Chapter 7, working-class and poor people are significantly more likely to get arrested, get convicted, go to prison, and receive the death penalty than are upper-class people (Reiman, 1998). Research also shows that those at lower levels of the stratification system are more likely to die prematurely as a result of homicide, accidents, or inadequate health care than are people at higher levels (Kearl, 1989). The death rate for U.S. residents with family incomes of less than $9,000 a year is three times higher than that of people with family incomes of more than $25,000 a year (Pear, 1993). Lack of health care causes three times more deaths than AIDS (Navarro, 1992).

People in the upper reaches of the class structure are able to run important political and economic institutions by controlling the government, large corporations, the majority of privately held corporate stock, the media, universities, councils for national and international affairs, and so on (Domhoff, 1998). Hence, members of this class enjoy political and economic power to a degree not available to members of other classes.

However, the existence of an upper class doesn't necessarily imply that other classes are totally powerless (Domhoff, 1998). Even members of the most powerless class can develop the capacity to disrupt the system. Strikes and revolutions often change the power structure to some extent. Under certain circumstances the voting masses may also place legislative restraints on the actions of the upper class.

People's social class standing also provides them with an understanding of the world and where they fit into it compared to others. Class is a statement about self-worth and the quality of one's life:

> It's composed of ideas, behavior, attitudes, values, and language; class is how you think, feel, act, look, dress, talk, move, walk; class is what stores you shop at, restaurants you eat in; class is the schools you attend, the education you attain; class is the very jobs you will work at throughout your adult life. Class even determines when we marry and become mothers. . . . We experience class at every level of our lives; class is who our friends are, where we live . . . even what kind of car we drive, if we own one. . . . In other words, class is socially constructed and all-encompassing. (Langston, 1992, p. 112)

Thus, when we talk about social class, we're just as likely to be referring to people's mannerisms, speech patterns, and lifestyles as we are their net worth. In 1998, for example, the town of Wilson, North Carolina, voted to prohibit people from keeping old sofas on their front porches (Bragg, 1998). Many people saw this policy as a clash of class lifestyles. For generations, poor people in the area—unable to purchase expensive outdoor furniture and unwilling to part with old but still usable indoor furniture—have kept their worn-out sofas and chairs on the porch, where they can still be used. But more affluent residents saw the practice as "low class" and approved the ban to make neighborhoods more cosmetically presentable.

People's perceptions of where they are in the system also affect their beliefs about the nature of inequality. Those at the lower end are likely to see stratification as unfair (Robinson & Bell, 1978) and may even express animosity toward those above them (Halle, 1984). However, upper-class people are likely to see stratification as a hierarchy of positions in which opportunities for success and advancement are fairly distributed on the basis of merit. In other words, one's ambition, effort, and intellect alone are responsible for her or his success. As you will see later in this chapter, however, the lack of success may be caused as much by external, societal factors as by personal failings.

Micro-Macro Connection
Mass Media and Images of Social Class

In Chapters 3 and 5 you saw that the mass media play a significant role in shaping reality and in socialization. You shouldn't be surprised, then, to learn that the media help to foster people's conceptions of class, wealth, and poverty (Mantsios, 1995).

Even though more than 50% of the adult working population in the United States are manual, unskilled, or semiskilled workers (Navarro, 1992), the media tend to ignore the poor and the working class (Mantsios, 1995; Parenti, 1996). In the affluent, middle-class worlds of television and film, poor and working-class people typically are depicted in such minor roles as waiters, service people, attendants, and the like (Parenti, 1996). A study of prime-time network television series between 1946 and 1990 found that in only 11% of the series were heads of households portrayed as working class—that is, holding occupations as blue-collar, clerical, or semiskilled service workers. Middle-class families were featured in 70% of the shows (Butsch, 1995).

When working-class people are shown, their depiction is often unflattering. The blue-collar heads of households that have existed on prime-time television throughout the years are typically portrayed as dumb, immature, or irresponsible buffoons. *The Honeymooners, All in the Family, Married with Children,* and *The Simpsons* are the most famous examples. Films such as *Saturday Night Fever, Working Girl,* and *Good Will Hunting* often portray working-class men as macho exhibitionists (Ehrenreich, 1995). On confrontational television talk shows such as *Jerry Springer* the odd personal problems of working-class guests are displayed for the condescending amusement of viewers.

In the news media, too, stories about poor people are rare. Fewer than 1 in 500 articles in the *New York Times* and 1 in 1,000 articles in the *Readers Guide to Periodic Literature* concern poverty (Mantsios, 1995). When the news media do turn their attention to the poor, the portrayals are often negative or stereotypical, as when local TV stations run the usual human interest stories about the "less fortunate" in soup kitchens and homeless shelters during the holidays. Frequently the poor are portrayed in grouped, statistical terms, such as annual fluctuations in the numbers of people in poverty or on welfare. Such coverage ignores the individual suffering and personal indignities of poverty. The more detailed stories about poor people tend to focus on welfare cheats, drug addicts, street criminals, and aggressive panhandlers.

Such images reinforce a perception that poverty is an aberration or something caused by poor people themselves (Mantsios, 1995). The message is often that we ought to blame those below us in the class structure for our society's most pressing problems. We learn to fear being victimized by the poor, and we learn to resent "welfare mothers" and blue-collar unions for our own declining purchasing power and economic insecurity.

In contrast, the media tend to focus much of their favorable attention on the concerns of the wealthy and the privileged. Television air time is filled with advertisements for luxury cars, cruise vacations, diamond pendants, and other things that only the wealthy can hope to afford. The news media devote a significant amount of broadcast time and print space to daily business news and stock market quotations (Mantsios, 1995), even though most U.S. families don't own any stock (Croteau & Hoynes, 2000). On a recent radio news show, an investment broker advised listeners to maintain two separate bank accounts: one for bills and mortgage, the other to "play" the stock market. Notice how such advice assumes that people have extra cash in their savings to play with. Some cable television networks report exclusively on stock market issues. International news and trade agreements are reported in terms of their impact on the business world, not on ordinary working people.

Furthermore, if you take a peek at the "style" sections of a large newspaper, you'll likely find the focus on high-priced fashion, costly vacation spots, investment opportunities in foreign real estate, dining at expensive restaurants, and etiquette for lavish, formal dinner parties.

The media also regularly provide information on individuals who have achieved supersuccess. We receive regular reports about the multimillion-dollar contracts of professional athletes, film stars, and TV personalities. Society pages and gossip columns keep those in the upper class informed of one another's doings and entice the rest of us to admire their achievements.

If people come to believe that having such a lavish lifestyle is desirable, those who don't earn enough to support that lifestyle often feel compelled to borrow to buy their own "entry-level luxury car," suburban palace, designer clothes, top-of-the-line sporting goods, rent-a-maid, and so on. This sort of "affluence" is precarious, frequently maintained by going deeper into debt by using credit cards and borrowing. Over the past 10 years the percentage of families with debt payments over 40% of their income has increased from 10% to 13% (Stevenson, 2000). As the economy weakens, the extra work that has allowed consumers to pay off such high debt will be harder to come by. But when you are exposed to media images of likeable and attractive people surrounded by the accoutrements of upper-class life, it is all too easy to justify going into debt to purchase those things for yourself so you can "keep up with the Joneses."

The mass media clearly shape how people think about each other and about the nature of society. By celebrating the lifestyles of the upper and middle class, the media create the impression that the interests and worries of the well-off are, or should be, important to everyone. Consequently, class differences and conflicts are concealed or rendered irrelevant. Yes, we're all concerned about economic issues. But whether that concern revolves around profit margins and stock dividends or around job security and the source of our next meal clearly depends on our class standing.

Sociological Perspectives on Stratification

Sociologists have long been interested in figuring out why societies are stratified. Two perspectives—the structural-functionalist perspective and the conflict perspective—offer insights into the sources and purposes of social inequality. They are often presumed to be competing views, but we can actually use them together to deepen our understanding of why social inequality exists, how it develops, and why it is so persistent.

The Structural-Functionalist View of Stratification

From a structural-functionalist perspective, the answers lie in a society's inevitable need for order. Because social inequality is found in some form in all societies and thus is apparently unavoidable, inequality must somehow be necessary for societies to run smoothly.

As with bureaucracies, the efficient functioning of society requires that various tasks be allocated through a strictly defined division of labor. If the tasks associated with all social positions in a society were equally pleasant, were equally important, and required the same talents, who got into which position would make no difference. But structural-functionalists argue that it does make a difference. Some occupations, such as teaching and medicine, are more important than others and require greater talent and training. Society's dilemma is to make sure that the most talented people perform the most important tasks. One way to ensure this distribution of tasks is to assign higher rewards—better pay, greater prestige, more social privileges—to some positions in society so that they will be attractive to the people with the necessary talents and abilities.

Presumably, if these talented people were not offered sufficiently high rewards, they would have no reason to take on the difficult and demanding tasks associated with important positions. Why would people go through the agony and costs of many years of medical school without some promise of compensation and high prestige? Those who rise to the top are seen as the most worthy and deserving, because they're the ones who can do the most good for society (K. Davis & Moore, 1945).

But the functional importance of a position is not enough to warrant a high place in the stratification system. If a position is easily filled, it need not be heavily rewarded, even though it is important (K. Davis & Moore, 1945). Imagine what our society would be like without people who remove our trash. Not only would our streets be unsightly, but our collective health would suffer, too. Therefore, garbage collectors serve a vital social function. They don't get paid very much, however, and trash removal certainly isn't a highly respected occupation.

Why aren't garbage collectors higher up in the hierarchy of occupations? According to the structural-functionalist perspective, it is because we have no shortage of people with the skills needed to collect garbage. Physicians also serve the collective health needs of a society. But because of the skills and training needed, society must offer rewards high enough to ensure that qualified people will want to become doctors.

The structural-functionalist perspective gives us important insight into how societies ensure that all positions in the division of labor are filled. Every society, no matter how simple or complex, differentiates people in terms of prestige and esteem and possesses a certain amount of institutional inequality. Critics argue, however, that this explanation doesn't address the fact that stratification can be unjust and divisive, a source of social *disorder* (Tumin, 1953).

One look at the salary structure in our society reveals obvious instances of highly rewarded positions that are not as functionally important as positions that receive smaller rewards. Entertainers and professional athletes are among the highest-paid people in U.S. society. The heavyweight boxer Lennox Lewis, for example, can make several million dollars for a few minutes' worth of punching someone else's face. Entertainers such as Oprah Winfrey, Tom Cruise, Jim Carrey, and Barbra Streisand are among the wealthiest of Americans. In 2000, the baseball player Alex Rodriguez signed a contract that pays him $252 million over 10 years, $2 million more than the owner paid for the entire franchise and stadium in 1998! You might say that boxers, singers, actors, comedians, and baseball players serve important social functions by providing the rest of us with a recreational release from the demands of ordinary life, and the best entertainers and athletes do have rare skills indeed. However, society probably can do without another music album, TV show, or pay-per-view prizefight more easily than it can do without competent physicians, scientists, computer programmers, teachers, or even trash collectors.

Furthermore, the structural-functionalist argument that only a limited number of talented people are around to occupy important social positions is probably overstated. Many people have the talent to become doctors. What they lack is access to training. And why are some people—women and racial minorities—paid less for or excluded entirely from certain jobs? The debates over equal employment opportunity and equal pay for equal work are essentially debates over how the functional importance of certain positions is determined.

Finally, when functionalists claim that stratification serves the needs of society, we must ask, Whose needs? A system of slavery obviously meets the needs of one group at the expense of another, but that doesn't make it acceptable. In a class-stratified society, those individuals who receive the greatest rewards have the resources to make sure they continue receiving such rewards. Over time, the competition for the most desirable positions will become less open and less competitive. The offspring of "talented"—that is, high-status—parents will inevitably have an advantage over equally talented people who are born into less successful families. Social background and not personal aptitude may become the primary criterion for filling important social positions (Tumin, 1953). For instance, both presidential candidates in the 2000 election, George W. Bush and Al Gore, came from powerful and well-to-do political families.

The Conflict View of Stratification

Conflict theorists argue that social inequality is neither a necessity nor a source of social order. They see it as a reflection of the unequal distribution of power in society and as a primary source of conflict, coercion, and unhappiness. Stratification ultimately rests on the unequal distribution of resources—some people have them, others don't. Important resources include money, land, information, education, health care, safety, and adequate housing.

Resources are an especially important source of power when they are scarce. Sometimes their scarcity is natural, such as the amount of land available to control. Other times, however, the scarcity of a resource is artificially created. For instance, in 1890, the founder of DeBeers, the South African company that currently controls two-thirds of the international diamond market, realized that the sheer abundance of diamonds in southern Africa would make them virtually worthless on the international market. So he decided to carefully limit the number of diamonds released for sale each year. This artificially created rarity, coupled with a carefully cultivated image of romance (in 1938 DeBeers launched an advertising campaign designed to convince millions of couples that the larger the diamond on an engagement ring, the greater their love) is what made diamonds so expensive and what continues to make companies such as DeBeers so powerful today (Harden, 2000).

Those high in the stratification system can control these resources because they are the ones who set the rules. According to conflict theorists, a system of stratification allows members of the dominant group to exploit those in subordinate positions as consumers, renters, employees, and so on, thereby reinforcing their own superiority over others.

Stratification virtually guarantees that some groups or classes of people (those who have less) will always be competing with other groups or classes (those who have more). The conflict perspective takes it as a fundamental truth that stratification systems serve the interests of those at the top and not the survival needs of the entire society. The dominant classes can manipulate both the economic system and the political system to maintain advantages over others and to protect their interests. What the conflict perspective gives us that the structural-functionalist perspective doesn't is an acknowledgment of the interconnected roles that economic and political institutions play in creating and maintaining a stratified society.

The Marxian Class Model. Karl Marx and Friedrich Engels (1842/1982) are the original proponents of the view that societies are divided into conflicting classes on the basis of two criteria: ownership of the **means of production**—land, commercial enterprises, factories, and wealth—and the ability to purchase and control the labor of others. Marx and Engels felt that in modern societies, two major classes emerge: **capitalists** (or bourgeoisie), who own the means of production and are able to purchase the labor power of others, and **workers** (or proletariat), who neither own the means of production nor have the ability to purchase the labor power of others. Workers, instead, must sell their own labor power in order to survive. Some workers, including store managers and factory supervisors, may control other workers but their power is minimal compared to that exerted over them by those in the capitalist class. Marx and Engels supplemented this two-tiered conception of class by adding a third tier, the **petite bourgeoisie**, which is a transitional class of people who own the means of production but don't purchase the labor power of others. This class consists of self-employed skilled laborers and businesspeople who are economically self-sufficient but don't have a staff of subordinate workers (Robinson & Kelley, 1979). Exhibit 10.1 diagrams the relationships among these three classes.

Exhibit 10.1 **Marx's Model of Class**

	Control labor of others	Do not control labor of others
Own means of production (land, factories, etc.)	*Capitalists*	*Petite bourgeoisie*
Do not own means of production	*Workers*	*Workers*

Capitalists have considerable sway over what will be produced, how much will be produced, and who will get how much of it. Such influence allows them to control other people's livelihoods, the communities in which people live, and the economic decisions that affect the entire society. In such a structure, the rich inevitably tend to get richer, to use their wealth to create more wealth for themselves, and to act in ways that will protect their interests and positions in society.

Ultimately the wealthy gain the ability to influence important social institutions such as the government, the media, the schools, and the courts. Those in power have access to the means necessary to create and promote a reality that justifies their exploitative actions. Their version of reality is so influential that even those who are harmed by it come to accept it. Marx and Engels called this phenomenon **false consciousness**. False consciousness is crucial because it is the primary means by which the powerful classes in society prevent protest and revolution. As long as large numbers of poor people continue to believe that wealth and success are solely the products of individual hard work and effort rather than structured inequalities in society—that is, believe what in the United States has been called the American Dream—resentment and animosity toward the rich will be minimized because people will perceive the inequalities as fair and deserved (Robinson & Bell, 1978).

A Neo-Marxian Model of Stratification. In Marx's time, the heyday of industrial development in the mid-19th century, ownership of property and control of labor in a capitalist system were synonymous. Most jobs were either on farms or in factories. Lumping all those who didn't own productive resources into one class and all those who did into another made sense. However, the nature of capitalism has changed a lot since then. Today a person with a novel idea for a product or service, a computer and a telephone line can go into business. Corporations have become much larger and more bureaucratic, with a long, multilevel chain of command. Ownership of corporations lies in the hands of stockholders who often have no connections at all to the everyday workings of the business. Thus ownership and management are separated. The powerful people who run large businesses and control workers on a day-to-day basis are frequently not the same people who own the businesses.

In light of changing realities, conflict sociologists such as Ralf Dahrendorf (1959) began arguing for an explanation of class stratification that focuses primarily on differing levels of authority among the members of society. What's important is not just who owns the means of production but who can exercise authority over others. **Authority** is the possession of some status or quality that compels others to obey (Starr, 1982). A person with authority has the power to order or forbid behavior in others (Wrong, 1988). Such commands don't require the use of force or persuasion, nor do they need to be explained or justified. Rulers have authority over the ruled, as do teachers over students, employers over employees, and parents over children. These authority relationships are not fixed, of course: Children fight with their parents, students disagree with their teachers, and workers protest against their bosses. But though the legitimacy of the authority may sometimes be called into question, the ongoing dependence of the subordinates maintains it. The worker may disagree with the boss, and the student may disagree with the teacher—but the boss still signs the paycheck and the teacher still assigns final grades.

Like Marx and Engels, Dahrendorf believed that relations between classes inherently involve conflicts of interest. Rulers often maintain their position in society by ordering or forcing people with less authority to do things that benefit the rulers. But by emphasizing authority, Dahrendorf argued that stratification is not an exclusively economic phenomenon. Instead, it derives from the social relations between people who possess different degrees of power.

Dahrendorf's ideas on the motivating force behind social stratification have since been expanded. Sociologist Erik Olin Wright and his colleagues (E. O. Wright, 1976; E. O. Wright et al., 1982; E. O. Wright & Perrone, 1977) have developed a model that incorporates both the ownership of means of production and the exercise of authority over others. The capitalist and petit bourgeois classes in this scheme are identical to Marx and Engels's. What is different is that the class of people who do not own society's productive resources (Marx and Engels's worker class) are divided into two classes: managers and workers (see Exhibit 10.2).

Wright's approach gives us a sense that social class is not simply a reflection of income or the extent to which one group exercises authority over another. A lawyer, plumber, or cook, for instance, could conceivably fall into any of the four class categories. They may own their own businesses and hire assistants (which would place them in the capitalist class), work for a large company and have subordinates (placing them in the manager class), work for a large company without any subordinates (placing them in the worker class), or work alone (placing them in the petite bourgeoisie) (Robinson & Kelley, 1979).

Wright's approach also emphasizes that class conflict is more than just a clash between rich and poor. Societies have, in fact, multiple lines of conflict—economic, political, administrative, and social. Some positions, or what Wright calls *contradictory class locations*, fall between two major classes. Individuals in these positions have

Exhibit 10.2 **Wright's Model of Class**

	Exercise authority	Do not exercise authority
Own means of production	*Capitalists*	*Petite bourgeoisie*
Do not own means of production	*Managers*	*Workers*

trouble identifying with one side or the other. Managers and supervisors, for instance, can ally with workers because both are subordinates of capitalist owners. Yet because managers and supervisors can exercise authority over some people, they also share the interests and concerns of owners. During labor disputes in professional sports, for example, coaches often struggle with the dilemma of whether they represent the interests of the owners or the players.

Inequality in the United States

One of the ideological cornerstones of U.S. society is the belief that all people are created equal and that nothing but personal shortcomings can impede a person's progress. After all, the United States is billed as the "land of opportunity." Our collective folklore is filled with stories of disadvantaged individuals who use their courage and resolve to overcome all adversity. We don't like to acknowledge that class inequality exists. To paraphrase one author, the idea of class has typically been the skunk at the garden party of U.S. culture (Moberg, 2000). But sociologists tell us that our place in the stratification system can determine the course of our lives, in sometimes obvious and sometimes subtle ways.

Consider, for instance, something I know you're familiar with: admission to college. We usually assume that admissions decisions are based on a student's merit. To get into a top college, you generally need high academic achievement and aptitude. Aside from your high school grades, your score on the SAT is also taken as a key indicator of your intellectual potential. What could be fairer than to use these sorts of objective measures to determine who gets an elite education, which will open doors for a lifetime?

Would it disturb you to know that your SAT score may depend as much on your parents' financial achievements as on your own intellectual achievements? Simply coming from a well-to-do family doesn't guarantee a high score on the SAT, but it can help. If you were fortunate enough to attend high school in an affluent, upper-class neighborhood, chances are your school offered SAT preparation courses. In some of these schools, students take practice SAT exams every year until they take the real one in their senior year. Even if a school doesn't provide such opportunities, private lessons from test preparation coaches—which can cost as much as $500 an hour for weekly sessions over the course of an academic year—are available to those who can afford them. Wealthy high schools are also significantly more likely to offer advanced placement courses—another important tool that college admissions officers use to measure applicants—than mid-level or poor high schools (Berthelsen, 1999).

The advantages that such resources provide require some sacrifice from many middle-class families and are obviously out of the reach of lower-class students in poorer school districts—all of whom might be just as intelligent and just as motivated as their wealthier counterparts. So is it the fault of individuals without the means or opportunity to prepare for the SAT that they often end up in less prestigious colleges and fail to reach the upper echelons of U.S. society? In this section you'll learn more about the profound effect that social class can have on everyday life.

How U.S. Society Is Stratified

Some sociologists have concluded that people in the United States aren't particularly class conscious: They don't recognize the class system, they don't think of themselves in terms of class membership, and they don't define their lives in class-related ways (see, for example, Hurst, 1979). Research suggests, however, that Americans are in fact acutely aware of class distinctions and are quite willing to identify their position within the class system.

Sociologists Mary R. and Robert W. Jackman (1983) asked a national sample of more than 1,900 U.S. adults the following question: "People talk about social classes such as the poor, the working class, the middle class, the upper-middle class and the upper class. Which of these classes would you say you belong to?" (p. 14). They found that all but 3.5% of the sample identified themselves with one of the class categories provided. However, only 7.6% perceived themselves as poor, and a little more than 9% perceived themselves either as upper-middle or upper class. The vast majority of people considered themselves either working class (36.6%) or middle class (43.3%). More recently, the National Opinion Research Center found that 44.9% of respondents identified themselves as working class and 45.3% as middle class (cited in Miller & Ferroggiaro, 1995).

The point is that although the lines between levels aren't all that clear, people in the United States implicitly acknowledge the existence of social classes in society. In fact, these distinctions go beyond differences in wealth and income. People create and maintain class boundaries through their perceptions of moral, cultural, and lifestyle distinctions between classes (Lamont, 1992).

The Upper Class. The upper class in the United States is a small, exclusive group that occupies the highest levels of status and prestige. For some, membership in the upper class is relatively new, acquired through personal financial achievement. For instance, Michael Jordan, one of the wealthiest people in the United States, came from fairly humble origins. He became part owner and president of a professional basketball team and is involved in many other lucrative enterprises. Such individuals may have been born into poor or working-class families but they have been able to climb the social ladder and create a comfortable life. These individuals are sometimes called "the new rich."

Others, however, are born into wealth gained by earlier generations in their families (Langman, 1988). Their formidable wealth and pedigree provides them with insulation from the rest of society. And their position in society is perpetuated through a set of exclusive clubs, resorts, charitable and cultural organizations, and social activities that provide members with a distinctive lifestyle and a perspective on the world that distinguishes them from the rest of society.

Sociologists G. William Domhoff (1983, 1998) and C. Wright Mills (1956) have made the case that members of the upper class can structure other social institutions to ensure that their personal interests are met and that the class itself endures. For example, the educational system plays not only a key socializing role (see Chapter 5) but also an important role in perpetuating or reproducing the U.S. class structure. In public schools, working-class and poor kids are subtly taught their place through authority relationships with teachers and principals so that they will be prepared for the subordinate work positions they will probably occupy in the future (Bowles & Gintis, 1976).

Members of the highest reaches of the upper class, in contrast, often spend their childhoods in private schools, their adolescence in boarding schools, and their college years in heavily endowed private universities (Domhoff, 1998). Elite private boarding schools have been called "educational country clubs," where children from such families as the Rockefellers, Kennedys, and Vanderbilts go to get socially polished for admission to exclusive colleges (Cookson & Persell, 1985). In addition to the standard curriculum, these schools teach vocabulary, inflection, styles of dress, aesthetic tastes, values, and manners (Collins, 1971). Required attendance at school functions; participation in esoteric sports such as lacrosse, squash, and crew; the wearing of school blazers or ties; and other "character-building" activities are designed to teach young people the unique lifestyle of the ruling class. In many ways, boarding schools function like such "total institutions" as prisons and convents (Goffman, 1961), isolating members from the outside world and providing them with routines and traditions that are highly effective agents of socialization.

In a study of more than 60 elite boarding schools in the United States and Great Britain, Peter Cookson and Caroline Persell (1985) showed how the philosophies, programs, and lifestyles of boarding schools help transmit power and privilege. The prep school experience forms an everlasting social, political, and economic bond among all graduates, and the schools act as gatekeepers into prestigious universities. After attending these universities, boarding school graduates connect with one another at the highest levels in the world of business, finance, and government. Said the director of development at Choate, an elite prep school in Connecticut:

> There is no door in this entire country that cannot be opened by a Choate graduate. I can go anywhere in this country and anywhere there's a man I want to see . . . I can find a Choate man to open that door for me. (quoted in Cookson & Persell, 1985, p. 200)

The privileged social status that is produced and maintained through the elite educational system practically guarantees that the people who occupy key political and economic positions will form a like-minded, cohesive group with little resemblance to the majority whose lives depend on their decisions.

The Middle Class. In discussing the U.S. class system, it is tempting to focus attention on the very top or the very bottom, overlooking the chunk of the population that falls somewhere in the ill-defined center of the U.S. class structure: the middle class. But the middle class has been important in defining U.S. culture: its moods, political direction, lifestyles, values, habits, and tastes. Today every other class is measured and judged against the values and norms of the middle class. It is a universal class, a class that supposedly represents everyone (Ehrenreich, 1990). Not surprisingly, the middle class is a coveted political constituency. Liberal and conservative politicians alike court it. Policies are proclaimed on its behalf.

But the lofty cultural status of the middle class in U.S. society belies the difficulties it experiences. Many Americans who consider themselves middle class report being worried about job security, taxes, unemployment, the cost of living, U.S. economic competitiveness, and high interest rates (cited in Francis, 1998). According to a national survey conducted by the Pew Research Center, only about a third of U.S. adults say they earn enough money to lead the kind of life they want, and about two-thirds worry that good jobs will move overseas and that workers here will be left with jobs that don't pay enough (Kohut, 1999). These concerns appear to be justified. According to some experts, many families with healthy incomes are still living close to the financial edge, one layoff or medical emergency away from financial crisis (Meckler, 1999).

The United States enjoyed a well-publicized, sustained economic recovery in the late 1990s. Average household incomes began to rise slowly but steadily (as depicted in Exhibit 10.3). However, most of the increases in household income can be explained not by higher wages but by people working longer hours (Uchitelle, 1999). Furthermore, not all U.S. residents have benefited from this growth. The minimum wage has increased 90 cents an hour since 1996, helping to push up the earnings of the lowest wage earners. And incomes of those households in the highest income brackets have, as always, surged. But the median wage—the wage earned by those right in the middle of the pack—was actually 17 cents an hour lower in 1998 than it was in 1989. Adjusted for inflation, incomes have fallen for the bottom 60% of U.S. households over the past

● Exhibit 10.3 **Growth in Median Household Incomes**

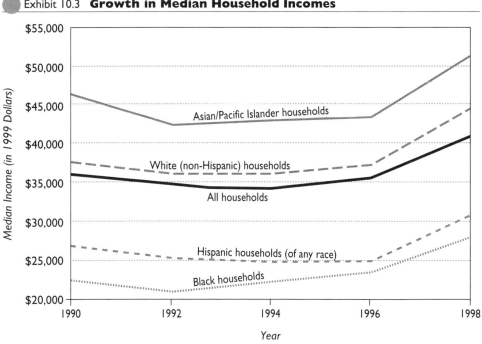

Note: Median means that half of the households have a higher income, half a lower income.

Source: U.S. Bureau of the Census, 2000a.

seven years. Between 1981 and 1999, middle-class families experienced a 340% increase in bankruptcies (Sullivan, Warren, & Westbrook, 2000). According to the National Association of Realtors, nearly half of U.S. families don't earn enough to qualify for a mortgage on a $119,000 median-priced home (cited in Roberts, 1997).

Furthermore, middle-income jobs actually became scarcer in the 1990s. Corporate downsizing has nibbled into stable, white-collar, middle-class occupations. Many of the largest and best-known companies in the United States have eliminated huge numbers of jobs over the past several years. For instance, between 1992 and 1996, AT&T, IBM, General Motors, Union Carbide, and GTE each cut their workforces by 25% or more (Rifkin, 1995; Uchitelle & Kleinfield, 1996). In 1998 Boeing announced a plan to cut 28,000 jobs. Even solid high-tech companies such as Hewlett-Packard and Intel eliminated thousands of middle-class jobs from their payrolls in the late 1990s and early 2000s due to slowdowns in the personal computer market.

The Working Class. Members of the working class—people who work in factory, clerical, or low-paying sales jobs—are especially susceptible to downturns in the economy. Most working-class people have only a high school education and earn an hourly wage. Although they may earn enough money to survive, they typically don't earn enough to accumulate significant savings or other assets. Under the best circumstances, they usually have difficulty buying a home or paying for a child's education. When times are bad, they live their lives under the constant threat of layoffs, plant closings, and unemployment. In recent years, many large companies have shut down their factories in the unionized industrial centers of the Midwest and shifted production to the South—where unions are weaker and wages are lower—or shifted them overseas (Cooper, 1998b). The attacks of September 11, 2001, led directly or indirectly to the layoffs of tens of thousands of working-class Americans (as well as members of other social classes) in the airline, hotel, and tourist industries.

When jobs are plentiful, as they were at the end of the 20th century, most people who lose a job will eventually find another one (Uchitelle, 1998). But the nature of those replacement jobs has deteriorated. Between 1963 and 1978, only 23% of the new jobs that were created paid poverty-level wages; however, during the 1980s and 1990s, more than half of the new full-time jobs that were created were unskilled, unstable positions paying below the poverty line (B. Harrison & Bluestone, 1988; J. E. Schwarz & Volgy, 1993). U.S. Department of Labor statistics show that only about 35% of laid-off full-time workers end up in equal- or better-paying jobs when they return to work (Uchitelle & Kleinfield, 1996). And the proportion of workers in jobs that last at least 10 years fell from 41% in 1979 to 35.4% in 1996 (Francis, 1998).

To survive psychologically in a world of such economic instability, many working-class people begin to define their jobs as meaningless and irrelevant to their core identity. Instead of focusing on the dreariness or the insignificance of their work, they may come to view it as a noble act of sacrifice. A bricklayer put it simply: "My job is to work for my family" (Sennett & Cobb, 1972, p. 135). Framing their work as sacrifice allows them to slip the bonds of the disappointing present and orient their lives toward their children's and grandchildren's future, something that gives them a sense of control they can't get through their jobs.

But it is especially difficult for working-class parents to sacrifice "successfully." Upper-class and middle-class parents make sacrifices so that their children will have a life *like* theirs. Working-class parents sacrifice so that their children will *not* have a life like theirs. Their lives are not a "model" but a "warning." The danger of this type of sacrifice is that if the children do fulfill the parents' wishes and rise above their quality of life, the parents may eventually become a burden or an embarrassment to them. Thus people who struggle to make ends meet are sometimes caught in a vicious trap.

The Poor. In an affluent society such as the United States, the people at the very bottom of the social class structure face constant obstacles and indignities in their everyday lives. You've heard the old saying "Money can't buy happiness." The implication is that true satisfaction in life is more than just a matter of being wealthy. Yet such a saying provides little comfort to people who can't pay their bills, don't know where their next meal is coming from or whether their job will even exist tomorrow, suffer from ill health, or have no home. Poverty pervades every aspect of a person's life. The entertainer Pearl Bailey perhaps summed it up best: "I've been rich and I've been poor. Rich is better."

The most publicly visible consequence of poverty is homelessness. No one knows for sure exactly how many homeless people live in the United States. Estimates range from 750,000 to 2 million (National Alliance to End Homelessness, 2000). According to a 1995 survey of 29 major cities, 46% of homeless people are single men, 14% are single women, 36.5% are families with children, and 3.5% are children on their own. One out of every four homeless people is a child, one out of five is employed, and fewer than half are substance abusers (cited in Worsnop, 1996b). The fastest-growing segment of the homeless population is families with children.

Shelters for the homeless are available but they are few and far between, overcrowded, and plagued by drugs, violence, and crime. An estimated 24% of requests for emergency shelter by homeless families go unmet each year (Worsnop, 1996b). By the way, it's no longer just unemployed or minimum wage earners who are homeless. In Silicon Valley, where the median family income is the highest in the nation and in the late 1990s an average of 63 people became millionaires every day, people earning $50,000 a year are increasingly seeking the services of homeless shelters (Nieves, 2000).

No matter where it exists, the reasons for homelessness in the United States are institutional ones: stagnating wages, changes in welfare programs, and perhaps most important, the lack of affordable housing. During the 1980s and 1990s most of the country's largest cities experienced massive reductions in low-income housing (rooming houses, single-room occupancy hotels, and the like), ranging from 12% to 58%. The problem seems to be getting worse. The Department of Housing and Urban Development found that, between 1991 and 1995, the number of low-rent apartments in suburban areas around the country decreased by 900,000, whereas the number of "very-low income" families in need of such housing grew by 370,000 (Janofsky, 1998b). By 1997, another 372,000 affordable rental units were lost (Stout, 1999).

According to the government, housing is considered "affordable" if it costs 30% of a household's income. The typical poor family spends twice that—about 60% of its after-tax income—on housing. By comparison, the average middle-class homeowner spends only 23% of his or her after-tax income on house payments. The nationwide median housing wage—the minimum amount of money a person would have to make to afford rental housing—is $11.08 an hour, more than twice the federal minimum wage. Indeed, nowhere in the United States is the minimum wage enough to afford adequate housing (National Low Income Housing Coalition, 1999).

A lack of affordable housing isn't the only thing that worsens the lives of the homeless. A fair amount of evidence suggests that the general public severely stigmatizes homeless people (Phelan, Link, Moore, & Stueve, 1997) and that tolerance of homelessness is wearing thin (Smolowe, 1993). More and more cities are imposing harsher restrictions on homeless people in an effort to reduce their visibility and force them to go elsewhere. Consider these examples:

- In many areas, city planners "sleep-proof" or "bum-proof" benches—for instance, by nailing pieces of wood to the bench or shaping them like barrels so people can't lie down—to discourage homeless people from sleeping in bus shelters.
- In a Los Angeles park, a sprinkler system comes on at random intervals throughout the night to prevent homeless people from sleeping there. Janitors in New York City's Grand Central Station accomplish the same thing by spreading ammonia on the floor.
- Tampa, Florida, has ordered that the homeless not be served food in public parks; Tucson, Arizona, is considering privatizing sidewalks so businesses can shoo away homeless people on their "property" (Kilborn, 1999a).

Related to homelessness and poverty is the problem of physical health. According to the World Health Organization (1995), poverty is the single greatest cause of ill health in the world today:

> Poverty is the main reason why babies are not vaccinated, why clean water and sanitation are not provided, why . . . drugs and other treatments are unavailable and why mothers die in childbirth. It is the underlying cause of reduced life expectancy, handicap, disability, stress, suicide, family disintegration, and substance abuse. (p. 1)

Poor people, and in particular homeless people, are more likely to suffer from such medical problems as trauma, infection, chronic disease, and malnutrition (Siwek, 1992). With each step down the income ladder comes an increased risk of headaches, varicose veins, respiratory infection, hypertension, emotional distress, low-birth-weight babies, and heart disease (Shweder, 1997).

The medical treatment poor people receive is generally worse than others get. More than 44 million U.S. residents are uninsured—roughly 16% of the population—and nearly one-third of all poor people lack medical insurance (Pear, 1999b). Even when they have insurance, poor people receive less preventive medical care and less effective management of chronic diseases than wealthy people do (Leary, 1996). To make matters worse, the nation's largest health maintenance organizations decided in 1998 to cut managed care programs for the poor and elderly, citing losses in income because of low government payments (Kilborn, 1998).

Because of the limitations in medical care, poor people die younger. At age 25, U.S. women with incomes above $50,000 can expect to live 4 years longer than women with incomes below $5,000. For men, the difference is 10 years. Advances in medical technology that have increased life expectancy affect mainly the middle and upper classes, not the poor (Colburn, 1992; Pear, 1993).

The educational deck also seems to be stacked against poor people. In a society where social status is usually based on credentials, chances of success in life are strongly determined by educational attainment (Jencks et al., 1979). However, poverty adversely affects the development of linguistic, educational, and job-related skills necessary for succeeding in school. Teachers become frustrated and do not teach; children become cynical and do not learn. Even if they graduate from high school, most poor children cannot afford to attend college. Those who do are more likely to attend community colleges or state universities, which lack the quality and prestige of their more expensive counterparts (A. M. Cohen & Brawer, 1982).

For many people, the worst schools can produce feelings of powerlessness that continue throughout their lives (Bowles & Gintis, 1976). Discipline and hierarchy, two crucial characteristics of a free market economy, are taught early in the education system. The "successful" students are the ones who learn to submit to authority. But poor children's prior socialization—their manner of speech, dress, and action—does not fit that of the teachers and the school administration at large, so the children are subtly made to feel inadequate. Instead of developing as competent, hopeful members of society, many poor young people become resigned to their fate. Some become openly hostile to the educational system; others turn to crime (for instance, selling illegal drugs) as an alternative means of earning money. Thus the educational system often serves to seal the fate of the poor instead of helping them succeed within the U.S. class system.

What Poverty Means in the United States

The word *poverty* has become all too commonly used in the English language. Politicians typically include it in their laundry lists of issues they say they plan to address if elected. Social researchers devote their careers to examining and explaining whom it affects and why it occurs. People point to it as the major cause of other social problems, such as violent crime and drug abuse.

But how exactly is poverty defined? In common usage, poverty is usually conceived in economic terms, as the lack of sufficient money to ensure an adequate lifestyle. Sociologists, though, often make a distinction between absolute and relative poverty. The term **absolute poverty** refers to the minimal requirements a human being needs to sustain a reasonably healthy life. The term **relative poverty** refers to one's economic position compared to the living standards of the majority in a given society. Absolute poverty means not having enough money for minimal food, clothing, and shelter, but relative poverty is more difficult to define. It reflects culturally defined aspirations and expectations. An annual family income of $5,000, which constitutes abject poverty in the United States, is perhaps five times higher than the average income in many developing countries. Life in a U.S. slum might be considered luxurious compared to the plight of tens of millions of starving people in other parts of the world.

The Poverty Line. The U.S. government uses an absolute definition of poverty to identify those people who need assistance to survive. The official **poverty line** identifies the amount of yearly income a family requires to meet its basic needs. The line is based on pretax money income only, which does not include food stamps, Medicaid, public housing, and other noncash benefits (U.S. Bureau of the Census, 1999a). The figure does vary according to family size and it is adjusted each year to account for inflation. But it doesn't take into account geographical differences in cost of living. In 2000 the official poverty line for a family of four was an annual income of $17,463.

The cutoff line for determining poverty is established by the U.S. Department of Agriculture and computed from something called the Thrifty Food Plan. This plan, developed in the early 1960s, is used to calculate the cost of a subsistence diet, which is the bare minimum a family needs to survive. The plan does not identify a healthy, nutritious diet: People are likely to become malnourished if they rely on the plan long term (Beeghley, 1984). This cost is then multiplied by 3 because research at the time showed that the average family spent one-third of its income on food each year. The resulting amount was adopted in 1969 as the government's official poverty line. The formula itself and the basic definition of poverty have remained the same for about four decades.

Many policymakers, sociologists, and concerned citizens question whether the current poverty line provides an accurate picture of basic needs in the United States. Several things have changed since the early 1960s. By 1990, for instance, food costs had dropped to one-sixth of the average family's budget because the price of other things, such as housing and medical costs, had inflated at much higher rates (Cloward & Piven, 1993). In addition, there were fewer dual-earner or single-parent families in the past, meaning that fewer families had to pay for child care at that time. In short, today's family has many more expenses and therefore probably spends a greater proportion of its total income on nonfood items. The consequence is that the official poverty line is probably set too low today and therefore underestimates the extent of poverty in this country.

Deciding who is and isn't officially poor is not just a matter of semantics. When the poverty line is too low, we fail to recognize the problems of the many families who have difficulty making ends meet but who are not officially defined as poor. A needy family making slightly more than the poverty line may not qualify for a variety of public assistance programs, such as housing benefits, Head Start, Medicaid, or Temporary Assistance for Needy Families. As a result, their standard of living may not be as good as that of a family that earns slightly less and therefore qualifies for these programs.

Interestingly, the government seems to agree implicitly that the poverty line is too low. The U.S. Bureau of the Census (2000b) defines individuals or families who earn between 100% and 125% of the poverty line as the **near-poor.** Families are eligible for food stamps if they earn up to 130% of the poverty line. Pregnant women and children younger than the age of 6 are eligible for Medicaid if their families earn up to 133% of the poverty line (DeParle, 1990).

Life on the edge of poverty is precarious. When nothing out of the ordinary happens, the near-poor can manage. But an unexpected event—a sickness, an injury, the breakdown of a major appliance or automobile—can send them into poverty. It has been estimated that about one-quarter of Americans hovering above the poverty line will fall below it at some point in their lives, and then they have some difficult decisions to make. Imagine being a poor single mother with a sick child. One trip to the doctor might cost an entire week's food budget or a month of rent. Dental work or an eye examination is easily sacrificed when other pressing bills need to be paid. If she depends on a car to get to work and it breaks down, a few hundred dollars to fix it might mean not paying the electric bill that month and having less money for other necessities. When gasoline prices skyrocketed to close to $2 a gallon in the summers of 2000 and 2001, many poor families found that they had to cut down on food purchases so they could afford to drive their cars to work.

Because of such situations, economists and advocates for the poor are calling for a revision of the poverty line. In fact, the U.S. Bureau of the Census is now experimenting with a new formula for determining the poverty line that would more accurately reflect contemporary spending patterns. Instead of simply using a subsistence food budget as the basis for the definition of poverty, this new formula would also consider expenses for housing, health care, transportation, utilities, child care, and personal expenses. It's estimated that this revised poverty line would be about $3,000 higher for a family of four than the current one.

The Poverty Rate. Raising the official poverty line by $3,000 would have a dramatic effect on the number of people defined as officially poor, perhaps raising the national poverty rate from 11.8% to over 14% (U.S. Bureau of the Census, 2001a). The **poverty rate,** the percentage of U.S. residents whose income falls below the official poverty line, is the measure that the U.S. government uses to track the success of its efforts to reduce poverty. Exhibit 10.4 shows how the poverty rate has fluctuated over the past few

Exhibit 10.4 **Historical Trends in the U.S. Poverty Rate**

Source: U.S. Bureau of the Census, 1998c.

decades. Although the rate decreased to 11.8% in 1999, its lowest point since 1979, over 32 million U.S. residents still live in poverty (U.S. Bureau of the Census, 2001a). But don't expect the poverty line to be redefined anytime soon. The resulting increase in the poverty rate not only would bring obvious political costs to whatever administration happens to be in office but would certainly cause a demand for increased spending on social welfare programs—something few people in government are willing to consider, given the ongoing public pressure to reduce government spending.

When used to describe national trends in poverty, the overall poverty rate can obscure important differences among subgroups of the population. For example, although two out of every three poor people in the United States are white, the poverty rate for whites of European descent (9.8%) is considerably lower than that for nonwhite Hispanics (22.8%) and African Americans (23.6%). The poverty rate in the South (13.1%) and West (12.6%) is significantly higher than the rate in the Midwest (9.8%) and Northeast (10.9%). Finally, poverty is higher in rural areas (16.8%) than in cities (13.9%) (Pear, 1998b; U.S. Bureau of the Census, 2001a).

Although racial and ethnic minorities have consistently been rated among the poorest Americans, other groups have seen their status change over time. Before Social Security was instituted in 1935, many of the most destitute were those over 65. As recently as 1970, 25% of U.S. residents over the age of 65 fell below the poverty line. Today, only 9.7% of the people in this age group are poor (Pear, 1998; U.S. Bureau of the Census, 2001a). Exhibit 10.5 shows how the poverty rate among older Americans has declined.

Taking their place among the poor, however, are women and children. The poverty rate for families headed by a single mother is 30.4%, compared to about 10.2% for all other families (U.S. Bureau of the Census, 2001a). Over half of poor families are

Exhibit 10.5 **Historical Trends in Poverty by Age**

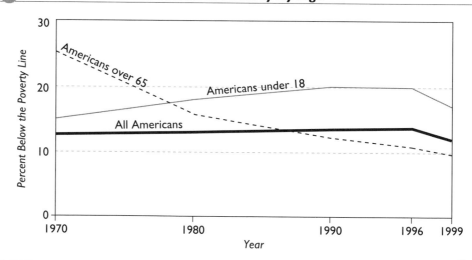

Source: U.S. Bureau of the Census, 2000b.

headed by single women (Pear, 1998). The risk of poverty increases dramatically when these women lack education. For example, 70% of young single mothers without a high school diploma are poor (Mishel, Bernstein, & Schmitt, 1997). Perhaps the most striking feature about the increase of women in poverty is that they are largely people who were not born into poverty but were instead forced into it by unemployment, illness, and especially divorce (Sidel, 1986).

Although the rate of child poverty has declined a bit since the mid-1990s, 17% of U.S. residents under the age of 18 are poor (see Exhibit 10.5) and children under 6 are the poorest age group in the nation (Pear, 1998; U.S. Bureau of the Census, 2001a). Children under 18 represent 26% of the U.S. population but constitute 39% of those living in poverty. During the booming 1990s the number of children living in working-poor families increased 30% (Koch, 2000a). The figures are especially bad for children of color: 36.4% of Hispanic children and 36.8% of African-American children live in poor households.

The 17% poverty rate among U.S. children is the highest of any industrialized country. For instance, in Australia 14% of children are poor. Great Britain and Italy have rates below 10%. In Denmark, Switzerland, and Sweden, around 3% of all children live in poverty (Mishel, Bernstein, & Schmitt, 1997).

One of the key reasons why so many U.S. children are poor is their family structure. Nearly half of all poor children live in a female-headed household (U.S. Bureau of the Census, 1999a). Children living with unmarried mothers are about five times more likely to be poor than children living with married parents (Lewin, 1998c). In most other industrialized countries, mothers receive help with child care, so they can earn more to support their children.

Why Poverty Persists

Even in the best of times, a prosperous country such as the United States has a sizable population of poor people. Why, in such an affluent society, is poverty a permanent fixture? To explain the persistence of poverty, we must look at enduring imbalances in income and wealth, the structural role poverty plays in larger social institutions, and the dominant cultural beliefs and attitudes that help support it.

Enduring Disparities in Income and Wealth. One reason why poverty is so persistent in the United States is the way that income and wealth are distributed. Although the strong economy of the late 1990s did lift many U.S. residents out of poverty, the wide income gap between the richest and poorest segments of the population actually grew substantially (see Exhibit 10.6). In 1999 the annual income of the top 20% highest-paid U.S. households averaged $135,401; the annual income of the 20% lowest-paid households averaged $9,940 (U.S. Bureau of the Census, 2000a). The richest 2.7 million U.S. residents—the top 1%— have as many after-tax dollars as the poorest 100 million people (cited in Johnston, 1999).

Between the late 1970s and the late 1990s, the income of the richest U.S. residents increased by 30%, but the poorest U.S. residents saw their incomes shrink by 21%. Workers in the middle range experienced a mere 2% increase (Cooper, 1998b). In

Exhibit 10.6 **The Increasing Gap in Incomes**

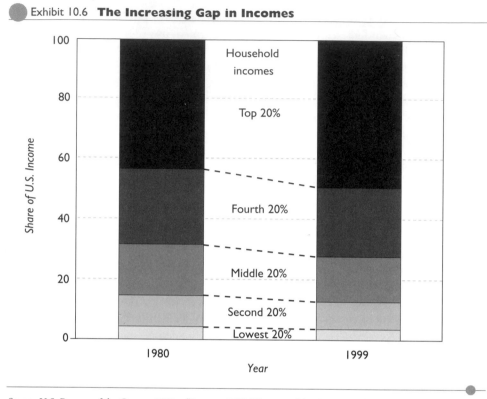

Source: U.S. Bureau of the Census, 2000a, "Income 1999," Bureau of the Census Web site, www.census.gov/hhes/income/income99/99tablef.html, November 20, 2000.

1997, earnings for top U.S. executives increased by 21%, but rank-and-file workers received only 3% raises on average. In 1980, executives made 42 times more than factory workers; in 1998, they made 419 times more (Wolfe, 1999). In fact, the average corporate chief executive now makes more in a single day than the average American worker makes in a typical *year* (Leonhardt, 2000). We may want to believe that personal effort and hard work solely determine our success, but it's hard to imagine that a CEO of, say, a TV manufacturing company works 400 times harder than a person who is making the TVs.

Although most U.S. residents paid more taxes as a percentage of income during the 1990s than in previous decades, many of the wealthiest citizens paid less. For instance, according to the Internal Revenue Service, nearly 2,400 individuals and couples with the highest incomes paid no federal income taxes at all in 1993, and 18,000 other people with high incomes paid only 5% of their income in taxes (Johnston, 1997). Even President Bush's much-publicized $1.35 trillion tax relief bill of 2001 primarily benefits the wealthy. The vast chunk of people, who earn between $23,000 and $55,000 a year and pay more than 40% of all federal income taxes, will receive little tax relief. And if this disparity isn't bad enough, the IRS is more likely to audit someone with an annual income under $25,000 than a person with an income over $100,000 (Johnston, 2000).

The United States has the greatest income inequality between poor and wealthy citizens of any industrialized nation. In Finland, the lowest-earning 20% of households earn 11% of the country's income—compared to 3.6% in the United States. In Japan, chief executives in manufacturing companies earn only 10 times more than their workers do. But to be fair, the gap between rich and poor is worse in developing countries. For example, the richest 20% of Brazilians earn 64% of the income, whereas the poorest 20% earn 2.5% (Romero, 1999). Similar disparities exist in other Latin American countries and in most of sub-Saharan Africa.

Disparities in income lead to even more striking disparities in wealth. A lifetime of high earnings and inheritance from privileged parents creates an advantage in ownership of durable consumer goods such as cars, houses, and furniture and of financial assets such as stocks, bonds, savings, and life insurance. In 1994 the most prosperous 20% of U.S. households held 78% of the nation's wealth (up from 76% in 1984). Their average net worth was about $871,463. And the wealthiest 1% of U.S. households owned 40% of the wealth (Bradsher, 1995b). At the same time, the average family in the poorest 20% of the population had a net worth of –$7,075, meaning the family owed more than it owned. This debt was twice as large as it had been in 1984. On average, the share of the nation's wealth held by the poorest 20% of families was actually below zero (–0.64%) (Bradsher, 1996). Bill Gates, chief executive of Microsoft, is worth an estimated $85 billion—equivalent to the entire net worth of the bottom 40% of U.S. households (Cooper, 1998b).

Such enormous disparities in wealth have a way of preserving themselves. As incomes of well-to-do U.S. citizens continue to rise, charities are reporting that individuals are donating less (Kilborn, 1999b). In fact, of those who made the *Forbes* list of the 400 wealthiest U.S. citizens, only 15% also made the *American Benefactor* list of the 100 most generous U.S. citizens (Rottenberg, 1997).

As a result, the United States is one of the most stratified of all industrial nations in regard to wealth. In Great Britain, for example, the wealthiest 1% of the population owns only 18% of the wealth—compared to 40% in the United States—despite Great Britain's long tradition of an elite aristocracy (Bradsher, 1995a).

The large economic gap between rich and poor in the United States challenges the notion that we live in a society based on equality. As disparities in income and wealth grow, so too, does the gap in quality of life and access to opportunity between those at the top of society and those at the bottom.

Micro-Macro Connection
Falling through the Net

As we've seen in previous chapters, the Internet is revolutionizing the way people all around the world live their lives. But not everyone is participating equally in the revolution. In the United States, the higher a family's income, the more likely it is that the family will own or use a computer. Wealthier school districts have equipment that is unavailable to poorer ones. And although computers and peripheral technological gadgets get cheaper each year, they are still priced well out of the reach of many people. As Exhibit 10.7 shows, Internet use is much greater for households with higher

Exhibit 10.7 **Internet Use and Income in U.S. Households**

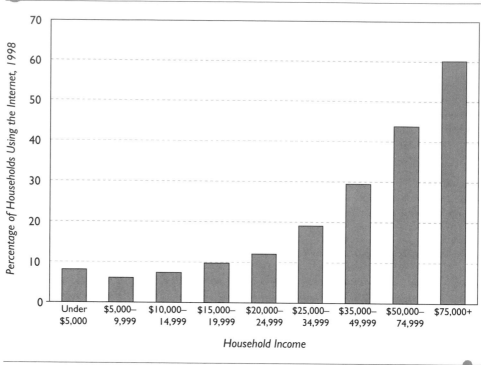

Source: U.S. Department of Commerce, 1999, *Falling through the net: Defining the digital divide: A report on the telecommunications and information technology gap in America.* www.ntai.doc.gov, accessed December 20, 2000.

incomes than for those at the bottom of the hierarchy. Many U.S. residents don't even have the phones on which Internet services depend. In an effort to alleviate the problem, many communities now provide public computer terminals that people can use in libraries, banks, community centers, and grocery stores.

Lack of money is not the only barrier. Geographical differences in telecommunication access are particularly striking. Most rural regions of the United States lack access to high-speed, broadband Internet service, which is necessary for extensive graphics and real-time audio and video. Such high-speed Internet capability is not just a matter of speed and convenience. It is crucial for communities trying to attract new businesses and retain old ones, and therefore has an indirect effect on people's quality of life.

Persistent racial and ethnic differences compound social class and geographical differences in computer access. In 1998, 47% of whites in the United States owned a home computer, compared to 23% of African Americans (Papadakis, 2000). And 73% of white college and high school students have access to a home computer, compared to 32% of African-American students. These racial gaps cannot be explained by differences in income alone, as Exhibit 10.8 shows. In households with annual incomes between $15,000 and $35,000, more than 32% of white families own computers, com-

Exhibit 10.8 **Computers in the Home by Income and Race**

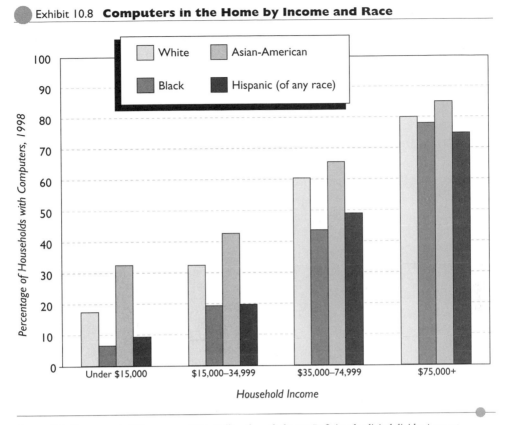

Source: U.S. Department of Commerce, 1999, *Falling through the net: Defining the digital divide: A report on the telecommunications and information technology gap in America.* www.ntai.doc.gov, accessed December 20, 2000.

pared with only 19% of black and Latino families in the same income bracket. The Internet-access gap between blacks and whites actually widened by 53% between 1997 and 1998 and 56% between Latinos and whites (cited in Koch, 2000b).

To many the "digital divide" has become one of society's most pressing civil rights issues. At one level it denies certain groups access to important technological skills, such as knowledge of computers and comfort navigating the Internet, that are now required for many entry-level jobs. But the gap poses other, less noticeable, obstacles to upward mobility. For instance, millions of job advertisements are available only on-line and more and more universities are providing application, registration, and course materials on-line. Furthermore, many products available over the Internet are less expensive than those available in traditional stores. In 2000, Congress approved a bill that allows consumers and businesses to sign contracts on-line that are just as binding as contracts signed in ink. Now people will be able to sign legally enforceable electronic contracts for such things as insurance and bank loans, which may be discounted because of the reduced paperwork involved. As long as these economic opportunities remain out of the reach of some people, the technological divide will help stratify the United States into a society of informational haves and have-nots.

The Social "Benefits" of Poverty. You will recall the structural-functionalist assertion that stratification and inequality are necessary because they ensure that the most qualified and valuable people in society will occupy the most important positions. Social conditions exist and persist only if they are functional to society in some way. But functional for whom? If you were to survey people on the street and ask them if poverty is a good or bad thing, they would all, I'm sure, say, "Bad." Yet according to sociologist Herbert Gans (1971, 1996), within a free market economy and competitive society such as the United States, poverty plays a necessary institutional role. Although structural-functionalism has often been criticized for its propensity to justify the status quo, Gans combines it with conflict thinking to identify several economic and social "functions" served by poverty that benefit all other classes in society.

Economically, poverty benefits the rest of society in a variety of ways. First, poverty provides a ready pool of low-wage laborers who are available to do society's "dirty work." Poor people will work at low wages primarily because they have little choice. They will do the dangerous, undignified, or menial jobs that others won't do but that are necessary to keep businesses running, such as housekeeping, hospital cleaning, garbage collection, and manual labor. When large numbers of poor people compete for scarce jobs, business owners can pay lower wages.

Poverty also creates occupations and services that either serve the poor or protect the rest of society from them: police officers, penologists, social workers, lawyers, pawnshop owners, and so on. Even drug dealers and loan sharks depend on the presence of a large population of poor people willing to pay for their illegal services.

On an organizational level, the welfare system supports a network of private-sector businesses that make enormous profits by providing the system with a wide range of goods and services. When you hear people use the term *welfare dependency*, they are probably referring to the alleged long-term reliance of some welfare recipients on government aid or food stamps. But we can also talk about people or organizations whose livelihood depends on the existence of this vast welfare system. For instance, everyone who works in the system needs to have an office or clinic space in which to work, as well as supplies, equipment, and furnishings. Bankers, real estate developers, office system suppliers, computer manufacturers, and the construction and building industries profit each time a new welfare office, mental hospital, jail, unemployment office, or public housing project for the poor is needed (Bedard, 1991).

Another economic function of poverty is that poor people purchase goods and services that would otherwise go unused: secondhand goods; day-old bread, fruits, and vegetables; deteriorated housing; dilapidated cars; incompetent physicians; and so forth. Consider the following example of a company benefiting from its ability to sell a faulty product to the poor:

> At regular intervals, pineapple juice canneries must clean out the pipes that carry the juice from the crushing to the canning rooms. To do this, a salt solution is forced through the pipes and then flushed out before the new canning process starts again. A few years ago, one large cannery went through this cleaning operation and began running juice again before it was discovered that the pipes had not been totally purged of the salt solution. But, by that time, thousands of gallons of pineapple juice, all of it slightly salty, had already been processed and canned. The cans were sold, unlabeled, at a very low price to a food distributor who specializes in handling off-brand and reject merchandise for sale in poor neighborhoods and communities. The distributor put labels on the cans and retailed them for about half the usual price for that size, making a very good profit for himself. Across the label was printed "No Sweetener Added," certainly an accurate statement of the juice's condition. (Jacobs, 1988, pp. 123–124)

Clearly, this merchandise would have had little or no monetary value outside the poverty market.

The poor also serve several less-obvious social functions. They act as a visible reminder to the rest of society of the "legitimacy" of the conventional values of hard work, thrift, and honesty. By violating, or seeming to violate, these mainstream values, the poor reaffirm these virtues. If poor people are thought to be lazy, their presence reinforces the ethic of hard work; if the poor single mother is condemned, the two-parent family is legitimated as the ideal (Gans, 1996).

When large numbers of poor people are considered "unworthy" or "undeserving," they can sometimes serve as scapegoats for society's institutional problems. The alleged laziness of the jobless poor and the anger aimed at street people and beggars distract us from the failure of the economic system to adequately deal with the needs of all citizens. Likewise, the alleged personal shortcomings of slum dwellers and the homeless deflect attention from shoddy practices within the housing industry (Gans, 1996).

The poor also provide a reference point against which others can compare themselves. Charity events allow upper- and middle-class people to symbolically demonstrate their concern and philanthropy and reinforce their feelings of moral superiority. Finally, the poor provide the manual labor that enables societies to produce many impressive achievements in which all take national pride, from railroads to wilderness parks.

This explanation of poverty can easily be dismissed as cold and heartless. We certainly don't want to admit that poor people allow the rest of us to have comfortable and pleasant lifestyles. Yet this explanation is quite compelling. Just as society needs talented people to fill its important occupational positions, it also needs a stable population of poor people to fill its "less important" positions. After all, someone needs to clean toilets or work the night shift at the local mini-mart. What would society be like if it fostered full equality? Who would do the dirty work?

If we are truly serious about reducing poverty, we must find alternative ways of performing the societal functions it currently fulfills. But such a change will assuredly come at a cost to those who are now able to take advantage of poverty's presence. In short, poverty will be eliminated only when it becomes dysfunctional for people who aren't poor.

The Ideology of Competitive Individualism. Poverty also persists because of cultural beliefs and values that support the economic status quo. An important component of this value system in U.S. society is the belief in **competitive individualism** (Feagin, 1975; M. Lewis, 1978; Neubeck, 1986). As children, most of us are taught that nobody deserves a free ride. The way to be successful is to work hard, strive toward goals, and compete well against others. We learn that we are fully responsible for our own economic fates. Stories of such people as Abraham Lincoln and Henry Ford, who rose above terrible conditions to make it to the top, reinforce the notion that anybody can be successful if he or she simply has the desire and puts in the necessary effort. All one needs to do is take the initiative. As one recent TV ad says, "On the road to life, there are passengers and there are drivers."

The dark side of the U.S. belief in competitive individualism is that it all too easily explains why rewards are distributed unequally and why there is poverty. If people who are financially successful are thought to deserve their success, because of individual hard work and desire, then the people who fail and are suffering financially must also deserve their plight—because of their *lack of* hard work and desire. If a poor person is suffering, she or he must have done something to deserve it, and that "something" is either a lack of ability, a defective trait, or a lack of desire to succeed. People get unequal rewards because some are born smarter, stay in school longer, or work harder.

People in the United States have an intense need to believe that good things happen to good people and bad things happen to bad people (J. Huber & Form, 1973; Lerner, 1970). The belief in competitive individualism gives people the sense that they can control their own fate. Individual opportunity is the presumed birthright of every American. So while grudgingly acknowledging the existence of unequal outcomes, people can justify poverty and inequality by emphasizing equal chances. To take or not to take advantage of these chances is up to the individual. In this way the cultural ideology of poverty both explains and justifies the system of stratification.

However, such a belief system doesn't take into consideration that the competition itself is perhaps not fair. Competitive individualism assumes that opportunities to learn a trade, skill, or profession are available to everyone. Every person is supposed to have the chance to "be all that he or she can be." But the system may be rigged to favor those who already have power and privilege.

The Culture of Poverty. A variation of the belief in competitive individualism is the argument that the poor as a group possess beliefs, norms, values, and goals that are significantly different from the rest of society and that perpetuate a particular lifestyle that keeps them poor. Oscar Lewis (1968), the chief proponent of this **culture-of-poverty thesis,** maintained that poor people, resigned to their position in society, develop a unique value structure to deal with the improbability that they will become successful by the standards of the larger society. This culture is at odds with the dominant culture—in the United States, the middle-class belief in self-discipline and hard work.

Although the culture of poverty may keep people trapped in what appears (to the outside observer) to be an intolerable life, it nevertheless provides its own pleasures. Street life in the ghetto is exhilarating compared to a world where jobs are dull, arduous, and difficult to obtain and hold (P. Peterson, 1991). It is more fun to hang out, tell exaggerated stories, and exhibit one's latest purchases and conquests than it is to work and struggle in the "conventional" world. This extreme "present-orientedness"—the inability to live for the future (Banfield, 1970)—and not the lack of income or wealth is the principal cause of poverty, according to this view.

Once the culture of poverty comes into existence, Lewis argued, it perpetuates itself. This way of life is remarkably persistent: You can take the child out of the ghetto, but you can't take the ghetto out of the child. Furthermore, it is passed down from generation to generation. By age 6 or 7 most children have absorbed the basic values and attitudes of their subculture, rendering them unable to take advantage of any opportunities that may present themselves later in life. Others have argued that a poor family with a history of welfare dependence tends to raise children who lack ambition, a solid work ethic, and self-reliance (Auletta, 1982).

Critics of the culture-of-poverty thesis point out that to generate such a persistent culture of poverty, a society must have a large group of the permanently poor. However, government statistics show that only a little over half of U.S. residents living in poverty in a given year are found to be poor the next, and considerably fewer than half remain poor over many years (Duncan, 1984; Sherraden, 1988). In a given two-year period, only 4.8% of all poor people are poor for the entire 24 months. Moreover, the average duration of poverty is less than 5 months (U.S. Bureau of the Census, 1999b). In short, people tend to move in and out of poverty, undermining any single, long-standing, poverty-based lifestyle and value system that might exist.

Contrary to popular belief, not all poor people receive public assistance, either. In 1997 only about 34% received food stamps, 45% participated in Medicaid, 27% participated in school lunch programs, and 21% received some kind of housing assistance (U.S. Bureau of the Census, 2000b). As with poverty in general, welfare recipients move in and out of the system, making it difficult to sustain a tradition of dependence across generations.

Critics of the culture-of-poverty approach also contend that the behavior of poor people is largely caused by institutional impediments, such as a tradition of racial or ethnic prejudice and discrimination, residential segregation, limited economic opportunities, and occupational obstacles against advancement (Wilson, 1980). Poor African Americans, for example, still struggle to overcome the disadvantages of the slavery and Jim Crow laws that subjugated their ancestors. Other root causes of poverty include a growing lack of affordable housing and a changing economy that has all but eliminated entire classes of well-paying, low-skilled jobs.

Despite the lack of supportive evidence, the culture-of-poverty explanation obviously remains popular. Many people strongly believe that the poor live by a different set of moral standards and therefore will remain in poverty unless forced to change their values. Like competitive individualism, however, this ideology protects the nonpoor, the larger social structure, and the economic system from blame.

Today, the argument that hard work is the tried and true way from poverty to wealth dominates much of the debate. After all, if poverty is a "way of life," then giving poor people enough money to raise them out of poverty is not the answer; changing their troublesome culture is. Said one sociologist sarcastically, "By liquidating the lower-class culture we can liquidate the lower class, and, thereby, bring an end to poverty" (Ryan, 1976, p. 123). Ironically, the amount of money the government spends on welfare programs is less than half the amount it spends on assistance programs that serve predominantly middle-class recipients, such as Social Security, disability insurance, unemployment insurance, and Medicare (U.S. Bureau of the Census, 1998c).

Micro-Macro Connection
Welfare Reform

In 1994, about 5 million U.S. citizens were on government assistance. Today that figure is less than 3 million (DeParle, 1999). You might think that the booming economy of the late 1990s is what helped to reduce U.S. citizen's dependence on government assistance, but much of the reduction is actually due to a new welfare system, which began in 1996. This most recent program of "welfare reform" includes a mandatory work requirement after two years of receiving assistance (or enrollment in vocational training or community service), a five-year lifetime limit to benefits for any family, a transformation of welfare from a federal entitlement to a "block grant" that each state decides how to spend, a massive reduction in food stamps, and other cuts that concentrate on legal immigrants, the disabled, and the elderly poor (McCrate & Smith, 1998; Shalala, 1996). The law also requires states to provide child care and health care for working mothers, but it doesn't specify how long states must offer such support to each recipient (K. M. Harris, 1996).

These changes have brought some improvements in the lives of poor people. Every state has seen an increase in the number of former welfare recipients who are employed. Some states are spending the surplus money on transportation for these new workers, job placement, and programs that let welfare recipients keep more of their benefits even while earning paychecks (DeParle, 1997). A few states are paying women—often welfare recipients themselves—to set up family day care centers in their homes. In allowing women to earn a living by caring for the children of others, these states create jobs for welfare mothers and pave the way for other mothers to go to work (Kilborn, 1997). In Minnesota, welfare reform increased the number of former welfare recipients who were able to secure jobs. These people experienced a significant increase in their incomes (Pear, 2000a).

But other evidence suggests that welfare reform has not been an unqualified success. A study by the Center on Budget and Policy Priorities (1999) found that sharp reductions in government cash and food assistance support exceeded any increases in family earnings, causing very poor female-headed families to lose ground. Another study found that people in so-called workfare programs started out at very low wages and increased their salaries by an average of only 6 cents an hour every year (cited in Sexton, 1997). An examination of welfare reform in New York City found that, though the welfare population declined sharply in the past few years, workfare programs have provided limited job training for many of the poorly skilled and poorly educated individuals on public assistance. Much of the available work is so menial that it offers few, if any, skills that employers demand. After three months off welfare, fewer than one-third of former welfare recipients had found full- or part-time work (Finder, 1998). Moreover, the city lacks child care for 61% of the children whose mothers participate in workfare, further limiting the effectiveness of the program (Swarns, 1998).

In addition, close to 1 million poor parents lost their Medicaid health insurance coverage as a consequence of welfare reform. In most cases, parents who were forced off of welfare had to take low-paying jobs that didn't offer health benefits. Those who did find jobs that offered insurance were often unable to pay the premiums (Pear, 2000b). And it's estimated that about a million additional toddlers and preschoolers are in day care—which in many cases is of poor quality—as a result of welfare revisions that require their mothers to work (Lewin, 2000b). As desirable as it is to reduce the need for government assistance, we cannot assume that all those who leave the welfare rolls are experiencing a better life.

Global Development and Inequality

As you've seen elsewhere in this book, it is becoming increasingly difficult to understand life in one society without understanding that society's place in the larger global context. The trend toward globalization (see Chapter 9) may have brought the world's inhabitants closer together but they are not all benefiting equally. Nations have differing amounts of power to ensure that their interests are met. The more developed and less developed countries of the world experience serious inequalities in wealth that have immediate consequences for their citizens.

The Global Economic Gap

The average per capita yearly income in Western Europe, the United States, Canada, and Japan is about $22,000; in the less developed countries of South America, Asia, and Africa it is a little over $300 (Bradshaw & Wallace, 1996). Thus wealthy countries constituting 20% of the world's population account for 65% of the world's income. In contrast, less affluent, developing countries account for 67% of the world's population but only 18% of its income (McMichael, 1996). The richest three *individuals* in the world have assets that exceed the gross domestic product of the 48 least developed *countries* (Crossette, 1998). And consider these other eye-opening statistics:

- Wealthy countries consume 85% of the world's supply of paper, 79% of its steel, 80% of all commercial energy, and 45% of all meat and fish (Crossette, 1998; Kerbo, 1991; Schor, 1991).
- Grains fed to U.S. livestock equal the amount of food consumed by the combined human populations of India and China (McMichael, 1996).
- A single child born in Western Europe, Japan, or the United States uses as much of the earth's resources as an entire village of African children (Steiner, 1998b).

- Americans spend about $8 billion a year on cosmetics—$2 billion more than the estimated annual amount needed to provide basic education for everyone in the world (Crossette, 1998).
- Europeans spend about $2 billion a year more on ice cream than the estimated amount needed to provide clean water and safe sewers for the world's population (Crossette, 1998).

The gap in the quality of everyday life is particularly striking. Only about 20% of school-aged children in poor countries are enrolled in secondary school, compared to 90% in affluent countries. In wealthy countries, 40% of college-aged people go to college; in poor countries only 3% do. The number of children who die before the age of 5 is nearly 20 times higher in poor countries than in rich ones (Bradshaw & Wallace, 1996).

Medical treatment is especially stratified. For instance, the vast majority of HIV-infected people around the world don't have access to the effective, but extremely expensive, drug treatments that are now available in the West. Consequently, though AIDS cases and AIDS deaths are dropping in Western industrialized countries, they are increasing dramatically in less developed countries. According to the United Nations, of the 34 million people worldwide infected with the HIV virus, 30 million are poor by world standards: living on less than $2 a day (cited in McNeil, 2000b). Impoverished countries in sub-Saharan Africa alone account for 69% of the world's victims of HIV and AIDS (Gordimer, 2000). In Botswana and Zimbabwe, for instance, one out of every four adults is infected, and in some major cities 70% of women in prenatal clinics test positive for HIV (L. K. Altman, 1998). In 1999 alone, more than 2 million Africans died of AIDS. That's more than five times the number of AIDS-related deaths in the United States in nearly two decades (Will, 2000). And it's estimated that between one-half and two-thirds of 15-year-olds in these African countries will eventually die of AIDS (L. K. Altman, 2000). The epidemic is growing out of control because AIDS in the developing world can't be addressed the way it is in the West:

> One cannot simply put baskets of condoms in all the gay bars and clean needles in all the methadone clinics or even send speakers to all the high schools. . . . For one, much of the world at risk of AIDS can't read. Most of the world at risk has never used a condom. . . . And most of the world with AIDS thinks it doesn't have the disease and doesn't know anyone who does, because 95 percent of those infected in the third world have never been tested. . . . And most of the world cannot afford the drugs that Americans can. (McNeil, 2000b, p. 1)

More generally, overall life expectancy in rich countries approaches 80 years; in poor countries it is barely above 50. Let me express the discrepancies in another way: In the space of a day, passengers flying from Japan to Mozambique leave the country with the world's highest life expectancy (81 years)—and land in one with the world's lowest (about 31 years). A flight between France and Côte d'Ivoire takes only a few hours, but it spans more than 37 years of life expectancy. A short air trip between Miami, Florida, and Haiti represents a life expectancy gap of more than 31 years (U.S. Bureau of the Census, 1995b, 2000b).

Explanations for Global Stratification

How has global stratification come about? The conflict perspective explains not only stratification within a society but also stratification between societies. One way a country can use its power to control another is through **colonization**—invading and establishing control over a weaker country and its people in order to expand the colonizer's markets. Typically, the native people of the colony are considered lower in status and are forced to give up their culture. Labor, cultural treasures, and natural resources are extracted to enhance the power and wealth of the colonizing country. The colony serves as a source of raw materials and a market for high-priced goods. Much of North and South America, Africa, and Asia were at one time or another under the colonial control of European countries such as Great Britain, France, Spain, Holland, and Portugal. The United States once controlled territories in Central and South America.

Although the direct conquest and subjugation of weak countries are rare today, wealthy countries are still able to exploit them for commercial gain. Powerful countries can use weaker countries as a source of cheap raw materials and cheap labor. Because of their access to better technology, wealthy nations are able to produce higher-quality goods at lower prices than are poor nations (D. A. Smith, 1993). This advantage allows them to have a more favorable balance of trade and ultimately gives them greater control of the world's financial resources (Wallerstein, 1974).

Powerful nations, like powerful ruling classes, seek to retain their favored positions while keeping other nations in their place. In a global economy, such dominance is accomplished through financial pressure—such as when powerful industrialized countries set world prices on certain goods—rather than brute force (Chase-Dunn & Rubinson, 1977). Because their economic base is weak, poor countries often have to borrow money or buy manufactured goods on credit from wealthy countries. The huge debt they build up locks them into a downward spiral of exploitation and poverty. As a result, they cannot develop an independent economy of their own and thus remain dependent on wealthy ones for their very survival (Frank, 1969). In short, just as upper-class people can exploit and exercise power over lower-class people within a society, so, too, can wealthy countries exploit poor ones in the global marketplace.

Global Financial Organizations

It's not just powerful countries that have the ability to hold poor nations in their grip. Several international financial organizations play a significant role in determining the economic and social policies of developing countries. The World Bank funds reconstruction and development in these countries through investments and loans. Similarly, the International Monetary Fund (IMF) tries to foster economic growth and international monetary cooperation through financial and technical assistance. The World Trade Organization (WTO) oversees the rules of trade between nations.

Although these organizations have improved the standard of living in some poor countries by providing the funds for such projects as new roads or water treatment plants, the countries that receive their aid often end up even more bankrupt and impoverished than before. For instance, when poor countries are unable to pay their foreign debts, the World Bank and the IMF provide new credit. But they do so with certain conditions attached. The conditions, often referred to as "structural adjustments" typically reflect a Western-style, free-market approach that includes reducing government spending, eliminating barriers to foreign ownership, privatizing public services, and demanding high interest rates (Brutus, 1999).

Conditions such as these have at times threatened the sovereignty and integrity of recipient nations:

- In Haiti, the IMF and World Bank blocked the government from raising the minimum wage and insisted that government services, such as sanitation and education, be cut in half. The desperate Haitian government complied, despite the fact that the life expectancy is 49 years for Haitian men and 53 years for women, that 45% of Haitians are illiterate, and that infant mortality is about 10%.
- In Mexico, the World Bank advised the government to abolish constitutionally guaranteed free education at the national university, making it virtually impossible for poor Mexicans to go to college.
- In Zimbabwe, the World Bank persuaded the government to shift production supports from food crops such as corn to export crops such as tobacco. As a result, malnutrition increased and infant mortality doubled (Brutus, 1999; U.S. Network for Global Economic Justice, 2000).

You can see that global financial relationships between international lending institutions and poor countries are a double-edged sword. The countries certainly receive much-needed and often life-saving financial assistance. But in the process they sometimes become even more dependent and powerless.

Multinational Corporations

Global stratification has been made even more complex in recent years by the growth of massive multinational corporations. Because of their access to economic and political resources, wealthy companies in the United States and elsewhere can go outside their country's borders to pursue their financial interests if domestic opportunities aren't promising. They can invest their money in more lucrative foreign corporations or establish their businesses or factories abroad. The 100 largest U.S. multinationals—well-recognized companies such as Exxon, IBM, Mobil, and Dow Chemical—earn well over half of their revenues from foreign sales (Braun, 1997).

With their ability to quickly shift operations to friendly countries, multinational corporations find it easy to evade the governance of any one country. Their decisions reflect corporate goals and not necessarily the well-being or interests of any particular country. In fact, the largest multinational corporations are wealthier than most countries in the world, as Exhibit 10.9 shows.

From a structural-functionalist perspective, a U.S. company locating a factory in a poor country would seem to benefit everyone involved. The host country benefits from the creation of new jobs and a higher standard of living. The corporation, of course, benefits from increased profits. And the country in which the corporation is based benefits from lower consumer prices for the products that would cost more if

Exhibit 10.9 **The Economic Power of Multinational Corporations**

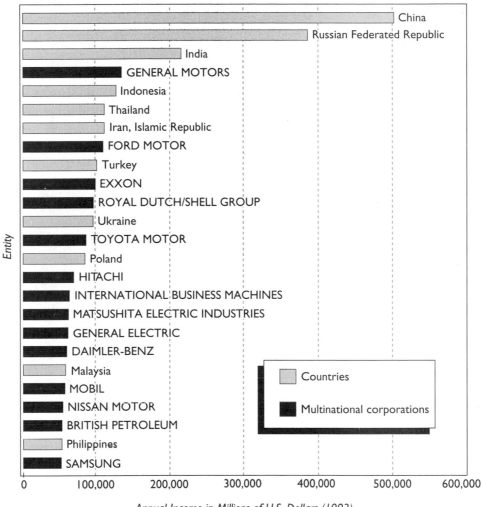

Annual Income in Millions of U.S. Dollars (1992)

Note: Highly industrialized, wealthy countries have been excluded.

Source: Bradshaw & Wallace, 1996, p. 49.

manufactured at home. Furthermore, the entire planet benefits because these firms form allegiances to many different countries and therefore might help pressure them into settling their political differences peacefully.

Multinational corporations are indeed a valuable part of the international economy. However, conflict theory argues that in the long run multinationals can actually perpetuate or even worsen global stratification. One common criticism of multinationals is that they exploit local workers and communities. Employees in foreign plants or factories often work under conditions that wouldn't be tolerated in wealthier countries.

The most obvious inequity is the wage people earn. Whereas the hourly wage of an auto worker in the United States is more than $20, the wage of an auto worker in Taiwan or South Korea is less than $3 (Braun, 1997). In 1996 the National Labor Committee discovered that clothes for Disney, London Fog, Bradlees, and Ralph Lauren were being produced in Burma by workers who earned about 6 cents an hour ("Sweatshops 'R' us," 1996). More than a third of Nike's clothing and athletic shoes are manufactured in Indonesia, where workers are paid the minimum wage of $2.20 a day—a wage level it took workers four years of violent struggle to achieve. In Vietnam, Nike factory workers make $30 a month (Herbert, 1996).

In addition, environmental regulations and occupational safety requirements, such as protection against dangerous conditions or substances—which drive up the cost of finished products—sometimes don't exist in other countries. Hence local workers may become sicker and the environment more polluted when foreign manufacturers set up facilities. For instance, U.S., Canadian, Australian, and European mining companies are digging mines of unprecedented size and destructiveness around the world. Many of these projects have caused not only significant deforestation but also the release of cyanide, arsenic, lead, and copper into nearby water supplies ("Tarnished gold," 1999). A 1997 report found that factory workers in one Southeast Asian plant were exposed to carcinogens that exceeded local standards—less stringent than U.S. standards—by 177 times, and 77% of the employees suffered from respiratory problems (Greenhouse, 1997).

Conditions in foreign factories were so bad and criticisms from human rights organizations so strong that a 1997 presidential task force created a code of conduct on wages, working conditions, and child labor for apparel factories that U.S. companies own and operate around the world. And in 1998 Nike bowed to international pressure and became one of the first major multinational corporations to pledge to end child labor and apply stringent U.S. health and safety standards to its factories abroad (Cushman, 1998).

The host countries themselves are equally likely to be exploited. The money that multinational corporations earn is rarely reinvested in the host country. In fact, 85% of the profit from exported products ends up in the hands of the multinational corporations, bankers, traders, and distributors (Braun, 1997). For example, in Brazil, one of the world's largest agricultural exporters, shipments abroad of fruits, vegetables, and soybeans have grown considerably over the past several decades. During the same period, however, the number of Brazilians who were undernourished grew from one-third to two-thirds of the population (Braun, 1997).

Multinational corporations can also perpetuate global inequality by their decisions on when to develop certain products and where to market them. A case in point is the global pharmaceutical industry. North America, Japan, and Western Europe account for 80% of world drug sales, whereas Africa accounts for about 1% (cited in McNeil, 2000a). A significant proportion of medical research today is devoted to developing drugs that are likely to sell in these lucrative markets. These drugs are usually either "blockbuster" drugs (those that can earn upward of $1.5 billion a year) or "lifestyle" drugs (those that enhance the lives of generally healthy people). The astounding popularity—and profit-making capacity—of the anti-impotence drug Viagra and the baldness drugs Propecia and Rogaine are recent examples. Impotence and baldness can be characterized as lifestyle troubles or embarrassing inconveniences but certainly not life-threatening illnesses.

This trend has global significance. Of the drugs introduced between 1975 and 1997 by the world's largest pharmaceutical companies, only 1% were created to combat diseases such as the tuberculosis, malaria, sleeping sickness, and acute lower-respiratory infections that kill or cripple millions each year in Africa, Asia, and South America. In developing countries, three times as many people each year die from these potentially curable diseases as from AIDS (Silverstein, 1999). The last truly new drug to treat tuberculosis—a disease that kills two million people a year, mostly in poor, developing countries—was invented over 30 years ago (McNeil, 2000a).

But not all multinationals are hard-hearted organizations that ignore the physical well-being of their workers abroad, the well-being of the workforce at home whose jobs are being exported to other countries, or the health and welfare of poor people in developing nations. For many multinationals, relocating manufacturing facilities to another country where labor is less expensive is a necessary response to global economic pressures as well as the demands of domestic consumers for inexpensive products. But those processes that drive corporate decisions do sometimes drive individuals out of work, contribute to environmental and health problems, and reinforce global inequality.

Micro-Macro Connection
The Global Tobacco Epidemic

When sales at home lag, multinationals are likely to turn to the foreign marketplace to boost sales. Consider the production and sale of cigarettes. In recent years, tobacco use has been declining in many countries of North America and Western Europe. The United States in particular has witnessed a fervent antismoking movement. Many states have enacted restrictive smoking ordinances, and class action suits against tobacco companies are piling up. U.S. cigarette consumption has undergone a 15-year decline. Worldwide, though, 1.1 billion people smoke—about one-third of the global population aged 15 and older (World Health Organization, 1996). And most of these smokers live in poor, developing countries.

Indeed, in many developing countries in Eastern Europe, Latin America, Africa, and Asia, tobacco use has increased dramatically over the past two decades, especially among young people and women. In China, for example, per capita consumption of cigarettes increased 260% between the early 1970s and the early 1990s. Today, 70% of Chinese men are regular smokers (Rosenthal & Altman, 1998). And about 300 million smokers in China consume an average of 1,900 cigarettes per smoker each year (World Health Organization, 1996). In the 1970s, the countries with the highest rate of adult cigarette consumption were Canada, Switzerland, Australia, and Great Britain. But in the 1990s, smoking was highest in Poland, Greece, Hungary, Japan, and the Republic of Korea. In the 2000s, 70% of the world's cigarettes will be smoked in developing countries.

Not surprisingly, U.S. tobacco companies have devoted substantial marketing attention abroad. In the developing countries of the world, the U.S. cigarette has become a coveted symbol of affluence and sophistication. And U.S. companies are not bashful about exploiting this lucrative market:

- In Taiwan, teenagers are offered free admission to a popular disco for five empty packs of Winstons.
- In Malaysia, where all tobacco advertising is banned, "cigarette girls" hand out free Salems to concert goers.
- On the streets of Manila, "jump boys" as young as 10 hop in and out of traffic selling Marlboros and Lucky Strikes to passing motorists.
- In the discos and coffee shops of Seoul, young Koreans light up U.S. brands that a decade ago were illegal to possess.
- Downtown Kiev has become the Ukrainian version of Marlboro Country, with the gray cityscape punctuated with colorful billboards of Western sunsets and chiseled cowboy faces.

Exports now account for 33% of total U.S. cigarette production, up from 8% in 1984 (McGinn, 1997). The United States is the world's leading exporter of manufactured cigarettes. In 1994 the Phillip Morris Company alone sold about 350 billion cigarettes outside the country (Frankel, 1996). Thanks to these foreign markets, U.S. tobacco companies have been able to make larger profits than ever before, despite the fact that they're being besieged at home by antismoking activists, government regulators, and plaintiffs' lawyers.

For the most part, these companies have exported cigarettes with the implicit support of the U.S. government, which sees the global tobacco market as a free trade issue rather than a health issue. Ironically, while one arm of the government has been warning the U.S. population about the dangers of smoking and enacting restrictive advertising and marketing policies for more than a decade, another arm has been helping the cigarette industry recruit a new generation of smokers abroad. In the late 1980s, a group of influential politicians, including Jesse Helms, Bob Dole, and Al Gore, wrote a letter to the president of South Korea demanding that U.S. tobacco companies be allowed to distribute, advertise, and promote cigarettes in Korea without discriminatory taxes. In 1990 then–Vice President Dan Quayle summed up the government's role in protecting tobacco companies' economic interests:

> I don't think it's any news to North Carolina tobacco farmers that the American public as a whole is smoking less. We ought to think about the exports. We ought to think about opening up markets, breaking down the barriers. (quoted in Frankel, 1996, p. A24)

What will be the long-term effect of the globalization of cigarettes on people's everyday lives? According to some experts, smoking is responsible for 3 million deaths per year worldwide, and in 30 years the number will likely approach 10 million. About 25% of all male deaths in developing countries are caused by smoking, a figure that reaches 33% among middle-aged men (World Health Organization, 1996). And the percentage of tobacco-related deaths among women continues to increase rapidly. In

China alone, 2,000 people each day die from smoking-related illness, a figure that is expected to increase to 8,000 by the middle of the next century unless public health measures are taken (Rosenthal & Altman, 1998). If current trends continue, about 800 million of the world's 2 billion children will become smokers, and according to the World Health Organization, tobacco will eventually kill one-third of them. Within 25 years, tobacco-induced illness is expected to replace infectious disease as the leading threat to human health worldwide (McGinn, 1997).

CONCLUSION

In Chapter 1, I pondered the question of how free we really are to act as we wish. I described some of the personal, interpersonal, and structural considerations that limit or constrain our choices. In this chapter you have seen that this fundamental issue is affected by social stratification and inequality. Certain groups of people have a greater capacity to control their own lives than others. Our position in the stratification system can determine not only our ability to influence people and exert authority but a whole host of life chances as well, from financial stability to housing, education, and health care. The unequal distribution of economic resources, whether between wealthy and poor individuals in the same society or between wealthy and poor countries worldwide, has created a seemingly indestructible culture of haves and have-nots.

The profound imbalances in wealth, power, and prestige that exist in the United States are especially ironic given how loudly and frequently U.S. citizens sing of their cultural commitment to the values of equality and justice. Nevertheless, the U.S. system is set up, like most others in the world, to promote, enhance, and protect the interests of those who reside at or near the top of the stratification system. Authority, wealth, and influence grant rights that are unknown to the vast majority of people.

It's rather shocking that in a country as wealthy as the United States, a comfortable and stable life is well beyond the reach of tens of millions of people. Constant media images of wealth remind poor and working-class people that they are outsiders who can only watch and long to be part of that affluent world.

We speak of the poor as if they were an unchanging and faceless group to be pitied, despised, or feared. To talk of the "poverty problem" is to talk about some depersonalized, permanent fixture on the U.S. landscape. But poverty is people. It's people standing in soup kitchen lines and welfare lines. It's people living in rat-infested projects. It's people sleeping on sidewalks. It's people struggling to acquire things the rest of society takes for granted. It's people coming up short in their quest for the American Dream.

When we look at the institutional causes of poverty, we see that the personality or "cultural" traits often associated with poverty—low ambition, rejection of the work ethic, inability to plan for the future—might be better understood as consequences of poverty rather than causes of it. As long as the structural obstacles to stable employment, adequate wages, and a decent education continue to exist, so will the characteristic hopelessness associated with poverty.

YOUR TURN

Even people whose income is well above the poverty line can sometimes find it difficult to make ends meet. Imagine a family of four living in your hometown. Suppose that both parents work, that one child is 7 years old and in elementary school, and that the other is 3 and must be cared for during the day.

Make a list of all the goods and services this family needs to function at a minimum subsistence level—that is, at the poverty line. Be as complete as possible. Consider food, clothing, housing, transportation, medical care, child care, entertainment, and so on.

Estimate the minimum monthly cost of each item. If you currently live on your own and must pay these expenses yourself, use those figures as a starting point (but remember that you must estimate for a family of four). If you live in a dorm or at home, ask your parents (or anyone else who pays bills) what their expenses are for such goods and services. Call the local day care center to see what it charges for child care. Go to the local supermarket and compute the family food budget. For those expenses that aren't divided on a monthly basis (for example, the purchase of clothing and household appliances), estimate the yearly cost and divide by 12.

Once you have estimated the total monthly expenses, multiply by 12 to get the subsistence budget for the family of four. If your estimate is higher than the government's official poverty line (around $17,463), what sorts of items could you cut out of the budget for the family to be defined as officially poor and therefore eligible for certain government programs? By looking for ways to cut expenses from your minimal subsistence budget, you will get a good sense of what everyday life in poverty is like.

Describe the quality of life of this hypothetical family that makes too much to be officially poor and too little to sustain a comfortable life. What sorts of things are they forced to do without that a more affluent family might simply take for granted (for example, annual vacations, discretionary income, a second car, eating out once a week)? What would be the impact of poverty on the lives of the children? How will the family's difficulty in meeting its basic subsistence needs translate into access to opportunities (education, jobs, health care,) for the children later in life?

Note: This exercise is adapted from M. V. Miller, 1985.

CHAPTER HIGHLIGHTS

- Stratification is a ranking of entire groups of people, based on race, gender, or social class, that perpetuates unequal rewards and life chances in society.

- Social class is the primary means of stratification in many societies, including the United States. Contemporary sociologists are likely to define one's class standing as a combination of income, wealth, occupational prestige, and educational attainment. Social class is more than an economic position; it is a way of life that affects how we experience every facet of our lives.

- The structural-functionalist explanation of stratification is that higher rewards, such as prestige and large salaries, are afforded to the most important positions in society, thereby ensuring that the most qualified individuals will occupy the highest positions. Conflict theory argues that stratification reflects an unequal distribution of power in society and is a primary source of conflict and tension.

● The official U.S. poverty line, the dollar cutoff point that defines the amount of income necessary for subsistence living, may actually be set too low, thereby underestimating the proportion of the population that is suffering financially.

● Poverty persists because it serves economic and social functions. The ideology of competitive individualism—that to succeed in life all one has to do is work hard and win in competition with others—creates a belief that poor people are to blame for their own suffering. In addition, poverty receives institutional "support" from a distribution of wealth and income that is growing increasingly unequal.

● Stratification exists not only among different groups within the same society but also among different societies within a global community. Wealthy nations are better able to control the world's financial resources than poor nations are.

KEY TERMS

absolute poverty Inability to afford the minimal requirements for sustaining a reasonably healthy existence

authority Possession of some status or quality that compels others to obey one's directives or commands

capitalist Someone who owns means of production and is able to purchase the labor power of others; a member of the bourgeoisie

caste system Stratification system based on heredity, with little movement allowed across strata

colonization Process of expanding economic markets by invading and establishing control over a weaker country and its people

competitive individualism Cultural belief that those who succeed in society are those who work the hardest and have the best abilities and that those who suffer don't work hard enough or lack necessary traits or abilities

culture-of-poverty thesis Belief that poor people, resigned to their position in society, develop a unique value structure to deal with their lack of success

estate system (feudal system) Stratification system in which high-status groups own land and have power based on birth

false consciousness Situation in which people in the lower classes come to accept a belief system that harms them; the primary means by which powerful classes in society prevent protest and revolution

lower class (underclass) In a society stratified by social class, a group of people who work for minimum wage or are chronically unemployed; the "poor"

means of production Land, commercial enterprises, factories, and wealth that form the economic basis of class societies

middle class In a society stratified by social class, a group of people who have an intermediate level of wealth, income, and prestige, such as managers, supervisors, executives, small business owners, and professionals

near-poor Individuals or families whose earnings are between 100% and 125% of the poverty line

petite bourgeoisie Class of people who own means of production but don't purchase the labor power of others

poverty line Amount of yearly income a family requires to meet its basic needs, according to the federal government

poverty rate Percentage of people whose income falls below the poverty line

relative poverty Individual's economic position compared to the living standards of the majority in the society

slavery Economic form of inequality in which some people are legally the property of others

social class Group of people who share a similar economic position in a society, based on their wealth and income

social mobility Movement of people or groups from one class to another

socioeconomic status Prestige, honor, respect, and lifestyle associated with different positions or groups in society

stratification Ranking system for groups of people that perpetuates unequal rewards and life chances in society

upper class In a society stratified by social class, a group of people who have high income and prestige and who own vast amounts of property and other forms of wealth, such as owners of large corporations, top financiers, rich celebrities and politicians, and members of prestigious families

worker Individual who neither owns means of production nor has the ability to purchase the labor power of others and who must instead sell his or her own labor to survive

working class In a society stratified by social class, a group of people who have a low level of wealth, income, and prestige, such as industrial and factory workers, office workers, clerks, and farm and manual laborers

Images of Social Class
Douglas Harper

Social classes exist in the United States, notwithstanding our egalitarian ideals. Just consider how people in the three different social classes depicted here experience some of the same things.

BARBARA NORFLEET

BILL OWNES

● **Housing density and conditions**

BRUCE DAVIDSON

Consider particularly the lives of the children. What have these children already learned about their social roles? What would happen if the children from one setting were placed into a different class location?

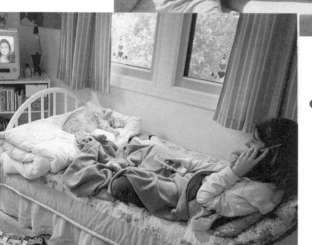

● **Children's postures and possessions**

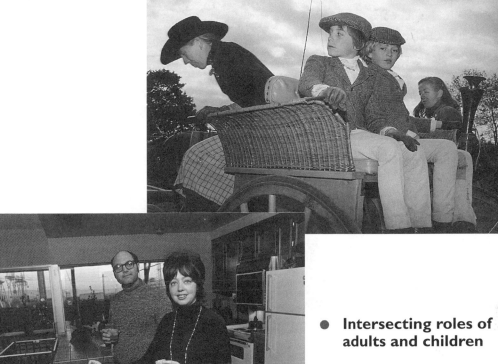

BARBARA NORFLEET

BILL OWENS

HERMAN LEROY EMMET

● **Intersecting roles of adults and children**

As you look at these photographs, examine the clothes that people wear and the possessions that surround them. Try to infer from the photographs what their typical activities are. Then study the body language of the people in the three class settings. How do they face the camera and one another? Do posture, expression, and emotion seem to be functions of social class?

BARBARA NORFLEET

• **Settings for social life**

BILL OWENS

EUGENE RICHARDS

● **Interior spaces**

The United States is often billed as a society in which all who apply themselves can be socially mobile. As you consider these photographs, ask yourself whether effort alone would be enough to move people from one class to another. Finally, think about the structural and historical forces in society that created the context for class-based experiences.

BARBARA NORFLEET

● **Water and recreation**

BILL OWENS

HERMAN LEROY EMMET

The Architecture of Inequality: Race and Ethnicity

In the months leading up to the 1996 presidential primary elections in the United States, the rumor mills buzzed with assessments of the political aspirations of the retired chairman of the Joint Chiefs of Staff, General Colin Powell. Was he going to run for president? He was painted by many—in particular, by conservative Republicans—as a veritable savior for the country and the Republicans' best chance for regaining the White House. Each day brought a new rumor or revelation about Powell's intentions. In the end, he didn't run.

Speculation surfaced again in 2000, when Powell's name was mentioned prominently and repeatedly as a possible running mate for the Republican presidential candidate, George W. Bush. Again the enthusiasm was unbridled. The conservative political adviser and television commentator, Mary Matalin, summed up the feelings of many Republicans when she said, "Is there anybody else the party would rather see there than Colin Powell?" ("Expectation shadows Gen. Powell," 2000). When it became clear he had no interest in being vice president, attention turned immediately to the possibility of a Cabinet position for him if Bush won the election. The country, it seemed, was unwilling to give up on the idea of General Powell serving somewhere in the highest reaches of the government. Ultimately President Bush named Powell secretary of state, a key post in his cabinet and fourth in line of succession to the presidency.

Democratic societies have always had popular but reluctant public figures in whom the voting populace invests its political hopes and dreams. Retired military figures—including George Washington, Ulysses Grant, and Dwight Eisenhower—have been especially attractive to the public. What made General Powell's situation particularly noteworthy was the relative lack of attention paid to the fact that he is an African American. If you had told a U.S. abolitionist in the 1860s, or even a civil rights worker in the 1960s, that someday millions of people in the United States, even conservatives, would pin their hopes for the country on a black man running for president or vice president or serving in the Cabinet, he or she might have laughed in your face. Even 15 or 20 years ago, it probably would have been inconceivable. But there

Powell was, making speeches to large, enthusiastic audiences and giving interviews on national television, further fueling speculation about his political future.

People's desire to see Powell in public office made me think about the tremendous gains that racial and ethnic minorities have made in the last few years, not only politically, but educationally, economically, and culturally. The percentage of African-American and Hispanic college graduates has risen steadily over the past 10 years, as has the proportion of minority people who could be considered middle or upper class. In 1995, the poverty rate among African Americans dipped below 30% for the first time since the U.S. Bureau of the Census began keeping tabs on it in 1955, and it continues to fall; between 1996 and 1997, the poverty rate for Hispanic families showed the largest 1-year drop since 1977; Asian Americans continue to have the highest levels of economic and educational attainment of any racial group in the country (Pear, 1998; U.S. Bureau of the Census, 1997a, 2000b). Once desolate inner-city neighborhoods have come to life. African Americans sit on the Supreme Court and, along with Latinos, serve in presidential cabinet positions. More Latinos, Asian Americans, and Native Americans are in elected offices than ever before. The African-American influence in pop culture is global—it's not uncommon to see teenagers in Japan who tan themselves deep brown, tease their hair into afros, and listen to rap music. In the early 2000s, Latino musicians such as Ricky Martin, Marc Anthony, and Carlos Santana achieved remarkable cross-over success. One popular book has even proclaimed that racism in the United States is, for all intents and purposes, over (D'Souza, 1995).

Yet as I think back to the color-blind enthusiasm that surrounded General Powell's every move, my mind keeps pulling me toward a different reality. Despite progress, African Americans, Hispanics, and Native Americans still remain the poorest and most disadvantaged of all groups in the United States; their average annual income is still only slightly over half that of whites (U.S. Bureau of the Census, 1999b). And 36.4% of African-American children and 33.6% of Hispanic children live in poverty—compared to 14.4% of white children (U.S. Bureau of the Census, 2000b). Only 56% of all Hispanic students complete high school (U.S. Bureau of the Census, 2000b). A third of all black men between the ages of 20 and 29 are embroiled in the criminal justice system. African Americans have the lowest life expectancy; highest rate of infant mortality; highest rate of most cancers, diabetes, high blood pressure, and kidney failure; highest rate of new AIDS cases; and highest rate of death from treatable illness, gunshot wound, and drug-induced or alcohol-induced cause of any racial or ethnic group in the country (Institute of Medicine, 1999a; Stolberg, 1998b; U.S. Bureau of the Census, 1997b; Zaldivar, 1998).

I also thought of specific events over the past few years that belie the image of racial progress and harmony:

- The handcuffed Haitian immigrant who was sodomized with a broom stick by police officers in a precinct bathroom and the unarmed West African immigrant who was fatally shot over 40 times by four police officers.
- The white supremacist whose shooting spree in Illinois and Indiana left a black man and an Asian college student dead and nine others injured.
- The white woman in California who repeatedly ran over a Latino man with her car and then referred to the man's body afterward as "dead road kill."

- The black man and white woman who, while walking down a street in Fayetteville, North Carolina, were shot and killed by white supremacists looking for "niggers" to torment.
- The Asian-American man in California who was stabbed to death while roller-blading. Police say the two young men arrested had Nazi paraphernalia and white supremacist posters in their apartment.
- The black man in Texas who was dragged behind a car driven by two white men until his body was torn apart.
- Days after the September 11, 2001, attacks, mosques were vandalized, Muslims were verbally and physically harassed, and several "Arab-looking" people were killed by angry whites.

How far have we really come? Which is the real United States? Is it the one that Martin Luther King Jr. dreamed about in 1963, a place where race and ethnicity are losing their status as major criteria for judging the content of a person's character? Or is it the one perpetually plagued by economic inequality, prejudice, and hatred?

In the previous chapter I examined the class stratification system. But social class isn't the only thing that influences social status and life chances. This chapter focuses on another important determinant of social inequality: race and ethnicity.

Race and Ethnicity: More than Just Biology

Race is typically viewed as a category of people labeled and treated as similar because of common inborn biological traits, such as skin color; color and texture of hair; and shape of eyes, nose, or head. Race is usually thought to be a fixed and immutable biological characteristic that can easily be used to separate people into distinct groups. But the concept really isn't so straightforward. For instance, people who consider themselves "white" may actually have darker skin and curlier hair than some people who consider themselves "black." Australian Aboriginals have black skin and negroid facial features but have blond, wavy hair. The black-skinned !Kung of Africa have epicanthic eye folds, a characteristic typical of Asian peoples. Scholars can't even agree on how many human races exist—estimates range from 4 to more than 40.

Not surprisingly, there is no universal definition of race. South Africa has four legally defined races—black, white, colored, and Indian—but in England and Ireland the term *black* is used to refer to all people who are not white. In one small Irish town that is experiencing an unprecedented influx of refugees, anyone who is not Irish—let alone not white—is considered black. As one resident puts it, "Either Romanians or Nigerians, we don't know the difference. They're all the same. They're all black" (quoted in Lyall, 2000, p. A6). Conversely, an African American visiting Tanzania is likely to be considered white by the African blacks there (Njeri, 1990). Brazilians have three primary races—*branco* (white), *prêto* (black), and *pardo* (mulatto)—but identify dozens of more precise terms to categorize people based on minute differences in skin color, hair texture and length, and facial features. These socially constructed categories don't denote discrete racial groupings. Instead they tend to blend fluidly into one another (Marger, 1994).

The complex issue of defining race points up a complicated biological reality. Since the earliest humans appeared, they have consistently tended to migrate and interbreed. Some surveys estimate that at least 75% of U.S. blacks have some white ancestry (cited in L. Mathews, 1996). The famous naturalist Charles Darwin (1871/1971) wrote that despite external differences, it is virtually impossible to identify clear, distinctive racial characteristics. Indeed, there is no gene for race—no gene that is 100% of one form in one race and 100% of a different form in another race (Brown, 1998).

Race is therefore a more meaningful social category than it is a biological one. That is, the characteristics selected to distinguish one group from another have less to do with innate physical differences than with what a particular culture defines as socially significant. In the United States, for instance, Jews, the Irish, and Italians were once seen as members of inferior races who came to be seen as "white" when they entered the mainstream culture and gained economic and political power (Bronner, 1998a). In South Africa under apartheid, wealthy Japanese businesspeople enjoyed the status of honorary white (R. Chambers, 1997). Similarly, as Brazilians climb the class ladder through educational and economic achievement, their racial classification changes, as illustrated by popular Brazilian expressions such as "Money whitens" or "A rich Negro is a white man, and a poor white man is a Negro" (Marger, 1994, p. 441).

In short, racial categories are not natural, biological categories. They are created, inhabited, transformed, applied, and destroyed by people (Omi & Winant, 1992). What ties people together in a particular racial group is not a set of shared physical characteristics—because there aren't any physical characteristics shared by all members of a particular racial group—but the shared experience of being identified by others as members of that group (Piper, 1992).

Despite the ambiguities and inconsistencies, racial identity remains important because of its connection to **ethnicity**—the sense of community that derives from the cultural heritage shared by a category of people with common ancestry (Marger, 1994). Your history, style, values, language, tastes, and habits may be more important indicators of your ethnic identity than skin color or other anatomical features. For example, Caribbean blacks are quite different ethnically from African blacks and often take great pains to avoid being identified as "black" (Gladwell, 1996).

To many, the very survival of an ethnic group depends on a shared identity. Thus individuals who seem to stray from their ethnic roots may be severely criticized. The debate over what constitutes an African-American identity was crystallized during the 1991 confirmation hearings on Judge Clarence Thomas's nomination to the U.S. Supreme Court. Some African Americans criticized Thomas for playing down the importance of his race until he was accused of sexual harassment by Professor Anita Hill. Then he linked his own predicament to the injustices historically inflicted on black men. Moreover, many African Americans questioned his "blackness"—his ethnic loyalty—because he embraces conservative political attitudes and is married to a white woman. Said one observer of the Thomas–Hill hearings: "I saw a black woman, and a white man in black skin" (quoted in L. Williams, 1991a). Such a statement is interesting sociologically because it illustrates that one can be racially black but still have one's ethnic "blackness" called into question for beliefs, actions, and attitudes that don't conform to those of most group members. Even today, many African Americans criticize

Justice Thomas for not fulfilling his presumed responsibilities as the nation's sole black Supreme Court justice (Cose, 1998). The issue of ethnic identity is even more critical for multiracial individuals.

Micro-Macro Connection
Politics and Multiracial Identity

Since the era of slavery the United States has adhered to the "one-drop rule" regarding racial identity (F. J. Davis, 1991). The term dates back to a common law in the South that a "single drop of black blood" made a person black. In the 19th century being a quarter black was as inconceivable as being a quarter pregnant. The U.S. Bureau of the Census long considered a person black if he or she had any known black African ancestry. Sociologists call this a *hypodescent* rule, meaning that racially mixed people are always assigned the status of the subordinate group (F. J. Davis, 1991).

People in the United States still tend to see race in categorical terms: black or white, red or yellow, brown or black. Even when faced with ambiguities, such as individuals with mixed-race backgrounds, U.S. residents still try to put people into specific categories. Most multiracial people have experienced being arbitrarily assigned a racial identity by a school principal or an employer that may differ from the identity of other members of their families or may differ from their identity in other settings.

But the dramatic growth in the number of multiracial children being born has upset traditional views of racial identity. In 1992 the U.S. Bureau of the Census reported that for the first time in history the number of biracial babies increased at a faster rate than the number of single-race babies (Marmor, 1996). And more and more people of mixed racial heritage are fighting against the one-drop rule and refusing to identify themselves as one race or another.

In the mid- to late-1990s, these individuals began lobbying Congress and the Bureau of the Census to add a multiracial category to the 2000 census. They argued that such a change would add visibility and legitimacy to a racial identity that has heretofore been ignored. Some even argued that a multiracial category might soften the racial lines that divide the country (Stephan & Stephan, 1989). When people blend several races and ethnicities within their own bodies, race becomes a meaningless concept, thereby presenting a biological solution to the problem of racial injustice (White, 1997).

But not everyone thought such a change was a good idea. Many civil rights organizations objected to the inclusion of a multiracial category. They worried that it would reduce the number of U.S. citizens claiming to belong to long-recognized minority groups, dilute the culture and political power of those groups, and make it more difficult to enforce civil rights laws (Mathews, 1996). Job discrimination lawsuits, affirmative action policies, and federal programs that assist minority businesses or that protect minority communities from environmental hazards all depend on official racial population data from the census. Furthermore, people who identify themselves as biracial or multiracial are sometimes perceived by members of racial groups as sellouts who avoid discrimination by taking advantage of the confusion their mixed identity creates (L. O. Graham, 1995).

In the end, the civil rights organizations won. For the 2000 census, the government decided not to add a multiracial category to official forms. Instead it adopted a policy allowing people, for the first time, to identify themselves on the census form as members of more than one race. The new guidelines specify that those who check "white" and another category will be counted as a member of the minority (Holmes, 2000). Preliminary 2000 census data show that 2% of the population—or close to 7 million people—identify themselves as belonging to one or more races. As you might expect, most of the people choosing this option are young. People under the age of 17 were four times as likely as people over 50 to identify themselves as belonging to more than one race (cited in Schmitt, 2001b). The changes in the census form illustrate that when it comes to determining racial identity, politics, not biology, is the determining factor.

Oppression and Inequality: Stories through the Years

A quick glance at the history of the United States reveals a record of not just freedom, justice, and equality but also conquest, discrimination, and exclusion. Racial and ethnic inequality has manifested itself in such phenomena as slavery and fraud; widespread economic, educational, and political deprivation; the violent and nonviolent protests of the civil rights movement; and racially motivated hate crimes. Along the way such injustices have affected people's access to the basic necessities of life, including housing, health care, a stable family life, and a means of making a decent living.

Every racial or ethnic minority has its own story of persecution. When they first arrived in significant numbers in the United States, white European immigrants—Irish, Italians, Poles, Jews, Greeks—were all objects of varying degrees of hatred, suspicion, and discrimination. Jews, for instance, were refused admission to many U.S. universities until the middle of the 20th century. The National Origins Act of 1924 placed restrictions on immigration from southern Europe (mainly Greece and Italy) until the 1960s. Newspaper want ads from the 19th century routinely carried the message "No Irish need apply."

Because these groups had the same skin color as the dominant white Protestants, however, they were able eventually to overcome most of these obstacles and gain entry into mainstream society. But for people of color—namely, Native Americans, Hispanics, African Americans, and Asian Americans—racial equality and destigmatization have been more difficult to achieve.

Native Americans

The story of Native Americans has been one of racially inspired massacres, the takeover of their ancestral lands, confinement on reservations, and unending governmental manipulation. Successive waves of westward expansion in the 18th and 19th centuries pushed them off any land that white settlers considered desirable. Native Americans "started off with everything and have gradually lost much of what they had to an advancing alien civilization" (U.S. Commission on Human Rights, 1992). A commonly held European belief that Native Americans were "savages" who should be displaced to make way for white civilization provided the ideological justification for conquering them.

According to the Fourteenth Amendment to the U.S. Constitution "All persons born or naturalized in the United States, and subject to the jurisdiction thereof, are citizens of the United States and of the state wherein they reside." But despite the broad wording of this amendment, Native Americans were excluded from citizenship. In 1884 the U.S. Supreme Court ruled that Native Americans owed their allegiance to their tribe and so did not acquire citizenship on birth. Not until 1940 were all Native Americans born in the United States considered U.S. citizens (Haney López, 1996).

Despite their history of severe oppression, though, Native Americans have shown a remarkable ability to endure and in some cases to shrewdly promote their own economic interests. In the Pacific Northwest, for instance, some Indian tribes have been successful in protecting their rights to lucrative fishing waters (F. G. Cohen, 1986). Casinos and resorts have made some tribes wealthy. Elsewhere, organizations have been formed to advance the financial concerns of Native Americans in industries such as gas, oil, and coal, where substantial reserves exist on Indian land (Snipp, 1986). However, intense struggles between large multinational corporations and Native American tribes continue today over control of these reserves.

Hispanic Americans

The history of Hispanics in this country has been diverse. Some groups have had a relatively positive experience. For instance, when Fidel Castro came to power in Cuba in the late 1950s, Cuban immigrants flooded into this country. Because they were fleeing a Communist political regime at odds with U.S. political ideals, their initial entry into this country was met with enthusiasm (Suarez, 1998). Many of the early immigrants were wealthy business owners who were able to set up lucrative businesses, particularly in south Florida. Today, Cuban-American families are the most financially successful of any Hispanic group.

But other Hispanic groups have experienced extreme hostility and oppression. For instance, when the United States expanded into the Southwest, white Americans moved into areas that were already inhabited by Mexicans. After a war that lasted from 1846 to 1848, Mexico lost half its national territory, including what is now Arizona, California, Colorado, New Mexico, Texas, Nevada, and Utah, as well as parts of Kansas, Oklahoma, and Wyoming.

In theory, Mexicans living on the U.S. side of the new border were to be given all the rights of U.S. citizens. In practice, however, their property rights were frequently violated, and they lost control of their mining, ranching, and farming industries. The exploitation of Mexican workers coincided with a developing economic system built around mining and large-scale agriculture, activities that demanded a large pool of cheap labor (J. Farley, 1982). Workers often had to house their families in primitive shacks with no electricity or plumbing for months on end while they performed seasonal labor.

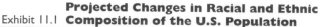

Exhibit 11.1 **Projected Changes in Racial and Ethnic Composition of the U.S. Population**

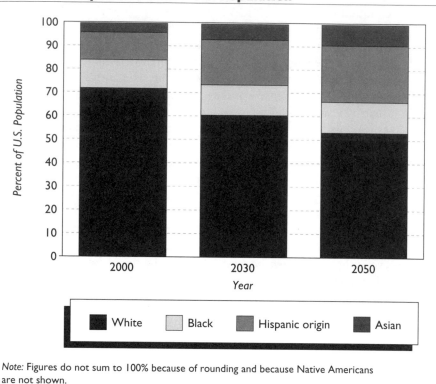

Note: Figures do not sum to 100% because of rounding and because Native Americans are not shown.

Source: U.S. Bureau of the Census, 2000b.

Today the status of Hispanics is mixed. Preliminary figures from the 2000 census show that Hispanics now make up roughly the same proportion of the U.S. population as blacks (cited in Schmitt, 2001b) and will soon outnumber them (see Exhibit 11.1). Larger numbers mean more political clout and a greater influence on the culture. Indeed, most large cities already have successful Spanish-language TV stations, radio stations, and newspapers.

Economically, though, the situation is less rosy. The average annual income for Hispanic individuals and families is still substantially lower than that of whites (U.S. Bureau of the Census, 2000b). Hispanic children are significantly more likely to drop out of school than white, Asian-American, or African-American children.

African Americans

The experience of African Americans has been unique among ethnic groups in this country because of the direct and indirect influences of slavery. From 1619, when the first black slaves were sold in Jamestown, Virginia, to 1865, when the Thirteenth

Amendment was passed outlawing slavery, several million blacks in this country endured the brutal reality of forced servitude. Slave owners controlled every aspect of a slave's life. They determined which slaves could marry and which marriages could be dissolved. The economic value of children (that is, future slaves) meant that slave owners had an interest in keeping slave marriages intact. But even the possibility of stable family life was an illusion. When economic troubles forced the sale of slaves to raise money, slave owners were not opposed to separating the very slave families they had once advocated. The threat of separation hung over every slave family.

Even after slavery was abolished, the conditions of life for U.S. blacks showed little improvement. "Jim Crow" laws established rigid lines between the races. In 1896 the U.S. Supreme Court ruled that racial segregation was constitutional. Unequal access to public transportation, schools, hotels, theaters, restaurants, campgrounds, drinking fountains, the military, and practically every other aspect of social life continued until the middle of the 20th century.

The quality of life for most African Americans remains below that of whites. In 1999 the average annual income for black households was $27,910, compared to $44,366 for whites (U.S. Bureau of the Census, 2000a). Nevertheless, blatant discrimination has declined in the last four decades, and some economic, educational, and political advances have been made. For instance, between 1987 and 1992, the number of black-owned businesses grew 46% while the total number of U.S. businesses grew only 26% (Key, 1996). The 1999 average annual income of $27,910 represents a 20% increase over 1993. As one author put it, "It's the best time ever to be black in America. . . . But not everyone's celebrating" (Cose, 1999, p. 29).

Asian Americans

Asian Americans have also experienced treatment over the years that calls into question the U.S. declaration that all people are created equal. Chinese men came to this country in the second half of the 19th century to work in the mines and on the expanding railroad system. But from the outset they were treated with hostility. The image of the "yellow peril" was fostered by rampant fears that hordes of Chinese would take scarce jobs and eventually overrun the white race. U.S. law prevented Chinese laborers from becoming permanent citizens, from bringing their wives with them, and from marrying whites. Eventually, laws were passed that put limits on and even prohibited Chinese immigration.

Early Japanese Americans faced similar circumstances. Like the Chinese, Japanese families created tight-knit, insulated communities where they were able to pool money and resources and achieve relative success. But their perceived success motivated lawmakers to enact the National Origins Act of 1924, which barred all further Japanese immigration. Hostility toward the Japanese reached a peak in 1941, following Japan's attack on Pearl Harbor. President Franklin Roosevelt signed an executive order authorizing the relocation and internment of Japanese immigrants and U.S. citizens of Japanese descent in camps surrounded by barbed wire, watch towers, and armed guards.

The irony of race for Chinese, Japanese, Koreans, Vietnamese, Cambodians, Laotians, Indians, and other Asian groups is that they are often perceived as "model minorities," or "America's greatest success story." Almost twice as many Asian Americans as whites complete college. The average income for Japanese and Chinese Americans is actually higher than that of the population as a whole (U.S. Bureau of the Census, 2000b).

But the expectations and resentment associated with being the "model minority" can be just as confining and oppressive as those created by more negative labels. During the mid-1980s, some university administrators openly worried about what they perceived as the overrepresentation of Asian students among their student bodies. The University of California at Berkeley, Stanford University, and Brown University used discriminatory quotas or increased the English-language-proficiency requirements for admission in order to limit the enrollment of Asian-American applicants. Asian Americans are often featured in news stories about successful high-tech companies, but they continue to face widespread discrimination in the workplace. In 2000 a U.S. Department of Energy investigation found that shortly after a Taiwan-born scientist at a nuclear weapons lab was dismissed for security violations, Asian-American employees at these labs nationwide faced systematic harassment and denial of advancement because they were suspected of spying. And one study shows that anti-Asian hate crimes are increasing (Noble, 1995).

From this brief historical overview you can see that opportunities to achieve "life, liberty, and happiness" have always been distributed along racial and ethnic lines in this country. Although some groups have been able to transcend the status of "despised minority," others continue to suffer.

Racial and Ethnic Relations

U.S. society's long history of racial tension is unlikely to fade away entirely any time soon. Increasing numbers of racial and ethnic minorities and an influx of non–English-speaking immigrants are heightening competition and conflict with the majority over scarce economic resources.

Racism is the belief that humans are subdivided into distinct groups so different in their social behavior and mental capacities that they can be ranked as superior or inferior. The presumed inferiority and superiority is then used to legitimate the unequal distribution of society's resources, such as various forms of wealth, prestige, and power (Marger, 1994). Racism can be expressed at the personal level through individual attitudes and behavior, at the cultural level in language and collective ideologies, and at the macro-structural level in social institutions.

Personal Racism

Personal racism is the expression of racist attitudes or behaviors by individual people. This is the most obvious form of racism, and it includes the use of derogatory names, biased treatment during face-to-face contact, avoidance, and threats or acts of violence. Personal racism receives the most media attention when it is violent and brutal, such as racially motivated hate crimes or the organized hatred of white supremacist groups. However, subtle forms of personal racism, such as the high school guidance counselor who steers minority students away from "hard" subjects toward those that do not prepare them for higher-paying jobs, are much more common. Whether blatant or subtle, personal racism rests on two important psychological constructs—stereotypes and prejudice.

Stereotypes. The word **stereotype** was first used by the political commentator Walter Lippmann in 1922. He defined it as an oversimplified picture of the world, one that satisfies our need to see our social environment as a more understandable and manageable place than it really is (Lippmann, 1922). It is the overgeneralized belief that a certain trait, behavior, or attitude characterizes all members of some identifiable group.

Casual observations easily refute the accuracy of common racial or ethnic stereotypes. Not all African Americans are on welfare, not all Jews are greedy, not all Italians belong to the Mafia, not all Asian Americans are excellent math students, not all Muslims are terrorists, and so on. Overgeneralizations such as these can never be true for every member of that group.

Yet despite their obvious inaccuracy stereotypes remain a common part of our everyday thinking. We all know what the stereotypes are, even if most of us choose not to express them or act on them. Thus, the modern view of stereotypes is that they are natural categories and an essential, universal aspect of human thought (Hamilton, 1981). Our brains have a tendency to divide the world into distinct categories: good and bad, strong and weak, them and us (Rothenberg, 1992). By allowing us to group information into easily identifiable categories, stereotypes make the processing of information and the formation of impressions more efficient. As you saw in Chapter 6, our lives would be utterly chaotic if we weren't able to quickly categorize people in terms of sex, race, age, ethnicity, and so on.

What's important to remember, though, is that the actual content of stereotypes is by no means natural; it must be learned. One of the most potent sources of racial and ethnic stereotypes is the media. Television, films, and literature provide large audiences with both real and fantasized images of racial, religious, and ethnic groups that inform many people's attitudes and beliefs. Consider the skewed images of certain ethnic groups served up on television: the savage Indian, the Jewish-American princess, the fanatical Arab terrorist, and so on. Hispanics have historically been cast as "Latin lovers," "banditos," "greasers," or "lazy good-for-nothings" (Reyes & Rubie, 1994). Asians are frequently cast as camera-wielding tourists, scholastic overachievers, or sinister warlords.

Although all racial and ethnic groups suffer from stereotypical media portrayal, most of the scholarly focus concerns African Americans. Early television shows of the 1950s, including *Amos 'n Andy* and *The Beulah Show*, depicted blacks either as lazy clowns, opportunistic crooks, or happy, docile servants.

But by the 1970s *Sanford and Son, Good Times, What's Happening,* and the other so-called ghetto sitcoms were trying to represent African Americans more positively. They showed slums and housing projects as places where people could lead happy, loving, even humorous lives. When U.S. society itself could not achieve social reform through civil rights, television solved the problem by inventing symbols of black success and racial harmony (Gates, 1992). Shows such as *Julia* or *I Spy* in the 1960s; *Roots* and

The Jeffersons in the 1970s; *Benson, A Different World,* and *The Cosby Show* in the 1980s; *The Fresh Prince of Bel-Air, Family Matters,* and *Moesha* in the 1990s; and *Gideon's Crossing, Jamie Foxx, The Parkers,* and *Malcolm & Eddie* in the 2000s seemingly overcame these harmful stereotypes by depicting blacks as strong, smart, and successful. In addition, popular shows with predominantly white casts, such as *ER, Boston Public,* and *Law & Order,* depict successful black characters. These shows have played an unmistakable role in showing that blacks and whites often share the core values of U.S. culture.

But critics have charged that many of these recent portrayals are also fantasies, which may be just as harmful to African Americans as the negative stereotypes of the 1950s. They feel that the characters in some of these shows amount to what some call the "white Negro" in television. The message seems to be that the more black characters act like whites, the more acceptable they are to the viewing audience. For example, the George Jefferson character from the 1970s sitcom, *The Jeffersons,* began his TV existence as the working-class neighbor of Archie Bunker. But through dogged commitment to the U.S. values of hard work and determination, he and his family were able to "move up" into the new black upper class and, not surprisingly, into a white neighborhood. Indeed, working-class and poor African Americans—especially men—still tend to be depicted as a menace and a source of social disorganization, involved in such activities as crime, gang violence, drug use, homelessness, and general aimlessness (Gray, 1995).

Opportunities for black actors are becoming rarer. The number of prime-time, predominantly black television shows reached its peak in 1997 when there were 15 such series. Today there are only 6. And all of these are comedies. No predominantly black dramatic series has ever succeeded on network television (Moss, 2001). A report by the Screen Actors Guild found that more than half of all black actors on prime-time television appear on all-black, or mostly-black, comedy shows ("Limited black slots on TV," 2000).

Compounding the problem is the fact that the viewing audience remains largely segregated along racial lines. For instance, in 1998 the comedy show *Friends*—which stars an all-white cast—was the second-most-watched show in white households but ranked 91st among blacks (Sterngold, 1998). Conversely, the number 1 show in the country among black viewers, *The Parkers,* ranked 140th overall (Allan, 2000).

The news is not all bad, however. This racial divide is narrowing among young people. Offered both black shows and white, teenage viewers, unlike their parents, are willing to watch predominantly black shows (Hass, 1998). Hence we can hope that when today's teens grow into adults, they will bring with them a greater appreciation of racial and ethnic diversity, thus ensuring that certain aspects of black culture—language patterns, values, sense of humor, and tastes in fashion, music, and theater—will continue to be a vital aspect of the larger U.S. culture.

Claude Steele
Stereotypes and Educational Performance

A lot of scholarly work examines where racial stereotypes come from, but less attention has been paid to how they actually affect the person who is the object of the stereotypical thinking. According to social psychologist Claude Steele (1997), stereotypes function in the institutional setting of universities much like self-fulfilling prophecies.

Thus they may account for why some groups—blacks and Hispanics, in particular—don't fare as well academically as others.

Steele became interested in how stereotypes affect students when he found that 80% of black students at the University of Michigan, some of whom were extremely bright, were enrolled in remedial programs (Gose, 1995). Even with the extra help, however, their dropout rate far exceeded that of white students. He wondered whether many capable students were dropping out not because they were innately intellectually inferior (see Herrnstein & Murray, 1994) but because the institutional practice of enrolling them in remedial classes was essentially stereotyping them as "dumb." When people are confronted with a negative stereotype about their intellectual skills before they take tests, they tend to perform according to the stereotype (C. Steele, 1997; C. Steele & Aronson, 1995). Whether they believe the stereotype or not, the mere threat that they might be judged in terms of it is enough to hurt academic performance. Steele hypothesized that the gap between whites and blacks on standardized tests—which is estimated to be 15 points on IQ tests and 140 points on the SAT—would disappear if blacks were taught that they have the same academic potential as whites.

To test his ideas, Steele gave groups of black and white students at Stanford University portions of the Graduate Record Exam. In the section asking for personal information, half the tests asked the students to indicate their race; the other half did not. Steele found that the blacks asked to identify their race scored significantly lower than the whites who were asked their race. In contrast, blacks and whites who were not asked to identify their race scored about the same.

In another experiment, blacks who were told they were taking a test that would evaluate their intellectual skills scored much lower than whites. Blacks who were told the test didn't evaluate intellectual ability scored the same as whites.

Steele has put his ideas into practice in a first-year transition program at Stanford. Incoming students from a variety of racial and ethnic backgrounds participate in workshops and seminars about adjustment to college. The emphasis of the program is on intellectual challenge, not remediation. Students are not led to believe that they are in the program to compensate for some perceived intellectual deficiency. He has found that black students in the program earn slightly better grades than white students who aren't in the program (Gose, 1995). Steele's research shows how long-standing and well-meaning practices of large educational institutions, such as remedial education programs, may unintentionally harm the very people they are designed to help.

Prejudice and Discrimination. When stereotypes are the basis for a set of rigidly held, unfavorable attitudes, beliefs, and feelings about members of a racial or ethnic group, they constitute **prejudice** (Allport, 1954). A good example of how prejudice affects social interaction is one study in which a group of whites was shown a photograph of a white person holding a razor blade while arguing with a black person on a New York subway. Subjects were shown the picture for a split second and then asked to write down what they saw. More than half of them said they saw the black man holding the razor against the white man's throat (cited in Helmreich, 1992). The belief that all blacks are violent was so powerful that it distorted people's perceptions.

Prejudiced beliefs such as this would be of little significance if they didn't lead sometimes to discrimination. **Discrimination** is the unfair treatment of people based on some social characteristic such as race, sex, or ethnicity. The 1964 Civil Rights Act prohibits discrimination or segregation on the grounds of race, color, religion, or national origin. This act has produced tremendous progress in U.S. race relations. Nevertheless, discrimination—expressed as avoidance, suspicions of wrongdoing, denied privileges, and hate-inspired violence—still exists.

Discrimination extends to the highest levels of corporate America. In 1996 a former executive at Texaco revealed tapes of company officials using blatantly racist slurs and mocking symbols of Jewish and African-American holidays. The tapes exposed a strongly rooted racist corporate culture in which black employees were sometimes called "porch monkeys" or "orangutans," asked to caddie golf games for their white bosses, or given birthday cakes decorated with rude caricatures and watermelon seeds. In addition to these personal indignities, they were also paid significantly less than white employees. To avoid a protracted lawsuit, Texaco eventually agreed to give about 1,000 black employees an 11% pay raise, spend millions more on programs designed to "wipe out" discrimination, and let outsiders come in and keep watch on the company (J. Solomon, 1996).

Most of the time, though, discrimination is much more subtle; in fact, the person engaging in it may not even realize he or she is doing so. Psychologists Carl O. Word, Mark P. Zanna, and Joel Cooper (1974) created an experimental situation in which white subjects were led to believe they were interviewing applicants for a team position in a group decision-making experiment. Their behavior was secretly being observed by the researchers. The applicants, who were really confederates of the researchers, were both black and white.

The results showed that the "interviewers" treated black applicants very differently from white ones. For instance, they placed their chairs at a significantly greater distance from the black interviewees. They leaned forward less and made less eye contact with the black applicants. In addition, they ended the interview sooner and tended to trip over their words.

In a second experiment, Word, Zanna, and Cooper sought to determine the effect such behavior would have on the applicants. In this experiment, the interviewers were now confederates of the experimenters. These new interviewers were trained to mimic the behaviors found among interviewers in the first experiment. This time, applicants who encountered the "less friendly" behavior—that is, reduced eye contact, greater physical distance, and so on—performed less adequately and showed less composure during the interview than the others.

These experiments illustrate the subtle process by which racism sometimes operates, even in people who are not self-consciously racist. We are generally so unaware of our own nonverbal behavior that if we unwittingly give off signs of our dislike, we don't interpret others' subsequent behavior as reactions to our nonverbal cues. Rather, we attribute it to some inherent trait in them. We may unknowingly create the very actions that we then use as evidence of some flaw or deficiency in that group.

From the point of view of those discriminated against, these subtle forms of discrimination are harder to fight than the overt bigotry of the past. If you are excluded from a job because you're Asian or denied membership in a club because you're Jewish, you can fight to open those doors. Today, quite a few people have made it through these doors (Blauner, 1992). But once inside, they still have many interpersonal barriers to overcome.

As such subtle behavior becomes common among large numbers of people, prejudice and discrimination become mutually reinforcing. If one group is defined as inferior by another and treated that way, the resulting discrimination in the form of denied access to jobs and inferior education becomes self-fulfilling, producing the very inferiority that the group was believed to possess in the first place.

Note also that prejudice and discrimination can sometimes occur within a racial or ethnic group. For instance, some see prejudice between light-skinned and dark-skinned blacks as a worse problem than racial hatred expressed by whites. Skin tone has long been associated with social advantage in the black community (L. O. Graham, 1999). Studies have found that lighter-skinned blacks have higher educational attainment, more prestigious occupations, and higher annual incomes than darker-skinned blacks, regardless of their parents' socioeconomic status, sex, region of residence, age, or marital status (Hill, 2000; Keith & Herring, 1991). Light-skinned blacks sometimes show prejudice toward darker-skinned blacks. In turn, darker-skinned blacks sometimes accuse light-skinned blacks of using skin whiteners and hair straighteners to conform to white standards of beauty (F. J. Davis, 1991). The entertainer Michael Jackson has been severely criticized for removing most of his "black" physical features.

Cultural background may also make a difference. Many black immigrants from the West Indies refuse to call themselves "black" when they come to this country. West Indian immigrants generally make substantially more money than U.S. blacks, live in better neighborhoods, and have more stable families (Gladwell, 1996). They often try to distance themselves as much as possible from U.S. blacks, whom they feel are socially, culturally, and financially inferior. The effect, according to one observer, is to reinforce, even legitimate, prejudice against blacks:

> The success of West Indians is not proof that discrimination against American blacks does not exist. Rather, it is the means by which discrimination against American blacks is given one last, vicious twist: I am not so shallow as to despise you for the color of your skin, because I have found people your color that I like. Now I can despise you for who you are. (Gladwell, 1996, p. 79)

Not having experienced the debilitating effects of discrimination, West Indian immigrants often have difficulty, as do whites, understanding why other blacks have such a tough time "making it" in U.S. society.

Indeed, people who are members of a racial majority often have trouble appreciating the humiliating effects of everyday encounters with discrimination. They don't have to experience the petty indignities of racism, such as repeatedly being watched with suspicion in stores and on streets. Consequently, many whites in the United States think people of color are obsessed with race and ethnicity and find it difficult to understand the emotional and intellectual energy that minorities devote to the subject (Haney López, 1996).

In a society in which they are the statistical and cultural majority, U.S. whites rarely define their identity in terms of race. Whiteness is unmarkable and unexamined. It is so obvious and normative that white people's racial identity is, for all intents and purposes, invisible. Whites enjoy the luxury of **racial transparency** or "having no color" (Haney López, 1996). People in the United States are far more likely to hear "black" or "Asian" or "Latino" used as an adjective (for example, the black lawyer, the Latino teacher) than "white" (the white lawyer, the white teacher).

Whites aren't burdened by race in a way that forces this aspect of their identity into full view. Indeed, many whites become conscious of their racial identity only when they find themselves in the company of large numbers of people of a different race. In short, whites for the most part enjoy the privilege of not having to think about race, even though they have one. Such a luxury provides advantages to whites whether or not they approve of the way dominance has been conferred on them. In other words, whites need not be bigots nor feel racially superior or more deserving than others to enjoy the privileges that racial transparency brings.

Class, Race, and Discrimination. Some sociologists have argued that discriminatory treatment, as well as the unequal social and political status of some racial groups, is more a function of social class than of race. If this belief were true, the lives of middle- and upper-class members of racial minorities should be relatively free of discrimination. Yet they are not. For many highly successful minority professionals, lack of respect, faint praise, low expectations, shattered hopes, and even outright harassment and exclusion are common features of their lives. The result is often utter despair:

> I have done everything I was supposed to do. I have stayed out of trouble with the law, gone to the right schools, and worked myself nearly to death. *What more do they want?* Why in God's name won't they accept me as a full human being? Why am I pigeon-holed in a "black job"? Why am I constantly treated as if I were a drug addict, a thief, or a thug? Why am I still not allowed to aspire to the same things every white person in America takes as a birthright? Why, when I most want to be seen, am I suddenly invisible? (Cose, 1993, p. 1)

Sociologist Joe R. Feagin (1991) conducted in-depth interviews with 37 middle-class U.S. blacks to determine the extent of discrimination directed against them in public situations. These 37 people, who were all college educated and held professional or managerial jobs, reported a total of 62 discriminatory incidents in such public places as hotels, jewelry stores, and restaurants. The incidents consisted of avoidance, poor service, closer scrutiny, verbal epithets, "hate stares," and police threats and harassment. The events disturbed the subjects not only because of the racist attitudes that lay behind them but also because they had come to believe that their upward social mobility protected them from such treatment.

A 28-year-old New York lawyer said that when he walks into a store, the staff don't see his Ivy League university degrees, his status as an associate in his law firm—they see him only as a black man. Their response to his blackness strips him of his credentials and achievements (L. Williams, 1991b). Feagin concludes that the stigma of color is still very important in the lives of African Americans, including affluent ones. They remain vulnerable targets of deprivation and discrimination.

What whites may see as "minority paranoia" is a response to humiliation that has accumulated over the years and has become part of everyday life. One middle-class black woman interviewed by Feagin pointed out that whenever she leaves her home she must put on her "shield" and be prepared for the insults and discrimination she expects to receive in public places. Indeed, wealthy black residents of affluent neighborhoods all over the country complain that the police view them with suspicion simply because their skin color doesn't match the neighborhood.

The days of "No Negroes" and "No Indians" signs on public facilities may be gone, but less blatant contemporary expressions of personal racism serve as a constant reminder that at the outset of the 21st century, minorities are still being stereotyped, prejudged, and discriminated against on the basis of their race or ethnicity. Taken as individual incidents, racial slurs, "hate stares," and poor service in restaurants may seem to be just trivial inconveniences. However, these forms of discrimination reflect the reality to which racial and ethnic minorities of all classes are exposed on a daily basis.

Symbolic Racism. The nature of public attitudes in the United States toward racial and ethnic groups has changed over the past few decades, prompting many sociologists to rethink their ideas of what constitutes personal racism. A recent nationwide poll found that the proportion of U.S. residents who feel that race relations are improving and that progress has been made in reducing racial discrimination is the highest it's been in 10 years (Sack & Elder, 2000). Likewise, attitudes about absolute segregation in schools, housing, and jobs have improved markedly (Citrin, 1996; Schuman, Steeh, Bobo, & Krysan, 1997). However, whites are three times more likely than blacks to feel that too much is made out of problems facing blacks today, and blacks are twice as likely as whites to feel that whites still have a better chance of getting ahead (Sack & Elder, 2000).

Given these statistics, it's not surprising that blacks and whites feel very differently about concrete efforts to change the racial status quo (McClendon, 1985). Although most U.S. whites feel that schools should be integrated and that people of all races should have equal opportunities to enter any occupation, overwhelming majorities in national surveys oppose special government economic assistance to minorities and government efforts to desegregate schools, such as court-ordered busing. National polls show that 9 out of 10 whites oppose preferential hiring and promotion of blacks (Citrin, 1996) to offset ways in which blacks have been disadvantaged.

This paradox has led some to argue that a new form of racism has emerged (Sniderman & Tetlock, 1986). **Symbolic racism** is linked to the traditional forms of personal racism by negative feelings toward certain groups. However, symbolic racism is expressed not through direct prejudice and discrimination against individuals but indirectly, through opposition to programs that seek to improve the status of minorities in society (McClelland & Auster, 1990).

The symbolic racist tends to disagree strongly with a statement such as "Mexican Americans are not generally as smart as Anglos" but at the same time likely agrees with a statement such as "Mexican Americans are getting too demanding in their push for Spanish-language services." The symbolic racist would justify opposition to government programs for minorities on the seemingly benign grounds that one's rewards should be based exclusively on personal achievements and not race.

What complicates the situation is that this type of racism is often expressed by people who consider themselves liberal, unbiased, and nonprejudiced. They are likely to

> sympathize with the victims of past injustice; support public policies that, in principle, promote racial equality . . . ; identify more generally with a liberal political agenda; regard themselves as non-prejudiced and non-discriminatory; but, almost unavoidably, possess negative feelings and beliefs about [minority groups]. (Gaertner & Dovidio, 1990, p. 271)

The feelings common to symbolic racism are not hate or hostility but discomfort, uneasiness, and sometimes fear, which tend to motivate avoidance rather than outright negative acts. Symbolic racists are people who maintain that discrimination against a person because of his or her race or ethnicity is wrong but who nonetheless cannot entirely escape the cultural forces that give rise to racist beliefs in the first place.

You can see why symbolic racism can be more insidious than overt personal racism. Community and legal pressures can have a significant impact on traditional expressions of bigotry. However, such techniques do little to change the values of people who are acutely aware of the social undesirability and the unfairness of their feelings but who hold them anyway.

The changing face of racism has serious institutional consequences as well. When racism remains hidden, people are tempted to assume that it has disappeared, forestalling the perceived need to help groups that have traditionally been the objects of discrimination. Recent efforts to eliminate programs designed to help minorities exemplify this trend. Most whites in the United States believe that the socioeconomic status of blacks has vastly improved and see no need to continue federal programs to assist them (Kluegel & Smith, 1986). Many whites now believe that the only reason so many blacks are unsuccessful is that they lack motivation and aren't committed to the "white" values of hard work, individualism, delayed gratification, and so on (Schuman & Krysan, 1999). Although these beliefs are more subtle than overt acts of bigotry, they have the same effect: They promote prejudice toward individuals on the basis of stereotypes.

The Cultural Ideology of Racism

If I stopped here in my discussion of racism and its constituent elements, you might be inclined to consider it a phenomenon of individuals that could best be stopped by changing the way people think or by individual acts of kindness and respect. But the sociologically important thing about racism is that it exists not just in individuals' minds and actions but in a cultural ideology that both justifies the domination of some groups over others and provides a set of social norms that encourages differential treatment for these groups (O'Sullivan, See, & Wilson, 1988). From a conflict perspective, the cultural ideology of racism that exists in our language and in our prevailing collective beliefs helps to maintain racial and ethnic inequality.

Racism in Language. If we accept that the dominant white culture in the United States is still racist to some degree and in some form, then we would expect the language—the transmitter of culture—to be racist as well (Moore, 1992). Certainly racial slurs and derogatory words reflect underlying racism. But racism in language is often more subtle. Consider the use of common terms to refer to different racial groups. Today we use the general term *Native Americans* or *Indian* to refer to all indigenous peoples of the Americas regardless of their specific tribes. *Asian American* refers to a variety of peoples whose ethnic heritages and lifestyles are quite different from one another. Similarly, *Hispanic* refers to people whose backgrounds include such culturally diverse areas as Mexico, the Caribbean, Central America, and South America.

When the first Europeans "discovered" Africans, they were quick to label them all "black" (Omi & Winant, 1992). Not only did this term mask the fact that the Africans came from a variety of different ethnicities and cultures, but it also maximized the perceived differences between "black" Africans and "white" Europeans (Fairchild, 1985). Furthermore, the word *black* incorporates a large set of negative connotations within the English language. For instance, good guys wear white hats, and bad guys wear black hats. Among the definitions of *black* in *Webster's New Universal Unabridged Dictionary* are soiled and dirty, thoroughly evil, wicked, gloomy, marked by disaster, hostile, and disgraceful. The definition of *white*, in contrast, includes fairness of complexion, innocent, favorable, fortunate, pure, and spotless. The pervasive "goodness" of white and "badness" of black affects children at a very young age and provides white children with a false sense of superiority (Moore, 1992). For instance, young children know the difference between a black lie, which is harmful and inexcusable, and a white lie, which is small, insignificant, and harmless.

Also important are the political implications of racist terminology. Terms such as *culturally deprived, economically disadvantaged, underclass,* and *underdeveloped* sound non-prejudiced, but they can mislead and distort our awareness of social phenomena. To apply the label "culturally deprived" to a Hispanic person, for instance, is to symbolically reinforce the belief that the only culture that really matters is the dominant white one. Similarly, the use of the term *nonwhite* to describe people of color implies that white is the standard against which all others are measured.

Language is just a small part of the overall problem of racist ideology in U.S. society. It seemingly pales in comparison to more visible issues such as racial violence and economic discrimination. We must remember, however, that language filters our perceptions. It affects the way people think from the time they first learn to speak. Fortunately, efforts are being made today to address the issue of language and its crucial role in maintaining racism and oppression. People are becoming more aware of the capacity of words to both glorify and degrade (Moore, 1992).

The Myth of Innate Racial Inferiority. The cultural ideology of racism is also supported by theories positing that certain racial or ethnic groups are innately inferior. These theories have long been used to explain why certain racial groups, as a whole, lag behind others in such areas as educational achievement and financial success. They combine with the belief in competitive individualism (see Chapter 10) to provide "scientific" justification and a seemingly intellectual climate for the perpetuation of all forms of prejudice and discrimination.

Appeals to biology and nature have been used throughout history to define the existing stratification system as proper and inevitable (Gould, 1981). What would you think of a person who harbored the following beliefs about blacks?

> [Blacks] have less hair on the face and body. They secrete less by the kidnies, and more by the glands of the skin, which gives them a very strong and disagreeable odour. . . . They are at least as brave, and more adventuresome. But this may perhaps proceed from a want of forethought, which prevents their seeing a danger till it be present. . . . In imagination, they are dull, tasteless, and anomalous. . . . The improvement of the blacks in body and mind, in the first instance of their mixture with the whites, has been observed by every one, and proves that their inferiority is not the effect merely of their condition of life. . . . I advance it therefore . . . that the blacks . . . are inferior to the whites in the endowments both of body and mind.

A white supremacist? A raving bigot? An ignorant fanatic? How would your assessment of this person change if you found out that this passage was written by none other than Thomas Jefferson (Jefferson, 1781/1955, pp. 138–143)? In the 18th and 19th centuries, no white—not even one apparently committed to protecting people's right to "life, liberty and the pursuit of happiness"—doubted the correctness of natural racial rankings: Indians below whites, and blacks below everyone else. Other idols of Western culture—George Washington, Abraham Lincoln, Charles Darwin—held similar beliefs about the "natural inferiority" of some races, beliefs that were commonly accepted knowledge at the time but would at the very least be considered racially insensitive today.

The approval given by white scientists to conventional racial rankings arose not from objective data and careful research but from a shared worldview, a cultural belief that "saw" the "goodness" and inevitability of racial stratification. Such beliefs were then twisted into independent, "scientific" support. Scientists, like everybody else, have attitudes and values that shape what they see. Such thinking is not the result of outright dishonesty or hypocrisy; rather, it is the combination of the way human minds work and the generally accepted knowledge of the day.

The belief in innate racial inferiority is not just a historical curiosity. Several years ago, the idea reemerged in a book called *The Bell Curve: Intelligence and Class Structure in American Life* (Herrnstein & Murray, 1994). The authors argue that racial and ethnic differences in intelligence—as measured by IQ scores—must be due, at least in part, to heredity. The book set off a firestorm of debate that continues to this day.

From a conflict perspective, cultural beliefs about innate racial inferiority provide advantages for the dominant group. These beliefs discourage subordinate groups from attempting to question their disadvantaged status. In addition, they provide moral justification for maintaining a society in which some groups are routinely deprived of their rights and privileges. Whites could justify the enslavement of blacks, and Nazis could justify the extermination of Jews and other "undesirables," by promoting the belief that those groups were inherently subhuman.

Despite energetic searches over the centuries, a link between "inferior" race-based genes and intelligence, creativity, or other valued abilities has not been found (Hacker, 1992). For one thing, comparing racial groups on, say, intelligence overlooks the range of differences within and between groups. Many African Americans are more intelligent than the average white; many whites are less intelligent than the average Native American. Variations such as these are difficult to explain in terms of genetic superiority of one race. Moreover, such comparisons also ignore a problem I described earlier in this chapter: that race itself is a meaningless biological category. How can we attribute racial differences in intelligence to genetics when there is no gene for race?

A more sensible argument is that certain races or ethnic groups may do better in some areas than others because they grew up in environments that prepared them for these endeavors. The effect of the learning environment on intelligence was illustrated several years ago in a comparison of IQ scores. The researchers found that IQ scores for some groups have been rising for the past 50 years (cited in Goleman, 1984). Early tests of Jewish, Chinese, and Italian immigrants showed these groups to be far below average in intelligence, but their grandchildren generally had average or above-average IQ scores (Sowell, 1977). Such a large difference over the span of two generations cannot be explained by changes in heredity, which generally are expressed over many generations.

Nevertheless, the idea that racial inferiority is innate remains appealing. If observable, physical differences among races are inherited, why not differences in social behavior, intelligence, the ability to rule, and so on? Like the belief in competitive individualism we examined in the previous chapter, the belief in innate racial inferiority places the blame for suffering and economic failure on the individual rather than on the society in which that individual exists.

Micro-Macro Connection
Racial Superiority and the Dominant Black Athlete

The flip side of the belief in innate racial inferiority is the notion that some racial groups have a biologically rooted superiority in some areas of life. Take, for instance, the widely held belief that blacks are better athletes than whites. Today, athletes of African heritage dominate the highest levels of such sports as football, basketball, and track. In the United States, African Americans make up about 13% of the population but about 67% of professional football players, 80% of professional basketball players, and 93% of male track and field Olympic gold medalists (Price, 1997). Not surprisingly, many people simply assume that blacks must be stronger, swifter, and more coordinated than whites. As the saying goes, great athletes are born, not made.

This belief has roots that span centuries. Many 18th- and 19th-century scholars believed that black slaves were bred by their owners to be physically strong. They were often impressed by what they saw as the unique ability of black slaves to endure harsh working conditions and to withstand inhuman levels of physical pain. In recent decades such ideas have been given a distinctly scientific cast (Entine, 2000). For instance, some biologists argue that black athletes' muscles are better adapted to hot climates and therefore are better at providing energy quickly. Others have cited better power-to-weight ratios and longer Achilles tendons.

The world of sports is so tightly connected to the media nowadays that these beliefs about black athletic superiority have gained a sort of taken-for-granted legitimacy. Many black athletes, such as track star Carl Lewis and baseball player Barry Bonds, have publicly expressed their belief that black success in sports is caused by blacks' physical superiority to whites. White athletes, too, accept this belief as truth. Scott Brooks, a white professional basketball player, once said, "You have to be a realist. White people can't jump as high." Another white basketball player, Pete Chilcutt, made a similar observation: "There aren't many white guys who can jump the way they can" (quoted in Hoberman, 1997, p. xvi). A white basketball player for the Sacramento Kings was nicknamed "White Chocolate" because he played with a flair and an athleticism that over the years has come to be associated with black players.

These "positive" stereotypes, however, can quickly become negative. The sportscaster Brent Musburger once commonly referred to powerful black athletes as "thoroughbreds," a term that simultaneously identified their natural prowess and rendered them nonhuman. Such comments strengthen the notion that black athletes are athletically superior but intellectually inferior, physically advanced while mentally primitive. Physically outclassed white athletes, then, must rely on self-discipline, mental acuity, "a tireless work ethic," "fiery determination," or an unwavering attention to discipline and "fundamentals" in order to succeed.

Because of these pervasive stereotypes, the white public often tempers its admiration of black athletic prowess with contempt for what some consider a pretentious, undisciplined style. In the 1992 film *White Men Can't Jump,* a white basketball player tells a black player that blacks would "rather look good and lose than look bad and win."

From these ideas to the notion that black athleticism has the capacity to disrupt the fragile virtue of professional sports is but a short step. Consider one reporter's description of a quiet white home run hitter for the San Francisco Giants: "No earrings, no backward caps, no untucked jerseys, no haughty stares or trashy taunts"—all characteristics that some people associate with young black athletes (quoted in Hoberman, 1997, p. 51).

What's seen by many whites as a brash, arrogant style has produced a menacing stereotype. In 1997 basketball player Latrell Sprewell became a poster child for the image of the fearsome black athlete when he attempted to choke his coach. Mike Tyson accomplished the same thing when he bit the ear of an opponent during a boxing match. Calls for harsh sanctions and more severe discipline of athletes only partially covered the underlying racial undertones—that black athletes were out of control and threatening the integrity of sports.

Nevertheless, blacks do dominate professional sports in the United States. One sociological explanation of such domination is that it results not from innate physical superiority alone but from a complex set of societal conditions that channels a disproportionate number of talented blacks into athletic careers (Edwards, 1971). Sport has long been perceived as one of the few places African Americans could "make it big." A national survey found that by a margin of 3 to 1 over whites, blacks said that one of the most important reasons to play sports is "If I am successful at sports, I can make a lot of money" (cited in Price, 1997). Whereas children from other racial groups are being taught that a good education will pay off, many black children are being taught that a good education may not be enough to overcome the prejudice and discrimination inherent in the system. Hence they are more likely to be encouraged to hone their physical skills and will spend more time perfecting this resource. A high school basketball coach put it this way: "Suburban [white] kids tend to play for the fun of it. Inner-city kids look at basketball as a matter of life or death" (quoted in Price, 1997, p. 35).

Sport has always served as a source of tremendous pride in the black community. It's one of the few areas where African Americans can feel superior and gifted. The black athletic champion has become the defining symbol of African-American achievement. African Americans have always joyfully embraced such national sports heroes as Jesse Owens, Joe Louis, Jackie Robinson, Muhammad Ali, and Jackie Joyner-Kersee. More recently, the silhouette of Michael Jordan clutching a basketball in his outstretched arm as he soars high above the floor has become the universal symbol of black athleticism and excellence, not to mention the multibillion-dollar multinational corporation the image represents (Hoberman, 1997). Black sports heroes such as Michael Jordan are now embraced by Americans of all races without hesitation.

But revering the athletic accomplishments of a select few can also discourage academic and occupational achievement in favor of physical self-expression, thereby harming the black community in the long run. Because only an extremely tiny percentage of athletes can, in fact, ever "make it big," the notion of innate black athletic superiority can function as a subtle support system for continuing inequality.

Whether or not the emphasis on sports is a good thing and whether or not black athletes do have some anatomical advantage, we must always remember that so-called black athletic superiority is as much a social product as a biological one. Innate talent is never sufficient in itself to explain athletic excellence (D. F. Chambliss, 1989). If we rely simply on innate superiority to explain black success in sports, we would be overlooking the broader social structural context in which everyday life is embedded.

————————————————————————— ● ● ————————

Institutional Racism: Injustice Built into the System

Anyone can be personally racist, and any racial group can develop a set of beliefs or a vocabulary that denigrates outsiders. But one form of racism, less obvious and more dangerous perhaps, can work only to the advantage of those who wield power in society: institutional racism. **Institutional racism** consists of established laws, customs, and practices that systematically reflect and produce racial inequalities in society, whether or not the individuals maintaining these practices have racist intentions (J. M. Jones, 1986). Thus a society can be racist even if only a small proportion of its members harbor racist beliefs. Because African Americans, Hispanics, Native Americans, and other groups have historically been excluded from key positions of authority in social institutions, they often find themselves victimized by the routine workings of such structures.

Understanding institutional racism is a great test of the sociological imagination. Because it is a built-in feature of social arrangements, institutional racism is often much more difficult to detect than acts of personal racism. Consider one well-established practice for granting home mortgage loans. Many banks use zip codes to mark off the neighborhoods they consider high risk—that is, where property values are low and liable to drop even further. Mortgages tend to be unavailable or very difficult to obtain in these areas. Unfortunately, these are precisely the areas where minorities, with lower average incomes, can afford to purchase a home. Thus although individual bank officers are not denying loans to minority members—they are merely following their employers' policy—the result is the same.

Sometimes institutional discrimination is camouflaged behind claims that seem quite reasonable on their face. For instance, taxi companies protect the safety of their drivers by refusing service to what they consider to be dangerous neighborhoods. Similarly, home delivery businesses, such as pizza restaurants, often refuse to deliver to some neighborhoods. Domino's Pizza distributes software to its outlets to let them mark addresses on computers as green (deliver), yellow (curbside only), or red (no delivery). Businesses defend such policies as a rational response to the threat of sending easy-to-spot delivery personnel with cash into unsafe areas ("Pizza must go," 1996). Although such practices may be considered a "good" business policy and are not intentionally racist, their consequences are racist because high-risk neighborhoods tend to be inhabited predominantly by people of color. Institutional racism is difficult to address in these cases because no individual "bad guy," no identifiable bigot, is the source of the discrimination. Moreover, how does a company like Domino's determine the safety of a neighborhood? Arrest rates? Police stops? Subjective impressions? Any official statistics they rely on may be racially biased themselves, thereby perpetuating the discrimination.

Racism in one institution tends to be accompanied by racism in another. For instance, the traditional exclusion of certain racial and ethnic groups from the upper levels of education affects their economic opportunities, which in turn affects their access to basic necessities such as quality health care and housing (Wilson, 1987).

Residential segregation based on class and race is so prevalent in U.S. society that one sociologist refers to the situation as "American apartheid" (Massey, 1990). For instance, over 83% of Detroit-area blacks live in the central city (Russell Sage Foundation, 2000). Such segregation is highly resistant to change despite laws designed to prevent housing discrimination that have existed since the 1970s. White attitudes toward neighborhood integration have improved over the years, as Exhibit 11.2 indicates. Yet overall levels of segregation—especially between blacks and whites—have remained quite high (R. Farley & Frey, 1994). Hispanics are slightly less residentially segregated than blacks, and Asians are substantially less segregated than blacks—but they all still tend to live in racial or ethnic enclaves (Massey & Fischer, 1999). Residential segregation is not just about people living near others of the same race. Research indicates that it is associated with a variety of negative effects, such as a reduced likelihood of people running successful businesses (Fischer & Massey, 2000) and an increased likelihood of contracting certain deadly diseases (Collins & Williams, 1999).

● Exhibit 11.2 **Improving Attitudes Toward Racial Integration**

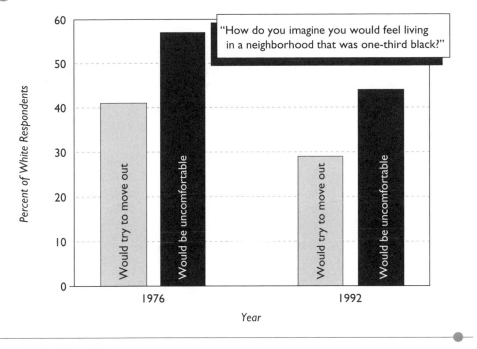

Source: Farley & Frey, 1994.

Moreover, although some minority families may be steered into less desirable neighborhoods, others are being steered out of the housing market entirely. For instance, the Bureau of the Census reports that 65% of U.S. whites own their own homes, compared to 45% of African Americans and Hispanic Americans. In 1999, a research organization in Washington, DC, sent pairs of white and minority members to seek mortgages from lenders throughout the nation. Each pair had the same income, assets, job, credit history, and neighborhood. The minorities were less likely to receive information about loan products, received less time from loan officers, and were quoted higher interest rates. A similar study found that African Americans were twice as likely as whites, and Hispanic Americans one-and-a-half times as likely, to be denied a conventional 30-year home loan (cited in Kilborn, 1999c). Concern over such discrepancies led the National Association of Realtors and the U.S. Department of Housing and Urban Development to enact a cultural awareness program for real estate agents, which will make them more aware of "racial steering" and help to increase minority opportunities in housing (Tahan, 1997).

Racism in the Economic System. Institutional racism is readily apparent throughout the U.S. economy. Consider participation in the labor force. Despite recent advances, workers from racial and ethnic minorities tend to be concentrated in lower-paying

● Exhibit 11.3 **Occupational Concentration by Race, Ethnicity, and Sex**

	Men	Women
White	Marketing, advertising, and public relations managers; engineers, architects, and surveyors; dentists; firefighters; construction supervisors; tool and die makers	Physical therapists; dental hygienists; secretaries; bookkeepers; accounting and auditing clerks
Black	Vehicle washers and equipment cleaners; bus drivers; concrete workers; guards; sheriffs, bailiffs, and other law enforcement personnel	Social workers; postal clerks; dietitians; child-care workers and teacher's aides; private household cooks and cleaners; nursing aides and orderlies
Hispanic	Janitors and cleaners; construction trades; machine operators; cooks; drivers; laborers and helpers; roofers; groundskeepers, gardeners, farm and agricultural workers	Private household cleaners and servants; child-care workers; janitors and cleaners; health service occupations; sewing machine operators
Asian	Physicians; engineers; professors; technicians; cooks; launderers; longshore equipment operators	Marine-life workers; electrical assemblers; dressmakers; launderers
Native American	Marine-life workers; hunters; forestry (except logging); fishers	Welfare aides; child-care workers and teacher's aides; forestry (except logging)

Source: National Committee on Pay Equity, 1995.

jobs (see Exhibit 11.3). African Americans make up 10% of the entire U.S. workforce, but they make up 31% of nursing aides and orderlies, 25% of all taxi drivers, 25% of hotel maids, and 22% of janitors and cleaners (National Committee on Pay Equity, 1995). They are severely underrepresented in the fields of law (3.2%), medicine (3.0%), and engineering (3.2%) (Hacker, 1992). Only about 25% of Hispanics have managerial, technical, and administrative jobs, compared to 50% of non-Hispanic whites (Valdivieso & Davis, 1991). In the high-tech manufacturing industries of Silicon Valley, California, people of color make up 26% of the total workforce but hold 80% of the lower-paying production jobs (Hossfeld, 1990). In Fortune 500 companies, 97% of senior managers are white (DeWitt, 1995).

Because minorities are occupationally concentrated in low-paying jobs and geographically concentrated in poor inner-city neighborhoods, they are particularly vulnerable to economically motivated business changes, such as plant shutdowns, the automation of lower-level production jobs, and corporate relocations. For example, when a factory in a predominantly black or Hispanic section of a city moves to an all-white suburb, minority employees tend to face greater problems than white employees in securing housing in the new location or experience higher transportation costs in commuting to it (Squires, 1980). Not surprisingly, with the exception of Asian Americans the rate of unemployment for people of color is twice as high as that of whites (U.S. Bureau of the Census, 2000b).

Institutional racism is not limited to the lower end of the economic spectrum, however. Members of racial minorities are sometimes reluctant to enter high-paying occupations previously closed to them because they anticipate that they will not be welcomed (Pettigrew & Martin, 1987; Sunstein, 1991). For instance, relatively few African Americans are likely to invest in the lengthy education needed to become a doctor as long as white patients remain uneasy about being treated by African-American doctors. In fact, in recent years, the number of African Americans applying to and being accepted by medical schools has decreased considerably (Noble, 1998). But with few African-American doctors practicing, white people may never have the chance to learn tolerance and acceptance. The result is a further perpetuation, perhaps even an increase, in discriminatory hiring practices.

We can see evidence of institutional racism in common employment policies, too, such as seniority rules. The people who have worked at a company the longest tend to get more benefits and higher salaries, even though their jobs might be no more demanding than those of more recent hirees. Moreover, the long-term workers have better job stability because seniority rules usually include a "last hired, first fired" provision. Again, nothing about these rules is inherently racist, but they have a racist effect when they are applied to jobs for which minorities have begun to be hired only recently. When an employer has to lay off workers, the newest employees, who are more likely to be minorities, will be the first to lose their jobs.

Members of racial and ethnic minorities also remain marginal participants in the economy as owners of their own small businesses. Loan companies usually demand a credit history, some form of collateral, and evidence of potential success before they will lend money to prospective businesses. These are standard practices, but they perpetuate racial stratification because members of groups that have been exploited in the past tend to have poor credit ratings and no collateral because of poverty. Admittedly, poor people are greater credit risks than those with economic resources, and businesses in poorer communities must pay more for insurance because of the greater likelihood of theft or property damage. Of course, the higher costs of doing business in a poor community usually make small business loans to minority members even more necessary.

Financial concerns, not some deep-seated racial hatred, are allegedly behind many other instances of discrimination by businesses:

- In 1999, a Miami restaurant was sued for its policy of adding an automatic 15% tip to the bills of black customers, a practice that was instituted because, according to the owner, "Blacks don't tip well" (Bragg, 1999).
- In 1999, the Adam's Mark Hotel in Daytona Beach, Florida, was charged with discriminating against African Americans who had gathered for the annual Black College Reunion. The lawsuit asserted that the hotel required black guests to wear orange wristbands to enter the hotel, and pay a $100 damage deposit, a $25 deposit to have the room telephone turned on, and a $300 deposit for access to minibars. None of these policies applied to whites staying in the hotel (Holmes, 1999).
- In the mid-1990s a group of black customers sued the Denny's restaurant chain, claiming that the restaurant required blacks to pay a cover charge or pay in advance for meals, refused to honor its free Birthday Meal offer to blacks, subjected blacks to racially derogatory remarks, threatened or forcibly removed black customers, and locked the doors so blacks couldn't enter. One Denny's manager was told by a supervisor that

> "A-A's"—in-house code for African-Americans—posed a problem because they could not be counted on to follow the protocols of restaurant-going; they offended other customers by being boisterous; they alienated waitresses by leaving skin-flinty tips; they cost the company money by skipping out on the bill.... "We were told we should take whatever measures we could to keep A-A's to a minimum.... [We] were to eliminate them from [the] restaurant. No questions asked. Just get it done." (H. Kohn, 1994, p. 44)

In all these cases senior executives, convinced that black customers were costing their companies money, issued orders that were widely interpreted by employees to mean they had to discriminate racially (H. Kohn, 1994). The companies claimed that their actions were motivated by business concerns. Hence they were not a matter of personal racism but a function of the competitive, profit-driven nature of the economic marketplace. You can see how racial and ethnic discrimination in business settings is sometimes difficult to overcome precisely because it may occur for reasons other than personal hatred. It is part of the taken-for-granted rules about doing business.

Interestingly, many *anti*racist actions may also be motivated by economic forces and not necessarily by personal desires to overcome racism. Network television in the 1990s had more series than ever featuring black characters. On the surface, the entertainment industry appeared to be finally eradicating a long tradition of racial inequality. However, a Nielsen study showed that black households average 70 hours a week of television watching compared with 47 hours in nonblack households (Hammer, 1992). The networks' decision to represent more blacks on television appears to be financially motivated. Similarly, TV stations are catering to the growing number of people who want to tune in to programs in Spanish and other languages besides English. In Los Angeles the number one station for viewers aged 18 to 34 during the 6 P.M. time slot is KMEX-TV, a station that broadcasts its shows exclusively in Spanish. In San Francisco

KTSF, an English-language station, now broadcasts a one-hour newscast in Cantonese every weeknight to appeal to the large concentration of Chinese Americans and Chinese immigrants in the city (Mogelonsky, 1998b).

As long as companies are motivated to maximize their own interests (and profits), they are likely to adapt to market tastes. To the extent that those tastes reflect underlying prejudice, discrimination will continue. This structural-functionalist explanation of institutional racism is important because it enables us to see why discrimination is so difficult to end. The problem is not individual bigotry; it is the mistreatment that has been built into the system so effectively that it is sometimes difficult to see, let alone remove.

Racism in the Health Care System. As I pointed out at the beginning of this chapter, the economic and educational advances of minority groups over the past decade or so have been tempered by continuing disadvantages in health and health care. As you can see in Exhibit 11.4, life expectancy and sickness clearly vary along racial/ethnic lines. To make matters worse, members of racial and ethnic minorities are also less likely than whites to have access to health insurance. Thirty-five percent of Hispanic Americans (especially those from Mexico and Central America) and 22% of African Americans lack health insurance (compared to 15% of non-Hispanic whites) (U.S. Bureau of the Census, 2000b).

We can't simply blame ruthless and bigoted doctors, nurses, medical researchers, or insurance agents for these differences. Instead, the heavy financial emphasis that drives the health care system creates a context ripe for institutional racism. For instance, transplant centers in some hospitals use a policy called the "green screen" to decide which patients should be excluded from their lists of eligible candidates for an organ transplant. A new liver can cost as much as $250,000, so most hospitals want some kind of evidence of insurance coverage up front. Because racial minorities are less likely than whites to have medical insurance, they are less likely to receive a referral for transplant surgery (Stolberg, 1998a). Likewise, the National Cancer Institute spends only 1% of its budget on studies of medically underserved ethnic groups, even though black women are 50% more likely to get breast cancer before they turn 35 than white women and 50% more likely to die from the disease before they turn 50 (Institute of Medicine, 1999; Jetter, 2000). In both these cases financial concerns and not outright racial prejudice lie at the heart of these policies.

Sometimes the institutional racism underlying threats to people's health is less obvious. For instance, people in neighborhoods where hazardous waste treatment plants or other sources of industrial pollution exist are disproportionately exposed to the unhealthful effects of air pollution, water pollution, and pesticides. The decisions on where to place such facilities are often based not on the racial makeup of an area but on such factors as the cost of land, population density, and geological conditions. However, because the less desirable residential areas (and hence more desirable industrial areas) are disproportionately inhabited by minorities and other poor people, these decisions have the effect of discriminating against them. The 437 counties and cities that failed to meet air-quality standards in 1990 were home to 80% of the nation's Hispanics, 65% of the African-American population, but only 57% of whites

Exhibit 11.4 **Life Expectancy by Race/Ethnicity at Age 20**

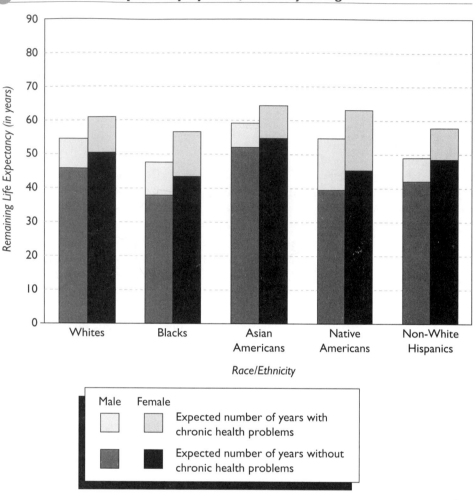

Source: M. D. Hayward & M. Heron, 1999, pp. 77–91.

(Cooper, 1998a). The nation's largest hazardous waste dump is located in Emelle, Alabama, a small rural community that is 90% black (Bullard & Wright, 1992).

More than 120 chemical plants—or one per mile—are situated along a stretch of the Mississippi River between Baton Rouge and New Orleans known as "cancer alley" (Cooper, 1998a). A study of toxic emissions in this area by the Environmental Protection Agency showed that 9 of the 10 major sources of industrial pollution are in predominantly black neighborhoods. In Carville, Louisiana, a town that is 70% black, 353 pounds of toxic material per person per year is released into the environment. The average in the rest of the state is 105 pounds (Cushman, 1993).

The broader racial assumptions that underlie the health care system can also create institutional racism. The most infamous example of such assumptions was the

Tuskegee study of black men with syphilis, which ran from the 1930s to the early 1970s. In 1932 the U.S. Public Health Service initiated a study in Tuskegee, Alabama, to determine the natural course of untreated syphilis in black men. In exchange for their participation, the 400 men—all poor and most illiterate—received free meals, free medical exams, and burial insurance. The men were never told they had syphilis. Instead, they were told that they had "bad blood" and would receive treatment. In reality, they received no treatment. When penicillin became available in the early 1950s—the most effective treatment for syphilis—the men were not treated. In fact, the Public Health Service actively sought to prevent treatment. Even as the men began to die or to go blind or insane, penicillin was withheld. As soon as the experiment was publicized in 1972, it was stopped. Since then, the federal government has paid out more than $9 million in damages to victims and their families and heirs.

The Tuskegee study was not driven by the outright prejudice of individual medical researchers but by scientific rationale and dominant, taken-for-granted medical "facts" of the time. Prevailing medical opinion in the 1930s was that blacks were born with strong sexual appetites and a lack of morality that made them particularly susceptible to venereal disease. This belief, coupled with the equally dominant belief that blacks wouldn't seek treatment even if it were available, led the researchers to conclude that this segment of the population would provide the best source of subjects for their study.

The legacy of the Tuskegee study has been a pervasive distrust of the health care system among many African Americans today. Indeed, this mistrust has been cited as one of the reasons why African-American patients have been slow to come for HIV testing and medical care (Richardson, 1997) and are less likely than whites to get surgery for early stages of lung cancer (Bach, Cramer, Warren, & Begg, 1999). Again, we see how the structure of social institutions can affect individual lives.

Racism in the Educational System. In 1954 the U.S. Supreme Court ruled, in *Brown* v. *Board of Education of Topeka*, that racially segregated schools were unconstitutional because they were inherently unequal. Nearly half a century later, a study by researchers at the Harvard Graduate School of Education found that 66% of all African-American public school students and 70% of Hispanic students still attend predominantly minority schools, defined as those schools with more than 50% of their enrollment made up of either African-American or Hispanic students. And about a third of black students attend schools in which 90% of the students are not white (Orfield & Yun, 1999). At the same time, most white students go to schools that are nearly all white, even in cities that have large minority populations. These figures represent the highest rates of school segregation reported in the last 25 years.

When African American and Latino students are segregated into schools where the majority of students are not white, they are likely to find themselves in schools where poverty is concentrated. This is not the case with segregated white students, whose majority-white schools almost always enroll high proportions of middle-class students (Orfield & Yun, 1999).

The racial mix of the classroom thus has important implications for the quality of the education that students receive. Concentrated poverty tends to be linked to lower educational achievement. Schools in poor communities lack the financial and therefore educational resources that schools in more affluent communities have (see Chapter 10). Poor schools offer fewer advanced courses, hire fewer teachers with credentials in the subjects they're teaching, and have more unstable enrollments, higher dropout rates, and more students with untreated health problems than wealthier schools. Furthermore, these districts face increasing financial pressures because of recent reductions in federal assistance programs. The rising cost of higher education also reduces the number of minority students who are able to attend college. Consequently, blacks and Hispanics continue to have lower levels of educational attainment than whites and Asian Americans (see Exhibit 11.5).

Lack of money isn't the only problem, though. Common practices within the educational system may perpetuate institutional discrimination. According to the National Coalition of Advocates for Students, poor, black, and Hispanic children are more likely

Exhibit 11.5 **Race, Ethnicity, and Educational Achievement**

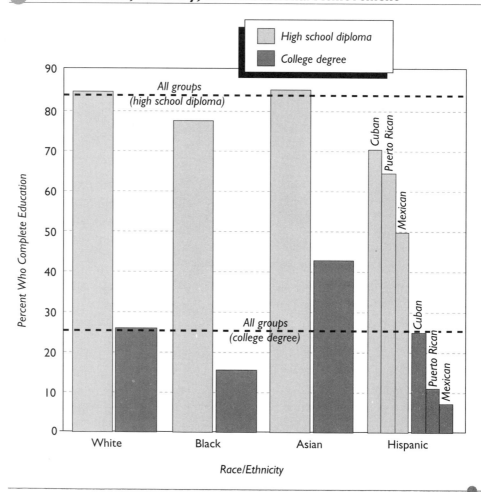

Source: U.S. Bureau of the Census, 2000b.

than middle-class white children to be physically punished, suspended, expelled, or forced to repeat a grade. These forms of treatment go beyond personal mistreatment and humiliation; they all increase the likelihood that a child will drop out of school (cited in Eitzen & Baca-Zinn, 1991).

Consider also the common use of standardized tests (IQ, SAT, and so on). Many elementary and secondary schools use standardized tests as the basis for tracking students—that is, assigning them to different educational programs based on their intellectual abilities. In principle, tracking allows every student to receive an education that is consistent with his or her talents. In practice, however, students from privileged backgrounds are likely to be placed in higher tracks, and those from less privileged backgrounds, who are disproportionately members of minority groups, are likely to be placed in lower tracks (Bowles & Gintis, 1976; Oakes, 1985).

Standardized tests supposedly measure innate intelligence and knowledge acquired in school. Many educational experts agree, however, that these tests are culture-bound, tapping an individual's familiarity with a specific range of white, middle-class experiences rather than indicating innate intelligence (Curran & Renzetti, 1990). Hence members of racial minorities consistently score lower on these tests than whites (Jencks & Phillips, 1998).

Standardized tests play a complicated role in U.S. society. Despite the potential for bias, more and more states in the country are requiring high school students to pass a standardized test to graduate. At the same time, though, many universities and other educational organizations have begun seeking alternative ways to determine eligibility for admission. For instance, some universities now use a "strivers" approach whereby college applicants who score between 1,000 and 1,200 on the SAT—a borderline range for many selective colleges—but manage to exceed the historical average for students from similar backgrounds by at least 200 points would be deemed "strivers" and given special consideration (K. J. Cooper, 1999). The Texas legislature went a step further, ordering the University of Texas system to accept all students who graduate in the top 10% of their class, regardless of their SAT scores. And the American Bar Association is searching for ways to reduce reliance on the Law School Admissions Test (LSAT) (Bronner, 1997). In 1999 a U.S. district court judge ruled that the NCAA could no longer use SAT scores to determine athletic eligibility. The court concluded that the test is culturally biased and therefore discriminates against underprivileged students. And in 2001 the president of the University of California proposed that the massive state university system he oversees end its use of all standardized aptitude tests as a requirement of admission (Schemo, 2001).

These changes indicate a significant effort to undermine the sort of institutional racism that is, according to some sociologists, the largest barrier to racial equality that exists in this country today (Jencks & Phillips, 1998).

Racism in the Legal System. Despite a decline in the overall crime rate in recent years, about 5,000 out of every 100,000 African-American men are in prison or jail. By comparison, the prison rate for the general population in the United States is 500 per 100,000 (Cockburn, 1995). Nearly twice as many African-American men and women as whites are in prison for drug offenses, even though there are five times as many white drug users as black ones (Human Rights Watch, 2000).

One reason for this imbalance is certainly the personal biases of individual police officers, attorneys, and judges. A 2000 U.S. Department of Justice report found that at every step of the juvenile justice system black and Hispanic youths are treated more severely than whites charged with similar crimes. They are more likely to be arrested, held in jail, sent to juvenile or adult court for trial, convicted, and given longer prison sentences. For those charged with violent crimes, blacks were nine times as likely as whites to be sent to prison. The average length of incarceration for similar offenses was 254 days for blacks, 305 days for Latinos, and 193 days for whites. For those youths charged with drug offenses, blacks were 48 times more likely than whites to be sentenced to prison (cited in Butterfield, 2000b).

But we must also examine the possibility that racial discrimination in the law exists at the institutional level. Consider, for instance, discrepancies in prison sentences for the possession and use of cocaine. Although the two types of cocaine—powdered and crack—cause similar physical reactions, the sentences for those convicted of selling them are vastly different. The average length of a sentence for selling crack cocaine is 133 months; for powdered cocaine it is 94 months. According to federal law, it would take 500 grams of powdered cocaine (or 5,000 doses) to draw the same mandatory minimum sentence of 5 years in prison that a person convicted of possessing 5 grams (or 10 doses) of crack cocaine would get (The Sentencing Project, 2000). Crack is the only drug that carries a mandatory prison sentence for possession without the intent to sell it.

Many law enforcement officials argue that the different levels of punishment are justified because crack cocaine is more closely associated with violence than powdered cocaine and more dangerous to the user. However, a study of the physiological and psychoactive effects of different forms of cocaine found they are so similar as to make the existing discrepancy in punishment "excessive" (cited in Wren, 1996).

Some sociologists argue that the problems associated with crack have as much to do with poverty, unemployment, and homelessness as with the drug itself (Duster, 1997). And others point to the skewed racial distribution of the users of crack versus the users of powdered cocaine. The common perception is that the typical user of powdered cocaine is a white suburbanite and that the typical crack user is a young, urban black man. Official crime statistics support this perception. In 1994, 89.7% of those convicted of crack possession were black and Hispanic; only 10% were white. By contrast, 26.7% of those convicted of powdered cocaine possession were black, 15% were Hispanic, and 58% were white (The Sentencing Project, 2000).

In this federal drug policy we see a clear example of institutional racism. Regardless of intent, the consequences of this law are discriminatory. Blacks are serving longer prison sentences for drug offenses not because of personal racism but because they are more likely to use a drug that is punished more severely than any other.

Micro-Macro Connection
Driving while Black

Law enforcement agencies around the country—such as police departments, state patrols, the Drug Enforcement Administration, even the U.S. Customs Service—have come under attack in recent years for their policies of "racial profiling": the use of racial and ethnic stereotypes in traffic enforcement or other investigative stops. In Texas, for example, black and Hispanic motorists are more than twice as likely as non-Hispanic whites to be searched during traffic stops (cited in Yardley, 2000a). Many African Americans complain about being stopped for the "offense" of DWB—"driving while black."

Police often explain their use of race in deciding what drivers or pedestrians to stop by pointing to statistics showing that African Americans and Hispanics are more likely than whites to be arrested and convicted of the most common street crimes. Hence, they have argued, it is statistical reality, not racism, that directs their attention to people of color. According to the police chief of Los Angeles, who happens to be black,

> It's not the fault of the police when they stop minority males or put them in jail. It's the fault of the minority males for committing the crime. In my mind it is not a great revelation that if officers are looking for criminal activity, they're going to look at the kind of people who are listed on crime reports. (quoted in Goldberg, 1999, pp. 53–54)

For decades, the courts have allowed such practices. But public attitudes toward racial profiling are starting to shift. Increasingly, targets of the practice are filing and winning discrimination suits. In 1998 a civil rights group and 11 black motorists filed a lawsuit charging that the Maryland State Police used a "race-based profile" in stopping drivers along a stretch of interstate highway and searching their cars and belongings for drugs and weapons (Janofsky, 1998a). The state of Maryland agreed to stop the practice, although recent evidence shows that a disproportionate number of motorists stopped on state highways in Maryland—more than two-thirds—continue to be people of color (Jost, 2000).

In a 1999 settlement, New Jersey officials acknowledged in court that state troopers had unfairly singled out black and Hispanic motorists in traffic stops. Several former troopers testified that they would park alongside the turnpike and shine their headlights into passing cars, looking for black drivers to pull over. They would then radio ahead to fellow officers down the road, letting them know that a "carload of coal" or a group of "porch monkeys" was headed their way (Hosenball, 1999).

To date, 5 states have passed laws banning racial profiling and 15 others are considering doing so. In 1999, the International Association of Chiefs of Police formally condemned the practice. Perhaps a comprehensive institutional response can eventually eliminate this type of institutional racism.

Ways to Overcome Institutional Racism. The irony of institutional racism is that although it may not be the result of conscious bigotry on the part of individual people and therefore not motivated by outright personal hatred, it is likely to be more harmful than personal racism in the long run and more difficult to stop. If tomorrow all people in the United States were to wake up with all hatred, prejudice, and animosity toward other groups gone from their hearts and minds, institutional racism would still exist:

> All that is needed for job opportunities to remain unequal is for employers to hire those with the most conventional training and experience and to use machines when they seem more . . . economical than manual labor. All that is needed to ensure that

poor children get an inferior education is to continue . . . using class-biased tests, . . . rewarding children who conform to the teachers' middle-class concepts of the "good student," and paying disproportionately less for education. In other words, all that is needed to perpetuate discrimination in the United States is to pursue a policy of "business as usual." (Eitzen & Baca-Zinn, 1989, pp. 218–219)

So overcoming institutional racism takes more than the goodwill of individual people. In fact, because it is a structural problem, it requires a structural solution. You have already seen how the educational system and the legal system are undertaking limited measures to overthrow certain types of institutional racism. However, the most far-reaching structural solution to the problem of institutional racism has been a governmental policy referred to as **affirmative action.** Affirmative action is a program that seeks out members of minority groups for educational or occupational positions from which they had previously been excluded. The assumption is that past discrimination has left certain people ill equipped to compete as equals today. Another assumption is that organizations will not change racist policies unless they are forced to do so.

Although once considered a promising solution to institutional racism, today affirmative action is highly controversial. Many consider it demeaning to the people it is supposed to help and unfair to everybody else. Contrary to popular belief, however, the goal of affirmative action is not to undermine standards by favoring the unqualified. Employers are not compelled to institute hiring quotas or to compromise standards to meet affirmative action goals. They are simply required to gather all relevant information on all qualified applicants, to interview minority candidates, and to make sure minorities have access to job information. Government agencies and private firms doing business with the government, for instance, are required to publicly announce job openings at least 45 days prior to the cutoff day for applications (Cherry, 1989).

Quotas are only a last resort, reserved for situations in which organizations are not making good-faith efforts to seek out qualified minority candidates. If a firm announces a job opening in newspapers that reach only the white community or uses discriminatory procedures to eliminate minorities from employment, the government can then impose quotas.

Affirmative action policies have been used successfully in several areas of social life. Cities have been ordered to bus children to schools outside their neighborhoods to eliminate school segregation. Businesses, unions, universities, and local governments accused of discrimination in hiring or admission have been sued under the 1964 Civil Rights Act. In part because of such action, more than 40% of U.S. colleges and universities reported enrollment gains among African Americans and Hispanics in the mid-1990s (cited in Worsnop, 1996a). People of color now hold a greater percentage of management, white-collar, and upper-level blue-collar jobs than ever before. Even young black men—historically the most economically disadvantaged and alienated group in the United States—are working in record numbers (Nasar & Mitchell, 1999). Wages and salaries relative to those of whites have also improved. Exhibit 11.6 shows the changes in household income of blacks and whites between 1970 and 1997.

Despite such successes, affirmative action has come under fire as a form of "reverse discrimination." Critics argue that the constitutional protection of each person's

Exhibit 11.6 **Household Income by Race**

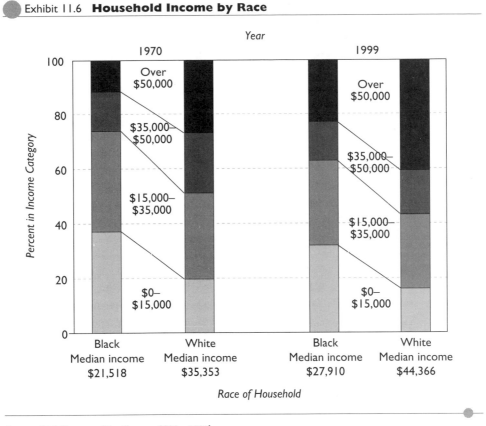

Sources: U.S. Bureau of the Census, 2000a, 2000b.

right to life, liberty, and property means that all groups, including those whose rights have never been violated or neglected, must have their opportunities safeguarded and must be treated equally. Hence any preferential treatment of any group, even one whose rights have been historically unrecognized, amounts to a form of discrimination, usually against white males. Critics suggest that "reverse discrimination" will create a "white backlash" and undermine the main goal of affirmative action, which is to reduce prejudice.

The catalyst for these criticisms was a case that went to the Supreme Court in 1978. Alan Bakke, a white male student, was twice denied admission into a California medical school. He claimed that less qualified applicants had been accepted under a special admissions program that saved 16 out of 100 places for minorities. The U.S. Supreme Court ruled in favor of Bakke, although it also stated that race or ethnicity could be used as one of several factors in evaluating applicants. The Court reversed itself a year later, however, when it ruled that private employers could legally give special preference to black workers to eliminate "manifest racial imbalance" in jobs traditionally restricted to whites.

After nearly three decades of affirmative action, many whites have come to believe it should be abolished (Citrin, 1996). They argue that enough has been done for minorities and that now the deck is stacked against them. People in the United States have never disagreed more about whether past discrimination entitles racial and ethnic minorities to preferential treatment in education or hiring. More than three-fourths of whites now feel that qualified blacks should not receive preference over equally qualified whites in such matters as getting into college or getting jobs (Citrin, 1996).

Several recent legislative decisions have also threatened the continued existence of affirmative action. In 1996 California voters approved Proposition 209, a referendum that banned the consideration of race, ethnicity, and sex in the public sector, including college admissions. Prior to the ban, African Americans, Hispanics, and Native Americans made up 23.1% of admitted first-year students in the University of California system. The first year after the ban went into effect, that figure fell to 10.4% (Bronner, 1998b). The Law School of the University of California at Berkeley saw an 81% decrease in black admissions. And of the 14 black students admitted in 1997, none decided to actually enroll (Applebome, 1997).

Similarly, in 1996 the U.S. Supreme Court let stand a lower court ruling that the University of Texas Law School couldn't use race as a factor in admissions. The Court implied that race-based affirmative action plans—even if used for the purpose of correcting racial imbalances—are discriminatory and therefore unconstitutional. The following year there was an 80% drop in black and Hispanic admissions at the University of Texas.

Even some members of the African-American community argue that affirmative action is at best a mixed blessing and may actually hurt those groups it is intended to help. For instance, black students attending predominantly white universities often find that many of their white classmates assume they were admitted because of affirmative action and not because of their qualifications. Furthermore, some sociologists point out that affirmative action has enhanced the opportunities of middle-class blacks but has done nothing to help the millions of poor blacks who have seen their economic situations worsen (Wilson, 1990). Others point out that many of the continuing problems blacks face today are a product of the cultivation and exploitation of the status of "victim." They argue that programs such as affirmative action simply reinforce feelings of inferiority, discourage initiative, and encourage blacks to claim victimization (S. Steele, 1990).

In a society with a tradition of racial stratification, what is the best way to overcome institutional and personal inequality? Does it take discriminating in the opposite direction to "make things equal," or is it enough simply to treat people equally from this point on?

Imagine a fictitious final game of the NCAA Basketball Championship Tournament between University A and University B. The rules of the game clearly favor University A. Its team is allowed five players on the court, but team B is allowed only four. Team A gets 4 points for every basket made; team B gets 2. Team A is given 2 points for each free throw made; team B gets 1. Team A is allowed to physically impede the progress of the opposing players without being called for a foul, and so on.

At halftime team A leads team B by a score of 70 to 15. During halftime the NCAA Rules Committee, responding to pressure from the referees, the fans, and players from both teams, decides that the current rules have made the game completely unfair and have harmed the interests of team B. The committee declares that from now on the game will use a new system of rules that makes the game more just. Each team will have the same number of players on the court and receive the same number of points per basket. The inequality of the game has been successfully eliminated, and fairness rules the day.

But there's a slight problem—the score is still 70 to 15! In other words, just because opportunities have been equalized doesn't mean that disadvantages of the past have been entirely erased. Such is the problem we face today. We can legislate hiring or admission polices that do away with unfair advantages to any group, but is that action enough to address a long history of exclusion? For a long time to come, members of certain groups will continue to be underrepresented in traditionally white positions. Can U.S. citizens achieve complete equality without forcing those who have benefited historically to give up some of their advantages? The answer to this question is complex, controversial, and emotionally charged and will have a great impact on the nature of U.S. race relations in the 21st century.

Global Perspectives on Racism

Given the focus of this chapter so far, you might be tempted to conclude that racism and racial inequality are purely U.S. phenomena. Certainly these problems are most obvious in a society such as the United States, which is so ethnically and racially diverse and which has had such a long history of bitter racial conflict. But racial and ethnic tension is the worldwide rule, not the exception. The result is prejudice and discrimination in many societies.

Discrimination

Like disadvantaged racial and ethnic groups in the United States, minority groups in other countries suffer discrimination that ruins their opportunities for success. For instance, in Eastern European countries such as Slovakia, Romania, Hungary, and the Czech Republic discrimination against the Roma—or Gypsies—is the norm. They have been despised for centuries as thieving subhumans with no allegiance to the law. They are stereotyped as loud, dirty, indecent, and sloppy. In 1998 city officials in Usti nad Lbem, Czech Republic, proposed that a 15-foot wall be built to separate the Gypsies who live there from the rest of the townspeople. According to a poll of Czech attitudes, 39% of the population feel that "only force is effective" in dealing with Gypsies (cited in Erlanger, 2000). As a result of such attitudes, Gypsies suffer disproportionately from poverty, interethnic violence, discrimination, illiteracy, and disease. Unemployment among European Gypsies is about 70% (cited in Perlez, 1998). Only 15% of Gypsy children attend kindergarten (cited in Erlanger, 2000).

In Mexico, all citizens are considered legally equal under the country's constitution. The National Commission of Human Rights has never received a racial discrimination complaint. Yet it is a society deeply divided along racial lines, particularly between dark-skinned people of Indian descent and light-skinned people of Spanish descent. Most Mexicans are of mixed lineage, so that nearly all of them could be considered at least part Indian. Nevertheless, the degree of "Indianness," or the darkness of one's skin, determines one's status in Mexican society. Because darkness is associated with low status, many Mexicans, especially in the larger cities, use hair dyes, skin lighteners, and blue or green contact lenses to appear more European (DePalma, 1995).

The desire to appear European is understandable. Mexicans who are considered Indians are the object of severe discrimination. Although 1 in 10 Mexicans is purely Indian, no Indians serve in the presidential cabinet and only a handful are in the congress. More than 80% of Mexico's Indian communities suffer high levels of poverty. Nearly half of all Indians are illiterate, and only 14% complete sixth grade. The Indians refer to themselves as "Mexico's most forgotten people" (DePalma, 1996).

The 1994 armed uprising by Mayan Indians in the state of Chiapas was an attempt to force the government to acknowledge its unjust treatment of its Indian people. The Mayans were protesting against years of poverty and their long-standing status as second-class citizens. The catalyst for the uprising was the Mexican government's signing of the North American Free Trade Agreement (NAFTA), which ended state subsidies for the crops that the Indians depend on for their survival. Despite this rebellion, racism in Mexico remains largely unaddressed, and the cultural assault on people of Indian descent continues.

In some countries, prejudice and discrimination against a particular minority group have nothing to do with actual racial differences. For instance, the Burakumin, who represent about 2% of the Japanese population, are the most disadvantaged minority in Japan. They are biologically, religiously, and ethnically indistinguishable from other Japanese. Nevertheless, many Japanese people consider the Burakumin a completely different race. Their low status dates back to the 17th century, when their occupations dealt with killing animals and disposing of their remains, which violated Buddhist principles. These jobs were necessary for society but considered so degrading that only "subhuman" outcasts would do them, forever contaminating those who engaged in them (Kristof, 1995).

The innate inferiority of the Burakumin remains beyond question to many Japanese. Burakumin are widely believed to be mentally weak, aggressive, impulsive, and dirty (Neary, 1986). Before marrying someone or hiring a new employee, some Japanese will have a detective agency check the background of a person for Burakumin ancestors. In the past, some shopkeepers accepted money from Burakumin customers in baskets with long handles and then washed the coins afterward (Mihashi, 1987).

The treatment and perception of the Burakumin have recently improved somewhat. Today almost two-thirds say they've never encountered discrimination, although many children are never told by their parents that they are Burakumin. More than 70% now marry non-Burakumin, and most believe they are treated fairly by the police (Kristof, 1995). The Japanese government has invested large sums of money to improve Burakumin neighborhoods so they are no longer unlivable slums.

As welcome as these measures are, the Burakumin still suffer from institutional discrimination. They have the lowest income and educational attainment in Japanese society and the highest rates of poverty, crime, alcoholism, single parenthood, and welfare dependency. And like minority groups in the United States, their dependence on government assistance has created resentment from a public that believes they are getting special, undeserved help.

Ethnic Conflict

You can see that in Eastern Europe, Mexico, and Japan—as in most other countries—racism has deep historical roots. Sociologists once believed that such traditions would gradually succumb to the global forces of industrialization and modernization, which would create racially diverse societies where people's loyalty would be directed to the national society rather than their racial or ethnic community (Deutsch, 1966). But the opposite has happened. At a time when people from every corner of the globe are linked technologically, economically, and ecologically and when mass migrations mix people from different races, religions, and cultures in unprecedented numbers, racial and ethnic hostilities are at an all-time high (Barber, 1992).

Ethnic conflict today typically has little to do with material or economic interests. It tends to center on less tangible resources such as power, security, respect, or social status. Ethnic groups fight about such abstractions as identity and cultural recognition. Conflicts usually arise from distorted images between groups, which create deep emotions, extreme opinions, and ultimately explosions of violence (H. D. Forbes, 1997).

Judging by what we see going on in the world today, we might conclude that hostility between groups is among the most universal of human feelings (Schlesinger, 1992). Look at the front page of the newspaper and you will see stories of conflict and violence between Jews and Palestinians in Israel, Hutus and Tutsis in Rwanda and Burundi, Serbs and Muslims in Bosnia, Serbs and ethnic Albanians in Kosovo, English-speaking Canadians and French-speaking Canadians in Quebec, Tamils and Sinhalese in Sri Lanka, Azerbaijanis and Armenians or Russians and Chechens in the former Soviet Union, Javanese and ethnic Chinese in Indonesia, and Hindus and Sikhs in India. Racial and ethnic hatred around the world costs the lives of millions of people each year.

Immigration and global financial instability can sometimes cause strains between racial and ethnic groups. When people's survival is threatened, they often blame others for their problems, particularly newly arrived others who look and act differently. In Great Britain, France, and Germany, for example, loud and sometimes violent resentment is directed toward immigrants from Africa, Eastern Europe, and Asia. In the United States, such animosity is likely to be directed toward immigrants from Latin America and Asia (see Chapter 13 for more detail).

But global forces don't always increase racial tension and inequality. In South Africa, for example, the end of apartheid was the result of an international boycott of companies that did business there. In the 1980s the global media brought the world pictures and stories of the brutal treatment of South African blacks. When consumers in the United States and other industrial nations stopped buying products from companies that held investments in South Africa, the companies began to withdraw their money. The minority white government felt the sting as domestic economic problems mounted. As a result of these pressures, the white population of South Africa voted to abolish apartheid. Shortly thereafter, the first black president, Nelson Mandela, was elected. In 1996 a new constitution was adopted that officially and peacefully completed South Africa's transition from white supremacy to nonracial democracy. The document renounces the racism of the past and guarantees all South Africans broad freedoms of speech, movement, and political activity (Daley, 1996). Although serious inequalities and animosities remain, the country is well on its way toward unity and stability.

CONCLUSION

On April 16, 1963, Reverend Martin Luther King Jr. allowed himself to be arrested and jailed for leading a civil rights demonstration in Birmingham, Alabama. Birmingham at the time was perhaps the most thoroughly segregated city in the country. Not only were blacks subjected to daily doses of fear, violence, and humiliation, but they also had to constantly fight what Dr. King called "a degenerating sense of nobodiness." Torn between the brutal reality of a racist society and a fierce optimism for the future, he wrote from his jail cell,

> Let us all hope that the dark clouds of racial prejudice will soon pass away and the deep fog of misunderstanding will be lifted from our fear-drenched communities and in some not too distant tomorrow the radiant stars of love and brotherhood will shine over our great nation with all of their scintillating beauty. (King, 1991, p. 158)

Close to 40 years later, Dr. King's words continue to fall on deaf ears. Our society—like most societies around the globe—still struggles with the debilitating effects of personal and institutional discrimination based on race, religion, and ethnicity. In the United States, lynchings and state-supported segregation have given way to a quiet, almost polite racism that resides not in bloodshed and flagrant exclusion but in the day-to-day workings of our major social institutions. Despite recent gains, minority groups still suffer noticeable disadvantages in economics, education, politics, employment, health care, vulnerability to crime, and so on. When opportunities to learn, legislate, and make a living are unequally distributed according to race, all facets of life remain unequal.

Four decades after racial segregation was ruled unconstitutional in the United States, the complete integration of such fundamental social institutions as public schools, government, and business remains largely unachieved. And some are questioning the very value of integration.

One reason why race relations are so problematic today is that public debate over the issue confuses the various types of racism. One person might use *racism* to refer to personal forms of bigotry; another might use the term to refer to broader forms of institutional racism. Different types of racism require different solutions. We cannot put an end to economic deprivation or massive residential segregation by trying to convince people not to stereotype other groups.

I realize this chapter has been rather depressing. After reading it, you may have a hard time imagining a multiracial society without racial or ethnic stratification. We must remember, however, that differences do not have to imply inequality. The transformation from difference to disadvantage is a social construction. The people of every society decide which differences should be irrelevant and which should be the primary criteria for making social and legal distinctions between groups of people. The good news is that because we construct these differences, we can tear them down.

YOUR TURN

In this chapter I examined the personal and institutional forms that racism takes. A curious and disturbing feature of prejudice is that many of our beliefs and attitudes about other racial or ethnic groups are formed without any direct contact with members of those groups. The media—most notably television—play a significant role in providing the public with often inaccurate and oversimplified information about racial and ethnic groups that indirectly shapes public attitudes.

For one week, observe several prime-time television shows that feature prominent African-American, Hispanic, and Asian characters. The shows can be either comedies or dramas. Note the number of characters on each show who are people of color. Pay particular attention to the way the characters are portrayed. What is their apparent social class standing? How does their behavior conform to common stereotypes associated with members of these groups? How frequently do their words or actions refer to their own race? Do the plots of the shows revolve around what you might consider "racial" themes? That is, how often does the issue of race come up during the course of the show?

Expand your analysis to examine the role of race in stand-up comedy. What proportion of comedians of color use race as part of their act compared to white comedians? Is there a danger in such comedians as Chris Rock, Martin Lawrence, Margaret Cho, and John Leguizamo playing on racial stereotypes in their acts?

Interpret your observations sociologically. What are the implicit messages communicated by the portrayal of racial/ethnic minorities? What role does humor play in reinforcing or fighting prejudice? Are characters who do not act in stereotypical ways conforming instead to a white, middle-class standard? If so, how will this portrayal ultimately affect public perceptions of race?

CHAPTER HIGHLIGHTS

● The history of race in U.S. society is an ambivalent one. Famous sayings about equality conflict with the experiences of most racial and ethnic minorities—experiences of oppression, violence, and exploitation. Opportunities for life, liberty, and the pursuit of happiness have always been distributed along racial and ethnic lines.

● Personal racism is manifested in the form of bigotry, prejudice, and individual acts of discrimination. Symbolic racism is not expressed directly but rather indirectly, through avoidance of minorities or opposition to programs designed to improve the status of minorities in society.

- Racism can also be found in a language and cultural ideology that justifies a set of social norms prescribing differential treatment of certain groups.

- Institutional racism exists in established institutional practices and customs that reflect, produce, and maintain racial inequality. Institutional racism is more difficult to detect than personal racism and hence is more difficult to stop. Because such racism exists at a level above personal attitudes, it will not disappear simply by reducing people's prejudices.

- Racial and ethnic conflict is not just an American phenomenon. It is a global reality.

KEY TERMS

affirmative action Program designed to seek out members of minority groups for positions from which they had previously been excluded, thereby seeking to overcome institutional racism

discrimination Unfair treatment of people based on some social characteristic, such as race, ethnicity, or sex

ethnicity The sense of community that derives from the cultural heritage shared by a category of people with common ancestry

institutional racism Laws, customs, and practices that systematically reflect and produce racial and ethnic inequalities in a society, whether or not the individuals maintaining these laws, customs, and practices have racist intentions

personal racism Individual's expression of racist attitudes or behaviors

prejudice Rigidly held, unfavorable attitudes, beliefs, and feelings about members of a different group, based on a social characteristic such as race, ethnicity, or sex

race Category of people labeled and treated as similar because of some common biological traits, such as skin color, texture of hair, and shape of eyes

racial transparency Tendency for the race of a society's majority to be so obvious, normative, and unremarkable that it becomes, for all intents and purposes, invisible

racism Belief that humans are subdivided into distinct groups that are different in their social behavior and innate capacities and that can be ranked as superior or inferior

stereotype Overgeneralized belief that a certain trait, behavior, or attitude characterizes all members of some identifiable group

symbolic racism Form of racism expressed subtly and indirectly through opposition to programs that seek to improve the status of racial and ethnic minorities in a society

12 The Architecture of Inequality: Sex and Gender

Sexism at the Personal Level

The Ideology of Sexism: Biology as Destiny

Institutions and Women's Inequality

The Global Devaluation of Women

At a women's rights convention held in Seneca Falls, New York, participants created a modified version of the Declaration of Independence. They called it the Declaration of Sentiments and Resolutions. Here are some excerpts from that document:

> We hold these truths to be self-evident: that all men and women are created equal. . . . The history of mankind is a history of repeated injuries . . . on the part of man toward woman, having in direct object the establishment of an absolute tyranny over her:
>
> - He has compelled her to submit to laws, in the formation of which she had no voice.
> - He has monopolized nearly all profitable [occupations], and from those she is permitted to follow, she receives but a scanty remuneration. He closes against her all the avenues to wealth and distinction which he considers most honorable to himself.
> - He has endeavored, in every way that he could, to destroy her confidence in her own powers, to lessen her self-respect, and to make her willing to lead a dependent and abject life.
>
> In view of their social degradation and in view of the unjust laws above mentioned, and because women do feel themselves aggrieved, oppressed, and fraudulently deprived of the most sacred rights, we insist that they have immediate admission to all the rights and privileges which belong to them as citizens of the United States.

The women who wrote this declaration were not the women's liberationists of the 1960s and 1970s or the radical feminists of the 1990s and 2000s. They were participants in the first convention in support of women's rights ever held in the United States—in 1848.

Many people are inclined to believe that the battle against sexual inequality is a relatively recent phenomenon that emerged along with the civil rights movement of the 1960s and the so-called sexual revolution of the 1970s. We tend to think that women of the past were either content with their second-class status or unaware that it could be otherwise. As you can see from the preceding declaration, though, 150 years ago U.S. women were anything but passive, ignorant victims of discrimination. They were as angry, humiliated, and frustrated by social mistreatment as many women are today. The purpose of their struggle—to overcome economic, legal, and social inequality—was as relevant and urgent in 1848 as it is in the 21st century.

Along with economic and racial inequality, sexual inequality has been a fundamental part of the historical development of the U.S. identity and a fundamental part of many movements toward democracy around the world. It has influenced the lives and dreams of individual people, shaped popular culture, and created and maintained social institutions.

Chapter 5 discussed how we learn to become boys and girls, men and women within the appropriate social and cultural context. Being placed in a gender category affects everything we do in life. But gender is more than just a source of personal identity that sets societal expectations; it is a location in the stratification system and a major criterion for the distribution of important resources in most societies. Therefore, sex or gender is perhaps the most important determinant of stratification worldwide.

In this chapter I explore the lives and experiences of women living in societies constructed, for the most part, by and for men. Several important questions are addressed: What are sexism and gender discrimination? How are they expressed and felt at the personal level? How is inequality based on sex and gender supported by cultural beliefs and symbols? At the institutional level, how is it related to family and work roles? What are its legal and economic consequences?

Sexism at the Personal Level

What do you think of when you hear the word *sexism*? The husband who won't let his wife work outside the home? The construction worker who whistles and shouts vulgar comments at female passersby? The office worker who tells lewd jokes about women? Perhaps even the woman who mocks men's interpersonal skills? Sexism is all those things, to be sure. But sociologically speaking, **sexism** refers to a system of beliefs that assert the inferiority of one sex and that justify discrimination based on gender—that is, on feminine or masculine roles and behaviors. At the personal level, sexism refers to attitudes and behaviors communicated in everyday interaction.

In a male-dominated society, or **patriarchy**, cultural beliefs and values give higher prestige and importance to men than to women. Throughout such a society, girls and women are affected by inequality in everything from the perceptions, thoughts, and social interactions of individuals to the organization of social institutions. Above all, sexual inequality in a patriarchy provides men with privileged access to socially valued resources and furnishes them with the ability to influence the political, economic, and personal decisions of others. Matriarchies, which are societies that give preference to women, are rare in the contemporary world. Even the most modern, democratic societies tend to be patriarchal to some degree.

Research on U.S. gender stereotypes, for instance, has shown that they have changed little over the years (D. L. Berger & Williams, 1991). Women are consistently perceived as more passive, emotional, easily influenced, and dependent than men (Broverman, Vogel, Broverman, Clarkson, & Rosenkrantz, 1972; Deaux & Kite, 1987;

Tavris & Offir, 1984). Others have noted the myriad ways personal sexism is expressed in U.S. society, both overtly and subtly, through physical domination, condescending comments, sabotage, and exploitation (Benokraitis & Feagin, 1993). One study found that although some forms of personal sexism are motivated by hostility, others are motivated by benevolence, as when men assume women are helpless and thus fell compelled to offer help (Glick & Fiske, 1996). Such attitudes and behaviors not only place women in a lower-status position compared to men but also channel them into less advantageous social opportunities.

Men, of course, aren't the only ones who can be personally sexist. Certainly many women dislike men, judge them on the basis of stereotypes, hold prejudiced attitudes toward them, consider them inferior, and even discriminate against them socially or professionally. For instance, in 1995, eight men sued Jenny Craig, Inc., a weight loss company, charging that they were denied promotions or fired because they were men. We must keep in mind, though, that male sexism occupies a very different place in society from female sexism. The historical balance of power in patriarchal societies has allowed men as a group to subordinate women socially and sometimes legally to protect male interests and privileges. Because men tend to dominate society, their sexism has more cultural legitimacy and more serious consequences than women's sexism.

Sexism and Social Interaction

Everyday social interaction is fraught with reminders that women play a subordinate role in our society. Men often have a hard time understanding women's reactions to everyday encounters between the sexes because, just as white people enjoy racial transparency (see Chapter 11), members of the dominant sex take for granted the social arrangements that serve their interests.

For example, consider the following tongue-in-cheek quote from a female newspaper columnist:

> By whistling and yelling at attractive but insecure young men, we women may actually help them feel better about themselves, and give them new appreciation of their bodies. Some might say women were descending to the level of male street-corner oafs, but I'm willing to take that risk. If, with so little effort, I can bring joy to my fellow man, then I am willing to whistle at cute guys going down the street. (Viets, 1992)

If you're a man, you may wonder why the columnist is bothering to make fun of "wolf whistles." The answer simply is that this behavior means different things to men and women. Unsolicited sexual attention may be an enjoyable, esteem-enhancing experience for men, but it doesn't have the weight of a long tradition of subordination attached to it, nor is it linked in any way to the threat of violence. Men aren't **objectified**—that is, treated like objects rather than people—in the same way that women are. In other words, for men a whistle is just a whistle. Their entire worth is not being condensed into a crude assessment of their physical appearance. Women, who still must fight to be taken seriously in their social, private, and professional lives, may interpret whistles and lewd comments as attempts to reinforce their low status in the stratification system. These actions serve as a reminder that their social value continues to be based primarily on their looks. Men have the luxury of knowing that such objectification is not a problem for them.

Communication patterns also show the effects of unconscious sexism. Research in the symbolic interactionist tradition suggests that women and men carry on conversations in different ways (Parlee, 1989; Tannen, 1990). For instance, women are more likely than men to use a tag question at the end of a statement: "She's a good professor, *don't you think?*" They are also more likely to use such modifiers and hedges as *sort of* and *kind of* and to be excessively polite and deferential in their speech (Lakoff, 1975). Such techniques may make the speaker sound less powerful and therefore call into question the credibility and qualifications of women who happen to occupy positions of authority. Imagine if your math professor always said things like "The answer to the problem is $3x + y$, *isn't it?*" Or if your boss said, "We're going to pursue the Johnson account, *is that OK?*"

The implicit, nonverbal messages of social interaction—body movements, facial expressions, posture—also have more serious implications and consequences for women than for men. Nonverbal cues play an important role not only in preserving social order but also in providing people with information about their social worth. Nonverbal behavior also serves to keep women "in their place." In India, for instance, crowded buses and trains are frequently the site of "Eve-teasing"—a euphemism for the common practice of men fondling and groping women they happen to be pressed up against in the crowd. The fact that men can more freely touch women than vice versa serves as a reminder that women's bodies are not considered entirely their own.

In this society, femininity is typically gauged by how little space women take up; masculinity is judged by men's expansiveness and the strength of their gestures. Women's bodily demeanor tends to be restrained and restricted (Henley, 1977). What is considered "ladylike"—crossed legs, folded arms—is also an expression of submission. Men's freedom of movement—feet on the desk, legs spread, straddling a chair—conveys power and dominance.

Interactional norms such as these place women who are in authoritative positions in a no-win situation. If, on the one hand, they meet cultural definitions of femininity by being passive, polite, submissive, and vulnerable, they fail to meet the requirements of authority. If, on the other hand, they exercise their authority by being assertive, confident, dominant, and tough, their femininity is called into question (J. L. Mills, 1985). Such dilemmas confront women in business, the professions, and perhaps most dramatically, the masculine culture of the military.

Laura Miller
Gender, Power, and Harassment in the Military

Over the past few years, we've heard many stories about the sexist behavior and gender discrimination that female cadets, soldiers, and pilots have had to endure in the U.S. military. In 2000, the only female three-star general in the army filed a sexual harassment complaint against another general. She retired a few months later. Many others have been humiliated, beaten, tortured, even in one case set on fire. A panel of senior U.S. Army officials concluded in 1997 that the military leadership was responsible for misconduct against women that had become pervasive in the entire system.

The U.S. military has been predominantly male for most of its history, except for female medical, clerical, and logistical personnel. Men still make up the vast majority of the armed forces and hold all the highest positions of authority. Depending on the branch of service, women today make up between 5% and 17% of active-duty personnel ("A glance at women," 2001).

Some women have been able to climb the military ladder and achieve the rank of lieutenant, captain, major, or even general. These women create a special dilemma for male soldiers because female officers simultaneously occupy a subordinate position (because they are women) and a superior position (because they are commanding officers in a highly stratified military hierarchy). So how do lower-level male soldiers—whose gender grants them power but whose military rank makes them inferior—respond?

Sociologist Laura Miller (1997) set out to answer this question by engaging in field research at eight U.S. Army posts and two national training centers. She also lived with U.S. Army personnel overseas, in Somalia and Haiti. In addition, she collected survey data from over 4,000 American soldiers, both enlisted personnel and officers. On the basis of her research, Miller draws a distinction between *sexual* harassment (unwanted sexual comments or advances) and the more common *gender* harassment (harassment that is used to enforce traditional gender roles or is used in response to the violation of those roles). She considered such statements as "Women can't drive trucks" or "Women can't fire heavy artillery" to be gender harassment. Gender harassment is also often used against men, as when they fail to live up to the masculine ideal and are called "ladies" or "girls" by their comrades or commanding officers.

Many of the men Miller studied strongly believed that they are the disadvantaged gender in the military. They were convinced that women's physical training requirements are easier than men's, that women are able to "get away with more," and that women receive special breaks, such as avoiding demanding physical duty because of menstrual cramps. As one enlisted man stated, "They want equal rights, but don't want to do what it takes to become equal" (quoted in L. Miller, 1997, p. 48). In short, many male soldiers had come to believe that any woman's power in the military is gained illegitimately.

As a result, many men resorted to subtle forms of gender harassment to express their disapproval of women's power positions in the military. Because of the ubiquitous military stratification system and their abiding loyalty to the "chain of command," these men were unlikely to use traditional forms of harassment against superior female officers, such as blatant sexual comments or sexual advances. Nor were they likely to overtly disobey orders. Instead, they often used what sociologists refer to as *weapons of the weak*—strategies that subordinates employ to resist oppression from above. Such techniques include foot-dragging, feigned ignorance, gossip and rumors, and sabotage. According to one male officer interviewed by Miller, most soldiers at one time or another try to undermine the authority of their female superiors.

Because of the recent rash of publicity concerning sexual harassment, the military has taken steps to control such behaviors and has shown, through publicized sanctions against offenders, a decreasing tolerance of this problem. However, these improvements do not mean that female military personnel now work in a supportive environment. Gender harassment is more subtle, and therefore more difficult to trace, than sexual harassment. Furthermore, this study shows us that positions of power are not sufficient to guarantee respect and authority. Rather, it shows that harassment lies at the crossroads of power and gender.

———————————————————————————— ●● ————————————

Violence against Women

The epitome of sexual domination expressed at the personal level is, of course, sexual violence. Forcible rape exists throughout the world, in the most democratic societies as well as in the most repressive.

In the United States, rape is the most frequently committed but least reported violent crime (U.S. Department of Justice, 2001). According to the National Crime Victimization Survey—an annual assessment of crime victimization carried out by the U.S. Bureau of Justice Statistics—more than 333,000 women are raped or sexually assaulted annually, three times the 93,000 incidents of rape that were officially reported to the police in 1998 (U.S. Bureau of the Census, 2000b). Such violence is especially prevalent on college campuses, where about 3% of college women experience a completed or attempted rape during a typical college year. Of these incidents about 90% of the victims knew their attackers (U.S. Bureau of Justice Statistics, 2001). Rape also has one of the lowest conviction rates of any violent crime. According to a report by the Senate Judiciary Committee (1993), 98% of rape victims never see their attacker caught, tried, and imprisoned. And of those rapists who are convicted, close to 25% never go to prison and another 25% receive sentences in local jails where the average sentence is 11 months.

Rape as a Means of Social Control. According to conflict theory, sex stratification has long distorted our understanding of rape. Throughout history, women have been viewed socially and legally as the property of men, either their fathers or husbands. Thus in the past rape was seen as a crime against men or, more accurately, against men's property (S. Griffin, 1986). Any interest a husband took in a sexual assault on his wife probably reflected a concern with his own status, the loss of his male honor, and the devaluation of his sexual property.

According to some feminist theorists, men have also used rape and the threat of rape throughout history to exert control over women (Brownmiller, 1975). The mere existence of rape limits women's freedom of social interaction, denies them the right of self-determination, makes them dependent on men, and ultimately subordinates them (S. Griffin, 1986). All forms of oppression—whether against ethnic Albanians in Kosovo, peasants in South America, or women in the United States—employ the threat of violence to ensure compliance (Sheffield, 1987). The subordination of women depends on the power of men to intimidate and punish them sexually.

The fear of rape goes beyond simply making life uncomfortable for women. It also affects them economically by restricting opportunities. Women may avoid some neighborhoods with affordable housing because of potential danger. If a woman has a job that requires night work, she may be forced to buy a car to avoid walking at night or using public transportation. The threat of sexual assault limits where and when she is able to work, thereby limiting her money-earning choices and perhaps keeping her financially dependent on others.

Women are also harmed by the larger cultural ideology surrounding rape and rapists. I think most of us are inclined to believe that men who rape must be insane or abnormally violent. The stereotypical image is one of the sex-crazed stranger hiding in bushes or in the back seat of a parked car. He is the wild-eyed psychopath bent on harming and humiliating women because of some deep-seated psychological or hormonal defect. All one has to do to avoid being raped, then, is to avoid strange guys. In 1997 the state of Montana reinforced this belief when it approved the use of "chemical castration," an injection of the drug Depo-Provera, for convicted rapists and other sex offenders. The logic was that the substance, which reduces testosterone levels, would solve the problem of rape by reducing the abnormal sex drives of these individuals, thereby rendering them harmless.

However, rapists as a group have not been shown to have higher levels of testosterone or, for that matter, to be any more disturbed or crazy than nonrapists (S. Griffin, 1986; Warshaw, 1988). Most rapists are quite "normal" by usual societal standards. In fact, about three-quarters of them are friends, acquaintances, or relatives of their victims (U.S. Bureau of the Census, 2000b). But when rape is perceived as the fault of a small number of physically or psychologically defective strangers, it doesn't have any effect on the dominant culture and established social arrangements. In other words, rape isn't considered the fault of society, it's the fault of flawed individuals who can't abide by society's rules. This assumption may explain why date or acquaintance rape, marital rape, and other forms of sexual violence that don't fit the typical image have, until quite recently, been ignored or trivialized.

We must therefore examine the crime of rape within a broader cultural context that encourages certain types of behavior between men and women (Jackson, 1995). When we do this, rape becomes less an act of deviance and more an act of overconformity to cultural expectations; less an act of defective individuals and more an act of "normal" men taking cultural messages to their violent extreme. As one author wrote, rape is the "All-American crime," involving precisely those characteristics traditionally regarded as desirable in American men: strength, power, domination, and control (S. Griffin, 1989).

Victim Blaming. Globally, cultural beliefs about gender, sexuality, and intimacy influence societal and legal responses to rape and rape victims:

- In 1999 the highest appeals court in Italy overturned a rape conviction because the victim wore tight jeans. The court ruled that it is impossible to take off tight jeans "without the collaboration of the person wearing them," implying that the woman must have been a consenting participant in a sexual encounter rather than a victim of a violent crime ("Italy," 1999, p. A8).
- In Peru, a man who rapes a woman—whether he knows her or not—can be absolved of all charges if he offers to marry her. As one Peruvian man put it, "Marriage is the right and proper thing to do after a rape. A raped woman is a used item. No

one wants her. At least with this law the woman will get a husband" (quoted in Sims, 1997, p. A8).

- In Kenya, 300 boys at a boarding school raped 71 girls in a dormitory. Several of the victims died as a result. The vice principal explained, "the boys never meant any harm against the girls, they just wanted to rape" (quoted in Cooper, 1999, p. 355).

The United States has a more sympathetic response to rape victims. But the legal response still tends to be consistent with men's interests, focusing on women's complicity or blameworthiness. In rape cases, unlike any other crime, victims typically must prove their innocence rather than the state having to prove the guilt of the defendant. No wonder that more than 70% of the rape victims in one study said they were concerned about their families discovering they had been raped, and about 66% worried that they might be blamed (cited in Johnston, 1992).

The conflict perspective provides one explanation for the widespread tendency to blame women: The common definition of rape is based on a traditional model of sexual intercourse—penile-vaginal penetration—rather than on the violent context within which the act takes place. Rape is still largely viewed in terms of women's sexuality rather than men's coercion (Sheffield, 1987).

The exclusive focus on the sexual component of the crime requires that information about the circumstances of the act and about the relationship between the people involved be taken into consideration—all of which tends to put female rape victims at a disadvantage. Research consistently shows that observers attribute more blame to victims and minimize the seriousness of the assault when the perpetrator is an acquaintance, date, or steady partner (Bell, Kuriloff, & Lottes, 1994). Such attitudes can influence court decisions. One study of convicted rapists found that those who assaulted strangers received longer prison sentences than rapists who were acquaintances or partners of their victims, regardless of the amount of force used or physical injury to the victim (McCormick, Maric, Seto, & Barbaree, 1998).

Consider also situations where husbands are accused of raping their wives. Rape laws in many states in the United States, and in most countries around the world, include what is commonly known as the "marital rape exemption." These laws typically define rape as "the forcible penetration of the body of a woman, *not the wife of the perpetrator*," making rape in marriage a legal impossibility (Russell, 1998, p. 71). In 8 states, husbands cannot be prosecuted for raping their wives unless they are living apart or legally separated. In 26 other states, they can be prosecuted in some circumstances but are totally exempt in others. For example, in some states rape imposed by force but without the wife's suffering additional degrees of violence, such as kidnapping or being threatened with a weapon, is not considered a crime (Russell, 1998). At present, only 15 states have abolished the marital rape exemption entirely (Burgess-Jackson, 1998). When the American Law Institute—an organization devoted to clarifying and simplifying the law through legislative reform—most recently revised the Model Penal Code provisions on rape, it decided to preserve language that exempts husbands from rape charges:

> The problem with abandoning the [marital] immunity in many . . . situations is that the law of rape, if applied to spouses, would thrust the prospect of criminal sanctions

into the ongoing process of adjustment in the marital relationship. . . . Retaining the spousal exclusion avoids this unwarranted intrusion of the penal law into the life of the family. (quoted in Siegel, 1996, p. 2174)

Even when rape victims are not married to their attackers, they are expected to provide some evidence that they were "unwilling" and tried to resist. No other serious crime requires that the victim prove lack of consent. People aren't asked if they wanted their car stolen or if they consented to being robbed. Until very recently the rape laws in several states still included what are called "corroboration rules," which required that rape charges be confirmed by evidence other than the victim's testimony (Tong, 1984).

If women cannot prove that they resisted or cannot find someone to corroborate their story, consent may be presumed. Anything short of vigorous and repeated resistance can call the victim's motives into question. In 1992 in Austin, Texas, a man forcibly entered a woman's apartment. The woman fled and locked herself in the bathroom. He broke down the door, held a knife to her, and demanded sex. Fearing for her life, not only because of the knife but also because of the chances of contracting a sexually transmitted disease, she begged the man to put on a condom. He agreed and went on to assault her for over an hour. The next day he was arrested for burglary with intent to commit sexual assault. In a sworn deposition he admitted that he had held a knife to her and had had sex with her. But the grand jury originally refused to indict the man because the victim's act of providing a condom was taken to mean consent. Only after widespread public outrage was the man tried, convicted, and sentenced to 40 years in prison.

Not only are women sometimes accused of not doing enough to stop rape, they are occasionally suspected of actually doing something to invite or "precipitate" it (Amir, 1971). Many people regard situations in which a woman places herself at risk—by hitchhiking, acting seductively, wearing "provocative" clothing, or telling dirty jokes—as a form of victim-precipitated rape. Accused rapists have been acquitted in cases in which victims had been raped during beer-drinking parties, had willingly entered a car with several men, had hitchhiked, or had gone dancing with the men who later assaulted them (Wood, 1975).

Research reveals a pervasive cultural belief that women provoke rape. One survey of 400 teens (Goodchilds, Zellman, Johnson, & Giarusso, 1988) found that approximately 50% of the boys and about 30% of the girls felt it was acceptable for a man to force sex on a woman when

- She is going to have sex with him and changes her mind.
- She has "led him on."
- She gets him sexually excited.
- They have dated for a long time.
- She lets him touch her above the waist.

In another study, male and female high school students were given a list of statements and asked to indicate the extent to which they agreed with them (Kershner, 1996). Of the male and female subjects, 52% agreed that most women fantasize about being raped by a man, 46% felt that women encourage rape by the way they dress, and 53% said they felt that some women provoke men into raping them. Moreover, 31% agreed that many women falsely report rapes, and 35% felt that the victim should be required to prove her innocence during a rape trial. Research has linked such attitudes to the heightened risk of rape and sexual assault on college campuses (Ching & Burke, 1999).

The important sociological point of these findings is that many men and even some women don't always define violent sexual assault as wrong. They think it is what men are expected to do under certain circumstances. These views have become so entrenched that many women have internalized the message, blaming themselves for their own victimization. Outside of fear, self-blame is the most common reaction to rape and is more frequent than anger (Janoff-Bulman, 1979). When rape victims say such things as "I shouldn't have walked alone," "I should have locked my windows," or "I shouldn't have worn that dress to the party," they are at least partly taking the blame for a crime they didn't commit.

The crucial consequence of victim blaming is that women must bear much of the responsibility for preventing rape. I frequently pose this question to students in my classes: What can people do to stop rape from occurring? Their responses always echo the standard advice: Don't hitchhike. Don't walk alone at night. Don't get drunk at parties where men are present. Don't initiate sex play. Don't engage in foreplay if you have no intention of "going all the way." Don't miscommunicate your intentions. Don't wear provocative clothing. Don't accept invitations from strangers. All these are sensible things to do. But note how these suggestions focus exclusively on things that *women* should avoid to prevent rape and say nothing about the things *men* can do to stop it.

I don't mean to imply that one ought to ignore this advice. It certainly makes sense, given all the violence in today's society, to communicate intentions clearly and not to put oneself in dangerous situations. Indeed, some authors argue that if women don't take responsibility for protecting themselves, they're perpetuating the image of women as helpless, passive victims (Roiphe, 1993). The implication of such instructions, however, speaks volumes about the nature of rape and the place of women in society. Confining discussions of rape prevention to women's behavior suggests that if a woman doesn't take these precautions, she is "inviting trouble." And "inviting trouble" implies that violent male behavior either is a natural response or is likely to happen if certain things aren't done to discourage it. Hence, a woman cannot dress the way she wants, walk where and when she wants, talk to whom she wants, or change her mind about having sex without putting herself at risk.

Without a fundamental restructuring of society, no significant reduction in rape is likely to occur. Such a change would require a transformation of male–female relationships and childhood socialization, as well as a more equitable sharing of political and economic power. Some progress is being made: The recent increase in attention paid to rape, particularly to acquaintance or date rape, has increased public awareness. Myths are being debunked, the sexual exploitation of women in the media is being protested, and the rules governing admissible evidence in rape trials are being changed. However, as long as we have a deeply ingrained sexist ideology that objectifies women and glorifies male assertiveness, so, too, will we have sexual violence.

The Ideology of Sexism: Biology as Destiny

The domination of one group over another is always endorsed by a set of beliefs that explains and justifies that domination. We saw in the previous chapter that racism is often justified by the belief in innate racial inferiority. With sexism, it is the belief that men and women are biologically, naturally different.

For 19th-century physicians, few facts were more incontestable than the fact that women were the products and prisoners of their anatomy, more specifically their reproductive systems (Scull & Favreau, 1986). Everything about women that made them different from men—their subordinate place in society, the predominance of the emotional over the rational, their capacity for affection, their love of children and aptitude for child rearing, their "preference" for domestic work, and so on—could be explained by the existence and functioning of their uterus and ovaries (Ehrenreich & English, 1979; Scull & Favreau, 1986).

Scholars at the time warned that young women who studied too much were struggling against nature, would badly damage their reproductive organs, and would perhaps even go insane in the process (Fausto-Sterling, 1985). So the exclusion of women from higher education was not only justifiable but necessary for health reasons and for the long-term good of society.

In 1900 the president of the American Gynecological Society stated that "many a young [girl's] life is battered and forever crippled on the breakers of puberty" (quoted in Ehrenreich & English, 1979, p. 110). Such beliefs about the undesirable effects of women's normal biological functioning are not just a thing of the past. The Board of Trustees of the American Psychiatric Association continues to debate the inclusion of a psychiatric diagnosis called "premenstrual dysphoric disorder" in its official manual of mental disorders. (At the time of this writing it appears in the manual as a "proposed category in need of further investigation.") Indisputably, women around the world experience irritability, moodiness, and other symptoms related to hormonal cycles. The issue, however, is whether these symptoms ought to be labeled as a medical problem (Lander, 1988). To do so fosters a belief that women's bodies are weak and in need of medical attention and promotes the selling of drugs to healthy women (C. A. Bailey, 1993; Figert, 1996).

Some structural-functionalist sociologists have also used the observable physical differences between men and women to explain sexual inequality. The fact that men tend to be physically stronger and that women bear and nurse children has created many culturally recognized and necessary sex-segregated social roles, especially at work and in the family (Parsons & Bales, 1955). This specialization of roles is the most effective way to maintain societal stability, structural-functionalists believe. By giving birth to new members, by socializing very young children, and by providing affection and nurturing, women make invaluable contributions to the reproduction of society. The common occupations that women have outside the home—teacher, nurse, day care provider, maid, social worker, and so on—tend simply to be extensions of their "natural" tendencies.

Similarly, men's physical characteristics better suit them for the roles of economic provider and protector of the family. If it's true that men are "naturally endowed" with such traits as strength, assertiveness, competitiveness, and rationality, then they are best qualified to enter the serious and competitive world of work and politics (Kokopeli & Lakey, 1992). As one social scientist matter-of-factly put it less than three decades ago, men inevitably occupy the most prestigious positions in society because they possess more testosterone—the hormone most of us associate with aggression—and therefore have a competitive advantage over women in the occupational market-place (S. Goldberg, 1974). In short, men are assumed to be the natural power wielders and societal leaders. One study, however, has found that the higher the level of test-osterone in men, the lower their occupational status (Dabbs, 1992).

The problem with depicting masculinity and femininity as natural, biological phe-nomena is that it confuses sex with gender. The underlying assumption of sexist ideol-ogy—that gender is as unchangeable as sex—overlooks extensive similarities between the sexes and extensive variation within each sex. The distributions of men and women on most personality and behavioral characteristics generally overlap. For in-stance, men as a group do tend to be more aggressive than women as a group. Yet some women are much more aggressive than the average man, and some men are much less aggressive than the average woman. Indeed, social circumstances may have a greater impact on aggressive behavior than any innate, biological traits. Some studies show that when women are rewarded for behaving aggressively, they can be just as violent as men (Hyde, 1984).

Furthermore, the reliance on biology ignores the wide cultural and historical variation in conceptions of masculinity and femininity. For instance, although every known society has a division of labor based on sex, what's considered "men's work" and "women's work" differs. In most societies men fish, hunt, clear land, and build boats and houses; but in some societies women regularly perform these tasks. In most societies women do the cooking; but in some societies cooking is typically a male re-sponsibility (Eitzen & Baca-Zinn, 1991).

Although women have become prominent in the U.S. workforce, many people still believe that they are less capable than men in performing certain tasks outside the home (Wagner, Ford, & Ford, 1986). Some people in the United States still may find fe-male doctors or dentists unusual and debate the role of female soldiers in combat. The controversy in both the Episcopal and Catholic churches over whether or not women should be ordained as ministers illustrates the depth and intensity of people's feelings about gender-appropriate career pursuits.

Moreover, the qualities we consider naturally feminine are usually seen as less so-cially valuable than those considered masculine. Girls do suffer sometimes when their behavior is considered "boylike." But for a boy to be called a girl is the ultimate school-yard insult, because it implies weakness, frailty, and lack of ability. Even today, many men can be easily whipped into anger by accusations of femininity, as when coaches call their male players "girls" or "ladies" to draw out their aggressiveness.

This devaluation of femininity even influences the cultural value of certain emo-tions. We think of love as involving emotional expressiveness, verbal self-disclosure, and affection (Cancian, 1987). Clearly these are qualities associated with women. The desirable masculine traits—independence, competitiveness, emotional inexpressive-ness—usually imply the antithesis of love. Not coincidentally, U.S. society tends to glorify achievement and downplay emotional expression as overly sentimental and fool-ish. Women are encouraged to specialize in and be emotionally responsible for roman-tic relationships, whereas men are expected to specialize in work activities, which are more highly regarded in society. When love is perceived in such a way, men's power over women is strengthened.

In sum, the biological rationale for gender inequality is difficult to justify. Tech-nological advances—including bottled baby formula, contraceptives that reduce women's childbearing and child-rearing responsibilities, and technological and social advances that lessen the need for sheer physical strength—have made the biological imperative for gender-based role responsibilities obsolete (Gough, 1971). Nevertheless, as long as people believe that gender-linked roles and societal contributions are deter-mined by nature, they will continue to accept inequality in women's and men's oppor-tunities, expectations, and outcomes. If people consider it "natural" for women to play nurturing, weak, and dependent roles, then structurally limiting women to such posi-tions seems neither unfair nor oppressive.

Institutions and Women's Inequality

The subordination of women that is part of the workings of social institutions (or **institutional sexism**) has far greater consequences for women as a group than does per-sonal sexism. As you've seen throughout this book, the experiences of individuals must always be located within an institutional structure. Media representations, the legal sys-tem, the family, and the organization of work all have a role in producing and main-taining gender inequality. Historically, men have developed, dominated, and inter-preted most institutions. The only institution in which women have had a central role is the family, but as you'll see, even that role has traditionally been a subordinate one.

When sexism in social institutions becomes part of the ongoing operation of large-scale organizations, it perpetuates and magnifies women's disadvantages, making social equality all the more difficult to attain. Consider, for instance, the institution of health care. Physicians can specialize in *women's* health care—but not in *men's*. Obste-tricians and gynecologists deal exclusively with the reproductive and sexual matters of female patients. Women are typically treated as special cases because they are different from men (Rothman & Caschetta, 1999). It's not surprising, then, that outside of ob-stetrics and gynecology there is a general lack of research data on women and a limited understanding of women's health needs. Because their menstrual cycles are said to complicate research, women have historically been excluded from medical studies in areas such as heart disease, diabetes, and arthritis. The problem became so bad that in 1993 Congress passed a law stipulating that women must be included in clinical trials in numbers sufficient to provide evidence of the different ways men and women re-spond to drugs and other treatments. Nevertheless, a 2000 study found that many re-searchers are not complying with the law, perpetuating a lack of understanding of how men and women respond differently to certain drugs, surgical treatments, and changes in diet or behavior (Pear, 2000c).

Not only are social institutions sexist—in that women are often segregated, ex-ploited, or excluded—but they are also gendered. In other words, institutions and organizations themselves incorporate values and practices based on traditional expectations for women and men (Kimmel, 2000). And more often than not, they incorporate masculine values. Take sports, for example. Most of us would agree that to compete successfully an athlete must be aggressive, strong, and powerful—attributes typically associated with masculinity. By celebrating these traits, a sport such as football symbolically declares itself an arena that women cannot or should not enter (except, of course as spectators or cheerleaders). But even such sports as gymnastics and figure skating that have traditionally valued more "feminine" traits, such as grace, beauty, and balance, have changed their rules recently to accommodate more power and strength. Simply being graceful and having a good sense of balance is no longer enough for a woman to be a world-class gymnast or skater. She must also exhibit explosive acrobatic power. Indeed, the recent growth in the popularity of women's team sports in this country (basketball, soccer, softball, and so on) coincides with the increasing presence of such traditionally male traits as physical strength and competitive vigor in female athletes. Yet traditional attitudes die slowly. One of the greatest achievements in American female sports history, the U.S. soccer team winning the 1999 World Cup, may be best remembered for the player who took her shirt off to celebrate the victory.

Similarly, most bureaucracies in institutional areas such as business, politics, and the military operate according to masculine principles:

> This "masculine ethic" elevates the traits assumed to belong to men . . . to necessities for effective organizations: a tough-minded approach to problems; analytic abilities to abstract and plan; a capacity to set aside personal, emotional considerations in the interests of task accomplishment; a cognitive superiority in problem-solving and decision making. (Kanter, 1975, p. 43)

Thus successful leaders and organizations are usually portrayed as aggressive, goal oriented, competitive, and efficient—all characteristics associated with masculinity in this society. Rarely are strong governments, prosperous businesses, or efficient military units described as supportive, nurturing, cooperative, kind, and caring (Acker, 1992). This sort of bias pervades other institutions as well.

Sexism and the Media

You saw in Chapter 5 that the media's portrayal of men and women contributes to early gender socialization. But the media as an institution can also contribute to the cultural devaluation of women and perpetuate gender inequality.

Worldwide, men tend to control the creation and production of media images. The vast majority of film producers and directors are men. The upper levels of corporate media organizations and top newspaper management positions are also almost entirely male (Croteau & Hoynes, 2000). Because women tend not to be in positions of control, they're less likely than men to be prominently featured in film, print, and television. For instance, one study of gender and global media found that women are featured in less than 20% of news stories around the world. The news coverage of women that does exist tends to focus on their family roles or issues of physical appearance (Steeves, 1993).

A glimpse at the portrayal of modern women in U.S. advertising, fashion, television, music videos, and films reveals a dual stereotype (Sidel, 1990). On the one hand, we see the successful woman of the 21st century: the perfect wife/mother/career woman, the triumphant professional who leaps gracefully about the pages of fashion magazines. Like the high-powered female lawyers and doctors we're likely to see on television, she is outgoing, bright, attractive, and assertive. No occupation is beyond her reach.

On the other hand, we see the stereotypical image of the "exhibited" woman: the seductive sex object displayed in beer commercials, magazine advertisements, soap operas, and the swimsuit issue of *Sports Illustrated*. According to a study by the National Commission on Working Women, television continues to present stereotypes that show women as shallow, vain, and materialistic characters whose looks still count for more than their brains (cited in Sidel, 1990). The "sex object" is the most dangerous media image of all because conventional physical beauty is her only attribute: "Women are constantly exhorted to emulate this ideal, to feel ashamed and guilty if they fail, and to feel that their desirability and lovability are contingent upon physical perfection" (Kilbourne, 1992, p. 349).

Not surprisingly, then, televised beauty pageants, the epitome of the exhibition of women, continue to be popular in this country. Tens of thousands of women compete in local and state pageants for a shot at the title of Miss America. An estimated 55 million people, 75% of whom are women, tune in each year to watch the pageant (Sidel, 1990). Many women watch to find out what an attractive female is supposed to look like (Freedman, 1986).

The image of beauty presented by the exhibited woman is artificial and largely unattainable, however. For instance, researchers at Johns Hopkins University compiled data on the heights and weights of Miss America pageant winners between 1922 and 1999. They found that the weights of these women have been steadily decreasing, reaffirming the cultural value of thinness (Rubinstein & Caballero, 2000). Recent winners have had a height-to-weight ratio that places them in a range of what the World Health Organization defines as "undernourished."

Aside from the occasional powerful female character—like Xena the Warrior Princess or Buffy the Vampire Slayer—the portrayal of women on prime-time television also remains rather traditional and stereotypical. Despite the fact that women make up a majority of the population, most characters on prime-time television are male (D. Smith, 1997). Although fewer women are portrayed as housewives than in the past, men are still more likely to be shown working outside the home (41% of male characters versus 28% of female characters). Similarly, an analysis of over 1,600 television commercials showed that female characters were less prevalent, more likely to be shown in families, and less likely to be employed outside the home than male characters (Coltrane & Adams, 1997).

On television, women express emotions much more easily and are significantly more likely to use sex and charm to get what they want than men. Physical attractiveness continues to be the preeminent quality for women, although they are more likely than before to be shown using their intelligence and self-reliance.

Media images continue to encourage women to view themselves as in constant need of alteration, improvement, and disguise. One survey of students in Chicago-area schools found that more than half of the fourth-grade girls were dieting and that three-quarters felt they were overweight (cited in Kilbourne, 1992). A *Glamour* magazine survey found that more than 75% of the respondents considered themselves overweight. What is more telling is that nearly half of the women in the *Glamour* survey were in reality underweight yet reported feeling too fat and wanting to diet. Sticklike standards of beauty—exemplified by the popular television character Ally McBeal—have become an ideal that many young women are ready to starve themselves to attain. These media messages can be lethal. By conservative estimates, one in five young U.S. women today has a serious eating disorder.

In sum, young women today are not only expected to achieve educationally and economically at unprecedented levels, they also must look sexy doing it. These images create the illusion that success or failure is purely a personal, private achievement and ignore the complex social, economic, and political forces that continue to prevent real-life women from achieving success.

Sexism and the Law

Historically, women have also been denied many of the legal rights that men take for granted. In the past, when women got married, they lost many of the rights they enjoyed as single women: legal title to their property, the right to execute contracts, and so forth. Husbands could chastise their wives, force them to stay at home, and even rape them without legal sanction. Such laws were based on the English common law doctrine of "coverture," under which a married woman's legal identity was submerged into that of her husband (Baron, 1987).

We don't have to go back a century to find attempts at limiting the legal rights of U.S. women. In 1981 a bill called the Family Protection Act was introduced in the U.S. Congress. Although the bill was never passed, its objective was to dismantle many of the legal achievements of the women's movement. Among its proposals were eliminating federal laws supporting equal education, forbidding the "intermingling of the sexes in any sport or other school-related activities," requiring marriage and motherhood to be taught as the proper career for girls, denying federal funding to any school using textbooks portraying women in nontraditional roles, repealing all federal laws protecting battered wives from their husbands, and banning all federally funded legal aid for any women seeking abortion counseling or divorce (Faludi, 1991). In addition, through an extra tax on spouses who file separate income tax returns, the bill encouraged a family structure with a working husband and nonworking wife (Ruether, 1980).

To counteract a long history of legal inequality, the U.S. Congress has passed many laws aimed at improving the situation of women. In addition to its central focus on eliminating segregation, the 1964 Civil Rights Act contained provisions forbidding sexism in employment. The 1972 Educational Amendments Act included a section forbidding sexual discrimination in all federally funded institutions of education. Obstacles to equality have also been removed in other areas, such as housing, eligibility for credit, and hiring practices. The 1993 Family and Medical Leave Act guarantees some working mothers (as well as fathers) up to 12 weeks of unpaid sick leave per year to care for a new child or a sick relative.

Courts in the United States have also made several noteworthy decisions that address women's concerns. In 1993 the U.S. Supreme Court ruled that victims of workplace harassment could win lawsuits without having to prove that the offensive behavior left them psychologically damaged—which in the past meant either a documented nervous breakdown or psychiatric hospitalization—or unable to do their jobs. Now workers need prove only that as a result of harassment the workplace environment "would reasonably be perceived as hostile or abusive" (Greenhouse, 1993). In 1996 the Court ruled that all-male public colleges and universities have to admit women.

But these court decisions and laws haven't been entirely effective. In the United States and elsewhere, occupations are still highly segregated along gender lines; female workers still earn a fraction of what male workers earn; and a woman's right to control her own body through legal contraception and abortion continues to be challenged.

Such lack of progress extends from home and work arenas to educational institutions and sports arenas. Close to three decades ago, Title IX of the Educational Amendments Act mandated that schools receiving federal money ban sex discrimination and that women's athletic programs in schools be equitable with men's. Since then, women's sports have become much more visible and legitimate. Female athletes can now find lucrative work in professional sports leagues. The basketball player, Chamique Holdsclaw, and the soccer player, Mia Hamm, now earn millions of dollars in endorsements. Nevertheless, women's athletics still lag behind men's. From 1992 to 1997, funding for women's athletics programs rose from an average of $263,000 a year to $663,000 a year. But during that same span, funding for men's programs increased from an average of $1.5 million to more than $2.4 million (Chambers, 1997). Since Title IX, the number of women's collegiate teams has doubled. But during the same period, the proportion of women who coach these teams has steadily declined. Thirty years ago, 90% of women's teams were coached by women; today that figure is about 46% (cited in Navarro, 2001).

Even laws explicitly designed to protect women's rights have created unforeseen disadvantages. Divorce laws in the United States, which were revised in the 1970s to make the termination of marriages less combative and more equitable, have actually increased the number of women who become poor after a divorce (Arendell, 1984; Weitzman, 1985). Divorced husbands typically experience an increase in their standard of living, but divorced wives—who are likely to have physical custody of children—suffer a decrease (Peterson, 1996). In California, for instance, after no-fault divorce laws were enacted only 13% of mothers with preschool children received spousal support (cited in Tavris, 1992). The situation for divorced women, particularly older women, was so bad that the California legislature had to pass the Displaced Homemakers Relief Act, which required judges to consider the future earning potential of each spouse before awarding a settlement.

Furthermore, not all legislation aimed at giving women equal legal rights has been supported by the public. In 1982 the Equal Rights Amendment, which would have prohibited state and federal laws that create unequal opportunities for men and women, was defeated. The defeat of the ERA is a classic example of how powerful the control of perceptions of reality and definitions of situations can be, as discussed in Chapter 3. The amendment consisted of a single sentence: "Equality of rights under the law shall not be denied or abridged by the United States or any State on account of sex." Opponents claimed the amendment would destroy society by, among other things, integrating public bathrooms, forcing women to fight in the military, and disrupting the family. One group called the amendment one of "the most destructive pieces of legislation ever to pass Congress" and referred to feminists as "moral perverts" and "enemies of every decent society" (Spretnak, 1982). Supporters of the ERA can take some comfort in the fact that, despite the act's demise, women's opportunities have expanded over the past two decades.

Sexism and Family

Much of the gender inequality found in the law revolves around the traditional family role of women as keepers of the household and as producers, nurturers, and socializers of children. Although in other times and places women have had different levels of responsibility for homemaking, they have always retained responsibility for reproduction; it is one of the few areas where women can exert tremendous societal influence (Rowland, 1990).

Reproductive Rights and Responsibilities. Motherhood has always been considered the pinnacle of a woman's social identity and her God-given and socially expected duty. This role can be the source of pride, joy, and a sense of accomplishment, but it can also be the source of pain, exploitation, and discrimination.

Consider how our society allocates responsibility for preventing pregnancy. Birth control techniques have been around for centuries (condoms, withdrawal, abortion, and so on) (Schwartz & Rutter, 1998). But not until the 1960s did innovations such as the intrauterine device (IUD) and the birth control pill give women themselves significant control over reproduction. This gain in control, however, was tempered by a parallel increase in responsibility. Women have always borne the greater burden of unwanted pregnancy, but now they also have almost exclusive responsibility for taking steps to prevent it. Women have become the gatekeepers of sexuality. Hence the issue of reproductive control has come to be seen as a women's issue and not a human issue (Schwartz & Rutter, 1998).

Women's right to choose *not* to bear children, through universal access to safe, legal contraception and abortion, has been the most visible aspect of the fight over reproductive rights. However, the issue of reproductive choice is much more complicated. Although most cultures continue to hold reproduction in high esteem and encourage most married women to "be fruitful and multiply," the reproductive capacities of some women—namely, poor or minority women—are often blamed by politicians and social critics for an increase in poverty and an alleged rise in immorality in society (Thomas, 1998). Poor women—both married and nonmarried—may be accused of bearing children for the purposes of increasing a welfare check, of being sexually out of control, and of causing their own poverty (Murray, 1994).

In several states, lawmakers have passed or attempted to pass legislation requiring poor women to use certain contraceptives, sterilization, or family planning services as a condition for receiving public assistance (Thomas, 1998). In 1990 a Kansas representative introduced a bill to authorize free Norplant implants (a contraceptive device that consists of tiny rods surgically implanted under the skin of a woman's arm, which remains effective for five years) and $500 "insertion bonuses" for all poor women on welfare. By 1995, 70 similar bills had been proposed in 35 states, most offering financial incentives to women on welfare who use Norplant or making its use a condition of receiving welfare payments.

Technological advances in infertility treatments have also complicated the issue of reproductive rights for women. Recent developments such as fertility drugs, artificial insemination, in vitro fertilization, and surrogate motherhood have allowed thousands of infertile women to conceive children. Although access to such procedures is limited primarily to the affluent—some procedures can cost as much as $20,000—these techniques have the potential of increasing reproductive choices and opportunities (B. K. Rothman, 1987; Rowland, 1990). Ironically, such advances, coupled with the U.S. culture's inability to accept infertility, may actually take reproductive control away from women who choose not to have children. If infertility is seen as a "curable" condition, those who don't enthusiastically pursue all possible "cures" can be looked at with suspicion.

Increased technological intervention into the processes by which women conceive has also allowed the medical profession to solidify its control over the reproductive process (Rowland, 1990; Woliver, 1989). Because of the cultural value placed on having children, fertility research has faced virtually no criticism and has been allowed to expand with little community debate (Rowland, 1990). After all, who would criticize research that could provide infertile couples with the miracle of a baby? Consequently, the predominantly male field of high-tech fertility is flourishing. In only a decade the industry has grown from 30 clinics to more than 300. It is a $350-million-a-year business that is largely exempt from government regulation and immune to the downward pressure on costs that insurance companies exert (Gabriel, 1996). At some hospitals, fertility doctors earn more than the hospitals' presidents.

Unfortunately, women are the ones who serve as experimental subjects in this research. Instead of being seen as individual people, they often become objects, "alternative reproductive vehicles," "human incubators," or "uterine environments" within which "harvested" eggs can be planted (Raymond, 1993). Women must also face most of the emotional and physical risks, including infection, painful side effects, permanent physical injury, and the heartbreak of failure.

Another reproductive issue that affects women disproportionately is the growing institutional emphasis on fetal rights. Women, far more than men, are seen to have a moral, societal, and legal responsibility to ensure a healthy birth. Consequently, pregnant women are sometimes denied the rights of bodily integrity and self-determination that all other competent adults in this society are granted (Tavris, 1992). For example, a Washington, DC, judge ordered a pregnant woman seriously ill with cancer to undergo a cesarean section against her wishes and those of her husband, her parents, and her doctor, in order to save the life of her 25-week-old fetus. She and the fetus died during the procedure, which was performed hastily, before her lawyers could appeal. In addition, since the late 1980s hundreds of women have been prosecuted for behavior while pregnant that posed a danger to their fetuses, the vast majority of cases involving the use of illegal drugs (Terry, 1996). Even more have been jailed during pregnancy (referred to as "protective incarceration") or deprived of custody of their newborns (D. E. Roberts, 1991).

From an institutional perspective, making pregnant women solely responsible for the well-being of fetuses allows us to ignore other dangers and other threats to children that lie outside the mother's body—poverty, inadequate health care, limited access to prenatal care, poor housing, environmental hazards, racism, and so on.

Housework and the Domestic Division of Labor. One of the major consequences of the Industrial Revolution of the 18th and 19th centuries was the separation of the workplace and the home. Prior to industrialization, most countries were primarily agricultural. People's lives centered around the farm, where husbands and wives were partners not only in making a home but also in making a living (Vanek, 1980). The farm couple was interdependent; each needed the other for survival. It was taken for granted that women provided for the family along with men (Bernard, 1981). Although the relationship between husbands and wives on the farm was never entirely equal—wives still did most if not all of the housekeeping and family care—complete male dominance was offset by women's indispensable contributions to the household economy (Vanek, 1980).

With the advent of industrialization, things began to change. New forms of technology and the promise of new financial opportunities and a good living drew people (mostly men) away from the farms and into cities and factories. For the first time in history, the family economy in some societies was based outside the household. Women no longer found themselves involved in the day-to-day supervision of the family's business as they had once been. Instead, they were consigned to the only domestic responsibilities that remained necessary in an industrial economy: the care and nurturing of children and the maintenance of the household. Because this work was unpaid and because visible goods were no longer being produced at home, women quickly found that their work was devalued (Hareven, 1992).

It's important to note however, that men weren't the only ones who left home each day to work in factories. At the turn of the century, hundreds of thousands of children worked in mines, mills, and factories (Coontz, 1992). And contrary to popular belief, one-fifth of U.S. women worked outside the home in 1900 (Staggenborg, 1998). Moreover, the separation of work and home varied along class lines. Poor women rarely had the luxury of being stay-at-home spouses and parents. In 1880 in the United States, for example, 73% of single black women and 35% of married black women reported paid jobs—compared to 23% of single white women and 7% of married white women (Kessler-Harris, 1982).

Today the devaluation of "women's work" is the result of a separation of the public and private spheres (Sidel, 1990). As long as men dominate the public sphere, the marketplace and the government, they will wield greater economic and political power within society and also be able to translate that power into authority at home.

"Women's work" within the relatively powerless private sphere of the home will continue to be hidden and be considered of little social value.

According to conflict theory, the problem is not that housewives don't work; it's that they work for free outside the mainstream economy, in which work is strictly defined as something one is paid to do (Ciancanelli & Berch, 1987; Voyandoff, 1990). Ironically, however, domestic work is actually invaluable to the entire economic system. If a woman were paid the minimum going rate for all her labor as mother and housekeeper—child care, transportation, errands, cleaning, laundry, cooking, bill paying, grocery shopping, and so on—her yearly salary would be over $35,000, more than the average salary of male full-time workers ("Mom's market value," 1998). But because societal and family power are a function of who brings home the cash, such work does not afford women the prestige it might if it were paid labor.

Despite significant shifts in attitudes toward gender roles and the accelerated entry of women into the paid labor force in the past few decades, housework continues to be predominantly female (Baxter, 1997; Brines, 1994). Husbands do play a more prominent role in the raising of children than they did two decades ago, and they've increased their contribution to housework (Bianchi, Milkie, Sayer, & Robinson, 2000). However, research consistently shows that U.S. women still spend more time on housework and child-rearing activities than men do (Cowan, 1991; Levant, Slatter, & Loiselle, 1987), although the gap is shrinking. On average, men are responsible for between 20% and 35% of the domestic work (Shelton & John, 1996).

Moreover, the household work that husbands do tends to be quite different from the work that wives do. Men's chores have typically been infrequent, irregular, or optional:

> They take out the garbage, they mow the lawns, they play with children, they occasionally go to the supermarket or shop for household durables, they paint the attic or fix the faucet; but by and large, they do not launder, clean, or cook, nor do they feed, clothe, bathe, or transport children. These . . . most time-consuming activities . . . are exclusively the domain of women. (Cowan, 1991, p. 207)

From a structural-functionalist perspective, one could argue that traditional gender disparities in household responsibilities actually reflect an equitable, functional, interdependent division of labor. That is, the husband works in the paid labor force and supports the family financially; the wife takes care of the household work and child care. Each person provides essential services in exchange for those provided by the other. If both partners work full time, as is the case for most U.S. couples today, we would expect housework to be shared equally.

But research in this area indicates that the gender discrepancy in housework responsibilities does not diminish when women work full time. Several national studies have found that, on average, U.S. women who work full time outside the home spend more than 33 hours a week on housework compared to 18 hours a week for their working husbands (Lennon & Rosenfield, 1994; South & Spitze, 1994). The discrepancy is especially large among married couples, as Exhibit 12.1 shows.

Because working women continue to be primarily responsible for housework, they often end up working what amounts to two full-time jobs. Even when a husband is

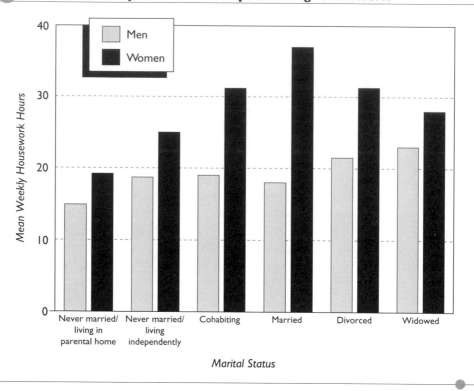

Exhibit 12.1 **Discrepancies in Time Spent Doing Housework**

Source: South & Spitze, 1994.

unemployed, he does much less housework than a wife who puts in a 40-hour week. Interestingly, couples who profess egalitarian, nonsexist values experience this discrepancy. Husbands who say that all the housework should be shared still spend significantly less time doing it than their wives (Blumstein & Schwartz, 1983).

Men's aversion to housework may be so intense that it can sour a relationship. The more housework married men do, the more conflict there is in the marriage (Blumstein & Schwartz, 1983). Such a pattern may serve as a significant barrier to the reorganization of gender roles within the family. The fact that housework is still predominantly women's work gives us some sense of how pervasive and powerful our sexist ideology continues to be.

Sexism and Education

Another institutional setting in which gender inequality exists is education. Globally, girls lag behind boys in educational opportunities. In most countries they are less likely than boys to be enrolled in school. Consequently two-thirds of illiterate people in the world are female (Jacobsen, 1994).

In the United States, girls tend to do better in school than boys. U.S. boys are more likely than girls to repeat a grade, drop out, be put in special education, or be diagnosed as having an emotional problem, a learning disability, or attention-deficit disorder (Lewin, 1998b). Nevertheless, schools still tend to promote male experiences by encouraging curiosity, independence, and initiative in boys and restrict female experiences by discouraging exploration and stressing "proper" behavior in girls (Block, 1983). Consequently, despite their poorer overall academic performance relative to girls, boys have higher expectations and higher self-esteem than girls, a gap that widens with each passing year in the school system. According to one study, around the ages of 8 and 9 about two-thirds of both boys and girls report feeling confident and positive about themselves. By high school, however, the percentage drops to 29% for young women (Freiberg, 1991).

As girls make the transformation from childhood to adolescence, they are faced with a conflict between the way they see themselves and the way others, particularly teachers, see them (Gilligan, 1990). In fact, gender biases in the way male and female students are treated continue to permeate the institution of education:

> Sitting in the same classroom, reading the same textbook, listening to the same teacher, boys and girls receive very different educations. From grade school through graduate school female students are more likely to be invisible members of classrooms. Teachers interact with males more frequently, ask them better questions, and give them more precise and helpful feedback. Over the course of years the uneven distribution of teacher time, energy, attention, and talent . . . takes its toll on girls. Since gender bias is not a noisy problem, most people are unaware of the secret sexist lessons and quiet losses they engender. (Sadker & Sadker, 1999, p. 343)

Concern over these tendencies has led some school districts around the country to create sex-segregated classrooms—particularly in math and science—where girls are able to work without the anxiety and threats to esteem they often feel in sex-mixed classrooms (Hancock & Kalb, 1996). Although many girls prefer such classes and report feeling more confident in them about traditionally male subjects, it's unclear whether they are emerging with measurably better academic skills (Lewin, 1998a).

Similar gender-typed patterns continue through high school. Teenage boys derive their prestige almost exclusively from athletics. Indeed, boys' sense of their own masculinity tends to be derived from participation in organized sports (Messner, 1990). Boys are also likely to be encouraged by counselors and teachers to formulate ambitious career goals. In contrast, prestige and popularity for teenage girls are more likely to come from their physical appearance and from having a boyfriend (Lott, 1987). As a consequence, according to the College Board, the gap between boys' SAT scores and girls' SAT scores has not closed over the past three decades (King, 1999). Not surprisingly, girls' career aspirations tend to be lower than those of their male classmates (Bridges, 1988) despite girls' academic achievement, which is usually higher than that of boys.

Since 1980, more women have been enrolled in U.S. colleges than men (although more men than women go on for advanced degrees) (U.S. Bureau of the Census, 2000b). However, many of the majors that lead to high-paying or high-prestige careers remain predominantly male (engineering, economics, mathematics, earth sciences, and so on), whereas women are concentrated in such fields as nursing, literature, education, and library science. But other fields, such as medicine, law, and business, have become "desegregated" in recent years (Brint, 1998). Hence there is reason to believe that in the future gender will become a less significant factor in determining people's educational tracks.

Sexism and the Economy

Because of their difficulty converting educational achievements into high pay, women have historically been prevented from taking advantage of the occupational opportunities and rewards that most men have had free access to. Although the size of the gap varies, in most countries around the world, women have higher poverty rates than men (Casper, McLanahan, & Garfinkel, 1994). Today women continue to have much less earning power in the labor market than men (Blood, Tuttle, & Lakey, 1992).

The unequal economic status of women not only results from personal expressions of sexism but is tied to larger economic structures and institutional forces. The standard assumptions that drive the typical workplace often work against women. Think of the things one generally has to do in order to be considered a good worker by a boss—work extra hours, travel to faraway business meetings, go to conferences, attend training programs, be willing to work unpopular shifts, or entertain out-of-town clients. These activities assume people have the time and the freedom from familial obligations to do them. Because women, especially mothers, still tend to have the lion's share of responsibility at home, they have more difficulty making time for these activities and therefore are less able to "prove" to management that they are good, committed employees. Because of built-in assumptions about what one needs to do to get ahead, women are less likely than men to possess the qualities commonly associated with an "ideal worker."

Consider the different reactions employers commonly have toward their male and female employees getting married. For a man, marriage is likely to be seen as a "stabilizing" influence. From the point of view of management, his "settling down" will make him a better, more dependable worker. He might even need a raise, because fatherhood is probably looming not far down the road.

But for women, marriage is still likely to be seen as disruptive to their careers. The employer may jump to the conclusion that a newly married woman will soon be seeking maternity leave or quitting altogether. Rather than making her a more dependable worker, marriage actually may make her less dependable in the eyes of management. These beliefs can subtly influence hiring and promotion decisions even in those employers who advocate gender equality (Reskin & Hartmann, 1986).

Gender Segregation in the Workplace. In view of the persistence of institutional sexism, U.S. women have made remarkable progress in overcoming traditional obstacles to employment. Today, 69% of single women and 61% of married women work in the paid labor force and close to half of all U.S. workers today are female. In addition, 36% of all U.S. businesses are owned by women (U.S. Bureau of the Census, 2000b).

Exhibit 12.2   **American Women in Managerial and Professional Jobs**

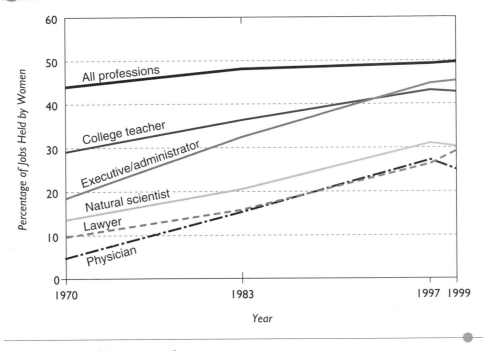

Source: U.S. Bureau of the Census, 2000b.

These workers make a significant economic contribution to their families. In one U.S. survey, more than 50% of employed women said they provided at least half of their household income, and 18% said they were their household's sole provider (cited in Lewin, 1995a). The increase in female labor force participation has been particularly dramatic in such male-dominated fields as engineering, medicine, law, and administration. For instance, in 1983 15% of lawyers in the United States were women; by 1999 29% of lawyers were women. During that same period, the proportion of female physicians increased from 16% to 24.5% (U.S. Bureau of the Census, 2000b). Exhibit 12.2 shows the increase in the percentages of U.S. women holding positions in a variety of professional occupations.

Although such figures are encouraging, segregation in the workplace on the basis of gender is still the rule and not the exception. According to the U.S. Bureau of the Census (2000b), women constitute 99% of all secretaries, 93% of all registered nurses, 97% of all child care workers, 99% of all dental hygienists, and 75% of all teachers, excluding those in colleges and universities. Despite their increased presence in traditionally male occupations, women still account for only 17% of all dentists, 25% of all physicians, 11% of all engineers, 29% of all lawyers and judges, and 17% of all police officers. About two-thirds of U.S. men and women would have to change jobs today to achieve equal gender distribution across occupations, a figure that was the same in 1900 (Philipson, 1993).

Most of the changes that have taken place in the gender distribution of different occupations have been the result of women entering male lines of work. Although women have entered traditionally male occupations at a steady clip since the 1970s, men have not noticeably increased their representation in female-dominated occupations. The number of male nurses, kindergarten teachers, librarians, and secretaries has increased only minimally, if at all (U.S. Bureau of the Census, 2000b). One study found that some men would rather suffer unemployment than accept "women's jobs," even if they were high-paying ones, because of the potential damage to their sense of masculinity (Epstein, 1989).

This kind of "one-way" occupational shift may cause problems in the long run. Historically, when large numbers of women enter a particular occupation previously closed to them, the number of men in that occupation decreases. Given the fact that greater value is usually awarded to male pursuits, such occupations become less prestigious as men leave them. In fact, the higher the proportion of female workers in an occupation, the less both male and female workers earn in that occupation (Reskin & Padavic, 1994).

But greater female entry into a traditionally male line of work doesn't necessarily mean gender equality either. A report by the American Bar Association states that the average annual incomes of women lawyers are significantly lower than men's at every level of experience and in all types of legal practice (cited in N. Bernstein, 1996). Female lawyers are often given low-status projects to work on, which are not only less interesting but also a professional dead end. Hence, their rate of promotion is lower than that of their male counterparts, and they remain underrepresented in such high positions as judges on the federal courts, district courts, and circuit courts of appeals.

Gender segregation within occupations is still strong. For instance, though half of all assemblers in the U.S. manufacturing industry are now women—a fact that suggests occupational integration—they comprise 75% of electrical assemblers but only 17% of motor vehicle assemblers, which is a higher-paying job (Reskin & Hartmann, 1986). Furthermore, when women occupy managerial positions in manufacturing plants, the workers they supervise are predominantly female (Carrington & Troske, 1998). In the field of medicine, female physicians are substantially overrepresented in such specialties as pediatrics, obstetrics, and gynecology and underrepresented in more prestigious and lucrative areas such as neurosurgery. For instance, 70% of obstetrics/gynecology residents today are women (Lewin, 2001). Similarly, women who work as sales clerks in department stores are likely to be in the lower-paying departments (for example, clothing and housewares), whereas men are likely to be in the more lucrative departments (for example, furniture and large appliances). In 1997, Home Depot, the home improvement discount chain, paid $87.5 million to settle a lawsuit brought by female employees who claimed they were systematically relegated to cash register jobs rather than given higher-paying sales positions.

Such within-occupation segregation reinforces gender stereotypes. A study of jobs in a McDonald's restaurant found that despite roughly the same number of male and female workers, most of the women worked at the counter or the drive-up window and most of the men worked at the grill. Many of the workers found this arrangement unremarkable. They simply assumed that women were more interested in working with people and that the job requirements of smiling and showing deference to customers were best suited to a feminine style of interaction (Leidner, 1991).

In sum, we continue to have one set of jobs that employs almost exclusively women and another that employs almost exclusively men. Such segregation has consequences that extend beyond its mere existence (Reskin & Hartmann, 1986). When people are allocated jobs on the basis of gender rather than ability to perform the work, chances for self-fulfillment are limited. Society also loses because neither men nor women are free to do the jobs for which they might best be suited. Gender segregation thus represents a failure of the economy to use the available labor force most efficiently. However, segregation is most harmful to individual women, because the occupations they predominantly hold tend to be less desirable than those held predominantly by men. In particular, occupational segregation contributes to the lower wages earned by women.

The Wage Gap

> The Lord spoke to Moses and said, "When a man makes a special vow to the Lord which requires your valuation of living persons, a male between twenty and sixty years old shall be valued at fifty silver shekels. If it is a female, she shall be valued at thirty shekels." (Leviticus 27:1–4)

You don't have to go back to the Bible to find evidence of the practice of setting women's pay at about three-fifths that of men's. Even though the 1963 Equal Pay Act guaranteed equal pay for equal work in the United States, and Title VII of the 1964 Civil Rights Act banned job discrimination on the basis of sex (as well as race, religion, and national origin), the gender gap in earnings persists. In 1973, for instance, U.S. women on average earned only 56.6 cents for every dollar a man earned. Advances in work experience and job-related skills have enabled some women—particularly middle- and upper-class women—to improve their income levels relative to men's. However, obvious discrepancies remain. In 1998, the average earnings for all U.S. men working full time, year-round was $36,476. All women working full time, year-round earned an average salary of $26,324 per year (U.S. Bureau of the Census, 2000a). To put it another way, for every dollar a U.S. white man earns, a woman still earns only about 72 cents. The differences are even more pronounced for African-American women, who earn 63 cents for every dollar a white man earns, and Hispanic women, who earn just 53 cents. Some sociologists argue that the wage gap has narrowed somewhat in recent years not because women's earning power has improved but only because men's has worsened (Bernhardt, Morris, & Handcock, 1995).

I should point out that the wage gap is a global phenomenon. To varying degrees, in every country around the world, men earn more than women. In the developing countries of Latin America, Africa, and Asia, women commonly earn 25% or less of what men earn (Tiano, 1987). In Korea and Japan, women earn barely half of men's income. The recent economic crisis in Asia has put an even tighter squeeze on the earnings of Asian women. In some countries, however, such as France, Sweden, Australia, and Denmark, the wage gap is actually much narrower than it is in the United States, with women earning 80% to 90% of what men earn (Reskin & Padavic, 1994).

Multinational corporations frequently export a wage gap abroad by paying female factory workers in developing countries as little as half of what they pay men. In many countries, women comprise more than three-quarters of unskilled assembly workers. This preference for women is sometimes rationalized by the belief that they have a high tolerance for monotonous work, an inherent dexterity that suits tasks involving tiny parts, and a docile nature that allows them to withstand the pressure of closely supervised production (Tiano, 1987).

Why does the wage gap continue to exist? One reason, of course, is occupational segregation and the types of jobs women are most likely to have. Studies suggest that occupational segregation accounts for about 40% of the gender differences in average earnings (Reskin & Hartmann, 1986). For the five "most female" jobs in the United States (that is, those more than 96% female)—which are secretary, receptionist, preschool teacher, dental assistant, and private house cleaner—the average weekly salary is $336. For the five "most male" jobs (those less than 3% female)—which are airplane pilot, aerospace engineer, aircraft mechanic, firefighter, and miner—the average weekly salary is $862 (U.S. Bureau of Labor Statistics, 1999; U.S. Bureau of the Census, 1998b).

Some economists and policymakers argue that the wage gap is essentially an institutional by-product that exists because men on the whole have more work experience, more training, and higher education than women. However, gender differences in education, labor force experience, and seniority—factors that might justify discrepancies in salary—account for less than 15% of the wage gap between men and women (National Committee on Pay Equity, 1999). For instance, the average income of full-time female workers in the United States is significantly lower than that of men with the same level of education or training. In fact, women with a bachelor's degree can expect to earn only slightly more than men with only a high school diploma (mean annual earnings of $31,452 for college-educated women compared to $28,742 for high school–educated men). Similarly women with doctoral degrees (mean annual earnings of $54,552) actually earn slightly less than men with bachelor's degrees (mean annual earnings of $55,057) (U.S. Bureau of the Census, 2000b). These statistics are depicted in Exhibit 12.3.

Broader economic causes also contribute to the wage gap. Because of the types of occupations women tend to have, their labor force participation is more likely to be determined by the fluctuating needs of the economy. More than two-thirds of temporary and part-time workers in this country are women ("Ten facts about women workers," 1997). During hard times, these workers are the first ones pushed out of employment—not because they're women but because their jobs are the most expendable.

One possible remedy for the wage gap is increasing women's access to occupations that have traditionally been closed to them. As I noted earlier, this is already happening, to a certain degree, although gender segregation is still the rule, not the exception.

A second solution is symbolized by the commonly heard phrase "equal pay for equal work." This approach seeks to overcome situations in which men and women in the same job, with the same seniority, performing the same work equally well, are paid differently. Such gaps would seem easy enough to spot and address. However, they still persist. For instance, female servers in restaurants make about $50 a week less than male servers; female secretaries make about $100 less per week than male secretaries.

Exhibit 12.3 **The Gap between Women's and Men's Pay**

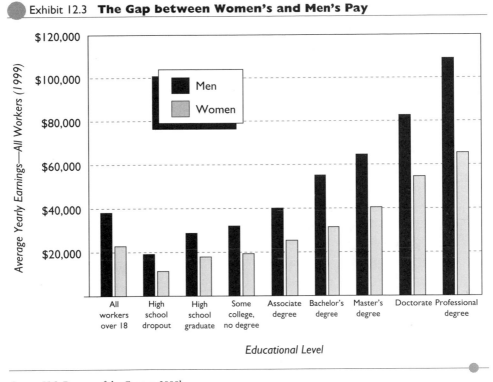

Source: U.S. Bureau of the Census, 2000b.

Female lawyers make about $300 less per week and female doctors $500 less per week than men (National Committee on Pay Equity, 1999).

A third, more controversial, approach is **comparable worth,** or **pay equity.** The principle behind this remedy is that the pay for particular jobs shouldn't be less simply because those jobs happen to be filled predominantly by women. Unlike "equal pay for equal work," comparable worth advocates claim that *different* jobs that are of equal value to society and require equal levels of training ought to have equal pay. This principle rejects the premise that women's work is inherently worth less than men's. The ultimate goal is to raise the wages of underpaid, female-dominated occupations (England, 1999). Various states have established job evaluation formulas to determine the comparability of certain occupations and whether wage disparities are discriminating against women. But political opposition to comparable worth policies has seriously weakened such initiatives on the national level and it remains a strategy with mixed results.

The Global Devaluation of Women

At first glance, women may seem to be making tremendous advances worldwide—becoming more economically independent, better educated, and more involved in national politics than ever before. Over the past several decades women in most regions of the world have increased their representation in most sectors of the paid labor force (see Exhibit 12.4).

Exhibit 12.4 **Women's Participation in Major Occupational Groups, by Region**

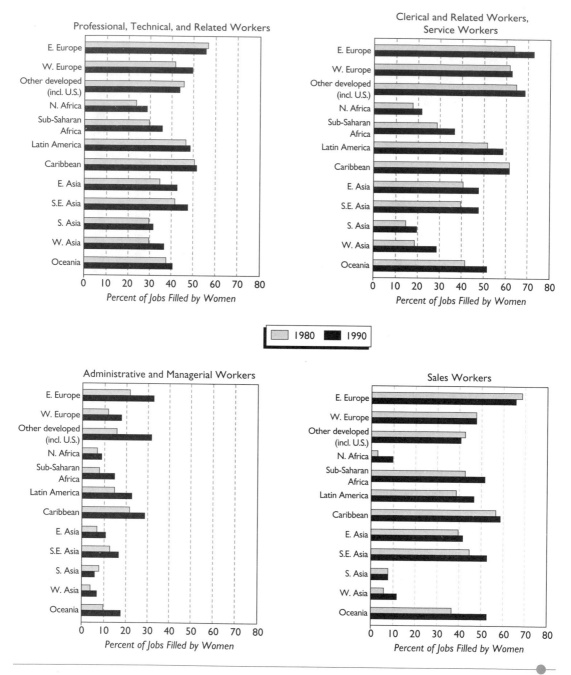

Source: United Nations, 1995.

Nevertheless, anthropologists agree that most societies around the world devalue women to some extent (Stockard & Johnson, 1992). Sociological research supports that view. Women represent 70% of the 1.3 billion people living in poverty worldwide, even though they work an average of 13% more hours than men in every country, not to mention their unpaid labor in the home ("Vital signs," 1995). About 585,000 women around the world die each year in pregnancy and childbirth, and perhaps as many as 18 million more suffer debilitating illnesses or injuries as a consequence of childbearing (Crossette, 1996b). Women make up the vast majority of global factory workers in multinational corporations, often working under unsafe and unhealthy conditions at extremely low pay. And violence against women and girls—from sexual abuse and wife battering in the United States to wife burning in India and "honor killings" of rape victims in the Middle East—remains a global epidemic.

In some societies female devaluation is pervasive and has extreme consequences. For example, in 1996 the Taliban, a radical fundamentalist Islamic movement, took control of Afghanistan. Before the takeover, women accounted for 70% of Afghanistan's teachers, 50% of its civil servants, and 40% of its physicians. The Taliban immediately issued edicts forbidding women to work outside the home, attend school, or leave their homes unless accompanied by a husband, father, brother, or son. They were not permitted to wear white socks—because white is the color of the Taliban flag—or to wear shoes that make noise as they walk. Such restrictions had a profound effect on women's physical and mental health. About 62% of Afghani women experienced a decline in access to health care after the takeover. Most were so frightened of being flogged or beaten in the streets that they were often reluctant to seek what little help was available to them. One study found that 86% of Afghan women showed signs of anxiety, and 97% demonstrated evidence of major depression (Rasekh, Bauer, Manos, & Iacopino, 1998).

In many developing countries, families short on food commonly make sure that male children get more food than female children, even though their nutritional needs are the same. As a result, girls tend to grow up sicker. Many female babies are so undernourished that they die within the first year (Bryjak & Soroka, 1992). In addition, land laws often dictate that a family's property can be passed down only through males. A daughter's inheritance automatically goes to her husband on marriage. Furthermore, widows often have no inheritance rights in property owned by their husbands and thus may lose their homes, the land they've worked on, and their household possessions when their husbands die (Owen, 1996).

In Ghana, girls are routinely given by their families to work as slaves in religious shrines as a way of appeasing the gods for crimes committed by relatives. In one case, a girl was enslaved to atone for the rape that led to her birth (her father had raped a young niece). Once given to a priest, the girl is considered his property and he is free to do as he wishes with her (French, 1997).

The cultural devaluation of women worldwide often turns violent:

- In many Arab countries women suspected of being adulterous are sometimes killed by their own relatives to cleanse the family's honor. In fact, women accused of sexual misconduct are often jailed, not to punish them but to protect them from being killed by their own families (Jehl, 1999). In Pakistan, women are often killed for marrying against their father's wishes.

- In Bangladesh, some men—usually spurned suitors—throw acid on the faces of women. Those who survive the attacks are typically left hideously deformed. One woman was forced by her parents to marry her attacker because they felt no one else would want to marry her. Most attackers are never arrested, and most who are arrested are never tried (Bearak, 2000).

- One of the most pernicious forms of wife abuse—known locally as "bride burning" or "dowry death"—takes place in India (Heise, 1989; Van Willigen & Channa, 1991). Dowry traditionally encompassed the gifts that a woman received from her parents on marriage. Even though it was officially banned in 1961, dowry is still an essential part of premarital negotiations and now encompasses the wealth that the bride's family pays the groom. Young brides, who by custom live with their new husbands' parents, are commonly subjected to severe abuse if promised money is not paid. Sometimes dowry harassment ends in suicide or murder. In 1998 about 7,000 wives—an average of 19 a day—were killed by their husbands for not providing adequate dowries ("Bridal dowry in India," 2000).

But the public devaluation of women can sometimes hide a very different private reality. In India, for instance, rural, lower-caste women still occupy the lowest rungs of society. Yet approximately one million of these women have been elected in recent years to the 500,000 or so *panchayat*, or village councils, that were established in 1993 to help rural villages deal with local political issues (Dugger, 1999b).

Likewise, Japanese women have historically occupied a visibly subservient position in society and in families. A woman may still walk several steps behind her husband so as not to offend his dignity by stepping on his shadow (Kristof, 1995). Wives are legally prohibited from using different surnames from their husbands'. Women in the workforce suffer discrimination in hiring, salary, and promotion despite an equal opportunity law. Yet even though women are still expected to clean, cook, and tend to the needs of their husbands within the home, many Japanese wives dominate their husbands completely, often referring to them as "oversize trash." Typically, they control the household finances, giving their husbands monthly allowances as they see fit. Many wives refuse to give their husbands cash cards for the family account. If a man wants to withdraw money from the account, the savings bank will usually phone the wife to get her approval. Japanese men are even starting to take on some of the housework responsibilities, a development that would have been unthinkable a decade ago. One man summed up the situation this way: "Things go best when the husband is swimming in the palm of his wife's hand" (quoted in Kristof, 1995, p. A6).

To some extent, the improvement of women's lives in some parts the world can be attributed to the forces of globalization, which are spreading democratic values and humanitarian principles. However, the globalization of the world economy also helps create a market for the international exploitation of women. In many poor countries—especially those in the former Soviet bloc—forcing naïve and desperate women into prostitution has become one of the fastest-growing criminal enterprises. As many as 500,000 women are estimated to be trafficked each year into Western Europe alone

(Specter, 1998b). Desperately seeking solutions to their hopelessness, these women are easily lured by ads that claim to be recruiting young women for work abroad as models, secretaries, dancers, and so on. In the interest of helping their families, they go. The prostitution rings are able to thrive because local police forces are not interested in stopping the flow of young foreign women into their countries. In many of these receiving countries prostitution is not illegal; in others it may be illegal, but enforcement is inconsistent and punishment light. Without any other means of support and often without knowledge of the native language, these women become completely dependent on men who are perfectly willing to exploit them.

A more positive example of the effects of globalization on women's lives is the international movement for women's rights. The effort to focus attention on violence against women and to pressure governments to pass protective laws has gained strength in recent years. In the past few years, several countries (for example, Egypt) have outlawed the traditional practice of female genital mutilation. Ironically, the United States has maintained an ambivalent stance toward this movement. It is the only developed country in the world that has not ratified the U.N. Convention on the Elimination of All Forms of Discrimination Against Women, despite its advocacy of human rights worldwide. Opponents in the United States feel that such a treaty would set a dangerous precedent by overruling local, state, and federal law.

CONCLUSION

Inequality based on gender goes beyond the degrading media and cultural images of women, the face-to-face interactions that reinforce the devaluation of women, and the stereotypes of individual people. It is woven into the institutional and cultural fabric of society. It is commonplace throughout the world and is as much a part of the U.S. scene as baseball, apple pie, and the Fourth of July. Every woman has felt sexism at some level, whether as personal violence, sexually suggestive leers and comments, fear of going out at night, job discrimination, legal obstacles, or subtle encouragement toward "appropriate" sports, hobbies, and careers.

Men tend to benefit from living in a society where language, identity, intimacy, history, culture, and social institutions are built on gender distinctions, even if the men themselves do not support such inequality. Thus, most men don't see gender inequality as their problem; it's a "women's issue." Like most people whose interests are being served by the system, men are largely unaware of the small and large advantages the social structure provides them (W. J. Goode, 1981). Therefore men are less likely to see a need for large-scale social change.

So the first step toward gender equality is that men will have to come to understand their role in the process, even in the absence of blatant, personal sexism. All men are tacitly involved in the oppression of women each time they automatically giggle at sexist jokes, mistake female doctors for nurses, see women in purely physical terms, expect less from women on the job or in school, or expect more of them at home.

The next step will require a fundamental transformation of institutional patterns and cultural values. Such a solution sounds too massive to be possible. But today we are seeing early steps in that direction: changing conceptions of family roles, women's increasing (though not yet equal) labor force participation, their growing (but not yet equal) political power, and greater awareness of sexual exploitation and violence worldwide. How far these changes will take us in the future remains to be seen.

YOUR TURN

To understand how beliefs are translated into action, examine how sexism influences people's activities. One fruitful area of examination is the home. Locate a few of each of the following types of couples in which both partners work full time outside the home:

- Newly married without children (married less than 1 year)
- Married without children (married 10 years or more)
- Married (older or younger) with at least one child living at home
- Cohabiting (heterosexual or homosexual)
- Remarried

Ask each person in the couple to make a list of all the household chores that need to be done during the course of a week. Ask each to be as specific and exhaustive as possible (for example, "cleaning windows" rather than "cleaning the house"). After the lists are completed, ask each person to indicate which of these tasks he or she is primarily responsible for, which his or her partner is responsible for, and which are shared. Ask the participants also to estimate the total amount of time spent each week on all these tasks combined. Finally, ask them if they work for pay as well and, if so, about how many hours they work during a typical week. (*Note:* To ensure that you're gauging each individual's perceptions, interview each partner separately.)

Compare people's responses to see if you can find any differences—in terms of time spent doing housework and the number of tasks for which each one is responsible—between

- Partners in the same couple
- Men and women
- Younger and older couples
- Married and cohabiting couples
- Couples with and without children at home
- Married and remarried couples
- Heterosexual and homosexual couples

Do women who work outside the home still bear the primary responsibility for housework? Is the traditional gender division of labor not the case for certain types of couples? How does the presence of children affect the household division of labor? If partners in the same couple have different ideas about housework responsibilities, to what do you attribute this lack of agreement? Describe the tensions that men and women experience when trying to balance work and home responsibilities.

CHAPTER HIGHLIGHTS

● Personal sexism is most apparent during the course of everyday interaction in the form of communication patterns and gestures. It can be particularly dangerous when expressed in the form of sexual harassment and sexual violence.

● Gender stratification is perpetuated by a dominant cultural ideology that devalues women on the basis of inherent biological differences between men and women. This ideology overlooks the equally important role of social forces in determining male and female behavior.

● Institutional sexism exists in the media, in the law, in the family, in the educational system, and in economics. Women have entered the paid labor force in unprecedented numbers but they still tend to occupy jobs that are typically considered "female" and still earn significantly less than men.

● Not only are social institutions sexist in that women are systematically segregated, exploited, and excluded, they are also "gendered." Institutions themselves are structured along gender lines so that traits associated with success are usually stereotypically male characteristics: tough-mindedness, rationality, assertiveness, competitiveness, and so forth.

● Despite recent advances worldwide, women still tend to suffer physically, psychologically, economically, and politically in most societies.

KEY TERMS

comparable worth (pay equity) Principle that women and men who perform jobs that are of equal value to society and that require equal training ought to be paid equally

institutional sexism Subordination of women that is part of the everyday workings of economics, law, politics, and other social institutions

objectification Practice of treating people as objects

patriarchy Male-dominated society in which cultural beliefs and values give higher prestige and value to men than to women

sexism System of beliefs that asserts the inferiority of one sex and that justifies gender-based inequality

Gender and Sex in Italian Ads

Douglas Harper

In the past 10 years I have been invited to the University of Bologna on several occasions to teach and do research. During those visits I have had the opportunity to photograph Italian advertising displays. I was struck by how gender is portrayed in advertisements there and wondered about both the effectiveness of the ads and their commentary on the status of men and women in modern Italy. I also wondered how these ads would be perceived by U.S. audiences.

Professor Patrizia Faccioli, a sociologist at the University of Bologna, joined me in exploring this question. We presented photographs of Italian advertising displays to a small number of U.S. and Italian women and then recorded and analyzed their responses. Here I share typical responses to five of the images.

We asked our subjects the following questions:

- Does the ad work for you? Does it compel you to buy the object advertised (or participate in the activity advertised)? What about the ad makes it successful or unsuccessful for you?
- What is the relationship between the men and women in the ad?
- Which gender has greater power in the ad? What is the source of that power?
- Does this ad challenge your identity? Does it make you angry, happy, entertained, glad to be a woman? What other feelings does the ad evoke?

As you look at the ads, think about how you might respond to these questions. Do the images present gender roles that reinforce your own taken-for-granted assumptions? What messages do these ads offer about men and women? After viewing these ads, would you be likely do buy the products or participate in the activities the ads offer? And finally, what is your view of Italy after considering its some of its advertising?

We learned three things from this exercise. First, the way that ads portraying female–male relationships are read is partly a function of culture. Even though U.S. and Italian cultures are fundamentally similar, Italian and U.S. viewers found different elements of the ads effective or objectionable. The Italian viewers were more likely to ascribe an ambiguous meaning to something such as sexual violence, and they were more likely to admire a sexually ambiguous figure such as a transvestite for his courage rather than to scorn him for his sexual deviance.

Second, the same image can produce a vastly different response from within a culture. Many of the ads produced an equal number of strongly positive and strongly negative reactions within the U.S. audience.

Finally, the ads teach us something about the experience of being an Italian rather than from the United States. In Italian culture, sexuality and gender relationships are framed quite differently than in U.S. culture. Even a short analysis of these few responses to the advertising illuminates this difference.

ANTEPRIMA
PER IL CINEMA INDIPENDENTE ITALIANO

6ª RASSEGNA   5/9 LUGLIO 1988

- *Film Festival:* This poster, displayed throughout Bologna for several weeks, advertises a film festival. The positions of the male photographer and female subject reverse the expected pattern of male dominance in these roles.

Women from the United States were divided in their view of the effectiveness of this ad. Those who found the ad convincing felt that it advertised a film festival in which one would see unusual and exotic films:

- The ad is very creative. You aren't going to see the typical roles; it's not going to be the typical movie you'd see on the big screen. You're going to see some very creative, weird stuff. And then there's this little bird here, which is interesting. I don't know what that means.
- The half-clothed image of the woman is great. The suggestion of nudity but not complete nudity. There's a lot beyond that, that can go deeper. That's what they are saying about independent films. *(U.S.)*

However, an equal number of U.S. women were critical of the ad. For example,

- The photo seems pornographic, voyeuristic, harsh, smutty. I wouldn't go to the film festival because it seems it would be full of "shock-value" films. The man has real power because he is getting his kicks from seeing a naked woman. She thinks she has power because he desires her and is at her feet. But she isn't special. He would do the same to any naked woman. I find the ad base and ugly and feel sorry for the woman, who looks used and abused. *(U.S.)*

Italian women, by and large, were less critical of the ad. Several viewers noted that the ad was aimed at a specific audience within Italy, for which nudity indicates artistic and cultural freedom:

- The ad is addressed to a well-educated public, interested in an alternative cinema. The woman fits the message. It is not a provocative nude, it's more an artistic nude. It's not the usual way in which ads use the nude. I like it, I would go to the cinema. *(Italian)*
- It's for a young and refined public. It's not scandalous, it's clean. I don't see any sin in it. There is no relationship between the man and the woman. He is photographing her, but she is looking at the public. She knows he's taking a picture of her, but she looks at us. She has an aggressive personality. I like all this. *(Italian)*

Le donne amano farsi ammirare.

● *Bananas:* This poster, which was ever-present for several weeks in the city of Bologna, sells lingerie by symbolizing sexual attraction (from the point of view of the male) and vulnerability (from the point of view of the female). The relationship between the man and woman is indicated by their postures, gestures, and expressions. The bananas hanging around the belt of the male model appear to be a humorous reference to the penis.

Once again, the U.S. audience was split in their reaction to the ad. Several women were charmed and identified with the strategies of sexual seduction that the ad implies. For example,

● Now this one is fun! I love it! It's soooo fun. It's so fun. It doesn't strike me as, you know, offensive. Their admiration is kind of equal. He's into her; she's into him. It's crazy. [The bananas are] total phallic symbols. It's funny. It's a little kinky. But it's fun. I like it. *(U.S.)*

The half of the U.S. women who were critical of the ad voiced opinions such as the following:

● The ad offends me. It makes me NOT want to buy it. Bananas remind me of penises, which seems like a goofy way to remind people of sex. Man has power over woman because he's clothed, and she's more naked and vulnerable. She's on display for his enjoyment. It makes me angry that women are abused in this way. *(U.S.)*

The Italian subjects were much more positive about the ad. All but one saw the ad as a game of mutual seduction. For example,

● The message is: if you would like to be appreciated, wear this stuff. All people love to be admired, the men too. . . . They are playing and enjoying. Maybe the bananas give a touch of originality and define the relationship as a game. The message suggests she is the winner and he is seduced: I think it's an equal relationship. The bananas remind me of the natives of any lost island, so that it confirms the message: he seems to be a slave to passion. He's a primitive, who doesn't resist to the impulses. She looks a self-confident woman, she's not afraid to show herself, she's brilliant. The slogan puts the passive and the active together: To be admired is passive, but to love to be admired is active. *(Italian)*

One Italian subject, however, disagreed:

● It's not difficult to decode the symbolic meaning of the bananas. Between them there is a banal relationship of reciprocal seduction, based on a playful situation. They seem to me to be two assholes dressed up in a manner which is supposed to make it interesting to buy the lingerie. It's not an explosive message; she looks like a retouched housewife. The photo is just a small, silly insult. . . . I pity them. The slogan "Women love to be admired" should be in the *Guinness Book of World Records* for its stupidity, in the sense that it's true and like all the obvious things could be omitted. *(Italian)*

● *Violence:* This store window display is one of the most ambiguous advertising signs in our study. The central message is male violence against women. The products that surround the image of the man and woman have no obvious relationship to the message of the image, and the small figure in the foreground is ambiguous.

No viewers from the United States found any redeeming value in the ad. For some, the ad appears to draw on inexplicable male attraction for violent domination of women:

● It seems that a lot of men are interested in sexual arousal by a suggestion of violence. I don't understand why. I couldn't begin to tell you why. But that's what it is. It seems like this is appealing more to men than to women, just because of that. *(U.S.)*

● This ad absolutely disgusts me! The man is totally dominating the woman. He wants to show her affection and she obviously does not feel the same way. He is forcefully grabbing her face, and she cannot stop it. Domestic abuse is a serious worldwide issue, and I certainly don't think it should be glorified as something sexy and racy. It is not. It makes me sick that women's clothes designers would use this along with their trendiest new clothes. *(U.S.)*

Italian women were less quick to typify the ad as simple male violence:

● I see a very passionate thing. His gesture seems aggressive; it gives the idea of an unbalanced relationship. Here the man has the power. She cares for him, he's not kind, but she stays there. Probably the relationship has its own balance. The shop window could be attractive because the gesture is violent but also passionate. The violence is always linked to the passion. If there were indifference, it would not be any violence. So, there is a strong emotion, and the product is presented in this way. She's a passive woman, more interested in her man than her job. *(Italian)*

Another linked the male violence to the woman's sexual potency. For this viewer, the objection is not to the violence implied by the ad but to the willingness of women to see themselves as a function of men's desires:

● It's the usual scene of passion, a little bit Latin. Maybe he wants her so much he is willing to be violent toward her. Maybe that's the message: a woman who kindles an uncontrollable wish. It's also a message which gives a male vision: the woman looks at herself through the man's eyes. Unfortunately, the male look is always the dominant one. So, that is the saddest thing: Women try to be pleasing to men and look at themselves through the men's eyes. *(Italian)*

● *Bicycle:* This display, in a perfume shop, included a contest to win a bicycle. The display suggests elegance, fashion, and independence to viewing publics in Italy and the United States. However, the bicycle itself represents fantasy for U.S. women and transportation for Italian women, perhaps recalling the reconstruction period in Italy following World War II. Finally, this ad lacks a male and thus does not present a relationship. Perhaps the absence of men is the message: the independence of women in the context of the missing men.

For women from the United States, the ad creates the fantasy of the liberated European woman:

● I love it. I like the ad; I like the bike. That would pull me in, because you don't intellectually think that "OK, if I buy perfume X, suddenly I am going to be this stylish, classically beautiful, film-star-looking person that buys that product and

that's what I want to be," but that's what happens. *(U.S.)*

● I guess you want to be playful enough to want to ride a bike but still have this elegant, striking look. I guess it makes sense—she has a classic line, and the woman in the picture [next to] her, La Perla, is a lot harsher but still absolutely gorgeous. *(U.S.)*

● I love this ad. It reminds me of France, where I studied. I like the idea of the bicycle. I really like this woman on the [bike]; she's well dressed. She looks like she's dressed for a career. You like the idea of the bike; she's in control of her own life. She's in control of her future. It reminds me of when I was in Europe, where people just hopped on their bikes and went places. There's a certain freedom, lack of female dependence there. She looks very confident, domineering. *(U.S.)*

412

● *Transvestite:* Here two copies of a self-made poster were posted alongside an ad for a skin product. The transvestite ad represents an ambiguous, elegant sexuality and offers sexual services. The skin care ad offers a lotion that promises a lovely body. The ads both play on the myth of sexual fulfillment through the consumption of purchasable goods.

U.S. women were offended by the blatant advertising of sexual services by a sexual deviant:

● I didn't know it was a transvestite until you told me. I just thought it was two beautiful women. But then that one's a transvestite and this one isn't. I think, "Oh my gosh, the non-transvestite is far more beautiful, far more attractive, far more interesting than the transvestite." It's kind of like yuck. *(U.S.)*

● The swimsuit ad is very classy, and I think it seems even classier when in juxtaposition with the trashy transvestite sign. *(U.S.)*

● As for the transvestite, that is not even worth mentioning. That's a horrible ad! *(U.S.)*

● The transvestite ad makes me angry because I don't think it should be publicly advertised. *(U.S.)*

Italians, however, interpreted the ads very differently. Several found a kind of relief in the image of the transvestite juxtaposed to the model:

● It is not offensive; it makes me laugh. I think it is brave. The transvestite ad is an admirable thing, a nice, original idea. *(Italian)*

● Parah is the classic photo on the beach, nothing new. It calls attention to the body, which is perfect, and secondarily there is the product. It's the image of a woman of yesterday, of the 1980s, probably a rich, bored housewife. Regarding the other, this manner of selling her/his body could be read in two ways. First, it's very ironic, open and clean, because of the phone number. It's a brave image. Second, reasoning on it, I can say I don't agree with the intent. I appreciate it because it is an intelligent image. I don't agree with the idea to put one's own body on sale. Anyway, in this case I'm more struck by the positive side. I see it as a brave, ironic, and therefore an intelligent thing. I'm not bothered. *(Italian)*

13 The Global Dynamics of Population: Demographic Trends

I admit it. I said them. I said those seven words people over 40 have been saying for centuries. The ones I once vowed I'd never say. The ones that, when uttered, permanently tag you as an over-the-hill relic: "*I just don't understand you kids today!*"

It all started when I was arguing with my two sons—one 14, the other 11—over what to watch on television. They wanted to watch the X Games on ESPN2; I wanted to watch a rerun of the sixth game of the 1975 World Series on ESPN Classic. I told them that my choice was a priceless piece of U.S. sports history, the best World Series game ever played. Besides, I didn't understand the allure of the X Games anyway. I know it's an annual alternative sports festival that began a few years ago as a sort of anti-Olympics novelty based on obscure recreational sports such as skateboarding, in-line skating, stunt biking, snowboarding, and so on. But I don't care to know the difference between a "frontside ollie" and a "50–50 grind." To me an "elephant glide" sounds like some sort of industrial-strength lubricant, and "getting clean air" means moving out of Los Angeles.

They told me that I was a dinosaur and that I had better wake up and smell the 21st century if I knew what was good for me. The X Games, they claimed, was the future. You know, they were right.

The X Games—both the winter and the summer version—has grown into an international mass marketing extravaganza, drawing hundreds of athletes from 27 nations who compete in dozens of events. The spectacle is now broadcast to more than 200 countries, and it has become the fastest-growing televised sports event for ESPN, the Disney-owned network.

The "extreme sports" included in the X Games are self-consciously thrilling, dangerous, subversive, and rebellious—just the sort of activities many communities around the country are now trying to ban. Extreme sports are part of a broader youth subculture with its own hard-edged—sometimes angry and sometimes threatening—language, fashion, and music. At a time when the trend in society is to eliminate risk (for instance, many communities have removed swings and monkey bars from playgrounds), the appeal of these sports lies not so much in grace, strategy, or face-to-face competition as in the chance of a wild catastrophe occurring. The athletes have tired of a bland and sometimes timid environment where individual expression is suppressed. As one X Games slogan goes, "If you're not living on the edge, you're taking up too much room."

Extreme athletes bear little resemblance to athletes in more traditional sports. They tend to despise rules, regulations, and standard conceptions of the competitive spirit. Indeed, most extreme sports don't have objectively measured results but are instead judged on their degree of risk and danger. The athletes take pride in their antiteam, individualistic attitude. They compete not to win but to have fun. "We hate the jock mentality," said one X Games participant. "And I think there are lots of kids who can relate more to snowboarders, surfers, and skaters than to some of the millionaire big-sport types" (quoted in Black, 1996, p. 56). Extreme sports prove that young people can be impressive athletes even when they have green hair and pierced tongues and wear pants seven sizes too big.

Ironically, although extreme sports appear solidly antiestablishment, they have clearly become a mainstream gold mine. Such corporate giants as Miller Beer, Taco Bell, IBM, Coors, Nike, AT&T, Old Spice Deodorant, Chevrolet, and Ricoh Copiers all prominently display their logos at X Games events or saturate TV commercial breaks with their advertisements. Corporate America has been scrambling to co-opt the language and the culture of extreme athletes in order to tap into a market that is booming. At the 2000 Super Show, the nation's biggest sporting goods trade show, ankle-high skateboarding shoes replaced Nike high-tops and cargo pants with extra pockets supplanted baggy basketball shorts emblazoned with Michael Jordan's silhouette as the top sellers ("Extreme sports dominate," 2000).

And it's not just sports. Record companies, clothes manufacturers, even Hollywood films (*American Pie, Varsity Blues, Cruel Intentions, She's All That, Boys and Girls, Save the Last Dance,* and *Saving Silverman* to name a few), are catering to the interests and tastes of the 70 or so million young people born between the late 1970s and the early 1990s.

What my sons didn't realize (they were too busy laughing at my ignorance) was that they had identified one of the most crucial dividing lines in society today. They and I may be members of the same family. We may have the same skin color, ethnicity, religion, and social class. And when they get older, we may even share the same views on political issues. But we're also members of two extremely different, sometimes conflicting, social groups that are distinguished by one simple and unchangeable fact: We are members of different **birth cohorts**—sets of people who were born during the same time period and who must face similar societal circumstances brought about by their position in the age structure of the population.

In the past several chapters I examined the various interrelated sources of social stratification: class, race, and gender. You have seen that the distance between the haves and the have-nots—both locally and globally—continues to grow wider as a result of their different levels of access to important cultural, economic, and political resources. But within the United States, as well as other societies, imbalances between various age groups will also be a defining feature of social life in the decades to come. Globally, population imbalances between richer and poorer societies underlie most if not all of the other forces for change that are taking placc today.

This chapter examines the relationship between broad population trends and everyday life. First I describe how the time in which we were born influences our everyday experiences. Next I look at three population trends occurring across the globe today—population growth, changing age structures, and migration. I then turn my focus to some of the key population trends in U.S. society. How are the changing age structure and the growing number of legal and illegal immigrants affecting the ability to provide people in the United States with the resources they need for a comfortable life? How are important social institutions functioning as a result of these population shifts?

The Influence of Birth Cohorts

You've no doubt asked yourself such questions as, What career will I pursue? Where will I live after I graduate? Will I be able to afford a house? Will I have a spouse? Children? The answers to these questions are obviously influenced by your personal desires, traits, values, ambitions, and abilities, not to mention your social class, gender, race, religion, and ethnicity. But they are also affected by your place in the population at a given point in time. The size of your birth cohort, relative to other cohorts, will be tremendously influential in determining the availability of affordable houses, high-paying jobs, attractive potential mates, and so on. Aside from its size, each birth cohort has other distinctive properties—such as ethnic composition, age-specific birthrates, and average life expectancies—that can set it apart from other cohorts.

Birth cohorts influence the everyday lives of individuals in two fundamental ways (Riley, 1971):

- People born at roughly the same time tend to experience life course events or social rites of passage—like puberty, marriage, childbearing, graduation, entrance into the workforce, and death—at roughly the same time. Sociologists call these experiences **cohort effects**.
- Members of the same birth cohort also share a common history. A cohort's place in time tells us a lot about the opportunities and constraints placed on its members. Historical events (wars, epidemics, economic depressions, and so on) and major social trends, called **period effects**, contribute to the unique shape and outlook of each birth cohort. Many historians, for instance, believe that a period of drought and famine caused the abandonment of the great cities of the Mayan civilization nearly a thousand years ago. Those who were young when this period began enjoyed comfortable lives, reveled in the high culture of the Mayans, and had tremendous prospects for the future. But for their children, born just a generation later, starvation, death, and social dislocation were basic facts of life (Clausen, 1986).

Cohort and period effects combine to profoundly influence the lives of individuals. Members of different birth cohorts experience the same major societal or world circumstances at different stages in their lives. Consider what people born in the 1920s have experienced: Their most vivid childhood memories are likely to be of growing up during the Depression era of the 1930s; they experienced World War II as teenagers, the Korean War as young adults, and the Vietnam War in middle age. They have also seen the advent of radio, television, the atomic bomb, space travel, telecommunications, and computers, not to mention dramatic changes in sexual, political, educational, and religious values (Clausen, 1986).

But it's not only exposure to events like these that shapes cohort histories, it's also how old people are when these events occur that distinguishes them from other cohorts (Soldo & Agree, 1988). For instance, the birth cohort that experienced the Great Depression during its peak childbearing years had the lowest birthrate of any cohort in the 20th century. Therefore, people born between 1900 and 1910 tended as a group to have smaller families to rely on and shared similar worries about how they would be cared for in their old age. These experiences contrast sharply with people born a mere 10 years later or earlier, who either were past their prime childbearing years during the Depression or were too young to have children at that time and who tended to have larger families when they entered adulthood after World War II (Soldo & Agree, 1988).

Cohort and period effects are also influential in forming your worldview and self-concept. Think how different your goals and ambitions would be had you experienced childhood during the Depression as opposed to a period of relative affluence, such as the late 1990s. Rights and privileges considered unattainable dreams by one cohort are likely to be taken for granted by a future one. Similarly, the differences in attitudes and values between people who became adults during the Vietnam War and people who became adults during the Persian Gulf War are a function not only of simple age differences but also of differences in prevailing social and historical conditions. Imagine how different your perceptions of the world and your ideas about solving international conflicts would be if your most vivid teenage memory was one of angry crowds jeering soldiers going off to fight an unpopular war as opposed to an image of proud crowds cheering soldiers going off to fight a popular one.

As we grow older, we develop and change in a society that itself is developing and changing. We start our lives in one historical period with a distinct age pattern of behavior and set of social norms, and we end our lives in another. Throughout most of the 20th century, for instance, each succeeding generation has received substantially more schooling than the previous one. Early in the century most people went to school for only 6 or 7 years, which yielded an adequate education for the sorts of jobs their parents and older siblings held. Today, most people are in school 12 years or longer. As a result, older cohorts on the whole tend to score substantially lower on standardized intelligence tests than younger ones. Because of such test results, social scientists long assumed that intelligence declined markedly with age. But we now know that these differences are not the result of aging but of changing societal values regarding education (Clausen, 1986).

Even the way people personally experience the aging process is affected by the character of their birth cohort and by the social, cultural, and environmental changes to which their cohort is exposed in moving through the life course. People are living longer, and advancements have been made in nutrition, education, sanitation, and other areas. As a result, cohorts experience the physical consequences of development in different ways (Riley, Foner, & Waring, 1988). For instance, the average age of menarche (a girl's first menstrual period) has gradually lowered from about 14 a century ago to between 12 and 13 today (Darton, 1991). Combined with changing social norms, values, and cultural beliefs, such a change inevitably speeds up the point at which young women become sexually curious and explorative.

In sum, to understand the impact cohorts exert on everyday life, we must place them within their relevant historical and social contexts. Birth cohorts are more than just a collection of individuals born within a few years of each other; they are distinctive generations tied together by historical circumstances, population trends, and societal changes. However, we must also realize that when many individuals in the same cohort are affected by social events in similar ways, the changes in their collective lives can produce changes in society. Each succeeding cohort leaves its mark on the prevailing culture. Each helps create and is shaped by its own *zeitgeist*—the intellectual, moral, and cultural spirit of the time (Mannheim, 1952). In other words, cohorts are not only affected by social changes but contribute to them as well (Riley, Foner, & Waring, 1988).

Baby Boomers

The birth cohort that has received the most national attention is, without a doubt, the baby boom generation, those 76 million or so people born between 1946 and 1964. They now make up almost one-third of the entire U.S. population. Preceded and followed by much smaller cohorts, they stand in sharp political, economic, and cultural contrast to those around them:

> They grew up as the first standardized generation, drawn together by the history around them, the intimacy of television, and the crowding that came from the sheer onslaught of other Baby Boomers. They shared the great economic expectations of the 1950's and the fears that came with *Sputnik* and the dawn of the nuclear era. They shared the hopes of John F. Kennedy's New Frontier and Lyndon Johnson's Great Society, and the disillusionment that came with the assassinations [of John Kennedy, Robert Kennedy, and Martin Luther King], Viet Nam, Watergate, and the resignation [of Richard Nixon]. (P. Light, 1988, p. 10)

The passing of this massive cohort through the life course has been described metaphorically as "a pig in a python." If you've ever seen one of those *Nature* shows on PBS where snakes devour and digest small animals, you can see how apt the metaphor is. As this cohort bulge works its way through the life course, it stretches the parameters of the relevant social institutions at each stage. Baby boomers packed hospital nurseries as infants; school classrooms as children; and college campuses, employment lines, and the housing market as young adults (P. Light, 1988).

The trend will continue into the future. By the year 2030 there will be more than 50 million retired baby boomers, about twice the number of retirees today. As they reach their golden years, those programs concerned with later life—pension plans, Social Security, medical and social care—will be seriously stressed. At the same time, though, they will represent a lucrative market for many businesses. The automobile industry, for instance, is currently looking for ways to make vehicles that suit the needs of older people, such as larger and lower doors, swiveling seats, and easy-to-use handles (Bradsher, 1999a). And sometime in the middle of the 21st century, there will no doubt be a huge surge in business for the funeral industry as this generation reaches the end of its collective life cycle (Schodolski, 1993).

Baby boomers have left a particularly influential mark on the institution of family. Their generation was the first to redefine families to include a variety of living arrangements, such as cohabitation, domestic partnerships, and never-married women with dependent children (Wattenberg, 1986). They were also the first to acknowledge the expectation of paid work as a central feature of women's lives. And they were the first to grow up with effective birth control, making delayed childbearing, voluntary childlessness, and our current low birthrate possible. Hence baby boomers are responsible for the smaller families we see in the United States today.

Consequently, as the baby boomers reach old age they will have fewer children to turn to for the kind of help they gave older generations in earlier years (Butler, 1989). Thus the baby boom elders will be more likely than previous generations were to turn to social service and health care organizations to care for them.

Generation X

Although baby boomers have dominated the cultural spotlight for decades, U.S. society has also taken notice of the next generation, known in the media as "Generation X." Today there are roughly 48 million U.S. residents who were born between the mid-1960s and 1980. The birthrate during the 1970s, when most of these individuals were born, was about half as large as it was during the post–World War II years of the baby boomers.

More Generation Xers are the product of divorced parents than any previous generation. Roughly 40% of them are children of divorce. As a result, they are emotionally conflicted about marriage. They are less likely to get married than other generations and more likely to delay marriage if they do. In 1970, 55% of U.S. men and 36% of U.S. women between the ages of 20 and 24 had never married. In 1994 the figures were 81% of men and 66% of women (U.S. Bureau of the Census, 1995b).

Even more Generation Xers were so-called latchkey children, the first generation of children to experience the effects of two working parents. For many of these children, childhood was marked by dependence on secondary relationships—teachers, friends, day care.

Many members of this cohort are angry that they have inherited a variety of gargantuan crises, from the national debt and the looming Social Security crisis to the degradation of the natural environment and growing urban decay. Resentful of the wasteful excesses of their elders, they are experiencing unprecedented apprehension about their own futures.

The Millennium Generation

The 70 to 80 million individuals born between 1979 and 1994 make up the next noticeable generation, known variously as the Millennium Generation, Generation Y, or Echo Boomers. This generation rivals the baby boom in size but is different in almost every other way. For one thing, unlike the baby boom, this cohort is not evenly distributed across the nation. Those states that have high foreign immigration, domestic in-migration, and large minority populations (for example, California, Florida, Texas) account for a relatively high proportion of the Millennium Generation (Faust, Gann, & McKibben, 1999). Consequently, according to the 2000 census, this cohort is more ethnically diverse than previous generations. For instance, over 35% of this group are not white, compared to 24% of baby boomers (Howe & Strauss, 2000). They are also more likely than preceding cohorts to grow up in a non-traditional family. One in four lives in a single-parent household; three in four have working mothers.

The Millennium Generation is also the first to claim computers as a birthright. Two-thirds of them use computers on a regular basis. Whereas the boomers and even some Generation Xers struggle to understand the basics of Windows 2000, these kids became computer literate in nursery school. It's estimated that they will spend one-third of their lives on the Internet (Hammel, 1999). Although this preoccupation with computers may create a generation less socially adept than those of the past, the exposure to other cultures that the Internet provides will make it significantly more worldly than any generation in history. And as the Millennium Generation enters and exits college, it will come to the workforce with unprecedented technological savvy.

Growing up in the affluent 1990s, many in this generation have positive feelings about their futures. Two-thirds of teenage respondents in a recent national survey indicated that they were very optimistic about their chances of having a good job, and many are confident that problems such as sexual harassment and economic discrimination against women are on their way out. But their optimism isn't just about personal interest. Asked to identify the most important concept that will guide their working lives, the most common response was "to help others who need help" (Mogelonsky, 1998a). This sort of altruism, if maintained into adulthood, could significantly alter the business environment of the future.

Although members of the Millennium Generation are quick to point out hypocrisy and superficiality (witness the success of the "Image Is Nothing" tag line in Sprite commercials), they may also be more socially conservative than prior generations. For instance, a nationwide study found that close to 70% of young people today support so-called zero tolerance policies in high school (cited in Howe & Strauss, 2000). According to the 1998 General Social Survey, over 80% of 18- to 24-year-olds said they'd get married if they found the right person, compared to 69% of 25- to 34-year-olds. In 1972 10% of respondents in the 18- to 24-year-old age group said that premarital sex was "always wrong"; in 1998 that figure had more than doubled. Similarly, the proportion who were sexually active decreased between 1996 and 1998 from 83.9% to 76.6% (cited in Stapinski, 1999). Indeed, rates of pregnancy, abortion and births for girls between 15 and 17 have all declined since 1990 (Howe & Strauss, 2000).

As this cohort ages and begins to control important social institutions, these attitudes and behaviors will shape reality for other cohorts in U.S. society.

Demographic Dynamics

Many aspects of our personal lives are influenced by our birth cohort, but our lives are also affected by society-wide and worldwide population trends. All of us are born, age, and eventually die. These seemingly private, biological events are part of the social fabric of all societies. Practically every sphere of activity is influenced by population trends.

The sociologists who study fluctuations in population characteristics are called **demographers**. Demographers examine several important and interrelated population processes to explain current social problems or to predict future ones: birth or fertility rates (changes in the number of children people are having), death or mortality rates (changes in people's life expectancy), and patterns of migration (the movement of people from one society to another). These three processes influence a population's growth, overall age structure, and geographic distribution.

Population Growth

The most fundamental population characteristic is, of course, size. No other phenomenon has the ability to touch the lives of everyone on the planet as profoundly as the growth of the human population. Changes in population size are a function of birth and death rates. As long as people are dying and being born at similar rates, the size of the population stabilizes (barring large changes due to migration). But when birthrates increase and death rates decrease, the population grows.

It took hundreds of thousands of years, from the beginning of humanity to the early 19th century, for the earth's population to reach 1 billion. However, it took only an additional hundred years to reach 2 billion. Then, 3 billion was reached 30 years later; 4 billion, 16 years later; and 5 billion, a little over 10 years after that. Today we have surpassed 6 billion and will exceed 7 billion by 2010. Exhibit 13.1 charts world population growth since 7000 B.C.

Exhibit 13.1   **World Population Growth since 7000 B.C.**

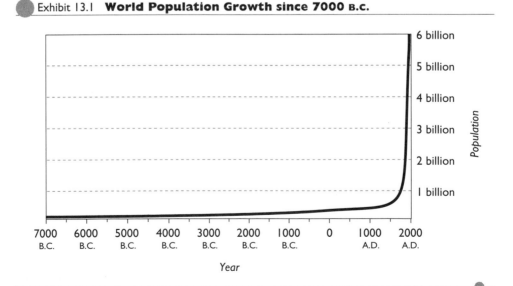

Year

Source: Farley, 1991.

Here's another way to look at it: Ten thousand years ago the world's population was 8 million; today it takes a little over a month for the population to grow by that much (J. E. Farley, 1991)!

Undeniably, the global population is growing at unprecedented speed. However, people disagree about the consequences of that growth. In the past, large numbers of people were seen as a precious resource. The Bible urged humanity to be fruitful and multiply. One 18th-century British scholar, referring to the strategic importance of a large population, called a high birthrate "the never-failing nursery of Fleets and Armies" (quoted in Mann, 1993, p. 49).

Although few people today sing the praises of massive population growth, some argue that it isn't particularly troublesome. A larger population creates greater division of labor and a larger market to support highly specialized services. More people are available to contribute to production.

Others, however, haven't been so optimistic. Population growth can compound, magnify, or even create a wide variety of problems, such as food shortages, pollution, housing shortages, high inflation, energy shortages, unemployment, illiteracy, and the loss of individual freedom (Weeks, 1995). Thousands of years ago, philosophers in ancient China worried about the need to shift the masses to underpopulated areas. The ancient Greek philosopher Plato said that cities with more than 5,040 landholders were too large (Mann, 1993). According to some contemporary demographers, global population growth will destroy the one-time bonanza of such environmental resources as fossil fuel, rich soil, and certain plant and animal species; widen the gap between rich and poor nations; perpetuate social and economic inequality within nations; give rise to racial and ethnic separatism, as we have seen recently in places such as Yugoslavia; and increase already high levels of world hunger and unemployment (Ehrlich & Ehrlich, 1993). When a particular population is excessively large, individuals are forced to compete for limited food, space, jobs, and salaries. People's ability to achieve the standard of living they feel they are entitled to is hampered by the size of the population.

On balance, the biggest problem seems to be that different countries are experiencing vastly different rates of growth. Populations in poor, developing countries are rapidly expanding, whereas those in wealthy, developed countries have either stabilized or are declining.

The annual rate of growth worldwide between 1990 and 2000 has been approximately 1.5%. But that figure masks dramatic regional differences (see Exhibit 13.2). Consider these facts:

- In Africa, the population increases 2.5% each year; Europe, in contrast, has seen a 0.1% annual *decline* in population (Cooper, 1998c).
- In 1950 half of the 10 most populous nations were industrial nations. By 2050 United Nations demographers predict that the United States will be the only developed country among the world's 20 most populous nations (cited in Crossette, 2001).
- Between 1995 and 2000, the countries that added the most people to the world's population were all in the less developed areas of Asia and Africa: India, China,

Exhibit 13.2 **World Population Growth by Region**

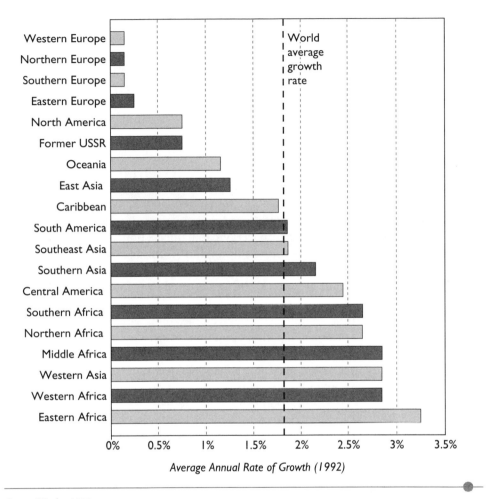

Average Annual Rate of Growth (1992)

Source: Weeks, 1995.

Pakistan, Indonesia, and Nigeria ("Six billion and counting," 1999). India and China alone accounted for over 20% of the increase.

• The United Nations (1999) predicts that 98% of global population growth over the next several decades will occur in less developed countries. Today 78% of the world's population resides in the developing countries of Africa, Asia, and Latin America. By the year 2030 that figure will rise to 86% ("World population growth," 1995).

• In 2000, all the countries of the European Union combined for an increase of 343,000 people; India achieved that figure in the first *week* of 2001 (cited in Crossette, 2001).

These imbalances will influence how people view one another; affect global and domestic policies; and determine the availability of food, energy, and adequate living space (P. Kennedy, 1993). When the most highly industrialized and economically productive societies begin to experience shrinking populations, their role as major global producers and consumers of goods is thrown into doubt. The result can be economic and political turmoil as other societies jockey for advantage.

The Demographic Transition.   In 1972 a group of researchers at the Massachusetts Institute of Technology predicted that because of rapid population growth, the world would run out of gold by 1981, oil by 1992, and usable farmland by 2000; civilization itself would collapse by 2075 (Mann, 1993). If Nigeria were to continue at its present rate of population growth (around 3.4% annually), in 140 years its population would be equal to that of the entire world today (Keyfitz, 1989). Needless to say, none of these things has happened or is going to happen. Sooner or later population growth will have to slow down. But why?

An 18th-century English clergyman named Thomas Malthus argued that populations always grow faster than food supplies. As the gap widens, starvation ensues. Famines, combined with wars, plagues, diseases, and the like, eventually act as natural limits to population growth. Malthus assumed that food supplies were the ultimate population check.

But Malthus couldn't have foreseen the ability of trade and technology to solve the food supply problem. Japan's population, for instance, would have started dying off long ago if it had to rely on its own food production instead of imports from other countries. In addition, agricultural progress over the last two decades has enabled societies to produce food more abundantly and more efficiently than was possible during Malthus's time. Global food production actually rose more than 10% between 1968 and 1990 (Mann, 1993). According to the World Resources Institute (2001), global agriculture has made remarkable progress since the 1970s in expanding world food supplies. Croplands and pasturelands support 1.5 billion more people today than they were able to support in 1970. Resources are becoming more accessible, average food consumption levels are improving, and life expectancy is increasing worldwide.

People in developing countries now consume almost a third more calories than they did in the early 1960s, meaning that fewer people die from starvation and malnutrition than ever before. The famines that we hear so much about today—in Ethiopia, Somalia, or Sudan, for example—have been largely the result of war and civil unrest rather than a scarcity of food (Cooper, 1998c). In fact, many of the nations that are experiencing famines today actually have food surpluses (Keyfitz, 1989).

A less grim and more popular theory of population growth and contraction than Malthus's theory is what demographers call the **demographic transition**. Underlying this model is the assumption that all societies go through similar stages of economic and social development. During the first, preindustrial stage of development, both birthrates and death rates tend to be quite high. People have lots of children during this stage, but life expectancy is so low that roughly the same number of people die as are born each year. Hence, the size of the population remains fairly stable.

The second stage occurs when societies begin to industrialize and living conditions improve. The first demographic indicator to improve is usually the death rate. New technology often means better food supplies and increased knowledge about disease. Societies learn how to keep their water supplies clean and how to dispose of garbage and sewage. But for a considerable time after the death rate begins to fall, the birthrate remains high. The result is a dramatic increase in the size of the population. Many demographers feel that most of the world's developing countries are in this second stage of demographic transition. In these countries women will bear an average of 3.3 children in their lifetimes, and the number is above 7.0 in Yemen, Angola, Oman, Ethiopia, Malawi, and Somalia (Cooper, 1998c). By comparison, the fertility rate in the United States is 2.05; in Japan it is 1.48; and in Italy, it is a minuscule 1.24 (Crossette, 1997a).

Why would poor parents in developing countries, who already face enormous difficulties, continue to produce more mouths to feed? Part of the reason is the lack of access to effective birth control. In Pakistan, for instance, only 12% of married women use some form of contraception (compared to 74% in the United States and 80% in France) (Elliot & Dickey, 1994). In addition, traditional beliefs about the importance of large families persist for some time during this stage of demographic transition. Established laws, customs, and religious norms often continue to exert strong influences on people's reproductive behavior. In developing nations, children are likely to be perceived as economic assets. They are the "social security" of traditional cultures and a form of savings few people can do without (Mann, 1993).

As countries modernize, they reach the third and final stage, which is marked by a reduced birthrate to accompany the low death rate. People moving into cities soon begin to realize that large families are an economic liability rather than an asset. They discover that raising large numbers of children in a crowded city is exceedingly difficult. Traditional and religious beliefs become weaker as a result. In addition, driven by relative prosperity and freedom, women in the developed world stay in school longer, put more emphasis on paid work, and marry later than women in developing countries. All these factors delay childbearing. Consequently, birthrates in the industrialized world are currently in rapid and sustained decline (Specter, 1998a).

Although the demographic transition model is useful in understanding the unequal rates of population growth, it has drawbacks. The model is based on processes of urbanization and modernization that characterized 18th-century Europe but may not apply to developing countries today. Death rates fall at a much more accelerated rate in today's developing countries than they did 200 years ago because immunizations, antibiotics, pesticides, and other health advances are likely to be imported from more advanced countries instead of arising from economic and scientific development within a country. As a result, declining mortality is not always associated with an increase in the standard of living, as it was in the past. And because birthrates don't tend to fall unless standards of living increase, the social pressures that drive down birthrates are also less of a factor in developing countries today. Hence, developing countries may be stalled in the second stage of the model, with less chance of moving to the final stage.

Signs indicate, however, that this assessment may be a bit pessimistic. Many people are beginning to seek more active ways to curb the global population explosion. Representatives from 182 nations attended the 1994 International Conference on Population and Development. Despite opposition from some Islamic countries and the Vatican, they agreed that promoting health care and reproductive education—particularly for women—is the best way to keep populations in developing countries in check (Ching,

1994). The conference draft plan stated, "Advancing gender equity and the empowerment of women is a cornerstone of population programs" (quoted in Elliott & Dickey, 1994, p. 22).

A study by the Population Crisis Committee (now called Population Action International) found that overall access to birth control has indeed increased worldwide ("World progress in birth control," 1993). Of the 87 developing nations studied, 57 had improved birth control substantially over the previous five years. Furthermore, 40% of the countries surveyed had decreased their average family size by a third, and another 42% exhibited smaller but still noticeable differences.

We must keep in mind, however, that although the rate of population growth may be declining, annual absolute numbers of people continue to mount in many countries and will continue to be large for several decades to come. When a country has a large and young population base, several generations may pass before a declining rate of growth can offset the sheer number of people produced by the high rates of the past. Even though individual people may be producing fewer children, so many of them are having kids that the population continues to grow anyway. For instance, 45% of the people living in sub-Saharan Africa are 15 years old or younger. With so many young people about to reach childbearing age, population growth will likely continue, no matter what the birthrate may be in the next several decades (Cooper, 1998c).

Politics, Culture, and Population Growth. You may be getting the impression that population growth is a "natural" process working relentlessly and inevitably on unsuspecting populations. Yet human intervention—government intervention, more specifically—has at times purposefully altered the size or even the configuration of a population for political or economic reasons.

Take China, for example. Because of its massive population of more than 1.2 billion and its limited resources, China's leadership has been struggling for decades to limit family size. One of every five humans alive today is Chinese, but China has only 7% of the earth's farmland, much of it of poor quality. In response, the government enacted a strict birth policy in the early 1970s. Couples had to wait until their mid-20s to marry. Provinces and cities were assigned yearly birth quotas. Neighborhood committees determined which married couples could have a baby and when they could start trying. The committees also oversaw contraceptive use and even recorded women's menstrual cycles (Ignatius, 1988). In some areas, groups of family planners visited each village once or twice a year and took all women who had already had children to a nearby clinic to be sterilized (Kristof, 1993a). In the 1990s, more than 80% of all Chinese couples of childbearing age were sterilized (Crossette, 1997a; Kristof, 1993a). Couples who had only one child were rewarded with salary bonuses, educational opportunities, and housing priorities. Penalties were imposed on couples who had more than one child, such as fines of more than a year's salary, lost access to apartments and schools, or dismissals from their jobs (Ignatius, 1988).

The effectiveness of China's birth policy has amazed demographers. Population targets have been reached that weren't expected until 2010. The average number of births per woman has decreased from more than seven in the 1960s to fewer than two in 1997. In contrast, the average woman in India, a country with similar population problems, still gives birth to four children in her lifetime.

However, the dramatic economic growth of China in recent years has eroded the old system of government control over people's private lives. Enforcement of the one-child policy has become looser, and in some areas couples are given somewhat more leeway in deciding how many children to have (Rosenthal, 1998). In large cities, the policy is still enforced, but in rural regions there is tremendous variation. For instance, in urban Beijing, one-third of 1% of newborns are third or later children, but in rural provinces the percentages are much higher, in some areas as high as 15% (Rosenthal, 2000). Almost all those births are technically illegal and therefore unlikely to be reported, which means that China's officially reported birth rate is probably lower than its actual birth rate.

Although countries such as China see their future in reducing the size of their populations, other countries are starting to worry that their populations aren't growing enough. The developed, industrialized countries of the world, which tend to have higher standards of living and superior health care, enjoy low mortality rates. But these countries have also experienced drastically lower fertility rates over the past 30 years, causing alarm among many governments. In Italy, which has the world's lowest fertility rate, government officials are looking for ways to help women have careers and children simultaneously. France and Sweden provide a range of government assistance for families willing to have additional children (Crossette, 1997a). In Taiwan, where the fertility rate dropped dramatically from 5.3 births per woman in 1963 to 1.8 in the mid-1990s (U.S. Bureau of the Census, 1995b; Weeks, 1995), the government has adopted a low-key "pro-baby" policy that, among other things, encourages early marriage and procreation and offers inexpensive specialist advice to infertile couples ("Taiwan's little problem," 1993). And in Japan, some companies will pay their employees bonuses—perhaps as much as $10,000—for each child they have (Sims, 2000).

At the same time that government policies are either encouraging or discouraging people to have children, cultural tradition continues to play a powerful role. In addition to exerting influence on family size, some cultures express a deep preference for male children. Rural residents in China, for instance, are allowed to have a second child if their first is either a girl or is handicapped. Sons are preferred in many traditional cultures because only they can perpetuate the family line. Sons also represent an economic asset to the family and a source of security for parents in old age (Heise, 1989).

Such devaluation of female children can lead to extreme acts. A few years ago I was stunned by the following passage in a newspaper article:

> At least 60 million females in Asia are missing and feared dead, victims of nothing more than their sex. Worldwide, research suggests, the number of missing females may top 100 million. (Kristof, 1991)

If tens of millions of people were missing because of a war, earthquake, tidal wave, or plague, we surely would have heard something about it. How could something so massive and hideous happen so quietly?

Before I address this question, let me describe how demographers arrive at such an estimate in the first place. These figures are based on a few fundamental facts about the natural sex configuration of human populations. Worldwide, 5% or 6% more male babies are born than female babies. But under normal circumstances males die at higher rates at every age thereafter. In the United States and Europe, the number of men and women evens out by the time a birth cohort reaches its 20s or 30s (Kristof, 1991). Later in life, though, the number of women is higher because women tend to live longer than men. The overall sex ratio in developed countries is approximately 105 women for every 100 men.

The figures in many developing countries contrast sharply with these demographic expectations. In India, for instance, the figure is only 92 females for every 100 males (Dugger, 2001). In China, it is 84 females for every 100 males (Kristof, 1993b). Similar shortages of women have been found in South Korea, Pakistan, Bangladesh, Nepal, and Papua New Guinea. Hence, the estimate of 100 million missing females represents the difference between the actual number of females in the world and the number that would be expected under normal demographic circumstances.

The "missing" females may include children of all ages who have been aborted, killed at birth, abandoned, neglected, given up for foreign adoption, or hidden (Kristof, 1993b). In South Korea, 1 out of 12 female fetuses—or 30,000 girls a year—is aborted because of its sex, even though disclosure of the sex of a fetus and abortion are against the law (WuDunn, 1997). In some Chinese provinces the infant mortality rate for girls is double that of boys ("6.3 brides for seven brothers," 1998). In other countries, girls die because they are given less food than boys or because family members view a sick daughter as a nuisance but view a sick son as a medical crisis requiring immediate attention. In Punjab, India, for instance, parents spend more than twice as much on medical care for boy infants as for girls (Heise, 1989).

Age Structure

In addition to population growth demographers also note the **age structure** of societies, the balance of old and young people. Age structure, like the size of a population, is determined by birth and death rates.

The proportion of the world's population over the age of 65 has been growing steadily for decades. In 1994, 357 million of the world's people were aged 65 and older. In 2000, about 418 million people were 65 and older (Kristof, 1996).

But as we saw with population growth, in general, the global growth of the elderly population is not spread evenly across countries. For developing countries where recent population growth is exceedingly rapid and where life expectancy remains low—as in Southeast Asia, Latin America, the Indian subcontinent, the Middle East, and especially Africa—the age structure is dominated by young people. The average age of the population in the four youngest countries in the world (Uganda, Niger, Yemen, and Congo Republic) is between 15 and 16 years ("A glimpse into how six billion live," 1999).

In contrast, those countries that are experiencing low birthrates coupled with increasing life expectancy have a very different age structure, as Exhibit 13.3 shows. More old people are living, and fewer young people are being born. The average age of the population in the world's four oldest countries (Italy, Japan, Germany, and Sweden) is about 40 years.

The global implications of these different age structures cannot be understated. When young people outnumber the elderly in a particular country, they are likely to achieve higher visibility and overwhelm such social institutions as the economy and the educational system (K. Davis, 1976). The resulting economic stresses can generate

Exhibit 13.3 **Changing Age Distributions in Less Developed and Developed Countries**

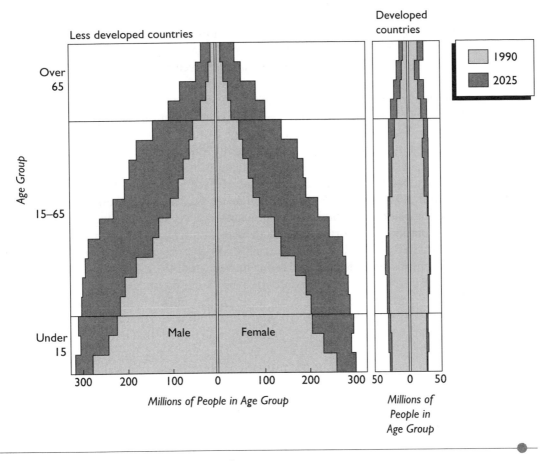

Source: Keyfitz, 1989. Used by permission of Ian Warpole.

political conflict as well. A steady decline in living standards usually means growing unrest, which can have an impact on the people who live in countries that depend on the troubled countries for certain resources, goods, or services.

The obvious consequence of today's population trends is that developing nations will have the burden of trying to support millions of people under the age of 15, whereas developed nations will have the burden of trying to support millions of people over the age of 65. As the prosperous societies of the world struggle with the problem of allocating more resources to the elderly, the rest of the planet must deal with the demands of growing numbers of children and infants.

Migration

In response to these problems, many people will be motivated to **migrate** or move to another place where prospects for a comfortable life are brighter. Throughout history humans have always had a tendency to move. Most scientists today believe that the first humans evolved in Africa and spread to all corners of the globe from there. Down the centuries migration has played a crucial role in history as people have contended for territory and the resources that go with it ("Workers of the world," 1998). Today, global television and the Internet expose people more quickly and more consistently than ever to appealing lifestyles found elsewhere. Large-scale migration, the third major demographic process, includes both in-country movement and cross-border movement.

Migration within a Society.   Migration trends within a country can have a considerable effect on social life. Consider the so-called Great Migration of African Americans from the rural South to the industrial North following the Civil War. Many former slaves, convinced there was no future for them in the Jim Crow South, migrated to the northern cities of New York, Philadelphia, Boston, Chicago, Detroit, Cleveland, and St. Louis, seeking a better life. In 1865, more than 90% of all African Americans lived in the South. By 1960 nearly 50% lived in the urban North (Smallwood, 1998). In Chicago alone the black population rose from 44,000 in 1910 to 110,000 in 1920 (P. Johnson, 1997). Blacks in the North were able to take advantage of opportunities unavailable to them in the South and establish the stable economic communities and strong political organizations that aided the civil rights movement of the 1950s and 1960s.

By 1980, however, many southern blacks were no longer seeing the decaying industrial centers of the North as an economic "promised land" and were choosing to remain in the South. And recently, more and more northern blacks have begun to move back to the South, reversing the migration pattern that had been in place for the better part of the century. This new trend is helping to redefine the South as relocated northern blacks incorporate their urban sensibilities and political savvy into everyday southern life.

Migration within developing countries is having an equally profound impact. In 1960 only a third of the world's population lived in cities; the United Nations estimates that by the year 2025 58% of the world's population and 54% of people in less developed countries will live in cities (Brockerhoff, 2000). In 2000 there were 292 cities in developed countries with over a million residents. Of the 10 largest "megacities"—urban areas with populations over 17 million—8 are in the developing world: Bombay, Lagos, Dhaka, São Paulo, Karachi, Mexico City, Delhi, and Jakarta (Brockerhoff, 2000).

This transformation illustrates more than just a shift of living tendencies; it has changed our assumptions about what urban living means worldwide. In the past, cities were meccas of great wealth, cultural activities, fine houses, impressive streets, and so on. Cities tended to have higher standards of living and better health conditions than rural areas. But when cities grow rapidly, as many are in the developing world, their economies and infrastructures can't keep up. As a result, contemporary urban life is associated with environmental and social devastation. In developing countries 90% of raw sewage from urban areas pours into streams and oceans. Of India's 3,000 cities, only 8 have full water-treatment plants (Crossette, 1996a). Cities have much higher rates of poverty, crime, violence, and sexually transmitted diseases than rural areas.

The sheer number of people crammed into large cities makes life difficult. At 11,480 people per square mile, you may think New York City is crowded. But it is a veritable open prairie compared to Bombay, India, which jams in 127,461 people per square mile (see Exhibit 13.4).

Exhibit 13.4 **Urban Overcrowding Worldwide**

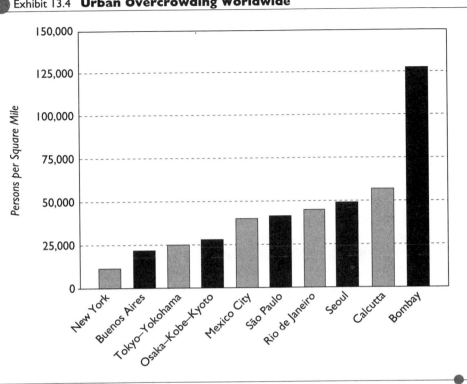

Source: U.S. Bureau of the Census, 1993c.

Migration from One Country to Another. Population movement from one country to another is equally significant. According to the United Nations, more than 120 million people worldwide—or 2% of the global population—live outside their countries of birth ("Workers of the world," 1998). Most have left their homelands in search of a better life somewhere else. In the process, they bring together an extraordinary diversity of ethnicities and cultures:

> A woman gynecologist from Romania sells bananas in a downtown supermarket [in the United States]. Polish engineers pick grapes in Swiss alpine vineyards. . . . Thai bar girls in Tokyo ride the Japanese economic boom together with 700,000 workers from Korea. . . . Among the 2.8 million foreign workers . . . in the Middle East last year were 17,000 Vietnamese. Hundreds of thousands of Indonesians harvest rubber and copra in Malaysia for the same pocketbook reasons that Mexicans pump gasoline in Los Angeles. In Germany, there are more than 1,000 mosques for resident Turkish workers. (McMichael, 1996, p. 187)

International migration is encouraged by disparities in opportunities. Poverty, political instability, war, famine, environmental deterioration, high unemployment, and the lure of high wages in richer countries continue to drive the world's poorest people to give up their life savings and risk death to find a better life in more prosperous nations. Consider, for instance, the economic pressures felt in Mexico. Between 1994 and 1995, the Mexican peso was devalued by 73%, throwing millions into unemployment and poverty. As Mexico's agricultural system modernizes, millions more will be forced off the land. Economists estimate that the country will need a million new jobs each year just to maintain the poor level of employment that exists today. Until employment opportunities improve, many Mexicans will continue to cross the border into the United States seeking work (Graham, 1996).

You might think that when people migrate from underdeveloped, overcrowded countries to more developed, technologically advanced countries, everyone would benefit. After all, migration lowers population pressures and unemployment at home while offsetting the problems of negative population growth and an aging workforce in developed countries. Indeed, low birthrates in Japan and Western Europe mean that the only way those countries will be able to sustain a stable population is through immigration. For example, the United Nations estimates that Italy will have to admit about 300,000 immigrants a year, Germany about 500,000, and Japan about 600,000 through 2025 simply to maintain their current workforces (Crossette, 2000b; French, 2000b).

From a sociological point of view, however, migration today doesn't mean moving to uncharted or newly developed areas, as in the past, but rather pushing into territories where people already live. People in receiving countries perceive the influx of immigrants and their economic impact in personal rather than societal terms. Instead of seeing immigrants for their contribution to the overall economy, the people already in residence see immigrants as an immediate threat. The immigrants are seeking to satisfy the same needs as everyone else. They require housing, education, and medical attention, all of which are in short supply. They also bring with them foreign habits, traditions, norms, and cultural ways.

Even though laws in most countries ban discrimination against foreigners, resentment and prejudice are deeply entrenched. In Great Britain the resentment is directed against immigrants from India and Pakistan; in France it's against Algerians and Moroccans; in Germany it's the Turks; in Sweden it's Iraqis and Kurds; in the United States it's immigrants from Latin America and Asia; and in Japan it's almost anyone not Japanese.

Despite the economic necessity of immigrants, many industrialized countries have tried to close their gates. In France, mounting resentment against Muslim Arab immigrants forced the government to place tight restrictions on immigration. One survey found that 76% of French citizens believe too many Arabs are in the country. In Italy, 75% of the population favor closing the borders to all new immigrants (Levin, 1993). Even Sweden, a country that has always preached racial tolerance, is developing segregated communities in the suburbs of Stockholm for many of its 800,000 immigrants (Hoge, 1998).

Immigration creates a variety of cultural fears: the fear that a nation can't control its own boundaries; the fear that an ethnically homogeneous population will be altered through intermarriage; the fear of an influx of a "strange" way of life with unfamiliar religious rituals and cultural habits; the fear that newcomers will encroach on property, clog the educational system, and suck up social benefits owned and largely paid for by "natives" (P. Kennedy, 1993). Many people also express concern that immigrants are responsible for outbreaks of such diseases as AIDS, tuberculosis, measles, and cholera, which strain health care systems and thus create even more resentment. Above all, they fear that immigrants and their offspring may one day become a statistical majority, rendering the "natives" powerless in their own country. Nevertheless, the trend toward immigration is unlikely to slow down as long as communication and transportation continue to shrink the globe and economic disparities between countries continue to exist.

The Impact of Population Trends in the United States

How are these demographic processes affecting the population in the United States? Talking about common effects is difficult because different ethnic, religious, and gender groups experience population trends differently. Hispanics, for instance, have a significantly higher birthrate than non-Hispanic whites. Catholics and Mormons have higher birthrates than people of other religions (Weeks, 1995). U.S. women, on average, can expect to live longer than U.S. men.

Nevertheless, two important demographic trends in the United States will exert a profound effect on the entire population in years to come—the growing proportion of nonwhite, non–English-speaking immigrants and their children, and the shifting age structure of the population, marked by a growing proportion of elderly and a shrinking proportion of young people. These two trends together strain the social fabric, raising questions about the fair distribution of social resources.

Immigration and the Changing Face of the United States

Because the U.S. population is growing at a manageable rate, U.S. residents may have trouble understanding the impact of population explosions in other countries on their everyday lives. But as populations burst the seams of national boundaries elsewhere, many of those seeking better opportunities end up in the United States. Some arrive legally by plane, boat, or train. Others arrive illegally by foot or are smuggled in the backs of trucks or the bottoms of cargo ships.

The Immigrant Tide. In the mid-1980s the U.S. Bureau of the Census predicted that by the year 2050 the United States would have a population of 300 million. In the early 1990s, however, the bureau revised its estimate, projecting instead a population of 383 million by 2050 (Pear, 1992). It has over 280 million today.

Part of the reason these projections were adjusted was that immigration increased more than had been anticipated. In the early 1990s, between 1 and 1.8 million documented immigrants were entering the country each year, although that figure had declined to about 660,000 by 1998 (U.S. Bureau of the Census, 2000b). In addition, according to Immigration and Naturalization Service estimates, more than 5 million illegal immigrants are currently living in the United States (U.S. Bureau of the Census, 1999b). One of every 10 U.S. residents today (28 million people) was born somewhere else. In California one out of every four residents is foreign born (U.S. Bureau of the Census, 1998a). The Bureau of the Census predicts that more than 90% of the growth

Exhibit 13.5 **Shifting Sources of Legal Immigrants to the United States**

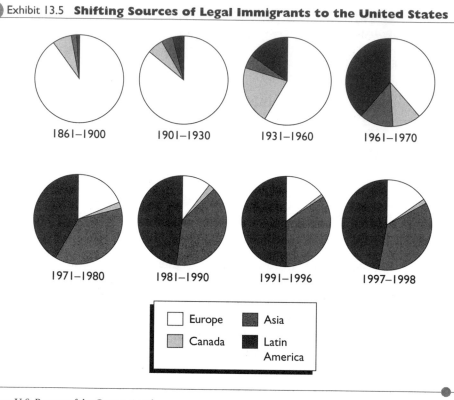

1861–1900	1901–1930
1931–1960	1961–1970
1971–1980	1981–1990
1991–1996	1997–1998

Legend:
- Europe
- Canada
- Asia
- Latin America

Source: U.S. Bureau of the Census, 2000b.

in the U.S. population by the year 2050 will have been caused by immigration that occurred after 1991 (cited in Honebrink, 1993).

This isn't the first time the U.S. population has been radically increased by a flood of immigration. In the first decade of the 20th century, nearly 9 million immigrants entered the country. What makes contemporary immigration different, though, is that relatively few of today's newcomers are of European descent (see Exhibit 13.5). In the late 19th century, 90% of the immigrants who came to the United States were from northern and southern Europe. But in 1997 only 14% were from Europe; 33% were from Asia and 44% from Latin America. The vast majority of undocumented immigrants who enter the country each year come from Latin America; more than half come from Mexico alone (U.S. Bureau of the Census, 2000b).

Not surprisingly, then, the racial and ethnic composition of the United States has changed more quickly and dramatically in the past decade than at any previous time in the 20th century. Experts estimate that by the year 2050 the proportion of U.S. whites will decrease by 9%, and Hispanics will see their share of the population increase by 119% and Asians, by 118% (cited in Begun, 2000).

Until quite recently, the non-European immigrant population was not spread equally across the country. Immigrants tended to settle in large urban areas that serve as ports of entry (New York, Los Angeles, Chicago, San Francisco, Houston, Miami, and so on). More than half of all Hispanics live in California and Texas. Of the 20 metropolitan areas with the largest proportion of Asian residents, 8 are in California and 6 are in the eastern corridor that runs from Boston to Washington, DC. In 2001 California became the first big state in which non-Hispanic whites are no longer the statistical majority. Hispanics will become an absolute majority there by 2040. As recently as 1970 the state was 80% white (cited in Purdum, 2000).

However, early figures from the 2000 U.S. Census show that Hispanic and Asian immigrants are settling in towns and cities all across the United States. Questions of how to integrate immigrants are being debated not just in California and New York, but in Illinois, Iowa, Georgia, and West Virginia as well (Sachs, 2001).

Globalization has changed the contemporary immigrant experience in the United States. Advances in technology and cheaper travel fares mean that today's immigrants are less likely than their earlier counterparts to sever all ties to their homelands. Many immigrants base themselves in the United States—getting a job, finding a place to live, and so on—but maintain vital ties to their homelands. Those with the economic means travel back and forth frequently between their country of origin and the United States.

The strains of high immigration levels are likely to continue for some time. Most people who immigrate to the United States are pulled by the lure of employment and a better life. Until population and economic pressures ease in other regions of the world, the United States will remain an appealing destination.

Social Responses to Immigrants. Immigrants often find that they are the targets of a variety of social anxieties, from economic tension to outright anger (Sontag, 1992). The problem is particularly acute in California. In a 1992 survey 76% of Californians felt there were too many immigrants entering their state, 78% said immigrants had become a financial burden on the state, and 80% thought steps should be taken to limit immigration (cited in Miles, 1992). In 1994 voters in California passed Proposition 187—a bill that makes illegal immigrants ineligible for public social services, public health services, and public school education at the elementary, secondary, and postsecondary levels. In 1998 a federal appeals court ruled that most of the initiative was unconstitutional.

The changing ethnic configuration of the U.S. population is not just heightening tensions between immigrant groups and whites but may also increase animosity between minority groups. To the extent that vast waves of immigration mean greater competition for unskilled jobs, those most affected by the presence of immigrants are often other people of color. For instance, janitorial companies serving downtown Los Angeles have almost entirely replaced their unionized black workforce with non-unionized, and therefore less expensive, immigrants from Latin America and Asia. African Americans are also losing jobs as gardeners, busboys, construction workers, and nannies (Miles, 1992).

New immigrants also face animosity from members of their own racial or ethnic groups who arrived earlier. According to the 1992 Latino National Political Survey, more than 70% of the respondents—which included people of Cuban, Mexican, and Puerto Rican descent—felt that too many Hispanic immigrants were coming into this country (Suro, 1992). About two-thirds felt that special preferences should not be given to Latin American immigrants. The researchers concluded that the strain of competing with recent Hispanic immigrants is felt as strongly by Hispanics as it is by whites and African Americans.

U.S. residents have always had a love–hate relationship with immigrants. In good times immigrants have been inexpensive and welcome contributors to the economy. Earlier in the century, their labor helped build roads and the U.S. rail system. Immigrants have filled unwanted jobs, opened businesses, and improved the lives of many U.S. residents by working cheaply as housekeepers, dishwashers, and gardeners. When times are bad, however, or when the political winds shift, many U.S. residents are inclined to shut the door and blame immigrants for many of the country's economic and social woes. Hatred directed toward Middle Eastern immigrants reached a peak in the months following the September 11 attacks in 2001.

Micro-Macro Connection
The Peculiar Politics of Immigration

In 1996 the conservative Republican Pat Buchanan ran his unsuccessful but influential presidential campaign on a theme that immigrants were overrunning the country and would soon "dilute" its European character. He called for the immediate deportation of all illegal aliens and advocated an impenetrable barrier along the border between the United States and Mexico to keep them out.

Harsh anti-immigrant rhetoric is not the exclusive domain of conservative politicians, however. For instance, in 2000 both major presidential candidates supported limits on immigration. Some Democratic politicians, such as California's Senator Dianne Feinstein, have also called on the government to seal the U.S. borders. Their concern is that immigration, both legal and illegal, hurts poor U.S. residents. According to one liberal journalist, competition with immigrants has accounted for roughly half the recent decline in wages among unskilled workers (Lind, 1996). The greatest gains in income by middle- and working-class U.S. residents came between 1920 and 1960, an era of immigration restriction. In addition, some environmentalist groups—typically associated with politically liberal causes—oppose unlimited immigration on the grounds that it will render an already overcrowded country unable to protect its environment (Holmes, 1995).

In 1996 the U.S. Senate passed a bill, the Immigration and Financial Responsibility Act, that authorized the hiring of an additional 4,700 U.S. border patrol agents, made it more difficult for those in the country illegally to gain employment, and set limits on social services available to illegal immigrants (W. Graham, 1996). Other legislation has been directed toward limiting the rights of immigrants who are in this country legally. Welfare reforms in 1996 slashed the number of legal immigrants who could use government services such as prenatal care, job training, college loans, Medicaid, and supplemental security income (Schmitt, 1996).

Not everyone involved in politics is so fervently anti-immigrant. Rather odd coalitions of groups at vastly different ends of the political spectrum lobby on behalf of immigrants. Some Christian fundamentalists, for instance, assert that proposals to restrict immigration for parents and siblings of naturalized U.S. citizens are "antifamily."

The National Rifle Association and the American Civil Liberties Union—as politically opposite as any two organizations could be—are both opposed to a proposal that immigrants be required to carry a national identification card containing a photograph and fingerprints. For many civil rights organizations and advocates for ethnic minorities, immigration is a human rights issue, and hostility toward immigrants is seen as fundamentally racist (Holmes, 1995).

In addition, more people now see the economic benefits of immigrants, legal and illegal. In a 1993 Gallup poll, 26% of respondents said that immigrants helped the economy; 64% said they hurt it. By 2000, 44% said that immigrants helped the economy and only 40% said they hurt it (cited in Schmitt, 2001a). Indeed, according to the National Academy of Sciences immigration produces substantial economic benefits for the United States, outweighing the slight reduction in wages and job opportunities it creates for low-skilled U.S. workers (cited in Pear, 1997). The academy estimates that immigration has added perhaps $10 billion a year to the nation's output. Others have argued that immigrants are directly responsible for the economic recoveries some areas have experienced in the late 1990s. In California, for example, the number of Hispanic-owned companies grew from 70,000 in 1982 to 280,000 in 1996. California immigrants are more likely to be self-employed, start their own businesses, and experience quick advances in income than their U.S.-born counterparts (Kotkin, 1996).

Furthermore, many wealthy owners of manufacturing facilities and agricultural businesses that employ large numbers of workers believe that the free flow of people across national borders leads to prosperity. Immigration, especially by easily exploited undocumented workers, provides abundant, cheap labor (W. Graham, 1996). As one journalist put it, if "the nation's estimated six million illegal immigrants were expelled tomorrow, thousands of hotels, restaurants, meat-packing plants, landscaping companies and garment factories would likely close" (Schmitt, 2001a, p. 1). In 2000, conservative business leaders and immigrants rights groups were successful in persuading Congress to pass a bill that would open the doors to tens of thousands of unskilled immigrant workers who could fill shortages at hotels and on farms (Sengupta, 2000).

This issue illustrates a clash of political and economic forces. To politicians of all stripes, immigration is a hot-button campaign issue. But as long as powerful business interests see a need for a pool of cheap, mobile labor that is willing to work outside union and regulatory constraints, attempts to "close the borders" will remain ineffective (R. L. Clark & Passel, 1993). Unless U.S. laws barring the employment of illegal immigrants are fully enforced, poor foreigners will continue to come here.

The "Graying" of America

At the same time that the United States must deal with the changing ethnic and racial configuration of its population, it also must address a monumental shift in its age structure. The age structure of a society is one of the key factors determining the need for various social resources. Very young people require physical care and protection. Use of educational resources is based, in large part, on the age of individuals. Workers at the beginning and end of their careers are more susceptible to unemployment than those at midcareer. And age is the major determinant of decisions to retire.

The age structure can even influence certain social problems in ways that are not immediately apparent. Take crime, for instance. According to the FBI, almost 50% more arrests were made in the United States in 1980 than in 1970. To some, this statistic showed that society had fallen apart. To others, it was proof that the country had turned into a police state. Actually, neither was true. The large baby boom cohort had reached its late teens and early 20s, a period in the life course when criminal activity is most common (L. E. Cohen & Land, 1987). The crime rates went up not because crime became a more desirable pursuit or because U.S. residents as a whole became less respectful of the law but simply because more people were at the age when criminal activity is statistically more likely to take place.

Perhaps the most important and most problematic demographic trend in the United States today involves the increasing average age of the population. Two hundred years ago, the median age for U.S. residents was 16; in 1980 it was 30; today it is about 35.8. It is expected to be over 38 by the middle of this century, as the massive baby boom cohort reaches old age (U.S. Bureau of the Census, 2000b).

Two developments in the past few decades have changed the age structure of the United States in dramatic ways (Preston, 1984). The first has been a decrease in the number of children being born. In 1960 there were approximately 24 births per 1,000 people in the population. By 2000 the rate had dropped to 14.2 per 1,000 (U.S. Bureau of the Census, 2000b). The U.S. fertility rate is below the level necessary to replace the current population in the next generation. Most of the conditions that have helped lower fertility—improved work conditions for women and more effective contraception, for example—are not likely to reverse in the future.

The other development has been a rapid increase in the number of people surviving to old age. Technological advances in medicine and nutrition have extended the lives of countless U.S. residents whose counterparts would have routinely died several decades ago. Life expectancy has risen from 67.1 for males and 74.0 for females in 1970 to 74.2 for males and 79.9 for females in 1997 (U.S. Bureau of the Census, 2000b). Between 1960 and 1980, the proportion of people over 65 grew by 54%. By 2030, the United States will have more old people than children (see Exhibit 13.6). The number of people over 85, an age group for which health care costs are exceptionally high, will grow fastest of all, doubling to 6.5 million by 2020 and soaring to 17.7 million by 2050 (Angier, 1995). More than 1 million people will be over the age of 100 by then as well (Rimer, 1998).

Why should we be concerned about the "graying" of the U.S. population? The answer is that a society with an aging population will inevitably experience increased demands for pensions, health care, and other social services catering to the needs of the elderly (OECD, 1988). One of the key concerns arising out of this trend is whether society, and in particular the working population, will be able and willing to bear the additional burden of caring for the growing number of elderly people.

This concern has led demographers to look at the statistical relationship between the elderly and the rest of the population (Kart, 1990). As you can see in Exhibit 13.7, a declining number of tax-paying workers aged 18 to 64 will be available to support each Social Security recipient. On average, 40 or so years from now workers may have to support twice as many older people (R. R. Peterson, 1996).

● Exhibit 13.6 **Changing Age Makeup of the U.S. Population**

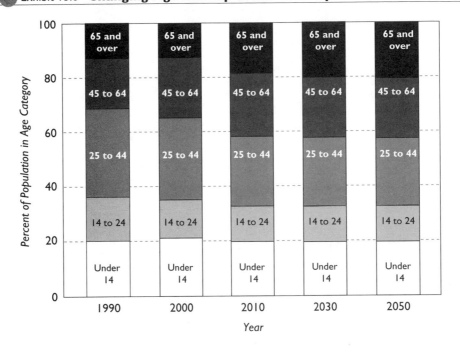

Note: Totals for some categories do not equal 100% due to rounding.

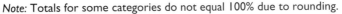

Source: U.S. Bureau of the Census, 2000b.

This figure is probably exaggerated, however. Not all people over 65 are retired, nor are they all in poor health. And not all people between the ages of 18 and 64 are working, nor are they all in good health (Friedland, 1989). Nevertheless, the retirements of older people will be directly or indirectly financed by the working-age population through Social Security and other pension programs. Unless the future's elderly are better able to support themselves financially than today's elderly, the government will have to play an even larger role, through tax dollars, in providing health care and other services.

The graying of the United States is also challenging employers to restructure the workplace. Many more workers have been choosing early retirement, and fewer young workers are available to replace them. As a result, the cost of labor is likely to go up in the future. Some employers will be forced to focus more attention on employee productivity, perhaps turning to machines to replace workers. On the positive side, however, because of the impending labor shortage employers will have to pay attention to the needs of their valuable employees and find better ways to attract and retain them. We may see more employers providing assistance with child and elder care. Employers may also have to find ways to keep older workers more interested in working than

Exhibit 13.7   **Declining Sources of Support for American Retirees**

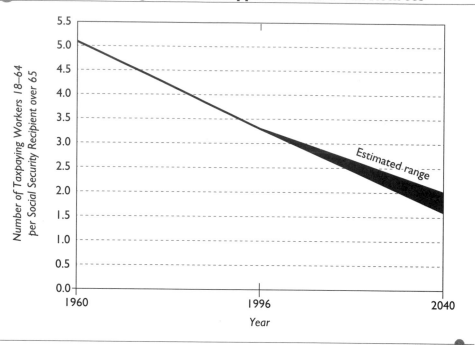

Source: R. R. Peterson, 1996.

retiring by offering bonuses for continued employment or by creating prestigious and well-paid part-time positions. Once again we see that structural forces and private experiences are interconnected.

CONCLUSION

The process of growing older is much more complex than simply adding a year to your age each birthday. It also involves the private experience of major world events, cultural trends, and shifts in population characteristics.

In discussing current and future demographic trends, I can't help but think about my own children. Their Millennium Generation cohort will be the first to reach the teen years during the 21st century. I wonder what kind of impact being born in the late 1980s and growing up in the 1990s and early 2000s will have on their lives. Will the world's population reach the predicted catastrophic proportions, or will we figure out a way to control population growth and enable all people to live quality lives? Will the growing ethnic diversity of U.S. society continue to create tension and conflict, or will people eventually learn how to be a truly multicultural nation? What will be their cohort's single, most definitive "punctuating" event: a war, an assassination, a severe economic depression, a terrorist attack, or some other unimaginable catastrophe? Or will it be world peace, an end to hunger and homelessness, a cure for AIDS?

I also wonder how well social institutions will serve my children's generation. What will their experience in higher education be like? Will jobs be waiting for them when they are ready to go to work? What will be their share of the national debt? How will they perceive family life? Will marriage be an outdated mode of intimacy by the time they reach adulthood? What will be a desirable family size?

As a parent, of course, I'm more than a little curious about how these questions will be answered. I want to know the answers right now! But as a sociologist I realize that they will emerge only from the experiences and interactions of my kids, and others their age, as they progress through their lives. Herein lies the unique and fundamental message of the sociological perspective. As powerful and relentless as the demographic and generational forces described in this chapter are in determining my children's life chances, the responsibility for shaping and changing this society in the 21st century ultimately rests in the hands of their generation. This topic—the ability of individuals to change and reconstruct their society—is the theme of the final chapter.

YOUR TURN

Demographers often use population pyramids to graphically display the age and sex distributions of a population (refer back to Exhibit 13.3). These pictures are often used to draw conclusions about a population's most pressing economic, educational, and social needs. To see what these pyramids look like for different countries, visit the Bureau of the Census Web site (www.census.gov/ipc/www/idbpyr.html).

Using information from the most recent U.S. census (available in the government documents section of your school's library or at www.census.gov), construct population pyramids for several different types of U.S. cities:

- A college town (for example, Ann Arbor, Michigan; Iowa City, Iowa)
- A military town (for example, Norfolk, Virginia; Annapolis, Maryland)
- A large urban city (for example, New York City, Chicago, Los Angeles)
- A small rural town
- An affluent suburb
- A city with a large elderly retirement community (for example, St. Petersburg, Florida; Sun City, Arizona)

Exhibit 13.8 is a form you can copy and then use to construct your population pyramids.

After constructing your population pyramids, describe how the age and sex profiles of these cities differ. What other characteristics of these cities would be different as a result of the shape of their populations? Consider the following:

- The nature of the educational system
- The types of businesses that would succeed or fail
- The sorts of recreational opportunities available
- The political issues considered important and the degree of citizen involvement in political activity
- The important health care issues

Exhibit 13.8 **Population Pyramid Form**

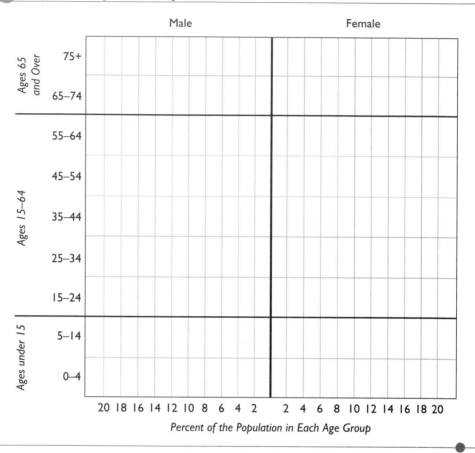

- The crime rates
- The divorce rates
- The suicide rates

From these differences, draw some general conclusions about how people's lives are influenced by the age and sex distribution of the population where they live.

CHAPTER HIGHLIGHTS

- Often overlooked in our quest to identify the structural factors that shape our everyday experiences are the effects of our birth cohort. Birth cohorts are more than just a collection of individuals born within a few years of each other; they are distinctive generations tied to-

gether by historical events, national and global population trends, and large-scale societal changes.

- The earth's population is growing at an unprecedented rate. But different countries experience different rates of growth. Poor, developing countries are expanding rapidly, while the populations in wealthy, developed countries have either stabilized or, in some cases, declined.

- When the population of a country grows rapidly, the age structure is increasingly dominated by young people. In slow-growth countries with low birthrates and high life expectancy, the population is much older on average.

- As conditions in developing countries grow worse, pressures to migrate increase, creating a variety of cultural, political, and economic fears in countries experiencing high levels of immigration.

- The changing age structure of the U.S. population—more older people and fewer younger people—suggests that the gap between rich and poor may increasingly become a gap between old and young.

KEY TERMS

age structure Population's balance of old and young people

birth cohort Set of people who were born during the same era and who face similar societal circumstances brought about by their shared position in the overall age structure of the population

cohort effect Phenomenon in which members of a birth cohort tend to experience a particular life course event or rite of passage—puberty, marriage, childbearing, graduation, entry into the workforce, death—at roughly the same time

demographer Sociologist who studies trends in population characteristics

demographic transition Stage of societal development in nonindustrialized countries marked by growing life expectancy and high birthrates; concept used to explain why populations in less developed countries grow faster than those in more developed countries

migration The movement of populations from one geographic area to another

period effect Phenomenon in which a historical event or major social trend contributes to the unique shape and outlook of a birth cohort

Funeral Rituals in the Netherlands

Marrie Bot

Rituals for the dead are typically dominated by religious beliefs and norms. In the Netherlands, however, rapid secularization and massive immigration have had a great impact on death ceremonies.

The sudden death of my father in 1984 made me reflect on death, funerals, and mourning rituals. I realized then how little is known about the manner in which the dead are cared for, among either the native Dutch population or the ethnic minorities who have settled in the Netherlands over the past decades. I began my project in 1990 by setting up a network of informants and mediators of 10 population groups. From 1990 to 1998 I attended more than 100 funerals of Roman Catholic, Protestant, Jewish, and secular Dutch groups. I also photographed the death rituals of many ethnic groups living in the Netherlands, including Creoles and Hindus from Surinam; Pakistani, Iranian, and Surinam-Javanese Muslims; Cape Verdeans; and Chinese.

These photos are from my book *A Last Farewell: Funeral and Mourning Rituals in the Multi-cultural Society of the Netherlands*. It shows the rituals and death customs from the moment the dead person is washed to the last mourning rituals, which are sometimes repeated many years after the death of a person. I also conducted a comprehensive study into the origin and the meaning of the different rituals.

● The deceased person, a young woman, is taken to the cemetery by a traditional Dutch funeral coach drawn by Friesian horses. In the past the entire cortege was made up of coaches, which have now been replaced by black funeral cars. The horse-drawn funeral coach is now only used when the relatives request it, usually for nostalgic reasons.

● At the end of the cremation ceremony of a 13-year-old boy, white balloons were sent up in the presence of his parents, brother, fellow pupils, and scouting friends.

● A man and a woman looked after a friend who suffered from Hodgkin's disease. After he died, they washed their friend themselves and dressed him in his favorite party suit. Because they did not want him to be laid out in an impersonal funeral parlor, they laid him in his own bed at home. From time to time during the days preceding the funeral ceremony, they sat with him and with other friends.

Although I was interested in the ethnic experience, I noticed that secularization has also changed funeral rituals in the Netherlands. Under the influence of the predominantly Protestant culture, Dutch death ceremonies were always very formal and sober. But by 1997 60% of the Dutch population had become secular, 19% Roman Catholic, and only 21% Protestant. Traditionally the dead were buried, but nowadays more than half of the population prefers cremation. And by the end of the 1980s AIDS and cancer patients were asking for personalized farewell rituals. The media reported on these new types of rituals, and planning one's own cremation or funeral became a generally accepted option.

The arrival of immigrants with their own diverse funeral and mourning rituals also caused many changes. The Dutch law regulating the disposal of the dead has been adjusted to meet the needs of these immigrant groups. Every population group in the Netherlands may now bury or cremate its dead as it sees fit.

Jewish Funeral Rituals

From the 16th century, Jews from southern and eastern Europe have emigrated to the Netherlands. More than 140,000 mainly poor Jews lived in the Netherlands around 1940, but most died in the German concentration camps during World War II. At the moment around 30,000 Jews live in the Netherlands. Only 25% belong to an orthodox or liberal religious community. The other Jews have assimilated and consider their Jewishness as a cultural identity based on ancestry.

For those who do observe the religious rules, the dead are buried at a Jewish cemetery, where graves are left eternally. At most Dutch cemeteries, graves are sometimes removed after 30 years.

The traditional Jewish mourning period lasts seven days to a year, depending on the relationship of the next of kin. The relatives must adhere to strict rules.

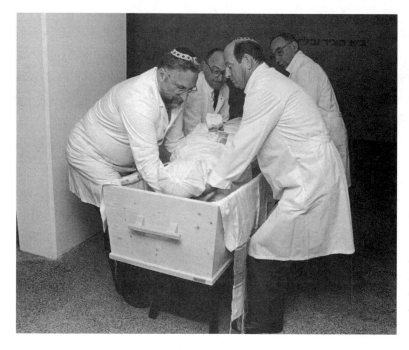

● Under traditional Jewish law, the dead are buried. The deceased person is immediately covered with a sheet. Nobody, not even a close relative, is allowed to see the dead person. Viewing the dead is common among other groups in the Netherlands. With the Jews, neither relatives nor the undertaker lay out the deceased; rather, a Jewish funeral association handles this task. Its members dress the deceased in white clothes, because after death everybody is the same to God, regardless of position in life.

Surinam-Creole Death Rituals

Creoles are the descendants of the African slaves in the former Dutch colony of Surinam. Many Surinam people emigrated to the Netherlands when Surinam became independent in 1975. Some 100,000 Creoles now live in the Netherlands, mainly in the large cities. They have assimilated into Dutch society but have kept many of their own cultural and religious traditions. Protestant-Christian and Winti beliefs play an important role in their funeral rituals.

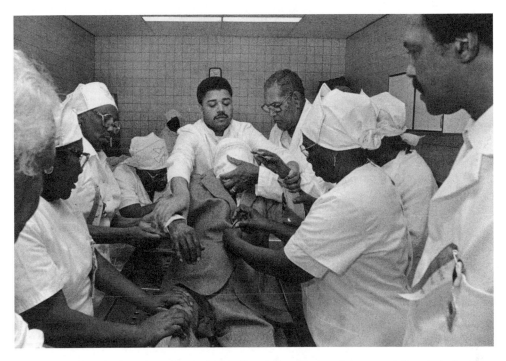

● When a Creole dies, the relatives hire a Creole brotherhood that specializes in laying out the dead. Their members, the *Dinari,* perform the washing and dressing rituals with great care in a funeral parlor. The deceased is asked for permission before each ritual is performed, while Creole and Christian songs are sung. The songs are alternated with the drinking of rum and brandy. The next of kin may not be present during these "secret" rituals.

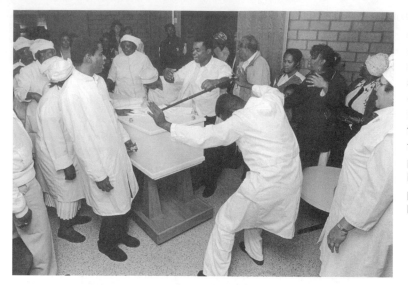

● At the wake, the deceased is carried into the room while the Dinari are singing and dancing. To the accompaniment of loud crying and lamenting, the relatives carry out the farewell rituals. However, no tears may fall on the dead person, because then his or her soul could not leave in peace, which would bring bad luck for the relatives.

● After the burial, the relatives and friends gather on the eighth day (*aiti dey*) and during the sixth week (*siksi wiki*) at home. A meal for the deceased is put outside, and in the living room a candle and a glass of water are put on a table laid with a white tablecloth. According to Winti belief, this arrangement will maintain the contact between the living and the soul of the dead and the spirits of the ancestors. All those present read from the Bible and sing Christian and Creole songs from 8 o'clock in the evening till 5 o'clock in the morning. After midnight the atmosphere can become more cheerful, and people drink, dance, and reminisce about the deceased.

448

Islamic Funeral Rituals

There are some 600,000 Muslims in the Netherlands. They come from a great many different countries, such as Turkey, Morocco, Pakistan (migrant workers), Surinam, Indonesia (a former Dutch colony), Iran, and many African countries (asylum seekers). They are a heterogeneous population, who combine the general rules of the Koran with their own cultural and religious traditions, which are expressed during the burial ceremonies.

Muslims are allowed to bury their dead at cemeteries in the Netherlands according to their rules: They can bury their dead within 24 hours, without a coffin, and at graveyards that are only for Muslims. The largest group of Muslims, the Turks and Moroccans, still prefer taking their dead to their native country and burying them there.

Death is the will of Allah, and therefore deep mourning may last only three days. The condolence reception is at the home of the deceased person's family. Most Muslims continue the death rituals for 40 days, however. On certain days the men read the Koran for the salvation of the soul of the deceased. After they have finished reading, relatives show their gratitude by offering them a large meal on behalf of the deceased. Women keep themselves apart in the kitchen or bedroom.

● Relatives or volunteers of the same gender as the dead person wash him or her following standard Islamic rules. The Surinam-Javanese in the photo are liberal and sometimes allow the washing rituals to be performed by someone of the opposite sex. The dead person must be wrapped in a white shroud, because after death everyone is the same to Allah.

● After the ritual washing, Pakistani men recite the death prayers, led by an imam. Women are not allowed to be present because the sexes are routinely segregated and also because their loud wailing and sobbing would disturb the peace of the dead. At the end of the ceremony, the men bid farewell by walking past the coffin.

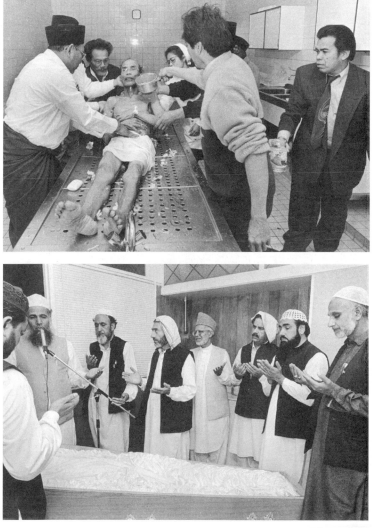

Chinese Ancestor Worship

At the beginning of the 20th century, the Chinese came to the Netherlands from China, Hong Kong, Surinam, Indonesia, and Vietnam. It is a diverse group consisting of some 60,000 people. Most Chinese keep themselves apart from mainstream Dutch society. They work mostly in restaurants owned by other Chinese and have relationships among themselves based on their country of origin and language.

The death cult plays an important role for all traditional Chinese. It is a combination of elements of the three Chinese religions: Taoism, Confucianism, and Buddhism. Faith teaches that the dead continue to live in the dangerous underworld while they are on their way to the Western Paradise. The dead continue to influence the lives of the relatives. The living have a lifelong obligation to help their ancestors on their journey to paradise by making sacrifices. They hope that their ancestors will show their gratitude by keeping them healthy, making them rich, and granting them sons.

● At the burial the relatives place a meal and incense at the grave, and they also burn paper clothes and large stacks of fake money called "hell bank notes." The son must conduct these rituals. Three times a year relatives visit the graves to honor all ancestors. The Surinam-Chinese family in the photo is making a threefold sacrifice at the Rotterdam cemetery—for the father in the grave, for their grandparents buried in Surinam, and for their great-grandfather in China.

Surinam-Hindu Death Rituals

The Surinam-Hindustani are descendants of the contract workers who were taken from north India (Hindustan) to Surinam around 1900. Since the independence of Surinam, some 100,000 Surinam-Hindustani have emigrated to the Netherlands. About 80% of them are Hindus, 16% Muslims, and 4% Christians.

The Surinam-Hindus live predominantly in the larger cities and have adopted the lifestyle and work pattern of the Western world. At home they adhere to the Hindu faith and rules, which are mainly practiced during the obligatory ceremonies, the *sanskaars*, connected to rites of passage. The rituals for the dead are most important. The deceased is carefully washed and smartly dressed in the funeral parlor by the relatives.

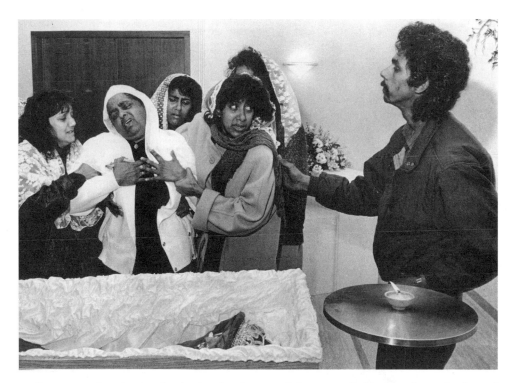

● Receptions for viewing the dead and making condolences are held every day in the funeral parlor until the day of the cremation. Just as at Creole funerals, the closest relatives participate in the ritual crying and wailing, and sometimes people faint. With orthodox Hindus, the son or husband carries out all the rituals for the deceased. On the day of the cremation his head is shaved, except for a small tuft of hair on the top, which is regarded as the seat of his wisdom. He is now clean and ready to perform his task.

● On the same day that the cremation takes place, the son, supervised by the Hindu priest called a *pundit,* carries out a sacrifice ritual lasting hours. Its purpose is to protect the deceased father until the moment of the cremation. One of the funeral parlors in Rotterdam has special facilities for Hindus and Chinese so that they can perform their fire offerings.

● The relatives, and often hundreds of friends of the deceased, bid a ritual farewell in the funeral parlor. These gatherings are often very emotional.

● During the year of mourning, the four offering rituals for the soul of the dead person are very important. On the tenth day and the thirteenth day, and in the sixth and twelfth months, the entire extended family gathers at the home of the deceased. This photo shows the offering ritual on the thirteenth day. The ceremony begins at 10 o'clock in the morning and continues till 3 o'clock in the afternoon. The home bar has been covered, as alcohol is banned during the mourning rituals. In this special case the brother of the deceased woman, who is divorced, conducts the offering rituals because the woman's son is still too young. Nevertheless, the boy's head was also shaven, and he had to participate in the ritual with his uncle on the tenth and thirteenth days.

The person making the offerings must carry out a number of complicated proceedings under the supervision of the pundit. He takes care that the deceased will have a new cosmic body and hence will be able to complete the difficult journey to *Yama,* the realm of the dead. There the deceased will be united with his or her ancestors and await reincarnation. During every ceremony, a meal for the deceased is put outside and gifts are offered to the pundit to help the deceased during his or her journey.

After the rituals the guests eat a special vegetarian meal and usually stay to chat for a long time.

Architects of Change: Reconstructing Society

Social Change

Social Movements

The Sociological Imagination Revisited

The 1992 film *Lorenzo's Oil* dramatized the true story of a couple, Augusto and Michaela Odone, who discovered that their son, Lorenzo, was suffering from a rare disease known as adrenoleukodystrophy (ALD). This disease destroys the protective coating around nerve fibers, progressively impairing victims' ability to talk, walk, and care for themselves. Death is slow, painful, and certain. Frustrated by doctors' overwhelming pessimism and inability to treat their son's disease, and having no scientific training whatsoever, the Odones launched a two-person crusade to find a treatment. They read obscure medical journals and managed to find a few medical and chemical experts who were willing to help them. They eventually discovered that a combination of two natural oils would stop the physical decline brought about by ALD. The film ends with a visual testimony to the many other children who used the Odones' oil preparation and were spared the debilitating effects of the disease.

As with all films derived from real-life events, however, there is some debate about whether the facts of Lorenzo's life and the actions of his parents were different from the film's portrayal. Nevertheless, the message is sociologically compelling: Two individuals were able to overcome the institutional indifference of the medical establishment to find their own solution to a seemingly insoluble problem.

The Odones succeeded in helping their son precisely because the massive health care system couldn't. From an institutional perspective, pharmaceutical companies see little profit in investing in so-called orphan diseases, ailments that affect only a small percentage of the total population. Furthermore, new drugs must be tested meticulously to determine their effectiveness and to identify all potentially dangerous side effects before they are made available to the public. A sharp line must be drawn between the need to satisfy the principles of sound scientific method and the desire to help individual people (D. J. Rothman & Edgar, 1992). As we have seen throughout this book, institutions must operate in a highly structured, standardized, and impersonal way, at a level above the interests and personalities of the individual people they are created to serve. Imagine the chaos that would ensue if the system were set up so that any parent with a sick child could compel pharmaceutical companies and medical researchers to concoct unique treatments. The entire health care system would quickly collapse.

But such institutional needs are often little comfort to the individuals whose lives operate under the influence of that institution. Lorenzo's story illustrates the inherent tension between individuals and institutions. Yet it also shows that individuals can overcome bureaucratic lethargy and actually change a part of their social structure. As a result of the Odones' actions, the standard medical approach to ALD will probably never be the same again.

The Odones aren't the only individuals who have succeeded in altering the health care system. Technology has dramatically increased people's access to medical information and research. More than 100,000 medical Web sites now offer information—some of it more trustworthy than others—on everything from common colds to exotic diseases. Such access is changing the way doctors and patients interact. In the past, only the most dedicated individuals, such as the Odones, were able to become highly involved and informed patients. Today, when a doctor mentions a diagnosis, many patients immediately rush to their computers to learn more about their conditions. When a doctor prescribes a drug, patients can go online to find information on its effectiveness and its side effects. And when they visit their doctors, more and more patients arrive with reams of printout bearing information gleaned from Web sites (Kolata, 2000). Any patient with access to the Internet can now take the initiative and influence the course of his or her treatment.

Furthermore, by working together individuals with common illnesses or common concerns have been able to overcome institutional obstacles and act as their own best advocates. For instance, in the early 1990s AIDS activists, frustrated by mounting deaths and a government drug-approval process that often required years to get drugs into the hands of the people who needed them, succeeded in changing the way AIDS drugs are developed and regulated. Potentially helpful treatments are now being produced more quickly (Arno & Feiden, 1992). More recently, AIDS activists have been successful in pressuring pharmaceutical companies to allow developing countries in sub-Saharan Africa to import cheaper, generic anti-AIDS drugs (Swarns, 2001). Unlike Lorenzo's parents, however, AIDS activists are members of an organized social movement.

This theme—the power of individuals acting collectively to influence the structural elements of their society—guides us through this final chapter of the book. I have spent the previous 13 chapters discussing how our society and everything in it is socially constructed and how these social constructions, in turn, impact the lives of individuals. At times the message has been pessimistic, even downright gloomy. You may well feel a little helpless when considering how much control culture, bureaucracies, institutions, and systems of social stratification have over our lives. And being upbeat is hard when talking about such things as poverty, racial and sexual inequality, and global population problems. It's only fitting, then, to end this book on a more encouraging note, with a discussion of social change and the ways individuals can reconstruct their society.

Social Change

Whether it occurs in our personal relationships, in our cultural norms and values, in our systems of stratification, or in our institutions, change is the preeminent characteristic of modern human societies. The world in which you are living at this precise moment is undoubtedly different from the one I experienced when I wrote this book. Everywhere you look—your relationships, your school, your job, your home, your entertainment equipment, your diet, your clothes, your government—institutional and cultural change is the rule, not the exception.

Consider U.S. family life over the past 40 or 50 years. Divorce rates skyrocketed, then stabilized. Women have entered the workforce in unprecedented numbers. People are waiting longer to get married, and once they do, they are having fewer children. Cultural concerns about gender equality have altered the way men and women relate to one another inside and outside the home. Social and sexual rules that once seemed permanent have disintegrated: Unmarried couples can live openly together, unmarried women can have and keep their babies, and remaining single and remaining childless have become acceptable lifestyle options (Skolnick & Skolnick, 1992). In short, today's American family bears little resemblance to the cultural ideal of the 1950s.

These changes have, in turn, affected other institutions. Because so many families are headed by dual-earner couples, children spend less time with their parents than they did in the past, forcing families to depend on others to care for their children: paid caregivers, friends, teachers. More parents than ever before now rely on professional day care centers to watch their preschool-age children. Many of these centers require that children be toilet trained in order to enroll, forcing many parents to exert premature pressure on their children to comply. As a result, many pediatricians report they are seeing more children with toilet training problems, such as lack of daytime and nighttime urine control (Goode, 1999a).

Schools are also being called on to address many of the problems that families used to deal with, by providing students with training in moral values, technological and financial "literacy," adequate nutrition, and practical instruction to help them avoid drug and alcohol abuse, teen pregnancy, and AIDS.

Not surprisingly, the very nature of childhood is also changing. Contemporary social critics argue that childhood has all but disappeared in the modern world. In the United States, children are exposed to events, devices, and ideas that would have been inconceivable to their baby boomer or Generation X parents. Parents and school officials place unprecedented pressures on children to perform and succeed:

> Preschoolers read, fifth graders take S.A.T.'s for admission to summer college programs and high school juniors are told they need three advanced-placement or college-level courses for Ivy League consideration. And they are urged to build a curriculum vitae that includes sports, student government, music, volunteer work, summer courses and internships. Children are drowning, up until midnight. (Gross, 1997, p. 22)

We read about 12-year-olds becoming pregnant and 7-year-olds being tried for such crimes as rape and drug smuggling. In Columbus, Ohio, an 8-year-old girl was charged with attempted murder for allegedly pouring poison into her great-grandmother's drink because the two didn't get along. In Pensacola, Florida, a 5-year-old girl faced assault charges for beating a 51-year-old school counselor. The 2000 National Longitudinal Study of Adolescent Health found that one in four young people between the ages of 12 and 17 has used a gun or knife—or has been in a situation where someone was injured by a weapon—in the past year ("Study finds increase in weapons use," 2000). No wonder that since the late 1980s 44 states have adopted new laws enabling courts to try more children as adults. Each year approximately 6,000 children are sent to adult prisons (Bradsher, 1999b). The situation is even worse in other parts of the world. For instance, a growing number of children are being drawn into combat as soldiers. According to the United Nations, more than 300,000 children under 18—some as young as 7—are taking part in armed conflicts in places such as the Sudan, Colombia, Angola, and Afghanistan ("UN to protect children," 1999).

Another noticeable change in contemporary society is the fundamental nature of work. If you had taken this course 30 years ago, your instructor would have needed only a few tools: a good collection of books on the subject, a manual typewriter, some pencils, a stack of carbon paper, and a love of the discipline. Good instructors today still need a love of the discipline (I hope), but it's becoming difficult to teach interestingly, effectively, and efficiently without taking advantage of state-of-the-art technology: a high-speed desktop computer, access to the Internet, electronic mail, online databases, computerized test banks, a video library, and access to photocopy and fax machines. My university offers financial incentives to professors who want to incorporate the latest technology into their courses. Technological advances have made inroads into almost every occupation—as well as almost every social institution.

As a result of substantive changes affecting many social institutions simultaneously, the United States and other technologically advanced societies have become what sociologists call **postindustrial societies.** Economies that once centered around farms or factories and the production of material goods now revolve around information and service industries, including communication, mass media, research and development, tourism, insurance, banking and finance, and computer systems. The everyday lives of ordinary people in these societies are qualitatively different from the lives of those in agricultural or industrial societies.

The Speed of Social Change

In the distant past, social change tended to be slow, almost imperceptible, during the course of one's lifetime. Family and community traditions typically spanned many generations. Although traditional societies still change relatively slowly, postindustrial societies are particularly fast moving. Just in writing this book, I've had to revise several examples at the last minute because some things are changing so abruptly.

You can see evidence of the accelerating pace of change in the way we characterize separate periods of history, each with its own distinct culture and social structure. We frame distant eras in chunks of time hundreds of years long: the Middle Ages, the Dark Ages, the 19th century, and so forth. More recent eras, however, are packaged in terms of decades: the Roaring Twenties, the turbulent 1960s, the self-centered 1980s. In fact, today a culture may adopt a new set of characteristics and a new identity in as little as half a decade. A few years ago I saw a movie called *The Wedding Singer,* which parodied the music, fashion, and attitudes of the late 1980s. I found tremendous humor in the film until I realized that it was treating an era when I was in graduate school as if it were ancient history! These days a popular way to tell people they are out of touch is to zing them with the insult, "That's so nineties!"

Because we live in a world that seems to be in a constant state of flux, we are often tempted to believe that rapid social change is an exclusively contemporary issue.

Keep in mind, however, that sociologists and other scholars have long expressed deep concern over the effects that social change has on people. The 19th-century sociologist Émile Durkheim argued that rapid social change creates a normative vacuum, what he called **anomie,** in which the old cultural rules no longer apply. When things change quickly—through sudden economic shifts, wars, natural disasters, population explosions, or rapid transitions from a traditional to a modern society—people become disoriented and experience anomie as they search for new guidelines to govern their lives.

Widespread anomie affects the larger society as well. When norms are disrupted by rapid social change, our naturally greedy impulses are unleashed. Without moral norms to constrain our unlimited aspirations and with too few resources to satisfy our unlimited desires, we are in a sense doomed to a frustrating life of striving for unattainable goals (Durkheim, 1897/1951). The result, Durkheim felt, is higher rates of suicide and criminal activity as well as weakened ties to family, neighborhood, and friends. But rapid change isn't always bad. Sometimes rapid change is necessary to effectively address shifting social conditions. For instance, over the span of a few years in the late 1990s school districts around the country drastically modified their curriculum in response to the sudden ascendancy of the Internet in students' everyday lives, forever changing the face of U.S. education. In the wake of the September 11, 2001, attacks, universities around the country scrambled to offer more courses on Islam and the politics of the Middle East.

The velocity of change today has affected the way sociologists go about their work, too. When U.S. society was understood to be relatively stable, sociological study was fairly straightforward. Most social researchers in the 1950s believed that one could start a 5- or 10-year study of some social institution, such as the family or higher education, and assume that that institution would still be much the same when the study ended (A. Wolfe, 1991). Today such assumptions about the staying power of institutions are dubious at best. There is no such thing as a permanent social institution. Thus sociologists, like everyone else in contemporary society, have had to adjust their thinking and their methods to accommodate the rapid pace of social change.

Causes of Social Change

The difficulty of pinning down any aspect of society when change is so rapid has led sociologists to study change itself. Following in the footsteps of Durkheim, they ask, What causes all these technological, cultural, and institutional changes? Sociologists who focus on change tell us it can be caused by a variety of social forces, including environmental and population pressures, cultural innovation, and technological and cultural diffusion.

Environmental and Population Pressures. As you saw in the previous chapter, the shifting size and shape of the population is enough by itself to create change in society. As populations grow, more and more people move either into urban areas where jobs are easier to find or into previously uninhabited areas where natural resources remain untapped.

Urbanization, which brings considerable change in societies and in people's lives, has always received a lot of attention from sociologists. But environmental sociologists have also begun to note the complex interplay between people, social structure, and natural resources as previously undeveloped territories are settled. Using these areas for food production has had many benefits for society, to be sure: Fewer and fewer people are dying from famine and malnutrition than ever before. But the positive effects of a growing global food supply have been tempered by the serious environmental damage that new production techniques have caused.

For instance, pesticide use has increased 17-fold over the past several decades, threatening the safety of water supplies. Some insects have developed resistances, which leads to increased pesticide use. New crops require irrigation, which has been accompanied by increased erosion and water runoff. As demand for meat products increases, cattle ranches expand, destroying natural habitats, displacing native animal species, and polluting water sources. The burning of forests to make room for farmland—not to mention the increasing consumption of coal, oil, and natural gas—has been implicated as one of the chief causes of global warming, a climatic condition that is beginning to change people's everyday lives around the world (Cooper, 1998c; Revkin, 1997). Some scientists blame global warming for recent increases in insect-borne diseases such as malaria in Asia, Rift Valley fever in Africa, cholera in Latin America, Hantavirus pulmonary disease in the Rocky Mountain states, and Lyme disease on the eastern seaboard of the United States (Stevens, 1998).

But more positive social change has also accompanied environmental pressures. For example, natural disasters such as earthquakes and tornadoes often inspire improvements in home safety products and architectural design that improve everyone's lives. Likewise, the degradation of the land, sea, and air by pollution has fostered innovative changes in individual and community behavior, such as recycling and conservation systems. In addition, it has motivated the development of environmentally safe products and services (low-watt light bulbs, low-flow shower heads, biodegradable detergent, and so on). The result is felt not only on an individual level but also on a societal level as so-called "green" businesses grow and develop around these innovations and attract investors.

Cultural Innovation. Sometimes change is spurred by scientific discoveries and technological inventions within a society. Consider the invention of corrective eyeglasses, which significantly extended the active lives of near- and far-sighted people and fostered the belief that physical limitations could be overcome with a little ingenuity. The discovery of fire, electricity, and disease processes changed the nature of human lives and cultures for all time. The invention of indoor plumbing, the internal combustion engine, television, the microchip, nuclear fusion, antibiotics, and effective birth control have been instrumental in determining the course of human history. Sometimes the smallest innovation has the largest impact: According to one author, without the machine-made precision screw—the most durable way of attaching one object to another—entire fields of science would have languished, routine maritime commerce would have been impossible, and there would have been no machine tools and hence no industrial products and no Industrial Revolution (Rybczynski, 1999).

Social institutions can sometimes be slow to adjust to scientific and technological innovation. Artificial insemination, in vitro fertilization, surrogate motherhood, and other medical advances in the area of infertility treatment have increased the number of people who can now bear children. Yet these technological developments were changing the face of parenthood well before society began to recognize and address the ethical, moral, and legal issues raised by them. For instance, surrogacy technology has divided motherhood into three separate roles, which can now be occupied by three separate people—the *genetic* mother (the one who supplies the egg from which the fetus develops), the *gestational* mother (the one who gives birth to the baby), and the *social* mother (the one who raises the child)—making legal parenthood unclear in some cases. Legal battles in divorce cases sometimes revolve around which partner is entitled to custody of frozen embryos conceived in a laboratory.

Technological innovations can also change people's behavior in unanticipated ways, as in the following cases (Kolata, 1997; Tenner, 1996):

- The invention of prepackaged sliced bread helped wipe out local bakeries.
- Safer skiing equipment encourages more reckless behavior, leading to an increase in accidents and avalanche fatalities.
- Low-tar, low-nicotine cigarettes encourage people to continue smoking.
- Automated teller machines have made banking more convenient, but lines at these machines in the evening are longer than they used to be at bank tellers' windows during working hours.
- The distractions caused by technological devices used in cars—cellular phones, navigation systems, e-mail systems, entertainment centers, even fax machines—may be responsible for as many as 1.5 million crashes each year.
- Some scientists argue that the emphasis on antibacterial cleanliness in wealthy, technologically advanced countries has been accompanied by an increase in asthma, hay fever, eczema, and other allergic diseases (Morse, 1998). Without contact with dirt and germs—which contain helpful microbes—people's immune systems don't develop the defenses necessary to fight off such diseases.

Similar problems have been created by changes in computer technology. Computers are indeed an indispensable tool in our postindustrial society and will no doubt have a lasting effect on the culture. They now keep track of vast quantities of crucial information in practically every sector of society, and they have all but eliminated the constraints of time and place, whether we're conversing with friends or doing business. But the convenience and unprecedented access to information computers provide us have come at a steep price. On a personal level, "Internet addiction" and carpal tunnel syndrome (a nerve disorder in the hands caused by too much keyboard use) are directly related to the spread of computers. According to some psychologists, cybersex addiction is quickly becoming a national epidemic.

Our reliance on computers also threatens to shatter the privacy of our personal lives. Sometimes that privacy is violated by direct surveillance. For instance, computer programs called "packet filters" enable people to eavesdrop on the millions of e-mail messages people send each other every day. Other times, private information is sold commercially. In 1998 some of the biggest commercial sites on the World Wide Web agreed to feed data about their customers' reading, shopping, and entertainment habits into a system that keeps track of more than 30 million Internet users, without their knowledge (Hansell, 1998). Although names, addresses, and other delicate information will not be divulged, critics fear that crucial pieces of private information, such as credit histories and medical records, will eventually be sold to telemarketing companies, insurance companies, and so on. Like the small villages of a bygone era, the global electronic village no doubt has its share of busybodies and nosy neighbors.

Furthermore, although high-tech electronic and telecommunications gadgets have had breathtaking effects on the way we communicate with others, they've also blurred the traditional boundary between home and work. Cell phones, pagers, and wireless e-mail have created a workday that never ends (Hafner, 2000). With all these devices, the unspoken expectation is that a person will always be reachable. Hence we no longer have any excuse to be "away" from work, not even while on vacation. If such technological intrusion continues, institutions such as the family are almost certain to change.

Diffusion of Technological and Cultural Practices. Another cause of social change is **cultural diffusion**: the process by which beliefs, technology, customs, and other cultural items are spread from one group or society to another. Most of the taken-for-granted aspects of our daily lives originally came from somewhere else. For instance, pajamas, clocks, toilets, glass, coins, newspapers, and soap were initially imported into Western cultures from other cultures (Linton, 1937). Even a fair amount of the English language has been imported; for example,

- *Anatomy* (Greek)
- *Bagel* (Yiddish)
- *Barbecue* (Taino)
- *Boondocks* (Filipino Tagalog)
- *Caravan* (Arabic)
- *Catamaran* (Tamil)
- *Coyote, poncho* (Spanish)
- *Dynamite* (Swedish)
- *Ketchup* (Chinese)
- *Medicine* (Latin)
- *Safari* (Swahili)
- *Sherbet* (Turkish)
- *Tycoon* (Chinese)
- *Vogue* (French)
- *Zero* (Arabic)

Diffusion often occurs because one society considers the culture or technology of another society to be useful. However, the diffusion process is not always friendly, as you may recall from the discussion of colonization in Chapter 10. When one society's territory is taken over by another society, the indigenous people may be required to adapt to the customs and beliefs of the invaders. When the Europeans conquered the New World, Native American peoples were forced to abandon their traditional ways of life and become more "civilized." Hundreds of thousands of Native Americans died in the process, not only from violent conflict but also from new diseases inadvertently brought by their conquerors. Whether diffusion is invited or imposed, the effect is the same: a chain reaction of social changes that affect both individuals and the larger social structure.

Social Movements

One danger of talking about the structural sources of social change or its cultural, environmental, and institutional consequences is that we then tend to see change as a purely macro-level, structural phenomenon, something that happens to us rather than something we create. But social change is not some huge, invisible hand that descends from the heavens to arbitrarily disrupt our routine way of life. It is, in the end, a phenomenon driven by human action.

Whether it takes the form of a million mothers marching on Washington, DC, to demand gun control legislation or thousands of students filling the streets of Seattle to protest the seamy side of globalization, collective action by large numbers of people has always been a major agent of social change. When people organize and extend their activities beyond the immediate confines of the group, they may become the core of a **social movement** (Zurcher & Snow, 1981).

Underlying all social movements is a concern with social change: the desire to enact it, stop it, or reverse it. That desire may be expressed through a variety of activities, from such peaceful activities as signing petitions, participating in civil demonstrations, donating money, protesting in the streets, and campaigning during elections to such violent activities as rioting and overthrowing a government.

Types of Social Movements

On the basis of their size and the magnitude of their goals, social movements can be categorized as either reform movements or revolutionary movements. A **reform movement** attempts to change limited aspects of a society but does not seek to alter or replace major social institutions. Take the U.S. civil rights movement of the 1960s. It did not call for an overhaul of the U.S. economic system (capitalism) or the political system (two-party democracy). Instead, it advocated a more limited change: opening up existing institutions to full and equal participation by members of minority groups (DeFronzo, 1991). Similarly, the anti–Vietnam War movement sought to change government policy rather than change the form of government itself. Other recent examples of reform movements include the women's movement, the nuclear freeze movement, the labor union movement, and the environmental movement.

Because reform movements seek to alter some aspect of existing social arrangements, they are always opposed by some people and groups. Thus reform movements inevitably spawn **countermovements** designed to prevent or reverse the changes sought or accomplished by an earlier movement. Countermovements are most likely to emerge when the reform movements against which they are reacting become large and effective in pursuing their goals and therefore come to be seen as threats to personal and social interests (Chafetz & Dworkin, 1987; Mottl, 1980).

For instance, the emergence in the 1980s and 1990s of the conservative social movements often called the new religious right was provoked by a growing perception among its members of enormous social upheaval in U.S. society: a breakdown of traditional roles and values and a concerted challenge to such existing institutions as education, religion, and the family. Although members of the new religious right blame these changes on the civil rights, antiwar, student, and women's movements of the 1960s and 1970s (Klatch, 1991), they perceive the women's movement as particularly corrosive. Indeed, the leaders of the new religious right were the first to articulate, in modern times, the notion that the push for women's equality is responsible for the unhappiness of many individual women and the weakening of the American family (Faludi, 1991). The high divorce rate and the increased number of working mothers are often mentioned as proof that the moral bases of family life are eroding (Klatch, 1991).

Through organizations such as the Eagle Forum, the Christian Coalition, the Family Research Council, the National Right to Life Committee, the Traditional Values Coalition, and many smaller groups around the United States, the new religious right has sought to restore the faith, morality, and decency it feels U.S. citizens have lost in recent years. In 1995 the Christian Coalition alone had 1,100 chapters across the country and more than a million members. Its thousands of full-time Christian radio stations and cable television networks reach tens of millions of households.

Over the past few decades the new religious right has successfully shifted the political and social mood of the country. It first gained legitimacy in 1980, when Ronald Reagan and several senate candidates it supported won election. It reasserted its influence in 1994 with the takeover of Congress by conservative Republicans. And it gained even more power and visibility with the election of George W. Bush in 2000, who promoted many religious right themes in his campaign and who on his election appointed a hero of the movement, John Ashcroft, as U.S. attorney general. But many of its most notable triumphs have been at the state and local levels, where it has succeeded in influencing public school curricula as well as antiabortion and anti–gay rights legislation. For instance, even though the majority of U.S. citizens still favor the legal right to abortion, virtually every state in the nation has enacted new restrictions on abortion since 1996. Consequently, fewer and fewer medical schools now teach their students how to perform abortions. In 1991 only 12% of obstetrics and gynecology programs taught abortion, and the percentage has shrunk each year since (Hitt, 1998).

Both the women's movement and the new religious right remain active, creating numerous colorful conflicts in the national political arena. However, it is important to remember that both are pursuing their interests within the existing social system—as do all reform movements and countermovements. In contrast, **revolutionary movements** attempt to overthrow the entire system itself, whether it be the government or the existing class structure, in order to replace it with another (Skocpol, 1979). The American Revolution of 1776, the French Revolution of 1789, the Russian Revolution of 1917, the Iranian Revolution of 1979, and the Afghan Revolution of 1996 are examples of movements that toppled existing governments and created a new social order. Although revolutionary change in basic social institutions can be brought about through nonviolent means (peaceful labor strikes, democratic elections, civil disobedience, and so on), most successful revolutions have involved some level of violence on the part of both movement participants and groups opposing revolution (DeFronzo, 1991).

The Development of a Social Movement

Whatever type they are, social movements occur when unsatisfied people see their condition as resulting from society's inability to meet their needs. Movements typically develop when certain segments of the population conclude that society's resources—access to political power, higher education, legal justice, medical care, a clean and healthy environment, and so on—are distributed unequally and unfairly (R. Brown, 1986). People come to believe that they have a moral right to the satisfaction of their unmet expectations and that this satisfaction cannot or will not occur without some effort on their part. This perception is often based on the experience of past failures of working within the system.

As individuals and groups who share this sense of frustration and unfairness interact, the existing system begins to lose its perceived legitimacy (Piven & Cloward, 1977). In large numbers, individuals who ordinarily might have considered themselves helpless come to believe that they have the capacity to change things and significantly alter their lives and the lives of others. For example, in 2000 tens of thousands of janitors all around the country went on strike to demand health insurance and better wages. In Chicago they blocked downtown traffic. In Los Angeles they walked off their jobs. In New York they marched down Park Avenue. In San Diego some went on a hunger strike. In several cities the janitors won new contracts. Leaders of the movement hope it will motivate other low-wage workers, such as hotel maids and hospital aides, to fight for higher pay.

Ideology. A successful social movement must have an **ideology**, a coherent system of beliefs, values, and ideas that justifies its existence (R. W. Turner & Killian, 1987; Zurcher & Snow, 1981). An ideology fulfills several functions. First, it helps frame the issue in moral terms. Once people perceive the moral goodness of their position, they become willing to risk arrest or worse for the good of the cause; to not act would therefore be immoral. Second, it defines the group's interests and helps to identify people as either supporters or enemies, creating identifiable groups of "good guys" and "villains." Finally, an ideology provides participants with a collective sense of what the specific goals of the movement are or should be.

Consider the antiabortion movement. Its ideology rests on several assumptions about the nature of childhood and motherhood (Luker, 1984). For instance, it assumes that each conception is an act of God, and so abortion violates God's will. The ideology also states that life begins at conception, the fetus is an individual who has a constitutional right to life, and every human life should be valued (Michener, DeLamater, & Schwartz, 1986). This ideology reinforces the view that abortion is immoral, evil, and self-indulgent.

Misdirected or ill-conceived ideologies can sometimes break a social movement. For instance, organized opposition to the 1991 Persian Gulf War was ineffective primarily on ideological grounds. Antiwar activists were committed to an ideological script that had been used successfully in the movement against the war in Vietnam 20 years earlier: Portray the United States as the hostile aggressor (Goertzel, 1993).

But given the reports of Iraqi atrocities and the unsavory actions of Saddam Hussein, the activists had trouble convincing the public that the actions of the U.S. military were wrong. Indeed, 90% of U.S. citizens supported President George H. W. Bush's handling of the crisis. There was no "innocent victim" the United States was attempting to destroy, as had been the case in Vietnam. The leadership of the U.S. Army was quite reluctant to go to war, and there was considerable public reluctance as well. In addition, the congressional vote authorizing the use of force passed by only a narrow margin.

This 1990s antiwar movement was therefore caught between two conflicting ideological positions: opposing Iraqi aggression but painting the United States as the bad guy. By acting only against U.S. military action, those involved in this antiwar movement became unwitting allies of Saddam. In a speech broadcast on CNN on January 28, 1991, he stated,

> All the people of Iraq are grateful to all the noble souls amongst the United States people who are coming out into the street demonstrating against this war. We follow with keenness this sublime level of humanity, which comes out to counter the policies of aggression. (quoted in Goertzel, 1993, p. 143)

If the antiwar movement had focused on legislators who favored stronger economic sanctions against Iraq rather than military intervention, it might have been more effective. But this approach would have required the antiwar movement to abandon its "United States as the hostile aggressor" ideological stance. The movement failed to make a clear distinction between opposition to war and selective opposition to only those wars conducted by the United States (Goertzel, 1993).

Although ideology might be what attracts people to a movement, the ideology must be spread through social networks of friends, family, co-workers, and so on (Zurcher & Snow, 1981). For some people, in fact, the ideology of the movement is secondary to other social considerations. Potential participants in a social movement usually are unlikely to join without being informed about it and introduced to it by someone they know. The ideological leaders of a social movement might want to believe that participants are there because of "the cause," but chances are that participants have a friend or acquaintance who convinced them to be there (Gerlach & Hine, 1970; Stark & Bainbridge, 1980).

Sometimes the activities required to promote or sustain a particular movement run counter to the ideological goals of the movement itself. The leaders of successful political revolutions, for example, soon realize that to run the country they now control, they must create highly structured bureaucracies not unlike the ones they have overthrown.

Individuals in reform movements may also have to engage in behaviors that conflict with the ideological tenets of the movement. The new religious right movement's pro-family, pro-motherhood positions are clearly designed to turn back the feminist agenda. However, early in the movement it became clear that to be successful it would have to enlist high-profile women to campaign against feminist policies. New religious right women frequently had to leave their families, travel the country to make speeches, and display independent strength—characteristics that were anything but the models of traditional womanhood they were publicly promoting.

Ironically, social movements sometimes require the involvement of individuals from outside the group of people whose interests the movement represents. Those individuals who are the most deprived and most in need of massive changes in social arrangements are not necessarily those who are most likely to subscribe to the ideology that sustains the movement. For example, many of the people who risked their lives marching in protests in Alabama and Mississippi during the civil rights movement of the 1950s and 1960s were middle-class white college students from the North.

People who are already disadvantaged may also lack the money, time, skills, and connections that successful movements require. For instance, the people who would stand to benefit the most from environmental improvement—individuals in poor, polluted communities—have historically been uninvolved in the environmental movement. They are often skeptical of the environmentalists, who they feel are taking away their jobs rather than protecting their interests. Recently, however, many members of poor communities have joined the environmental movement, motivated not by a desire to "save the earth" but by an ideology that is more relevant to their everyday lives.

Robert Bullard and Beverly Wright
The Environmental Justice Movement

In Chapter 11 I mentioned that environmental degradation disproportionately affects minority communities. Urban black ghettoes, rural Hispanic "poverty pockets," and economically destitute Native American reservations face the worst environmental devastation in the United States. In Los Angeles, more than 71% of the African Americans and 50% of the Hispanics live in areas with the most polluted air, compared to only 34% of the white population (Bullard, 1993). A report by the Commission for Racial Justice (1987) concluded that the racial makeup of a community is the best predictor of where toxic waste sites in the United States are located.

For the most part, African Americans and other people of color have been underrepresented in the mainstream environmental movement. The ideological supporters of this movement tend to be middle- and upper-middle-class whites whose neighborhoods are relatively unpolluted. They are likely to focus on such goals as wilderness and wildlife preservation, wise resource management, and population control (Bullard, 1993). The environmental degradation of poor, minority communities has been largely overlooked.

The most polluted communities are often on the brink of economic catastrophe, places where providing jobs for residents is of utmost concern. But in many instances bringing jobs to the community has been achieved only at great risk to the health of the workers and the surrounding area. For instance, in 1998 the Louisiana chapter of the National Association for the Advancement of Colored People (NAACP) supported the construction of a $700 million plastics plant in St. James Parish, which it knew could pose dangerous health risks to the neighborhoods nearby. However, at the time the region suffered an unemployment rate of 12% and a poverty rate of 44%. The president of the NAACP said, "Poverty has been the No. 1 crippler of poor people, not chemical plants" (quoted in Cooper, 1998a, p. 532).

Nobody wants garbage dumps, landfills, incinerators, or polluting factories in their backyards. But if these are the only ventures that will provide steady employment for residents, poor communities are left with little choice but to support them. The result has been a form of blackmail: You can get a job but only if you're willing to do work that will harm you, your family, and your neighbors (Bullard, 1993).

This issue is not limited to the United States. In the developing world, the desire for clean air and water to protect public health often conflicts with the need for jobs to help struggling workers survive. In 2000, for instance, thousands of people in New Delhi, India, took to the streets in violent protests, demanding that polluting local factories remain open after the Indian Supreme Court took steps to close them. Many of the protestors were sole breadwinners who were barely able to support their families on the $35 to $50 a month they earned in the local factories (Dugger, 2000).

Hence one of the biggest obstacles to getting people in poor, minority communities involved in the environmental movement has been an economic one: the fear of job loss or plant closure. How do you get people to protest against a polluting factory when that factory is their only hope for economic survival? To answer this question, sociologists Robert D. Bullard and Beverly H. Wright (1992) examined environmental activism within African-American communities in the South, the region of the United States with the largest ecological disparities between black and white communities. They interviewed activist leaders in five communities involved in environmental disputes: Institute, West Virginia; Alsen, Louisiana; Emelle, Alabama; and black neighborhoods in Houston and Dallas, Texas. In addition, they examined newspaper articles, editorials, and feature stories concerning the disputes.

In the 1980s and early 1990s, communities such as these began to challenge both the industrial polluters and the often indifferent mainstream environmental movement by actively fighting environmental threats in their neighborhoods. The key, according to Bullard and Wright, was that these challenges framed environmental degradation within a social justice ideology rather than an exclusively ecological one. In other words, they were able to band together to fight for their own interests by painting pollution and environmental danger as a form of racial discrimination. The communities argued that environmental quality was a basic civil right of all individuals. Consequently, they adopted the confrontational strategies of the earlier civil rights movement. For instance, all the communities used local protest demonstrations, petitions, and press lobbying to publicize their plight.

Bullard and Wright found that all these movements were spearheaded by local people—church leaders, community improvement workers, and civil rights activists—who had very little previous experience with environmental issues. Many of them had worked in other organizations that fought discrimination in housing, employment, and education. Local people played a pivotal role in organizing, planning, and mobilizing opposition activities. Mainstream environmental leaders, referred to as "outside elites," played only a minor role. Indeed, many residents were suspicious of the motives of outside environmentalists and the largely white national environmental movement.

All the environmental justice movements that Bullard and Wright examined achieved some level of success:

- In West Dallas, people were able to convince the city and state to join in a lawsuit against an industrial polluter that routinely pumped more than 269 tons of lead particles into the air each year. The plant was eventually shut down, and some residents won a $20 million out-of-court settlement against the company.
- In Houston, the city council, after intense pressure from the African-American community, passed a resolution opposing the placement of a garbage dump nearby. However, a federal court ruled against the plaintiffs, and the dump was eventually built. Nevertheless, the city council passed ordinances that prohibited city-owned solid waste trucks from dumping at the controversial site and regulated the distance between the landfill and schools, parks, and playgrounds.
- In Alsen, Emelle, and Institute, protesting residents convinced government officials to fine facilities for pollution and safety violations. In addition, they extracted some concessions from the firms, such as technical modifications, updated pollution monitoring systems, and reduced emission levels.

The movement has had some national success as well. In 1994 President Bill Clinton issued an environmental justice executive order in which he called on each federal agency to identify and address the disproportionately high and adverse health effects of its programs, policies, and activities on minority and low-income populations. Environmental justice advocates say that even though the new policy didn't change any laws, it was a major step forward in protecting the civil rights of poor, minority communities.

We're unlikely to see a massive influx of people of color into national environmental groups in the near future. However, multiracial, grassroots environmental groups have been the fastest-growing segment of the environmental movement over the past decade. These groups are increasingly forming alliances with one another and with other community-based groups to increase their power (Bullard, 1993). The days are long gone when minority communities would remain silent or refuse to question the nature of new jobs being promised them by companies manufacturing dangerous products (D. E. Taylor, 1993). And the successes of these groups have caught the attention of mainstream environmental organizations, which now provide support in the form of technical advice, expert testimony, direct financial assistance, fund-raising, research, and legal assistance. The environmental community and the social justice community are beginning to take steps toward reducing the artificial barriers that have historically kept them apart.

Rising Expectations. You might think that major social movements, particularly revolutionary ones, would be most likely to occur when many people's lives were at their lowest and most desperate point. Certainly huge numbers of disadvantaged people who see little chance that things will improve, and who perceive the government as unwilling or unable to meet their needs, are necessary for any massive movements for change (Tilly, 1978).

But some sociologists argue that social movements are actually more likely to arise when social conditions are beginning to improve than when they are at their worst (C. Brinton, 1965; Davies, 1962). Constant deprivation does not necessarily make people want to revolt. Instead, they are more likely to be preoccupied with daily survival than with demonstrations and street protests. Improvements in living conditions, however, show those who are deprived that their society is capable of being different, raising their expectations and sparking a desire for large-scale change. When these expectations aren't met, deprived people become angry. The gap between what they expect and what they have now seems intolerable. Although they may actually be better off than they had been in the past, their situation relative to their expectations now appears much worse (Davies, 1962). Such frustration makes participation in protest or revolutionary activity more likely.

Consider the short-lived prodemocracy movement in China in 1989. During the early 1980s the Chinese government began to introduce economic reforms that opened up markets and created faster growth. It also enacted political reforms that provided citizens with more freedom. The lives of ordinary Chinese were improving, but only slightly and not quickly enough. Because they could now imagine even greater freedom and democracy, young people began to actively protest for more reforms. The result was a wide-scale student movement. The government quickly and violently squashed the movement, although after a while it did continue to gradually liberalize Chinese society.

Resource Mobilization. At any given point, numerous problems in a society need fixing and people's grievances remain more or less constant from year to year. Yet relatively few major social movements exist at any one time. If widespread dissatisfaction and frustration were all that is needed to sustain a social movement, "the masses would always be in revolt" (Trotsky, 1930/1959). What prompts a social movement to get started, gain support, and achieve its goals?

According to *resource mobilization theory*, the key ingredient is effective organization, which keeps a movement going and enables it to be successful. No social movement can exist unless it has an organized system for acquiring money, labor, participants, legal aid, access to the media, and so on (McCarthy & Zald, 1977). How far a movement goes in attaining its goals depends on its ability to expand its ranks, acquire large-scale public support, and transform those who join into committed participants (Zurcher & Snow, 1981).

For example, in many societies people have been systematically harassed, sometimes even beaten or killed, by deranged admirers or jilted lovers. This problem didn't attract prolonged public attention in the United States until the late 1980s and early 1990s, when we began to hear about high-profile celebrities being harassed by fans. Only then did the public recognize "stalking" as a serious social problem in need of immediate attention. The murder of actress Rebecca Shaeffer in 1989 by an obsessed fan mobilized such powerful organizations as the Screen Actors Guild to provide the resources necessary to publicize the problem in the media. Daytime talk shows were filled with celebrities telling frightening stories of being stalked. Antistalking laws finally came into being when other organizations in the victims' rights movement and the battered women's movement linked this problem to their causes (Lowney & Best, 1995).

Most large, long-term social movements involve a national, even international coalition of groups. Such widespread organization makes the movement more powerful by making the mobilization of resources, in the form of people and fund-raising, more efficient. For example, most of us first heard of the movement against corporate globalization in 1999 when thousands of people in Seattle protested a meeting of the World Trade Organization. News reports of the event gave the impression that the protesters were a bunch of renegade anarchists who spontaneously took to the streets to arbitrarily vandalize corporate giants such as McDonald's and Starbucks. Although a few of the protesters were, in fact, excessively destructive, the vast majority consisted of long-time nonviolent supporters of the movement. The mobilization that was required to get so many people out was accomplished by various established organizations, such as the AFL-CIO, Sierra Club, Humane Society, Global Exchange, Public Citizen, and the Rainforest Action Network. In fact, more than 1,200 labor, environmental, consumer, religious, farm, academic, and human rights groups from over 90 nations had already been working to halt the expansion of the WTO long before the Seattle protest took place (Nichols, 2000; Rothschild, 2000).

Moreover, those movements that historically have lasted longest—the women's movement, the civil rights movement, and the environmental movement—are those that are supported by large organizations. The National Organization for Women, the NAACP, the Sierra Club, and the like have full-time lobbyists or political action committees that connect them to the national political system. Few movements can succeed without such connections because achieving social change often requires changing laws or convincing courts to interpret laws in particular ways.

Another important feature of highly organized social movements is an established network of communication (McCarthy & Zald, 1977). The ability to quickly mobilize large numbers of people for, say, a march on the nation's capital depends on the ability to tell them what is going to happen and when and where it will happen. Web sites, phone systems, direct mailing systems, and networked computers are all used by modern movements. Movements need an effective system of mass communication both for getting information to all participants and for recruiting and fund-raising (Tarrow, 1994).

The mass media play an equally important role in the success of a social movement by helping validate and enlarge the scope of its cause. In other words, the media serve as a vital political tool in constructing a particular social reality useful to the movement. The media spotlight sends the message that the movement's concerns are valid and that the movement is an important force in society. A protest march with no media coverage at all is a nonevent. Media recognition is often a necessary condition before those who are the targets of influence respond to the movement's claims and demands (Gamson & Wolfsfeld, 1993).

Movements that succeed in enacting substantial social change are not necessarily those with the most compelling ideological positions or the greatest emotional appeal (Ferree, 1992). Instead, they are the ones with the necessary high-level organization and communication networks to mobilize supporters and the necessary media access to neutralize the opposition and transform the public into sympathizers.

Bureaucratization. It makes sense that the most successful social movements are the best organized. However, high-level organization can backfire if it leads to the rigidity and turf wars common to any bureaucracy. When organizations within a movement differ in their philosophies and tactics, tremendous infighting and bickering may break out among organizations ostensibly working toward the same goal.

For instance, the U.S. civil rights movement during the 1950s and 1960s included many diverse, seemingly incompatible organizations. The National Association for the Advancement of Colored People (NAACP) was large, racially integrated, legalistic, and bureaucratic in form; the Student Non-Violent Coordinating Committee (SNCC) was younger and more militant in its tactics and after a while excluded whites from participation; the Southern Christian Leadership Conference (SCLC) was highly structured, had a religious ideology, and was dominated by male clergy; the Black Muslims and the Black Panthers advocated extreme, sometimes violent methods to achieve civil rights. The ideologies and methods of these diverse civil rights groups often conflicted, which arguably slowed down the extension of civil rights to African Americans.

No matter what their shape, size, or motive, social movements require sustained activity over a long period (R. W. Turner & Killian, 1987). Thus unlike riots, which are of limited duration, social movements may become permanent, bureaucratic fixtures in the political and social environment. Ironically, a social phenomenon whose goal is the large-scale alteration of some aspect of society can, in time, become part of the establishment it seeks to change.

In addition, people who devote their lives to the movement come to depend on it for their own livelihood. Hence social movements organized for the purposes of enacting social change actually provide structure and order for the lives of their members, acting as sources of opportunities, careers, and rewards (Hewitt, 1988).

Political Opportunity Structure. Social movements also depend on conditions outside their reach. One such condition is the structure of existing political institutions. Political systems are more or less vulnerable and more or less receptive to challenge at different times (McAdam, McCarthy, & Zald, 1988). These ebbs and flows of political opportunities produce cycles of protest and movement activity. Movements won't develop if the political structure does not provide some opportunity for change: "Rational people do not often attack well-fortified opponents (Tarrow, 1994, p. 86). When political systems are firm, unyielding, and stable, people have to deal individually with their problems or air their grievances through existing channels. But when a system opens up and people realize it is vulnerable—that they can actually make a difference—movements are likely to develop.

Sometimes these opportunities are unintentional and exist quite independently from the actions of movement members. For instance, similar antinuclear movements arose about the same time in the 1970s in West Germany and France. Both had similar ideologies and used similar techniques. However, the German movement flourished and remains highly influential in German politics today. The French movement was weak and ineffectual and quickly died off. Why were the outcomes of these two movements so different? In West Germany, the government procedure for reviewing nuclear power facilities provided opportunities for those opposed to nuclear power to legally intervene. The procedure in place in France was closed and unresponsive to public sentiment (Nelkin & Pollack, 1981). Similarly, the emergence in the 1970s of the contemporary environmental movement in the United States was possible because government agencies were already sympathetic to environmental concerns (Gale, 1986).

The idea that unintentional political opportunities can encourage social movements for change was dramatically supported by the 1989 prodemocracy movement in the former Soviet Union and Eastern Europe. In the mid-1980s, the Soviet government under Mikhail Gorbachev embarked on a massive program of economic and structural reforms (*perestroika*) as well as a relaxation of constraints on freedom of expression (*glasnost*). The ensuing liberties encouraged open criticism of the political order and created new opportunities for political action (Tarrow, 1994). Protest movements took advantage of these opportunities, leading to the sometimes violent struggles for independence on the part of small, ethnically homogeneous republics that we saw during the 1990s and continue to see today. In other words, only when the political structure became less repressive could these monumental changes take place.

Political instability can sometimes spawn less dramatic reform movements. The changing fortunes of a government can create uncertainty among supporters and encourage challengers to try to take advantage of the situation. Consider once more the civil rights movement in the United States in the 1950s and 1960s. During the 1950s, as the first, early calls for racial equality were being heard, many conservative southern Democrats defected to the Republican Party, where their segregationist leanings met with more sympathy. The ensuing decline of southern white support for the Democratic Party, coupled with the movement of African Americans to large cities in the North, where they were more likely to vote, forced the Democrats to seek black support in the presidential election of 1960. The black vote is widely credited with John Kennedy's narrow victory that year (McAdam, 1982). Hence the Kennedy administration (and later the Johnson administration) felt compelled to campaign for civil rights (Tarrow, 1994). Increased political power, in turn, enhanced the bargaining position of civil rights forces, culminating in two landmark pieces of legislation: the Civil Rights Act of 1964 and the Voting Rights Act of 1965.

At other times, existing political regimes intentionally create or actively support structural opportunities for change. For example, in the 1980s the Reagan administration accepted political support from Christian fundamentalist groups and organizations. In return, it made some efforts to limit abortion access and to appoint judges who opposed legal abortions. These reforms, in turn, encouraged the growth and development of the pro-life movement (R. Garner, 1996).

Similarly, the U.S. anti–drunk driving movement is strong and influential today because it enjoys substantial support from federal, state, and local governments; state and federal highway agencies; and state and local police departments (McCarthy & Wolfson, 1992). When in the 1980s the movement advocated a national drinking age of 21, many state legislatures balked, fearing a backlash from powerful alcohol producers, distributors, and retailers. However, the federal government enacted legislation threatening to withhold significant amounts of federal highway funds from states that didn't establish the 21-year-old drinking age. This proved to be a strong incentive for states to pass such a law.

Political opportunities provide the institutional frame within which social movements operate. Movements form when ordinary citizens respond to changes in the opportunity structure that lower the costs of involvement and reveal where the authorities are vulnerable. Unlike money and power, these conditions are external to the movement. If political opportunities exist, then even groups with fairly mild grievances or few resources can develop a successful movement (see also Jenkins & Perrow, 1977). In contrast, groups with deep grievances and ample resources—but few political opportunities—may never get their movements off the ground (Tarrow, 1994).

The Sociological Imagination Revisited

In the summer of 1981 I had the good fortune to visit Florence, Italy. While there, I made a point of visiting the Galleria dell' Accademia, the museum where one of my favorite works of art, Michelangelo's statue of David, resides. The statue stands in a bright rotunda at the end of a long hallway. To my eye it is truly a masterpiece of sculpture, nearly flawless in its detail.

I stood there admiring this amazing work of art for close to two hours. Afterward, as I contentedly made my way back down the hallway, I noticed a series of sculptures that had escaped my attention when I first entered the museum. I found out that they, too, were created by Michelangelo. What made them particularly interesting was that they were all unfinished. Some were obviously near completion, but others looked to me like shapeless blocks of granite.

There was something astounding in these pieces. As I looked closer, I could see the actual chisel marks that the great sculptor had made. I imagined the plan Michelangelo had in his head as he worked. I envisioned him toiling to bring form to the heavy stone. These imperfect slabs of rock showed evidence of human creation in a way that the perfect, finished statue of David never could. At that moment I saw Michelangelo as a real person who fashioned beauty from formlessness. I began to admire the genius of the creator and not just the creation. I went back to look at David again with a newfound appreciation.

Society isn't nearly as perfect as Michelangelo's David, yet we can still fall into the trap of seeing social structure as a product that exists on its own and not as something that people have collectively chiseled. We sometimes forget that many of the realities of our lives that we take for granted were the result, at some point in history, of the handiwork of individuals. One generation's radical changes become another's common features of everyday life. The fact that you can't be forced to work 70 or 80 hours a week, can't be exposed to dangerous working conditions without your knowledge, and are entitled to a certain number of paid holidays a year are a result of the actions of real people in early labor union movements.

Because we take many of our freedoms, rights, and desires for granted, we may not only overlook the struggles of those who came before us but also downplay the extent to which inequities and injustices existed in the past. For instance, many young women today have never even considered that they are only a generation or so removed from a time when they might have been prohibited from attending the college or pursuing the career of their choice; when they might have been expected to abandon their own dreams and ambitions to provide the support their husbands needed to succeed; or when they might have had to take sole responsibility for household chores and their children's daily care while their husbands focused on work and the outside world. Like most beneficiaries of past movements, young women today simply take their freedoms and opportunities for granted, sometimes even expressing contempt for the women's movement responsible for the rights they so casually enjoy (Stacey, 1991).

The irony of social movements, then, is that the more profound and far-reaching their accomplishments, the more likely we are to eventually forget the efforts of the individuals who produced them. Like Michelangelo's David, these achievements begin to exist independently of the individuals and groups who created them. Changing mainstream society is the ultimate goal of any social movement, but the cultural and historical price is that the efforts and sacrifices made by real individuals to re-create our society will ultimately fade into collective oblivion.

Fundamentally, not only the nature of social movements but also the nature of human society itself—whether stable or in flux—must be understood by examining what people do and think. We must remember that societies remain stable because enough individuals define existing conditions as satisfactory and that societies change because enough individuals define situations that were once tolerable as problems that must be acknowledged and solved. As one author wrote regarding the antiwar movement of the 1960s and 1970s:

> Ten years and 12 days after the first busloads of demonstrators rolled into Washington to protest U.S. involvement in Indochina, the last planeloads of Americans left Saigon. . . . The standard American histories of the Vietnam War, when they are culled from the memoirs of the generals and politicians . . . are unlikely to record this coincidence. But the decisions about the pursuit of those generals' and politicians' objectives in Indochina were not made only in their carpeted offices. They were also made in the barracks, in the schools, in the streets, by the millions of Americans—Blacks and whites, students, workers, nuns and priests, draftees and draft resisters—who made up the Anti-War Movement. (Cluster, 1979, p. 131)

Some influential acts of individuals may at first blush appear rather insignificant. Early in 1960, four black students at North Carolina Agricultural & Technical State University in Greensboro engaged in a series of discussions in their dormitory rooms about the state of the civil rights movement. They came to the conclusion that things weren't progressing quickly enough in the still-segregated South and that it was time for action. They decided to go to the lunch counter at the local Woolworth's store and order coffee and doughnuts. In the 1960s South, public eating facilities that weren't for blacks only were forbidden by law to serve blacks.

After purchasing some school supplies in another part of the store, the four students sat down at the lunch counter and placed their orders. As anticipated, the reply was "I'm sorry, we don't serve you here" (McCain, 1991, p. 115). They remained seated for 45 minutes, citing the fact that they had been served in another part of the store without any difficulty. They were subjected to the verbal taunts, racial slurs, and even violence of angry whites in the store. Nevertheless, they returned the next week with more demonstrators. Word of their actions spread quickly. Within two months, similar sit-ins had taken place in nine states and 54 cities in the South as well as several areas in the North, where sympathetic pickets of stores took place. The sit-ins eventually proved to be one of the most effective tactics of the civil rights movement.

Some social observers argue that many of the political movements for change that burst onto the scene in the 1960s—including the women's movement, the antiwar movement, and the student free speech movement—could trace their philosophical and tactical roots to this small act by four students (Cluster, 1979). More recently, college students have staged sit-ins to protest the conditions of clothing and footwear factory workers overseas. As a result, industry giants such as the Gap and Nike have cut back on child labor, reduced the use of dangerous chemicals, and required fewer employees to work 80-hour weeks (Greenhouse, 2000). Now, maybe the participants in these movements would have developed such tactics on their own, even if in 1960 the four students *had* been served coffee and doughnuts at Woolworth's. The point is, though, that the collective movement that arose from the actions of these seemingly insignificant individuals in 1960 had an enormous impact on the massive changes that occurred in the United States over the next 40 years and probably beyond.

We re-create society not only through acts of defiance and organized social movements but also through our daily interactions. The driving theme throughout this book has been that society and its constituent elements are simultaneously human creations and phenomena that exist independently of us, influencing and controlling our private experiences at every turn.

Organizations and institutions exist and thrive because they implicitly or explicitly discourage individuals from challenging the rules and patterns of behavior that characterize them. Imagine what would happen to the system of higher education if you and others like you challenged the authority of the university. You could establish a new order in which students would dictate the content of courses, take control of the classroom, abolish grading or any other evaluative mechanism used for assessing student performance, do away with tuition, and so on. But because you have an education and a career to gain from the institutional structure as it stands, you're not very likely to do something to jeopardize it.

Are we then to believe that we are all leaves in the wind, buffeted here and there by the powerful and permanent forces of a structure that dwarfs us? To some extent the answer is yes. I subscribe to the sociological imagination and strongly believe that to fully understand our lives we must acknowledge that processes larger than ourselves determine some of our private experiences. Along the way, though, we sometimes lose sight of our important role as shapers of society:

> We know when to tear down a building that has ceased to serve any useful function and may even be a source of danger. However, we sometimes rattle around in dusty old social institutions that are cracked and crumbling simply because we fail to realize that it is within our power to step beyond the confines of this structure and build others. . . . What may have served as a useful basis for achieving some particular end becomes an ideology and an end in itself. When this occurs our social constructions may cease to serve any useful function but we may persist in maintaining them simply because they have become permanent, hardened features of our social landscape. (Kollock & O'Brien, 1993, p. 503)

Although society presents itself as largely unchangeable, U.S. culture is based at least in part on the "can do" attitude. I recall, as a child in 1969, sitting in a darkened living room with my parents on a warm July evening. The only light in the room came from the gray-blue glow of the television. I watched with great amazement the fuzzy, almost imperceptible image of astronaut Neil Armstrong taking the first tentative steps on the moon and stating, "That's one small step for man, one giant leap for mankind." I didn't realize then how far beyond the space program the power of that statement stretched. But since then I have come to realize that people do influence the world in which they live.

CONCLUSION AND FAREWELL

Sociology is not one of those disciplines that draws from a long-standing body of scientific facts and laws. We do have some good explanations for why certain important social phenomena happen, and we can make reasonable predictions about future developments. But sociology is not inherently a discipline of answers. It's a discipline of questions, one that provides a unique and useful method for identifying the puzzles of your life and your society.

This discipline scrutinizes, analyzes, and dissects institutional order and its effects on our thinking. It exposes the vulnerable underbelly of both objective and official reality and, by doing so, prods us into taking a closer look at ourselves and our private worlds, not an easy thing to do. Sociology makes everyday life an unsafe place. I don't mean that it makes people violent or dangerous, I mean that it makes perceptions of social stability unstable or at least fair game for analysis. It's not easy to admit that our reality may be a figment of our collective minds and just one of many possible realities. We live under a belief system that tells us that our unchallenged assumptions are simply the way things are.

Sociology is thus a "liberating" perspective (Liazos, 1985). It forces us to look at the social processes that influence our thoughts, perceptions, and actions and helps us see how social change occurs and the impact we can have on others. In doing so, sociology also points out the very limits of liberation. We are aware of the chains that restrict our "movements," but we also have the tools to break those chains. The sociological imagination goes beyond a description of powerful social forces to a questioning of them and ultimately a push toward social action. Sociology gives us a glimpse of the world both as it is and as it could be. To be a sociologically astute observer of the world as it is, you must be able to strip away fallacies and illusions and see the interconnected system underneath. Only then can you take full advantage of your role as a co-creator of society.

I leave you with one final thought: If you now look at your life and the lives of those around you differently, if you now question things heretofore unquestionable, if you now see where you fit in the bigger societal picture, if you now see orderly patterns in areas you previously thought were chaotic or chaos in areas you previously thought were orderly, then you are well on your way to understanding the meaning—and the promise—of sociology.

YOUR TURN

Reading about people taking an active role in reconstructing a part of their personal lives or of their society is one thing, but it's quite another to see such people in action. Most communities contain people who were at one time active in a major movement for social change: the labor movement, the antiwar movement, the women's movement, the civil rights movement, the antiabortion movement, and so forth. Find a few people who were involved in one such movement. Ask them to describe their experiences. What was their motive for joining the movement? What sorts of activities did they participate in? What were the goals they wanted to accomplish? Looking back, do they feel the movement accomplished those goals? If not, why not? What else needs to be done?

For purposes of historical comparison, see if you can identify a movement that is currently under way in your community. It might be a drive in support of a broad societal concern, such as environmental or drunk-driving awareness or a group organized to address an issue of local interest, such as the construction of a new skate park or an attempt to stop the construction of a factory or business.

Try to attend a gathering in which the movement is involved. It might be an organizational meeting, a town council meeting, a protest march, a fund-raiser, or a demonstration. What happened at the gathering? What seemed to be the overall atmosphere? Was it festive? solemn? angry? businesslike? Was any opposition present?

Interview some of the participants. Ask them the same questions you asked the participants who were in past movements. Do people get involved in social movements for the same reasons they did in the past?

Most social movement organizations now have their own Web sites on the Internet. Visit some of these sites to get a sense of the kinds of information these organizations provide. Do they tend to be primarily informational, focusing on the history and current state of the issue at hand, or are they primarily recruitment tools, designed to attract new participants and financial donors? How are these sites presented? Do they appeal to emotions, or do they rely on factual argument? Do these Web sites contain links to the sites of other organizations that have similar ideologies?

Relate your observations from the interviews and the Internet to the discussion of social movements in this chapter. What are the most effective tactics and strategies? How are resources mobilized? Why do some movements succeed and others fail?

CHAPTER HIGHLIGHTS

- Whether at the personal, cultural, or institutional level, change is the preeminent feature of modern societies.

- Social change is not some massive, impersonal force that arbitrarily disrupts our routine way of life; it is a human creation.

- Social change has a variety of causes: adaptation to environmental pressures, internal population changes, technological discoveries and innovations and the importation of cultural practices from other countries.

- Social movements are long-term collective actions that address an issue of concern to large numbers of people.

- Societies remain stable because enough people define existing conditions as satisfactory, and they change because enough people define once-accepted conditions as problems that must be solved.

KEY TERMS

anomie Condition in which rapid change has disrupted society's ability to adequately regulate and control its members and the old rules that governed people's lives no longer seem to apply

countermovement Collective action designed to prevent or reverse changes sought or accomplished by an earlier social movement

cultural diffusion Process by which beliefs, technology, customs, and other elements of culture spread from one group or society to another

ideology Coherent system of beliefs, values, and ideas

postindustrial society Society in which knowledge and the control of information are more important than agriculture or manufacturing and production

reform movement Collective action that seeks to change limited aspects of a society but does not seek to alter or replace major social institutions

revolutionary movement Collective action that attempts to overthrow an entire social system and replace it with another

social movement Continuous, large-scale, organized collective action motivated by the desire to enact, stop, or reverse change in some area of society

Imagining Futures
Douglas Harper

Sociologists recognize that films and other forms of popular culture reflect how at least some people define the world in a particular era or place. They also influence what people think about and come to accept as social alternatives. In this way what begins as entertainment may end up defining our imagination and thus our sense of the possible.

It is sometimes shocking to look back in history at visions of the future, for they sometimes foretell what, indeed, has taken place. It is also startling to look at contemporary films as serious statements about possible futures for you and your children.

Consider Fritz Lang's 1925 film *Metropolis*. The German filmmaker offered a mythical urban utopia that excited public imagination: airplanes flying among glittering skyscrapers, sleek modern buildings connected by aerial roadways, telephone with video communication, robots that could emulate human emotions and replace them in the workplace. Lang understood, however, that someone would have to manufacture and maintain the technological marvels of his metropolis. In the first scene of the movie, workers descend to the underground to perform these tasks. When they complete their shift, they descend to an even greater depth to their living quarters. A largely unidentified middle class inhabits the wonderful city aboveground; the workers seldom even venture to the surface to see the world they have made.

● The film *Metropolis* presents a vision of the modern city based on subterranean worlds of workers. In the left frame below, the workers descend to their factories and living quarters. In the right frame below we see the Robot, who has been designed to replace the workers and their political agitation.

At the time Lang made *Metropolis*, Europeans were trying to make sense of two events: a war that technology made so terrible as to render it our first "world" war; and the first large-scale Communist victory, in the Soviet Union. The social inequality of Metropolis threatened the social order, just as it had in the Soviet Union before the advent of communism. Lang's solution was to send a gentle woman reformer to the workers to preach patience, exhorting them to wait for a "negotiator." By the end of the film, however, the workers have destroyed most of the city, and the Master of Metropolis has responded with his own terror directed against the working class. It takes his son to become "the heart which binds the mind and the hands." In the last scene the son actually joins the hands of his father with the doltish foreman, who appears as a modern-day peasant. Thus Lang's society preserves social classes but softens inequality with "understanding." But the masses are not sufficiently advanced to take part in the technological marvels. The son asks the father, "It was their hands that built this city of ours . . . but where do hands belong in your scheme?" The father responds, "In their proper place, the depths!"

● The son of the Master of Metropolis recoils in shock as workers killed in an industrial accident are removed from the subterranean factory.

This is a fascist vision. The masses are to be inspired by grandiose architecture, mass gatherings, and fiery, emotional speeches. Their position as workers and soldiers is not to be questioned. Democracy is out of the question.

A similarly fascist vision emerged in one form or another in all industrializing countries during the era *Metropolis* was being made but emerged most dramatically in Nazi Germany. Consider next Leni Riefenstahl's 1934 documentary *Triumph of the Will* (which recorded the Second Party Congress of the German National Socialists) to see how this fascist imagery was developed in a film depicting reality.

The film is a direct descendent of Lang's *Metropolis*; in nine short years the future has been achieved. The outside pavilions and halls in which the rally took place were designed by the architect Albert Speer to create the mass experience integral to fascist culture. Much of the film shows Hitler and other Nazi leaders reviewing thousands of representatives of one group after another, all united under the banners of the new society. The party leaders elevate work to a near-sacred status at the same time they have eliminated basic political rights. At one point in the film, Hitler cries out,

> My labor servicemen! For the first time, you report for review before me . . . and before all the German people. You represent a great idea . . . work will no longer be divisive . . . but will bind us together. No German will now look on manual labor as inferior . . . to any other kind of labor. The whole nation will enter your school. The time will come when no German will be part of our community unless he has first been a part of your community!

By 1934 the people of Germany had traded their brief experience with democracy for the fascist social order portrayed by Lang. The vision offered by *Triumph of the Will* led to 50 million deaths during World War II.

● These two frames from *Triumph of the Will* show the marching masses. The first frame is an ironically beautiful silhouette of the fascist salute. The second frame presents future soldiers, in an era still ostensibly of peace, marching with spades and shovels instead of rifles.

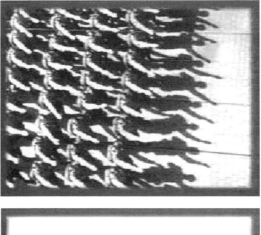

● The fascist order reserved a place for all workers: A cook prepares soup for hundreds of thousands of participants at the Nuremberg rally.

● The rally itself was a spectacular presentation of the Nazi Party. Hitler himself is dwarfed by the architecture and symbolism designed for the rally, presented with other party leaders on dramatically lit platforms above the tens of thousands of cheering Nazis.

The power of film to shape imaginations did not end there. Perhaps the darkest vision during the cultural revolutions of the 1960s was the film *A Clockwork Orange*, by Stanley Kubrick from the novel by Anthony Burgess. Set at an undetermined future date, the film concerns the antics of antihero Alex and his band of hooligans. The larger themes are sex, violence, and the power of the state.

Alex and his hooligans rape for pleasure. But society has turned the female body and male sexual anatomy into furniture and art. Kubrick's film is ironic in this regard: it is critical of the marketing of nudity, sex, and violence but is also guilty of it. Alex and his friends also mutilate and kill for pleasure. The film makes it clear that violence is integral to the larger society as well. For example, the conditioning methods used by the state to rehabilitate Alex draw on culturally resonant images from the Holocaust, certainly the greatest organized violence in history.

● *A Clockwork Orange* ironically criticizes society's fascination with sex and violence but was noteworthy for its own graphic depiction of both.

● Alex enforces his control of his gang by beating them up. Later, after his "rehabilitation," two members of his former gang who have become police beat and nearly drown him.

● Alex reads the Bible in prison, pretending to be reformed while imagining himself as a guard beating Christ on the way to the Crucifixion. Even religion is saturated by and condones violence, the film implies.

From the beginning of the film, the moral authority of the state seems to have eroded. Society's permissiveness is represented by sexual pop art and clubs in which drinks are laced with amphetamines. When Alex is caught, he is sent to a conventional prison, where he is conditioned to become violently ill when he has aggressive or sexual urges. These methods are psychologically intrusive. In the end, however, Alex is "rehabilitated" (his conditioning removed) to his previously violent state and once again unleashed on the public. He is then used by the state as a symbol of its enlightenment.

● Alex ironically becomes a hero of government critics (one whom Alex had crippled and whose wife he had killed). But his unlikely supporter is eventually committed to a mental institution and thus silenced.

A Clockwork Orange won several awards and four Academy Award nominations, including Best Picture. The future it described was maniacally sexual and violent, with complicity of the state. In the thirty-some years since its release, its dark vision of morality and social control has become much less like the future and more like the present.

Other visions of the future have focused on technology. *Bladerunner* (1984) introduced a theme that has returned in several contemporary films, where the lines blur between humans and their creations. In *Bladerunner* the "replicants" have advanced to the point of developing emotions and self awareness. The self-awareness leads to rebelliousness, and so the replicants, reason the humans, must be killed. The human assassin (the Bladerunner), however, falls in love with a replicant as he is in the process of killing the others. The final replicant the Bladerunner hunts, about to perish from a built-in self-destruct mechanism, actually saves the Bladerunner (who is about to fall from a building) and says he just wanted what we all want: to express his emotions and experiences, and to be understood. The audience sympathy thus transfers from the humans to the beings they have created, as it does in the first version of this theme: *Frankenstein.*

Other films explore variations on this theme. The *Terminator* series, for instance, introduces the modern "friendly robot" who is empathic and heroic. We have no trouble seeing him as a viable character, even when he is reduced to an arm and bubbling metal. The point being made by these filmmakers is that in the future, human creations will become more human than we are ourselves. As humans we will inevitably fail; our greed, potential for violence, and dishonesty will always dominate our instincts of altruism and love.

● *Terminator 2* begins in Los Angeles in 2029 A.D., some thirty years after society has been thrown into chaos by a nuclear blast. Humans and technologically advanced machines are at war over the remains. But one terminator robot (played by Arnold Schwarzenegger) is sent back in time by the humans to save the boy who is destined to become their leader. Eventually this "good" terminator destroys the even more advanced "bad" terminator, who had been sent by the machines to assassinate the boy. His battle won, the "good" terminator insists on being destroyed himself to remove from earth all terminator computer chips. As he disappears into a vat of molten metal, he raises his thumb to signal his faith that all will be well for the humans he leaves behind. In a final voiceover, the boy's mother says, "The unknown future rolls toward us. I face it for the first time with a sense of hope. Because if a machine, a terminator, can learn the value of human life, maybe we can, too."

The other common technological theme posits humans with some machine or computer parts. For example, in the "cyperpunk" novels of William Gibson, the best of which was the first of a trilogy written several years ago, *Neuromancer*, the Internet was a reality one could actually "enter," once humans had become part computer. Gibson's vision of human–machine interface has become so common in film that we no longer recoil. We have, it seems, redefined the acceptable limits of machine intervention in the human body.

The societies of the future characterized by advanced technologies are of two sorts. The first is a projection of our current culture into future settings; the crew of the first *Alien* movie are working class characters who would be comfortable subjects of a Bruce Springsteen song. The high school portrayed in *Starship Troopers* is pure 1950s, down to the biology lab in which a futuristic "bug" is dissected. The other vision, however, presents social chaos beneath the technological marvels. If there is a government, it exists to spy on and control the masses. More typically the technology is a kind of veneer over a dark world (often these films are filmed in rainy night settings), where an individual survives on the basis of his or her cunning and violence. Most often social anarchy lurks in the background, shored up by technological means of social control and the state's own capacity for violence.

Contemporary films about the future rarely present a utopian vision, it seems. Perhaps cheery films would be less interesting, and perhaps the imagination of the artists is simply not receptive to utopia. As a result, however, the future is usually presented to us in dark, violent, and pessimistic terms. We are left to wonder, Will the role of these filmmakers in defining our imagination actually lead us in the direction of their visions?

References

Acitelli, L. 1988. "When spouses talk to each other about their relationship." *Journal of Social and Personal Relationships, 5,* 185–199.

Acker, J. 1978. "Issues in the sociological study of women's work." In A. H. Stromberg & S. Harkees (Eds.), *Women working.* Palo Alto, CA: Mayfield.

———. 1992. "From sex roles to gendered institutions." *Contemporary Sociology, 21,* 565–569.

Aday, D. P. 1990. *Social control at the margins.* Belmont, CA: Wadsworth.

Adler, J. 1994. "Kids growing up scared." *Newsweek,* January 10.

Ahrons, C. R., & Rodgers, R. H. 1987. *Divorced families: A multidisciplinary developmental view.* New York: Norton.

Ainlay, S. C., Becker, G., & Coleman, L. M. 1986. *The dilemma of difference.* New York: Plenum.

Alessio, C., & Condor, B. 1999. "Ritalin: The eye of the storm." *Indianapolis Star,* March 28.

The Alibi Agency. 2001. "Objectives of the Alibi Agency." www.alibi.co.uk. Accessed June 15, 2001.

Allan, M. D. 2000. "'Parkers' illustrates racial gap." *Indianapolis Star,* June 2.

Allon, N. 1982. "The stigma of overweight in everyday life." In B. B. Wolman (Ed.), *Psychological aspects of obesity.* New York: Van Nostrand Reinhold.

Allport, G. 1954. *The nature of prejudice.* Reading, MA: Addison-Wesley.

Altman, L. K. 1998. "Parts of Africa showing H.I.V. in 1 in 4 adults." *New York Times,* June 24.

———. 2000. "U.N. warning AIDS imperils Africa's youth." *New York Times,* June 28.

Amato, P. R. 2000. "The consequences of divorce for adults and children." *Journal of Marriage and the Family, 62,* 126–288.

American Association of University Women. 1991. *Shortchanging girls, shortchanging America: A call to action.* Washington, DC: Author.

American Psychiatric Association. 1994. *Diagnostic and statistical manual of mental disorders* (4th ed.). Washington, DC: Author.

American Society of Plastic and Reconstructive Surgeons. 2001. "Cosmetic procedures—Trends: 1992, 1994, 1996, 1997, 1998, 1999." www.plasticsurgery.org/mediactr/stats.htm. Accessed February 22, 2001.

American Sociological Association. 1999. "After the fall: The growth rate of sociology BAs outstrips other disciplines, indicating an improved market for sociologists." A.S.A. Research Brief. Washington, DC.

Amir, M. 1971. *Patterns of forcible rape.* Chicago: University of Chicago Press.

Ammerman, N. T. 1987. *Bible believers: Fundamentalists in the modern world.* New Brunswick, NJ: Rutgers University Press.

Amnesty International. 1998. "International standards on the death penalty." Report ACT 50/10/98 www.web.amnesty.org/ai.nsf/index/ACT5001098.htm. Accessed June 22, 2001.

Anderson, E. 1990. *Streetwise: Race, class and change in an urban community.* Chicago: University of Chicago Press.

Andrews, E. L. 1992. "Broadcasters, to satisfy law, define cartoons as education." *New York Times,* September 30.

Angier, N. 1995. "If you're really ancient, you may be better off." *New York Times,* March 27.

———. 1997a. "Sexual identity not pliable after all, report says." *New York Times,* March 14.

———. 1997b. "New debate over surgery on genitals." *New York Times,* May 13.

———. 2000. "Cell phone or pheromone? New props for the mating game." *New York Times,* November 7.

Applebome, P. 1996a. "Crime fear is seen forcing changes in youth behavior." *New York Times,* January 12.

———. 1996b. "Holding parents legally responsible for the misbehavior of their children." *New York Times,* April 10.

———. 1997. "In 2 law schools, black enrollment scarcely exists." *New York Times,* June 28.

Archer, D. 1985. "Social deviance." In G. Lindzey & E. Aronson (Eds.), *Handbook of social psychology* (3rd ed., Vol. 2). New York: Random House.

Arendell, T. 1984. "Divorce: A woman's issue." *Feminist Issues, 4,* 41–61.

———. 1995. *Fathers and divorce.* Thousand Oaks, CA: Sage.

Argyle, M. 2000. "The laws of looking." In J. Spradley & D. W. McCurdy (Eds.), *Conformity and conflict.* Boston: Allyn and Bacon.

Ariès, P. 1962. *Centuries of childhood: A social history of family life.* New York: Vintage.

Armstrong, P. J., Goodman, J. F. B., & Hyman, J. D. 1981. *Ideology and shop-floor industrial relations.* London: Croom Helm.

Arno, P. S., & Feiden, K. L. 1992. *Against the odds: The story of AIDS drug development, politics and profits.* New York: HarperCollins.

Aronowitz, S., & DiFazio, W. 1995. *The jobless future: Sci-tech and the dogma of work.* Minneapolis: University of Minnesota Press.

Astbury, J. 1996. *Crazy for you: The making of women's madness.* Melbourne: Oxford University Press.

Auletta, K. 1982. *The underclass.* New York: Random House.

Babbie, E. 1986. *Observing ourselves: Essays in social research.* Belmont, CA: Wadsworth.

———. 1992. *The practice of social research.* Belmont, CA: Wadsworth.

Baca-Zinn, M., & Eitzen, D. S. 1996. *Diversity in families* (4th ed.). New York: HarperCollins.

Bach, P. B., Cramer, L. D., Warren, J. L., & Begg, C. B. 1999. "Racial differences in the treatment of early-stage lung cancer." *New England Journal of Medicine, 341,* 119–205.

Bagdikian, B. H. 1991. "Missing from the news." In J. H. Skolnick & E. Currie (Eds.), *Crisis in American institutions.* New York: HarperCollins.

———. 2000. *The media monopoly* (6th ed.). Boston: Beacon Press.

Bailey, B. L. 1988. *From front porch to back seat: Courtship in 20th century America.* Baltimore: Johns Hopkins University Press.

Bailey, C. A. 1993. "Equality with difference: On androcentrism and menstruation." *Teaching Sociology, 21,* 121–129.

Bailey, W. C. 1990. "Murder, capital punishment, and television: Execution publicity and homicide rates." *American Sociological Review, 55,* 628–633.

Bald, M. 2000. "Disputed dams." *World Press Review.* December.

Ballard, C. 1987. "A humanist sociology approach to teaching social research." *Teaching Sociology, 15,* 7–14.

Bandura, A., & Walters, R. H. 1963. *Social learning and personality development.* New York: Holt, Rinehart & Winston.

Banfield, E. 1970. *The unheavenly city.* Boston: Little, Brown.

"Baptists seek to 'convert' Mormons." 2000. *New York Times.* January 22.

Barber, B. 1992. "Jihad vs. McWorld." *Atlantic Monthly,* March, pp. 53–65.

Barker, C. 1997. *Global television.* Oxford, England: Blackwell.

Baron, A. 1987. "Feminist legal strategies: The powers of difference." In B. Hess & M. M. Ferree (Eds.), *Analyzing gender: A handbook of social science research.* Newbury Park, CA: Sage.

Barry, D. 2000. "What to do if you're stopped by the police." *New York Times,* February 27.

Baxter, J. 1997. "Gender equality and participation in housework: A cross-national perspective." *Journal of Comparative Family Studies, 28,* 220–247.

Beaman, A. L., Klentz, B., Diener, E., & Svanum, S. 1979. "Objective self-awareness and transgression in children: A field study." *Journal of Personality and Social Psychology, 37,* 1835–1846.

Bearak, B. 2000. "Women are defaced by acid and Bengali society is torn." *New York Times,* June 24.

Becker, H. 1963. *The outsiders.* New York: Free Press.

Becker, H. S., & Geer, B. 1958. "The fate of idealism in medical school." *American Sociological Review, 23,* 50–56.

Bedard, M. 1991. "Captive clientele of the welfare supersystem: Breaking the cage wide open." *Humanity and Society, 15,* 23–48.

Beeghley, L. 1984. "Illusion and reality in the measurement of poverty." *Social Problems, 31,* 322–333.

Begley, S. 1994. "One pill makes you larger, and one pill makes you small . . ." *Newsweek,* February 7.

Begun, B. 2000. "USA: The way we'll live then." *Newsweek,* January 1.

Belkin, L. 1990. "Airport anti-drug nets snare many people fitting 'profiles.' " *New York Times,* March 20.

Bell-Rowbotham, B., & Lero, D. 2001. "Responses to extension of parental leaves." Centre for Families, Work, and Well-Being. www.uoguelph.ca/cfww/response.htm. Accessed July 10, 2001.

Bell, D. J., & Bell, S. L. 1991. "The victim–offender relationship as a determinant factor in police dispositions of family violence incidents: A replication study." *Policing and Society, 1,* 225–234.

Bell, S. T., Kuriloff, P. J., & Lottes, I. 1994. "Understanding attributions of blame in stranger rape and date rape situations: An examination of gender, race, identification, and students' social perceptions of rape victims." *Journal of Applied Social Psychology, 24,* 171–734.

Bellah, R., Madsen, R., Sullivan, W. M., Swidler, A., & Tipton, S. M. 1985. *Habits of the heart.* New York: Harper & Row.

Belluck, P. 1998a. "Black youths' rate of suicide rising sharply." *New York Times,* March 20.

———. 1998b. "Forget prisons. Americans cry out for the pillory." *New York Times,* October 4.

———. 2001. "A nation's voices: Concern and solace, resentment and redemption." *New York Times,* January 20.

Benokraitis, N. V., & Feagin, J. R. 1993. "Sex discrimination: Subtle and covert." In J. Henslin (Ed.), *Down-to-earth sociology* (7th ed.). New York: Free Press.

Ben-Yehuda, N. 1990. *The politics and morality of deviance.* Albany: State University of New York Press.

Berg, B. 1992. "The guilt that drives working mothers crazy." In J. Henslin (Ed.), *Marriage and family in a changing society.* New York: Free Press.

Berger, D. L., & Williams, J. E. 1991. "Sex stereotypes in the United States revisited: 1972–1988." *Sex Roles, 24,* 413–423.

Berger, P. L. 1963. *Invitation to sociology.* Garden City, NY: Anchor.

Berger, P. L., & Kellner, H. 1964. "Marriage and the construction of reality: An exercise in the microsociology of knowledge." *Diogenes, 46,* 1–23.

Berger, P. L., & Luckmann, T. 1966. *The social construction of reality.* Garden City, NY: Anchor.

Berke, R. L. 1998. "Flurry of anti-gay remarks has G.O.P. fearing backlash." *New York Times,* June 30.

Bernard, J. 1972. *The future of marriage.* New York: Bantam.

———. 1981. "The good provider role: Its rise and fall." *American Psychologist, 36,* 1–12.

Bernhardt, A., Morris, M., & Handcock, M. S. 1995. "Women's gains or men's losses? A closer look at the shrinking gender gap in earnings." *American Journal of Sociology, 101,* 302–328.

Bernstein, M. F. 1996. "Racial gerrymandering." *Public Interest,* Winter, pp. 59–69.

Bernstein, N. 1996. "Equal opportunity recedes for most female lawyers." *New York Times,* January 8.

Berscheid, E., & Walster, E. 1974. "Physical attractiveness." In L. Berkowitz (Ed.), *Advances in experimental social psychology.* New York: Academic Press.

Bertenthal, B. I., & Fischer, K. W. 1978. "Development of self-recognition in the infant." *Developmental Psychology, 14,* 44–50.

Berthelsen, C. 1999. "Suit says advanced-placement classes show bias." *New York Times,* July 28.

Bertram, E., & Sharpe, K. 1998. "The unwinnable drug war." In H. A. Widdison (Ed.), *Social Problems 98/99.* Guilford, CT: Dushkin.

Best, J. 1993. *Threatened children: Rhetoric and concern about child-victims.* Chicago: University of Chicago Press.

Bianchi, S. M., Milkie, M. A., Sayer, L. C., & Robinson, J. P. 2000. "Is Anyone Doing the Housework? Trends in the Gender Division of Household Labor." *Social Forces, 79,* 191–228.

Birenbaum, A., & Sagarin, E. 1976. *Norms and human behavior.* New York: Praeger.

Bjerklie, D., Cole, P. E., & Cray, D. 1995. "Age of the road warrior." *Time,* Spring Special Issue.

Black, K. 1996. "Extreme prejudice." *Rolling Stone,* September 5.

Blackman, A. 1994. "When violence hits home." *Time,* July 4.

Blakeslee, S. 1998. "Placebos prove so powerful even experts are surprised." *New York Times,* October 13.

Blau, P. M., & Duncan, O. D. 1967. *The American occupational structure.* New York: Wiley.

Blau, P. M., & Meyer, M. W. 1987. "The concept of bureaucracy." In R. T. Schaeffer & R. P. Lamm (Eds.), *Introducing sociology.* New York: McGraw-Hill.

Blauner, R. 1964. *Alienation and freedom.* Chicago: University of Chicago Press.

———. 1992. "The ambiguities of racial change." In M. L. Anderson & P. H. Collins (Eds.), *Race, class and gender: An anthology.* Belmont, CA: Wadsworth.

Block, J. H. 1983. "Differential premises arising from differential socialization of the sexes: Some conjectures." *Child Development, 54,* 1335–1354.

Blood, P., Tuttle, A., & Lakey, G. 1992. "Understanding and fighting sexism: A call to men." In M. L. Anderson & P. H. Collins (Eds.), *Race, class and gender: An anthology.* Belmont, CA: Wadsworth.

Blumstein, P., & Schwartz, P. 1983. *American couples.* New York: Morrow.

Bohlen, C. 1989. "Holtzman may appeal probation for immigrant in wife's slaying." *New York Times,* April 5.

Bonner, R., & Fessenden, F. 2000. "States with no death penalty share lower homicide rates." *New York Times,* September 22.

Bonner, R., & Lacey, M. 2000. "Pervasive disparities found in the federal death penalty." *New York Times,* September 12.

Bonnie, R. J., & Whitebread, C. H. 1974. *The marijuana conviction.* Charlottesville: University of Virginia Press.

Booth, A., Johnson, D. R., Branaman, A., & Sica, A. 1995. "Belief and behavior: Does religion matter in today's marriage?" *Journal of Marriage and the Family, 57,* 661–671.

Bowker, L. H. 1993. "A battered woman's problems are social, not psychological." In R. J. Gelles & D. R. Loeske (Eds.), *Current controversies on family violence.* Newbury Park, CA: Sage.

Bowles, S., & Gintis, H. 1976. *Schooling in capitalist America: Educational reform and the contradictions of economic reform.* New York: Basic Books.

Bradshaw, Y. W., & Wallace, M. 1996. *Global inequalities.* Thousand Oaks, CA: Pine Forge Press.

Bradsher, K. 1993. "Mark Twain would understand the water crisis that's corrupting Iowans." *New York Times,* July 22.

———. 1995a. "Gap in wealth in U.S. called widest in west." *New York Times,* April 17.

———. 1995b. "Sluggish income figures show modest gains for some groups." *New York Times,* October 6.

———. 1996. "Rich control more of U.S. wealth, study says, as debt grows for poor." *New York Times,* June 22.

———. 1999a. "As buyers age, car designers make subtle shifts." *New York Times,* March 1.

———. 1999b. "Fear of crime trumps fear of lost youth." *New York Times,* November 21.

Bragg, R. 1998. "Proposal to ban sofas from porches creates culture clash." *Indianapolis Star,* January 4.

———. 1999. "Restaurant's added gratuity leads to discrimination claim." *New York Times,* November 10.

Bramlett, M. D., & Mosher, W. D. 2001. "First marriage dissolution, divorce, and remarriage: United States." Centers for Disease Control and Prevention Advance Data #323, May 31, 2001.

Braun, D. 1997. *The rich get richer: The rise of income inequality in the United States and the world.* Chicago: Nelson-Hall.

"Bridal dowry in India." 2000. *Morning Edition,* National Public Radio. www.npr.org/programs/morning. June 19.

Bridges, J. S. 1988. "Sex differences in occupational performance expectations." *Psychology of Women Quarterly, 12,* 75–90.

Brines, J. 1994. "Economic dependency, gender and the division of labor at home." *American Journal of Sociology, 100,* 652–688.

Brinkley, J. 2000. "C.I.A. depicts a vast trade in forced labor." *New York Times,* April 2.

Brint, S. 1998. *Schools and societies.* Thousand Oaks, CA: Pine Forge Press.

Brinton, C. 1965. *The anatomy of revolution.* New York: Vintage.

Brinton, M. 1988. "The social-institutional bases of gender stratification." *American Journal of Sociology, 94,* 300–334.

Brockerhoff, M.P. 2000. "An urbanizing world." *Population Bulletin, 55,* 1–4.

Bronner, E. 1997. "Colleges look for answers to racial gaps in testing." *New York Times,* November 8.

———. 1998a. "Inventing the notion of race." *New York Times,* January 10.

———. 1998b. "U of California reports big drop in black admission." *New York Times,* April 1.

Brooke, J. 1998. "Homophobia often found in schools, data show." *New York Times,* October 14.

Brosch, E. 1998. "No place like home." *Harper's,* April.

Broverman, I., Vogel, S., Broverman, D., Clarkson, F., & Rosenkrantz, P. 1972. "Sex role stereotypes: A current appraisal." *Journal of Social Issues, 28,* 59–78.

Brown, L. R., & Flavin, C. 1999. "A new economy for a new century." In L. R. Brown, C. Flavin, & H. French (Eds.), *State of the world: A Worldwatch Institute report on progress toward a sustainable society.* New York: Norton.

Brown, P. 1998. "Biology and the social construction of the 'race' concept." In J. Ferrante & P. Brown (Eds.), *The social construction of race and ethnicity in the United States.* New York: Longman.

Brown, R. 1986. *Social psychology.* New York: Free Press.

Browne, B. A. 1998. "Gender stereotypes in advertising on children's television in the 1990s: A cross-national analysis." *Journal of Advertising, 27,* 8–7.

Brownmiller, S. 1975. *Against our will: Men, women and rape.* New York: Simon & Schuster.

———. 1984. *Femininity.* New York: Fawcett.

Brutus, D. 1999. "Africa 2000 in the new global context." In T. J. Gallagher (Ed.), *Perspectives: Introductory sociology.* St. Paul, MN: Coursewise Publishing.

Bryjak, G. J., & Soroka, M. P. 1992. *Sociology: Cultural diversity in a changing world.* Boston: Allyn and Bacon.

Bullard, R. D. 1993. "Anatomy of environmental racism and the environmental justice movement." In R. D. Bullard (Ed.), *Confronting environmental racism.* Boston: South End Press.

Bullard, R. D., & Wright, B. H. 1992. "The quest for environmental equity: Mobilizing the African-American community for social change." In R. E. Dunlap & A. G. Mertig (Eds.), *American environ-*

mentalism: The U.S. environmental movement, 1970–1990. Philadelphia: Taylor & Francis.

Bullington, B. 1993. "All about Eve: The many faces of United States drug policy." In F. Pearce & M. Woodiwiss (Eds.), *Global crime connections.* Toronto: University of Toronto Press.

Burawoy, M. 1979. *Manufacturing consent.* Chicago: University of Chicago Press.

Burgess-Jackson, K. 1998. "Wife rape." *Public Affairs Quarterly, 12,* 1–2.

Butler, R. 1989. "A generation at risk: When the baby boomers reach Golden Pond." In W. Feigelman (Ed.), *Sociology full circle.* New York: Holt, Rinehart & Winston.

Butsch, R. 1995. "Ralph, Fred, Archie and Homer: Why television keeps recreating the white male working-class buffoon." In G. Dines & J. M. Humez (Eds.), *Gender, race and class in media.* Thousand Oaks, CA: Sage.

Butterfield, F. 1995. "More blacks in their 20's have trouble with the law." *New York Times,* October 5.

———. 1997. "Crime keeps on falling, but prisons keep on filling." *New York Times,* September 28.

———. 1998. "Behind the death row bottleneck." *New York Times,* January 25.

———. 1999. "Eliminating parole boards isn't a cure-all, experts say." *New York Times,* January 10.

———. 2000a. "Often, parole is one stop on the way back to prison." *New York Times,* November 29.

———. 2000b. "Racial disparities seen as pervasive in juvenile justice." *New York Times,* April 26.

Cahill, S. 1999. "Emotional capital and professional socialization: The case of mortuary science students (and me). *Social Psychology Quarterly, 62,* 10–16.

Cameron, D. 1999. "You don't have to be nice here, but it helps to pretend: Language, gender, and emotional labor in the new workplace." Paper presented at DePauw University Colloquium Series, Greencastle, Indiana, April 28.

Campbell, A. 1987. "Self-definition by rejection: The case of gang girls." *Social Problems, 34,* 451–466.

Campbell, A., Converse, P. E., & Rodgers, W. L. 1976. *The quality of American life.* New York: Russell Sage Foundation.

Cancian, F. 1987. *Love in America: Gender and self-development.* New York: Cambridge University Press.

Caplan, P. J. 1995. *They say you're crazy: How the world's most powerful psychiatrists decide who's normal.* Reading, MA: Addison-Wesley.

Caplow, T., Hicks, L., & Wattenberg, B. J. 2001. *The first measured century.* Washington, DC: AEI Press.

Carr, J. 1988. *Crisis in intimacy.* Pacific Grove, CA: Brooks/Cole.

Carrington, W. J., & Troske, K. R. 1998. "Sex segregation in U.S. manufacturing." *Industrial Labor Relations Review, 51,* 445–464.

Carter, H., & Glick, P. C. 1976. *Marriage and divorce: A social and economic study.* Cambridge, MA: Harvard University Press.

Casper, L. M., McLanahan, S. S., & Garfinkel, I. 1994. "The gender-poverty gap: What we can learn from other countries." *American Sociological Review, 59,* 594–605.

Center on Budget and Policy Priorities. 1999. "Average incomes of very poor families fell during early years of welfare reform, study finds." www.cbpp.org/—9wel.htm. Accessed June 23, 2000.

Cetron, M. J., Rocha, W., & Luckins, R. 1991. "Into the 21st century: Long-term trends affecting the United States." In L. Cargan & J. H. Ballantine (Eds.), *Sociological footprints* (5th ed.). Belmont, CA: Wadsworth.

Chafetz, J. S. 1978. *A primer on the construction and testing of theories in sociology.* Itasca, IL: Peacock.

Chafetz, J. S., & Dworkin, A. G. 1987. "In the face of threat: Organized anti-feminism in comparative perspective." *Gender and Society, 1,* 33–60.

Chalfant, H., & Prigoff, J. 1987. *Spraycan art.* New York: Thames and Hudson.

Chambers, M. 1997. "For women, 25 years of Title IX has not leveled the playing field." *New York Times,* June 18.

Chambers, R. 1997. "The unexamined." In M. Hill (Ed.), *Whiteness: A critical reader.* New York: New York University Press.

Chambliss, D. F. 1989. "The mundanity of excellence: An ethnographic report on stratification and Olympic swimmers." *Sociological Theory, 7,* 70–86.

Chambliss, W. 1964. "A sociological analysis of the law of vagrancy." *Social Problems, 12,* 66–77.

Chambliss, W., & Nagasawa, R. H. 1969. "On the validity of official statistics: A comparative study of white, black and Japanese high-school boys." *Journal of Research in Crime and Delinquency, 6,* 71–77.

Chapman, G. 1996. "The Internet: Promise and peril in cyberspace." *Microsoft Encarta Encyclopedia.*

Charon, J. 1992. *Ten questions: A sociological perspective.* Belmont, CA: Wadsworth.

Chase-Dunn, C., & Rubinson, R. 1977. "Toward a structural perspective on the world system." *Politics and Society, 7,* 453–476.

Cherlin, A. 1978. "Remarriage as an incomplete institution." *American Journal of Sociology, 84*, 634–650.

———. 1992. *Marriage, divorce, remarriage.* Cambridge, MA: Harvard University Press.

Cherlin, A., Furstenberg, F. F., Chase-Landale, P. L., Kiernan, K. E., Robins, P. K., Morrison, D. R., & Teitler, J. O. 1991. "Longitudinal studies of effects of divorce on children in Great Britain and the United States." *Science, 252*, 1386–1389.

Chernin, K. 1981. *The obsession: Reflections on the tyranny of slenderness.* New York: Harper & Row.

Cherry, R. 1989. *Discrimination: Its economic impact on blacks, women and Jews.* Lexington, MA: Lexington Books.

Ching, C. L., & Burke, S. 1999. "An assessment of college students' attitudes and empathy toward rape." *College Student Journal, 33*, 573–584.

Ching, F. 1994. "Talking sense on population." *Far Eastern Economic Review,* October 6.

"Christian faith in the age of Prozac." 1995. *Harper's,* December.

Ciancanelli, P., & Berch, B. 1987. "Gender and the GNP." In B. B. Hess & M. M. Ferree (Eds.), *Analyzing gender: A handbook of social science research.* Newbury Park, CA: Sage.

Cicirelli, V. G. 1983. "Adult children and their elderly parents." In T. H. Brubaker (Ed.), *Family relationships in later life.* Beverly Hills, CA: Sage.

Citrin, J. 1996. "Affirmative action in the people's court." *Public Interest,* Winter, pp. 39–48.Clarity, J.F. 1999. "Lost youth in Ireland: Suicide rate is climbing." *New York Times,* March 14.

Clark, B. 1960. "The 'cooling out' function in higher education." *American Journal of Sociology, 65*, 569–576.

Clark, R. L., & Passel, J. S. 1993. "Studies are deceptive." *New York Times,* September 3.

Clausen, J. A. 1986. *The life course: A sociological perspective.* Englewood Cliffs, NJ: Prentice Hall.

Clifford, M. M., & Walster, E. 1973. "The effect of physical attractiveness on teacher expectations." *Sociology of Education, 46*, 248–258.

Clinard, M. B., & Meier, R. F. 1979. *Sociology of deviant behavior.* New York: Holt, Rinehart & Winston.

Cloward, R., & Piven, F. F. 1993. "The fraud of workfare." *The Nation,* May 24, pp. 693–696.

Cluster, D. 1979. *They should have served that cup of coffee.* Boston: South End Press.

Cobb, N. J., Stevens-Long, J., & Goldstein, S. 1982. "The influence of televised models on toy preference in children." *Sex Roles, 8*, 1075–1080.

Cockburn, A. 1995. "The white man's answer." *The Nation,* November 27, pp. 656–657.

Coe, R. M. 1978. *Sociology of medicine.* New York: McGraw-Hill.

Cohen, A. K. 1955. *Delinquent boys: The culture of the gang.* New York: Free Press.

———. 1966. *Deviance and control.* Englewood Cliffs, NJ: Prentice Hall.

Cohen, A. M., & Brawer, F. 1982. *The American community college.* San Francisco: Jossey-Bass.

Cohen, F. G. 1986. *Treaties on trial: The continuing controversy over Northwest Indian fishing rights.* Seattle: University of Washington Press.

Cohen, L. E., & Land, K. C. 1987. "Age structure and crime: Symmetry vs. asymmetry and the projection of crime rates through the 1990's." *American Sociological Review, 52*, 170–183.

Colburn, D. 1992. "A vicious cycle of risk." *Washington Post Health Magazine,* July 28.

Collins, C., & Williams, D. R. 1999. "Segregation and mortality: The deadly effects of racism." *Sociological Forum, 14*, 49–23.

Collins, R. 1971. "Functional and conflict theories of educational stratification." *American Sociological Review, 36*, 1002–1019.

———. 1981. "On the microfoundations of macrosociology." *American Journal of Sociology, 86*, 984–1014.

Coltrane, S., & Adams, M. 1997. "Work-family imagery and gender stereotypes: Television and the reproduction of difference." *Journal of Vocational Behavior, 50*, 32–47.

Comer, J. P., & Poussaint, A. F. 1992. *Raising black children.* New York: Plume.

"Coming to a neighborhood near you." 2001. *The Economist,* May 5–May 11.

Commission for Racial Justice. 1987. *Toxic waste and race.* New York: United Church of Christ.

Conrad, P. 1975. "The discovery of hyperkinesis: Notes on the medicalization of deviant behavior." *Social Problems, 23*, 12–21.

Cookson, P., & Persell, C. 1985. *Preparing for power.* New York: Basic Books.

Cooley, C. H. 1902. *Human nature and social order.* New York: Scribner's.

Coontz, S. 1992. *The way we never were.* New York: Basic Books.

Cooper, K. J. 1999. "Admissions models for inclusion." *Black Issues in Higher Education, 16*, 3–5.

Cooper, M. H. 1994. "Prozac controversy." *CQ Researcher,* August 19.

———. 1998a. "Environmental justice." *CQ Researcher,* June 19.

———. 1998b. "Income inequality." *CQ Researcher,* April 17.

———. 1998c. "Population and the environment." *CQ Researcher,* July 17.

———. 1999. "Women and human rights." *CQ Researcher,* April 30.

Corcoran, M., Duncan, G. J., & Hill, M. S. 1986. "The economic fortunes of women and children: Lessons from the panel study of income dynamics." In B. C. Gelpi et al. (Eds.), *Women and poverty.* Chicago: University of Chicago Press.

Cose, E. 1993. *The rage of the privileged class.* New York: HarperCollins.

———. 1998. "The obligations of race." *Newsweek,* August 10.

———. 1999. "The good news about black America." *Newsweek,* June 7.

Coser, L., & Coser, R. 1993. "Jonestown as a perverse Utopia." In K. Finsterbusch & J. S. Schwartz (Eds.), *Sources: Notable selections in sociology.* Guilford, CT: Dushkin.

Coulson, M. A., & Riddell, C. 1980. *Approaching sociology.* London: Routledge & Kegan Paul.

Cowan, R. 1991. "More work for Mother: The postwar years." In L. Kramer (Ed.), *The sociology of gender.* New York: St. Martin's Press.

Cowley, G. 1997. "Gender limbo." *Newsweek,* May 9.

Crandall, C. S., & Martinez, R. 1996. "Culture, ideology, and antifat attitudes." *Personality and Social Psychology Bulletin, 22,* 1165–1176.

Cranz, G. 1998. *The chair: Rethinking culture, body, and design.* New York: Norton.

Critser, G. 2000. "Let them eat fat: The heavy truths about American obesity." *Harper's Magazine,* March.

Cross, G. 1997. *Kids' stuff: Toys and the changing world of American childhood.* Cambridge, MA: Harvard University Press.

Cross, J., & Guyer, M. 1980. *Social traps.* Ann Arbor: University of Michigan Press.

Crossette, B. 1996a. "Hope, and pragmatism, for U.N. cities conference." *New York Times,* June 3.

———. 1996b. "New tally of world tragedy: Women who die giving life." *New York Times,* June 11.

———. 1997a. "How to fix a crowded world: Add people." *New York Times,* November 2.

———. 1997b. "What modern slavery is, and isn't." *New York Times,* July 27.

———. 1998. "Kofi Annan's astonishing facts!" *New York Times,* September 27.

———. 2000a. "Burgers are the globe's fast food? Not so fast." *New York Times,* November 26.

———. 2000b. "Europe stares at a future built by immigrants." *New York Times,* January 2.

———. 2001. "Against a trend, U.S. population will bloom, UN says." *New York Times,* February 28.

Croteau, D., & Hoynes, W. 2000. *Media/Society: Industries, images, and audiences.* Thousand Oaks, CA: Pine Forge Press.

Crowley, G. 1994. "The culture of Prozac." *Newsweek,* February 7.

———. 1997. "Do kids need Prozac?" *Newsweek,* October 20.

Cummings, B. 1992. *War and television,* London: Verso.

Curra, J. 2000. *The relativity of deviance.* Thousand Oaks, CA: Sage.

Curran, D. J., & Renzetti, C. M. 1990. *Social problems.* Boston: Allyn and Bacon.

Cushman, J. H. 1993. "U.S. to weigh Blacks' complaints about pollution." *New York Times,* November 19.

———. 1998. "Nike pledges to end child labor and apply U.S. rules abroad." *New York Times,* May 13.

Dabbs, J. M. 1992. "Testosterone and occupational achievement." *Social Forces, 70,* 813–824.

Dahrendorf, R. 1959. *Class and class conflict in industrial society.* Stanford, CA: Stanford University Press.

Daley, S. 1996. "A new charter wins adoption in South Africa." *New York Times,* May 9.

———. 2000. "More and more, Europeans find fault with U.S." *New York Times,* April 9.

Darton, N. 1991. "The end of innocence." *Newsweek* (special summer issue).

Darwin, C. 1971. *The descent of man.* Adelaide, Australia: Griffin Press. (Original work published 1871)

Davies, J. C. 1962. "Toward a theory of revolution." *American Sociological Review, 27,* 5–19.

Davis, A. J. 1984. "Sex-differentiated behaviors in nonsexist picture books." *Sex Roles, 11,* 1–16.

Davis, F. J. 1991. *Who is black?* University Park: Pennsylvania State University Press.

Davis, J. A., & Smith, T. 1986. *General social survey cumulative file 1972–1982.* Ann Arbor, MI: Inter-University Consortium for Political and Social Research.

Davis, K. 1937. "The sociology of prostitution." *American Sociological Review, 2,* 744–755.

———. 1976. "The world's population crisis." In R. K. Merton & R. Nisbett (Eds.), *Contemporary social problems.* New York: Harcourt Brace Jovanovich.

Davis, K., & Moore, W. 1945. "Some principles of stratification." *American Sociological Review, 10,* 242–247.

Deaux, K., & Kite, M. E. 1987. "Thinking about gender." In B. B. Hess & M. M. Ferree (Eds.), *Analyzing gender: A handbook of social science research.* Newbury Park, CA: Sage.

DeFronzo, J. 1991. *Revolutions and revolutionary movements.* Boulder, CO: Westview.

Denzin, N. 1977. *Childhood socialization: Studies in the development of language, social behavior, and identity.* San Francisco: Jossey-Bass.

———. 1989. *The research act: A theoretical introduction to sociological methods.* Englewood Cliffs, NJ: Prentice Hall.

DePalma, A. 1995. "Racism? Mexico's in denial." *New York Times,* June 11.

———. 1996. "For Mexico's Indians, new voice but few gains." *New York Times,* January 13.

DeParle, J. 1990. "In debate over who is poor, fairness becomes the issue." *New York Times,* September 3.

———. 1997. "U.S. welfare system dies as state programs emerge." *New York Times,* June 30.

———. 1998. "In booming economy, poor still struggle to pay the rent." *New York Times,* June 16.

———. 1999. "States struggle to use windfall born of shifts in welfare law." *New York Times,* August 29.

Derber, C. 1979. *The pursuit of attention.* New York: Oxford University Press.

Deutsch, K. W. 1966. *Nationalism and social communication.* Cambridge, MA: MIT Press.

DeWitt, K. 1995. "Panel's study cites job bias for minorities and women." *New York Times,* November 23.

Diekmann, A., & H. Engelhardt. 1999. "The social inheritance of divorce: Effects of parent's family type in postwar Germany." *American Sociological Review, 64,* 78–93.

Diller, L. H. 1998. *Running on Ritalin.* New York: Bantam.

DiMaggio, P. J., & Powell, W. W. 1983. "The iron cage revisited: Institutional isomorphism and collective rationality in organizational fields." *American Sociological Review, 48,* 147–160.

———. 1991. "Introduction." In W. W. Powell & P. J. DiMaggio (Eds.). *The new institutionalism in organizational analysis.* Chicago: University of Chicago Press.

Dion, K. 1972. "Physical attractiveness and evaluations of children's transgressions." *Journal of Personality and Social Psychology, 24,* 207–213.

Dion, K., Berscheid, E., & Walster, E. 1972. "What is beautiful is good." *Journal of Personality and Social Psychology, 24,* 285–290.

Dobash, R. E., & Dobash, R. P. 1979. *Violence against wives: A case against the patriarchy.* New York: Free Press.

"Doctors implicated in Tutsi genocide." 1996. *The Lancet, 347,* 684.

Domhoff, G. W. 1983. *Who rules America now? A view from the eighties.* Englewood Cliffs, NJ: Prentice Hall.

———. 1998. *Who rules America? Power and politics in the year 2000.* Mountain View, CA: Mayfield.

Donahue, B. 1998. "For new sports, ESPN rules as the X-treme gatekeeper." *New York Times,* March 11.

Donath, J. S. 1997. "Identity deception in the virtual community." In P. Kollock & M. Smith (Eds.), *Communities in cyberspace.* Berkeley: University of California Press.

Dowd, M. 2000. "Nymphet at the net." *New York Times,* June 4.

Doyle, R. 1994. *Atlas of contemporary America.* New York: Facts on File.

Drucker, S. 1996. "Who is the best restaurateur in America?" *New York Times Magazine,* March 10.

D'Souza, D. 1995. *The end of racism.* New York: Free Press.

Dugger, C. W. 1996. "Immigrant cultures raising issues of child punishment." *New York Times,* February 29.

———. 1999a. "India's poorest are becoming its loudest." *New York Times,* April 25.

———. 1999b. "Lower-caste women turn village rule upside down." *New York Times,* May 3.

———. 1999c. "Massacres of low-born touch off a crisis in India." *New York Times,* March 15.

———. 2000. "A cruel choice in New Delhi: Jobs vs. a safer environment." *New York Times,* November 24.

———. 2001. "Abortion in India is tipping scales sharply against girls." *New York Times,* April 22.

Duke, S. B. 1994. "Casualties of war." *Reason, 25,* 20–27.

Duncan, G. J. 1984. *Years of poverty, years of plenty.* Ann Arbor: University of Michigan Press.

Durkheim, E. 1951. *Suicide.* New York: Free Press. (Original work published 1897)

———. 1954. *The elementary forms of religious life* (J. Swain, Trans.). New York: Free Press. (Original work published 1915)

Duster, T. 1997. "Pattern, purpose, and race in the drug war." In C. Reinarman & H. G. Levine (Eds.), *Crack in America.* Berkeley: University of California Press.

Ebaugh, H. R. F. 1988. *Becoming an ex.* Chicago: University of Chicago Press.

Eckholm, E. 2001. "Psychiatric abuse by China reported in repressing sect." *New York Times,* February 18.

Edney, J. 1979. "Free riders en route to disaster." *Psychology Today,* August, pp. 80–102.

Edney, J. J., & Harper, C. S. 1978. "The commons dilemma: A review of contributions from psychology." *Environmental Management, 2,* 491–507.

Edwards, H. 1971. "The sources of black athletic superiority." *Black Scholar,* November.

Egan, T. 1995. "Many seek security in private communities." *New York Times,* September 3.

———. 1999a. "Less crime, more criminals." *New York Times,* March 7.

———. 1999b. "The war on crack retreats, still taking prisoners." *New York Times,* February 28.

Ehrenreich, B. 1989. *Fear of falling: The inner life of the middle class.* New York: HarperPerennial.

———. 1990. "Is the middle class doomed?" In B. Ehrenreich (Ed.), *The worst years of our lives.* New York: HarperPerennial.

———. 1995. "The silenced majority: Why the average working person has disappeared from American media and culture." In G. Dines & J.M. Humez (Eds.), *Gender, race, and class in media.* Thousand Oaks, CA: Sage.

Ehrenreich, B., & English, D. 1979. *For her own good: 150 years of the experts' advice to women.* Garden City, NY: Anchor.

Ehrlich, P. R., & Ehrlich, A. H. 1993. "World population crisis." In K. Finsterbusch & J. S. Schwartz (Eds.), *Sources: Notable selections in sociology.* Guilford, CT: Dushkin.

Eitzen, D. S., & Baca-Zinn, M. 1989. *Social problems.* Boston: Allyn and Bacon.

———. 1991. *In conflict and order: Understanding society.* Boston: Allyn and Bacon.

Elder, G. H., & Liker, J. K. 1982. "Hard times in women's lives: Historical influences across 40 years." *American Journal of Sociology, 88,* 241–269.

Elliot, M., & Dickey, C. 1994. "Body politics." *Newsweek,* September 12.

"Employers hit with $4.5 million in 1998 FMLA penalties." 1999. *HR Focus,* November.

"Employers offer gays more benefits." 2000. *New York Times,* September 25.

Engelhardt, T. 1992. "The Gulf War as total television." *The Nation,* May 11, pp. 613–617.

England, P. 1999. "The case for comparable worth." *Quarterly Review of Economics and Finance, 39,* 74–55.

English, C. 1991. "Food is my best friend: Self-justifications and weight loss efforts." *Research in the Sociology of Health Care, 9,* 335–345.

Entine, J. 2000. *Taboo: Why black athletes dominate sports and why we're afraid to talk about it.* New York: Public Affairs.

Epstein, C. F. 1989. "Workplace boundaries: Conceptions and creations." *Social Research, 56,* 571–590.

Erikson, K. 1966. *Wayward puritans.* New York: Wiley.

Erlanger, S. 2000. "Across a new Europe, a people deemed unfit for tolerance." *New York Times,* April 2.

Etzioni, A. 2000. "E-communities build new ties, but ties that bind." New York Times, February 10.

Evans-Pritchard, E. E. 1937. *Witchcraft, oracles and magic among the Azande.* Oxford, England: Oxford University Press.

Evered, R. 1983. "The language of organizations: The case of the Navy." In L. R. Pondy, P. J. Frost, G. Morgan, & T. C. Dandridge (Eds.), *Organizational symbolism.* Greenwich, CT: JAI Press.

Ewing, W. 1992. "The civic advocacy of violence." In M. S. Kimmel & M. A. Messner (Eds.), *Men's lives.* New York: Macmillan.

"Expectation shadows Gen. Powell." 2000. AP Online. www.ap.org. April 13.

"Extreme sports dominate gear market." 2000. AP Online. www.ap.org. February 11.

"Facts about figures, The." 1996. *People,* June 3.

Faludi, S. 1991. *Backlash: The undeclared war against women.* New York: Crown.

Farb, P. 1983. *Word play: What happens when people talk.* New York: Bantam.

Farley, J. 1982. *Majority–minority relations.* Englewood Cliffs, NJ: Prentice Hall.

———. 1991. *Sociology.* Englewood Cliffs, NJ: Prentice Hall.

Farley, J. E. 1991. *American social problems: An institutional analysis* (2nd ed.). Upper Saddle River, NJ: Prentice Hall.

Farley, R., & Frey, W. H. 1992. *Changes in the segregation of whites from blacks during the 1980s: Small steps toward a more racially integrated society.* Ann Arbor: Population Studies Center, University of Michigan.

———. 1994. "Changes in the segregation of whites from blacks during the 1980s: Small steps toward a more integrated society." *American Sociological Review, 59,* 23–45.

Faust, K., Gann, M., & McKibben, J. 1999. "The boomlet goes to college." *American Demographics, 21,* 4–5.

Fausto-Sterling, A. 1985. *Myths of gender: Biological theories about women and men.* New York: Basic Books.

———. 1993. "How many sexes are there?" *New York Times,* March 12.

Feagin, J. R. 1975. *Subordinating the poor.* Englewood Cliffs, NJ: Prentice Hall.

———. 1991. "The continuing significance of race: Anti-black discrimination in public places." *American Sociological Review, 56,* 101–116.

Featherstone, M. 1990. *Global culture: Nationalism, globalization and modernity.* Newbury Park, CA: Sage.

Federal Bureau of Investigation. 1991. *Uniform crime reports for the United States.* Washington, DC: U.S. Government Printing Office.

Fein, E. B. 1997. "Lack of common language can hinder care at hospitals." *New York Times,* November 23.

Felmlee, D., Sprecher, S., & Bassin, E. 1990. "The dissolution of intimate relationships: A hazard model." *Social Psychology Quarterly, 53,* 13–30.

Ferree, M. M. 1992. "The political context of rationality." In A. D. Morris & C. M. Mueller (Eds.), *Frontiers in social movement theory.* New Haven, CT: Yale University Press.

Festinger, L., Riecken, H., & Schacter, S. 1956. *When prophecy fails.* New York: Harper & Row.

Figert, A. 1996. *Women and the ownership of PMS.* New York: Aldine de Gruyter.

Fincham, F., & Bradbury, T. N. 1987. "The impact of attributions in marriage: A longitudinal analysis." *Journal of Personality and Social Psychology, 53,* 510–517.

Finder, A. 1998. "Evidence is scant that workfare leads to full-time jobs." *New York Times,* April 12.

Fine, G. A. 1990. *Talking sociology.* Boston: Allyn and Bacon.

Finke, R., & Stark, R. 1992. *The Churching of America, 1776–1990: Winners and Losers in Our Religious Economy.* New Brunswick, NJ: Rutgers University Press.

Finnegan, W. 1998. *Cold new world: Growing up in a harder country.* New York: Random House.

Fischer, M. J., & Massey, D. S. 2000. "Residential segregation and ethnic enterprise in U.S. metropolitan areas." *Social Problems, 47,* 40–24.

Forbes, H. D. 1997. *Ethnic conflict: Commerce, culture and the contact hypothesis.* New Haven, CT: Yale University Press.

Francis, D. R. 1998. "Workers' wages are up, but security eludes many." *Christian Science Monitor,* September 4.

Frank, A. G. 1969. *Capitalism and under-development in Latin America.* New York: Monthly Review Press.

Frankel, G. 1996. "U.S. aided cigarette firms in conquests across Asia." *Washington Post,* November 17.

Franklin, C. W., II. 1988. *Men and society.* Chicago: Nelson-Hall.

Fraser, L. 1999. "Thigh anxiety." *Utne Reader,* July–August.

Freedman, R. 1986. *Beauty bound.* Lexington, MA: Lexington Books.

Freemantle, D. 1998. *What customers like about you: Adding emotional value for service excellence and competitive advantage.* London: Nicholas Brealey.

Freiberg, P. 1991. "Self-esteem gender gap widens in adolescence." *APA Monitor, 22,* 29.

French, H. W. 1997. "The ritual slaves of Ghana: Young and female." *New York Times,* January 20.

———. 1999a. "'Japanese only' policy takes body blow in court." *New York Times,* November 15.

———. 1999b. "Japan's troubling trend: Rising teenage crime." *New York Times,* October 12.

———. 2000a. "Japan unsettles returnees, who yearn to leave again." *New York Times,* May 3.

———. 2000b. "Still wary of outsiders, Japan expects immigration boom." *New York Times,* March 14.

Friedland, R. 1989. "Questions raised by the changing age distribution of the U.S. population." *Generations, 13,* 11–13.

Frieze, I. H., Parsons, J. E., Johnson, P. B., Ruble, D. N., & Zellman, G. L. 1978. *Women and sex roles: A social psychological perspective.* New York: Norton.

Furstenberg, F. F., & Cherlin, A. J. 1991. *Divided families.* Cambridge, MA: Harvard University Press.

Furstenberg, F. F., & Nord, C. 1985. "Parenting apart: Patterns of childrearing after marital disruption." *Journal of Marriage and the Family, 47,* 893–904.

Gabriel, T. 1996. "High-tech pregnancies test hope's limit." *New York Times,* January 7.

Gaertner, S., & Dovidio, J. 1990. "The aversive form of racism." In A. G. Halberstadt & S. L. Ellyson (Eds.), *Social psychology readings: A century of research.* New York: McGraw-Hill.

Gailey, C. W. 1987. "Evolutionary perspectives on gender hierarchy." In B. B. Hess & M. M. Ferree (Eds.), *Analyzing gender: A handbook of social science research.* Newbury Park: Sage.

Gaines, D. 1991. *Teenage wasteland: Suburbia's dead-end kids.* New York: Pantheon.

Gale, R. P. 1986. "Social movements and the state: The environmental movement, countermovement and governmental agencies." *Sociological Perspectives, 29,* 202–240.

Galles, G. M. 1989. "What colleges really teach." *New York Times,* June 8.

Gamson, W. A., Fireman, B., & Rytina, S. 1982. *Encounters with unjust authority.* Homewood, IL: Dorsey Press.

Gamson, W. A., & Wolfsfeld, G. 1993. "Movements and media as interactive systems." *Annals of the American Academy of Political and Social Science, 528,* 114–125.

Gans, H. 1971. "The uses of poverty: The poor pay for all." *Social Policy,* Summer, pp. 20–24.

———. 1996. "Positive functions of the undeserving poor: Uses of the underclass in America." In J. Levin & A. Arluke (Eds.), *Snapshots and portraits of society.* Thousand Oaks, CA: Pine Forge Press.

Garner, R. 1996. *Contemporary movements and ideologies.* New York: McGraw-Hill.

Garson, B. 1988. *The electronic sweatshop.* New York: Penguin.

Gates, H. L. 1992. "TV's black world turns—but stays unreal." In M. L. Anderson & P. H. Collins (Eds.), *Race, class and gender: An anthology.* Belmont, CA: Wadsworth.

Gaubatz, K. T. 1995. *Crime in the public mind.* Ann Arbor: University of Michigan Press.

"Gay men and lesbians find a home on Internet services." 1996. *New York Times,* June 16.

Gelles, R. J., & Cornell, C. P. 1990. *Intimate violence in families.* Newbury Park, CA: Sage.

Gergen, K. J. 1991. *The saturated self.* New York: Basic Books.

Gerlach, P., & Hine, V. H. 1970. *People, power, change: Movements of social transformation.* Indianapolis: Bobbs-Merrill.

Gerson, K. 1993. *No man's land: Men's changing commitments to family and work.* New York: Basic Books.

Gibbons, D. C. 1992. *Society, crime and criminal behavior.* Englewood Cliffs, NJ: Prentice Hall.

Giddens, A. 1984. *The construction of society: Outline of the theory of structuration.* Berkeley: University of California Press.

———. 2000. *Runaway world: How globalization is reshaping our lives.* New York: Routledge.

Gillen, B. 1981. "Physical attractiveness: A determinant of two types of goodness." *Personality and Social Psychology Bulletin, 7,* 277–281.

Gillespie, C. K. 1989. *Justifiable homicide.* Columbus: Ohio State University Press.

Gilligan, C. 1990. "Teaching Shakespeare's sister: Notes from the underground of female adolescence." In C. Gilligan, N. P. Lyons, & T. J. Hanmer (Eds.),

Making connections. Cambridge, MA: Harvard University Press.

Gillings, A. 1996. "Sleeping with the enemy?" *Village Voice,* July 2.

Gitlin, T. 1979. "Prime time ideology: The hegemonic process in television entertainment." *Social Problems, 26,* 251–266.

Gladwell, M. 1996. "Black like them." *The New Yorker,* April 29, May 6.

"A glance at women in the military." 2001. Associated Press Online. May 9.

Glantz, S. A. 1996. "The anti-smoking campaign that tobacco loves." *Harper's,* July, pp. 26–28.

Gleason, H. A. 1961. *An introduction to descriptive linguistics.* New York: Holt, Rinehart & Winston.

Glenn, N. 1982. "Interreligious marriage in the United States: Patterns and recent trends." *Journal of Marriage and the Family, 44,* 555–566.

Glick, P., & Fiske, S.T. 1996. "The ambivalent sexism inventory: Differentiating hostile and benevolent sexism." *Journal of Personality and Social Psychology, 70,* 49–12.

"A glimpse into how six billion live." 1999. *New York Times,* September 19, p. 1.

Godson, R., & Olson, W. J. 1995. "International organized crime." *Society, 32,* 18–29.

Goertzel, T. G. 1993. "Some observations on psychological processes among organized American opponents to the Gulf War." *Political Psychology, 14,* 139–146.

Goetting, A. 1982. "The six stations of remarriage: Developmental tasks of remarriage after divorce." *Family Relations,* April, pp. 213–222.

Goffman, E. 1952. "On cooling the mark out: Some aspects of adaptation to failure." *Psychiatry, 15,* 451–463.

———. 1959. *The presentation of self in everyday life.* Garden City, NY: Doubleday.

———. 1961. *Asylums.* Garden City, NY: Anchor.

———. 1963. *Stigma: Notes on the management of spoiled identity.* Englewood Cliffs, NJ: Prentice Hall.

———. 1967. *Interaction ritual.* Chicago: Aldine-Atherton.

Goldberg, C. 2001. "In some states, sex offenders serve more than their time." *New York Times,* April 22.

Goldberg, J. 1999. "The color of suspicion." *New York Times Magazine,* June 20.

Goldberg, S. 1974. *The inevitability of patriarchy.* New York: Morrow.

Goldberg, S., & Lewis, M. 1969. "Play behavior in the year-old infant: Early sex differences." *Child Development, 40,* 21–31.

Goleman, D. 1984. "Rethinking IQ tests and their value." *New York Times,* July 22.

———. 1989. "Sensing silent cues emerges as key skill." *New York Times,* October 10.

———. 1990. "The group and the self: New focus on a cultural rift." *New York Times,* December 25.

———. 1991a. "Parents' warmth is found to be key to adult happiness." *New York Times,* April 18.

———. 1991b. "When ugliness is only in the patient's eye, body image can reflect a mental disorder." *New York Times,* October 2.

———. 1993. "Therapists find some patients are just hateful." *New York Times,* May 4.

———. 1995. "Making room on the couch for culture." *New York Times,* December 5.

"Good fences." 1998. *The Economist,* December 19.

Goodchilds, J., Zellman, G., Johnson, P., & Giarusso, R. 1988. "Adolescents and the perceptions of sexual interaction outcomes." In A. W. Burgess (Ed.), *Sexual assault.* New York: Garland.

Goode, Erich. 1989. *Drugs in American society.* New York: McGraw-Hill.

———. 1994. *Deviant behavior.* Englewood Cliffs, NJ: Prentice Hall.

Goode, Erica. 1999a. "Pediatricians renew battle over toilet training." *New York Times,* January 12.

———. 1999b. "Study finds TV trims Fiji girls' body image and eating habits." *New York Times,* May 20.

Goode, W. J. 1971. "World revolution and family patterns." *Journal of Marriage and the Family, 33,* 624–635.

———. 1981. "Why men resist." In B. Thorne & M. Yalom (Eds.), *Rethinking the family: Some feminist questions.* New York: Longman.

———. 1993. *World changes in divorce patterns.* New Haven, CT: Yale University Press.

Gordimer, N. 2000. "Africa's plague, and everyone's." *New York Times,* April 11.

Gordon, M. M. 1964. *Assimilation in American life.* New York: Oxford University Press.

Gose, B. 1995. "Test scores and stereotypes." *Chronicle of Higher Education,* August 18.

Gough, K. 1971. "The origin of the family." *Journal of Marriage and the Family, 33,* 760–770.

Gould, S. J. 1981. *The mismeasure of man.* New York: Norton.

———. 1997. "Dolly's fashion and Louis's passion." *Natural History,* June.

Gove, W., Hughes, M., & Geerkin, M. R. 1980. "Playing dumb: A form of impression management with undesirable effects." *Social Psychology Quarterly, 43,* 89–102.

Gove, W., Style, C. B., & Hughes, M. 1990. "The effect of marriage on the well-being of adults." *Journal of Family Issues, 11,* 34–35.

Gracey, H. L. 1991. "Learning the student role: Kindergarten as academic boot camp." In J. Henslin (Ed.), *Down-to-earth sociology.* New York: Free Press.

Graham, L. 1995. *On the line at Subaru-Isuzu.* Ithaca, NY: ILR Press.

Graham, L. O. 1999. *Our kind of people: Inside America's black upper class.* New York: HarperCollins.

Graham, W. 1996. "Masters of the game." *Harper's,* July.

Gray, H. 1995. "Television, black Americans, and the American dream." In G. Dines & J. M. Humez (Eds.), *Gender, race and class in media.* Thousand Oaks, CA: Sage.

Greeley, A. M., & Hout, M. 1999. "Americans' increasing belief in life after death: Religious competition and acculturation." *American Sociological Review, 64,* 81–35.

Greenberg, J. 1998. "Israel battles new foreign foe: Music." *New York Times,* December 20.

Greencastle Banner Graphic. 1992. Letter to the editor. March 7.

Greenhouse, L. 1986. "The rise and rise of McDonald's." *New York Times,* June 8.

———. 1990. "Use of illegal drugs as part of religion can be prosecuted, high court says." *New York Times,* April 18.

———. 1993. "Court, 9–0, makes sex harassment easier to prove." *New York Times,* November 10.

———. 1996. "Christian Scientists rebuffed in ruling by Supreme Court." *New York Times,* January 23.

———. 1997. "Nike shoe plant in Vietnam is called unsafe for workers." *New York Times,* November 8.

———. 2000. "Anti-sweatshop movement is achieving gains overseas." *New York Times,* January 26.

Greider, W. 1997. *One world, ready or not: The manic logic of global capitalism.* New York: Simon & Schuster.

Griffin, S. 1986. *Rape: The power of consciousness.* New York: Harper & Row.

———. 1989. "Rape: The all-American crime." In L. Richardson & V. Taylor (Eds.), *Feminist frontiers II.* New York: Random House.

Griswold, W. 1994. *Cultures and societies in a changing world.* Thousand Oaks, CA: Pine Forge Press.

Gross, E. 1984. "Embarrassment in public life." *Society, 21,* 48–53.

Gross, E., & Etzioni, A. 1985. *Organizations and society.* Englewood Cliffs, NJ: Prentice Hall.

Gross, E., & Stone, G. P. 1964. "Embarrassment and the analysis of role requirements." *American Journal of Sociology, 70,* 1–15.

Gross, J. 1997. "Wall Street's frenetic? Try the eighth grade." *New York Times,* October 5.

———. 1998. "In quest for the perfect look, more girls choose the scalpel." *New York Times,* November 29.

Gusfield, J. R. 1963. *Symbolic crusade: Status politics and the American temperance movement.* Urbana: University of Illinois Press.

Haas, L. L. 1995. "Household division of labor in industrial societies." In B. B. Ingoldsby & S. Smith (Eds.), *Families in multicultural perspective.* New York: Guilford.

Haberman, C. 2000. "Attica: Exorcising the demons, redeeming the deaths." *New York Times,* January 9.

Hacker, A. 1992. *Two nations: Black and white, separate, hostile, unequal.* New York: Scribner's.

Hafferty, F. W. 1991. *Into the valley: Death and socialization of medical students.* New Haven, CT: Yale University Press.

Hafner, K. 1999. "In real life's shadow, virtual life can pale." *New York Times,* August 26.

———. 2000. "For the well-connected, all the world's an office." *New York Times,* March 30.

Hagan, J. 1985. *Modern criminology: Crime, criminal behavior and its control.* New York: McGraw-Hill.

Hall, P. 1990. "The presidency and impression management." In J. W. Heeren & M. Mason (Eds.), *Sociology: Windows on society.* Los Angeles: Roxbury.

Hall, R. M., & Sandler, B. R. 1985. "A chilly climate in the classroom." In A. G. Sargent (Ed.), *Beyond sex roles.* St. Paul, MN: West.

Hall, W. 1986. "Social class and survival on the S.S. Titanic." *Social Science and Medicine, 22,* 687–690.

Halle, D. 1984. *America's working man: Work, home, and politics among blue-collar property owners.* Chicago: University of Chicago Press.

Hallin, D. C. 1986. "We keep America on top of the world." In T. Gitlin (Ed.), *Watching television.* New York: Pantheon.

Hamilton, D. L. 1981. *Cognitive processes in stereotyping and intergroup behavior.* Hillsdale, NJ: Erlbaum.

Hamilton, K., & Weingarden, J. 1998. "Lifts, lasers and liposuction: The cosmetic surgery boom." *Newsweek,* June 15.

Hamilton, V. L., & Sanders, J. 1995. "Crimes of obedience and conformity in the workplace: Surveys of Americans, Russians, and Japanese." *Journal of Social Issues, 51,* 67–88.

Hammel, S. 1999. "Living their lives online." *U.S. News & World Report,* November 29.

Hammer, J. 1992. "Must Blacks be buffoons?" *Newsweek,* October 26.

Hancock, L., & Kalb, C. 1996. "A room of their own." *Newsweek,* June 24.

Haney López, I. F. 1996. *White by law: The legal construction of race.* New York: New York University Press.

Hansell, S. 1998. "Big web sites to track steps of their users." *New York Times,* August 16.

Harden, B. 2000. "Africa's gems: Warfare's best friend." *New York Times,* April 6.

Hardin, G., & Baden, J. 1977. *Managing the commons.* New York: Freeman.

Hareven, T. K. 1978. *Transitions: The family and the life course in historical perspective.* New York: Academic Press.

———. 1992. "American families in transition: Historical perspectives on change." In A. S. Skolnick & J. H. Skolnick (Eds.), *Family in transition* (7th ed.). New York: HarperCollins.

Harper, D. 1996. Personal communication.

"Harper's Index." 1996. *Harper's,* July.

———. 1998a. *Harper's,* January.

———. 1998b. *Harper's,* May.

Harris, J. R. 1998. *The nurture assumption.* New York: Free Press.

Harris, K. M. 1996. "Life after welfare: Women, work, and repeat dependency." *American Sociological Review, 61,* 407–426.

Harris, M. 1964. *Patterns of race in the Americas.* New York: Norton.

Harrison, B., & Bluestone, B. 1988. *The great U-turn: Corporate restructuring and the polarizing of America.* New York: Basic Books.

Harrison, R. J., & Bennett, C. E. 1995. "Racial and ethnic diversity." In R. Farley (Ed.), *State of the Union: America in the 1990s.* New York: Russell Sage Foundation.

Hartmann, H., Kraut, R. E., & Tilly, L. A. 1989. "Job content: Job fragmentation and the deskilling debate." In D. S. Eitzen & M. Baca-Zinn (Eds.), *The reshaping of America.* Englewood Cliffs, NJ: Prentice Hall.

Hass, N. 1995. "Margaret Kelly Michaels wants her innocence back." *New York Times Magazine,* September 10.

———. 1998. "A TV generation is seeing beyond color." *New York Times,* February 22.

Hayward, M. D., & Heron, M. 1999. "Racial inequality in active life among adult Americans." *Demography, 36,* 7–1.

Headlam, B. 2000a. "Barbie PC: Fashion over logic." *New York Times,* January 20.

———. 2000b. "Boys will be boys, and sometimes girls, in online communities." *New York Times,* May 25.

Heaton, T. B., Jacobson, C. K., & Fu, X. N. 1992. "Religiosity of married couples and childlessness." *Review of Religious Research, 33,* 24–55.

Heise, L. 1989. "The global war against women." *Washington Post Magazine,* April 9.

Helmreich, W. B. 1992. "The things they say behind your back: Stereotypes and the myths behind them." In H. F. Lena, W. B. Helmreich, & W. McCord (Eds.), *Contemporary issues in sociology.* New York: McGraw-Hill.

Henley, N. 1977. *Body politics.* Englewood Cliffs, NJ: Prentice Hall.

Henriques, D. B. 1999. "New take on perpetual calendar." *New York Times,* August 24.

Henslin, J. 1991. *Down-to-earth sociology.* New York: Free Press.

Henslin, J., & Biggs, M. A. 1978. "Dramaturgical desexualization: The sociology of the vaginal examination." In J. Henslin & E. Sagarin (Eds.), *The sociology of sex: An introductory reader.* New York: Schocken.

———. 1996. "Nike's pyramid scheme." *New York Times,* June 10.

———. 1999. "A brewing storm." *New York Times,* February 11.

Herman, N. J. 1993. "Return to sender: Reintegrative stigma-management strategies of ex-psychiatric patients." *Journal of Contemporary Ethnography, 22,* 29–30.

Herrnstein, R. J., & Murray, C. 1994. *The bell curve: Intelligence and class structure in American life.* New York: Free Press.

Hewitt, J. P. 1988. *Self and society: A symbolic interactionist social psychology.* Boston: Allyn and Bacon.

Hewitt, J. P., & Stokes, R. 1975. "Disclaimers." *American Sociological Review, 40,* 1–11.

Hill, M. E. 2000. "Color differences in the socioeconomic status of African American men: Results from a longitudinal study." *Social Forces, 78,* 1437–1460.

Hill, N. E. 1997. "Does parenting differ based on social class? African American women's perceived socialization for achievement." *American Journal of Community Psychology, 25,* 67–97.

Hiller, E. T. 1933. *Principles of sociology.* New York: Harper & Row.

Hilliard, D. C. 1994. "Televised sport and the (anti) sociological imagination." *Journal of Sport and Social Issues, 18,* 88–99.

Hills, S. 1980. *Demystifying social deviance.* New York: McGraw-Hill.

Hilts, P. J. 1995. "Pessimism is hazardous to health, a study says." *New York Times,* November 29.

Hirschi, T. 1969. *Causes of delinquency.* Berkeley: University of California Press.

Hitt, J. 1998. "Who will do abortions here?" *New York Times Magazine,* January 18.

Hoberman, J. M. 1997. *Darwin's athletes: How sport has damaged Black America and preserved the myth of race.* Boston: Houghton Mifflin.

Hochschild, A. R. 1983. *The managed heart.* Berkeley: University of California Press.

———. 1997. *The time bind: When work becomes home and home becomes work.* New York: Metropolitan Books.

Hodson, R. 1991. "The active worker: Compliance and autonomy at the workplace." *Journal of Contemporary Ethnography, 20,* 47–78.

Hoffman, J. 1997. "Crime and punishment: Shame gains popularity." *New York Times,* January 16.

Hoge, W. 1998. "Sweden, the world's role model, now drifting as currents change." *New York Times,* August 10.

Holmes, S. A. 1995. "The strange politics of immigration." *New York Times,* December 31.

———. 1998. "Klan case transcends racial divide." *New York Times,* November 20.

———. 1999. "Blacks sue, saying hotel discriminated." *New York Times,* May 21.

———. 2000. "New policy on census says those listed as white and minority will be counted as minority." *New York Times,* March 11.

Holtzworth-Munroe, A., & Jacobson, N. S. 1985. "Causal attributions of married couples: When do they search for causes? What do they conclude when they do?" *Journal of Personality and Social Psychology, 48,* 1398–1412.

Honebrink, A. 1993. "Migrants create a new world order with their feet." *Utne Reader,* May–June, pp. 46–49.

Hosenball, M. 1999. "It is not the act of a few bad apples." *Newsweek,* May 17.

Hossfeld, K. J. 1990. "'Their logic against them': Contradictions in sex, race and class in Silicon Valley."

In K. Ward (Ed.), *Women workers and global restructuring.* Ithaca, NY: ILR Press.

House, J. 1981. "Social structure and personality." In M. Rosenberg & R. H. Turner (Eds.), *Social psychology: Sociological perspectives.* New York: Basic Books.

Howard, J. A., & Hollander, J. 1997. *Gendered situations, gendered selves.* Newbury Park, CA: Sage.

Howe, N., & Strauss, W. 2000. *Millennials rising: The next great generation.* New York: Vintage.

Huber, B. 1994. "Internal memorandum." American Sociological Association, Washington, DC. February.

Huber, J., & Form, W. H. 1973. *Income and ideology.* New York: Free Press.

Human Rights Watch. 2000. "Punishment and prejudice: Racial disparities in the war on drugs." *HRW report.* www.hrw.org. Accessed June 8, 2000.

Humphreys, L. 1970. *The tearoom trade: Impersonal sex in public places.* Chicago: Aldine-Atherton.

Hunt, J. 1985. "Police accounts of normal force." *Urban Live, 12,* 315–341.

Hunter, J. D. 1991. *Culture wars: The struggle to define America.* New York: Basic Books.

Hurst, C. 1979. *The anatomy of social inequality.* St. Louis: C. V. Mosby.

Hyde, J. S. 1984. "How large are gender differences in aggression? A developmental meta-analysis." *Developmental Psychology, 20,* 722–736.

Iggers, J. 1997. "How the new market-driven journalism is turning our stories into industrial waste." *Utne Reader,* September–October.

Ignatius, A. 1988. "China's birthrate is out of control again as one-child policy fails in rural areas." *Wall Street Journal,* July 14.

"Impact of the family and medical leave law." 1997. *World Almanac.* Mahwah, NJ: World Almanac Books.

Inciardi, J. A. 1992. *The war on drugs II.* Mountain View, CA: Mayfield.

Institute of Medicine. 1999a. "To err is human: Building a safer health care system." Committee on Quality of Health Care in America. Washington, DC: National Academy Press.

————. 1999b. "The unequal burden of cancer: An assessment of NIH research and programs for ethnic minorities and the medically underserved." www2.nas.edu.whatsnew/29aa.html. January 20.

"Is there a Santa Claus?" 1897. *New York Sun,* September 21.

"Italy: Rape ruling protested." 1999. *New York Times,* February 12.

Jackall, R. 1988. *Moral mazes: The world of corporate managers.* New York: Oxford University Press.

Jackman, M. R., & Jackman, R. W. 1983. *Class awareness in the United States.* Berkeley: University of California Press.

Jackson, S. 1995. "The social context of rape: Sexual scripts and motivation." In P. Searles & R. J. Berger (Eds.), *Rape and society.* Boulder, CO: Westview Press.

Jacobs, A. 1999. "Gay couples are divided by '96 immigration laws." *New York Times,* March 23.

Jacobs, P. 1988. "Keeping the poor, poor." In J. H. Skolnick & E. Currie (Eds.), *Crisis in American institutions.* Glenview, IL: Scott, Foresman.

Jacobsen, J. P. 1994. *The economics of gender.* Cambridge, MA: Blackwell.

Jacquet, C. H., & Jones, A. M. 1991. *Yearbook of American and Canadian churches.* Nashville: Abingdon.

Janoff-Bulman, R. 1979. "Characterological versus behavioral self-blame: Inquiries into depression and rape." *Journal of Personality and Social Psychology, 37,* 1798–1809.

Janofsky, M. 1998a. "Maryland troopers stop drivers by race, suit says." *New York Times,* June 5.

————. 1998b. "Shortage of housing for poor grows in U.S." *New York Times,* April 28.

Jaynes, G. 1982. "Suit on race recalls lines drawn under slavery." *New York Times,* September 30.

Jefferson, T. 1955. *Notes on the state of Virginia.* Chapel Hill: University of North Carolina Press.

Jehl, D. 1999. "Arab honor's price: A woman's blood." *New York Times,* June 20.

Jencks, C. 1994. *The homeless.* Cambridge, MA: Harvard University Press.

Jencks, C., Bartlett, S., Corcoran, M., Crouse, J., Eaglesfield, D., Jackson, G., McClelland, K., Mueser, P., Olneck, M., Schwartz, J., Ward, S., & Williams, J. 1979. *Who gets ahead?* New York: Basic Books.

Jencks, C., & Phillips, M. 1998. *The black-white test score gap.* Washington, DC: Brookings Institute.

Jenkins, H. 1999. "Professor Jenkins goes to Washington." *Harper's Magazine,* July.

Jenkins, J. C., & Perrow, C. 1977. "Insurgency of the powerless: Farm worker movements (1946–1972)." *American Sociological Review, 42,* 249–268.

Jensen, C., & Project Censored. 1995. *The news that didn't make the news—and why.* New York: Four Walls Eight Windows.

Jetter, A. 2000. "Breast cancer in Blacks spurs hunt for answers." *New York Times,* February 22.

Johnson, D. 1996a. "No-fault divorce is under attack." *New York Times,* February 12.

———. 1996b. "Students still sweat, they just don't shower." *New York Times,* April 27.

Johnson, R. 1987. *Hard time: Understanding and reforming the prison.* Pacific Grove, CA: Brooks/Cole.

Johnston, D. 1992. "Survey shows number of rapes far higher than official figures." *New York Times,* April 24.

———. 1997. "More U.S. wealthy sidestepping I.R.S." *New York Times,* October 5.

———. 1999. "Gap between rich and poor found substantially wider." *New York Times,* September 5.

———. 2000. "I.R.S. more likely to audit the poor and not the rich." *New York Times,* April 16.

Jones, A. 1980. *Women who kill.* New York: Fawcett Columbine.

Jones, E. E., Farina, A., Hastorf, A. H., Markus, H., Miller, D. T., & Scott, R. A. 1984. *Social stigma: The psychology of marked relationships.* New York: W. H. Freeman.

Jones, E. E., & Pittman, T. S. 1982. "Toward a general theory of strategic self-presentation." In J. Suls (Ed.), *Psychological perspectives on the self* (Vol. 1). Hillsdale, NJ: Erlbaum.

Jones, J. M. 1986. "The concept of racism and its changing reality." In B. P. Bowser & R. G. Hunt (Eds.), *Impacts of racism on white Americans.* Beverly Hills, CA: Sage.

Juergensmeyer, M. 1996. "Religious nationalism: A global threat?" *Current History,* November.

Kagan, J. 1976. *Raising children in modern America: Problems and prospective solutions.* Boston: Little, Brown.

Kagay, M. R., & Elder, J. 1992. "Numbers are no problem for pollsters. Words are." *New York Times,* August 9.

Kain, E. 1990. *The myth of family decline.* Lexington, MA: Lexington Books.

Kalmijn, M. 1994. "Assortive mating by cultural and economic occupational status." *American Journal of Sociology, 100,* 422–452.

Kanter, R. M. 1975. "Women and the structure of organizations: Explorations in theory and behavior." In R. M. Kanter & M. Millman (Eds.), *Another voice.* Garden City, NY: Doubleday.

———. 1977. *Men and women of the corporation.* New York: Basic Books.

Kanter, R. M., & Stein, B. A. 1979. *Life in organizations: Workplaces as people experience them.* New York: Basic Books.

Karabel, J. 1972. "Community colleges and social stratification." *Harvard Educational Review, 42,* 521–559.

Kariya, T., & Rosenbaum, J. E. 1987. "Self-selection in Japanese junior high schools: A longitudinal study of students' educational plans." *Sociology of Education, 60,* 168–180.

Karp, D. A., & Yoels, W. C. 1976. "The college classroom: Some observations on the meanings of student participation." *Sociology and Social Research, 60,* 421–439.

Karraker, K. H., Vogel, D. A., & Lake, M. A. 1995. "Parents' gender stereotyped perceptions of newborns: The eye of the beholder revisited." *Sex Roles, 33,* 687–701.

Kart, C. S. 1990. *The realities of aging.* Boston: Allyn and Bacon.

Katz, J. 1975. "Essences as moral identities: Verifiability and responsibility in imputations of deviance and charisma." *American Journal of Sociology, 80,* 1369–1390.

Kaufman, M. 1987. *Beyond patriarchy: Essays by men on pleasure, power, and change.* Toronto: Oxford University Press.

Kearl, M. C. 1980. "Time, identity and the spiritual needs of the elderly." *Sociological Analysis, 41,* 172–180.

———. 1989. *Endings: A sociology of death and dying.* New York: Oxford University Press.

Kearl, M. C., & Gordon, C. 1992. *Social psychology.* Boston: Allyn and Bacon.

Keith, V. M., & Herring, C. 1991. "Skin tone and stratification in the Black community." *American Journal of Sociology, 97,* 760–778.

Kelley, J., & DeGraaf, N.D. 1997. "National context, parental socialization, and religious belief: Results from 15 nations." *American Sociological Review, 62,* 63–59.

Kelley, R. D. G. 1996. "Freedom riders (the sequel)." *The Nation,* February 5.

Kennedy, P. 1993. *Preparing for the 21st century.* New York: Random House.

Kerbo, H. R. 1991. *Social stratification and inequality.* New York: McGraw-Hill.

Kershner, R. 1996. "Adolescent attitudes about rape." *Adolescence, 31,* 29–33.

Kessler, S. J., & McKenna, W. 1978. *Gender: An ethnomethodological approach.* Chicago: University of Chicago Press.

Kessler-Harris, A. 1982. *Out to work: A history of wage-earning women in the United States.* New York: Oxford University Press.

Key, P. 1996. "Black expo looks back to its source." *Indianapolis Star,* July 7.

Keyfitz, N. 1989. "The growing human population." *Scientific American,* September.

Kilborn, P. T. 1993. "New jobs lack the old security in time of 'disposable workers.'" *New York Times,* March 15.

————. 1997. "Child-care solutions in a new world of welfare." *New York Times,* June 1.

————. 1998. "Largest H.M.O.'s cutting the poor and the elderly." *New York Times,* July 6.

————. 1999a. "Gimme shelter: Same song, new tune." *New York Times,* December 5.

————. 1999b. "Prosperity yields a lag in charity toward the poor." *New York Times,* December 12.

————. 1999c. "Bias worsens for minorities buying homes." *New York Times,* September 16.

Kilbourne, J. 1992. "Beauty and the beast of advertising." In P. S. Rothenberg (Ed.), *Race, class and gender in the United States.* New York: St. Martin's Press.

Kimmel, M.S. 2000. *The gendered society.* New York: Oxford University Press.

King, M. L., Jr. 1991. "Letter from Birmingham City jail." In C. Carson, D. J. Garrow, G. Gill, V. Harding, & D. Clark Hine (Eds.), *The Eyes on the Prize civil rights reader.* New York: Penguin.

King, P. A. 1999. "Science for girls only." *Newsweek,* June 21.

Kirk, S. A., & Kutchins, H. 1992. *The selling of DSM: The rhetoric of science in psychiatry.* Hawthorne, NY: Aldine de Gruyter.

Klatch, R. 1991. "Complexities of conservatism: How conservatives understand the world." In A. Wolfe (Ed.), *America at century's end.* Berkeley: University of California Press.

Klawitter, M. M. 1994. "Who gains, who loses from changing U.S. child support policies?" *Policy Sciences, 27,* 197–219.

Kleck, R. 1968. "Physical stigma and nonverbal cues emitted in face-to-face interaction." *Human Relations, 21,* 19–28.

Kleck, R., Ono, H., & Hastorf, A. 1966. "The effects of physical deviance and face-to-face interaction." *Human Relations, 19,* 425–436.

Kleck, R., & Strenta, A. 1980. "Perceptions of the impact of negatively valued physical characteristics on social interaction." *Journal of Personality and Social Psychology, 39,* 861–873.

Kluckholm, C. 2000. "Queer customs." In G. Massey (Ed.), *Readings for Sociology.* New York: Norton.

Kluegel, J. R., & Smith, E. R. 1986. *Beliefs about inequality: Americans' views of what is and what ought to be.* New York: Aldine de Gruyter.

Kobrin, F. E. 1976. "The fall in household size and the rise of the primary individual in the United States." *Demography, 31,* 127–138.

Koch, K. 1999. "Rethinking Ritalin." *CQ Researcher,* October 22.

————. 2000a. "Child poverty." *CQ Researcher,* April 7.

————. 2000b. "The digital divide." *CQ Researcher,* January 28.

Kocieniewski, D. 1999. "New Jersey's state police enlist hotel workers in war on drugs." *New York Times,* April 29.

Kohlberg, L. A. 1966. "A cognitive-developmental analysis of children's sex-role concepts and attitudes." In E. Maccoby (Ed.), *The development of sex differences.* Stanford, CA: Stanford University Press.

Kohn, H. 1994. "Service with a sneer." *New York Times Magazine,* November 6.

Kohn, M. L. 1979. "The effects of social class on parental values and practices." In D. Reiss & H. A. Hoffman (Eds.), *The American family: Dying or developing.* New York: Plenum.

Kohut, A. 1999. "Globalization and the wage gap." *New York Times,* December 3.

Kokopeli, B., & Lakey, G. 1992. "More power than we want: Masculine sexuality and violence." In M. L. Anderson & P. H. Collins (Eds.), *Race, class and gender: An anthology.* Belmont, CA: Wadsworth.

Kolata, G. 1996. "Boom in Ritalin sales raises ethical issues." *New York Times,* May 15.

————. 1997. "Accidents much more likely when drivers hold a phone." *New York Times,* February 13.

————. 2000. "Web research transforms visit to the doctor." *New York Times,* March 6.

Kolbert, E. 1996. "But don't sweat or be too short." *New York Times,* September 29.

Kollock, P., & O'Brien, J. 1993. *The production of reality.* Newbury Park, CA: Pine Forge Press.

"Korean girls take poison to aid kin." 1989. *Hartford Courant,* March 3.

Kotkin, J. 1996. "New fuel for California's engine." *Wall Street Journal,* March 25.

Kovel, J. 1980. "The American mental health industry." In D. Ingleby (Ed.), *Critical psychiatry.* New York: Pantheon.

Kramer, P. 1997. *Listening to Prozac.* New York: Penguin.

Kristof, N. D. 1991. "Stark data on women: 100 million are missing." *New York Times,* November 5.

———. 1993a. "China's crackdown on births: A stunning and harsh success." *New York Times,* April 25.

———. 1993b. "Peasants of China discover new way to weed out girls." *New York Times,* July 21.

———. 1995. "Japanese outcasts better off than in past but still outcasts." *New York Times,* November 30.

———. 1996. "Aging world, new wrinkles." *New York Times,* September 22.

Kunkel, D. 1998. "Policy battles over defining children's educational television." *The Annals of the American Academy of Political and Social Science, 557,* 3–4.

Kurtz, L. R. 1995. *Gods in the global village.* Thousand Oaks, CA: Pine Forge Press.

Kurz, D. 1998. "Old problems and new directions in the study of violence against women." In R. K. Bergen (Ed.), *Issues in intimate violence.* Thousand Oaks, CA: Sage.

Kushner, D. 2000. "Untangling the Web's languages." *New York Times,* April 20.

Labalme, J. 1995. "Parents opposed removal of life support." *Indianapolis Star,* December 1.

Labaton, S. 1996. "The packaging of a perpetrator." *New York Times,* September 15.

Labaton, S., & Bergman, L. 2000. "Documents indicate Ford knew of defect but failed to report it." *New York Times,* September 12.

Lakoff, R. 1975. *Language and woman's place.* New York: Harper & Row.

Lamont, M. 1992. *Money, morals & manners: The culture of the French and American upper-middle class.* Chicago: University of Chicago Press.

Lander, L. 1988. *Images of bleeding: Menstruation as ideology.* New York: Orlando.

Landler, M. 1996. "Corporate insurer to cover cost of spin doctors." *New York Times,* September 10.

Langman, L. 1988. "Social stratifcation." In M. B. Sussman & S. K. Steinmetz (Eds.), *Handbook of marriage and the family.* New York: Plenum.

Langston, D. 1992. "Tired of playing monopoly?" In M. L. Anderson & P. H. Collins (Eds.), *Race, class and gender: An anthology.* Belmont, CA: Wadsworth.

Larson, L. E., & Goltz, J.W. 1989. "Religious participation and marital commitment." *Review of Religious Research 30,* 387–400.

Lasch, C. 1977. *Haven in a heartless world.* New York: Basic Books.

Lauer, R., & Handel, W. 1977. *Social psychology: The theory and application of symbolic interactionism.* Boston: Houghton Mifflin.

Lawson, C. 1992. "Who believes in make-believe? Not these new toys." *New York Times,* February 6.

———. 1993. "Stereotypes unravel, but not too quickly, in new toys for 1993." *New York Times,* February 11.

Leape, L. L., & Bates, D. W. 1995. "Systems analysis of adverse drug events." *Journal of the American Medical Association, 274,* 35–43.

Leidner, R. 1991. "Serving hamburgers and selling insurance: Gender work and identity in interactive service jobs." *Gender and Society, 5,* 154–177.

Leinberger, P., & Tucker, B. 1991. *The new individualists: The generation after the organization man.* New York: HarperCollins.

Lekachman, R. 1991. "The specter of full employment." In J. H. Skolnick & E. Currie (Eds.), *Crisis in American institutions.* New York: HarperCollins.

Leland, J. 1996. "Tightening the knot." *Newsweek,* February 19.

Lemert, E. 1972. *Human deviance, social problems, and social control.* Englewood Cliffs, NJ: Prentice Hall.

Lennon, M. C., & Rosenfield, S. 1994. "Relative fairness and the division of housework." *American Journal of Sociology, 100,* 506–531.

Leonhardt, D. 2000. "Executive pay drops off the political radar." *New York Times,* April 16.

Lerner, M. 1970. "The desire for justice and reactions to victims." In J. Macauley & L. Berkowitz (Eds.), *Altruism and helping behavior.* New York: Academic Press.

Levant, R. F., Slatter, S. C., & Loiselle, J. E. 1987. "Fathers' involvement in housework and child care with school age daughters." *Family Relations, 36,* 152–157.

Levin, J. 1993. *Sociological snapshots.* Newbury Park, CA: Pine Forge Press.

Levine, H. G. 1992. "Temperance cultures: Concern about alcohol problems in Nordic and English-speaking cultures." In G. Edwards et al. (Eds.), *The nature of alcohol and drug-related problems.* New York: Oxford University Press.

Lewin, T. 1994. "Outrage over 18 months for man who killed his wife in 'heat of passion.'" *New York Times,* October 21.

———. 1995a. "Study says more women earn half their household income." *New York Times,* May 11.

———. 1995b. "Workers of both sexes make trade-offs for family, study shows." *New York Times,* October 29.

———. 1998a. "All-girls schools questioned as a way to attain equity." *New York Times,* March 12.

———. 1998b. "How boys lost out to girl power." *New York Times,* December 13.

———. 1998c. "Study finds that youngest U.S. children are poorest." *New York Times,* March 15.

———. 1999. "Father awarded $375,000 in a parental leave case." *New York Times,* February 3.

———. 2000a. "Disabled student is suing over test-score labeling." *New York Times,* April 11.

———. 2000b. "Study finds welfare changes lead a million into child care." *New York Times,* February 4.

———. 2001. "Women's health is no longer a man's world." *New York Times,* February 6.

Lewis, M. 1978. *The culture of inequality.* New York: New American Library.

Lewis, M. M. 1948. *Language in society.* New York: Social Science Research Council.

Lewis, O. 1968. "The culture of poverty." In D. P. Moynihan (Ed.), *On understanding poverty: Perspectives from the social sciences.* New York: Basic Books.

Lewis, P. H. 1998a. "Forget big brother." *New York Times,* March 19.

———. 1998b. "Too late to say 'extinct' in Ubykh, Eyak or Ona." *New York Times,* August 15.

Liazos, A. 1985. *Sociology: A liberating perspective.* Boston: Allyn and Bacon.

Light, K., with introduction by R. Rodriguez. 1988. *To the promised land.* New York: Aperture.

Light, P. 1988. *Baby boomers.* New York: Norton.

"Limited black slots on TV." 2000. *New York Times,* February 26.

Lind, M. 1996. "Huddled excesses." *The New Republic,* April 1.

Lindesmith, A. R., Strauss, A. L., & Denzin, N. K. 1991. *Social psychology.* Englewood Cliffs, NJ: Prentice Hall.

Link, B. G., Mirotznik, J., & Cullen, F. T. 1991. "The effectiveness of stigma coping orientations: Can negative consequences of mental illness labeling be avoided?" *Journal of Health and Social Behavior, 32,* 302–320.

Linton, R. 1937. "One hundred percent American." *American Mercury, 40,* 427–429.

Lippmann, L. W. 1922. *Public opinion.* New York: Harcourt Brace Jovanovich.

Lips, H. M. 1993. *Sex and gender: An introduction.* Mountain View, CA: Mayfield.

Loe, V. 1997. "New nuptial license gets cool reception." *Indianapolis Star,* September 21.

Lofland, L. H. 1973. *A world of strangers: Order and action in urban public space.* New York: Basic Books.

Lopez, G. A. 1991. "The Gulf War: Not so clean." *Bulletin of the Atomic Scientists, 47,* 30–35.

Lorber, J. 1989. "Dismantling Noah's Ark." In B. J. Risman & P. Schwartz (Eds.), *Gender in intimate relationships: A microstructural approach.* Belmont, CA: Wadsworth.

Lott, B. 1987. *Women's lives: Themes and variations in gender learning.* Pacific Grove, CA: Brooks/Cole.

Loury, G. C. 1985. "Beyond civil rights." *New Republic,* October.

Lowney, K. S., & Best, J. 1995. "Stalking strangers and lovers: Changing media typifications of a new crime problem." In J. Best (Ed.), *Images of issues: Typifying contemporary social problems.* New York: Aldine de Gruyter.

Luker, K. 1984. *Abortion and the politics of motherhood.* Berkeley: University of California Press.

Lyall, S. 2000. "Irish now face the other side of immigration." *New York Times,* July 8.

Lytton, H., & Romney, D. M. 1991. "Parents' differential socialization of boys and girls: A meta-analysis." *Psychology Bulletin, 109,* 267–296.

MacAndrew, C., & Edgerton, R. B. 1969. *Drunken comportment: A social explanation.* Chicago: Aldine-Atherton.

MacDonald, K., & Parke, R. D. 1986. "Parent–child physical play: The effects of sex and age on children and parents." *Sex Roles, 15,* 367–378.

Mann, C. C. 1993. "How many is too many?" *Atlantic Monthly,* February.

Mannheim, K. 1952. "The problem of generations." In P. Kecskemeti (Ed. and Trans.), *Essays on the sociology of knowledge.* London: Routledge & Kegan Paul.

Mannon, J. 1997. *Measuring up.* Boulder, CO: Westview.

Mantsios, G. 1995. "Media magic: Making class invisible." In P. S. Rothenberg (Ed.), *Race, class and gender in the United States* (3rd ed.). New York: St. Martin's Press.

"Many victims of violence hurt by someone they knew." 1997. CNN Online. www.cnn.com. August 24.

Marger, M. N. 1994. *Race and ethnic relations: American and global perspectives.* Belmont, CA: Wadsworth.

Marmor, J. 1996. "Blurring the lines." *Columns,* December.

"Marriage and divorce." 1996. *CQ Researcher,* May 10.

Marriot, M. 1998. "Internet unleashing a dialogue on race." *New York Times,* March 8.

Martin, D. 1997. "Eager to bite the hands that would feed them." *New York Times,* June 1.

Martin, K. A. 1998. "Becoming a gendered body: Practices of pre-schools." *American Sociological Review, 63,* 494–511.

Martin, M. K., & Voorhies, B. 1975. *Female of the species.* New York: Columbia University Press.

Martin, T. C., & Bumpass, L. L. 1989. "Recent trends in marital disruption." *Demography, 26,* 37–51.

Marx, K. 1963. *The 18th Brumaire of Louis Bonaparte.* New York: International Publishers. (Original work published 1869)

Marx, K., & Engels, F. 1982. *The communist manifesto.* New York: International Publishers. (Original work published 1848)

Massey, D. 1990. "American apartheid: Segregation and the making of the underclass." *American Journal of Sociology, 96,* 329–357.

Massey, D., & Fischer, M. J. 1999. "Does rising income bring integration? New results for Blacks, Hispanics, and Asians in 1990." *Social Science Research, 28,* 316–326.

Mathews, L. 1996. "More than identity rides on a new racial category." *New York Times,* July 6.

Matthews, J. 1989. "Rescue plan for Africa." *World Monitor,* May, pp. 28–36.

Mauro, J. 1994. "And Prozac for all . . . " *Psychology Today, 27,* 44–52.

"MBA vs. prison." 1999. *American Prospect,* May–June.

McAdam, D. 1982. *Political process and the development of black insurgency, 1930–1970.* Chicago: University of Chicago Press.

McAdam, D., McCarthy, J. D., & Zald, M. N. 1988. "Social movements." In N. J. Smelser (Ed.), *Handbook of sociology.* Newbury Park, CA: Sage.

McCain, F. 1991. "Interview with Franklin McCain." In C. Carson, D. J. Garrow, G. Gill, V. Harding, & D. Clark Hine (Eds.), *The Eyes on the Prize civil rights reader.* New York: Penguin.

McCall, G. J., & Simmons, J. L. 1978. *Identities and interactions.* New York: Free Press.

McCarthy, J. D., & Wolfson, M. 1992. "Consensus movements, conflict movements, and the cooptation of civic and state infrastructures." In A. D. Morris & C. M. Mueller (Eds.), *Frontiers in social movement theory.* New Haven, CT: Yale University Press.

McCarthy, J. D., & Zald, M. N. 1977. "Resource mobilization and social movements: A partial theory." *American Journal of Sociology, 82,* 1212–1241.

McCarthy, T. 2001. "He makes a village." *Time,* May 14.

McClelland, K. E., & Auster, C. J. 1990. "Public platitudes and hidden tensions: Racial climates at predominantly white liberal arts colleges." *Journal of Higher Education, 61,* 607–642.

McClendon, M. J. 1985. "Racism, rational choice and white opposition to racial change: A case study of busing." *Public Opinion Quarterly, 49,* 214–233.

McCormick, J. S., Maric, A., Seto, M. C., & Barbaree, H. E. 1998. "Relationship to victim predicts sentence length in sexual assault cases." *Journal of Interpersonal Violence, 13,* 41–20.

McCrate, E., & Smith, J. 1998. "When work doesn't work: The failure of current welfare reform." *Gender and Society, 12,* 61–80.

McDonald's Corporation. 2001. "McDonald's announces supplementary financial data." Press release. www.mcdonalds.com/corporate/press/financial/2001/02132001/index.html. Accessed March 8, 2001.

McGinn, A. P. 1997. "The nicotine cartel." *World Watch,* July–August.

McGinnis, J. 1997. "Attention deficit disorder." *Wall Street Journal,* September 18.

McKenry, P. C., & Price, S. J. 1995. "Divorce: A comparative perspective." In B. B. Ingoldsby & S. Smith (Eds.), *Families in multicultural perspective.* New York: Guilford Press.

McLoyd, V. C., Cauce, A. M., Takeuchi, D., & Wilson, L. 2000. "Marital processes and parental socialization in families of color: A decade review of research." *Journal of Marriage and the Family, 62,* 107–094.

McMichael, P. 1996. *Development and social change: A global perspective.* Thousand Oaks, CA: Pine Forge Press.

McNeil, D. G. 2000a. "Drug companies and the third world: A case study of neglect." *New York Times,* May 21.

———. 2000b. "Writing the bill for global AIDS." *New York Times,* July 2.

McPhee, J. 1971. *Encounters with the archdruid.* New York: Noonday.

Mead, G. H. 1934. *Mind, self and society.* Chicago: University of Chicago Press.

Meckler, L. 1999. "Millions living close to the edge of a financial precipice." *Indianapolis Star,* July 9.

Mehan, H., & Wood, H. 1975. *The reality of ethnomethodology.* New York: Wiley.

Menand, L. 1996. "How to make a Ph.D. matter." *New York Times Magazine,* September 22.

Merton, R. 1948. "The self-fulfilling prophecy." *Antioch Review, 8,* 193–210.

———. 1957. *Social theory and social structure.* New York: Free Press.

Messick, D. M., & Brewer, M. B. 1983. "Solving social dilemmas: A review." In L. Wheeler & P. Shaver (Eds.), *Review of personality and social psychology.* Beverly Hills, CA: Sage.

Messner, M. 1990. "Boyhood, organized sports, and the construction of masculinities." *Journal of Contemporary Ethnography, 18,* 41–44.

Meyer, J. W., & Rowan, B. 1977. "Institutionalized organizations: Formal structure as myth and ceremony." *American Journal of Sociology, 83,* 340–363.

Miall, C. E. 1989. "The stigma of involuntary childlessness." In A. S. Skolnick & J. H. Skolnick (Eds.), *Family in transition.* Boston: Little, Brown.

Michaels, K. 1993. "Eight years in Kafkaland." *National Review, 45,* 36–38.

Michener, H. A., DeLamater, J. D., & Schwartz, S. H. 1986. *Social psychology.* San Diego: Harcourt Brace Jovanovich.

Mies, M. 1982. *The lace makers of Narsapur.* London: Zed Press.

Miles, J. 1992. "Blacks vs. browns." *Atlantic Monthly,* October.

Milgram, S. 1974. *Obedience to authority.* New York: Harper & Row.

Milkie, M. A. 1999. "Social comparisons, reflected appraisals, and mass media: The impact of pervasive beauty images on black and white girls' self-concepts." *Social Psychology Quarterly, 62,* 19–10.

Miller, A. G., Collins, B. E., & Brief, D. E. 1995. "Perspectives on obedience to authority: The legacy of the Milgram experiments." *Journal of Social Issues, 51,* 1–19.

Miller, C. L. 1987. "Qualitative differences among gender-stereotyped toys: Implications for cognitive and social development." *Sex Roles, 16,* 473–488.

Miller, J. 1984. "Culture and the development of everyday explanation." *Journal of Personality and Social Psychology, 46,* 961–978.

Miller, L. 1997. "Not just weapons of the weak: Gender harassment as a form of protest for army men." *Social Psychology Quarterly, 60,* 32–51.

Miller, M. C. 1996. "Free the media." *The Nation,* June 3.

Miller, M. V. 1985. "Poverty and its definition." In R. C. Barnes & E. W. Mills (Eds.), *Techniques for teaching sociological concepts.* Washington, DC: American Sociological Association.

Miller, S. M., & Ferroggiaro, K. M. 1995. "Class dismissed?" *The American Prospect, 21,* 10–04.

Miller, T. M., Coffman, J. G., & Linke, R. A. 1980. "Survey on body-image, weight and diet of college students." *Journal of the American Dietetic Association, 77,* 561–566.

Millman, M. 1980. *Such a pretty face.* New York: Norton.

Mills, C. W. 1940. "Situated actions and vocabularies of motive." *American Sociological Review, 5,* 904–913.

———. 1956. *The power elite.* New York: Oxford University Press.

———. 1959. *The sociological imagination.* New York: Oxford University Press.

Mills, J. L. 1985. "Body language speaks louder than words." *Horizons,* February.

Mishel, L., Bernstein, J., & Schmitt, J. 1997. *The state of working America 1996–1997.* Armonk, NY: Sharpe.

Moberg, D. 2000. "New concepts of class." *The Progressive, 64,* 4–3.

Moffatt, M. 1989. *Coming of age in New Jersey.* New Brunswick, NJ: Rutgers University Press.

Mogelonsky, M. 1998a. "Teens' working dreams." *American Demographics, 20,* p. 14.

———. 1998b. "Watching in tongues." *American Demographics,* April.

Mokhiber, R. 1999. "Crime wave! The top 100 corporate criminals of the 1990s." *Multinational Monitor,* July–August, 1–9.

———. 2000. "White collar crime spree." *Multinational Monitor,* July–August, p. 38.

Molloy, B. L., & Herzberger, S. D. 1998. "Body image and self-esteem: A comparison of African-American and Caucasian women." *Sex Roles, 38,* 631–643.

Molotch, H., & Lester, M. 1974. "News as purposive behavior: On the strategic use of routine events, accidents, and scandals." *American Sociological Review, 39,* 101–112.

———. 1975. "Accidental news: The great oil spill as local occurrence and national event." *American Journal of Sociology, 81,* 235–260.

"Mom's market value." 1998. *Utne Reader,* March–April.

Moore, R. B. 1992. "Racist stereotyping in the English language." In M. L. Anderson & P. H. Collins (Eds.), *Race, class and gender: An anthology.* Belmont, CA: Wadsworth.

Morgan, G. 1986. *Images of organizations.* Newbury Park, CA: Sage.

Morgan, M. 1982. "Television and adolescents' sex role stereotypes: A longitudinal study." *Journal of Personality and Social Psychology, 48,* 1173–1190.

———. 1987. "Television sex role attitudes and sex role behavior." *Journal of Early Adolescence, 7,* 269–282.

Morse, M. 1998. "Get down and dirty." *Utne Reader,* January–February.

Moss, R. F. 2001. "The shrinking life span of the black sitcom." *New York Times,* February 25.

Mottl, T. L. 1980. "The analysis of countermovements." *Social Problems, 27,* 620–635.

Mowlana, H., Gerbner, G., & Schiller, H. I. 1992. *Triumph of the image: The media's war in the Persian Gulf—A global perspective.* Boulder, CO: Westview.

Murdock, G. P. 1949. *Social structure.* New York: Macmillan.

———. 1957. "World ethnography sample." *American Anthropologist, 59,* 664–687.

Murray, C. 1994. "What to do about welfare." *Commentary,* December, pp. 26–34.

Murty, K. S., Roebuck, J. B., & Armstrong, G. R. 1994. "The black community's reaction to the 1992 Los Angeles riot." *Deviant Behavior, 15,* 85–104.

Mydans, S. 1995. "A shooter as vigilante, and avenging angel." *New York Times,* February 12.

Nanda, S. 1990. *Neither man nor woman: The Hijras of India.* Belmont, CA: Wadsworth.

———. 1994. *Cultural anthropology.* Belmont, CA: Wadsworth.

Nasar, S., & Mitchell, K. B. 1999. "Booming job market draws young black men into the fold." *New York Times,* May 23.

National Alliance to End Homelessness. 2000. "Facts about homelessness." www. naeh.org/back/factsus.htm. Accessed June 22, 2001.

National Center for Education Statistics. 1989. *1989 education indicators.* Washington, DC: U.S. Government Printing Office.

———. 1999. *The digest of education statistics.* Washington, DC: U.S. Government Printing Office.

———. 2000. "Education indicators: An international perspective." http://nces.ed.gov/pubs/eiip/eiipid24.html. Accessed December 28, 2000.

National Committee on Pay Equity. 1995. "The wage gap: Myths and facts." In P. S. Rothenberg (Ed.), *Race, class and gender in the United States.* New York: St. Martin's Press.

———. 1999. "The wage gap: 1998." www.feminist.com/fairpay. Accessed July 1, 2000.

National Low Income Housing Coalition. 1999. "Out of reach: The gap between housing costs and income of poor people in the United States." www.nlihc.org/OOR99/index.htm. Accessed June 20, 2000.

Navarro, M. 2001. "Women in sports cultivating new playing fields." *New York Times,* February 13.

Navarro, V. 1992. "The middle class—A useful myth." *The Nation,* March 23.

Nelkin, D., & Pollack, M. 1981. *The atom besieged.* Cambridge, MA: MIT Press.

Neubeck, K. 1986. *Social problems: A critical approach.* New York: Random House.

Newman, C. 2000. "The enigma of beauty." *National Geographic,* January.

Nichols, J. 2000. "Now what? Seattle is just a start." *The Progressive,* January.

Nickler, P. A. 1999. "A tragedy of the commons in coastal fisheries: Contending prescriptions for conservation, and the case of the Atlantic bluefin tuna." *Boston College Environmental Affairs Law Review, 26,* 54–77.

Niebuhr, G. 1996. "Public supports political voice for churches." *New York Times,* June 25.

———. 1998a. "As the old-line Anglican churches wilt, those in Africa flower profusely." *New York Times,* August 2.

———. 1998b. "Makeup of American religion is looking more like a mosaic, data say." *New York Times,* April 12.

Nieves, E. 2000. "Homeless on $50,000 a year in luxuriant Silicon Valley." *New York Times,* February 20.

Njeri, I. 1990. *Every good-bye ain't gone.* New York: Random House.

Noble, H. B. 1995. "Attacks against Asian-Americans are rising." *New York Times,* December 13.

———. 1998. "Struggling to bolster minorities in medicine." *New York Times,* September 29.

Nossiter, A. 1997. "Judge rules against Alabama's prison 'hitching posts.'" *New York Times,* January 31.

Oakes, J. 1985. *Keeping track: How high schools structure inequality.* New Haven, CT: Yale University Press.

OECD (Organization for Economic Co-operation and Development). 1988. *Aging populations: The social policy implications.* Washington, DC: Author.

Oldham, C. 2000. "Women have more top jobs in Fortune 500 than in '95." *Dallas Morning News,* November 13.

Olsen, M. 1965. *The logic of collective action.* Cambridge, MA: Harvard University Press.

Olson, E. 1998. "U.N. surveys paid leave for mothers." *New York Times,* February 16.

Omi, M., & Winant, H. 1992. "Racial formations." In P. S. Rothenberg (Ed.), *Race, class and gender in the United States.* New York: St. Martin's Press.

Onishi, N. 2001. "On the scale of beauty, weight weighs heavily." *New York Times,* February 12.

Orfield, G., & Yun, J. T. 1999. "Resegregation in American schools." *Harvard Civil Rights Project Report.* Cambridge, MA.

O'Sullivan See, K., & Wilson, W. J. 1988. "Race and ethnicity." In N. Smelser (Ed.), *Handbook of sociology*. Newbury Park, CA: Sage.

Owen, M. 1996. *A world of widows*. London: Zed Books.

Owens, B. 1973. *Suburbia*. San Francisco: Straight Arrow Press.

Papadakis, M. C. 2000. "Complex picture of computer use in the home emerges." *National Science Foundation Issue Brief*. www.nsf.gov/sbe/srs/issuebrf/sib00314.pdf. Accessed June 22, 2001.

Parenti, M. 1986. *Inventing reality*. New York: St. Martin's Press.

———. 1995. *Democracy for the few*. New York: St. Martin's Press.

———.1996. "The make-believe media." In M. J. Carter (Ed.), *Society and the media*. New York: HarperCollins.

Parker, S., Nichter, M., Nichter, M., Vuckovic, N., Sims, C., & Ritenbaugh, C. 1995. "Body image and weight concerns among African American and white adolescent females: Differences that make a difference." *Human Organization, 54*, 103–114.

Parlee, M. B. 1989. "Conversational politics." In L. Richardson & V. Taylor (Eds.), *Feminist frontiers II*. New York: Random House.

Parsons, T. 1951. *The social system*. New York: Free Press.

———. 1971. "Kinship and the associational aspect of social structure." In F. L. K. Hsu (Ed.), *Kinship and culture*. Chicago: Aldine-Atherton.

Parsons, T., & Bales, R. F. 1955. *Family, socialization and interaction process*. Glencoe, IL: Free Press.

Parsons, T., & Smelser, N. 1956. *Economy and society*. New York: Free Press.

Payer, L. 1988. *Medicine and culture*. New York: Penguin.

Pear, R. 1992. "New look at U.S. in 2050: Bigger, older and less white." *New York Times*, December 4.

———. 1993. "Wide health gap, linked to income, is reported in the U.S." *New York Times*, July 8.

———. 1997. "Academy's report says immigration benefits the U.S." *New York Times*, May 18.

———. 1998. "Black and Hispanic poverty falls, reducing overall rate for nation." *New York Times*, September 25.

———. 1999a. "Mental disorders common, U.S. says; many not treated." *New York Times*, December 13.

———. 1999b. "More Americans were uninsured in 1998, U.S. says." *New York Times*, October 4.

———. 2000a. "Changes in welfare bring improvements for families." *New York Times*, June 1.

———. 2000b. "A million parents lost Medicaid, study says." *New York Times*, June 20.

———. 2000c. "Studies find research on women lacking." *New York Times*, April 30.

Pearce, L. D., & Axinn, W. G. 1998. "The impact of family religious life on the quality of mother–child relations." *American Sociological Review, 63*, 81–28.

Perin, C. 1988. *Belonging in America*. Madison: University of Wisconsin Press.

Perlez, J. 1991. "Madagascar, where the dead return, bringing joy." *New York Times*, August 31.

———. 1998. "A wall not yet built casts the shadow of racism." *New York Times*, July 2.

Perlman, D., & Fehr, B. 1987. "The development of intimate relationships." In D. Perlman & S. Duck (Eds.), *Intimate relationships: Development, dynamics and deterioration*. Newbury Park, CA: Sage.

Perrow, C. 1986. *Complex organizations: A critical essay*. New York: Random House.

Pescosolido, B. A. 1986. "Migration, medical care and the lay referral system: A network theory of role assimilation." *American Sociological Review, 51*, 523–540.

Pescosolido, B. A., & Georgianna, S. 1989. "Durkheim, suicide, and religion: Toward a network theory of suicide." *American Sociological Review, 54*, 33–48.

Pescosolido, B. A., Grauerholz, E., & Milkie, M. A. 1997. "Culture and conflict: The portrayal of Blacks in U.S. children's picture books through the mid- and late-twentieth century." *American Sociological Review, 62*, 443–464.

Peters, T. J., & Waterman, R. H. 1982. *In search of excellence*. New York: Harper & Row.

Petersilia, J. 1985. *Probation and felony offenders*. Washington, DC: U.S. Department of Justice.

Peterson, J., & Kim, P. 1991. *The day America told the truth*. Englewood Cliffs, NJ: Prentice Hall.

Peterson, P. 1991. "The urban underclass and the poverty paradox." In C. Jencks & P. Peterson (Eds.), *The urban underclass*. Washington, DC: Brookings Institution.

Peterson, P. G. 1996. "Will America grow up before it grows old?" *Atlantic Monthly*, May.

Peterson, R. D., & Bailey, W. C. 1991. "Felony murder and capital punishment: An examination of the deterrence question." *Criminology, 29*, 367–395.

Peterson, R. R. 1996. "A re-evaluation of the economic consequences of divorce." *American Sociological Review, 61*, 528–536.

Peterson, S. B., & Lach, M. A. 1990. "Gender stereotypes in children's books: Their prevalence and influence in cognitive and affective development." *Gender and Education, 2,* 185–197.

Petrunik, M., & Shearing, C. D. 1983. "Fragile facades: Stuttering and the strategic manipulation of awareness." *Social Problems, 31,* 125–138.

Pettigrew, T. F., & Martin, J. 1987. "Shaping the organizational context for black American inclusion." *Journal of Social Issues, 43,* 41–78.

Pfohl, S. J. 1994. *Images of deviance and social control.* New York: McGraw-Hill.

Phelan, J., Link, B. G., Moore, R. E., & Stueve, A. 1997. "The stigma of homelessness: The impact of the label 'homeless' on attitudes toward poor persons." *Social Psychology Quarterly, 60,* 323–337.

Philipson, I. J. 1993. *On the shoulders of women: The feminization of psychotherapy.* New York: Guilford Press.

Phillips, P., & Project Censored. 1997. *The news that didn't make the news—and why.* New York: Seven Stories Press.

———. 2000. *Censored 2000: The year's top 25 censored stories.* New York: Seven Stories Press.

"Physical traits affect earning power, study says." 1994. *New York Times,* July 13.

Pierre-Pierre, G. 1998. "The white wife." *Essence,* July.

Piper, A. 1992. "Passing for white, passing for black." *Transition, 58,* 4–32.

Piven, F. F., & Cloward, R. A. 1977. *Poor people's movements: Why they succeed, how they fail.* New York: Vintage.

"Pizza must go through: It's the law in San Francisco, The." 1996. *New York Times,* July 14.

Pollitt, K. 1991. "Fetal rights: A new assault on feminism." In J. H. Skolnick & E. Currie (Eds.), *Crisis in American institutions.* New York: HarperCollins.

Popenoe, D. 1993. "American family decline, 1960–1990: A review and appraisal." *Journal of Marriage and the Family, 55,* 527–555.

Pratkanis, A., & Aronson, E. 1991. *Age of propaganda.* New York: Freeman.

Preston, S. H. 1984. "Children and the elderly in the U.S." *Scientific American,* December, pp. 44–49.

Price, S. L. 1997. "Whatever happened to the white athlete?" *Sports Illustrated,* December 8.

Pugliesi, K. 1987. "Deviation in emotion and the labeling of mental illness." *Deviant Behavior, 8,* 79–102.

Purdum, T. S. 1997. "Registry laws tar sex-crime convicts with broad brush." *New York Times,* July 1.

———. 2000. "Shift in the mix alters face of California." *New York Times,* July 4.

Purdy, M. 1997. "Wave of new laws seeks to confine sexual offenders." *New York Times,* June 29.

Putnam, R. D. 1995. "Bowling alone: America's declining social capital." *Journal of Democracy, 6,* 65–78.

Quinney, R. 1970. *The social reality of crime.* Boston: Little, Brown.

Rasekh, Z., Bauer, H. M., Manos, M. M., & Iacopino, V. 1998. "Women's health and human rights in Afghanistan." *Journal of the American Medical Association, 280,* 449–455.

Raymond, J. 1998. "Say what? Preserving endangered languages." *Newsweek,* September 14.

Raymond, J. G. 1993. *Women as wombs.* New York: HarperCollins.

Reich, R. 1998. "The care and feeding of the rich." *New York Times,* April 5.

Reiman, J. 1998. *The rich get richer and the poor get prison.* New York: Macmillan.

Reinarman, C. 1994. "The social construction of drug scares." In P. A. Adler & P. Adler (Eds.), *Constructions of deviance.* Belmont, CA: Wadsworth.

Reinarman, C., & Levine, H. G. 1997. "Crack in context: America's latest drug demon." In C. Reinarman & H. G. Levine (Eds.), *Crack in America.* Berkeley: University of California Press.

Reinharz, S. 1992. *Feminist methods in social research.* New York: Oxford University Press.

Rennison, C. M., & Welchans, S. 2000. "Intimate partner violence." *United States Bureau of Justice Statistics Special Report.* Washington, DC: U.S. Government Printing Office.

Renzetti, C. M., & Curran, D. J. 1989. *Women, men and society: The sociology of gender.* Boston: Allyn and Bacon.

Reskin, B., & Hartmann, H. 1986. *Women's work, men's work: Sex segregation on the job.* Washington, DC: National Academy Press.

Reskin, B., & Padavic, I. 1994. *Women, men and work.* Newbury Park, CA: Pine Forge Press.

Revkin, A. C. 1997. "Who cares about a few degrees?" *New York Times,* December 1.

Reyes, L., & Rubie, P. 1994. *Hispanics in Hollywood: An encyclopedia of film and television.* New York: Garland Press.

Rheingold, H. 1994. *The virtual community.* New York: Harper Perennial.

Richardson, L. 1997. "An old experiment's legacy: Distrust of AIDS treatment." *New York Times,* April 21.

Riesman, D. 1950. *The lonely crowd.* New Haven, CT: Yale University Press.

Rifkin, J. 1995. *The end of work.* New York: Putnam.

Riley, M. W. 1971. "Social gerontology and the age stratification of society." *The Gerontologist, 11,* 79–87.

Riley, M. W., Foner, A., & Waring, J. 1988. "Sociology of age." In N. J. Smelser (Ed.), *Handbook of sociology.* Newbury Park, CA: Sage.

Riley, M. W., Johnson, M., & Foner, A. 1972. *Aging and society III: A sociology of age stratification.* New York: Russell Sage Foundation.

Rimer, S. 1998. "Tradition of care thrives in black families." *New York Times,* March 15.

Ritzer, G. 2000. *The McDonaldization of society.* Newbury Park, CA: Pine Forge Press.

Roberts, A. R. 1996. "Battered women who kill: A comparative study of incarcerated participants with a community sample of battered women." *Journal of Family Violence, 11,* 291–304.

Roberts, D. E. 1991. "Punishing drug addicts who have babies: Women of color, equality and the right of privacy." *Harvard Law Review, 104,* 1419–1482.

Roberts, S. 1995. "Alone in the vast wasteland." *New York Times,* December 24.

———. 1997. "Another kind of middle-class squeeze." *New York Times,* May 18.

Robinson, R. V., & Bell, W. 1978. "Equality, success and social justice in England and the United States." *American Sociological Review, 43,* 125–143.

Robinson, R. V., & Kelley, J. 1979. "Class as conceived by Marx and Dahrendorf: Effects on income inequality and politics in the United States and Great Britain." *American Sociological Review, 44,* 38–58.

Rodin, J. 1985. "The application of social psychology." In G. Lindzay & E. Aronson (Eds.), *The handbook of social psychology.* New York: Random House.

Roehling, M. V. 1999. "Weight-based discrimination in employment: Psychological and legal aspects." *Personnel Psychology, 52,* 969–1017.

Roethlisberger, F. J., & Dickson, W. J. 1939. *Management and the worker.* Cambridge, MA: Harvard University Press.

Roiphe, K. 1993. *The morning after: Sex, fear and feminism on campus.* Boston: Little, Brown.

Roland, A. 1988. *In search of self in India and Japan.* Princeton, NJ: Princeton University Press.

Romero, S. 1999. "Cashing in on security woes." *New York Times,* July 24.

Rosen, J. 1997. "Abraham's drifting children." *New York Times Book Review,* March 30.

Rosenblatt, P. C., Karis, T. A., & Powell, R. D. 1995. *Multiracial couples.* Thousand Oaks, CA: Sage.

Rosenthal, E. 1998. "For one-child policy, China rethinks iron hand." *New York Times,* November 1.

———. 2000. "Rural flouting of one-child policy undercuts China's census." *New York Times,* April 14.

Rosenthal, E., & Altman, L. 1998. "China, a land of heavy smokers, looks into abyss of fatal illness." *New York Times,* November 20.

Rosenthal, R., & Jacobson, L. 1968. *Pygmalion in the classroom.* New York: Holt, Rinehart & Winston.

Ross, C. E., Mirowsky, J., & Goldstein, K. 1990. "The impact of family on health: The decade in review." *Journal of Marriage and the Family, 52,* 1059–1078.

Rossi, A. 1968. "Transition to parenthood." *Journal of Marriage and the Family, 30,* 26–39.

Rossi, P., Waite, E., Bose, C. E., & Berk, R. E. 1974. "The seriousness of crimes: Normative structure and individual differences." *American Sociological Review, 39,* 224–237.

Rothenberg, P. S. (Ed.). 1992. *Race, class and gender in the United States.* New York: St. Martin's Press.

Rothman, B. K. 1987. "Reproduction." In B. B. Hess & M. M. Ferree (Eds.), *Analyzing gender: A handbook of social science research.* Newbury Park, CA: Sage.

Rothman, B. K., & Caschetta, M. B. 1999. "Treating health: Women and medicine." In S. J. Ferguson (Ed.), *Mapping the social landscape: Readings in sociology.* Mountain View, CA: Mayfield.

Rothman, D. J. 1994. "Shiny happy people." *New Republic,* February 14.

Rothman, D. J., & Edgar, H. 1992. "Scientific rigor and medical realities: Placebo trials in cancer and AIDS research." In E. Fee & D. M. Fox (Eds.), *AIDS: The making of a chronic disease.* Berkeley: University of California Press.

Rothschild, M. 2000. "Soothsayers of Seattle." *The Progressive,* January.

Rottenberg, D. 1997. "100 most generous Americans." *American Benefactor,* Fall.

Rowland, R. 1990. "Technology and motherhood: Reproductive choice reconsidered." In C. Carlson (Ed.), *Perspectives on the family: History, class and feminism.* Belmont, CA: Wadsworth.

Rubin, J. Z., Provenzano, F. J., & Luria, Z. 1974. "The eye of the beholder: Parents' views on sex of newborns." *American Journal of Orthopsychiatry, 44,* 512–519.

Rubin, L. 1976. *Worlds of pain.* New York: Basic Books.

———. 1994. *Families on the fault line.* New York: HarperCollins.

Rubinstein, S., & Caballero, B. 2000. "Is Miss America an undernourished role model?" *Journal of the American Medical Association, 283,* 1569.

Ruether, R. 1980. "Politics and the family: Recapturing a lost issue." *Christianity and Crisis, 40,* 261–267.

Rusbult, C. E., Zembrodt, I. M., & Iwaniszek, J. 1986. "The impact of gender and sex-role orientation on responses to dissatisfaction in close relationships." *Sex Roles, 15,* 1–20.

Russell, D. E. H. 1998. "Wife rape and the law." In M. E. Odem & J. Clay-Warner (Eds.), *Confronting rape and sexual assault,* Wilmington, DE: SR Books.

Russell Sage Foundation. 2000. "Multi-city study of urban inequality." www.russellsage.org/special_ interest/point_5_residential.htm. Accessed May 31, 2000.

Ryan, W. 1976. *Blaming the victim.* New York: Vintage.

Rybczynski, W. 1999. "One good turn." *New York Times Magazine,* April 18.

Sachs, S. 2001. "A hue, and a cry in the heartland." *New York Times,* April 8.

Sack, K. 1997. "Blacks strip slaveholders' names off schools." *New York Times,* November 12.

Sack, K., & Elder, J. 2000. "Poll finds optimistic outlook but enduring racial division." *New York Times,* July 11.

Sadker, M., & Sadker, D. 1999. "Failing at fairness: Hidden lessons." In S. Ferguson (Ed.), *Mapping the social landscape.* Mountain View, CA: Mayfield.

Safire, W. 1995. "News about Jews." *New York Times,* July 17.

Sapir, E. 1929. "The status of linguistics as a science." *Language, 5,* 207–214.

———. 1949. *Selected writings* (D. G. Mandelbaum, Ed.). Berkeley: University of California Press.

Saul, L. 1972. "Personal and social psychopathology and the primary prevention of violence." *American Journal of Psychiatry, 128,* 1578–1581.

Saunders, J. M. 1991. "Relating social structural abstractions to sociological research." *Teaching Sociology, 19,* 270–271.

Schacter, S. 1951. "Deviation, rejection, and communication." *Journal of Abnormal and Social Psychology, 46,* 190–207.

Schemo, D. J. 2001. "Head of U. of California seeks to end SAT use in admissions." *New York Times,* February 17.

Schlesinger, A. 1992. *The disuniting of America.* New York: Norton.

Schmitt, E. 1996. "Provisions on legal immigrants jeopardize bill on illegal aliens." *New York Times,* May 28.

———. 2001a. "Americans (a) love (b) hate immigrants." *New York Times,* January 14.

———. 2001b. "For 7 million people in census, one race category is not enough." *New York Times,* March 13.

Schodolski, V. J. 1993. "Funeral industry, pitching videos, 2-for-1 specials to baby boomers." *Indianapolis Star,* December 26.

Schooler, C. 1996. "Cultural and social structural explanations of cross-national psychological differences." *Annual Review of Sociology, 22,* 323–349.

Schor, J. B. 1991. "Global equity and environmental crisis: An argument for reducing working hours in the north." *World Development, 19,* 73–84.

Schuman, H., & Krysan, M. 1999. "A historical note on whites' beliefs about racial inequality." *American Sociological Review, 64,* 84–55.

Schuman, H., Steeh, C., Bobo, L., & Krysan, M. 1997. *Racial attitudes in America: Trends and interpretations.* Cambridge, MA: Harvard University Press.

Schur, E. M. 1984. *Labeling women deviant: Gender, stigma and social control.* New York: Random House.

Schwalbe, M. 1998. *The sociologically examined life.* Mountain View, CA: Mayfield.

Schwartz, P., & Rutter, V. 1998. *The gender of sexuality.* Thousand Oaks, CA: Sage.

Schwartz, R. D., & Skolnick, J. H. 1962. "Two studies of legal stigma." *Social Problems, 10,* 133–138.

Schwarz, J. E., & Volgy, T. J. 1993. "Above the poverty line—but poor." *The Nation,* February 15.

Scott, J. 2000. "Florida face-off." *New York Times,* December 3.

Scott, M., & Lyman, S. 1968. "Accounts." *American Sociological Review, 33,* 46–62.

Scull, A., & Favreau, D. 1986. "A chance to cut is a chance to cure: Sexual surgery for psychosis in three nineteenth century societies." In S. Spitzer & A. T. Scull (Eds.), *Research in law, deviance and social control* (Vol. 8). Greenwich, CT: JAI Press.

Segall, A. 1987. "Sociocultural variation in sick role behavioral expectations." In H. D. Schwartz (Ed.), *Dominant issues in medical sociology.* New York: Random House.

Senate Judiciary Committee. 1993. "The response to rape: Detours on the road to equal justice." www. inform.umd.edu/EdRes/Topic/WomensStudies/ GenderIssues/Violence+Women/ResponsetoRape/ full-text. Accessed January 18, 2001.

Sengupta, S. 2000. "Full employment opens the door." *New York Times,* June 18.

Sennett, R. 1984. *Families against the city: Middle-class homes in industrial Chicago.* Cambridge, MA: Harvard University Press.

Sennett, R., & Cobb, J. 1972. *Hidden injuries of class.* New York: Vintage.

Sentencing Project, The. 2000. "Crack cocaine sentencing policy: Unjustified and unreasonable." *Sentencing Project briefing sheet.* www.sentencingproject.org/brief/1003.htm. Accessed June 26, 2000.

"Sex offender's case denied in court." 2001. Associated Press Online. January 16.

Sexton, J. 1997. "For some, work may not mean self-sufficiency." *New York Times,* April 21.

Shakin, M., Shakin, D., & Sternglanz, S. H. 1985. "Infant clothing: Sex labeling for strangers." *Sex Roles, 12,* 955–964.

Shalala, D. 1996. "Welfare reform: We must all assume responsibility." *Chronicle of Higher Education,* October 4.

Sheffield, C. J. 1987. "Sexual terrorism: The social control of women." In B. B. Hess & M. M. Ferree (Eds.), *Analyzing gender: A handbook of social science research.* Newbury Park, CA: Sage.

Shelton, B. A., & John, D. 1996. "The division of household labor." *Annual Review of Sociology, 22,* 299–322.

Sherraden, M. 1988. "Rethinking social welfare: Toward assets." *Social Policy,* Winter, pp. 37–43.

Shibutani, T. 1961. *Society and personality: An interactionist approach to social psychology.* Englewood Cliffs, NJ: Prentice Hall.

Shon, S. P., & Ja, D. Y. 1992. "Asian families." In A. S. Skolnick & J. H. Skolnick (Eds.), *Family in transition.* New York: HarperCollins.

Shorto, R. 1997. "Belief by the numbers." *New York Times Magazine,* December 7.

Shotland, R. L., & Straw, M. K. 1976. "Bystander response to an assault: When a man attacks a woman." *Journal of Personality and Social Psychology, 34,* 990–999.

Shweder, R. A. 1997. "It's called poor health for a reason." *New York Times,* March 9.

Sidel, R. 1986. *Women and children last.* New York: Penguin.

———. 1990. *On her own: Growing up in the shadow of the American Dream.* New York: Penguin.

Siegel, R. B. 1996. "The rule of love: Wife beating as prerogative and privacy." *Yale Law Journal, 105,* 2116–2207.

Silverman, D. 1982. *Secondary analysis in social research: A guide to data sources and methods with examples.* Boston: Allen & Unwin.

Silverstein, K. 1999. "Millions for Viagra, pennies for the poor." *The Nation,* July 19.

Simons, M. 2001. "An awful task: Assessing 4 roles in death of thousands in Rwanda." *New York Times,* April 30.

Simpson, I. H. 1979. *From student to nurse: A longitudinal study of socialization.* Cambridge, England: Cambridge University Press.

Sims, C. 1997. "Justice in Peru: Rape victim is pressed to marry attacker." *New York Times,* March 12.

———. 2000. "Japan's employers are giving bonuses for having babies." *New York Times,* May 30.

Singleton, R., Straits, B. C., & Straits, M. M. 1993. *Approaches to social research.* New York: Oxford University Press.

"Site warns of new neighbors who are sex offenders." 2001. News Bytes News Network. June 13.

Siwek, J. 1992. "Plight of the homeless shows flaws in the system." *Washington Post Health Magazine,* July 28.

"Six billion and counting." 1999. *New York Times,* September 19, p. 5.

"6.3 brides for seven brothers." 1998. *The Economist,* December 19.

Skocpol, T. 1979. *States and social revolutions: A comparative analysis of France, Russia and China.* New York: Cambridge University Press.

Skolnick, A. S. 1981. "Married lives: Longitudinal perspectives on marriage." In D. H. Eichorn et al. (Eds.), *Present and past in middle life.* New York: Academic Press.

———. 1991. *Embattled paradise.* New York: Basic Books.

———. 1996. *The intimate environment: Exploring marriage and the family.* New York: HarperCollins.

Skolnick, A. S., & Skolnick, J. H. (Eds.). 1992. *Family in transition* (7th ed.). New York: HarperCollins.

Smallwood, A. D. 1998. *The atlas of African-American history and politics: From the slave trade to modern times.* New York: McGraw-Hill.

Smith, D. 1997. "Study looks at portrayal of women in media." *New York Times,* May 1.

Smith, D. A. 1993. "Technology and the modern world system: Some reflections." *Science, Technology and Human Values, 18,* 186–195.

Smolowe, J. 1993. "Giving the cold shoulder." *Time,* December 6.

Sniderman, P. M., & Tetlock, P. E. 1986. "Symbolic racism: Problems of motive attribution in political analysis." *Social Forces, 42,* 129–150.

Snipp, C. M. 1986. "American Indians and natural resource development." *American Journal of Economics and Sociology, 45,* 457–474.

Snow, D. A., & Machalek, R. 1982. "On the presumed fragility of unconventional beliefs." *Journal for the Scientific Study of Religion, 21,* 15–26.

Soldo, B. J., & Agree, E. M. 1988. "America's elderly." *Population Bulletin, 43,* 1–45.

Solomon, J. 1996. "Texaco's troubles." *Newsweek,* November 25.

Sontag, D. 1992. "Across the U.S., immigrants find the land of resentment." *New York Times,* December 11.

———. 1997. "For some battered women, aid is only a promise." *New York Times,* February 14.

Sorohan, E. G. 1995. "Soundbite." *Training and Development, 49,* 11–12.

South, S. J., & Lloyd, K. M. 1995. "Spousal alternatives and marital dissolution." *American Sociological Review, 60,* 21–35.

South, S. J., & Spitze, G. D. 1994. "Housework in marital and nonmarital households." *American Sociological Review, 59,* 327–347.

Sowell, T. 1977. "New light on black IQ." *New York Times Magazine,* March 27.

Specter, M. 1998a. "Population implosion worries an aging Europe." *New York Times,* July 10.

———. 1998b. "Traffickers' new cargo: Naïve Slavic women." *New York Times,* January 11.

Spretnak, C. 1982. "The Christian Right's 'holy war' against feminism." In *The politics of women's spirituality.* New York: Anchor.

Sproull, L., & Kiesler, S. 1991. *Connections: New ways of working in the networked organization.* Cambridge, MA: MIT Press.

Squires, G. D. 1980. "Runaway factories are also a civil rights issue." *In These Times,* May, pp. 14–20.

Stacey, J. 1991. "Backward toward the postmodern family." In A. Wolfe (Ed.), *America at century's end.* Berkeley: University of California Press.

Staggenborg, S. 1998. *Gender, family, and social movements.* Thousand Oaks, CA: Pine Forge Press.

Stapinski, H. 1999. "Y not love." *American Demographics, 21,* 6–8.

Staples, B. 1999. "The final showdown on interracial marriage." *New York Times,* July 6.

Staples, R. 1992. "African American families." In J. M. Henslin (Ed.), *Marriage and family in a changing society.* New York: Free Press.

Staples, R., & Mirande, A. 1980. "Racial and cultural variations among American families: A decennial review of the literature on minority families." *Journal of Marriage and the Family, 42,* 157–173.

Stark, R., & Bainbridge, W. S. 1980. "Networks of faith: Interpersonal bonds and recruitment in cults and sects." *American Journal of Sociology, 85,* 1376–1395.

Starr, P. 1982. *The social transformation of American medicine.* New York: Basic Books.

Steele, C. 1997. "A threat in the air: How stereotypes shape intellectual identity and performance." *American Psychologist, 52,* 613–629.

Steele, C., & Aronson, J. 1995. "Stereotype threat and the intellectual test performance of African Americans." *Journal of Personality and Social Psychology, 69,* 797–811.

Steele, S. 1990. *The content of our character: A new vision of race in America.* New York: HarperCollins.

Steeves, L. H. 1993. "Gender and mass communication in a global context." In P. J. Creedon (Ed.), *Women in mass communication.* Thousand Oaks, CA: Sage.

Steiner, A. 1998a. "As the world turns." *Utne Reader,* January–February.

———. 1998b. "One for the planet." *Utne Reader,* July–August.

Steinmetz, S. K., Clavan, R., & Stein, K. F. 1990. *Marriage and family realities: Historical and contemporary perspectives.* New York: Harper & Row.

Stephan, C. W., & Stephan, W. G. 1989. "After intermarriage: Ethnic identity among mixed-heritage Japanese-Americans and Hispanics." *Journal of Marriage and the Family, 51,* 507–519.

Stephens, G. 1994. "The global crime wave." *The Futurist, 28,* 22–28.

Stephens, W. N. 1963. *The family in cross-cultural perspective.* New York: University Press of America.

Sterngold, J. 1998. "Prime-time TV's growing racial divide frustrates industry's blacks." *New York Times,* December 29.

Stevens, W. K. 1998. "Warmer, wetter, sicker: Linking climate to health." *New York Times,* August 10.

Stevenson, R. W. 2000. "Fed reports family gains from economy." *New York Times,* January 19.

Stewart, A. J., Copeland, A. P., Chester, A. L., Malley, J. E., & Barenbaum, N. B. 1997. *Separating together: How divorce transforms families.* New York: Guilford Press.

Stewart, J. E. 1980. "Defendant's attractiveness as a factor in the outcome of criminal trials: An observational study." *Journal of Applied Social Psychology, 10,* 348–361.

Stinnett, N., & DeFrain, J. 1985. *Secrets of strong families.* Boston: Little, Brown.

Stockard, J., & Johnson, M. M. 1992. *Sex and gender in society.* Englewood Cliffs, NJ: Prentice Hall.

Stokes, R., & Hewitt, J. P. 1976. "Aligning actions." *American Sociological Review, 41,* 837–849.

Stolberg, S. G. 1998a. "New cancer cases decreasing in U.S. as deaths do, too." *New York Times,* March 13.

———. 1998b. "Live and let die over transplants." *New York Times,* April 5.

———. 1999. "Science looks at Littleton and shrugs." *New York Times,* May 9.

Stone, G. P. 1981. "Appearance and the self: A slightly revised version." In G. P. Stone & H. A. Farberman (Eds.), *Social psychology through symbolic interaction.* New York: Wiley.

Stout, D. 1999. "Odds worsen in hunt for low income rentals." *New York Times,* September 24.

Straus, M. A. 1977. "A sociological perspective on the prevention and treatment of wife beating." In M. Roy (Ed.), *Battered women.* New York: Van Nostrand.

———. 1991. "Physical violence in American families: Incidence, rates, causes, and trends." In D. Knudsen & J. Miller (Eds.), *Abused and battered.* Chicago: Aldine-Atherton.

———. 1993. "Physical assaults by wives: A major social problem." In R. Gelles & D. Loeske (Eds.), *Current controversies on family violence.* Newbury Park, CA: Sage.

Straus, M. A., & Gelles, R. J. 1986. "Societal change in family violence from 1975 to 1985 as revealed by two national surveys." *Journal of Marriage and the Family, 48,* 465–479.

———. 1990. "How violent are American families? Estimates from the National Family Violence Resurvey and other studies." In M. A. Straus & R. J. Gelles (Eds.), *Physical violence in American families.* New Brunswick, NJ: Transaction.

Straus, M. A., Gelles, R. J., & Steinmetz, S. K. 1980. *Behind closed doors.* New York: Bantam.

Strom, S. 1999. "In Japan, mired in recession, suicides soar." *New York Times,* July 15.

Strube, M. J., & Barbour, L. S. 1983. "The decision to leave an abusive relationship: Economic dependence and psychological commitment." *Journal of Marriage and the Family, 45,* 785–793.

Stryker, J. 1997. "The age of innocence isn't what it once was." *New York Times,* July 13.

Stryker, S. 1980. *Symbolic interactionism.* Menlo Park, CA: Benjamin/Cummings.

"Study finds increase in weapons use." 2000. *New York Times,* November 30.

Suarez, Z. 1998. "The Cuban-American family." In C. H. Mindel, R. W. Habenstein, & R. Wright (Eds.), *Ethnic families in America: Patterns and variations.* Upper Saddle River, NJ: Prentice Hall.

Sullivan, T. A., Warren, E., & Westbrook, J. L. 2000. *The fragile middle class: Americans in debt.* New Haven, CT: Yale University Press.

Sunstein, C. 1991. "Why markets don't stop discrimination." In E. F. Paul, F. D. Miller, & J. Paul (Eds.), *Reassessing civil rights.* Cambridge, MA: Blackwell.

Suro, R. 1992. "Poll finds Hispanics desire to assimilate." *New York Times,* December 15.

Sutherland, E., & Cressey, D. 1955. *Criminology.* Philadelphia: Lippincott.

Swanson, G. 1992. "Doing things together: On some basic forms of agency and structuring in collective action and on some explanations for them." *Social Psychology Quarterly, 55,* 94–117.

Swarns, R. L. 1998. "Mothers poised for workfare face acute lack of day care." *New York Times,* April 14.

———. 2001. "Drug makers drop South Africa suit over AIDS medicines." *New York Times,* April 20.

"Sweatshops 'R' us." 1996. *The Nation,* November 11.

Sweet, J. A., & Bumpass, L. L. 1987. *American families and households.* New York: Russell Sage Foundation.

Sykes, G., & Matza, D. 1957. "Techniques of neutralization: A theory of delinquency." *American Sociological Review, 22,* 664–670.

Szasz, T. 1990. *Insanity: The idea and its consequences.* New York: Wiley.

Tahan, R. 1997. "Realtors to receive cultural training." *Indianapolis Star,* November 16.

"Taiwan's little problem." 1993. *The Economist,* June 5.

Talbot, M. 2000a. "A mighty fortress." *New York Times Magazine,* February 27.

———. 2000b. "The placebo prescription." *New York Times Magazine,* January 9.

Tannen, D. 1990. *You just don't understand: Women and men in conversation.* New York: Ballantine.

"Tarnished gold." 1999. *Harper's Magazine,* October.

Tarrow, S. 1994. *Power in movement.* New York: Cambridge University Press.

Tauber, M. A. 1979. "Parental socialization techniques and sex differences in children's play." *Child Development, 50,* 225–234.

Tavris, C. 1992. *The mismeasure of woman.* New York: Touchstone.

Tavris, C., & Offir, C. 1984. *The longest war: Sex differences in perspective.* New York: Harcourt Brace Jovanovich.

Taylor, D. E. 1993. "Environmentalism and the politics of inclusion." In R. D. Bullard (Ed.), *Confronting environmental racism.* Boston: South End Press.

Taylor, R. J., Chatters, L. M., Tucker, M. B., & Lewis, E. 1990. "Developments in research on black families: A decade review." *Journal of Marriage and the Family, 52,* 993–1014.

Taylor, S. J., & Bogdan, R. 1980. "Defending illusions: The institution's struggle for survival." *Human Organization, 39,* 209–218.

Teachman, J. D. 1991. "Contributions to children by divorced fathers." *Social Problems, 38,* 358–371.

"Ten facts about women workers." 1997. *World Almanac.* Mahwah, NJ: World Almanac Books.

Tenner, E. 1996. *Why things bite back.* New York: Knopf.

Terry, D. 1995. "Heat death toll rises to 436 in Chicago." *New York Times,* July 20.

———. 1996. "In Wisconsin, a rarity of a fetal-harm case." *New York Times,* August 17.

Thoits, P. 1985. "Self-labeling process in mental illness: The role of emotional deviance." *American Journal of Sociology, 91,* 221–249.

Thomas, S. L. 1998. "Race, gender and welfare reform: The antinatalist response." *Journal of Black Studies, 28,* 419–446.

Thompson, P. 1989. *The nature of work.* London: Macmillan.

Thompson, T. L., & Zerbinos, E. 1995. "Gender roles in animated cartoons: Has the picture changed in 20 years?" *Sex Roles, 32,* 651–673.

Thomson, D. S. 2000. "The Sapir-Whorf hypothesis: Worlds shaped by words." In J. Spradley & D. W. McCurdy (Eds.), *Conformity and conflict.* Boston: Allyn and Bacon.

Thorne, B., & Luria, Z. 1986. "Sexuality and gender in children's daily worlds." *Social Problems, 33,* 176–190.

Thorne, B., & Yalom, M. 1982. *Rethinking the family: Some feminist questions.* New York: Longman.

Thornton, A. 1989. "Changing attitudes toward family issues in the United States." *Journal of Marriage and the Family, 51,* 873–893.

Thornton, A., Axinn, W. G., & Hill, D. H. 1992. "Reciprocal effects of religiosity, cohabitation, and marriage." *American Journal of Sociology, 98,* 62–51.

Thornton, A., & Camburn, D. 1989. "Religious participation and adolescent sexual behavior and attitudes." *Journal of Marriage and the Family, 51,* 64–53.

Tiano, S. 1987. "Gender, work and world capitalism: Third world women's role in development." In B. B. Hess & M. M. Ferree (Eds.), *Analyzing gender: A handbook of social science research.* Newbury Park, CA: Sage.

Tilly, C. 1978. *From mobilization to revolution.* Reading, MA: Addison-Wesley.

Timms, E., & McGonigle, S. 1992. "Psychological warfare." *Indianapolis Star,* April 5.

Tittle, C. R. 1969. "Crime rates and legal sanctions." *Social Problems, 16,* 40–23.

Tobin, J. J., Wu, D. Y. H., & Davidson, D. H. 1989. *Preschool in three cultures: Japan, China and the United States.* New Haven, CT: Yale University Press.

Tong, R. 1984. *Women, sex and the law.* Totowa, NJ: Rowman & Allanheld.

"Too many biologists spoil the broth." 1998. *Newsweek,* October 5.

"Top 10 drugs prescribed to kids without pediatric labeling." 1999. *FDA Consumer,* May–June.

Treaster, J. B., & Petersen, M. 1997. "Florida report concludes that Prudential Insurance cheated customers for 13 years." *New York Times,* December 22.

Trent, K., & South, S. J. 1989. "Structural determinant of the divorce rate: A cross-societal analysis." *Journal of Marriage and the Family, 51,* 391–404.

Trepanier, M. L., & Romatowski, J. A. 1985. "Attributes and roles assigned to characters in children's writing: Sex differences and sex role perceptions." *Sex Roles, 13,* 263–272.

Triandis, H. C., McCusker, C., & Hui, C. H. 1990. "Multimethod probes of individualism and collectivism." *Journal of Personality and Social Psychology, 59,* 1006–1020.

Trotsky, L. 1959. *The history of the Russian Revolution* (F. W. Dupee, Ed.). Garden City, NY: Doubleday. (Originally published 1930)

Trudgill, P. 1972. "Sex, covert prestige and linguistic change in the urban British English of Norwich." In B. Thorne & N. Henley (Eds.), *Language and society.* Cambridge, England: Cambridge University Press.

Tumin, M. 1953. "Some principles of stratification: A critical analysis." *American Sociological Review, 18,* 387–393.

Turkle, S. 1994. "Constructions and reconstructions of self in virtual reality: Playing in the MUDs." *Mind, Culture and Activity, 1,* 158–167.

Turner, J. H. 1972. *Patterns of social organization.* New York: McGraw-Hill.

Turner, R. W., & Killian, L. M. 1987. *Collective behavior.* Englewood Cliffs, NJ: Prentice Hall.

Turning Point Project. 1999. "Global monoculture." *New York Times,* November 15.

Ubel, P., Zell, M. M., Miller, D. J., Fischer, G. S., Peters-Stefani, D., & Arnold, R. M. 1995. "Elevator talk: Observational study of inappropriate comments in a public space." *American Journal of Medicine, 99,* 190–194.

Uchitelle, L. 1993. "Use of temporary workers is on rise in manufacturing." *New York Times,* July 6.

———. 1998. "Downsizing comes back, but the outcry is muted." *New York Times,* December 7.

———. 1999. "Rising incomes lift 1.1 million out of poverty." *New York Times,* October 1.

Uchitelle, L., & Kleinfield, N. R. 1996. "On the battlefields of business, millions of casualties." *New York Times,* March 3.

"UN to protect children in conflicts." 1999. *New York Times,* August 26.

United Nations. 1995. *The world's women 1995: Trends and statistics,* New York: Author.

———. 1999. "Comprehensive tables." *World population prospects: The 1998 revision,* volume I. UN Population Division. Sales no. E.99.X111.9.

United States [U.S.] Bureau of Justice Statistics. 1983. *Report to the nation on crime and justice: The data.* Washington, DC: U.S. Government Printing Office.

———. 1993. *Sourcebook of criminal justice statistics—1992.* Washington, DC: U.S. Government Printing Office.

———. 2001. "The sexual victimization of college women." BJS Press release. 222.ojp.usdoj.gov/bjs/pub/press/svcw.pr. Accessed January 28, 2001.

United States [U.S.] Bureau of Labor Statistics. 1985. *Handbook of labor statistics.* Washington, DC: U.S. Government Printing Office.

———. 1989. *Handbook of labor statistics.* Washington, DC: U.S. Government Printing Office.

———. 1999. "Median weekly earnings of full-time wage and salary workers by detailed occupation and sex." *Current Population Statistics.* http://ferret.bls. census.gov/macro/171996/empearn/aat39.txt. Accessed June 20, 2000.

United States [U.S.] Bureau of the Census. 1993. *Census and you, 28.* January, p. 1.

———. 1994. *Statistical abstract of the United States.* Washington, DC: U.S. Government Printing Office.

———. 1995a. "Population projections of the United States by age, sex, race and Hispanic origin: 1995–2050." *Current Population Reports,* Series P25, 1130.

———. 1995b. *Statistical abstract of the United States.* Washington, DC: U.S. Government Printing Office.

———. 1997a. "Income up, health coverage down, and poverty unchanged." *Census and you.* November.

———. 1997b. *Statistical abstract of the United States.* Washington, DC: U.S. Government Printing Office.

———. 1998a. "Foreign-born population reaches 25.8 million, according to Census Bureau." Census Bureau press release http://www.census.gov/Press-Release/cb9–7.html.

———. 1998b. "Historical income tables." Tables H-1, H-2, H-3. www.census.gov/hhes/income/histinc/index.html.

———. 1998c. *Statistical abstract of the United States.* Washington, DC: U.S. Government Printing Office.

———. 1999a. "Poverty in the United States." *Current Population Reports,* P6–07. Washington, DC: U.S. Government Printing Office.

———. 1999b. *Statistical abstract of the United States.* Washington, DC: U.S. Government Printing Office.

———. 2000a. "Income 1999." Census Bureau web site. www.census.gov/hhes/income/income99. Accessed January 4, 2001.

———. 2000b. *Statistical abstract of the United States.* Washington, DC: U.S. Government Printing Office.

———. 2001a. "Poverty in the United States: 1999. p6–20. www.census.gov/hhes/www/povty99.html. Accessed February 18, 2001.

———. 2001b. "Profile of general demographic characteristics for the United States: 2000." Table DP-1. www.census.gov/Press-Release/www/2001/tables/dp_us_2000.pdf. Accessed May 15, 2001.

United States [U.S.] Commission on Human Rights. 1992. "Indian tribes: A continuing quest for survival." In P. S. Rothenberg (Ed.), *Race, class and gender in the United States.* New York: St. Martin's Press.

United States [U.S.] Department of Agriculture. 2001. "USDA estimates child rearing costs." USDA News Release #0097.01. www.usda.gov/news/releases/2001/06/0097.htm. Accessed June 17, 2001.

U.S. Department of Commerce. 1999. *Falling through the net: Defining the digital divide: A report on the telecommunications and information technology gap in America.* www.ntia.doc.gov. Accessed November 20, 2000.

United States [U.S.] Department of Health, Education and Welfare. 1973. *Work in America: Report of a special task force to the Secretary of Health, Education and Welfare.* Cambridge, MA: MIT Press.

United States [U.S.] Department of Health and Human Services. 1988. "The health consequences of smoking." In *Nicotine addiction: A report of the Surgeon General.* Washington, DC: U.S. Government Printing Office.

United States [U.S.] Department of Justice. 2001. "Criminal victimization in United States, 1999 statistical tables." NCJ 184938. www.ojp.usdoj.gov/bjs/pub/pdf/cvus99.pdf. Accessed January 28, 2001.

[United States] U.S. Network for Global Economic Justice. 2000. "False profits: Who wins, who loses when the IMF, World Bank, and WTO come to town." www.50years.org/april16/booklet.html. Accessed June 22.

United States [U.S.] Sentencing Commission, 1998. *Sourcebook of federal sentencing statistics.* www.ussc.gov./ANNRPT/1998/Sbtoc98.htm. Accessed June 20, 2001.

Valdivieso, R., & Davis, C. 1991. "U.S. Hispanics: Challenging issues for the 1990's." In J. Skolnick & E. Currie (Eds.), *Crisis in American institutions.* New York: HarperCollins.

van den Haag, E. 1975. *Punishing criminals: Concerning a very old and painful question.* New York: Basic Books.

Vanek, J. 1980. "Work, leisure and family roles: Farm households in the United States: 1920–1955." *Journal of Family History, 5,* 422–431.

Van Willigen, J., & Channa, V. C. 1991. "Law, custom and crimes against women: The problem of dowry death in India." *Human Organization, 50,* 369–377.

Vaughan, D. 1986. *Uncoupling.* New York: Vintage.

———. 1996. *The* Challenger *launch disaster.* Chicago: University of Chicago Press.

Viets, E. 1992. "Give a whistle, he'll love it." *St. Louis Post-Dispatch,* November 29.

"Vital signs." 1995. *The Nation,* September 11.

Wagner, D. G., Ford, R. S., & Ford, T. W. 1986. "Can gender inequalities be reduced?" *American Sociological Review, 51,* 47–61.

Wallerstein, I. 1974. *The modern world system.* New York: Academic Press.

Walton, J. 1990. *Sociology and critical inquiry.* Belmont, CA: Wadsworth.

Warshaw, R. 1988. *I never called it rape.* New York: Harper & Row.

Wattenberg, E. 1986. "The fate of baby boomers and their children." *Social Work, 31,* 20–28.

Watzlawick, P. 1976. *How real is real?* Garden City, NY: Doubleday.

———. 1984. "Self-fulfilling prophecies." In P. Watzlawick (Ed.), *The invented reality: How do we know what we believe we know? Contributions to constructivism.* New York: Norton.

Webb, E. J., Campbell, D. T., Schwartz, R. D., Sechrest, L., & Grove, J. B. 1981. *Nonreactive measures in the social sciences.* Boston: Houghton Mifflin.

Weber, M. 1946. "Bureaucracy." In H. H. Gerth & C. W. Mills (Eds.), *From Max Weber: Essays in sociology* (pp. 196–244). New York: Oxford University Press.

———. 1947. *The theory of social and economic organization.* New York: Free Press.

———. 1968. *Economy and society* (G. Roth & C. Wittich, Eds.). New York: Bedminster Press.

———. 1970. *From Max Weber: Essays in sociology* (H. H. Gerth & C. W. Mills, Eds.). New York: Oxford University Press.

———. 1977. *The Protestant ethic and the spirit of capitalism.* New York: Macmillan. (Original work published 1904)

Weeks, J. 1995. *Population: An introduction to concepts and issues* (updated 5th ed.). Belmont, CA: Wadsworth.

Weitzman, L. 1985. *The divorce revolution: The unexpected consequences for women and children in America.* New York: Free Press.

Weitzman, L., Eifler, D., Hodada, E., & Ross, C. 1972. "Sex-role socialization in picture books for preschool children." *American Journal of Sociology, 77,* 1125–1150.

Wellman, B. & Gulia, M. 1999. "Net-surfers don't ride alone: Virtual communities as communities." In B. Wellman (Ed.), *Networks in the global village.* Boulder, CO: Westview.

Whalen, C. K., & Henker, B. 1977. "The pitfalls of politicization: A response to Conrad's 'The discovery of hyperkinesis: Notes on the medicalization of deviance.' " *Social Problems, 24,* 590–595.

White, J. E. 1997. "Multiracialism: The melding of America." *Time,* May 5.

White, L., & Brinkerhoff, D. 1981. "The sexual division of labor: Evidence from childhood." *Social Forces, 60,* 170–181.

Whorf, B. 1956. *Language, thought and reality.* Cambridge, MA: MIT Press.

Whyte, M. K. 1990. *Dating, mating and marriage.* New York: Aldine de Gruyter.

Whyte, W. H. 1956. *The organization man.* Garden City, NY: Doubleday.

Wilgoren, J. 2001. "Calls for change in the scheduling of the school day." *New York Times,* January 10.

Wilkerson, I. 1991a. "As interracial marriage rises, acceptance lags." *New York Times,* December 12.

———. 1991b. "Shift in feelings on the homeless: Empathy turns to frustration." *New York Times,* September 2.

Wilkinson, L. C., & Marrett, C. B. 1985. *Gender influences in classroom interaction.* Orlando, FL: Academic Press.

Will, G. 2000. "AIDS crushes a continent." *Newsweek,* January 10.

Will, J., Self, P., & Datan, N. 1976. "Maternal behavior and perceived sex of infant." *American Journal of Orthopsychiatry, 46,* 135–139.

Williams, C. 2000. "Suicide rate rises among young black males." *Indianapolis Star,* October 25.

Williams, L. 1991a. "In a 90's quest for black identity, intense doubts and disagreements." *New York Times,* November 30.

———. 1991b. "When blacks shop bias often accompanies sale." *New York Times,* April 30.

Wilson, W. J. 1980. *The declining significance of race.* Chicago: University of Chicago Press.

———. 1987. *The truly disadvantaged.* Chicago: University of Chicago Press.

———. 1990. "Race-neutral programs and the Democratic coalition." *American Prospect, 1,* 75–81.

———. 1996. *When work disappears.* New York: Knopf.

Wisotsky, S. 1998. "A society of suspects: The war on drugs and civil liberties." In H. A. Widdison (Ed.), *Social problems 98/99.* Guilford, CT: Dushkin.

Wolf, N. 1991. *The beauty myth: How images of beauty are used against women.* New York: William Morrow.

Wolfe, A. 1991. *America at century's end.* Berkeley: University of California Press.

———. 1998. *One nation, after all.* New York: Viking.

———. 1999. "The new politics of inequality." *New York Times,* September 22.

Wolfe, S. M. 1991. *Women's health alert.* Reading, MA: Addison-Wesley.

Woliver, L. R. 1989. "The deflective power of reproductive technologies: The impact on women." *Women and Politics, 9,* 17–47.

Wood, P. L. 1975. "The victim in a forcible rape case: A feminist view." In L. G. Schultz (Ed.), *Rape victimology.* Springfield, IL: Charles C Thomas.

Word, C. O., Zanna, M. P., & Cooper, J. 1974. "The nonverbal mediation of self-fulfilling prophecies in interracial interaction." *Journal of Experimental Social Psychology, 10,* 109–120.

"Workers of the world." 1998. *The Economist,* January 30.

World Health Organization. 1995. "World health report 1995—Executive summary." www.who.int.

———. 1996. "The tobacco epidemic: A global public health emergency." www.who.int.

World Monitor. 1992. "The Map." *World Monitor,* September 11.

"World population growth." 1995. *The Futurist,* January–February.

"World progress in birth control." 1993. *The Futurist,* August.

World Resources Institute. 2001. "Feeding the world." Sustainable Development Information Service. www.wri.org/trends/feeding.html. Accessed February 3, 2001.

"World view, A." 1998. *The Economist,* January 30.

Worsnop, R. 1996a. "Getting into college." *CQ Researcher,* February 23.

———. 1996b. "Helping the homeless." *CQ Researcher,* January 26.

Worthington, R. 1996. "Doctoral degree holders face daunting job shortages." *Indianapolis Star,* May 26.

Wren, C. S. 1996. "Study poses a medical challenge to disparity in cocaine sentences." *New York Times,* November 20.

———. 1997. "Phantom numbers haunt war on drugs." *New York Times,* April 20.

Wright, E. O. 1976. "Class boundaries in advanced capitalist societies." *New Left Review, 98,* 3–41.

Wright, E. O., Costello, C., Hachen, D., & Sprague, J. 1982. "The American class structure." *American Sociological Review, 47,* 709–726.

Wright, E. O., & Perrone, L. 1977. "Marxist class categories and income inequality." *American Sociological Review, 42,* 32–55.

Wright, J. D., & Wright, S. R. 1976. "Social class and parental values for children: A partial replication and extension of the Kohn thesis." *American Sociological Review, 41,* 52–37.

Wrong, D. 1988. *Power: Its forms, bases, and uses.* Chicago: University of Chicago Press.

WuDunn, S. 1996. "In Japan, even toddlers feel the pressure to excel." *New York Times,* January 23.

———. 1997. "Korean women still feel demands to bear a son." *New York Times,* January 14.

Wuthnow, R. 1994. *Sharing the journey.* New York: Free Press.

Xiao, H. 2000. "Class, gender, and parental values in the 1990s." *Gender & Society, 14,* 78–03.

Yardley, J. 2000a. "Studies find race disparities in Texas traffic stops." *New York Times,* October 7.

———. 2000b. "Unmarried and living together, till the sheriff do us part." *New York Times,* March 25.

Zaldivar, R. A. 1998. "Balancing the 'good' life with the risk." *Indianapolis Star,* August 2.

Zola, I. 1986. "Medicine as an institution of social control." In P. Conrad & R. Kern (Eds.), *The sociology of health and illness.* New York: St. Martin's Press.

Zuboff, S. 1988. *In the age of the smart machine.* New York: Basic Books.

Zuckoff, M. 2000. "Lawsuit accuses drug maker Eli Lilly of concealing Prozac data from trial." *Boston Globe,* June 8.

Zuger, A. 1999. "Take some strychnine and call me in the morning." *New York Times,* April 30.

Zurcher, L. A., & Snow, D. A. 1981. "Collective behavior: Social movements." In M. Rosenberg & R. H. Turner (Eds.), *Social psychology: Sociological perspectives.* New York: Basic Books.

Zweigenhaft, R. L. 1987. "Minorities and women of the corporation." In G. W. Domhoff & T. R. Dye (Eds.), *Power elites and organizations.* Newbury Park, CA: Sage.

Zwingle, E. 1999. "A world apart." *National Geographic,* August.

Credits

Exhibits

Exhibit 1.1: Adapted from a memo prepared by Bettina Huber of the Modern Language Association to the American Sociological Association and several other professional associations, February 1994. Reprinted by permission.

Exhibit 3.1: From *Word Play: What Happens When People Talk* by Peter Farb. Copyright © 1973 by Peter Farb. Reprinted by permission of Alfred A. Knopf, Inc. a division of Random House, Inc., and Brandt and Brandt Literary Agents.

Exhibit 11.3: From "The Wage Gap: Myths and Facts," in P. S. Rothenberg (Ed.), *Race Class and Gender in the United States*, 1995. Copyright © P. S. Rothenberg. Used by permission of the author and the National Committee on Pay Equity.

Exhibit 12.1: From "Housework in Marital and Non-marital Households," S. J. South and G. Spitze, 1994, *The American Sociological Review, 59*, pp. 327–347. Copyright © 1994 by the American Sociological Association. Reprinted by permission.

Exhibit 13.1: From *American Social Problems: An Institutional Analysis,* 2nd ed., by John E. Farley (p. 344). © 1991. Reprinted by permission of Pearson Education, Upper Saddle River, NJ.

Exhibit 13.2: Art adapted from *Population: An Introduction to Concepts and Issues,* 5th edition, by John R. Weeks. © 1994. Reprinted with permission of Wadsworth, an imprint of Wadsworth Group, a division of Thomson Learning. Fax 800-730-2215.

Exhibit 13.3: From art by Ian Worpole in "The Growing Human Population," Nathan Keyfitz, *Scientific American*, p. 122, September 1989.

Quotations

Chapter 3: From Letter to the Editor, 1992, *Greencastle Banner Graphic* (7 March). Copyright 1992. Reprinted by permission.

Chapter 7: From "Psychological Warfare" by E. Tims and S. McGonigle, 1992, *Indianapolis Star* (5 April), p. F4. Reprinted by permission of Knight-Ridder/Tribune News Services.

Chapter 11: From "Black Like Them" by M. Gladwell, 1996, *The New Yorker* (29 April and 6 May). Reprinted by permission of the author.

Chapter 12: From "Give Him a Whistle, He'll Love It" by Elaine Viets, 1992, *St. Louis Post Dispatch* (29 November). Copyright 1992. Reprinted by permission of the St. Louis Post Dispatch.

Quotations in the visual essay "Graffiti and the Eye of the Beholder": by Richard Rodriguez from *Pacific News Service Newsletter*, published by Pacific News Service; by Alex Alvarez from "In a City of Graffiti, Gangs Turn to Violence to Protect Their Art," by B. Drummond Ayres, Jr., *The New York Times* (13 March, 1994); from "Billboard Hijinks: Graffiti Groups (Pro and Con) Rally Against Chrysler," *San Francisco Bay Guardian* (4 May 1994).

Photographs in the Visual Essays

"A Matter of Sexual Identity" photo of Jim Morris by Corbis/UPI-Bettmann; photo of Jan Morris by David Hurn/Magnum; photo of Eva Robbins reprinted by permission of Eva Robbins; photo of Jane Fee by A/P Wide World Photos.

"Graffiti and the Eye of the Beholder" photos by James Prigoff, in Henry Chalfant and James Prigoff, *Spraycan Art*, New York: Thames and Hudson, 1987.

"Families on the Web" screen shots courtesy of Luc Pauwels, Brenda and Allen Lloyd, Jim Hilton, and Bruce Hallman. Photo on page 231 (bottom) courtesy of Susan and Kevin Kelly.

"The Trail of the Tomato" photos © Deborah Barndt/Tomasita Project.

"Images of Social Class" photos by: Bruce Davidson, *East 100th Street*, Cambridge, MA: Harvard University

Glossary/Index

A

abortion
  of female fetuses, 428
  social movements opposing, 464, 472

absolute poverty Inability to afford the minimal requirements for sustaining a reasonably healthy existence, 297

absolutism Approach to analyzing deviance that rests on the assumption that all human behavior can be considered either inherently good or inherently bad, 163–164

account Statement designed to explain unanticipated, embarrassing, or unacceptable behavior after the behavior has occurred, 153

achieved status Social position acquired through our own efforts or accomplishments or taken on voluntarily, 23, 280

adolescents
  contemporary changes in, 456–457
  suicide rate among, 10
  weight concerns among, 137
  See also children

advertisements, Italian, 408–413

affirmative action Program designed to seek out members of minority groups for positions from which they had previously been excluded, thereby seeking to overcome institutional racism, 364–367

Afghani women, 403

African Americans
  affirmative action and, 364–367
  civil rights movement of, 19, 471, 472, 474–475
  educational system and, 359–361
  environmental movement and, 466–468
  health care system and, 357–359

impression management among, 147–148
institutional racism against, 351–367
legal system and, 164, 361–362
migration of, 430
occupational concentration of, 354
political involvement of, 329–330
poverty and, 309, 330
prejudice and discrimination against, 336–337, 341–344
professional sports and, 349–351
racial profiling of, 362–363
residential segregation of, 351–353
skin-tone issues among, 343
socialization of, 118–119
stereotypes of, 339–340
teen suicide rate for, 10
  See also minority groups

African Rights (organization), 16

age distributions
  global view of, 428–429
  graphically displaying, 441–442
  in the United States, 437–440

age structure Population's balance of old and young people, 428–429

agricultural workers, 269–276

AIDS
  activists for treating, 455
  global epidemic of, 312

Albright, Madeleine, 135

alcohol use
  anti-drunk driving movement and, 473
  criminal behavior and, 179
  social behavior and, 36
  temperance movement and, 57

alibis, 154

Alien (film), 486

alienation, 12

aligning action Action taken to restore an identity that has been damaged, 153

Alvarez, Alex, 191

American Civil Liberties Union (ACLU), 24

American Psychiatric Association (APA), 58

ancestor worship, 79, 450

Anderson, Elijah, 147–148

anomie Condition in which rapid change has disrupted society's ability to adequately regulate and control its members and the old rules that governed people's lives no longer seem to apply, 458

antiabortion movements, 464, 472

anticipatory socialization Process through which people acquire the values and orientations found in statuses they will likely enter in the future, 107

antidepressants, 183–186

anti-drunk driving movement, 473

antinuclear movements, 472

antistalking laws, 470

antiwar movements, 465, 474

Applewhite, Marshall Herff, 112

Arab women, 403–404

architecture metaphor, 1

Armstrong, Neil, 476

arrest/conviction statistics, 165
  See also crime

As You Like It (Shakespeare), 144

ascribed status Social position acquired at birth or taken on involuntarily later in life, 23, 280

Ashcroft, John, 463

Asian Americans
  educational achievement of, 360
  historical overview of, 337–338
  immigration of, 434–435
  life expectancy estimates for, 358
  socialization of, 119
  See also minority groups

athletes
  African American, 349–351
  heroic symbols of, 40–41

attention deficit hyperactivity disorder (ADHD), 182–183

ethics in research, 74–75

ethnicity The sense of community that derives from the cultural heritage shared by a category of people with common ancestry, 332

conflicts based on, 369–370

family composition and, 221

impression management and, 146–148

interracial marriage and, 214–215

national inequality based on, 334–338

race linked to, 332–333

socialization and, 118–119

See also race

ethnocentrism Tendency to judge other cultures using one's own as a standard, 91

eugenics, 105

euphemisms, 52–53

European Gypsies, 367

European immigrants, 434

European Union, 423

Evans-Pritchard, E. E., 55

exogamy Marriage outside one's social group, 212

experiment Research method designed to elicit some sort of behavior, typically conducted under closely controlled laboratory circumstances, 67

extended family Family unit consisting of the parent–child nuclear family and other relatives, such as grandparents, aunts, uncles, and cousins, 201

extreme sports, 414–415

F

Faccioli, Patrizia, 408

faith, 54–56

false consciousness Situation in which people in the lower classes come to accept a belief system that harms them; the primary means by which powerful classes in society prevent protest and revolution, 288

families, 26, 200–229

child-rearing in, 204–205

contemporary changes in, 456

cultural variations in, 203–205

definitions of, 205–207, 228–229

divorce and, 202–203, 217–223

domestic violence in, 223–227

dual-earner parents in, 209–211

economic issues for, 208–211

extended vs. nuclear, 201

gender roles in, 211–212

historical trends of, 200–203

household structures and, 205

interfaith marriages and, 213–214

interracial marriages and, 214–215

law and, 207, 210–211

politics and, 207–208

poverty rate for, 300–301

privacy rights of, 29–31

reconstituted, 222–223

religion and, 208, 213–214

sexism and, 390–394, 406

social class and, 215–217

social diversity issues and, 212–215

social structure and, 207–217

Web sites of, 229, 231–235

working-class, 216–217

See also children; parents; social relationships

Families on the Fault Line (Rubin), 217

Family and Medical Leave Act (1993), 210, 388–389

Family Protection Act (1981), 388

farm workers, 269–276

fascism, 481, 482

Feagin, Joe R., 344

Federal Bureau of Investigation (FBI), 63

Federal Communications Commission (FCC), 58

Federal Crime Bill (1994), 171

Federal Trade Commission (FTC), 261

Fee, James/Jane, 132

Feinstein, Dianne, 436

fertility rate, 425, 427, 438

fertility technology, 391, 460

Festinger, Leon, 68

fetal rights, 391–392

feudal system. *See* estate system

field research Type of social research in which the researcher observes events as they actually occur, 67–69

Fight Club (film), 247

Fijian girls, 138

folkways Informal norm that is mildly punished when violated, 90

Food and Drug Administration (FDA), 61, 153

free-rider problem Tendency for people to refrain from contributing to the common good when a resource is available without requiring any personal cost or contribution, 243–244

Freud, Sigmund, 63

front stage Area of social interaction where people perform and work to maintain appropriate impressions, 144

funeral directors, 113–114

funeral rituals in the Netherlands, 444–453

future, visions of, 479–486

G

game stage Stage in the development of self during which a child acquires the ability to take the role of a group or community (the generalized other) and to conform his or her behavior to broad, societal expectations, 110

Gates, Bill, 303

gender Psychological, social, and cultural aspects of maleness and femaleness, 119

sex distinguished from, 119, 384

socialization process and, 119–123, 124–125, 127–128

stereotypes based on, 119–120, 125, 374

transgendering movement and, 131–132

See also sex

gender differences

housework and, 392–394, 406

labor force participation and, 73, 396–399

physical attractiveness and, 135–136

sexual advertisements and, 408–413

wage gap based on, 399–401

See also sexism

gender harassment, 377

gender roles

consumer products and, 121–123, 129

educational system and, 124–125

family and, 211–212

mass media and, 127–128

toy industry and, 121–123

gender segregation, 396–399